The Boundless Biddy Mason

The publisher and the University of California Press Foundation gratefully acknowledge the generous support of the Peter Booth Wiley Endowment Fund in History.

The Boundless Biddy Mason

AN ODYSSEY FROM SLAVERY TO FREEDOM ACROSS THE AMERICAN WEST

Kevin Waite

UNIVERSITY OF CALIFORNIA PRESS

University of California Press
Oakland, California

Library of Congress Cataloging-in-Publication Data

Names: Waite, Kevin (Historian) author

Title: The boundless Biddy Mason : an odyssey from slavery to freedom across the American West / Kevin Waite.

Description: Oakland : University of California Press, 2026. | Includes bibliographical references and index.

Identifiers: LCCN 2026009878 (print) | LCCN 2026009879 (ebook) | ISBN 9780520394728 cloth | ISBN 9780520394735 ebook

Subjects: LCSH: Mason, Biddy, 1818–1891 | African American midwives—California | Overland journeys to the Pacific—History—19th century | African American women—California | Enslaved women—United States | Frontier and pioneer life—California | LCGFT: Biographies

Classification: LCC E444.M38 W35 2026 (print) | LCC E444.M38 (ebook)

LC record available at https://lccn.loc.gov/2026009878

LC ebook record available at https://lccn.loc.gov/2026009879

Manufactured in the United States of America

GPSR Authorized Representative: Easy Access System Europe, Mustamäe tee 50, 10621 Tallinn, Estonia, gpsr.requests@easproject.com

35 34 33 32 31 30 29 28 27 26
10 9 8 7 6 5 4 3 2 1

Contents

List of Illustrations vii

Introduction 1

PART I SLAVERY

1. Mississippi Bound 13
2. Making a Patriarch 30
3. Overland 49
4. Children of Zion, Seed of Cain 69
5. California Bound 86
6. Hiding in Plain Sight 98
7. Unmaking a Patriarch 111
8. The Trial 128

PART II FREEDOM

9. The Decision 147
10. Freedwoman 160

11. Healer 176
12. Unionist 193
13. Reconstructing Los Angeles 215
14. Philanthropist 237
15. City-Builder 257
16. Matriarch 283

Epilogue: In Search of Biddy Mason 301

Acknowledgments 311
Notes 317
Bibliography 395
Index 431

Illustrations

FIGURES

Ruined courthouse of Hancock County, Georgia 14
Robert Mays Smith 31
Utah County slave schedule 84
Black and white miners in California gold country 91
Robert Smith's cattle brand 100
Santa Monica Mountains 118
Benjamin Ignatius Hayes 120
Elizabeth Flake Rowan 121
Los Angeles Plaza, ca. 1860s 129
Los Angeles panorama with county jail, late 1860s 131
Biddy Mason's X 169
Calle de los Negros 173
San Pedro Street with *zanja* 174
John S. Griffin 180

Robert Curry Owens, Biddy Mason's grandson, as a child 185
Drum Barracks 201
"History of Medicine in California" mural series by Bernard Zakheim 207
Deed to Biddy Mason's first property purchase 219
Women of the Mason-Owens family 221
Victims of the Los Angeles Chinese Massacre of 1871 238
Biddy Mason, ca. late 1870s 251
Biddy Mason's business block 260
Owens livery stable (and candy factory) in the Mason Block 261
Ellen Mason Owens Huddleston 265
First African Methodist Church of Los Angeles on Azusa Street 267
Robert Curry Owens 276
Los Angeles from Biddy Mason's Spring Street, 1890s 278
Biddy Mason's last will and testament 285
Interior of one of Robert C. Owens's properties 293
First AME of Los Angeles at Eighth and Towne 294
Headstone at Biddy Mason's burial site 302
Golden State Mutual Life Insurance mural by Charles Alston 306
Altar mural at First African Methodist Church of Los Angeles 306
Biddy Mason memorial wall by Sheila Levrant de Bretteville 307

MAPS

Biddy Mason's transcontinental journey, 1820s–1856 x
Early Black Los Angeles 262

For Rumi

BIDDY MASON'S TRANSCONTINENTAL JOURNEY

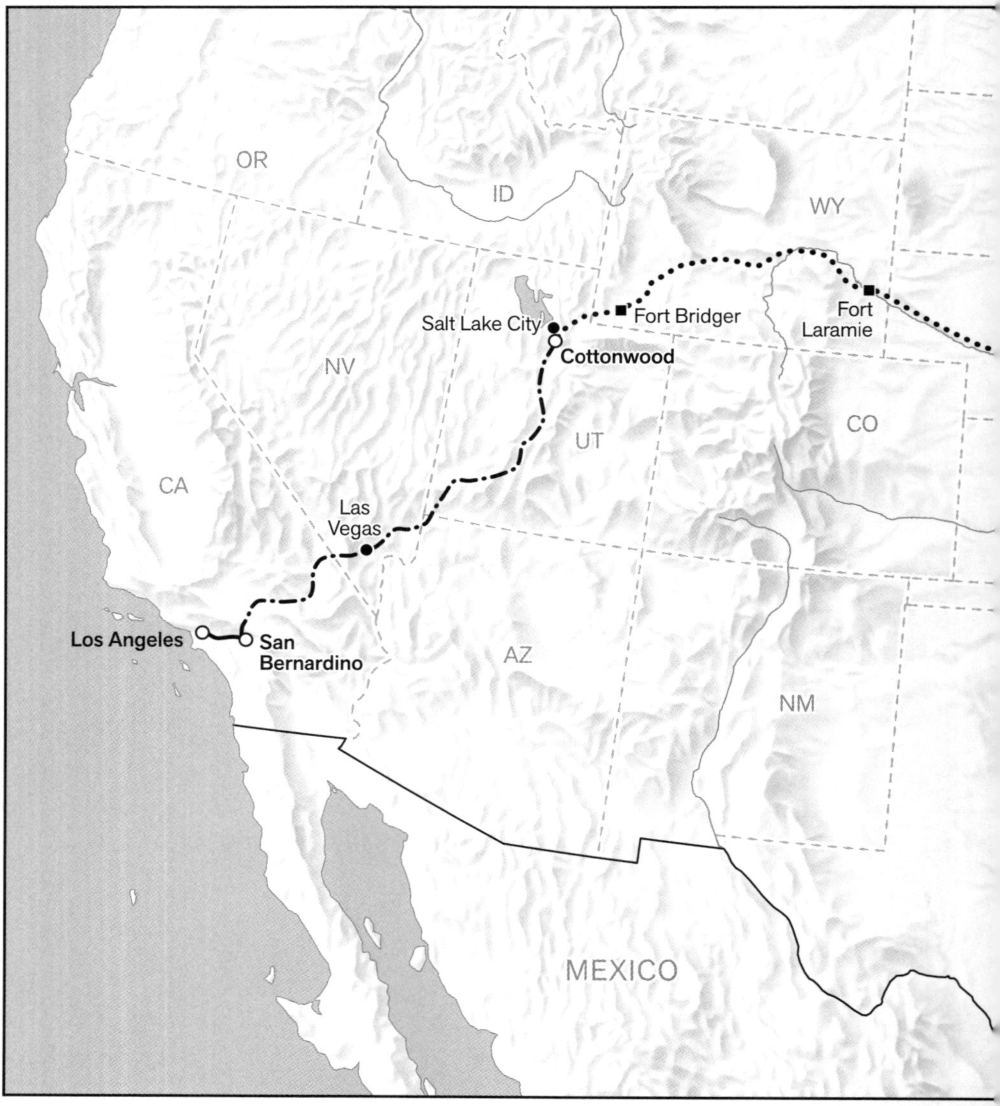

Map by Erin Greb.

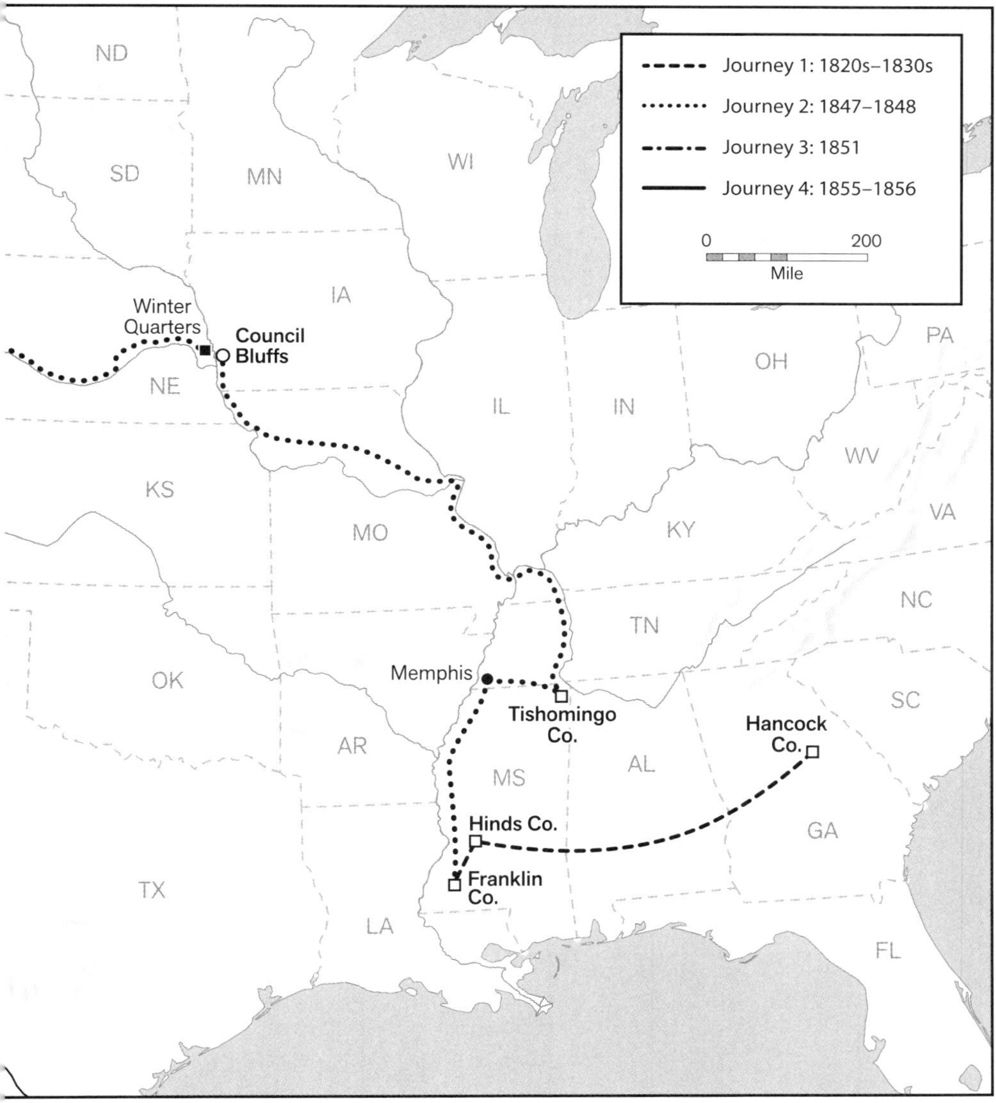

Journey 1: 1820s–1830s
Journey 2: 1847–1848
Journey 3: 1851
Journey 4: 1855–1856
0
200
Mile
ND
SD
MN
WI
IA
NE
KS
MO
IL
IN
OH
PA
WV
VA
KY
TN
NC
SC
OK
AR
MS
AL
GA
TX
LA
FL
Winter Quarters
Council Bluffs
Memphis
Tishomingo Co.
Hancock Co.
Hinds Co.
Franklin Co.

Introduction

Southern California's perennial sunshine rarely penetrated the ground-floor lockup of the Los Angeles county jail. On the best of days a dank stillness would have encased the adobe chamber and those confined within. And this was the worst of days. January 1856 brought freezing temperatures and a new set of inmates to the jail: a group of women and children, now huddled together on the earthen floor of their prison home. If they were lucky, the jailor may have provided a few spare blankets to cut the chill and some candles to illuminate the hollow chamber. The pity of the judge who imprisoned them here was cold comfort for a group of people who had little reason to trust any legal authority. The oldest among them, a woman named Biddy, perhaps offered a word of assurance here and there. She had, after all, survived worse in nearly four decades of enslavement. But even for her, hope was hard to find in that dark place.[1]

These prisoners—all of them Black, most of them minors, including Biddy's three daughters—were some of the first inmates of what would become the largest prison system in the country.[2] They found themselves there not because they had broken any laws or been charged with any offenses. Rather, they were there to launch a historic bid for freedom.

Biddy was no stranger to irony. Not only was she conducting a freedom suit from a prison cell, she had spent the previous five years in California in bondage—a slave in a free state. She was the property of a man named Robert Smith, who had transported Biddy and her daughters to California in 1851. Although California had technically abolished slavery in its 1849 constitution, no legal authority troubled Smith about his human property. He continued to profit from their labor as they worked his ranch, managed his household, and even delivered his neighbor's children. Smith's Black workforce grew to a total of fourteen people, making him the largest slaveholder anywhere on the Pacific Coast.[3]

Only when Smith attempted to leave California with his caravan of Black workers in early 1856 did legal authorities finally intervene. Shortly before the wagon company's planned departure for Texas, a sheriff's posse intercepted them, detained the enslaved people, and ordered Smith to appear before the First District Court of Los Angeles. The district judge confined Biddy and most of the Black children in the county jail, ostensibly for their own protection from their unscrupulous enslaver. Hence Biddy's long winter nights in prison as she awaited her family's fate.[4]

Smith's case rested on an insidious fiction. He had subjected Biddy and the others to "no greater control than his own children," he claimed. In fact, they had followed him "with their own consent."[5] Their migration to California was voluntary, Smith insisted, as was the planned trip to Texas. His argument would have been laughable, if not for the fact that Black Americans were barred from giving testimony against white people in California's courts and therefore from contradicting Smith's account. With the law on his side, Smith expected that Biddy and the others would be forced to follow him once again—from the cusp of freedom into the maw of slavery.

. . .

To Smith, Biddy was merely a piece of property. But to those who knew her, she was a mother, a midwife, a migrant, and a survivor. In time she would become an entrepreneur, a philanthropist, a religious leader, a matriarch, and a city-builder.

Biddy's multitudes are reflected in her sole surviving photographic portrait (as seen on the cover of this book).[6] Taken roughly two decades after her prison ordeal, the image reveals a still formidable figure, a woman unbroken by countless trials, staring straight into the camera's lens. Even in old age (by the standards of her time), she exhibits a vitality that shines through the faded ambrotype. She was later eulogized by a prominent Black writer as a woman of great physical strength.[7] But it wasn't bodily prowess alone, or even in the main, that sustained Biddy and her family. It was her resilience, her courage, her kindness, her faith.

She would need all those qualities and more. The road that led her to the Los Angeles courthouse snaked across roughly three thousand miles of American terrain, from Georgia to Mississippi to Utah to California, amounting to one of the longest forced migrations in US history. Biddy covered most of the journey on foot—the equivalent of about six million steps—herding animals at the rear of her owner's wagon company and choking her way through a moving screen of dust kicked up by the migrant caravan.[8] Along the way she passed crude wooden crosses planted in the earth, grim reminders that disease and disaster constantly stalked the trail. Yet through it all, she managed to keep her family alive and together.

Biddy's story doesn't end in a Los Angeles prison cell or on the road back to bondage in Texas. In fact, those long nights in the county jail marked the beginning of a new trail—a trail that finally forked from the path of slavery. Robert Smith exploited all the advantages that his whiteness and wealth afforded yet was ultimately outmanuevered by the Black women he claimed as property. Their courtroom victory in January 1856 led to one of the largest legal emancipations in American history, and certainly the largest anywhere west of Texas.[9] Biddy, her three daughters, and ten other women and children were, in the words of the California district judge, "free forever."[10]

But what would "freedom" mean? Biddy's new home was an unwelcoming, even dangerous place for people of color. Antebellum Los Angeles had a well-honed reputation for violence and mob rule, with a murder rate fifty times higher than that of New York City.[11] The Southern migrants who comprised a majority of the town's US-born population still viewed those like Biddy as property, not people.[12] When the Civil War reached the Pacific Coast, many of these Southern transplants rushed into the arms of the Confederacy. And in the Reconstruction years that followed, they spearheaded an anti-Black political backlash that drew envious accolades from rebels and revanchists across the country. Los Angeles remained, in many ways, the far western outpost of the rebel South.[13]

Unbowed by these obstacles, Biddy began a long, slow, improbable rise up the socioeconomic ladder of her adopted hometown. She took the last name Mason and formed a nursing practice to serve the needs of people across the city without regard for wealth, status, or race. With money earned from healing, she invested in Los Angeles real estate. And with money earned from real estate, she continued to heal Los Angeles through an array of philanthropic ventures. Even the erratic economy of nineteenth-century Los Angeles, gyrating from boom to bust, didn't destabilize Mason's investment strategy. The land she developed in downtown Los Angeles occupied a core part of what later became known as the "Wall Street of the West." By 1890 she was one of the wealthiest Black women west of the Mississippi. Estimates placed her net worth as high as $100,000 (nearly $4 million today).[14] That wealth would continue to grow after Mason's death, seeding the fortunes of a Black family dynasty in Los Angles.[15]

Even more durable than her fortune was her faith. To truly understand Mason and her transformational impact requires an appreciation of her Christian belief, which sustained her through decades of enslavement and continued to guide her in freedom. As soon as Mason was able, she co-founded Los Angeles's first Black house of worship, then bankrolled many of the church's operations through its unsteady early years. Today First African Methodist Episcopal Church of Los Angeles boasts a membership of nearly twenty thousand. Her faith also inspired decades of philanthropy, a far-reaching "gospel of giving."[16] At the heart of her ethic was a radical notion: that all those in need deserved care. Her philanthropic activities extended far beyond her own community to include Indigenous inmates, Chinese immigrants, and white laborers, along with countless other Angelenos. According to a biographer, writing decades after Mason's death, "The name of Biddy Mason is reverenced in the City of Los Angeles where her kindness to the poor is fresh in the minds of the public."[17]

Mason's success was singular but it wasn't solitary. *The Boundless Biddy Mason* is simultaneously the biography of an individual, of a community, and of a city in its formative years. The enslaved women and children who huddled together in the county jail in January 1856 became the freedpeople who transformed Los Angeles in the decades thereafter. They founded many of the first Black institutions in Southern California and formed the residential nexus of the city's permanent African American community. Los Angeles would become a magnet for Black refugees from the Jim Crow South, who sought the opportunities that Mason and her neighbors made possible. By the early twentieth century, LA boasted the highest rate of Black homeownership of any major city in the country.[18]

There were no shortcuts to success along Biddy Mason's long road. Hers was a journey of Odyssean proportions, a survival story on a continental scale. From Georgia to California. From slavery to freedom. From poverty to fortune. From dislocation to home.

. . .

Despite the scope of her journey and the scale of her success, much of Biddy Mason's life story is still unknown. She has never before been the subject of a book-length biography. There have been numerous shorter treatments of her story, including newspaper articles, blog posts, and microbiographies from major publishing houses. Yet many of those portrayals perpetuate misconceptions and reproduce common fictions about her life. The most recent publications are among the most erroneous. Amid growing interest in Black history, we still see only faintly one of the most remarkable African American figures in US history.[19]

Much of that oversight can be traced to the intrinsic challenges of the subject matter and the silences of the archive: "the wall of slavery" behind which so many Black Americans have vanished.[20] The authors of most early records on the subject were slaveholders themselves. As a rule, they didn't express interest in the humanity of those they held as chattel. To the men who owned her, Biddy was just a line in a ledger, another "hand" to work the earth. Biddy appears by name in a known record for the first time in 1848, roughly thirty years after her birth.[21] The lives of enslaved people, even those who later rose to prominence in freedom, come to us only in fragments.[22]

The trauma of enslavement imposes another obscuring layer over the historical record. A combination of forced illiteracy and acute suffering prevented the vast majority of enslaved people from recording their histories. True, some among the fortunate few who escaped from bondage documented their stories. But they were the exceptions. Rather than record their experiences, many freedwomen like Mason learned to conceal them, to cloak their inner selves from the intrusion of others. This was a survival strategy that gave them a degree of autonomy over their personal lives and shielded them from further interrogation. Mason rarely ever spoke about herself in the surviving documentation. Instead, she dedicated herself to others, asking no reward beyond the satisfactions of compassion.[23]

And then there's the problem of place. The most recognizable Black women of early American history—Phillis Wheatley, Sojourner Truth, Harriet Tubman—led the freedom struggle from the East, closer to the nation's political nerve center and cultural capitals.[24] Biddy Mason, however, accomplished her most lasting achievements in a frontier town at the far edge of American settlement. News from nineteenth-century Los Angeles, no matter how remarkable, rarely made national headlines. Biddy Mason became a household name among many Angelenos, but her fame didn't spread much further than that. The subsequent generation of historians barely bothered to look for Black Westerners. In the words of Walter Prescott Webb, the West was defined by its lack of "water, timber, cities, industry and Negroes."[25] Some of these geographic prejudices persist. California is all-too-often relegated to "regional" history, whereas what happens in, say, New York is deemed part of the national story.

The Boundless Biddy Mason challenges this pinched view of American history. It aims to broaden our field of vision and to center people and places often deemed marginal. After all, African American history runs the length of the continent, and its early pioneers could never be confined to a single region. This is not a work of hagiography by any measure, but it does seek to enlarge the American pantheon, to make space for an enslaved Black woman who traversed the country, outwitted her captors, foiled her detractors, and helped build a modern metropolis.

. . .

Just because much of Biddy Mason's life story is unknown does not mean that it is unknowable. Generations of historians, writers, and archivists have prepared the way for a deeper understanding of Mason and her world. The imprint of her life is evident, so long as we look closely—at the institutions she founded, the communities she built, the lives she touched, and the drama that unfolded around her.

The research for this book rests on a bedrock of scholarship—much of it overlooked and underappreciated—of an earlier generation of Black women writers and scholars. The historian Delilah Beasley, the journalist Charlotta Bass, and the archivist Miriam Matthews preserved the memory of Biddy Mason at a time when most Americans were inclined to forget. In her self-published *The Negro Trail Blazers of California* (1919), Beasley recorded an interview with Mason's eldest daughter in addition to other key biographical information. Bass's newspaper, *The California Eagle*, published tributes from those who knew and loved Mason. And Matthews, the first Black public librarian in Los Angeles, collected materials on Mason and her family that otherwise would have been lost to history.[26]

Thanks to them and those who came after, we can now speak of the Black West as a small yet growing field of study. For perfectly understandable reasons, African American history still has a strong Southeastern tilt. But a new generation of scholars have pushed the field toward new frontiers, exploring Black communities from Houston to San Francisco and a number of places in between.[27] The work on twentieth-century Black Los Angeles has blossomed recently.[28] And although we know far less about the community's nineteenth-century origins, there have been a few notable investigations into this earlier period.[29] Several studies of Biddy Mason's community—the work of Dolores Hayden, DeEtta Demaratus, Marne Campbell, Amy Tanner Thiriot, and Sarah Barringer Gordon—follow the trails blazed by Black writers and scholars a century earlier.[30]

Building on this pioneering work, I bring more than a decade of archival research into the history of slavery and emancipation in the West. *The Boundless Biddy Mason* draws on a host of previously underutilized and forgotten sources—court records, property deeds, tax assessments, census data, unpublished memoirs, and newspaper accounts—to peel away layers of misunderstanding and occlusion that have surrounded Mason's story. I attempt to assemble the shards of her life story into something akin to a biographical mosaic, a collection of fragments that, when taken together, constitute a whole.

There is much, however, that is simply unrecoverable. This book is written in a spirit of humility, in recognition of the vast unknowability of so much of the past. Readers looking for an intimate history of Biddy Mason's life will be disappointed. We know about the many people she aided, the institutions she sustained, and the city she helped build. But we understand very little about her inner life. There are no personal letters, diaries, or other writings in her hand. Her will is marked with an X. The identity of much of her family, including her parents and the fathers of her children, remains a mystery that may never be solved. Silence envelops much of her story.

But silences often speak. This is the paradox that a new generation of thinkers, Black feminist scholars foremost among them, have unpacked. They concede the limitations of the archive while also mining those deficiencies for new insights into the lives of the forgotten. What's absent from the historical record, these scholars show, can often tell us as much as what's there. To summon the lives of the enslaved, they make space for supposition and even imagination. I follow their methodologies in reconstructing the life of Biddy Mason, always careful to indicate when the paper trail runs thin and where informed speculation supplements the documentary evidence. I also rely heavily on historical context to explore the world that Mason shaped and which shaped her in turn. Thanks to these insights and techniques, honed by generations of scholars, the life of Biddy Mason is now recoverable as never before.[31]

. . .

The Boundless Biddy Mason expands outward from a single life to reconstruct a community, a city, and a nation during a period of revolutionary transformation. Improbable and often counterintuitive, Mason's story compels us to see once-familiar narratives in new ways: the rise and fall of American slavery; the conquest and settlement of the American West; the Civil War and Reconstruction; and the long struggle for African American rights.

This is a book about slavery—how the Southern plantation regime spread its tentacles across the continent in the mid-nineteenth century, infiltrating places now considered bastions of pluralism and progressivism. It did so primarily through peripatetic slaveholders like Robert Smith, the man who owned Biddy, her three daughters, and ten other women and children. He was the largest slaveholder in California by the mid-1850s, but he wasn't the only one. As many as fifteen hundred African Americans were forcibly transported from the slave states of the South to the frontier outposts of the West. They herded livestock, cultivated fields, tended to homesteads, and pulled gold from California's riverbeds—all to the profit of their enslavers. Often they labored beside Indigenous captives. The

American slave regime, as Biddy herself discovered, was as adaptable as it was expansive.[32]

This is a book about freedom—how Mason and other Black Americans ultimately dismantled that continental slave regime and built something far more enduring in its place. California was not born free through its putatively antislavery constitution. It was *made* free by people like Mason, whose historic courtroom victory in 1856 propelled a wave of self-emancipations that fatally weakened the institution of Black bondage in the West. That was just the beginning, however, of the long struggle for Black civil rights in California. To make their freedom meaningful, Mason and her peers erected churches, schools, and a new class of Black political leadership. It was a slow, grinding process, fraught with internal struggles and external obstacles. But by 1890, Mason could look with pride on what she had built: a Black community of more than one thousand in Los Angeles, endowed with the institutions and a collective spirit that would see them through the battles to come.

This is a book about hope—how families and communities struggled forward even when the struggle seemed lost. What makes Mason's accomplishments even more remarkable was her timing. Her twilight years witnessed the dawn of Jim Crow, the apartheid regime that marked the so-called nadir of American race relations and cast a pall on prospects for Black advancement across much of the country. Yet as Jim Crow sunk its talons into the South, Mason and her peers forged a new era of opportunity for African Americans in the West. Her good works provided a refuge, a place where Black people could dare to dream, a beacon for generations to come. And for us today her story offers a broader understanding of African American history. The view from Biddy Mason's Los Angeles presents luminous snapshots of Black progress in an era so often characterized by violence, retrenchment, and decline.[33]

This is a book about an iconic American place—how Los Angeles, through the efforts of founding mothers like Mason, rose from frontier backwater to a modern metropolis. The tumble-down cattle town she first encountered in 1856 bore no trappings of the city it would eventually become. Single-story timber buildings and a patchwork of adobe dwellings lined the narrow dirt streets. Saloons and gambling dens proliferated. Lynch mobs raged wantonly. By 1890, however, Los Angeles was a city transformed, the product of one of the great real estate booms in American history. Streetcars trundled down paved streets, electricity illuminated homes, water flowed through miles of pipes, and stately houses and brick business blocks sprouted like clover. The city we now recognize as LA was taking shape. Mason's property was at the heart of it all.

Above all, this a book about a remarkable individual—how one woman rose from nothing and lifted others as she climbed.[34] It's the odyssey of Biddy Mason's struggle to survive, to preserve her family against all odds, and at long last to find home on the far edge of the country that she traversed. Along the way there were dark days too numerous to count. Yet her courage never flagged when it mattered most. She battled the worst instincts of American life, those demons of division, exclusion, and exploitation that still today often crowd out the better angels of our nature. We need her story now, more than ever. Who better to renew our hope for a brighter tomorrow than someone who triumphed over our bleakest yesterdays?

To understand how she did it, we have to travel thousands of miles east and decades earlier, to the beginning of Biddy Mason's long road. There we'll find a bone-weary Black girl staggering along a muddy trail to Mississippi, into the rotten core of slavery, where tens of thousands went and few ever emerged.

A NOTE ON NAMES

For the first nine chapters of the book I refer to the subject of this biography simply as "Biddy." This is done not out of disrespect or to create a sense of casual familiarity but rather for the sake of historical continuity. Biddy lacked a last name until she adopted one in 1856. Reference to a surname before she selected one herself would be anachronistic. I therefore honor the name her family gave her (Biddy) in the first half of the book and the name *she* chose (Mason) in the chapters thereafter.

PART I Slavery

1 Mississippi Bound

They came, first by the hundreds and then by the thousands. Gangs of enslaved people, bound together by ropes and chains, could be found on nearly every road and waterway leading into Mississippi's cotton heartland in the early 1830s. Some arrived by boat, forced onto any brig, schooner, or steamship that would carry them. Others covered some of the journey by train, packed into cars like cattle. The majority came on foot in groupings known as coffles. Most coffles contained about thirty to forty enslaved people, though sometimes more than two hundred men, women, and children marched in a single cargo.[1]

Observers witnessed, often with a shudder, the ghostly spectacle of slave coffles moving across the Southern landscape. The men were generally chained together, with ropes around their necks and shackles around their hands, as women and children trudged beside them. Only the very young and the infirm were permitted to travel in the wagons that accompanied a coffle. Chains clattered as the enslaved shuffled toward market, "tramping through the waxy ground on foot and . . . shivering with cold," according to one horrified observer.[2] In this way a coffle could cover up to twenty-five miles a day. Crowds often gathered as these miserable parades passed. Some observers likened them to giant serpents, snaking their way

We'll probably never know if Biddy's birthplace, Hancock County, Georgia, once contained vital records related to her early life. The county courthouse and its archives burned in 2014, leaving this charred metaphor for the challenges of uncovering her story. Courtesy of Brian Brown.

westward. In truth they were more like funeral processions, rending the air with the sound of weeping and wailing as the despondent captives slogged toward "another land of sorrow in a far off southern country."[3]

The scene was so common that no one would have taken any notice of an exhausted Black girl, yet another involuntary migrant in the relentless human traffic, trudging along one of these highways of captivity. She was nearing the end of her five-hundred-mile forced journey from Hancock County, Georgia, where she had been born into bondage in 1818.

No records survive from that early stage in her life. We only know the year and place of her birth from testimony she later provided. The identity of her mother and father are mysteries. As for siblings, their names aren't recorded in any extant account. Nor do we know who owned her in Georgia or who first purchased her in Mississippi.[4] If any of the plantation records from her home county mentioned her by name, perhaps in a ledger or bill of sale, we'll likely never find out. Most such records were destroyed by fire. Like most enslaved African Americans, she lacked a legal family name. She was probably called Bridget at birth. But she always went by Biddy.[5]

Biddy's Mississippi ordeal involved a series of scarring experiences: transport, sale, and separation from the only family she had ever known. If she was spared the harshest plantation tasks during her childhood in Georgia, the same couldn't be said of her adolescence in Mississippi. She was now a field hand at the leading edge of the cotton frontier, where fortunes rose and fell as rapidly as human beings were bartered and discarded.

. . .

Biddy's forced migration belonged to what historians call the "Second Middle Passage," a terrestrial sequel to the aquatic first Middle Passage that carried captives from Africa to plantations across the Americas. Between 1800 and 1860 roughly one million enslaved Black people were forced on the internal trade from the seaboard states to the Southern interior. Like Biddy, most victims of the Second Middle Passage were bound for the rich cotton and sugar frontier in Louisiana, Alabama, and Mississippi.[6]

According to her later testimony, Biddy's forced journey from Georgia began when she was just five years old. She then disappears from all known historical records for a period of about fifteen years. Within that time she was sold and bought, perhaps multiple times.[7] The exchange could have taken place at any number of junctions—plantations, county courthouses, hamlets, or larger cities. Nearly every town in the region contained a slave pen or depot, where Black people were confined before being auctioned to the highest bidder. Wherever and whenever she was eventually purchased, Biddy's experiences would have followed a common pattern: inspection, sale, and finally relocation to her new farm or plantation.

First, she would have been closely assessed—perhaps even violated during her teenage years—by potential buyers. "The slaves were stripped naked, and carefully examined, as horses are," wrote an abolitionist observer at a Southern slave market. "Every part of their body, from their crown to their feet, was rigorously scrutinized."[8] Upon request, prospective buyers could examine a woman's genitals to check for venereal disease, a prolapsed uterus, or anything else that could conceivably impact their child-bearing potential. Many white men did more than merely examine, however. “The slave-pen is only another name for a brothel,” according to a Black man named John Brown, who was himself sold as an adolescent. “What passes behind the screen in the auction-room, or in the room where the dealer is left alone with the ‘chattels’ offered to him to buy,” Brown continued, “only those who have gone through the ordeal can tell.”[9]

The process reduced Biddy to a commodity in the eyes of her prospective buyers. The “flesh-mongers” of the South, according to Frederick Douglass, drove their slaves to market “to be sold like horses, sheep, and swine, knocked off to the highest bidder.”[10] In some instances sellers graded enslaved people using a scale that eerily prefigured the meat rating system from the US Department of Agriculture. The most valuable field hands received a rating of 1 or A1 Prime.[11]

Traders resorted to a number of ruses to boost the sale price of their human property. They dyed slaves’ hair, shaved gray whiskers, dressed them handsomely, and forced them to sing and dance to display a cheerful disposition. But heartbreak was hard to disguise. As William Wells Brown, an enslaved man forced to work in a New Orleans depot, recalled: “I have often set them to dancing when their cheeks were wet with tears.”[12] Some enslaved people were able to manipulate their own market value. For instance, they could complain of ailments or adopt a disagreeable attitude with prospective buyers. One way or another, however, they would be commodified and carried off.[13]

Once buyers completed their inspections, the purchasing began. Such scenes were social events for white Southerners. Lawmakers in the Louisiana state legislature, for instance, often left their seats to attend auctions in Baton Rouge. When Charles Ball was put up for sale in Columbia, South Carolina, on the Fourth of July, “a great crowd of people gathered . . . many of whom were intoxicated, and sang and shouted in honour of free government, and the rights of man.”[14] The irony was lost on the jubilant crowd. But it was agonizingly apparent to Ball as the auctioneer’s hammer fell and he, like Biddy, was carted away to an unknown future.

. . .

In the process of sale, Biddy was pried from her family and the broader Black community that had reared her from infancy. “There is not, beneath the sky, an enemy to filial affection so destructive as slavery,” wrote Frederick Douglass. It "does away . . . with families."[15] Indeed, roughly half of all enslaved families were shattered as a result of the interstate slave trade.[16] We don't know whether Biddy's was broken in Georgia or in Mississippi, or precisely when those family ties were forcefully sundered. But we do know that it was permanent. By the time she reached young adulthood, Biddy was utterly alone.

Forever after, those who had been amputated from their families as children could recall the sensations—the smells, the sights, the burning terror—of that moment.[17] Biddy would have been no different. "I can remember the scene as if it were but yesterday," Elizabeth Keckley wrote of the sale of her father. "How my father cried out against the cruel separation; his last kiss; his wild straining of my mother to his bosom; the solemn prayer to Heaven; the tears and sobs—the fearful anguish of broken hearts."[18] The cries from recently separated family members converted "the auction-room into a perfect Bedlam of despair," recalled the formerly enslaved John Brown. "I cannot think of it without a cold shiver."[19]

The trauma of separation left psychological scars impossible to measure. According to Henry Box Brown, who was pried from most of his family at an early age, the ordeal of sale "is a thousand fold more cruel and barbarous than the use of the lash which lacerates the back." For sale, Brown wrote, "lacerate[s] the soul."[20] After being ripped from her son and daughter, a woman named Eliza continued "talking of them—often *to* them, as if they were actually present," wrote Solomon Northup in *Twelve Years a Slave*.[21] Another mother continued to knit clothes for her long-lost children.[22] In the coming decades, Biddy would be uprooted multiple times, each experience a searing reminder of her family's fragility. The surname that she later selected for herself was likely an attempt to symbolically rebind the family ties that were sundered during her childhood and adolescence.

Enslaved families fought against their own destruction with whatever tools they could muster. Some Black people even killed to resist the sale of their loved ones. A man in Saint Louis, for example, emptied a double-barreled shotgun into his owner to keep his wife from the auction block. Others stabbed, kicked, clawed, and poisoned in desperate attempts to hold their families together. Violence against slave traders reached such a point in the 1830s that white people in Virginia began to fret over the long-term security of their most lucrative export.[23]

The most common modes of resistance were nonviolent. Flight was the preferred recourse for countless enslaved people. To guard against escape, slaveholders often concealed their plans for an upcoming auction, or imprisoned Black people in jails and pens prior to sale. Still, no amount of subterfuge could prevent the heart-wrenching protests of soon-to-be separated family members. "The greatest orator I ever heard was a woman," according to John Randolph of Roanoke, a slaveholding congressman. "She was a slave and a mother and her rostrum was an auction block."[24]

We can only speculate about what Biddy and her loved ones would have done to avoid separation. Like so many other enslaved parents, her mother or father may have implored their owner, slowed their work pace, broken tools, or fled the plantation altogether. These "weapons of the weak" were the only means available. To prevent the breakup of their family, however, was beyond their power.[25]

For enslaved families like Biddy's, the process of sale was catastrophic; for traders it was routine. One scholar calculated that between 1820 and 1860 an enslaved person was sold every 3.6 minutes in the South. More recent work suggests that the rate of sale may have been even higher. Fleshmongers auctioned off one of every three young enslaved people in the Upper South. In total two million Black people were bought and sold, most of them locally, in the forty years before the Civil War.[26]

Much of the Southern economy rested on the profits derived from these sales. By 1860 the South's four million enslaved people were worth a combined $3 billion. That amounted to three times the total capital invested in railroads across the country, seven times the amount invested in banks, seven times the value of all currency in circulation across United States, and roughly forty-eight times the total expenditures of the US government that year. By that point, human property was also worth more than the assessed value of all real estate within the slave South.[27]

The sale of human beings was just one peg of the slave economy, however. The exploitation of their labor was the other. Biddy's Mississippi ordeal had only just begun.

. . .

Biddy's forced removal coincided with, and indeed helped fuel, one of the great economic revolutions in world history. When she was born in

1818, American cotton had only recently begun its spectacular rise in the international marketplace. By the time she turned twenty—prime age for a field hand—the crop had claimed a dominant share of America's total trade. Soon the United States would account for nearly two-thirds of the world's cotton supply.[28]

White Americans had been experimenting with cotton in Mississippi since the 1790s. But only in the 1830s did a combination of cheap land, easy money, and mass importation of enslaved people spark what contemporaries called the "flush times" of the Southwest. By the end of the decade Mississippi grew more cotton than any other American state, nearly a quarter of the nation's total crop. Mississippi was the world's cotton heartland. And Biddy was in the thick of it.[29]

Biddy was just one of thousands of African Americans dragged into the state during the decade. Although Mississippi had banned the interstate slave trade in its 1832 constitution—in response to fears of slave rebellion—the clause was honored in its breach. In fact, more Black people were sold into the state after the constitutional ban than ever before. There were 65,000 enslaved people in Mississippi in 1830. Within six years the slave population surged by roughly 250 percent, to 164,000. Mississippi now had a Black majority.[30]

Forced importations followed forced deportations. The US policy of Indian Removal—that is, the expulsion of Native people from their homelands—devasted the Indigenous communities of Mississippi. Prior to 1830, the Choctaw and Chickasaw nations controlled the northern half of Mississippi, with the Choctaw alone occupying ten million acres. But the state and the federal government, spurred on by the rapacity of land-hungry settlers, forced most of Mississippi's Native residents to accept treaties and make the dangerous journey to Indian Territory. Tens of thousands of Indigenous people were exiled from Mississippi in the 1830s. They left behind friends, family, homesteads, livelihoods—and some of the finest cotton-growing land in the country.[31]

What resulted was a land rush, comparable to few other migrations in American history up to that point. The government set Mississippi land prices at just $1.25 an acre, creating a frenzy of speculation and settlement on former Native land and beyond. In 1833 alone the federal government sold more than one million acres in Mississippi, twice as much as in any other state. Buyers snapped up another three million acres in 1835. That was more land than had been sold in the entire country just a few years earlier.[32] Counties that hadn't existed prior to 1830 had Black majorities within several years.[33] Hinds County, where Biddy lived and labored by the mid-1830s, if not earlier, was an epicenter of this land rush and the cotton boom that followed.[34]

Those who witnessed the California gold rush roughly two decades later would claim Mississippi as its antecedent—with cotton, rather than gold, providing the lure. "Every road" leading to the region was "a vagrant stream of enterprise and adventure," according to one former resident. Slave ownership was "remunerating," he wrote, "as it had never been remunerated before," creating fortunes where none existed only a few years earlier. Amid this headlong rush, state banks printed bills by the sheet and "prices rose like smoke," he continued.[35]

But as with smoke, all that wealth could be blown away in an instant.

. . .

White Mississippians' prosperity rested on volatile foundations. Even the lustiest boosters and wealthiest opportunists couldn't entirely overlook the warning signs. Breakneck development had stirred a toxic brew of rampant speculation and violent exploitation, with few institutional restraints to check settlers' worst instincts. The result was a frontier where the venal and the predatory prospered—and the enslaved perished.[36]

The prospect of quick wealth drew a deep cast of unsavory characters: swindlers, counterfeiters, bandits, pettifoggers, horse thieves, land speculators, corrupt politicians, and, of course, hordes of slaveholders. The Southwest, according to one of the region's sharpest critics, was a land of "credit without capital, and enterprise without honesty."[37] Wealth was there for those who could seize it fastest. Although the famous French traveler Alexis de Tocqueville found much to admire in America, he detected a sinister edge in the nation's frontier settlements. "The Americans who . . . plunge into the western wilderness," he wrote, "are adventurers impatient of restraint, greedy of wealth, and frequently men expelled from the States in which they were born."[38]

The heedless rush to frontier riches produced perhaps the most vicious, degrading slave regime anywhere in the United States. As the enslaved themselves attested, conditions became progressively worse as one moved west. “The treatment of slaves is mildest near the borders, where the free and slave states join,” Moses Grandy wrote. “It becomes more severe, the further we go from the free states.”[39] In Mississippi the rations were leaner, the lodgings cruder, the punishments harsher. The most enduring (and misleading) images of the Old South feature stately, colonnaded plantation homes, on the model of Tara from *Gone with the Wind*. But Biddy’s experiences in Mississippi would have looked far more like the scenes of frontier squalor from William Faulkner’s *Absalom! Absalom!* than anything in Margaret Mitchell’s plantation romance.

When she arrived in Mississippi, Biddy would have encountered little more beyond miles of forest, canebrakes, and bayous. The job before her was to convert this thicketed and swampy landscape into acres of cotton fields. The work was backbreaking, as Louis Hughes, a contemporary of Biddy’s, recalled of his enslavement in Mississippi. “The trees, except the larger ones, were cut down, cut into lengths convenient for handling and piled into great heaps . . . and burned,” he wrote. “The undergrowth was grubbed out and also piled and burned.”[40] Other tasks included uprooting stumps, digging wells, and erecting fences.[41]

Material niceties in this pioneer stage of plantation development were few and far between. When not felling trees or grubbing the undergrowth, Biddy and others would have been forced to construct shelters for slaveholders and their families. The enslaved themselves generally lived in tents. Only after the land was cleared and their owners comfortably situated were the enslaved allowed to build their own crude and cramped shanties.[42]

Then the planting commenced. To satisfy Europe’s craving for cotton, enslaved people were driven to the limits of human endurance. Planters and overseers in the major cotton-producing regions, including Hinds County, were notorious for the punishments they inflicted in pursuit of profit.[43] John Brown discovered this when he was sold as a child from Virginia to a plantation in the Deep South. There, the daily routine of cotton picking became a Sisyphean ordeal. Every time he reached his daily cotton quota, the figure was raised. Every time he fell short, “the whip was liberally applied to keep me up to the mark.”[44] Suffering tracked the price of cotton. "When the price rises in the English market, even but half a farthing a pound," Brown recalled, "the poor slaves immediately feel the effects, for they are harder driven, and the whip is kept more constantly going."[45] This was Biddy's waking nightmare on the Mississippi cotton frontier.

. . .

Mississippi's harsh climate and brutal work regime produced conditions ripe for rebellion. And Mississippi's slaveholders knew it. Even as they repeated reassuring lies about their contented workforce, slaveholders fretted incessantly about the prospect of an uprising. As the *Vicksburg Register* put it in 1831, "We repose on a volcano."[46]

White anxieties stemmed from several factors, including simple arithmetic. Black people outnumbered white residents, sometimes overwhelmingly, in multiple Mississippi counties. In parts of cotton-rich Madison County, for instance, the ratio of slaves to slaveholders was roughly fifty to one. Control over Black laborers' movements was made difficult by the sparsely settled and widely scattered white population. The rush to seize land and plant cotton left Mississippi with few institutions like churches and schools. Neighbors were strangers to one another. In such an environment the paranoid style flourished.[47]

Biddy was just seventeen years old when lynch mobs raged across twelve Mississippi counties. The killings followed from a bestselling 1835 pamphlet, *A History of the Detection, Conviction, Life, and Designs of John A. Murel, the Great Western Land Pirate*, which confirmed what white Mississippians thought they knew: that their enslaved population was on the brink of rebellion, and that white banditti would stoke this unrest for their own criminal ends. With almost farcical melodrama, the pamphlet described a conspiracy by white outlaws to incite a slave insurrection while white provocateurs plundered Mississippi's plantations.[48] When whispers of the feared uprising reached central Mississippi in the summer of 1835, the killings quickly followed.

White mobs scoured the countryside for those they suspected of sowing insurrection. Makeshift vigilance committees passed summary judgment on the accused. Confessions from several enslaved people, extracted under torture, fueled an indiscriminate manhunt that raged for days. Members of the committees acted as judge, jury, and executioner. There were no appeals. On the Fourth of July the so-called Committee of Public Safety in Livingston hanged two suspected white conspirators. Vigilantes murdered an additional nine Black people that day.[49] Most victims were hanged, though some were tortured as well. In Yazoo County a mob apprehended a white teacher, guilty of nothing more than talking to an enslaved man. They stripped him, forced him facedown, tied each of his limbs to a peg in the ground, and proceeded to whip him—a torment known as "slicking." After receiving five hundred lashes, the teacher was hanged and decapitated. His head was sent to a local physician for dissection, and then thrown into the street to be devoured by swine.[50]

Henry Foote, a lawyer from Hinds County and future US senator, recoiled in horror as Mississippi devolved into bedlam. "Cries of alarm... literally rang through the whole community" as "suspected persons, both white and black, were apprehended everywhere."[51] Bodies could be seen hanging from the roadsides and in front of the victims' homes. The sight was "revolting to humanity," according to a young Illinois lawyer named Abraham Lincoln. "Dead men were seen literally dangling from the boughs of trees in numbers almost sufficient, to rival the native Spanish moss of the country, as a drapery of the forest," Lincoln exclaimed.[52]

The total death toll is impossible to determine, given the number of Black people who were murdered away from public view. At least a dozen were executed, though probably far more than that. Not until the Civil War would any part of the South witness a deadlier rash of extralegal violence.[53]

Biddy was likely living in Hinds County, a nerve center of the carnage. We have no evidence that she participated in any kind of violence against Mississippi's slave regime. But the color of her skin was enough to implicate her, especially as paranoia blanketed Mississippi in the summer of 1835. No enslaved person was safe from roving gangs of vigilantes who saw treason everywhere they looked. Biddy probably came face-to-face with violence of some sort. She may have witnessed one of dozens of atrocities perpetrated against enslaved people or been accosted herself. Black life was cheap in Mississippi.

In the space of a few years Biddy and 160,000 other enslaved people had transformed Mississippi from lonesome frontier to the beating heart of the cotton kingdom. And for that they received nothing but an accelerated labor regimen, deepening violence, and the ever-present threat of dislocation. Biddy escaped the slaughter of 1835, but she was still prisoner to the cotton regime. As were her children.

. . .

Three years after the insurrection scare that gripped the state, Biddy gave birth to her first child, a daughter, in Hinds County. She called her Ellen. Nothing about her origins suggested that Ellen would become, in time, one of the wealthiest and most respected African American women in the West. She was, after all, born a slave in an especially deadly section of the South's plantation belt. And unlike many enslaved children, Ellen most likely lacked the support of a father.[54]

The identity of Ellen's father remains a mystery. One tale has it that Biddy, while still in Georgia, managed to slip from her Hancock County plantation and make her way to Cherokee country, where she married a Native leader. The story does not account for the fact Biddy was forcibly relocated from Georgia when she was just five years old, and that she gave birth when most Cherokees had already been exiled to Indian Territory. The legend therefore is almost certainly that—a legend.[55]

The best evidence of Ellen's paternity comes from a later census record. Census takers were tasked with identifying the skin color of those they enumerated, using terms like "mulatto," and "yellow" for people of mixed-race heritage. The census of 1850 listed Biddy as "black" and Ellen as "mulatto." The categorization of skin color was of course highly subjective and wildly imprecise. But the different labels for mother and daughter strongly suggests that Ellen had a white father.[56]

In other words, Biddy was most likely the victim of rape.

The assailant could have been any number of men in Hinds County. Her enslaver (name unknown) is the likeliest suspect. "The greater part of slaveholders are licentious men," according to Henry Box Brown. The bond between husband and wife, Brown continued, "may be utterly disregarded, and their devoted attachment cruelly ignored at any moment a brutal slave-holder may think fit."[57] Slave drivers, overseers, and male family members of her owner may have also had access to Biddy. Or perhaps it was a member of the paramilitary patrols charged with policing Black movement in Hinds County. According to one formerly enslaved person, patrols "would come to our place of enjoyment and drive and whip the husbands away from the wives and use those same women for their own pleasure."[58] Resistance was almost impossible.

Enslaved women lived in constant fear of violation. Like Biddy, Harriet Jacobs suffered sexual abuse from a young age. Her legal owner "told me that I was made for his use, made to obey his command in *every* thing." She hid away in an attic crawl space for seven years to escape his assaults and the cruelty of his jealous wife. Only when Jacobs escaped to New York was she finally free of the "wrongs, and sufferings, and mortifications" peculiar to enslaved women. Biddy would endure these trials for nearly two decades before she found a safe haven of her own.[59]

The paternity of mixed-race children like Ellen was the poorly kept secret of the plantation South. "The mulattoes one sees in every family exactly resemble the white children," wrote the plantation diarist Mary Boykin Chesnut. "Every lady tells you who is the father of all the mulatto children in everybody's household," except of course for those in her own home. "Those . . . she seems to think drop from the clouds," Chesnut sniped.[60]

Fear of reprisal generally ensured the silence of Black women. Jilted plantation mistresses vented their frustrations on enslaved victims rather than their offending husbands. Some mistresses sold mixed-race children to avoid the reminder of their husbands' infidelity. Others made enslaved mothers' lives a daily torment. As described by Solomon Northup in *Twelve Years a Slave*, a slave woman named Patsey endured years of savage treatment from her jealous mistress. Patsey's crime was being the survivor of rape. Rather than admit that their husbands were violent predators, most slaveholding women instead insisted that white men were seduced by Black "jezebels." It was a palatable delusion for them. And one that cast women like Patsey, and perhaps Biddy as well, in the role of aggressor.[61]

Enslaved mothers and mixed-race children therefore often concealed the identity of fathers to shield their families from sale or other abuses. Although Candis Goodwin eventually discovered the identity of her white father, she preferred to keep that knowledge to herself. She instead maintained that a "tuckey buzzard lay me an' de sun hatch me."[62] An aviary origin story, after all, was better than the alternative. Biddy and Ellen, it seems, followed a similar line of self-defense, albeit without any fanciful touches. Neither of them divulged the identity of Ellen's father in any known interview or document.

Silence also reflected the emotional trauma of sexual assault. The psychological scars left by slavery—what historian Nell Irvin Painter calls "soul murder"—are impossible to fathom, much less describe. Elizabeth Keckley devoted just a few sentences to the birth of her only child in her autobiography. "I do not care to dwell upon this subject, for it is one that is fraught with pain." Keckley wrote. "Suffice it to say, that he [her owner] persecuted me for four years, and I-I- became a mother."[63] Her stuttered silence spoke volumes. Biddy's silence may have stemmed from a similarly traumatic experience, an experience too painful to communicate. And so, like many aspects of her early life, she kept that burden to herself.

. . .

The overlapping traumas of Biddy's early years—dislocation, physical violence, sexual abuse—forged a fierce and abiding attachment to those she could hold close. Pried from her family at a young age, Biddy, now a mother herself, fought against the ever-present specter of separation. Her continent-spanning odyssey from slavery to freedom is also the saga of a mother's love. Among the most touching tributes to Biddy, some penned decades later, are those from her own children and grandchildren, in recognition of what she gave and at what cost.[64]

Biddy provided whatever she could for her family, though the demands of plantation labor in Mississippi frequently robbed her of time with Ellen. When she gave birth, Biddy was roughly twenty years old—considered prime working age. Slaveholders, in a rush to wrench profits from the Mississippi frontier, spared no workers from the plantation's relentless needs, certainly not experienced young women like Biddy.

The so-called separate spheres that men and women were expected to occupy in nineteenth-century America didn't exist for enslaved African Americans. When a Swedish actress visited the slave states, she discovered that "black [women] are not considered to be of the weaker sex."[65] Across the South enslaved women could be seen clearing fields, hauling logs, plowing with mule and ox teams, hoeing with heavy instruments, digging ditches, building roads, and ubiquitously picking cotton. As the formerly enslaved Anne Clark recalled, "[I] ploughed, hoed, split rails. I done the hardest work a man ever did."[66] Biddy could have said the same.

Nor did their sex shield Black women from beatings and torture. Like African American men, they were whipped, caned, slapped, shackled, forced into stocks, branded with hot irons, and shot. Even pregnant women received savage beatings. As Moses Grandy recalled, "I seen the overseer beat them with raw hide, so that blood and milk flew mingled from their breasts." His own pregnant sister was so severely flogged that she went into labor prematurely.[67]

New mothers like Biddy could expect only a brief respite from hard labor. Some received a monthlong reprieve from cotton picking and were instead assigned to more sedentary domestic duties. Or they might perform lighter tasks in the fields, such as hoeing potatoes or pulling weeds. Slaveholders granted such concessions not from an abundance of mercy or compassion. Rather, they did so to ensure the survival of valuable enslaved offspring.[68]

All too soon, Biddy would have been driven back into the fields or the main plantation home. Enslaved women typically worked twelve-hour days, six days a week. But during the busy planting and harvest seasons, Biddy's days probably extended to thirteen or even sixteen hours. Such a regimen left precious little time to tend to infant Ellen. "During slavery it seemed lak yo' chillum b'long to ev'ybody but you," according to one formerly enslaved woman.[69] Frederick Douglass put it another way: "The slave-mother . . . has no control over [her children]; the master is even more than the mother, in all matters touching the fate of her child."[70]

As an infant, Ellen probably accompanied Biddy into the cotton fields. Babies were often nestled in boxes, pallets, or quilts at the end of cotton rows, where mothers and other field hands could keep occasional watch over them. Some mothers worked the fields with babies strapped to their bodies, an added burden for what was already backbreaking labor. "Many were the heart-sighs of these sorrowing mothers as they went to minister to their infants," according to Louis Hughes. "Sometimes the little things would seem starved, for the mothers could only stop their toil three times a day to care for them."[71] Infant mortality tracked the rhythms of the work year. Deaths typically peaked in September and October, the height of the cotton-picking season. That Ellen survived in sickly Hinds County in the late 1830s was due to a combination of factors: luck, vigor, and Biddy's tireless devotion to her child.[72]

Biddy's workday did not end when the sun went down and she returned from the fields. That was just the beginning of the "second shift," when enslaved women typically attended to all manner of domestic tasks. They cooked supper, washed and mended clothing, and cleaned their cabins. Often, planters provided their enslaved laborers with yards of cloth rather than readymade clothes. Black women were then required to work evenings to convert raw materials into clothing for their families.[73]

Because young mothers like Biddy worked such long days, childcare was often a communal endeavor. Only on the largest plantations were young children raised within specially-built nurseries. It's far more likely that Biddy kept Ellen by her side through much of the day and shared the responsibilities of childcare with other female members of her enslaved community. That community functioned as an extended family, giving ballast to Biddy who otherwise may have been cast adrift in Mississippi's capricious plantation regime.[74]

That community, however, was brittle. Having already been torn from her first home in Georgia, Biddy knew this as well as anyone. Not long after giving birth to Ellen, the ground was once again shifting under her feet.

. . .

Biddy had arrived in Mississippi during the state's boom years, when the price of land and slaves soared, and profits were pulled from the earth as fast as cotton could grow. But by the end of the decade, the outlook for Mississippi's parvenu planters had dimmed considerably. A crippling financial recession, known as the Panic of 1837, erased generations of wealth within months. Because much of Mississippi's capital rested on a speculative bubble—on wealth promised rather than profits earned, with large liens on yet-unplanted cotton crops—the state felt the full force of the crash. The value of slaves fell by half. The price of cotton, which likewise declined precipitously, didn't recover until the 1850s.[75] Hinds County, where Biddy was held in slavery, had been an epicenter of Mississippi's cotton boom. Now it was ground zero for a society in crisis.

The real victims of the panic weren't the enslavers facing foreclosure;

they were the enslaved facing sale. When Biddy's owner sought to recoup some of the losses he likely sustained during the Panic, the young mother and her daughter presented a simple solution to his financial difficulties. They could be sold together, therefore salving his conscience while also netting him a tidy profit—perhaps as much as $500.

He found a buyer in Franklin County, in southwest Mississippi, some thirty-five miles from the slave market of Natchez. Biddy's new owner was a transplanted South Carolinian with a thirst for land, wealth, and status, coupled with a wanderlust that would propel Biddy across the country and ultimately into a battle to reclaim her family from slavery.

2 Making a Patriarch

Robert Mays Smith was a man on the make. Ambitious and restless in equal measure, Smith sought fortune wherever he could find it. He would uproot his family multiple times, traversing the length of the continent and halfway back again, from South Carolina, to Mississippi, to Utah, to California, to Texas. Even in his later years the hardened look of a perpetual pioneer never left him. He stares from his final portrait with steely-blue eyes toward a distant horizon, as if still searching for that next best place.

Decades earlier, in the late 1830s, Smith had determined that place to be western Mississippi. There, he established a modest homestead with his wife and three young boys. A life of independent farming, however, was never Smith's primary ambition. He chased the white Southern dream: to grow rich off the coerced labor of others.

Smith had spent much of his life adjacent to great wealth, although personal prosperity eluded him thus far. Born in 1804 in Edgefield, South Carolina, he witnessed the transformation of his home county into a wealthy plantation district. While his immediate family lived humbly, his maternal grandparents hailed from the slaveholding elite. His grandfather, William Simon Dean, owned thirty-four enslaved people—a fig-

Robert Mays Smith, pictured here in old age in Texas, traversed the continent in search of fortune, built on the backs of enslaved people. Public domain.

ure that placed him firmly in the ranks of the planter class. Smith likely viewed slaveholding, and the patriarchal authority that came with it, as his birthright.[1]

Smith's marriage to Rebecca Dorn in the late 1820s provided an additional link to the planter elite. The Dorns, like the Deans, sat atop Edgefield's social hierarchy. Rebecca, one of ten Dorn children, was raised on a sixteen-hundred-acre plantation along Sleepy Creek. Thirty to forty enslaved people worked the fields and attended to the Dorn family needs within the household. According to census records, one of those laborers moved with the newly-wedded Robert and Rebecca when they established their own household in a neighboring part of Edgefield.[2]

They would not remain there for long. Smith yearned for a fortune already beyond his grasp in South Carolina, where acreage was expensive and the soil depleted. Mississippi, in contrast, offered cheap land and quick profits for those who could carve farmsteads from the wilderness. By 1830 the rush to the cotton frontier had already begun. The lean, square-jawed

Smith was eager to join. When, that same year, his grandfather died and left him an inheritance of $150, Smith suddenly had the means to relocate.[3]

The view from Robert and Rebecca's westward-bound wagon challenges one of the oldest and most enduring myths of the slave South. The quintessential slaveholder in the public imagination is a sedentary patriarch leading a life of stately leisure. Popular portrayals feature planters sipping mint juleps on their verandas or leafing through musty copies of Walter Scott's chivalric romances beneath the canopies of magnolia trees. The slaveholding South, according to this stereotype, was a quasi-feudal holdover ruled by a backward-looking social class, deliberately cloistered from the concerns of the modern world.[4]

Hard-driving opportunists like Smith, however, were more representative of the Old South. According to a leading historian on the subject, "The antebellum master class was one of the most mobile in history." Mississippi was made by the relentless movement and acquisitiveness of slaveholders. Robert, Rebecca, and tens of thousands of fellow settlers endured hardscrabble frontier conditions in pursuit of land and independence. They were as entrepreneurial and forward-looking as their Yankee counterparts. Upward and downward mobility—into and out of the slaveholding class—was common.[5]

Rebecca was one of those who fell from the slaveholding ranks, at least for a time. It was a jolting transition: from the luxuriant plantation grounds of her childhood home to a roughhewn cabin in Copiah County on Mississippi's southwestern frontier. For the next decade, Rebecca's days would be consumed by an unyielding cycle of cooking, cleaning, spinning, pregnancy, and childrearing. By 1838 she had given birth to one daughter, who died in childhood, and three sons, who survived.[6]

Shortly thereafter, the Smiths moved again—for at least the second or third time that decade. They settled in Franklin County, Mississippi, roughly fifty miles southwest of their previous homestead. Irrigated by the Homochitto River, Franklin sat squarely in Mississippi's cotton belt, where slaveholders monopolized the choicest lands and the highest political offices. The Smiths, however, remained part of the non-slaveholding yeomanry, a demographic that constituted about two-thirds of all white Southern families.[7]

Robert was determined to change that. Years of farming, along with some aid from planter relatives, had provided Robert and Rebecca with a modest foundation. Then the Panic of 1837 hit. The financial depression came as a mixed blessing for the Smiths. On the one hand, the panic sent crop prices tumbling, and thus ate into their main source of income. But the aftershocks of the depression also created opportunities: Enslaved laborers could be purchased for just half of what they cost a few years earlier.

The tax records for Franklin County reveal a new source of Smith family wealth by the turn of the decade. In 1840, Robert was listed as the owner of two enslaved people. A year later he had none, but then he rejoined the slaveholding ranks in 1842 when he acquired one person. Two years later, Smith was taxed for four slaves: two aged five to sixty, and two under five. By 1846 he had acquired an additional four people from the estate sale of Rebecca's father in South Carolina. Smith, in other words, had become a regular buyer and likely seller of slaves.[8]

One of those purchases included a woman named Biddy and her young family.

. . .

Biddy was no stranger to the experience of sale. This was the second or third time that she had been bought since being torn from her community in Georgia. Still, there was no acclimating to the trauma and terror of dislocation. Perhaps she had already heard rumors of the hard-driving man who now owned her—and what was in store. The only comfort she had were her two daughters, Ellen and a newborn baby girl named Ann.[9] For the time being at least, Biddy's family remained mostly intact.

The notable exception was Ann's father, who, as far as we can tell, never joined Biddy in the Smith household. Ann was Biddy's only child listed in the census as "Black," as opposed to "mulatto." That means that her father was probably also a person of color. And because Mississippi possessed a miniscule free Black population, her father was almost certainly enslaved. He might have been Biddy's husband, at least for a short period. In which case, Smith may have deliberately separated the couple, either because he couldn't afford to purchase Biddy's whole family or because he wanted her to himself. Any concrete information on the identity of Ann's father, however, eludes us. He slips from the historical record, just as he slipped—or was ripped—from his family's life.[10]

When Biddy arrived on the Smith farm sometime between 1843 and 1844, she would have faced a labor regimen as varied as it was oppressive. Although probably smaller in size than some of her previous worksites, Smith's land had no shortage of responsibilities to fill Biddy's days and nights. In fact, labor on small farms was generally less specialized and therefore often even more taxing than the work on large plantations. Smith would have forced Biddy into an array of jobs. Her experience in the cotton-growing regions of Mississippi was an asset in the fields. As a mother with caretaking and perhaps even medical experience, she would have also been valued in domestic settings, where she fell under the command of Rebecca.[11]

Domestic labor under the watchful eye of slaveholding mistresses was, according to numerous accounts, a harrowing ordeal. Rebecca was no exception. Raised on a South Carolina plantation, she had been trained to command others from an early age. Now with a labor force of her own, she probably wasted no time in bending Biddy's labors to her will and her needs. Reputedly subject to bouts of illness, Rebecca required careful attention from Biddy and other enslaved domestics. But her illnesses didn't dull her desire for control. As we shall see, she could prove every bit as imperious and cunning as her husband in her attempts to preserve the prerogatives of slaveholding.[12]

The exhausting labor regimen left Biddy with precious little time for the care of her daughters. Ellen, roughly five years old, would have looked after infant Ann for much of the day. Their greatest challenge was survival. Enslaved newborns died at twice the rate of white babies in the nineteenth century, and mortality rates remained frightfully high for Black youngsters in their subsequent years.[13] In addition to caretaking responsibilities, Ellen would have also performed numerous tasks around the Smith farm. Enslaved children like her watched over their owners' white infants. They fetched water and wood, raked leaves, and husked corn. They drove cows to pasture and fed chickens. They cleaned kitchens, washed clothes, and waited tables. They kept fires burning in winter and shooed flies from their owners in summer. They performed, in other words, the innumerable light jobs upon which the comfort of their enslavers depended. Ellen's childhood, if it ever existed, effectively ended by the time Smith purchased her.[14]

Biddy, Ellen, and Ann's living conditions could be characterized as something between crude and utterly abject. As recent arrivals in Franklin County, even Robert and Rebecca would have lived in a humble home of no more than several rooms. Biddy and her daughters were likely housed in an adjacent shanty, as cramped as it was drafty.[15] Frederick Law Olmsted, known today as the designer of New York's Central Park, captured the squalor of slave life on an antebellum Mississippi farm. "The negro cabins were small, dilapidated and dingy," he wrote. "The walls were not chinked, and there were no windows—which, indeed, would have been a superfluous luxury, for there were spaces of several inches between the logs, through which there was unobstructed vision." When Olmsted stepped inside such a cabin, he found the conditions even more deplorable. "Every thing within," he wrote, "was colored black by smoke."[16] Biddy and her daughters would have lived in similarly deprived conditions. After all, Robert Smith's pursuit of wealth depended on the labor, not the comfort, of his human chattel.

. . .

In 1846, Smith acquired an additional laborer and Biddy gained a lifelong companion who would eventually help define the meaning of freedom in the American West. Her name was Hannah. A light-skinned enslaved woman from South Carolina, Hannah was roughly twenty-four—Biddy's junior by about four years—when she arrived in Mississippi with her three children. Robert had purchased Hannah and her children directly from the estate of Rebecca's father, who died that year. Smith paid $1,210. The acquisition brought Robert's enslaved population to eight, and marked him as a man of some means.[17]

Smith's successes were built on Hannah's sorrows. The sale had ripped her from the only community she knew: an extended family of roughly three dozen enslaved people who worked the Dorn plantation in South Carolina. Most notably, the sale separated Hannah from her husband, Frank, with whom she had lived since she was sixteen. One of Rebecca's brothers purchased Frank in the same auction, which broke up the entire Black community of Sleepy Creek. Rebecca and her siblings divided the proceeds from the auction evenly among themselves.[18]

Hannah's connections to the Dorn family ran deep—deeper perhaps than any member of the family cared to admit. She was listed in the census as "yellow" and later described as "nearly white," suggesting mixed-race ancestry going back multiple generations. Hannah had the blood, yet none of the privileges, of slaveholding fathers and forefathers. It's plausible and even likely that Hannah's enslaved mother on the Sleepy Creek plantation had been raped by a member of the Dorn family or a white employee. John Dorn, the family patriarch, may have been the father. In which case Hannah would have been Rebecca's half-sister.[19] It was a tangled family tree, fertilized by coercion and violence, that resembled the famous mixed-race lineage of Thomas Jefferson and Sally Hemings.[20]

Whether or not they were related by blood, Hannah knew Rebecca well before she arrived on the Smith's Mississippi farm. In fact, she was said to have been Rebecca's personal attendant on the Dorn plantation. Presumably, Rebecca directed Robert to purchase her childhood slave from her father's estate sale. Hannah may also have labored in the Smith household when Robert and Rebecca were newly-married and living briefly in Edgefield. Perhaps she already bore the marks of Smith's mastery on her body. And she almost certainly knew of his restlessness, his desires, and his cruelty—the traits that would guide the next decade of their lives together.[21]

. . .

The composition of Robert's enslaved labor force was, from a certain perspective, peculiar. Of the eight people he held in bondage in 1846, only one was an adult male laborer (most likely a young man by the name of Rande).[22] Five of them—Biddy's two daughters and Hannah's three children—were under the age of ten. They were therefore of little use to Robert in the fields, the source of much of his wealth. Why, then, did his two biggest purchases of human property consist of mothers and their young children?

Biddy and Hannah were valuable laborers in their own rights, for one thing. Having come of age in the cotton kingdom, both women would have been trained to plant and harvest cash crops. They had also acquired the skills necessary to tend to Smith's growing family. Hannah would become a well-known midwife in California by the mid-1850s, and she almost certainly knew enough of the practice by the late 1840s to be useful to Rebecca in Mississippi. Biddy, who became even more famous for her midwifery and other medical knowledge in postbellum Los Angeles, acquired many of these skills while enslaved as well.[23]

But it wasn't their *production*, so much as their *reproduction*, that enriched Smith. As strong, healthy women in their twenties, Biddy and Hannah had years of childbearing ahead of them. Put another way, they were long-term investments. That investment paid dividends for the Smiths. Between them, Biddy and Hannah eventually produced eleven children. Those children would make Robert the largest slaveholder in the American Far West by the mid-1850s.

Fellow slave traffickers would have noted nothing unusual about the female-heavy composition of Smith's labor force. As one South Carolina physician wrote, "The principal value of the negro with us is his increase."[24] Sellers routinely advertised enslaved women's reproductive potential. Potential buyers in turn assessed Black women's bodies prior to purchase. They would often knead enslaved women's stomachs to ascertain how many children they might bear, or take them into private rooms to inspect them even more intimately. Biddy may have been examined and probed by Robert in a similar manner.[25]

The Southern obsession with Black women's reproduction is evident in the language slaveholders employed. Women of childbearing age were "breeders," while women who remained fertile into their thirties were called "breeding wenches." Slaveholders generally referred to the birth of Black children as "increase." Comparisons between livestock and enslaved mothers were common. "As much attention is paid to the breeding and growth of negroes as to that of horses and mules," according to one slaveholder.[26] Or as one formerly enslaved person lamented, "women wasn't nothing but cattle."[27] While the births of white family members were recorded in Bibles, births of enslaved children went in business ledgers.[28]

The American slave regime depended on those births. By 1808 the United States had outlawed the international slave trade. Although some traffickers continued to illicitly import captive Africans, the growth in the US slave population from the early nineteenth century on was attributable almost entirely to childbirth. The United States in fact was unique among slave societies in the Americas in that Black births outpaced Black deaths by a wide margin. In 1790 the US slave population stood at just under seven hundred thousand. Within twenty years it had risen to 1.2 million, a 70 percent increase. By 1860 that figure tripled to almost four million.[29]

Historians often refer to the growth of the American slave population as "natural increase." But there was little that was natural about this rate of reproduction. Although enslaved women like Biddy had a number of reasons to desire children, their pregnancies were often coerced by slaveholders.[30] Coercion sometimes took the form of incentives—as reprieves from oppressive daily routines. Pregnant women often performed lighter work and received better rations. Some even received gifts, such as clothing or cash, after the birth of a child. In rarer instances slaveholders permanently excused mothers from work after they had delivered a certain number of babies. "When the family increases to ten children living, I require no other labour from the mother than to attend to her children," one Georgia planter boasted of his supposed magnanimity.[31]

Other slaveholders, however, found beatings and threats to be more effective methods of boosting their chattel population. Forced couplings were common, as was the specter of sale for women who failed to produce offspring. After the sale of her lover, a woman named Lavinia was pressed to quickly marry another man on the plantation. When she refused, she was whipped "in such a manner that it was thought she would die."[32] Some slaveholders even took Black men on circuit to neighboring plantations, where they were compelled to have sex with the enslaved women there. One historian calls this "third-party rape."[33] Whether from personal experience or from the experiences of their loved ones, almost every enslaved person had stories of sexual abuse to tell. That was certainly the case for Biddy and Hannah.

. . .

Who fathered each child born to Hannah and Biddy after they arrived at Robert Smith's farm is nearly impossible to discern. What's clear, though, is that the Smith household was a site of terror for both women. Indeed, the surviving evidence strongly suggests that Hannah and Biddy were the repeated victims of sexual assault. Robert himself was likely their assailant. Indeed, Hannah later testified to the fact that at least one of her children, Henry, was fathered by Smith.[34]

Sexual access may have been one of the main reasons that Smith purchased Biddy and Hannah in the first place. Slaveholders often paid a premium to use Black women in such a fashion. By the 1850s a prime field hand could fetch roughly $1,800 on the New Orleans slave market. But the price for a single "fancy girl"—that is, a victim of the slave South's legal sex-trafficking industry—could reach as high as $5,000. Light-skinned women like Hannah were considered the most desirable and therefore the most expensive.[35]

Two years after her arrival on Smith's farm, Hannah gave birth to a daughter, Jane. Although many of her children were regarded as light-skinned, Jane was especially fair. According to a later report, she "cannot easily be distinguished from the white race."[36] Her father therefore was almost certainly white. Which means that he was probably Robert Smith himself. How can we know this? We can't. Hannah, like many victims of sexual assault, left no record of this particular trauma, even as she explicitly implicated Smith in one of her later pregnancies.

Several conditions suggest that Smith's sexual abuse of Hannah began at an early stage. Farmsteads in Franklin County, Mississippi, in the 1840s were remote and widely dispersed. Hannah, working long days on the farm, would have had limited contact with white men beyond the Smith household. The three Smith sons were all adolescents or younger when Jane was born, leaving Robert as the only adult white man in the family who had regular contact with Hannah. Furthermore, the slave cabins on small farms were generally located close to the main family home, providing Robert with close surveillance of—and easy access to—his labor force. True, he may have employed someone, giving that person access to Hannah as well. Nevertheless, the obvious culprit remains the man who owned her.

The same logic suggests that Smith fathered Biddy's third and final daughter, Harriet, born the same year as Jane. Harriet, like her older sister Ellen, was listed in the census as "mulatto."[37] If her father had been enslaved or a freeman, unless exceptionally light-skinned, Harriet probably would have been considered "black," like her mother. We can again infer that the father was white.

Biddy never formed a romantic attachment after the mid-1840s, as far as we can tell. Even as a freedwoman in Los Angeles, where more partners were available, she remained unmarried. There could be numerous reasons for this. As a tireless philanthropist and entrepreneur, she may have simply been too busy for romantic relationships. Furthermore, by remaining unmarried, Biddy maintained control over her earnings and property. She could dispense those assets as she wished, rather than subsuming them under the estate of a husband.

Trauma may also explain her decision not to marry. That was certainly the case with an enslaved woman named Rose Williams, who had been forced to bear the children of a man she didn't love in order to enrich her owner. When Rose resisted, her enslaver issued an ultimatum: If she failed to reproduce, her family members would be sold off. Rose was sixteen at the time. "After what I does for the massa," she explained, "I's never wants no truck with any man."[38] Biddy may well have felt the same.

Shared trauma, including sexual predation and forced separation from their families, forged enduring bonds between Biddy and Hannah. However unwelcome the source of that solidarity, it nurtured a friendship between the two women that spanned decades and persisted into subsequent generations. In slavery they helped raise one another's children, and in freedom those attachments held firm. Some of the foundational institutions of Black Los Angeles, including the first African American church and the community's school, drew strength from the multigenerational and interfamilial ties that Hannah and Biddy fostered, beginning decades earlier as young enslaved mothers in Mississippi.[39]

. . .

How to bear such suffering? Commodification, separation from family, sexual assault, physical abuse, frighteningly high mortality rates, and a relentless labor regimen—this is what characterized the first thirty-eight years of Biddy's life. In a world marked by dislocation, she could count on just a few abiding constants. The friendship of Hannah was one. The love of her daughters was another. Faith was a third.

Biddy's journey of faith—which would culminate in the founding of one of the most important Black churches in the American West—almost certainly began during her years in slavery. Her introduction to Christianity may have come as a child, while living in Georgia. More likely, however, is that Biddy received her first Christian instruction in Mississippi in the 1830s, when the plantation mission movement began in earnest. In the coming decades, Christian missionaries swept across the South, claiming nearly half a million Black church members by the late 1850s. Countless others, who didn't have the opportunity or the inclination to formally join a church, would have identified as Christian nonetheless. Biddy was probably among that number. She would join a Methodist church as soon as she won her freedom. Not coincidentally, the Methodists had been the most active evangelists in the antebellum era, with a dedicated "mission to the slaves."[40]

Why were white evangelicals so eager for Black converts? Primarily because conversion fed one of the central delusions of the slave regime: that human bondage was a "positive good," a blessing to slave and slaveholder alike. Or, in the words of one of the South's most influential preachers, slavery was an institution "full of mercy."[41] Furthermore, by preaching directly to enslaved people, white ministers and slaveholders could cherry-pick the biblical chapters and verses that best suited their agenda. Obedience was the New Testament virtue that they stressed above all others. The letters from the Apostle Paul, in particular, provided them with a scriptural defense of the slave regime. "Servants," Paul instructed, "be obedient to them that are your masters according to the flesh, with fear and trembling . . . as unto Christ."[42]

What enslaved people were told and what they believed were of course two very different things. They often recognized that the religious instruction they received from their owners was "a system of mere delusion, got up expressly for the purpose of deceiving the poor slaves," in the words of Henry Box Brown.[43] While slaveholders cited Paul and his emphasis on obedience, the enslaved celebrated Moses, who led his people from bondage. On their own time, enslaved elders, preachers, and exhorters crafted a distinct Christian message. They stressed dignity rather than subservience, resilience rather than meekness. At the heart of their message was a vital belief: slaveholding and Christianity were fundamentally incompatible. Slavery, in other words, was a heresy. This was the Christianity that Biddy embraced.[44]

Slaveholders understood the subversive power of the Christian message and therefore vigorously policed Black religion. In 1831 the Mississippi state legislature outlawed independent slave preaching. Slaveholders saw a potential uprising in any gathering of Black people without white oversight. Increasingly, enslaved Christians sought secluded places—gullies, ravines, woods, and thickets—known as "hush harbors" or "brush arbors," where they could practice their faith beyond the anxious gaze of their owners.[45] It's likely that Biddy's faith was similarly circumscribed.

Slaveholders were right to fear rebellion in the religiosity of the enslaved. But it was a rebellion of a different nature from the one they suspected. Black Christianity was not a direct revolt against the slaveholding class but rather a spiritual insurgency against the dehumanization intrinsic to the plantation regime.[46] Faith provided meaning and hope within a system designed to produce resignation and despair. On plantations and small farms alike, enslaved people stole away to pray together, sing together, and plan for better days to come. "It mattered not what their troubles had been during the week" or "how much they had been lashed," recalled Louis Hughes of Black life in Mississippi, "the prayer-meeting on Saturday evening never failed to be held." The sermons they preached and the hymns they sang came from those "inspired" and reflected a faith "tried and true," according to Hughes.[47] Above all, that faith fed the communal belief that they would one day transcend their earthly torments and break free of the chains that bound them. It was a belief Biddy carried forward.

. . .

Among those swept up in the religious enthusiasm cresting across America was an unemployed white Illinois schoolteacher named John Brown. Tall and wiry with lively blue-gray eyes, Brown (no relation to the abolitionist of Harpers Ferry fame) caught "the spirit" in 1841. When his schoolhouse burned down shortly thereafter, Brown took it as a sign and gave up teaching in favor of preaching. He set out for Kentucky with a fellow evangelist and a mere twenty-five cents between them. For the next several years Brown crisscrossed the frontier slave states, finding his most fertile fields in Alabama and Mississippi. There, he and his coreligionists claimed hundreds of converts. Robert and Rebecca Smith were two of them.[48]

Brown's mission was in some respects unremarkable in an era of religious enthusiasm and mass conversion. He was merely one among numerous circuit-riding preachers racing across the American frontier, from town to town and farm to farm. But in one crucial respect Brown and his many converts were strikingly different. They referred to themselves as "Latter-day Saints," or "Saints" for short. Outsiders called them "Mormons."[49]

Brown spoke to his Southern audiences of ancient miracles and miracles yet to come. His prophet was Joseph Smith (no relation to Robert), a struggling farmer-turned-divine messenger and church president. Around 1827, Joseph Smith unearthed a set of golden plates near his farm in upstate New York. They were covered in mysterious runes, which he transcribed and published in 1830 as *The Book of Mormon: An Account Written by the Hand of Mormon upon Plates Taken from the Plates of Nephi*.

The Book of Mormon is a six-hundred-page, thousand-year biblical epic set in the Western Hemisphere. It begins around 600 BC, when a prophet named Lehi leads a band of Israelites out of Jerusalem and eventually toward a new promised land, somewhere in the Americas. (Although the name "America" never appears in the *Book of Mormon*, Joseph Smith later confirmed that Lehi's destination was the future United States.) A family feud among Lehi's offspring descends into a long, bitter war between two factions, the Nephites and the Lamanites. The righteous (though occasionally wayward) Nephites ultimately perish at the hands of the Lamanites. Only the prophet Moroni survives, who reappeared in a vision before Joseph Smith some fourteen hundred years later, instructing him about the Nephites' forgotten history, inscribed on golden plates buried in rural New York. That history had been recorded by Moroni's father, Mormon, who serves as the main narrator for the book that bears his name.[50]

The Book of Mormon is more than a history lesson, however. It's also, like the Bible, a guide to righteous living. The book's central event is a visitation from the risen Christ. In America, Jesus delivers a reprise of the Sermon on the Mount and preaches of atonement for sin through his sacrifice. His Nephite disciples establish a New World Christian church. Those who would follow Jesus's American gospel—the Latter-day Saints—must restore this church and build a new Kingdom of God in anticipation of Christ's coming thousand-year reign.[51]

John Brown carried this message across the South, preaching in fields, homes, churches, schoolhouses, meeting houses, and wherever else listeners gathered. Some days he walked more than thirty miles to find a home that would welcome an itinerant Mormon. When heavy rains saturated northeast Mississippi, Brown waded through "water up to the waist" then hopped aboard a canoe to paddle "through the woods and brush to get to our appointment."[52] More often than not, he met skepticism if not outright hostility. Even members of his own family urged him "to quit preaching such foolish doctrine and go back home to my mother."[53] In Tuscaloosa County, Alabama, "a mob of some sixteen or eighteen men patrolled the neighborhood the evening of our arrival, threatening to lynch the elders and drive them out of the country."[54]

Brown's trials weren't unique for Mormon evangelists. Mobs greeted the Saints wherever they gathered, from New York to Ohio to Missouri to Alabama. One Protestant minister called the Book of Mormon "the greatest fraud of our time in the field of religion."[55] Critics became more imaginative, though no less cutting, in subsequent decades. The book was an "insipid mess of inspiration" and "chloroform in print," according to Mark Twain. "If Joseph Smith composed this book, the act was a miracle—keeping awake while he did it was, at any rate."[56]

Joseph Smith nevertheless inspired devotion from men like John Brown, who persisted against violence, both threatened and realized, to spread the word. Brown estimated that he personally baptized sixty Southerners and witnessed an equal number of conversions. A small handful of those baptisms were of enslaved African Americans.[57] He and his fellow missionaries also established a number of Mormon outposts, known as branches, across Mississippi and Alabama, and ordained elders to lead those branches.[58]

It was during Brown's Southern mission, though not by Brown's hand, that Robert and Rebecca Smith came into the faith. On February 11, 1844, a church elder led Robert into the shallows of a river in Franklin County, a tributary of the Mississippi. His baptism would have followed the standard ritual. "Robert Smith," the elder would have proclaimed, "having been commissioned of Jesus Christ, I baptize you in the name of the Father, and of the Son, and of the Holy Ghost. Amen." Robert would have held the elder's forearm as he was lowered fully into the water and ritually washed of his sins. Rebecca, though raised in a devout Baptist family, followed her husband into the river and into their new faith, much as she had followed him to the Mississippi frontier fifteen years earlier. Neither Biddy nor Hannah nor their children were baptized into the LDS Church.[59]

Biddy held fast to her own faith, though she probably looked on while Smith went under. As she stood there on the river's bank, a witness to Robert's spiritual rebirth, Biddy may have wondered if there was enough water in all the Mississippi to truly cleanse her owner of his sins.

. . .

What drew an ambitious young slaveholder like Robert Smith to the LDS Church? Conversion was risky business. Like all Mormons at the time, Robert would have to endure ridicule and even threats of violence in defense of his faith. Robert's brethren saw "all their relatives turned against them," according to the recollections of another Mississippi Mormon family. "They became outcasts among their own people."[60] The Saints had suffered particularly brutal treatment in the slave South. Less than a decade earlier, Mormon migrants had been accused of abolitionist sympathies and violently ousted from Missouri. Joseph Smith and other church leaders strenuously denied these allegations of abolitionism, but Mormons remained suspect in the eyes of many slaveholders.[61] Meanwhile, Mississippi was still recovering from a horrific wave of proslavery mob violence that had gripped large parts of the state in 1835.

And yet John Brown and his fellow missionaries baptized hundreds of people in the heart of the slave regime. Although non-slaveholding farmers made up the majority of his converts, Brown helped build the LDS Church in Mississippi and Alabama around members of the slaveholding class.[62] A central figure was William Crosby, whose planter father had left twenty-four enslaved laborers to his heirs. Many of the prominent Mississippi Saints were connected to William Crosby through either blood or marriage. John Brown himself joined the slaveholding class when he married Crosby's sister, Elizabeth, who owned several Black workers.[63] At the peak of his wealth, Crosby claimed the labor of a dozen enslaved African Americans. Of all the slaveholding Mormons, only Robert Smith would come to own more people.[64] Some Mississippi neighbors scoffed at men like Crosby and Smith. Others followed them into the faith.

What skeptics failed to appreciate was the spiritual hunger that the LDS Church satisfied—in free states and slave states alike. Religious experiments popped up like mushrooms on the fertile soil of revival America. Every "reading man," according to the American philosopher Ralph Waldo Emerson, had "a draft of a new community in his waistcoat pocket."[65] Yet amid the evangelical fervor of the Second Great Awakening, many seekers still felt a divine absence. They sought a richer, more direct experience of God—through dreams, visions, tongues, and other miracles—than most of the traditional Protestant denominations could provide. They knew they wanted something more; they simply lacked a name for it.[66]

Joseph Smith gave it to them. Mormonism promised a new Zion in America. Whereas most Christians confined the age of prophecy to a distant land and distant past—that is, Israel in the biblical era—Mormons brought it into the here and now. According to the Book of Mormon, America was the "choice land above all other lands," and its present-day inhabitants were the latest links in a glorious genealogy.[67] God spoke through Joseph, as He once did through the Old Testament patriarchs. In fact, the Book of Mormon was merely the first in a series of revelations and translations that brought the word of God directly to His chosen people. Joseph Smith continued to receive divine visitations from a who's who of biblical grandees: Moses, Elijah, John the Baptist, Peter, James, and John, among others.[68]

Robert Smith had been striving for more—wealth, land, slaves, and purpose—since he uprooted his young wife from their home in South Carolina roughly a decade earlier. On a certain level, the LDS Church appealed to his visions of grandeur. Whereas Protestants had ministers and churches, Mormons had priests and temples. But it was far more than titles or pomp that drew Robert to the faith. The Book of Mormon spoke to his enduring belief that something better lay just ahead. Like him, fellow Mormons pushed relentlessly toward new frontiers, in pursuit of what they called the New Zion. Mormonism thus endowed Robert Smith's pioneering ambitions with a sense of divine purpose and destiny.

Mormonism also granted immense power and prestige to patriarchs like Robert. Even before polygamy became official LDS policy, Mormons placed "an unremitting emphasis on male dominance," in the words of one scholar.[69] Joseph Smith built his church around an all-male hierarchy and promised them endless progression, even after death. Equally important, the church admitted all men (but only men) into the lay priesthood. When Mormon women claimed that they also had prophetic power, Joseph Smith dismissed their visions. "A woman," Smith declared in 1841, "has no right to found or organize a church."[70] The institution of polygamy—also known as "patriarchal marriage"—reinforced male authority and extended it over multiple wives and vast family networks. Robert never took additional wives, although he probably used Biddy and Hannah as concubines. Regardless, he wouldn't dispute the underlying patriarchal logic of polygamy. The first formal defense of plural marriage, published in 1842, reminded readers that the Tenth Commandment had placed wives alongside servants and livestock as a man's property.[71] Slaveholding preachers cited that same commandment—what one prominent minister called a "patriarchal catalogue of property, having God for its author"—to justify both slavery and male command over the household.[72]

It took more than a decade of crude living in frontier conditions, but Robert had finally attained much of what he sought. Wealth, independence, and mastery over others—precisely the things a Southern patriarch was supposed to possess—were now his. He was the father to a family of six. He was the owner of a rapidly increasing slave labor force. And he was now poised to take a leading position among a group known as the "Mississippi Saints."

. . .

And then the unthinkable happened. Just months after his baptism, Robert Smith's newly adopted church was in crisis. The news trickled down the Mississippi River, from the Mormon city of Nauvoo, where roughly twelve thousand Saints resided. When word reached the new converts in the South, most of them dismissed it as a pernicious rumor, concocted by their enemies to sow dissension among the faithful. But eventually they had to concede that what they heard was true: their prophet was dead.[73]

The details emerged later. Joseph Smith had been imprisoned in a two-story building in Carthage, Illinois, along with his brother Hyrum and two other church leaders. As they awaited a sentencing that would never come, an armed mob marched toward them. The vigilantes rubbed wet powder on their faces to hide their identities as they approached the jailhouse. They stormed the building, blasting shots through the door and into the room that held Joseph. The initial shots struck Hyrum, first in the face, then in the thigh, torso, and shin. Joseph, who was allowed to keep a side arm while imprisoned, had time to fire his pistol into the mob before rushing to the window in a desperate attempt to escape the assassins. Almost immediately, four shots ripped through his body as he tumbled from the building to the ground below.[74]

John Brown heard the news while riding circuit in central Mississippi. At first he refused to believe it. But finally he "became satisfied that it was a fact and I had no more desire to preach to the world." Along with William Crosby and several other Mississippi Saints, Brown rushed to Nauvoo. They had responded to a call for all able-bodied Mormon men to muster in the Mormon city in order "to defend the place . . . [and] to carry with them their arms and ammunition."[75]

Robert, however, opted to remain on his Mississippi farm for the time being. Perhaps he was reluctant to leave his large enslaved labor force to the care of his wife and four adolescent boys. He needed time to ponder his next move. Would he and his family join the main body of the Saints in Illinois, where they would find the fellowship of their brethren? Would they stay in Mississippi, where they had lately prospered? Or would they venture toward a new frontier, where perhaps an even greater fortune awaited?

How Robert Smith and his fellow Saints responded in that moment of crisis would define the next phase of Biddy's life, Hannah's life, and ultimately the contours of American slavery.

3 Overland

Love and terror—the two emotions often comingled for Biddy as she struggled to preserve her family amid Robert Smith's feverish quest for more. Those emotions reached a new pitch in late 1847 with the birth of her third child, a baby girl she named Harriet. Biddy barely had time to recover from childbirth or to revel in the tiny miracle of Harriet before Smith ordered the wagons loaded. They were moving once again. If Biddy pled to delay their departure for the sake of her infant, her appeals fell on deaf ears. Neither the fragility of her baby's life nor the fact that Hannah was now pregnant with her fourth child would deter Smith. His household would set out at the first blush of spring.

The directive had come from the LDS Church itself. Following the assassination of Joseph Smith, armed mobs had driven the Saints from their main settlement in Nauvoo, Illinois, by late 1846. Just a year earlier, Nauvoo held more than twelve thousand residents, surpassing Chicago to become one of the largest cities in the American West. But once anti-Mormon vigilantes finished their work, Nauvoo was little more than a ghost town, haunted by the stillborn vision of Zion. Exiled once again, the Saints went in search of a new homeland. They set their sights far beyond the American mobs that had hounded them at all their previous gathering places. They would journey together to a remote corner of the Great Basin in what's now the state of Utah.[1]

By the spring of 1848 the free and enslaved members of Robert Smith's household were bound for this new Zion as well. But for Biddy and Smith's other Black workers, there was little promise in the Mormon promised land. The trail ahead, lined with hastily erected headstones of unfortunate overlanders, was a potential killing field for Biddy's vulnerable family. Her road stretched for two thousand miles, from southwest Mississippi, across Tennessee, Kentucky, and Missouri, and finally along the Mormon Trail to the Great Salt Lake. It would be one of the longest continuous journeys made by any Black person in the history of American slavery.[2]

. . .

Before anyone set out, the would-be settlers had to overcome a series of crises: in leadership, logistics, public health, and even faith. Biddy and the other members of Robert Smith's household remained in Mississippi at this point. She therefore didn't witness the major movements within the LDS Church, primarily in Illinois, at the outset of the Mormon exodus in 1846. Still, those movements would set the course for her westward journey two years later.

The management of the church's crises fell on the broad shoulders of Brigham Young. After a short power struggle with several other aspirants, Young seized the mantle of the martyred prophet Joseph Smith and convinced a majority of Nauvoo's Mormons to follow him west. Like Joseph, Brigham had risen from rural poverty, compensating for a lack of formal education with religious zeal and sheer force of will. But in manner and appearance, Young was a marked departure from his predecessor. The barrel-chested Brigham was cruder, coarser, and more bellicose than the handsome, smooth-talking Joseph. Young often browbeat his followers and peppered his speech with the occasional profanity. ("Shit," both in noun and verb form, was a personal favorite.) He excused his bite as the natural by-product of his devotion. "If I did not feel so strenuous," Young remarked, "I should not use such language."[3]

Young's style would have been too piquant for, say, a traditional Protestant congregation; but for a people under duress, facing persecution to their rear and a yawning frontier before them, he was an ideal leader. Over the coming years, he marshalled tens of thousands of Mormons westward to build what they called their Kingdom in the Mountains. He ultimately laid claim to roughly one-sixth of the western United States, making him, in the words of a recent biographer, "the greatest colonizer in American history."[4]

One of the first major threats to Young's ambitions and the LDS Church itself was theological. Rumors of polygamy had swirled around the church for years and helped fuel the mob that murdered Joseph Smith. Even some devout Saints condemned the practice. Several of Brigham Young's rivals, including members of Joseph Smith's family, made opposition to polygamy central to their leadership claims. Although some Mormons followed these leaders into splinter sects, the vast majority of Nauvoo Saints clung to Brigham. Like Smith, Young attempted to keep the practice of plural marriage from the public eye. But his preference for secrecy didn't deter him from marrying nearly forty women by 1846, ranging in age from sixteen to sixty-six. Brigham Young was nothing if not prolific. He would acquire fifty-three wives and father fifty-six children over the course of his long life.[5]

Rumors of polygamy Brigham could handle; the weather was another matter. By spring 1846 the LDS Church was essentially an extended refugee camp, strung out across hundreds of miles of sodden terrain west of Nauvoo. The Saints had hoped to cross the Missouri River that season, in time to begin the journey toward the Rocky Mountains. But incessant rain saturated the trails as the migrants floundered in the mudflats of Iowa. Even sunshine brought peril. During a brief dry spell, hordes of rattlesnakes came out to sun themselves. As roughly twelve thousand exiles limped west from Nauvoo, it became increasingly clear that a mass migration beyond the Rockies would be impossible that year.[6]

Instead, thousands of Saints threw up shelter on the western bank of the Missouri River, at a place called Winter Quarters (now a suburb of Omaha). Winter Quarters was Nebraska's first city, although Mormons only intended it as a temporary waystation. It was situated on lands belonging to the Omahas and Otoes, with whom the Mormons negotiated treaties. Clustered in hundreds of longhouses, huts, caves, and hovels, the Saints were easy prey for disease and exposure. An epidemic ripped through the shantytown and surrounding settlements, killing roughly six hundred people by the end of 1846. Hundreds more died the following year.[7]

While most of the Saints huddled along the banks of the Missouri River to await a more suitable season for the overland journey, Brigham Young mobilized a small vanguard party to push west. They didn't have a precise destination, though most agreed that the Great Basin, a sparsely populated corner of Mexico's northern frontier, held the most promise. Young assured his followers that he would know Zion when he saw it.

. . .

Among the pioneers in that first Mormon overland expedition were a handful of enslaved Black men. Their journey was far longer, more arduous, and ultimately deadlier than the route taken by most of their white counterparts. Whereas a majority of LDS migrants left from Winter Quarters, all except one of the enslaved pioneers of 1847 set out from the Deep South before joining with the rest of the expedition in Nebraska. The Southern passage doubled the length of the journey. This was the same road that Biddy would travel the next year, under almost equally trying conditions.

Five Black men in total were selected to join the so-called Pioneer Camp: Green Flake, Hark (Lay) Wales, Oscar (Crosby) Smith, and two men named Henry and Jacob. Only Green Flake left from Winter Quarters. The rest departed from Mississippi. Some of them had converted to Mormonism. Membership in the LDS Church did not, however, alter their enslaved status.[8]

Their passage from the Deep South began in the bleak extremity of winter. They had no say in the matter. Their owners were obeying the instructions of their church leaders. And they were obeying the commands of their owners. Guided by John Brown, the missionary who had converted dozens of Southerners, they started out from southwest Mississippi in January 1847. The small party moved as quickly as possible in order to meet the main body of migrants at the Nebraska trailhead for a planned spring departure.[9]

The weather was cold and wet as they set out from Mississippi. It only got colder as they struggled northward. Brown called it "the severest trip I had undertaken." That meant something coming from a man who made thirteen overland crossings in his lifetime. "The negroes suffered most," Brown added. He didn't specify why, but it's easy enough to imagine the reasons. The four enslaved men were worked harder and outfitted worse than their white fellow travelers. Brown's personal slave, Henry, came down with pneumonia and died on the side of the trail in Missouri that winter. Jacob made it all the way to Winter Quarters before pneumonia took him as well. The two Black survivors joined Green Flake and roughly 150 white Mormons in the Pioneer Camp. Then they were forced west across the next one thousand miles of trail.[10]

Green Flake, Hark Wales, and Oscar Smith proved vital to the success of that journey. They drove wagons, wrangled livestock, and served the white members of the party. As the company approached the Great Basin, the trail became narrower and steeper. The three enslaved men cleared the path, removing rocks and hacking away willows to make way for the wagons. When Brigham Young fell dangerously ill on the final leg of the journey, the slaveholding John Brown formed an advance party with another elder, Orson Pratt. From a high mountain pass in late July 1847, Brown and Pratt finally caught sight of the Salt Lake Valley. Green Flake drove the first wagon into the canyon leading to their destination. This would be their place.[11]

It's often said that this vanguard party suffered no deaths along the trail, a feat that distinguishes the Mormon migrants from most overland companies and perhaps even signifies divine favor for their historic journey. But that's true only if Henry and Jacob aren't counted. They were certainly intended as members of the pioneer expedition when they were forced northward from Mississippi that winter. But when they lost their lives along the way, they also lost their place in history and memory. There is no mention of either of them on two grand monuments in central Salt Lake City, which do in fact honor Green Flake, Hark Wales, and Oscar Smith for their pioneering roles in that expedition. Instead, Henry and Jacob met the same destiny as countless Black pathbreakers before and after them: death and erasure. That miserable fate loomed over Biddy and her fragile young family as well, as they readied themselves for the long road ahead.[12]

. . .

Biddy would travel the same perilous path that these Black pioneers charted from Mississippi the previous year. Yet the Mormon gathering place in the Salt Lake Valley wasn't her original intended destination. While most of the Saints went west by divine mandate, Biddy's wagon company came to Utah only after Robert Smith had exhausted his alternatives.

Robert Smith had no intention of crossing the Rockies, at least not initially. According to one of his sons, Smith "had the Texas fever bad."[13] After a decade of independence, Texas had joined the Union as a slave state in 1846. Its cheap land and fertile soil beckoned ambitious slaveholders like Smith. Although the antislavery republic of Mexico sought to reclaim Texas, a string of US victories in the war against Mexico in 1846 and 1847 ensured that the Lone Star State would remain American—and slaveholding.[14]

Smith, Biddy, and the rest of the household set out for Texas in 1847, making it as far as Memphis before nature intervened and threw them on a radically different trajectory. Heavy rains had rendered the Mississippi River impassable that season. When the levee gave way and the river bottoms flooded, Smith decided to halt his westward journey for the year. He redirected his household to Tishomingo County, Mississippi, where he rented a farm and put his enslaved laborers to work. This is when Biddy gave birth to Harriet, her third daughter. Rebecca also gave birth that season—her sixth living child—named for the martyred LDS prophet, Joseph. Robert Smith was still a devout Mormon, even if he didn't see his future among the brethren.[15]

While wintering in Mississippi, Smith abandoned his Texas dream, for the time being at least. His decision was prompted by a group of US soldiers who passed his farm on their way home from the ongoing US war against Mexico. According to one of Robert's sons, the soldiers "stayed all night at our place," whispering about mountains of gold in California. (Although the historic discovery of gold at Sutter's Mill was still a year into the future, there was enough local knowledge of California's mineral wealth to make this story plausible.) That the United States had recently seized California from Mexico provided an additional incentive for Smith to migrate. Never one to miss out on a profit-making venture, Smith agreed to meet the former soldiers at Kanesville (now Council Bluffs, Iowa, just across the river from Winter Quarters) early the next spring. They would then proceed together to California.[16]

To fund the upcoming journey, Smith may have been advised to sell at least some of his slaves. After all, most of them were children with limited capacities for hard labor or rough travel. To that point in 1847, very few Americans had tested the viability of enslaved labor in the Far West. Many would argue that there were natural limits to slavery, that the institution couldn't survive past a certain line of longitude. Such prognosticators considered it foolish to transport valuable human property across thousands of miles of terrain into what they believed to be an unprofitable climate.[17]

If anyone tried to dissuade Smith, he didn't listen. Instead, he took a calculated gamble and kept all his Black laborers, including Hannah, pregnant with his tenth slave. He may have reasoned that to sell Biddy's or Hannah's children would break their spirits and thus their usefulness as workers. Plus, one or more of those children may have been his own. He probably also reckoned that his human investments would continue to pay dividends. Experience would prove him right.

. . .

By mid-March 1848 they were on their way. Their party consisted of nineteen people in three wagons. Nine of them—Robert, Rebecca, their six children, and a hired driver named John Cook—were white. The others—Biddy and her three daughters, Hannah and her three (soon four) children, and a young man named Rande—were enslaved. They also traveled with a small menagerie of animals: two yoke of oxen, one horse, eight mules, and seven cows. Another party of slaveholding Mormons, led by the tireless John Brown, set out from Franklin County that same month. The two Mississippi caravans traveled independently but most likely along the same route, separated by just a few days. They were both bound for the Iowa trailhead of Kanesville, a journey of roughly one thousand miles from their Mississippi launching points.

So long as the weather cooperated, Smith's company could cover about twenty miles per day. But a combination of bad roads and heavy rain turned much of the journey into a muddy slog. In Tennessee limey roads gave way to rolling hills, made slippery and slowgoing by early spring showers. A storm, which soon "assumed the character of a hurricane" according to John Brown, ripped through southern Tennessee in late March. The weather didn't improve much from there. "We had one of the most disagreeable times I ever saw," Brown wrote of his drenched party in central Tennessee. Wagon wheels and animal hooves churned the trail into a thick gumbo, which clung in large clumps to migrants' feet. Biddy's shoes, undoubtedly of an inferior quality, would have retained the mud and the damp from Tennessee to Kentucky to Missouri.[18]

Biddy spent much of the journey in the rear of the caravan, corralling the company's animals. She likely also helped haul the wagons across streams and bogs whenever necessary. The scarce space inside the three wagons was reserved primarily for the white people in the party. Biddy therefore probably pitched a tent on the side of the road at the end of each day's long march. The cold would have crept into her bones through the sodden earth and canvas, as she huddled close to her three daughters. This was the same route that claimed the lives of the two enslaved men, Henry and Jacob, the previous season. Biddy may not have known about their fate. But she certainly understood that this trail could kill.[19]

The journey was hard enough for a trail-tested adult like Biddy. But it was especially hazardous for the seven children under her care and Hannah's. Biddy's primary concern was Harriet, just months old at the time. Even more vulnerable was Hannah's infant, Jane, born along the trail that April. Hannah was probably allowed to recuperate in a wagon for a limited time after enriching Robert Smith with yet another slave. Biddy, however, almost certainly walked the entire distance. The care of Harriet could be delegated to Biddy's two other daughters, Ellen (roughly ten) and Ann (now about five). Biddy was needed for heavier tasks.

Biddy hobbled into Kanesville with the rest of the Smith party on May 17, 1848. She and her daughters had survived the first thousand miles of their overland journey. The next thousand miles of the trail yawned before them.

. . .

Biddy would walk that trail in the company of even more slaveholders and their human chattel. A week after Robert Smith's party rolled into Kanesville, John Brown's wagon train joined them. Together, they numbered twenty-eight wagons, fifty-six white Mormons, and thirty-four enslaved people. Camped on the bluffs above the Missouri River, the slaveholding overlanders were "quite an admiration," according to Brown.[20] Biddy now belonged to the single largest company of enslaved people to ever attempt a crossing of the Great Plains.

Smith had changed his plans once again. He now decided to join his brethren in the journey toward the Great Basin, rather than striking out independently for the rumored gold fields of California. Brown himself may have convinced (or shamed) Brother Smith to alter his course. After all, the Mormon Zion was the purified image of the vision—new beginnings, open land—that had already drawn Smith westward. Smith's vanity may have also played a part. With ten Black laborers to his name, he was the single largest slaveholder in the group. That distinction gave him a degree of status and authority among the Mississippi Saints. There was also safety in numbers. Westward-bound slaveholders often traveled and settled together. Doing so enabled them to communally police their enslaved laborers on otherwise open frontiers. Smith would need allies. As he soon discovered, his Black workers pursued freedom wherever and however they could.[21]

Before they set off, the Mississippi Saints made a register of all the people and property—and people *held* as property—in their unit. Biddy is listed alongside the other enslaved African Americans forced to make the journey. For an unknown reason her daughter Ann isn't on the list, though she was certainly on the trail. This was the first time that Biddy appeared by name in any extant historical record.[22]

Although Robert Smith was the largest single slaveholder in the group, the extended family of William Crosby accounted for the majority of the enslaved people in that party. William himself owned five people. Crosby's brother-in-law, John H. Bankhead, jointly owned eleven African Americans with his brother George. The Bankheads would have had another two enslaved laborers to their names, but it appears that John sold someone named Malinda and someone named Benjamin to help finance the trip.[23] Enslaved people had therefore already given their lives, their labor, and the value stored in their bodies to propel the Mormons westward.

Members of the newly-formed company faced their first challenge in Kanesville itself. They wanted to get clear of the shantytown, where migrants clustered and disease took root, as quickly as possible. But crowding and high winds at the ferry crossing along the Missouri River delayed their planned departure for days. In the meantime a fatal accident struck Smith's party.

The Mississippi Saints awoke one night to the sound of a single gunshot followed by "low, death-like groans." John Brown rushed to the scene to find John Cook, a white wagon driver in Smith's company, lying "partly on the ground and partly on Brother Crosby's lap." He was bleeding profusely. Cook had apparently been tending to one of the horses when his loaded pistol slipped from his shirt collar, where he had unwisely stashed it. The gun fell to the ground, muzzle pointing upward. When the butt of the pistol struck the earth, it discharged the "whole load in [Cook's] neck." Cook rushed ten paces to the fire and collapsed. "He exclaimed 'Oh, Lord!' once or twice," Brown recalled. "Beside this he said nothing more than to groan. He was dead in less than three minutes." The company commissioned a coffin, dug a grave on a bluff overlooking the Missouri River, and lowered Cook into the ground.[24]

Smith didn't tarry long over the gravesite. He replaced his dead trail-hand with another and procured an additional wagon for his company. After making these acquisitions and possibly uttering a few prayers over Cook's crude grave, there was nothing left to do but press on. On June 10, 1848, the Mississippi Saints finally crossed the Missouri River and broke trail.[25]

Biddy was now part of what would become "one of the largest peacetime mass migrations in human history," according to a leading scholar on the subject.[26] Between 1841 and 1869 roughly half a million people moved west over the Oregon, California, and Mormon Trails. Some sixty thousand of them were Latter-day Saints.[27] Overlanders often traveled in vast caravans of more than one hundred wagons, transporting entire communities in a single migration. These wagon companies were "villages on wheels," in the words of Wallace Stegner.[28]

Biddy's caravan, however, more closely resembled a plantation on wheels. Her journey was unique. Of all the overland companies across all those years, none contained more enslaved people than the Mississippi Saints in the summer of 1848. Over the coming decade, hundreds of Black bondspeople would be marched westward across the Great Plains, most of them bound for the gold fields of California. But they moved in smaller parties, generally not more than several of them in any given group. By comparison, Biddy's party set out with nearly three dozen enslaved people. Their forced migration would propel a small slice of Mississippi toward the Mormon promised land.[29]

. . .

Biddy reached the first landmark of the trail just a few days after setting out. It was a tall wooden pole with a white flag on top, rising above the north bank of the Platte River in what is now eastern Nebraska. A previous party of Mormon migrants had erected it there to mark their departure and the promise of the journey ahead. They called it a "liberty pole," a common symbol of freedom in early America.[30] Although liberty poles could be found throughout the United States, the Mormons didn't intend theirs as an expression of American patriotism or solidarity. This particular liberty pole celebrated their freedom *from* the United States, rather than *within* it.

This was no ordinary migration. It was a departure charged with profound sacred meaning—an Exodus. The Saints believed that they were reenacting one of the central dramas of the Old Testament: the flight of the ancient Israelites from the land of Pharoah. Like the Bible's chosen people, LDS migrants had faced captivity and persecution—from American mobs rather than Egyptian slave-drivers—before seeking salvation in a place of their own. And they followed their very own Moses, Brigham Young, on this divine errand toward a sacred land.

Mormon migrants treated the travails along the way as a providential reprise of the biblical Exodus. Every difficulty surmounted, every illness survived, every injury healed demonstrated evidence of God's blessing. When the Mississippi River froze over in the winter of 1846, enabling passage of the refugees from Nauvoo, it became the American Red Sea. Further west, the arid landscape along the trail naturally invited comparisons to the Israelites' desert journey. The Great Basin itself was a reasonable facsimile of the Holy Land. Mormons likened the Great Salt Lake to the Dead Sea and Utah Lake to the Sea of Galilee. They named the interlinking river the "Western Jordan," later shortened to the Jordan. Even the non-Mormon press could discern the biblical parallels. "This expedition of the Mormons has some analogy to that of the exodus of the Israelites from Egypt," reported the *New York Herald*.[31] Not one to minimize his own role in the drama, Young claimed to "feel all the time like Moses."[32]

For Biddy and the other Black Christians along the trail, however, "exodus" conjured a very different set of meanings. "There is no part of the Bible with which they are so familiar as the story of the deliverance of the children of Israel," wrote a US army chaplain of Black refugees during the Civil War.[33] The enslaved emphasized Moses's role as a liberator. "Exodus" meant emancipation. And therefore their LDS enslavers had it all backward. People like Robert Smith weren't latter-day Israelites; they were Pharoah on wagon wheels. Nor did any of the other biblical references align with what Biddy and her fellow Black Christians knew to be true. The "liberty pole" signified continued bondage, not newfound freedom. The Mississippi River was no Red Sea. The Great Basin was no Holy Land. The stream between Utah Lake and the Great Salt Lake was no River Jordan. And Brigham Young was certainly no Moses.[34]

Only rarely did African Americans transform the overland journey into an exodus from slavery. The greatest flight for freedom took place on July 4, 1854, roughly six years after Biddy's journey. While passing through Tabor, Iowa, five enslaved people slipped away from the wagon company of William Taylor Dennis, another Mormon migrant from Mississippi. Dennis organized a manhunt, but the freedom-seekers outmaneuvered their pursuers and eventually made their way to Canada, beyond the reach of any American slave-catcher.[35] Their flight, however, was a rare exception. For the vast majority of enslaved African Americans who traveled west, the overland trails were corridors of captivity, not gateways to freedom.[36]

Escape for Biddy and most enslaved overlanders was impossible. Sheer distance amid the enormous expanses of the Great Plains dissuaded all but the most stalwart or reckless from seeking freedom on the overland trails. Flight was a death sentence, if it didn't result in a speedy recapture. Furthermore, many enslaved overlanders had been pried from family and friends in the South. A return journey with their enslavers was a surer pathway back to their loved ones than a bold bid for freedom across the unknown vastness of the Plains.[37]

Biddy and Hannah faced an additional impediment to escape: they were mothers. Although Black women played crucial roles in the pursuit of freedom, as historian Stephanie Camp has shown, their child-caring responsibilities made them less frequent flight risks. True, one of the enslaved women who escaped to freedom in Iowa in 1854 was a mother. But her two children were old enough to join her in that flight. Biddy and Hannah, however, had infants in their care. By building an enslaved labor force of mostly women and children, Robert Smith had made a canny investment. Biddy and Hannah's children not only enriched him; they also foreclosed the possibility of escape—at least for the time being.[38]

If Smith or any other Mississippi Saint saw the irony in forcing enslaved people on a self-proclaimed exodus, there's no record of it. For Biddy, though, the constant invocations of "exodus" and "liberty" would have been cruel mockeries. Such terms threw into stark relief her status as chattel property. True, Biddy would eventually find freedom in the West, her personal exodus. But only after a prolonged ordeal in the American wilderness.

. . .

As Biddy's party headed west from the so-called liberty pole, they crossed a sequence of unfamiliar and often perilous landscapes. From Winter Quarters the trail cut across the Great Plains through present-day Nebraska and Wyoming before swinging southwest to Fort Bridger and through a series of white-knuckle mountain passes to the Salt Lake Valley. Nothing Biddy had seen in Georgia or Mississippi could have adequately prepared her for the road ahead.

More than twenty-four hundred Mormons, along with several dozen enslaved Black laborers, moved west that season. They divided themselves into three main camps. The Mississippi Saints traveled in the third camp, which included a total of 300 wagons and 526 migrants under the direction of elders Willard Richard and Amasa Lyman. Because the camp was too large and unwieldy to move as a single unit, they separated further into subunits known as "fifties" and "tens." Robert Smith and most of the other slaveholders fell under the ten commanded by John Brown, by now a veteran overlander. Biddy traveled by foot with this group for 130 bone-weary days.[39]

The terrain for the first several hundred miles proved merciful. Biddy's trail followed the broad sunken floodplain of the Platte Valley, which ran like a level highway to the West. Only occasionally did rolling bluffs, which hugged the Platte River's edge, intercede. Then members were required to help haul the wagons up and over the rises. The greatest dangers were stream crossings with shallow sandbars and quicksand pits that could snare migrants and their animals. Otherwise the path was clear, the grass plentiful, and timber in decent supply along the river's edge.[40]

Roughly 250 miles from Winter Quarters, Biddy's trail became drier, flatter, and featureless. "No place in the world looks more lonesome and discouraging than the wide prairies of this region," according to James Clyman, a famous overland guide. The landscape, he wrote, had a "perfect sameness."[41] For decades, maps had labeled this part of the continent the "Great American Desert," and Biddy probably wouldn't have disputed the appellation. Often dull, but occasionally dangerous, the trail was lined with sun-bleached bison bones and stalked by various hazards. Prairie fires consumed acres of grass, threatening the food source for the company's animals. Wolves tracked the wagon companies, waiting for weakened livestock to fall by the wayside. The wind whipped across the Plains with a dryness that parched travelers' lips and with a force to topple wagons. Without accessible timber the company had to burn buffalo chips for fuel.[42]

Mud was Biddy's constant companion along the trail from Mississippi; now it was dust. Descriptions of blinding, choking, omnipresent dust suffuse the diary entries of overlanders. One especially frustrated migrant cursed the "annoying... impalpable powder, put in motion by the trains, and blowing directly in our faces." Those caught in its path were saturated by dirt and made "ludicrous," he continued. "3 dark spots in the face"—two eyes and a mouth—"was all you could recognize of features."[43] To cope, travelers often wore scarves and handkerchiefs across their faces. Only those in the vanguard of their wagon company had the luxury of clean air. That was rarely, if ever, Biddy's position within the wagon train. She traveled to the rear, a silhouette behind a moving screen of sand and grit.[44]

. . .

American slavery, as Biddy's labor proved, was a mobile institution. She had by now worked and walked across a vast swath of the continent—from Georgia, Mississippi, Tennessee, Kentucky, Missouri, Iowa, and into present-day Nebraska and Wyoming. Her labor regimen diversified, and probably even intensified, as she moved west.

Biddy's experiences didn't accord with conventional wisdom about the geography of American slavery. Influential Americans across the political spectrum argued that the West was simply too arid to support chattel bondage. The institution of slavery would be excluded from the West by a fundamental and immutable law, Daniel Webster famously argued in the US Senate. “I mean the law of nature—of physical geography—the law of the formation of the earth,” he proclaimed.[45] Even the slaveholding president James K. Polk, who waged war against Mexico to seize vast portions of the North American West, conceded that slavery wouldn’t take root in the lands that his conflict had won.[46]

Polk may have argued otherwise if he saw Biddy at work. Her day began at sunup and encompassed a range of duties. Breakfast had to be made and camp had to be broken so that the company could hit the trail by an early hour. Biddy, Hannah, and their daughters probably collected buffalo chips for the morning’s fires and served dishes to the Smith family. Rande, the only adult male slave in Smith’s party, likely drove one of the wagons. Back in camp in the evening, Biddy would have performed similar tasks: corralling animals, building fires, making meals, and serving the white members of the caravan.[47]

Biddy’s primary responsibility, according to the account of her daughter Ellen, was with the company’s animals. She spent most of her days driving the livestock. Smith had seven cows that required close attention. The Mississippi Saints owned dozens of sheep between them, some of whom probably also fell under Biddy’s watch. She walked as many as twenty miles in a typical day, as she prodded and herded Smith’s animals. Migrant companies were, in the words of Black overlander Sylvia Estes (Stark), an “endless caravan of white-topped wagons,” a “moving, mooing mob.”[48] Biddy’s duty was to keep that mob moving.

It was considered one of the toughest jobs in any wagon company. A white migrant named Jesse Applegate captured the rigors of cattle-driving in an article for *Overland Monthly*. Applegate was up by 4 a.m. each day to corral the animals and prepare them for the road ahead. The company followed a standard order of procession. First came the wagons, driven by teamsters; then came the horses, generally docile and responsive; and finally, there were the cattle, “lazy, selfish and unsocial” moving only “in fear of the driver’s whip.” As the cows wandered off in search of fodder and water, the driver had to continuously press them back in line. Each one, after all, represented a substantial investment. “Although to all others the march furnishes some season of relaxation or enjoyment,” Applegate wrote, “for the cow-drivers there is none.” His days, like Biddy’s, were consumed by “tedious and vexatious labors.”[49]

Biddy wasn't the only Black cattle driver to be found on the trail. Other enslaved people in her Mississippi caravan probably joined her with the livestock in the rear, including a woman named Elizabeth Flake (later Rowan), who would one day help chart Biddy's path to freedom.[50] Their friendship may have begun on those long, dusty trails. Although largely invisible to their fellow travelers, Black cattle drivers like Biddy and Elizabeth occasionally drew condescending commentary from white overlanders. "There is a darkey in the company," one woman wrote during her 1854 journey along the Platte Valley. "He got his cattle in a mud hole and he had a fine time getting them out."[51]

All that wrangling left little time for what Biddy surely considered her most sacred duty: motherhood. On short breaks she would have been able to nurse her infant, Harriet, who was otherwise in the care of Biddy's two older daughters. Only at night were they all together. By daybreak she was back with the animals. However brief their time together, Biddy's transformative love kept her family going, from camp to camp and day after debilitating day.[52]

The hazards that Biddy encountered along the trail ranged from persistent nuisances, like the omnipresent dust, to deadly dangers. Rattlesnakes lurked in the tall grasses beside the trail, where Biddy would occasionally venture in pursuit of a wayward animal. Children and adults alike fell under wagon wheels and animal hooves, which could maim and even kill. Migrants drowned in streams and rivers at the numerous crossings along the trail. And although not a danger to Biddy herself, who almost certainly went unarmed, self-inflicted gunshot wounds were a common occurrence. Biddy had already witnessed one such death.[53]

The greatest killer was disease, and infants like Biddy's and Hannah's were the most vulnerable. Vitamin-deficient diets caused scurvy. Ticks, hiding in tall grasses, carried mountain fever. And polluted drinking water brought cholera. Cholera, in particular, turned the trail into a via dolorosa for thousands of migrants. It could ravage entire wagon companies in a single wave. When Alvin Coffey, an enslaved Black overlander, heard rumors of cholera along the trail, his party "drove night and day" to outpace the killer disease.[54] An estimated 4 to 6 percent of all overland migrants—perhaps as many as thirty thousand people in total—died along the way. By 1870 there were between five to ten graves for every mile of trail. The dead had to be buried deep in the earth to avoid disinterment by scavenging wolves.[55]

Indian attack loomed large in the fevered imaginations of American overlanders and achieved an outsized place in the lore of the trail. The Missouri River marked what was called the Permanent Indian Frontier. The length of the Mormon Trail ran through Indian Country, with only three white settlements dotted along the way. Encounter with Native people was nearly inevitable. Yet contrary to legend, it was almost always peaceful. Conflict with Native Americans accounted for fewer than four hundred of the total deaths along the trail. Rather than a source of bloodshed, Indigenous people were far more commonly the source of information, trade goods, and even medical aid.[56]

Long before the overland trails were overland trails, they were Native hunting and trading routes. Biddy's path passed through the strongholds of several Native nations: first the Pawnees, then the Otoes and Omahas, then the Sioux, then the Crows and Shoshones, and finally the Utes. Her party had at least two encounters during the journey from Winter Quarters. First they met a group of Omahas, who "behaved themselves very well," in the patronizing language of John Brown. Then they met several bands of friendly Sioux south of Fort Laramie.[57]

John Brown didn't record how these Native people responded to the numerous African Americans in the party, although later accounts give us an idea for what they may have thought. Some Native people regarded Black travelers as no more trustworthy than any other American—which is to say, not trustworthy at all. Other Indians, however, believed that Black people brought good fortune. So great was the power that some Indigenous people accorded to skin color that, on at least one occasion, a Black man earned his entire wagon company safe passage.[58] According to one oral history, the Shoshone were "fascinated" by the presence of Black people along the trail, who were regarded as "hard workers, always industrious, always doing something."[59] That certainly described Biddy.

Biddy's path crossed with Native communities at several formative junctures in her life. Her earliest encounters may have come while an adolescent in the slave South. She was forced into Mississippi at the same time that the Choctaw and Chickasaw nations were being forced out, as part of the federal policy of Indian Removal. Years later, as a freedwoman in Los Angeles, Biddy would apply her time-tested medical knowledge to incarcerated Indians in the county jail. Administering to LA's Native population was in fact the first work she would do by choice rather than by force. But Biddy had hundreds of miles yet to travel and years of slavery to endure before she would reach that point.

. . .

The last leg of Biddy's overland journey was the roughest and most dangerous. About five hundred miles from Winters Quarters, her party reached the adobe walls of Fort Laramie. Established in 1835 as a fur-trading outpost in the heart of Sioux country, Fort Laramie marked the end of the Plains portion of the journey and the beginning of the mountainous half. Even Horace Greeley, who would famously urge young men to "Go West," regarded this vast region as off-limits, a wasteland "of precipice and volcanic sterility." To send women and children there was "palpable homicide," he warned.[60] Nothing Biddy had seen before compared to the towering heights and the precipitous drops she was about to encounter.[61]

Whereas Biddy's party "lost nothing of any consequence" until this point, according to John Brown, their fortunes began to turn in the Black Hills just beyond Fort Laramie (not to be confused with the more famous Black Hills of South Dakota). They found "little or no feed" in that rugged country. The starving cattle "began to die," Brown reported. Aside from his human property, cattle were Robert Smith's most valuable assets. They were also Biddy's primary responsibility. With losses mounting, the company pressed ahead as quickly as it could.[62]

The path only became steeper, drier, and more forbidding as they cut southwest across present-day Wyoming. The Platte River was no longer their guide or (muddy) water source. They left the valley behind and entered a moonscape of high desert country broken by soaring ridges of granite. By September, Biddy's party began the long, hard climb up the Continental Divide through the South Pass (elevation 7,550 feet). Even in midsummer the ice along the trail at the South Pass could be "as thick as a dinner plate," according to the enslaved migrant Alvin Coffey.[63] This is where sickness struck the Pioneer Camp the previous year, as John Brown remembered well. Biddy and the rest of the company endured a long, waterless stretch as they made their way toward Fort Bridger and its cluster of Shoshone lodges.[64]

Just over one hundred miles now separated them from the Salt Lake Valley. But those miles were the cruelest yet. The Wasatch Range rose before them like a stone sentinel, guarding the eastern entrance to the Great Basin. To get there, Biddy's company traveled along the route that the Donner Party pioneered just two years earlier. That ill-fated wagon company had inched their way through the gulches of the Wasatch, enroute to California, where they spent a starving, snowbound winter on the slopes of the Sierra Nevada. Previous Mormon migrants, including enslaved ones like Green Flake, had helped clear the trail of rocks and undergrowth to make travel somewhat more comfortable.[65]

Even so, it was a back-breaking, gut-wrenching struggle through those high mountain passes. The final thirty-five miles were, by almost unanimous consent, the most challenging of the entire journey. The Mississippi Saints crept along the four-thousand-foot descent, made all the more treacherous by dense brush, boulders, tree stumps, rattlesnakes, and razor-sharp willows. Biddy probably remained in the rear of the caravan to steer the animals down gulches and past vertiginous drops-offs. She may have also joined with the men of the party on steeper stretches of the trail, as they pulled on ropes attached to the backs of the wagons, easing their descents.[66]

On October 16, 1848, the Mississippi Saints finally rolled into the valley, the Great Salt Lake glittering like a pale amethyst before them.[67] Biddy had been on the trail for roughly seven months. She had crossed the mudflats of Mississippi, the broad prairies of Nebraska, and the mountain passes of what would soon be called Utah. Her children and Hannah's, including their two infant daughters, all arrived safely.

. . .

There was little time to rest at the end of the long journey. The Mississippi Saints had to build quarters, and build them quickly, before the Great Basin's harsh winter set in. What the Mormons called Great Salt Lake City already teemed with several thousand residents housed in hundreds of adobe and log houses. Robert Smith searched for open land roughly ten miles to the southeast of the main settlement. He and the other Mississippi Saints eventually found it in a place called Cottonwood, a fertile stretch of land nestled between two streams at the foot of the Wasatch Range. The Mississippi slaveholders had traveled together and now they settled together—a people apart among a people apart. Smith soon set Rande, Biddy, Hannah, and at least some of their children to work.[68]

It was a lean, trying winter. Fortunately for the Saints, John Brown had transported several enslaved people into the valley the previous season, who had already prepared "a tolerable good crop of corn, enough to do us." By early December the snow started falling and continued for months. It lay nearly a foot deep "all over the valley," Brown wrote. The cold was unlike anything Biddy knew from Mississippi or Georgia. The migrants lived out of tents before finally completing their log houses. Brown's tent was heated by his stove. Biddy probably didn't have such a luxury.[69]

The slaveholding Saints may have been cold and hungry that first winter, but at least they were secure. They had found their Zion within the natural cloisters of the Great Basin. "This is the most safe and secure place the Saints could possibly locate themselves in," wrote an early Mormon settler. "Nature has fortified this place on all sides, with only a few narrow passes, which could be made impregnable without much difficulty."[70] For the Saints the Great Basin was a fortress sanctuary.

For the enslaved, however, it was a fortress prison. Biddy had walked roughly two thousand miles from the cotton fields of Mississippi yet seemingly not a step closer to freedom.

4 Children of Zion, Seed of Cain

Robert Smith had let his guard down. After successfully transporting ten enslaved people across the Great Plains and establishing himself as the largest slaveholder in the booming Mormon colony around the Great Salt Lake, he settled into a long winter in his new mountain retreat. Perhaps he had become complacent or self-satisfied. He may have even assumed his homestead, screened by soaring peaks and cloaked in a thick blanket of snow, was invulnerable to challenge. It wasn't until the snow began to melt around his land in spring 1849 that he discovered the first overt defiance of his mastery. His only enslaved male adult, a man named Rande, had taken flight.[1]

While the news of Rande's escape came as a bitter shock to Smith, Biddy and Hannah probably saw it coming. They may have even colluded. Flight across unfamiliar terrain, after all, required information, allies, and careful preparation. Unable to flee themselves with infant children, Biddy and Hannah likely took a vicarious pleasure in a plan to deprive their enslaver—the man who had just dragged them two thousand miles to a remote and unforgiving frontier—of a valuable asset. If they couldn't have freedom themselves, at least someone could.[2]

From Smith's farm at Cottonwood, Rande dashed ten miles northwest to Salt Lake City along a path now mercifully free of snow. There, he took shelter with at least two different white families. Rande selected his safe houses carefully. He probably probed the antislavery sentiments of various fellow travelers during the overland journey to ascertain who, if anyone, might provide sanctuary for a fugitive. A Black man named Jim may have also played an instrumental role, according to a contemporary report. Jim had escaped from his owner in Missouri in 1848 and joined the same wagon company to the Great Basin. Not inclined to linger among slaveholders any longer than he had to, Jim planned to travel with a migrant company to California that season. It seems Rande intended to join him.[3]

But not if Robert Smith had any say in the matter. The loss of Rande was a blow, not only to his pool of able-bodied workers but also to his reputation for mastery. And as a newcomer in a frontier settlement, reputation was currency. Rande's flight might also set a costly precedent by inspiring others to follow. To retrieve his absconded property, Smith enlisted the services of a fellow Mississippi Saint named Benjamin Matthews.[4]

Matthews tracked Rande to Great Salt Lake City. He wrote to Brigham Young in late March 1849 to report on what he had discovered. Rande was still in the city but "not Comatable [come-at-able?] yet." Worse, "there is people in the Company going to Calafornia [*sic*]" who were "interested" in smuggling him out of the Great Basin. Matthews may have had experience with slave-catching in Mississippi—many of his peers did—but the Salt Lake Basin wasn't the plantation South. He couldn't extort information at gunpoint or threaten Rande's suspected allies, common tactics of Mississippi slave patrollers. Those who harbored Rande were fellow Saints and therefore crucial contributors to the dream of a New Jerusalem. Slave-catching was a delicate business in Zion.[5]

Matthews never got his man. Rande slipped from the Great Basin, beyond the reach of Robert Smith and for that matter any further record keepers. Where he settled or whether he prospered, the extant documents don't say. But we know this much: he almost certainly did so as a free man. (Matthews later moved to California, where he was killed by a falling tree.)[6]

Rande wasn't the only freedom-seeker in Zion that season. The same day that the would-be slave-catcher Matthews wrote to Young, another Mississippi Mormon named Francis McKown inquired after a different fugitive. According McKown, one of his enslaved women had taken flight and sought refuge with none other than Brigham Young himself. It was a bold and politically shrewd move by the runaway woman (who is unnamed in the letter), forcing the LDS president to take a position on slave recapture.[7]

Her strategy didn't pay off, however. McKown assured Young that he wouldn't "Correct" his enslaved worker upon her safe return, but that he was dependent on her services as his cook and washer woman. "She was Borne mine and I raised hur," McKown asserted with standard slaveholding proprietorship. It seems that Young complied and returned her to bondage.[8]

One way or another, the first two recorded slave escapes in the Great Basin had therefore been settled. But a much bigger problem remained. Indeed, Rande's flight and the unnamed woman's recapture only deferred a broader reckoning over property rights and race—issues that had followed the Mormons west from Mississippi.

Biddy's years in the Great Basin marked a transformative period for both the LDS Church and the nation as a whole. Where in the West would slavery be allowed, and what protections, if any, could people like Biddy claim? These were the questions that bedeviled lawmakers across the country as Biddy entered her first planting season in the Salt Lake Valley. As she discovered, Brigham Young would address those questions by drawing an increasingly stark line between two groups of people. There were those like Robert Smith, who could be counted among the "children of Zion." Then there were those like Biddy, who were cursed as the "seed of Cain."[9]

. . .

Biddy's first challenge in the Great Basin was the land itself. She was no stranger to harsh frontiers, to be sure. She had been among the vanguard of enslaved laborers trafficked into Mississippi, where she carved cotton plantations from the wilderness during the state's boom years in the 1830s. She therefore knew how to build from the ground up. But the Salt Lake Valley's hard soil, high altitude, and extreme climate presented a different set of hardships. A biting cold had already crept over the land by the time she arrived, which quickly gave way to a snowbound winter. The spring brought a welcome thaw but also an intensified work regimen as the planting season began in earnest.

Biddy labored in the shadow of the Wasatch mountains, which loomed over the eastern edge of the Mississippi settlement at Cottonwood. Whether those peaks appear majestic or menacing depends on the condition of the viewer. For enslaved people, they were towering symbols of captivity. A Black man named Alex Bankhead recalled how bondspeople would gather in Salt Lake City to "discuss their condition, and gaze in wonderment at the lofty mountains, which reared their snowy peaks heavenward, and completely forbade them from ascertaining how they could make their escape back to the South, or to more congenial climes."[10] Rande was the only known Black freedom-seeker to successfully traverse the Great Basin. Not only did Biddy's mountainous environment preclude escape, it also robbed her of oxygen. Smith's farm was about 4,300 feet above sea level. Every one of Biddy's tasks was that much harder in the thin air of the Salt Lake Valley.[11]

Additional hazards came from above. A plague of crickets descended on the fledgling settlement in truly biblical quantities the summer before Biddy arrived. They devoured the ripening crops and pushed Great Salt Lake City to the brink of starvation. Only the providential arrival of a flock of seagulls, who gorged themselves on the crickets, saved the Mormons from calamity. Although the Saints hardly needed further evidence, here was yet another sign of God's favor. (In tribute to the settlement's winged saviors, Utah unveiled the Seagull Monument—probably the only major statue ever erected in honor of the otherwise unloved bird—in Temple Square in 1913. The California Gull became the Utah state bird in 1955.)[12]

With the aid of enslaved labor, the Saints gradually turned the landscape to their advantage. The sunbaked earth attained a plow-breaking hardness by midsummer. But the streams that flowed from the mountain valleys soon irrigated the Mormons' fields and softened the soil. Smith and the other Mississippi Saints selected their land wisely in a well-watered corner of the Salt Lake Valley, along the banks of the two Cottonwood Creeks. The nearby Great Lake, although lifeless, was an inexhaustible reservoir of salt, which could be used as a preservative as well as a supplement for livestock. The high bunch grass that covered the valley floor provided ample fodder for cattle, while plentiful sagebrush and shrub oak could be used for firewood. Like the other Cottonwood settlers, Smith probably built his home of timber hauled from the nearby canyons.[13]

Biddy would have helped gather these resources, in addition to performing numerous other tasks that sustained the Smith farm. Much of her work probably took place within the home. Rebecca Smith continued to depend on Biddy and Hannah. Like other enslaved people in Utah, Biddy would have risen early to begin the day's work: starting the fires, emptying chamber pots, sweeping floors, preparing meals, washing laundry, and managing the white children (four of whom were under the age of eight). Enslavers like Rebecca were objects of envy within the Salt Lake Valley, where days were long and a woman's work was never done. One of Brigham Young's wives longed for a Black worker of her own. "May God grant me a negro some day," she prayed.[14]

When not at the whim of their mistress, Biddy and Hannah could be found in the fields of Smith's eighty-acre farm, harvesting wheat, oats, and potatoes alongside Robert and his sons. Although the thermometer regularly climbed above 100 degrees in the summer, the heat wouldn't have deterred Smith from sending Biddy into the fields. After all, slaveholders like Smith typically viewed Black laborers as biologically suited to extreme heat. Biddy would have also spent part of her day with Smith's livestock—a herd of twenty-three cattle and eighteen working oxen by 1850—which were turned loose each evening and rounded up in the morning.[15] She probably knew the cattle better than Smith himself, having driven them across two thousand miles of open country. In short, Biddy's work regimen in the Great Basin was much the same as it had been in Mississippi: varied and relentless. As Alex Bankhead recalled, many of the enslaved people in Zion "were subjected to the same treatment that was accorded the plantation negroes of the South."[16]

All that work paid off—for Smith and other Mormon slaveholders. According to the 1850 census, ten households that relied on Black slave labor, including the Smiths, prospered in their early years of settlement. Between them, they had improved nearly three hundred acres of land and grew more than two thousand bushels of grain and corn. Their dairy operations proved particularly lucrative. Smith and the other enslavers produced more than four thousand pounds of butter and cheese. Individually they "produced more butter and cheese," according to historian Amy Tanner Thiriot "than dozens of their neighbors combined."[17] After just one year in Zion, the total assessed value of Smith's farm—not including the value of his human property—came to nearly $3,000, a considerable fortune for a once struggling migrant.[18] Who could claim that the Far West wasn't suited to slavery?

Biddy labored far from the public eye—in a satellite settlement of a deliberately cloistered colony in a remote corner of the United States. Nobody in Washington, DC, knew her name or even that she existed. And yet, as partisan rancor gripped the nation's capital, the looming crisis came to focus, inescapably, on the fate of Biddy and people like her.

• • •

Talk of disunion hung like a black cloud over Washington, DC, in early 1850 as Congress feuded over an irreconcilable question: Should Americans be allowed to take enslaved laborers into lands recently seized from Mexico, including California and the new Mormon colony in the Salt Lake Valley? Partisans refused to give ground. Southern fire-eaters preached secession. Lawmakers whispered of civil war. For a harrowing moment, it seemed that the first shots might be fired from the Senate floor.[19]

On April 3 a shouting match over the slavery controversy broke out between Senators Thomas Hart Benton of Missouri and Henry Foote of Mississippi, seated on opposite ends of the chamber. Benton pushed aside his chair and strode defiantly down the center aisle toward Foote, who drew his pistol. Panic swept the chamber as senators leapt to their feet and converged on the two combatants. Benton, never one to shy from a fight, bared his chest and dared Foote to shoot. "Let him fire!" he roared. "Stand out of the way and let the assassin fire!" Before Foote could indulge the offer, several senators pounced on him, wrestled him to the floor, and tore the pistol from his grip. Bloodshed was averted that day. But the political crisis hardly abated in the months or the years ahead.[20]

Some lawmakers attempted to diffuse the controversy by insisting that slavery would wither and die in the arid climate of Southwest. The westward expansion of slavery was essentially a nonissue, they argued. Representative James Brooks of New York scoffed at the idea of a slaveholder swapping his Southern cotton fields for a farm in the Great Basin. He mocked the "imminent danger" that "the planter may desert the rich bottom lands of the Mississippi . . . and rush with his slaves, from the cotton and sugar temptations of Texas, through the desert, over the Snowy mountains, to the great Salt Lake in Utah."[21]

Brooks may not have been so flippant had he witnessed Biddy's overland journey across a similar route or the profits pulled from Smith's farm that season. Indeed, most Southern lawmakers didn't fall for Brooks's argument, and they generally dismissed the notion that slavery obeyed strict "natural limits." Instead, they advocated for the westward expansion of slavery at all costs. As John C. Calhoun famously argued, the survival of the slaveholding class depended on the extension of human bondage into the West.[22] Senator Robert Toombs of Georgia later explained the slaveholding dilemma in Manichean terms: "We are constrained by an inexorable necessity to accept expansion or extermination."[23]

Robert Smith was at the vanguard of the slaveholding South's crusading mission: to extend human bondage as far as it would go. For the next decade and beyond, the region's foremost thinkers, men like Jefferson Davis, would rhapsodize about slavery's westward march. Smith was among the first to put theory to practice. While slaveholding politicians daydreamed about an enlarged dominion, Smith set his household in motion. With each turn of his company's wagon wheels, he and his fellow Mississippi Saints further extended slavery's western frontier. And now those Mississippi Saints—and, crucially, those who struggled against them—would determine whether that frontier could hold.[24]

. . .

Brigham Young and his advisers understood all too well how vexed the question of slavery had become.[25] Thomas Kane, the Mormons' greatest non-Mormon ally, urged Young to "refuse to take any action that can give official expression to your sentiments on this point."[26] Taking a stance would only invite further public scrutiny of the Saints' affairs, something that had rarely, if ever, worked to their benefit. Remaining silent on the issue of slavery while simultaneously harboring a community of slaveholders was easier said than done, however.

Young and his brethren had confronted that controversy from the very earliest days of the church.[27] More often than not, slavery was a thorn in the side and a prick to the conscience of a church that drew its membership overwhelmingly from the American North and northern Europe. Mormonism's foundational text contains an explicit critique of slaveholding, something the Bible lacks. Human bondage is one of the practices that distinguishes the idolatrous from the righteous in the Book of Mormon.[28] Not only does the Book of Mormon condemn slavery, it also insists that salvation is available to everyone, regardless of skin color. The Lord "denieth none that came unto him, black and white, bond and free, male and female," according to the central LDS text. "All are alike unto Him."[29] There were, from the beginning, "emancipatory possibilities in Mormonism."[30]

But in the face of violent persecution—rumors of LDS abolitionism had spurred the mobs that drove the Saints from Missouri in the 1830s, for instance—Mormons learned to tread carefully on the slavery question.[31] The prophet himself even offered olive branches to slaveholders where necessary. "The fact is uncontrovertable [*sic*]," Joseph Smith wrote in 1836, "that the first mention we have of slavery is found in the holy bible, pronounced by a man who was perfect in his generation and walked with God."[32] True, Joseph Smith would suggest a plan for gradual emancipation during his ill-fated 1844 presidential campaign. But compensation to slaveholders was a key part of that plan.[33] Robert Smith was baptized into the LDS Church that same year. If he read Joseph Smith's campaign manifesto, he wasn't overly troubled by it.[34]

Nor would he be troubled by the church's evolving positions on the slavery question in the years to come, which typically took the form of ambivalence or evasion. Utah's unofficial representative in Congress recommended that Young simply lie in the upcoming census of 1850. He suggested that "no person of African descent be reported as a slave," despite the fact that about sixty Black people were currently laboring in bondage within the territory. "I make this suggestion," he continued, "because a large majority of the members of both branches of Congress, and a vast majority of the jurists in the United States entertain the conviction that slavery does not, and cannot exist in the Territory . . . without the sanction of positive law, yet to be enacted."[35]

The future of Zion was at stake. Young coveted statehood, which would bring congressional representation and greater federal funding for his people's needs. He called the proposed state "Deseret"—a Book of Mormon term for "honeybee"—which encompassed most of present-day Utah, Nevada, and Arizona, along with portions of Wyoming, Colorado, New Mexico, California, and Oregon. Nobody could accuse Young of thinking small. Conspicuously, the proposed Deseret constitution lacked a statement on slavery. The omission was strategic. Young knew that any statehood bid required broad support within Congress, including from those on starkly opposing sides of the sectional divide.[36]

Young didn't get his way. Instead, the proposed state of Deseret became the US territory of Utah, named not for anything or anyone connected to the LDS faith but rather for the region's most powerful Native group, the Utes. As a territory, Utah was subject to federal oversight. The US president, rather than the president of the LDS Church, had the power to appoint territorial officers, including governor and the judges who comprised Utah's supreme court. Utah would have no representatives in either the US House or the Senate. Young had to content himself with a nonvoting delegate to represent Utah's interests in Washington, DC. He felt these constraints keenly. Securing statehood for Utah would remain one of his principal ambitions for years to come.[37]

Utah's territorial designation belonged to a broader package of bills, known as the Compromise of 1850. Congress remained deeply divided, but the bills gave each faction just enough to forestall political catastrophe. Crucially, California was admitted to the Union as a free state, despite roars of protest from Southern congressmen. In return, slaveholders gained a robust Fugitive Slave Act, which enabled them to enlist federal support to reclaim Black freedom-seekers from Northern states. The Compromise also stipulated that the status of slavery in the territories of Utah and New Mexico would be left to "popular sovereignty." That meant, in essence, that the voters of those territories would decide the issue for themselves.[38]

Mormons now had a momentous choice to make. Would slavery or freedom prevail across their broad swath of the American West?

. . .

For perhaps the first time in her life, Biddy found herself without a "master" in the winter of 1849–50. Robert Smith had been called on an expedition to explore the southern reaches of the territory alongside about fifty other LDS men, taking him nearly four hundred miles from Cottonwood in the teeth of the coldest season he had ever faced. That left thirty-nine-year-old Rebecca, who had just given birth a week before her husband's departure, to manage a household of ten enslaved people and her seven children. She may have reasonably wondered whether she, or her husband, would live to see the backside of this long, cruel winter.[39]

Yet if Biddy or Hannah expected the bonds of slavery to loosen during Smith's absence, they were likely disappointed. A lonely, postpartum Rebecca was still a formidable presence. She bore little resemblance to the soft, refined mistresses of plantation mythology. Rebecca was a seasoned overlander as well as a lifelong slaveholder who, unlike her husband, had been trained in the techniques of mastery from childhood. In the accounts of enslaved people, slaveholding mistresses often come off as more vicious than their husbands. Whereas male slaveholders often delegated punishments to overseers or family members, the work of mistresses "was done at close quarters, on a daily and intimate basis," in the words of historian Thavolia Glymph.[40] There's no reason to believe Rebecca wielded power gently. In fact, later evidence suggests that she commanded through fear.[41] If she suspected Biddy and Hannah of bearing some of her husband's children, her punishments may have taken on an especially hard edge, now that she had sole command of the household.

To cope, Biddy and Hannah could find comfort in their friendship, in their families, and in the broader Black community of Cottonwood. Roughly thirty African Americans lived in the tract of land between the two Cottonwood creeks, making it perhaps the densest assembly of enslaved people anywhere in the Far West at the time.[42] That community included Elizabeth Flake (later Rowan), whose friendship with Biddy may have blossomed as early as 1848 as they drove the company's livestock along the overland trail; Green Flake, one of the three surviving enslaved men in the first overland expedition to the Great Basin and an impassioned advocate for the growing African American community there; and Oscar (Crosby) Smith, who entered the Salt Lake Valley alongside Green Flake and would later join Biddy as a founding member of Los Angeles's first Black church.[43]

For Hannah, friendship with a man named Toby Embers ripened into romance during their time together in Cottonwood. They may have married sometime after their arrival in Utah, although they weren't permitted to live together. Embers was the property of Bishop William Crosby, while Hannah remained under Robert and Rebecca's control. Still, the Smiths would have permitted visits, given their financial stake in the union: any child born to Hannah would automatically become Robert's property.

In 1849, Hannah gave birth to her first child by Embers, a boy named Charles. Their second child, Martha, followed in 1855.[44]

When Robert Smith returned to Cottonwood from his winter expedition in February 1850, weary and bone-cold but alive, he took stock of his workforce. The birth of Charles brought his total back to ten slaves, after the escape of Rande. And Hannah, now in her late twenties, still had years of fertility ahead of her. What Smith likely didn't tally, however, was the hidden cost of a growing labor force. Sure, each additional enslaved child enriched him personally. But every birth also expanded and deepened Biddy and Hannah's community. Although their path to freedom was narrow, with the right allies behind them, they might yet chart it.

. . .

The Saints in the Great Basin still fancied themselves a people apart. Despite Utah's status as a federal territory governed by the United States, signs of the US government were hard to find in Brigham Young's mountain kingdom. Mormons processed their mail at the "Great Basin Post Office," rather than a US post office, and residents listed their address as "Great Salt Lake City, Great Basin, North America."[45] Utah even had its own military, the Nauvoo Legion. And yet, however hard they tried, the Saints couldn't escape the central problem of the United States: the controversies over slavery and race.

Young's hardening views threatened to exacerbate the situation. Although fiercely loyal to the legacy of the prophet, Young diverged from Joseph Smith on racial politics. To be sure, Young personally opposed an institution that reduced people to the status of property. But he never spoke against slavery in the way his predecessor did. Young's views on Black people ranged from exclusionary (they could never become full members of the church) to downright absurd ("mulattoes are like mules they can't have children").[46] He spoke of interracial mixing with particular vehemence. "If the white man who belongs to the chosen seed mixes his blood with the seed of Cain," he claimed, "the penalty under the law of God, is death on the spot."[47] Underwriting many of Young's racial attitudes was his belief in divine curses. Like many Americans, he held that Black people traced their ancestry to the biblical villains Cain and Ham. People like Biddy couldn't remove the curse of their forefathers themselves,

Young argued. Only God could. Until then, she and other Black people were destined to be "servants unto servants."[48]

Standing before the Utah legislature in January 1852, Young proclaimed that African-descended people—the "seed of Cain"—could not attain priesthood in the LDS Church. The priesthood, available to every other male above the age of twelve, was the very foundation of the Mormon church. By this point a small number of African Americans, including roughly a dozen enslaved people, had been baptized. Some, like Jane Manning James and a man named Abel, even achieved positions of honor within Mormon society. From this moment on, however, they were barred from the most sacred rituals of the LDS faith.[49]

The priesthood ban would have dire consequences for Black Mormons in the here-and-now and the hereafter. Without priesthood, African Americans weren't allowed to bless their newborn children or family members when they were ill. Black Mormons also couldn't receive temple sealings—that is, to be spiritually and eternally bound—to their own family. The Saints believed that families sealed together on Earth traveled together in the afterlife. Without those temple sealings, the highest realms of heaven were closed to Black Mormons. When one Black woman in Utah learned that she was unable to receive her endowments, she allegedly scratched at her arm until it bled. Was her blood "not as white as anyone's," she implored in despair.[50]

Biddy never converted to Mormonism and thus the ban had no direct effect on her. But it transformed the lives of Black Mormons within her community, including those she regarded as friends. The priesthood ban remained in effect for 126 years. Not until 1978 did the church finally lift it.[51]

• • •

One cold day in late January 1852, the same month that Young articulated the ban on Black priesthood, roughly forty men filed into a two-story granite and adobe building at the southwest corner of what is today Salt Lake City's Temple Square. They were members of Utah's territorial legislature, an august group that included many of "the chief men of Israel," in the words of the veteran missionary John Brown. Although Utah had been declared a territory two years earlier, this was the first session of its legislature. They were there to deliberate on a bill they would call "An Act in Relation to Service"—the first slave code ever introduced in the American Far West.[52]

Orson Pratt, an original member of the Quorum of Twelve Apostles, wasn't pleased. He rose from his seat to speak against the "preposterous" measure. "Shall we take then the innocent African that has committed no sin," he asked, "and damn him to slavery and bondage without receiving any authority from heaven to do [so]?" Permitting slavery within Zion was sheer hypocrisy, Pratt continued. The Saints had fled their own sort of "slavery" within the United States to secure their "religious [liberties]," he argued. And yet here they were imposing slavery on others within the promised land. "For us to bind the African because he is different from us in color," he thundered, "[is] enough to cause the angels in heaven to blush!"[53]

Pratt's objections fell on deaf ears. Brigham Young had already instructed his legislators on the fundamental principles: Race-based servitude had been decreed in heaven, and those on Earth were in no position to defy that arrangement.

Young enunciated his position in a series of speeches before the legislature in January and February as the bill was being drafted. "Inasmuch as I believe in the Bible, inasmuch as I believe in the ordinances of God, in the Priesthood and order, and decrees of God, I must believe in slavery," he said.[54] That didn't give slaveholders free rein, however. Young preached humanity in the treatment of "servants" (he generally avoided the term "slave"). "Servitude may and should exist" for the descendants of Ham, he argued. "Yet we should not fall into the other extreme, and make them as beasts of the field... nor yet elevate them, as some seem disposed, to an equality with those whom Nature and Nature's God has indicated to be their masters, their superiors."[55]

Brigham had spoken, and the legislature voted. On February 4, 1852, Young signed an "Act in Relation to Service" into law.

As far as slavery statutes went, Utah's law was comparatively mild. The bill provided more protections for the enslaved and mandated more obligations for their owners than any of the numerous slave codes in the American South. Mormon slaveholders had to first register their laborers with a probate court, where a "contract" would be drawn up. If a slaveholder was proven guilty of "cruelty or abuse, or neglect to feed, clothe, or shelter his servants in a proper manner," the so-called contract between master and slave could be rendered void. Those guilty of "carnal intercourse" with any of their enslaved workers forfeited "all claim" to their labor—a clause that *should* have worried Robert Smith. Slaveholders also had to provide at least eighteen months of education for the enslaved. And "masters" were subjected to fines or imprisonment if they transported slaves out of the territory against their "will." The new law therefore softened some of the cruelest features of human bondage.[56]

The comparatively flexible terms of the statute, however, made little difference to the enslaved people themselves. As experience would show, the notion of slave "consent" was a fiction if not an outright contradiction. Enslavers in Utah bought, sold, and transported Black laborers without regard for anyone's will but their own. Black people were routinely listed as movable property in Mormon consecration records. John Brown, for instance, valued his slave Betsy at $1,000 in 1857.[57] The law contained no mechanism for manumission. Furthermore, most enslavers simply didn't comply with the requirement that they register their "servants" in probate court, which provided the only recourse for the enslaved to contest mistreatment. Tellingly, the very few Mormons who did register their Black laborers listed them as "slaves," not "servants."[58] In short, many African Americans in Utah remained what they had been in the South: property.

Why the Utah legislature passed this code remains a matter of debate. The vast majority of Utah's population came from either the American North or northern Europe. And only one slaveholder—the indispensable John Brown—sat in the legislature that passed the act. No more than about one hundred enslaved African Americans would be taken into the territory that decade, and they were concentrated among a small number of slaveholders. (Robert Smith owned roughly 10 percent of the total enslaved population of Utah.) Why, then, didn't Young simply stay silent on the issue, as his own advisers had suggested?

Although small in number, those slaveholding Saints wielded disproportionate influence. The list of Mormon enslavers included the first mayor of Salt Lake City, Abraham O. Smoot; one of Utah's first delegates in Congress, William Hooper; the bishop William Crosby; the indefatigable missionary, pioneer, and now legislator, John Brown; and, of course, the largest Mormon slaveholder of them all, Robert Smith. Thanks to the unpaid labor that they commanded, Smith and his fellow slaveholding Saints were wealthy and only getting wealthier.[59]

"An Act in Relation to Service" also insulated Young from the unpleasant business of slave-catching. Just three years earlier, the flight of Rande and the unnamed woman belonging to Francis McKown had placed Young in a tight spot. Utah's slave statute delegated more authority to the territory's courts, so that Young would no longer have to personally adjudicate the claims of slaveholders within the Great Basin. He believed that the legislation would also relieve him of a related headache, as he saw it: the immigration of free Black people into the territory.[60]

Above all, "An Act in Relation to Service" enabled Brigham Young to maintain a delicate political balancing act between North and South. That balance was crucial to his continuing campaign for statehood. The 1852 bill protected the property rights of influential Mormon slaveholders while nonetheless signaling that Zion wasn't about to become a slaveocracy. Young's later comments, given in an interview to the prominent New York journalist Horace Greeley, are revealing. Slavery was a "divine institution," Young explained, "and not to be abolished until the curse pronounced on Ham shall have been removed from his descendants." Nevertheless, Young didn't believe that chattel slavery could flourish in Zion. Utah, he predicted, would eventually come into the Union as a free state.[61]

Whatever Brigham Young may have believed, slaveholders had scored key victories in the struggle for the American West by 1852. First, Robert Smith and his fellow Mississippi Saints successfully transported dozens of Black bondspeople across the country. Then they demonstrated that slave labor could pay at the far western reaches of American settlement. Then the Utah legislature, rather than condemning the practice or simply turning a blind eye, enshrined slavery in law. As every step in Biddy's journey had demonstrated, the American West was no landscape of freedom; it was another dominion of slavery.

. . .

Biddy didn't remain in Utah long enough to witness the passage of the territory's slave code. The previous spring, Robert Smith had elected to join a group of Saints bound for a new Mormon settlement several hundred miles west of the Great Basin.

Brigham Young had expected a small contingent of migrants to volunteer for the mission. When nearly 450 prospective settlers lined up in

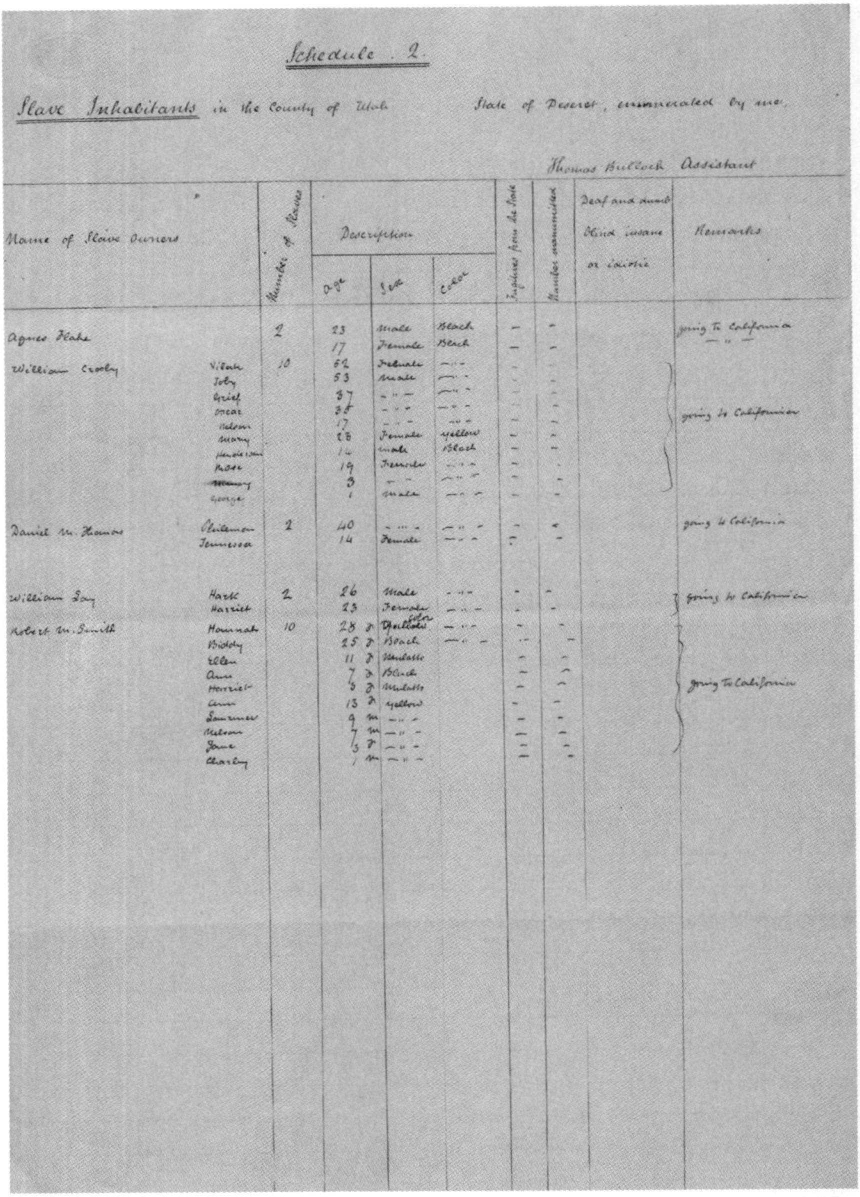

Schedule. 2.

Slave Inhabitants in the County of Utah State of Deseret, enumerated by me,

Thomas Bullock Assistant

Name of Slave Owners		Number of Slaves	Description: Age	Sex	Color	Fugitives from the State	Number manumitted	Deaf and dumb blind insane or idiotic	Remarks
Agnes Flake		2	23	Male	Black	—	—		going to California
			17	Female	Black	—	—		— " —
William Crosby	Vilate	10	62	Female	— " —	—	—		going to California
	Toby		53	Male	— " —	—	—		
	Grief		37	— " —	— " —	—	—		
	Oscar		35	— " —	— " —	—	—		
	Nelson		17	— " —	— " —	—	—		
	Mary		28	Female	yellow	—	—		
	Henderson		14	male	Black	—	—		
	Rose		19	Female	— " —	—	—		
	[illegible]		3	— " —	— " —	—	—		
	George		1	male	— " —	—	—		
Daniel M. Thomas	Philemon	2	40	— " —	— " —	—	—		going to California
	Tennessee		14	Female	— " —	—	—		
William Lay	Hark	2	26	Male	— " —	—	—		going to California
	Harriet		23	Female	— " —	—	—		
Robert M. Smith	Hannah	10	28 F	yellow color	— " —	—	—		going to California
	Biddy		25 F	Black	— " —	—	—		
	Ellen		11 F	Mulatto		—	—		
	Ann		7 F	Black		—	—		
	Harriet		5 F	Mulatto		—	—		
	Ann		13 F	yellow		—	—		
	Lawrence		9 m	— " —		—	—		
	Nelson		7 m	— " —		—	—		
	Jane		3 F	— " —		—	—		
	Charley		1 m	— " —		—	—		

The draft copy of the federal census slave schedule for Utah County, taken in early 1851, lists Biddy and other enslaved people "going to California" that spring. Church of Jesus Christ of the Latter-day Saints, Church History Library, Salt Lake City, Utah.

the spring of 1851, he was stunned. The outflow of so many Saints, while strengthening the missionary enterprise of the church, would also deplete the Salt Lake Valley of much-needed settlers and laborers.[62] However, he may have been pleased to see the backside of Smith and several other slaveholders. After all, it had only been twenty-four months since Rande made his escape from Smith, thereby raising thorny questions about the reach of slavery in Zion.

Many of those slaveholding migrants are recorded in a special section of the census that year. They're listed in one column. In the adjacent column are the names of the people they owned, twenty-six of them in total. Biddy's name appears by her children and the six others that Robert Smith claimed, including Hannah. Next to their names are three words that would define the next chapter of their lives: "Going to California."[63]

Robert Smith was on his way west once again, this time to establish a contradiction: a slaveholding colony in a free state.

5 California Bound

While the landscapes changed, the routine along the trail remained largely the same.[1] Break camp, corral the livestock, drive them roughly twenty miles through a moving screen of dust, avoid ingesting a lungful of the stuff in the process, rejoin the wagons, set up camp, cook, clean, snatch a few precious moments with family, and get to sleep before the whole ordeal repeated itself in the morning. This had been Biddy's daily grind for more than six months in 1848, from Mississippi to the Great Basin. And this was again her regimen from late March to June 1851, as Robert Smith went west once more in search of a new frontier.

The trail this time carried Biddy across four hundred miles of diverse and frequently forbidding terrain. Beginning from the high country of central Utah, her party pressed through early spring snows, inched along the mountain passes of the Great Basin, and then hobbled across long, sandy, waterless stretches of the Mojave Desert. Much of the journey followed the Old Spanish Trail, a route that linked the horse and mule markets of California to the settlements of New Mexico. Traders frequently traveled with Indigenous captives to sell at both ends of the route. The trade proved so lucrative that slave raiders—American, Mexican, and Indigenous alike—had stripped some Native communities in the Southwest of more than half their women and children. Biddy, in other words, followed an old slaver's trail.[2]

Although human trafficking was a common sight along the route, Biddy's migrant company stood out. This was an expedition rarely seen at such a scale, totaling 437 migrants, 150 wagons, 588 oxen, 336 cows, 21 calves, 107 horses, and 52 mules. At least two dozen migrants, or roughly 5 percent of total company, were enslaved. Ten of them—Biddy and her three daughters and Hannah and her five children—belonged to Robert Smith.[3] The Indigenous captives found along the Spanish Trail were generally treated as trade goods, a colonial currency of sorts. Biddy and her enslaved companions, however, went west as colonizers themselves, though certainly not of their own volition.

They were the involuntary agents of Brigham Young's grand imperial vision. Young sought to build more than just a city of God; he wanted an entire kingdom. Over the next ten years Mormon settlers would establish more than one hundred colonies and forts, dotted along a thousand-mile corridor from the Pacific to the Mountain West.[4] Young tasked his California-bound brethren with establishing an outpost that could serve as a waystation for converts arriving from across the Pacific world. But this was to be more than just a rest stop for Mormons enroute to Salt Lake City. Young envisioned it as an agricultural center in its own right. He saw "no reason why the sugar cane & cotton plant should not flourish" in Southern California.[5] If it could be done, cultivators like Robert Smith and enslaved laborers like Biddy were the ones to do it.

Although plantation crops never took root there, the colony flourished beyond Young's wildest expectations. Within a few years San Bernardino would grow into one of the most prosperous settlements in Southern California and the largest Mormon colony after Salt Lake City itself. Biddy and her enslaved compatriots were its unheralded pioneers.

· · ·

But first, Biddy would have to survive the journey there. Although she was a trail-tested veteran by this point, the route to San Bernardino presented challenges that few of her fellow travelers, slave or free, could have anticipated. Parley Pratt, one of the leaders of the expedition (and great-great-grandfather to Mitt Romney), referred to a long portion of the journey as "the hardest times I ever saw."[6]

They departed from Teeteetneet (now the city of Payson) on March 24, eluding the last gasps of winter, aside from a few final snowfalls that dropped in their way. For the first week of travel the company had plenty of fuel in the form of cedar and scrub pines as well as ample feed, thanks to the bunch grass that lined the trail. Long, monotonous days for Biddy were broken up by the occasional well-watered assembly point, where she may have been afforded a brief respite. By early May, the caravan had cleared much of Utah's rugged terrain and headed toward the grassy springs of Las Vegas. Biddy would've been glad to see the backend of the Wasatch Range with its towering peaks and its prolonged winters. What lay ahead, however, was hardly any improvement. She was bound for one of the hottest, driest, loneliest stretches of terrain anywhere in the country.

From Las Vegas the trail wound through majestic red rock cliffs, though few of the travelers had the energy or inclination to admire the view.[7] To Pratt, the landscape was a "most horrable desart [*sic*].... Consisting of mountains Ridges and plains of Naked Rock... destitute of Soil or fertility."[8] The party moved in smaller companies so as not to overtax the scant resources along the way. Feed and water, sometimes separated by dozens of miles, were rarely available in sufficient quantities to satisfy the migrants or their animals. Even when the party reached water, it was often alkaline and "unpleasant to drink," according to one weary traveler.[9] Another watering spot, according to Pratt, was as "palitable [*sic*] as a dose of Salts."[10] Thirst was Biddy's constant companion.

By late May the party had reached the scorching heart of the Mojave Desert. The terrain went from "wide plains of dreary cactuses" to "utterly herbless sand" to even more "sand, hopelessly deep and dry."[11] Biddy and the party often traveled through the night to avoid the midday heat and thereby conserve their water supply. Even so, oxen and cattle began to give out. The surviving animals and travelers stopped to rest every few minutes. Then they lumbered on. For one desolate stretch they traveled "without much intermission 2 days and 2 nights, during which we had no feed or water except that which we carried with us," Pratt wrote.[12]

Finally, by June, the wagon parties limped up and over the Cajon Pass to a predetermined meeting point within the San Bernardino Valley.

After two months of desert travel they had found their way at last to their Southern California destination.

And Biddy found herself on free soil.

. . .

Robert Smith knew this as well as anyone: California was a free state. Lawmakers had outlawed human bondage in California's 1849 constitution, which Congress approved the next year. Southerners like John C. Calhoun had spent much of that congressional session lamenting the imminent decline and fall of the plantation regime, now that California was closed to their peculiar institution.[13] So why would Smith take his ten bondspeople, in whom much of his wealth was stored, to a place that had outlawed that very form of property?

Despite the risks, California presented lures that Smith found impossible to resist. For starters there was the weather. Three snowbound winters in the high country of the Great Basin, including a treacherous expedition to the southern reaches of Utah, was more than enough for a South Carolina native like Smith. The snow still stood ten inches deep in Cottonwood, just days before his departure.[14] San Bernardino, in contrast, had mild winters, perennial sunshine, ample feed, and lengthy growing seasons.[15] Plus, Southern California didn't seem to house any of the crickets that periodically descended in biblical proportions on the fields around the Great Salt Lake.

There was also strength and comfort in numbers. Roughly half of the California-bound Mormons were Southern by birth. And many of those Southerners came by way of Mississippi.[16] They had traveled overland together, settled Cottonwood together, and now moved to California together. Above and beyond companionship, this Southern diaspora enabled tighter control over enslaved workers. Having lost his only adult male slave to flight in the Great Basin, Smith may have reasoned that his human property would be more secure in a region where white Southerners predominated. Indeed, if he could count on anyone to police his workforce, it was the Mississippi Saints. Other slaveholders in the West adopted similar settlement strategies, banding together for added security.[17]

Robert Smith also knew something that most Americans have since forgotten: California was a free state in name only.

Although the state constitution technically outlawed slavery, that ban was rarely enforced. California lawmakers lacked the means to actively monitor dozens if not hundreds of slaveholders, who often fortified themselves in remote locations. The problem wasn't just a shortage of resources, however; it was also a lack of will. Southern-born politicians and their allies occupied a disproportionate share of California's high offices. They predominated in the statehouse in Sacramento, dominated California's congressional delegation, packed its judicial posts, and monopolized the lucrative federal jobs in the state. "The State of California was as much under the control of the Southern wing of the Democratic party as South Carolina," wrote one early pioneer.[18]

Their outmatched political opponents marveled at how white Southerners, who accounted for only a third of the state's population at their demographic peak, managed it. A beleaguered California abolitionist theorized that enterprising Yankees had seized on the various business opportunities in the state, leaving politics and law to their Southern counterparts "who have nothing else to do."[19] There may have been a grain of truth to that. More to the point, slaveholders and their allies had built a well-oiled political machine that rewarded allies and punished renegades. The man pulling the levers was William Gwin, who owned two hundred enslaved people and vast tracks of land in Mississippi, even as he represented California in the US Senate. Gwin commanded fealty by distributing plum patronage jobs to his proslavery friends.[20]

With little to fear from the authorities, Southerners successfully imported hundreds of enslaved Black people into California, beginning in 1849. Most of them were forced to labor in gold country. Fortune proved an elusive idol for most miners, but slaveholding argonauts boosted their odds in proportion to the size of their workforce. Two enslaved Black men, for instance, dug up $5,000 for their owner in the space of two months.[21] Even if they didn't hit paydirt, enslaved people could earn vast sums for their owners in the impromptu slave markets of San Francisco and Sacramento. Some Black men were sold for as much as $3,000 to $4,000—quadruple what they might fetch from the auction blocks of Mississippi.[22] Others were used as collateral or even as the stakes in games of chance. Those who attempted to flee were often run down.[23]

With telling bluntness, an aspiring California master named Robert Givens shrugged off the risks of slaveholding in a free state. He urged his

Biddy was one of hundreds of enslaved Black people carried into California in the antebellum period. Two Black men (likely enslaved) work the gold diggings in El Dorado County in 1852. Courtesy of the California History Room, California State Library, Sacramento, California.

father in Kentucky to send one of the family's enslaved workers to gold country to assist him in his fledgling mining venture. "I don't consider there is any risk in bringing Patrick... as no one will put themselves to the trouble of investigating the matter," Givens wrote. "When he gets in, I should like to see any one get him out."[24] One of the nation's leading antislavery newspapers put it another way: "the only law [in California] is that of force."[25] It was a law Robert Smith knew well.

. . .

Biddy was trapped in a contradiction: a slave in a free state. Even her environment seemed to conspire in her captivity. To her west stretched a long, arid plain, running roughly seventy-five miles to the hard edge of the continent. To her north and east, the San Bernardino Mountains rose nearly twelve thousand feet above sea level. To her south were few settlements that could offer safe refuge, even if she did manage the impossible feat of escaping from Smith with her three daughters.[26]

Nor could she expect aid from the colony's leadership. The LDS apostles Amasa Lyman and Charles C. Rich shared much in common with the Southerners they had led into California. Lyman, one of the early lights of the church and close confidant of Joseph Smith, had earned the trust of the Mississippians through years of association. First, he served on a mission to the slave states, and then he settled among them in Cottonwood, Utah.[27] Rich, a Kentucky native, came by his Southern sympathies naturally. A lifelong soldier and colonizer, he led Mormon militias in Missouri, Nauvoo, and Utah, and established communities in Idaho and Iowa before agreeing to head up the San Bernardino settlement. (Although physically imposing at over six feet and somewhere between 200 and 225 pounds, Rich was soft-spoken by nature and rather inarticulate, according to some accounts. He proposed to his first wife by mail, sight-unseen. Another five wives followed from there—some with similarly abrupt courtships—who ultimately gave him fifty-one children.)[28]

Even before they found a site to occupy, Lyman and Rich appointed the ecclesiastical authorities of the settlement-in-waiting. William Crosby, the Mississippi patriarch who had brought ten enslaved people to Southern California, was named bishop, a role he held in the Cottonwood ward as well. Robert Smith became one of his two high counsellors. Thus, from the beginning, slaveholders and their allies occupied exalted positions within the colony's hierarchy.[29]

The colony had plenty of leadership; what it lacked was land. For the next three months Lyman and Rich went in search of a permanent Southern California home for their brethren. In September 1851, after several dead ends and stalled negotiations, they finally secured title to a large tract of land known as the Rancho San Bernardino. The rancho had been in the hands of the Lugo family since 1839, granted to them by the Mexican governor of California. The Lugos sold their title to Lyman and Rich for $77,500.[30]

For the cash-poor Mormon settlers this was an eye-watering sum. Their cumulative cash assets amounted to a mere $800. Considerably more than that was stored in the enslaved laborers of the colony. Biddy alone probably could have fetched $800 in certain markets. But patriarchs like Smith weren't looking to liquidate their human assets. Lyman and Rich managed to secure a loan to finance a portion of the purchase, albeit at a ruinous 30 percent annual interest rate. Although Biddy had no way of knowing it then, controversies emerging from this original land deal would open an opportunity to challenge Robert Smith and at last contest her enslavement.[31]

For the time being, however, the Mormon settlers were just glad to have a place to call their own. And no one could deny that it was a rich piece of land. "It is certainly one of the best, if not the very best tract of land in California," a local correspondent to the *Southern Californian* enthused, with just a touch of regional chauvinism.[32] The rancho's advantages included ample stores of timber from the San Bernardino Mountains, a reliable water supply from the Santa Ana River and nearby springs, a nearly inexhaustible source of feed on gently rolling fields of clover and mustard, and farmland that would soon produce some of the healthiest crops in Southern California. True, the dry heat of the valley could reach stifling heights in the summer. But the Saints were no strangers to a little discomfort.[33]

They began erecting their settlement as soon as the ink dried on the Lugo land deed. Speed was of the essence before the wetter winter season set in. Within two months they had constructed a town of roughly one hundred homes, a herculean feat that exemplified the sober work ethic and communitarian spirit for which Mormon colonists had become known.[34] It also exemplified the advantages, for white colonists, of forced labor. Many of the colony's two dozen enslaved workers contributed to the building effort.[35]

The Saints named their settlement San Bernardino after the original name of the Mexican land grant. They now laid claim to the first predominantly Anglo-American community in the southern half of the state.[36]

Before they could celebrate, however, word reached the colonists that multiple groups of California Indians were planning a coordinated attack on the LDS settlement. The Saints rapidly converted their town into an armed garrison. Within about three weeks they erected the largest fortress in Southern California. Again, the Saints were nothing if not efficient. Within high walls of willow and cottonwood, they had sealed themselves from the feared assault. They declared martial law and began drilling a militia of 150 men.[37]

The enslaved not only helped erect the fort; they also maintained order within the garrison. A man named Grief Embers, who may have been Hannah's brother-in-law, emerged as one of the central figures of the colony during those uneasy early days. One resident remembered Grief and his six-foot-long tin horn, which he used to muster the fort's militia. "He acted as a sort of bugler and blew his horn to assemble the men or for other purposes, according to different signal calls that were adopted and understood by all," the settler recalled. "Many times were all hands called out to the sound of Uncle Grief's horn."[38] Grief would later use the horn for less martial purposes. His bugling announced the beginning of major celebrations like the Fourth of July. Sources often refer to the instrument as the "bishop's horn," after Bishop William Crosby, the man who owned Grief.[39]

The feared Indigenous attack never materialized, and so the walls of the fort functioned primarily to keep Mormons in rather than to keep any enemies out. For two-and-a-half years nearly four hundred settlers squeezed into eight acres of space. Even the most vigilant housekeepers fought a rearguard action against the dirt and disorder that proliferated in such cramped quarters. "The wind blew so much, and the sand drifted in until it was inches deep on the floor," according to one family reminiscence.[40] For the vast majority of the Saints, early life in San Bernardino was lean, hard, and sustained at great personal sacrifice.[41]

. . .

Not for Robert Smith, however. While most of his brethren lived cheek-to-jowl within the fort, Smith stretched out on a choice piece of land on the southern bank of the Santa Ana River, roughly three miles from the main Mormon settlement. As one historian put it, Smith "had not come to California to live within other men's walls."[42] His decision would soon stir jealousy among the brethren. But no matter. Smith's grand ambitions of patriarchal authority and slaveholding mastery required room to roam.

The place Biddy now called home was once a mission rancho named Jumuba. One of the Lugo brothers, Jose Maria, had built a large adobe on the land, from which he reigned over his portion of the family's vast estate. Prior to that, Jumuba had been the site of Spanish missionary activity, and before that the land had sustained Indigenous people known as the Yuhaaviatam or "people of the pines."[43] Now it served Robert Smith.[44]

Robert had an eye for good land, honed from his experiences in homesteading across the length of the continent. His latest acquisition was his finest yet. Like his farm at Cottonwood, Jumuba was strategically situated near a river, on lush and gently rolling acreage. But unlike Cottonwood, Jumuba never suffered through snowbound winters. His wheat grew in abundance on his well-watered fields, supplied by the Santa Ana River and a fresh spring nearby. And his growing herd of cattle grazed on acres of mustard and clover that grew as high as the animals themselves.[45] As one visitor enthused about the setting along the Santa Ana River, "The groves, the running water, and the green river banks greet your eyes, and you remember the scriptural allusions to springs & streams in the desert."[46] Although Jumuba today sits at the site of an unlovely stretch of asphalt at the intersection of the I-10 and I-215 freeways, it would have been nothing short of idyllic when Smith settled there.[47]

Jumuba and the enslaved people who worked it had made Smith a rich man by the mid-1850s. Mormon tithing records reveal a portion of the wealth he had amassed. In addition to cash contributions, Smith gave butter and cheese from his dairy cows and wheat and flour from his fields. There were other settlers in the community who gave more, like William Crosby, but Smith sat comfortably in the upper echelon of contributors.[48] Daniel M. Thomas, another slaveholding settler in San Bernardino, noted that Smith "prosper[ed]...in the Land" with "flocks & herds" roaming his estate.[49]

Although Smith tithed like any good Mormon, he managed to avoid some of the other financial liabilities that burdened his brethren. Unlike a majority of the Saints in San Bernardino, Smith squatted on his land. As such, he owed no taxes on his ranch. Ironically, he also profited from California's antislavery constitution. Because California law didn't recognize slavery, California assessors couldn't tax enslaved property. That gave Smith a financial advantage over any planter in his native South, where enslaved people were taxed as items of personal property. The tax assessment records of San Bernardino show annual collections on Smith's wheat and dairy, but not on his most valuable assets: land and people. In other words, Smith had created a tax shelter for slavery on the ostensibly free soil of California.[50]

Beyond its fertility and low tax liability, Jumuba provided Smith with another thing he coveted: space. The lots available for purchase within San Bernardino measured just an acre in size.[51] Jumuba was orders of magnitude larger. Furthermore, it was situated several miles from the fort, giving Robert a degree of seclusion that his town-dwelling coreligionists lacked. Whereas the presence of Black laborers in San Bernardino occasionally attracted the notice of visitors to the colony, no traveler ever commented—at least not in any extant source—on Robert's enslaved workforce at Jumuba. To be sure, these visitors didn't present an active threat to the security of slaveholders in San Bernardino. Nonetheless, Smith prized privacy.[52]

That's because privacy was synonymous with autonomy. Those within the town of San Bernardino were routinely drawn into the collective enterprises on which the colony depended. Robert, however, played out his planter fantasies of the self-contained patriarch, reigning over acres of land and a large household of dependents. This had been the model of manly independence in his native South Carolina, something achieved by his grandfather and father-in-law. And now it was something he could boast for himself.[53]

By mid-decade, Robert Smith—or rather, his enslaved laborers—had transformed Jumuba into a peculiar hybrid. It was something between a slave plantation and a ranch, with cattle and wheat rather than cotton or sugar driving the workloads of the day. Jumuba, that is, fused the archetypal Southern and Western worlds that Robert had inhabited across decades of migration. He was now a prosperous planter-cum-ranchero, lording over his fiefdom on the banks of the Santa Ana River. Biddy, meanwhile, remained what she had always been: an enslaved woman with seemingly no way out.

6 Hiding in Plain Sight

By mid-decade, Robert Smith and his fellow LDS settlers in San Bernardino had achieved something unfamiliar: the respect of their non-Mormon neighbors. Many colonists still wore the scars inflicted by anti-Mormon mobs in New York, Ohio, Missouri, and Illinois. And now, suddenly, they found themselves the subjects of fawning attention in California. Visitors to San Bernardino enthused over numerous aspects of the Mormon enterprise: their location ("one of the most charming places in the country");[1] their farming ("agricultural wealth . . . that can scarcely be estimated");[2] their work ethic ("the most industrious beings on the face of the globe");[3] their future prospects (destined to become "the most beautiful city of California");[4] and perhaps unsurprisingly, their whiteness (unlike Los Angeles, San Bernardino wasn't "choked up with mongrel races of all colors").[5] Thousands of Saints had finally found their place.

And yet, in all that positive attention, a key ingredient to San Bernardino's success went unnoticed. The enslaved people who helped build the colony's roads, mill its lumber, work its fields, drive its livestock, and sustain its households were conspicuously absent from contemporary commentary (and from most historical accounts ever since). Robert Smith and his brethren had managed to build a slaveholding settlement—the most durable and prosperous ever erected in the American Far West, by almost any metric—without legal interference. San Bernardino was an unfree colony in a free state, hiding in plain sight.

. . .

Robert Smith's Jumuba ranch showcased the fortunes to be made from enslaved labor in Southern California. But what had become a triumph for Smith was, for Biddy, just another field to hoe, a herd to corral, and a household to oversee. Indeed, Robert's growing wealth brought a proliferating workload for her and the others. The tasks around the rancho would have filled every last hour of the day. First, the enslaved had to build homes for Robert's expanding family and for themselves. Then, they had to clear the land for his wheat fields and plant the first crop. And while the crops matured, they also had to oversee a growing stock of range cattle and dairy cows.[6]

Much of Biddy's work probably took place in the fields with the cattle. Next to his enslaved laborers and his land, Robert's livestock were his most valuable assets. No one knew these animals better than Biddy. She had driven them across thousands of miles of trail, steering them through nearly every topographical and environmental challenge the Western landscape had to offer. Safely settled on Jumuba, she would have continued to manage at least some of his stock. Given the size of the ranch and the heavy tasks involved—branding and driving the cattle, for instance—Biddy may have also worked alongside a staff of Indigenous or Mexican laborers, known as *vaqueros*. Cattle ranching was Southern California's biggest business, and thanks to Biddy's herding along the trail and now her work on Jumuba, Robert Smith could claim his share of the enterprise.[7]

According to his tithing records, Smith generated a sizable portion of his income from the produce of his livestock. Again, Biddy's labor would have been crucial. She or her daughters were probably responsible for milking Smith's cows and churning some of that milk into butter or converting it to cheese, which could be transported to Los Angeles for sale. Although the dairy would often spoil during the three-day journey between the two settlements, Angelenos continued to source their foodstuffs from Mormons like Smith. "This disadvantage . . . was in part com-

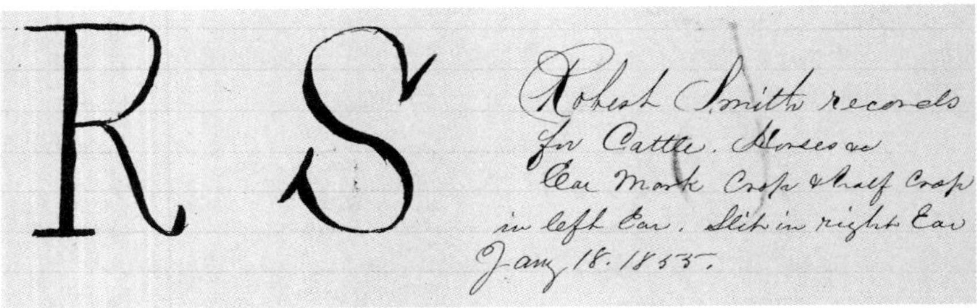

Robert Smith's cattle brand. Brand Book A, San Bernardino County Historical Archives.

pensated for by the economical advantage of the industry and thrift of the Mormons, and their favorable situation in an open, fertile country," one Los Angeles resident recalled. "They could afford to sell us their produce very reasonably."[8] San Bernardino dairy cows were generally regarded as superior to their Los Angeles counterparts. With eager buyers Mormons raised two thousand pounds of butter for sale in 1855 alone and another twenty-five hundred pounds of cheese.[9]

Jumuba also produced wheat in significant quantities. Biddy, by now a jill-of-all-trades, probably spent at least a portion of her day in the fields. She began pulling in healthy yields within just a few years. The thirty-three bushels of wheat and the nearly twenty dollars in flour that Smith tithed in 1853 speak to his prosperity—and the diversified workload of his enslaved laborers.[10]

Maintenance of the Smith home produced another bevy of tasks for the enslaved. As ever, they attended to Rebecca's domestic needs: cleaning, cooking, serving, washing, and childcare, among other jobs. Of Rebecca's seven children, four were under the age of nine by the time they settled in Jumuba. Childcare responsibilities alone probably involved multiple enslaved caretakers, either Biddy, Hannah, or likely some of their own children. Because Hannah gave birth around the same time as Rebecca, she may have been enlisted as a wet nurse for the youngest Smith child. Every hour spent with the Smith children was one less hour she and Biddy had with their own families.[11]

Biddy and Hannah also made money for Smith beyond the bounds of Jumuba. San Bernardino's multiplying projects—new homes, new roads, new mills, not to mention plenty of fieldwork and domestic tasks—created a labor shortage within the colony. Smith was happy to fill the void, for a price. Strong, seasoned workers like Biddy and Hannah could be hired out at a premium. This was a common practice throughout the slave South as well as within California's gold country. And Robert Smith wasn't one to miss a money-making opportunity.[12]

If the colony's cofounder, Amasa Lyman, had any aversion to slavery, he certainly didn't let that get in the way of his needs. "This morning went to [Brother] Robert Smith's to hire his colored woman to work for us," Lyman wrote in his diary in April 1854.[13] Who that woman was, Lyman didn't specify. Most likely it was Biddy or Hannah, as one of Lyman's wives had just given birth and she required a skilled caretaker and domestic worker. That summer, Lyman also hired some of Bishop William Crosby's enslaved laborers to help operate his lumber mill.[14]

Robert derived particular value from the medical skill of Biddy and Hannah. According to one of San Bernardino's early historians, Hannah "was the midwife of the colony . . . [who] responded to calls day or night."[15] Biddy, although not mentioned by name in the sources, almost certainly delivered some of San Bernardino's babies as well. Indeed, she later testified to the fact that her career as a midwife began in the early 1850s, while she lived in San Bernardino. She and Hannah would have honed their medical knowledge together, exchanging recipes for remedies and conferring on time-tested methods. Eventually this knowledge would enrich and empower Biddy. For the time being, however, it enriched only Robert.[16]

There was no shortage of work for skilled midwives in the mushrooming colony. More than twenty-five children were born to San Bernardino Mormons during the first spring and summer of settlement. The birthrate rarely slowed from there.[17] Frontier midwives like Biddy and Hannah did far more than deliver babies, though. They also provided prenatal advice, postpartum services, as well as general health care. Mormon families often hired midwives to stay in the home for up to ten days after delivery. It's doubtful, however, that Smith ever allowed his Mormon brethren to retain the services of Biddy or Hannah for so long, as valued as their expertise was. They were needed back on Jumuba.[18]

Biddy and Hannah enriched Smith, not only with each baby they delivered but also through the accumulated value of their medical knowledge. By the time they reached Southern California, Biddy was roughly thirty-three years old, considered past prime age for an enslaved woman. In fact, she had already exceeded the life expectancy of the average enslaved person in the South, a mere twenty-five years. Black people who survived to forty were considered elderly. In most cases a woman of Biddy's age would have depreciated sharply in the estimation of any prospective buyer. Yet given their medical skills, which came at a premium in San Bernardino, she and Hannah had probably appreciated in value. This explains why Smith would fight fiercely to keep them in bondage even as they approached "old age."[19]

While Robert Smith was profiting from the minds of his enslaved women, he also exploited their bodies. The pattern of predation that likely began in Mississippi continued in California. Of the three children that Hannah delivered while living there, only one of them, Martha, was claimed by her husband Toby. The other two, Marion and Henry, were most likely Smith's. In fact, Henry is explicitly identified as Smith's son in later records.[20] Hannah's teenage daughter, Ann, also gave birth to a baby named Mary during this time (father unknown). The arrival of those children brought the total number of Robert's enslaved property to fourteen people by early 1856. Through reproduction—some of it compelled—he had become the largest slaveholder in California.[21]

. . .

As the enslaved labored, San Bernardino flourished. In fact, the colony grew at a pace that no other settlement in Southern California ever had. When the Mormons arrived in 1851, San Bernardino was undeveloped ranchland belonging to a single family (although Indigenous people had, for untold generations, made a home there). Within just a few years the settlement's population had bulged to nearly three thousand to rival neighboring Los Angeles in size. According to a knowledgeable source, San Bernardino's cultivators also outproduced the agricultural yield of Santa Barbara, San Diego, and Los Angeles counties *combined*.[22]

Mormons began tilling the land as soon as they gained title to it. "Plowers are to be seen moving tirelessly through the ground in all directions," the colony's scribe reported proudly in December 1851.[23] The next fall, settlers held a harvest festival to celebrate their first bumper crop. "Every person upon the place White Black Red was . . . invited" to marvel at the superlative produce of Southern California: a twenty-four-pound cabbage, a sixteen-foot cornstalk, and melons the size of small children.[24] Mormons harvested much of that produce from what they called their Big Field (which eventually grew to several big fields), totaling about eight thousand acres by mid-decade.[25]

Wheat was San Bernardino's main cash crop. Cultivators harvested more than fifty thousand bushels of it in 1854 alone. They then milled it into a fine flour that elicited rave reviews from authorities across the region. San Bernardino "will defy competition in the manufacturing of flour, in quality, quantity, and cheapness," enthused the *Southern Californian*, which regarded the colony's flour as "probably the best brought to this market [Los Angeles]."[26] To irrigate their crop, Mormons diverted the valley's streams and creeks, creating "crop cultivation and related technology and practices on a larger scale than had ever before existed in California," according to the foremost historian of early San Bernardino.[27]

Another major source of revenue came from the export of lumber. First, colonists, slave and free alike, constructed a twelve-mile road into the San Bernardino Mountains to access the ample supplies of alder, hemlock, and sycamore there. Then they built six lumber mills to process the logs that they felled and hauled from the mountains. Each mill could churn out three hundred thousand board feet of lumber annually, a commodity that became known as "Mormon banknotes." Ox carts, loaded with these banknotes, fanned out across Southern California, underwriting much of the region's development. "San Bernardino . . . supplied all of our wants in the lumber line," wrote Harris Newmark of Los Angeles, a town that owed much of its construction to this supply of wood.[28]

Los Angeles grew incrementally that decade; San Bernardino grew rampantly. In spring 1854 residents finally moved out from the walls of their fort and into city lots. Within six months they had erected more than one hundred adobe and lumber homes, aligned on wide streets intersecting at right angles. The homes were fronted by flower gardens and ornamental trees, with room in the rear for orchards and vegetable patches. Irrigation canals ran along each street. The canopies of shade trees extended over the sidewalks. The cumulative result was a handsome, leafy town—a sanctuary both spiritual and ecological within inland California. Los Angeles appeared squalid and forlorn in comparison.[29] Alongside the handsome one-acre lots of San Bernardino, Lyman's residence stood out.

Two stories high and 125-feet wide, the adobe mansion contained sixteen rooms, divided into separate apartments for each wife. Admirers praised it as an "ornament to the city." Critics called it a harem.[30]

No single residence drew more praise than the colony's hotel, known as the San Bernardino House. And no single residence, aside from Smith's Jumuba ranch, more clearly exhibited the profits that could be wrenched from forced labor. The hotel's proprietor, Bishop William Crosby, owned ten enslaved people. Those laborers not only helped build the San Bernardino House, they staffed it and served its many visitors.[31] Some of those visitors commented on the presence of Black workers at the hotel, though they generally ignored, elided, or excused their unfree status. District Judge Benjamin Hayes, himself a former slaveholder, simply noted, "Negro servants. Good table."[32] Another visitor marveled at the leisure enjoyed by Mrs. Crosby and the reason for it: "Household work she did none; there were negroes to do that."[33]

When not working the hotel, Crosby's Black laborers played key roles elsewhere in San Bernardino. They erected some of the first homes in the settlement; they helped carve the main road to the San Bernardino Mountains; and they operated one of the colony's lucrative lumber mills. On their days off some of them would work for white settlers in exchange for extra food. All that labor left Toby Embers, who belonged to Crosby, with precious little time to visit Hannah and their two children on Jumuba.[34]

With demographic growth came political influence for San Bernardino's white colonists. Jefferson Hunt, a Kentucky native and LDS elder, won a seat in the California legislature in 1852. Acting on a petition first circulated by the slaveholding Mormon Daniel M. Thomas, Assemblyman Hunt convinced lawmakers in Sacramento to designate San Bernardino as a separate county. Previously, most of the valley had belonged to Los Angeles County. The newly-formed San Bernardino County measured more than twenty thousand square miles, roughly half the size of the state of New York, making it the largest county in the lower forty-eight states, which it remains to this day.[35]

Despite San Bernardino's breakneck growth, its leaders managed to preserve a degree of order that drew envious tributes from neighbors. "San Bernardino must be a model city, and it would be well if all the towns and cities in the State would take pattern in point of the neatness, order, and the industry of their inhabitants," reported the *Alta California* from

San Francisco.[36] Although the "Word of Wisdom"—the strict code of abstinence covering alcohol, tobacco, tea, and coffee—didn't become a Mormon commandment until the 1890s, San Bernardino was already trending toward temperance. Visitors marveled at the "absence of gambling houses, whisky shops, rows, riots and all their thousand concomitant evils."[37] The orderliness of San Bernardino garnered special attention from residents of Los Angeles, a town afflicted by one of the highest murder rates in the country.[38] Even the Spanish language press of Los Angeles joined in the praise for San Bernardino ("una sociedad bien organizada").[39] The Mormons never bothered to build a jail or a courthouse. The occasional prisoner was boarded in private quarters, while rented rooms in Crosby's hotel served as a makeshift courtroom. The minutes from San Bernardino's court of sessions make for painfully dull reading.[40]

. . .

San Bernardino drew praise for its rule of law even as the colony's leaders were actively flouting a key provision in the state constitution. Article I, Section 18 of the state's founding document reads, "Neither Slavery nor involuntary Servitude, unless for the punishment of crimes, shall ever be tolerated in this State."[41] And yet, with virtually no resistance and barely any commentary, Mormon migrants had managed to plant a slaveholding colony there.

Mormons weren't of course the only slaveholders in the state. White Southerners had been importing Black bondspeople into the region since the first months of the gold rush. But for its prosperity and longevity, slaveholding San Bernardino was unique. Enslaved African Americans typically entered California in a trickle, one or two at a time. With Mormons they came in a stream, more than two dozen in the first migrant party. And even though several LDS leaders spoke frankly about the presence of enslaved people in San Bernardino, the colony's slaveholding class had gone undisturbed.[42]

Others had attempted to launch large slaveholding enterprises in California. During the early stages of the gold rush, some mining companies held upwards of a dozen people in bondage. Thomas Jefferson Green, a Texas revolutionary turned California argonaut, led one of these outfits. Green and his enslaved miners worked the diggings around Rose's Bar in July 1849. But they were soon run off by a group of antislavery miners, who vowed bloodshed if the Black men didn't vacate their claims.[43] The venture of William F. English, a planter from Florida, was similarly short-lived and ill-fated. English had sailed to California with thirty-five enslaved laborers aboard his private steamship in 1850. He briefly operated a shipping and retail business out of San Francisco. Just eighteen months after his arrival, however, a fatal shooting accident put an end to English and his slaveholding operation.[44] Although a more diffuse enterprise, the miners of Burke and McDowell Counties, North Carolina, managed to transport an estimated two hundred enslaved Black men to work across California's gold country.[45]

For sheer audacity, none could match the ambitions of James Gadsden. Gadsden is best remembered for a land deal that bears his name, which transferred nearly thirty thousand square miles of northern Mexico to the United States in 1854. Before that he attempted an even bolder scheme in California. In 1851 he began conspiring with none other than Thomas Jefferson Green, now stripped of his human property, to establish a slaveholding colony in central California. Gadsden rallied more than one thousand white Southerners, who pledged a further two thousand enslaved laborers, toward the building of his California dream. He petitioned the California legislature for permission to settle in flagrant disregard of the constitution that these lawmakers had sworn to uphold. The plot received a hearing before dying quietly in the committee on federal relations.[46]

Mormons had succeeded where Gadsden only dared to dream. To do so, they relied on complicit lawmakers at multiple levels. The state legislature remained overwhelmingly Democratic, and largely proslavery, during these years. Meanwhile, William Gwin, the Mississippi planter-cum-California senator, paid a personal visit to San Bernardino in September 1854. If he encountered Biddy or any other enslaved people during his stay, Gwin would have been all too happy to look the other way.[47]

Perhaps even more important than the tacit support of national powerbrokers like Gwin was the collusion of local leaders like Daniel M. Thomas. Despite his thin resume—"a man of fair education, but without learning as a lawyer"—Thomas was installed as county judge of San Bernardino in 1853.[48] His was one of several appointments that gave slaveholding Saints a commanding share of the colony's highest offices. Another Mississippi Saint, John H. Holladay, became constable.[49] And Bishop Crosby continued to hold the highest ecclesiastical office, while Robert Smith served for several years as his high counsellor. Even the colony's cofounders, Lyman and Rich, benefited from enslaved labor. Furthermore, San Bernardino's leading political representative, Jefferson Hunt, was Southern by birth and partisan affiliation.[50] Virtually none of the major figures in San Bernardino had any interest in disrupting the status quo.

San Bernardino slaveholders also relied on misinformation. Most, if not all, of the enslaved people in the colony were illiterate. Aside from word of mouth from sympathetic parties, they had no way of learning that they now resided in a technically free state. Their owners aimed to keep it that way, according to Ralph Johnson, a descendent of one of the enslaved pioneers. "Many of the slaves brought to California continued in slavery because their masters kept them ignorant of the law," he said in a 1972 interview with a local historian. "They continued working for their master until information trickled down concerning their freedom."[51]

Robert Smith likely practiced another type of subterfuge. As Hannah's daughter Martha later recalled, the enslaved people under Robert's control lived in "terror" of the idea of independence.[52] Smith had doubtlessly intimidated them from pursuing freedom. He may have painted lurid images of the horrors that awaited Black mothers and their children when not under his care. This was a common tactic among Southern slaveholders, something Harriet Jacobs, after finally winning her freedom, recalled painfully: "If you were to hear the enormous lies [slaveholders] tell their slaves, you would have small respect for their veracity."[53]

To this day, the long-gone slaveholders of San Bernardino continue to deceive. Almost every major study of early San Bernardino maintains that Black people like Biddy were granted their freedom upon their arrival in California.[54] In doing so, historians parrot the fictions of the enslavers themselves. William Crosby apparently claimed that his "servants" had elected to work for him "voluntarily," while Robert Smith insisted that his Black bondspeople had followed him to California of their own free will.[55]

One simple fact gives the lie to the myth of "voluntary" Black labor in San Bernardino: Only when legal authorities finally challenged Smith did other Black people in the settlement dare to leave their enslavers. Until then, they remained bound to the families that had owned them for years. Even after the death of her legal owner in 1855, Elizabeth Flake remained with the white Flake family, with no apparent change in her enslaved status. For Elizabeth, Biddy, and the other Black workers of San Bernardino, California's so-called free soil was still the terrain of slavery.[56]

· · ·

Slaveholders like Robert Smith also took cover behind a different form of human bondage: the coerced labor of California Indians. Colonizers had been exploiting California's Indigenous population since before the Spanish established their first mission in 1769. Indeed, Native Americans had been held in bondage and bartered as trade goods for hundreds of years across the Americas, part of a tragic history described by scholar Andrés Resendez as "the other slavery."[57] When Americans rushed into California in 1849, rates of enslavement and murder soared. Between 1850 and 1863 roughly twenty thousand California Indians labored in bondage. They could be found from one end of the state to the other, including San Bernardino.[58]

Rather than attempt to curb Indigenous enslavement, California lawmakers licensed it. The "Act for the Government and Protection of Indians" may go down as the most tragic misnomer in California legal history. Passed in 1850, the statute legalized a wide array of coercive labor practices, including child servitude, debt bondage, and convict leasing. Indian minors were particularly vulnerable. Aspiring masters simply had to convince a sympathetic court that the relationship was "voluntary," and they could legally claim the labor of Indigenous children without compensation, until age fifteen for girls and eighteen for boys.[59]

Some enslavers didn't even bother with legal recourses, however. They raided Indian communities, murdered the adults, and abducted their orphans. The captives could be sold for around fifty dollars a head. Slave raiding fueled a vicious campaign against California Indians that can only be described as genocide. Between 1845 and 1870 the California Indian population plummeted from an estimated 150,000 to 30,000.[60] Although some lawmakers decried the practice—what one Indian superintendent called an "unholy traffic in human blood and souls"—their outrage fell on deaf ears in Washington, DC, and Sacramento. The trade in Indigenous slaves continued in California well into the next decade.[61]

The result was a sprawling landscape of Native slavery, according to Edward O. C. Ord, an Army engineer who made multiple surveys of

Southern California in the antebellum era. "Each of the large cattle ranchos near Los Angeles and San Bernardino has from fifteen to thirty Indians permanently occupied on it and they are numerously employed by the Mormons at San Bernardino," he reported. Although Ord admitted to using Indian servants himself from time to time, he was alarmed by the abuses he encountered in what he tellingly termed the "free? state" of California. "In this county, no one, not even the Indian agents, deny that the Indians are miserably abused by their own system." The Indigenous workers of the West were treated worse, he concluded, than the Black slaves of the South.[62]

Contemporary descriptions of Southern California's ranches bear an uncanny resemblance to Southern plantations. "The rich Dons who lived in this valley had a goodly number of vassals . . . little better than slaves," recalled one observer. Indigenous servitude enabled these "patriarchal" landholders to live "in stately pomp on his leagues of domain, unvexed by the doings of the outer world."[63] Historian Hubert Howe Bancroft made the comparison more explicit still. Shortly after the Civil War he visited the ranch of Cave Couts, a Tennessee transplant who exploited large numbers of Indigenous laborers on his San Diego ranch. "Everything about Guajorne [Couts's property] had the air of the home of a wealthy southern planter," Bancroft marveled.[64] Robert Smith therefore had plenty of models for patriarchal mastery in Southern California.

San Bernardino's settlers had become habituated—one might say morally inured—to the presence of laborers in various states of bondage. Whether captive Indians or enslaved African Americans, much of San Bernardino ran on coercion. Robert Smith was in fact a relative latecomer to the enterprise of labor exploitation in Southern California. Rancheros had for generations built their quasi-feudal dominions on the backs of uncompensated workers. Smith's labor force was distinctive in its composition—Black rather than brown—but not in its operation. He was simply doing what colonizers in California had long seen as their right: coercing the labor of those they deemed inferior.[65]

. . .

Robert Smith had crossed the continent in search of more—more land, more wealth, greater independence. And here along the banks of the

Santa Ana River in Southern California, he found it. Jumuba flourished as he drove his enslaved workers in a variety of enterprises, from ranching to wheat cultivation to midwifery. Even if Biddy had been informed of California's free-soil constitution, the document had little tangible meaning for her. Jumuba lay beyond the reach of anyone willing or able to enforce the state's antislavery law.

But internal frictions within San Bernardino were about to shake Robert Smith's world to its core and provide Biddy with her first real chance at freedom.

7 Unmaking a Patriarch

The honeymoon was over. By 1855 the prosperity and harmony that characterized the early days of San Bernardino's settlement—and drew flattering attention from even non-Mormon neighbors—had been usurped by a growing sense of unease. "The spirit of dissension and apostasy is daily becoming more evident," fretted San Bernardino's official secretary Richard Hopkins in August that year. "Some men who have occupied responsible stations in the church here are very violent against the authorities."[1]

The Mormon leadership had a name for their recent troubles: "R.M. Smith one of the High Council."[2] From his Jumuba ranch Robert Smith fueled a growing opposition movement at the southern fringes of the colony. Although he was hardly the only problem in the eyes of the church, Smith's dissent had become particularly worrisome. If one of their most trusted, most exalted, wealthiest brethren could stray, what did that augur for the rest of them? Soon, Smith's resistance to the LDS leadership would erupt into open conflict with far-reaching consequences.

Biddy may not have been privy to the delicate intricacies of Mormon politics, but she, like so many enslaved people, would have tracked developments much more shrewdly than her owner cared to admit. Smith did little to hide his growing agitation with his coreligionists. His frustrations guided nearly everything he did in 1855. And Biddy took note. Where there was misfortune for her enslaver, there might be opportunity for her family.[3]

. . .

Smith's problems, ironically, stemmed from his good fortune. He had grown wealthy and independent while the settlement's founders attempted to bring the colonists more tightly under their control. Land became the central bone of contention. What Smith had claimed they now coveted.

The root of the trouble lay in the terms of the original land grant, which had been transferred from the ownership of the Lugo family to Amasa Lyman and Charles C. Rich. For $77,500, Lyman and Rich had purchased a rancho that totaled somewhere between eighty thousand to one hundred thousand acres. Or so they thought. In actuality, the fine print of the original land grant entitled its owners to less than half that—roughly thirty-five thousand acres.[4]

Lyman and Rich depended on the sale of individual plots to cover the enormous debt they had incurred to acquire the land. Anything that fell outside of their thirty-five thousand acres could be purchased by settlers directly from the government at lower fixed prices. Although most San Bernardino Saints had been regularly contributing to the LDS Church in the form of tithes, those donations went to Salt Lake City, rather than to pay down the ranch debt. With significantly fewer acres to sell than they had once imagined, the colony itself was in jeopardy.[5]

Fortunately for Lyman and Rich, the US Land Commission allowed them to select any thirty-five thousand acres within the broader vicinity of their colony. Rather than claim those acres immediately, they waited to see where colonists settled. Presumably those would be the most fertile plots and therefore yield the best returns for the church. It so happened that some of the choicest lands were located just south of the Santa Ana River, several miles from the main settlement. At least one property in particular stood out: Robert Smith's Jumuba ranch.[6]

Smith, however, was not in a giving mood. He had always treated Jumuba as his private fiefdom. And while he regularly contributed tithes to the church, he wasn't about to offer his land to the colony. Jumuba lay beyond the original Mormon land claim, he insisted, and was therefore subject to squatters' rights, not to the inventive boundary lines that Lyman and Rich were now attempting to draw. Smith knew he had a good thing going. For years he had deliberately shielded his most valuable assets from taxation, and he wasn't inclined to pony up now. Why pay when you could simply squat? And why forfeit what you had already seized?[7]

The homesteads around Jumuba became the nerve center of a growing opposition movement, which manifested in rebellions against the colony's land policy and against the church leaders themselves. In spring 1855 the dissenters nominated two candidates for newly-created seats on the county board of supervisors. It was a minor contest with major implications. Customarily, elections in Mormon communities weren't elections as such. The church leadership put up a single slate of candidates, which voters were expected to affirm. As one San Bernardino settler recalled, "Their real government was a very thinly disguised hierarchy of the church, even if it could be called disguised at all."[8] To challenge the candidates handpicked by Lyman and Rich, even for a post as unsexy as the county board of supervisors, was to court excommunication.[9]

Which is precisely what happened. The opposition party was jeered and pelted by stones as they paraded through San Bernardino on the night before the election. Then they were beaten decisively at the polls. Then they were hauled before the church leadership to answer for their apostasy. When they refused to recant, they were disfellowshipped and finally excommunicated.[10]

Rather than chastening the dissenters, such retribution further entrenched the opposition. Smith wasn't among those disciplined for his politics in this instance, but the entire episode, which unfolded in parallel with his land dispute, pushed him further from the fold. Other prominent Saints "turned against the authorities," according to the colony's official secretary.[11] Meanwhile, a motley assortment of non-Mormons—dispirited goldseekers, speculators, squatters, and ne'er-do-wells of all varieties—filtered south of the Santa Ana River and rallied under the opposition banner.[12] Visitors to the colony detected an apprehensive, acquisitive spirit hanging over the community, often with a sinister edge.[13] As Edward Ord reported, San Bernardino "is surrounded with unscrupulous squatters and dissenters, anxious for an excuse to drive [Mormons leaders] from the country."[14]

Brigham Young looked on in disgust. From the start, Young had been a fair-weather and rather tight-fisted patron of the colony. Although he longed for an extensive kingdom for the faithful, he hoped to build it on a budget. He bemoaned the departure of so many Saints when the first colonists set out from Cottonwood for Southern California. His misgivings intensified as California's superior weather, longer growing seasons, and rumors of gold continued to lure much-needed colonists from the Great Basin. He repeatedly growled about "the scum, the half hearted, that float off upon the light air," and drifted toward California. By May 1855, San Bernardino had become "a cage of every unclean and hateful bird," he spat.[15] That one of Young's former wives fled Salt Lake City and settled in San Bernardino certainly didn't improve his opinion.[16]

By late 1855, Mormon San Bernardino was being squeezed from multiple angles. Dissent became increasingly difficult to ignore, given that the antiestablishment camp included some of the most powerful men in the colony. Meanwhile, the ranch debt hung like a cloud over the entire enterprise. Early San Bernardino had flourished through collective action and self-sacrifice. But within just a few years much of that communal spirit had disintegrated, leaving a fractured colony in its wake.

. . .

San Bernardino's leaders weren't the only ones after Robert Smith and his land. Nature itself seemed to be set against him.

As land disputes roiled and dissent intensified, a blight struck San Bernardino. It came in the form of rust, a fungal disease that periodically attacks wheat, barley, and rye. A year earlier, San Bernardino colonists had harvested a bumper crop of fifty thousand bushels of wheat. By spring 1855 the region's agriculturists faced "general ruin," with a four-thousand-acre enclosure in San Bernardino "entirely gone with the rust."[17] The rust compounded the problems caused by late rains from the year before, which damaged much of the crop.[18] One correspondent estimated that five-sixths of the entire San Bernardino crop had been destroyed, placing the Mormons "under great pecuniary embarrassments," according to another report.[19] On top of everything, one of the colony's sawmills burned to the ground at an estimated loss of $10,000 to $20,000.[20]

Then came a plague of a different nature. Hordes of grasshoppers, "like the locusts of Egypt," descended on Southern California's ranches. Landowners averted general disaster only because the grass dried up and thus became unpalatable to the grasshoppers.[21] A God-fearing man like Smith would have been hard-pressed to look past such an omen or to disregard its biblical echoes. He once hoped that by leaving the Great Salt Lake, he had escaped such visitations. But the locusts, it seems, followed him west. Even after the grasshoppers departed, the ranchers continued to suffer. Later in the year, a report from Los Angeles County confirmed the alarming news that "the stock is dying for want of grass."[22]

While some threats came from above, others came in the night. Thieves struck San Bernardino during these troubled years, and evidence suggests that they may have targeted Robert Smith. "The quiet little city of San Bernardino has been somewhat disturbed recently by several daring robberies," reported the *Los Angeles Star*. The crimes were allegedly committed by two horse thieves, a Black man and a Mexican man.[23] An earlier report noted that "Mr. Smith of San Bernardino, had two horses stolen from his stable."[24] As tempting as it is to imagine an interracial duo of Western Robin Hoods exacting justice on the largest slaveholder in the state, we lack sufficient evidence to confirm that Robert Smith was the target or that these particular men were the culprits. There was indeed another Mr. Smith in San Bernardino at the time. Yet even if Robert wasn't the mark, news of a Black desperado—who was briefly captured but then escaped from jail—would have been alarming enough for a man who currently held more than a dozen African Americans in bondage on his remote ranch.[25]

By the summer of 1855, Smith took stock of his rapidly deteriorating prospects. Rust had killed his crop, locusts had attacked his pastures, and thieves stalked the vicinity in search of horses to steal. In Robert's eyes, though, the most dangerous threat remained Lyman and Rich. Whereas bandits threatened his livestock, the colony's cofounders sought his livelihood. If he lost his ranch to them, he'd have nothing but a herd of cattle without pasture, seven children without a home, and thirteen (soon to be fourteen) enslaved people without a place to work them.

Robert didn't require any more convincing. He had had enough of San Bernardino and the people who ran it. And so he enacted a familiar routine: he marshaled his household, corralled his livestock, readied his wagons, and went in search of the next frontier.[26]

. . .

The West had always been his destination, the place where Robert Smith sought opportunity and fortune. First it was Mississippi during the flush times of the 1830s. Then it was Utah in the great Mormon migration of the late 1840s. And finally he came to Southern California, where for a time he thrived as a rancher and wheat farmer. But after about three thousand miles of migration, Smith had finally run out of continent. So he decided to double back and revive an old dream of his—Texas.

Texas had been the original plan when he first set out from Mississippi in 1847. But a swollen river had blocked his progress, and ultimately his LDS brethren convinced him to join them on the exodus to the Great Basin. Now that he had severed most of his ties with the church, Robert was free to make his own way once again.[27]

Texas had been a magnet for American slaveholders well before it was US territory. Some of the largest landholders in Mexican Tejas were migrants from the neighboring US slaveholding states. They poured into Tejas in the 1820 and 1830s, lured by cheap land on which to build cotton plantations. For each enslaved person they imported, they received an additional fifty acres. When they rebelled from Mexico and won independence in 1836, they placed slavery at the heart of their constitution.[28] For the next quarter century the exploitation of slave labor remained the surest path to prosperity in Texas. It was therefore a natural draw for someone like Robert Smith, who already had a large enslaved Black workforce with which to raise cotton, rear cattle, or simply sell.[29]

What made Texas alluring for Smith made it terrifying for Biddy. "[I] always feared this trip to Texas, since I first heard of it," she would later state.[30] For seventeen years and multiple relocations, she had somehow managed to hold her family together. Now, the specter of separation, the most traumatic experience of her adolescence, loomed large over the upcoming expedition. Had Smith wanted to sell any of his enslaved laborers in Utah or California, he would have found relatively few buyers. True, such transactions occurred in both places, but they were rare. In Texas, however, they were routine. And some of Smith's human property had only appreciated in value. Biddy's daughter Ellen and Hannah's daughter Ann had reached their most marketable years, measured by their productive and, crucially, their reproductive potential.

From Jumuba, Smith and his household traveled to Los Angeles, a three-day journey with numerous tests and snags along the way. The first twenty miles of trail wound through a waterless plain. The road was lined with "chaparral, a thicket of gnarled sage-brush," from which the howls of wolves emanated, according to a contemporary traveler. There were also the "scattered herds of wild-looking Spanish cattle" to contend with, who "pawed the ground and made eyes" at passing travelers. Not until they reached El Monte did the terrain finally soften. From there to Los Angeles it was an easy day's journey through rich pastureland populated with more docile animals. They made camp in the Santa Monica Mountains, to the west of Los Angeles.[31]

Altogether the journey amounted to a lengthy detour of at least sixty miles and several hard days of travel. Smith wanted to head east, so why start by going west? Surely he had learned his cardinal directions in his many years of pioneering.

Some accounts suggest that Smith was headed to the port of San Pedro, about thirty-five miles south of Santa Monica. Once there, he would board a ship, according to this theory, to ferry he and his household from California.[32] But such a possibility misses the fact that the ranchlands of central Texas were more easily reached by overland wagon roads than by ship from California. Plus, traveling by sea was an expensive mode of transportation, and Smith was husbanding his resources to buy as much land (and perhaps as many slaves) as possible in Texas.[33]

Rather, Smith went west for temporary refuge and resupply. He needed provisions and additional workers for the upcoming journey, and he could no longer trust his brethren in San Bernardino. Perhaps he had even been blackballed by the merchants there after he made his public break with Lyman and Rich. He therefore sought a neutral site to supply his wagons and hire trailhands.[34]

Smith bivouacked in the Santa Monica Mountains, rather than stay in Los Angeles, as a precaution. He cut a conspicuous figure with his retinue of more than a dozen enslaved Black people. Had Biddy or any others contemplated escape, Los Angeles would have been the place to do it, with its small but active free Black community. The Santa Monica Mountains, however, were sufficiently rugged, remote, and vast to deter either Biddy or Hannah's families from escaping together. (Today the Santa Monica Mountains National Recreation Area is the largest urban national park in the world.) Fearsome, potentially deadly animals—rattlesnakes, mountain lions, bobcats, coyotes, and bears—lurked and prowled in the canyons.[35]

Travelers pitch their tents near present-day Rustic Canyon in the Santa Monica Mountains. This was the approximate location of Robert Smith's encampment in the winter of 1855–56. William Godfrey, published by H. T. Payne, Santa Monica (Watering Place), ca. 1871, Philip D. Nathanson Collection of Southern California stereographs, approximately 1870s–1890s. Huntington Library, San Marino, California.

Together, Biddy and Hannah had five children and one grandchild under the age of eight. This was no country for young runaways.

Thus by late 1855, Biddy was pinned at the far edge of the continent. She had now covered more American terrain—roughly three thousand miles of forced overland travel from Georgia to California—than almost any other enslaved person of the era. Here, on this isolated stretch of coastline perched above the Pacific Ocean, her westward odyssey hit a natural terminus.

But where one trail ended, another began. Smith prepared the wagons for the next stage of the journey. Biddy was forced to confront the tragic prospect of another thousand-mile march along another dust-choked trail, and the likelihood of permanent separation from her daughters once they reached Texas. The long nights of December 1855 must have been some of the darkest of her entire life. She could only pray that someone could somehow intervene in time.

. . .

Biddy wasn't without her allies, however. As Robert primed his household for the journey, various forces were aligning against him. Biddy herself had likely set some of these forces in motion. Would her plans ultimately lead to her rescue? That she couldn't know. Her fate was in the hands of the same Southern California legal authorities who had turned a blind eye to the slaveholders in their midst for the previous four-and-a-half years.

The details of what came next are hazy. Some of the key sources have been either lost, deliberately obscured, or contested. Nevertheless, by following contextual clues, cross-referencing, and employing informed speculation where necessary, a coherent picture begins to emerge.

Biddy's rescue would depend on the cooperation of District judge Benjamin Ignatius Hayes. A slight, bookish man from Baltimore who once contemplated the priesthood, Hayes ventured west, first to Missouri in the 1840s and then to California, reasoning that frontier communities would have a need for lawyers. He arrived in Los Angeles in 1850 and immediately fell in love with the charm, the color, and the Catholic piety of the pueblo. His faith and facility with Spanish helped win over a crucial constituency, catapulting him to the district judgeship, one of the most powerful legal positions in Southern California, just two years after his arrival. Through his connections within the Democratic party, the dominant political force in Los Angeles, Judge Hayes held that seat for more than a decade. His jurisdiction extended across San Diego, Los Angeles, and San Bernardino Counties. As a result, he spent much of his time on circuit, traveling by horseback, stage, and steamer across Southern California, all while dodging the bandits and outlaws that preyed on travelers like him. When not on circuit, he spent much of his time pouring over his personal archive, what would become one of the finest private collections of California history ever assembled.[36]

Hayes was a study in contrasts and contradictions: a delicate, scholarly

Benjamin Ignatius Hayes in 1849, several years before he would become district judge for Los Angeles, San Bernardino, and San Diego Counties. "California Faces: Selections from the Bancroft Library Portrait Collection," Bancroft Library, University of California, Berkeley.

man who nevertheless maintained one of the most physically rigorous jobs in American jurisprudence; an amateur historian who loved nothing more than the solitary pursuit of knowledge in his private study and yet repeatedly and compulsively ventured into public life; a temperance champion who all-too-often sought solace at the bottom of a bottle; and a Southerner with a slaveholding past who would render the largest antislavery legal ruling in the history of the American West.[37]

Precisely how Hayes was drawn into Biddy's case is difficult to ascertain from the extant records. Someone—identity unknown—approached the judge in late 1855 with a formal complaint against Robert Smith. The original document has either been lost or was never recorded, so we don't know precisely what it specified. But from Hayes's subsequent writings, it's clear that the petitioner raised the issue of kidnapping. Thirteen women and children were being forced against their will on an overland

Elizabeth Flake Rowan played an instrumental role in Biddy and Hannah's quest for freedom in 1855–56. San Bernardino Historical and Pioneer Society.

trek to Texas. The petitioner sought legal intervention to prevent that from happening.[38]

The identity of this petitioner is one of the unsolved mysteries of Biddy's life story. That person is never named in any of the surviving legal documents from the case, most likely to protect them from retribution in a notoriously proslavery region. In his coverage of the case, Hayes only referred to them as the "affiant."[39]

Fortunately we have two surviving accounts from Biddy's family members—her daughter Ellen and her grandson Robert—that throw light on the subject. Unfortunately they offer conflicting interpretations.[40]

Ellen credits Elizabeth Flake Rowan with playing the key part. Elizabeth had indeed occupied a central role in much of San Bernardino's history. Like Biddy, she drove a team of cattle on the four-hundred-mile march from Salt Lake to Southern California. She then assisted in building some of the first homes for the settlement.[41] Before their departure Biddy or Hannah got word to Elizabeth, whom they had known for roughly eight years through numerous shared ordeals.[42] Benjamin Hayes happened to be in San Bernardino for a court session on October 15, 1855, around the time of Smith's exit. Elizabeth may have seized that brief window of opportunity to inform the judge directly of Smith's plans.[43]

A more romantic explanation comes from Biddy's grandson. According to his account, a free Black man named Charles Owens of Los Angeles had fallen in love with Biddy's daughter Ellen. When he learned that Ellen was to be carried off to Texas, he pleaded with his father, Robert Owens, to intervene. Acting at the behest of his lovestruck son, Robert Owens initiated a rescue operation, personally leading a posse of vaqueros into the Santa Monica Mountains in search of the rogue slaveholder.[44]

Like Ellen's account, the chronicle of Biddy's grandson has the ring of truth to it. The vital meeting between Ellen and Charles may have taken place when Robert Smith stopped in Los Angeles to stock up for the journey ahead. The Owens family happened to run a successful livery stable on San Pedro Street in Los Angeles. Even if Smith balked at the idea of patronizing a Black business, the Owens stables may have been his best option. Furthermore, Robert Owens wielded influence within the community, despite the color of his skin. He therefore had the means and the connections to intervene if he believed his son's future happiness was at stake.[45] The explanation also has the benefit of cinematic allure: star-crossed lovers, runaway slaveholders, and a healthy dash of derring-do.

The real explanation is, alas, more complicated. But it's also more satisfying.

. . .

The truth lies not in any single account or any individual actor. To bring California's largest slaveholder to justice was no small feat, especially within an apathetic, if not hostile, legal landscape. It required the coordinated efforts of multiple parties, including the enslaved and their free allies. Biddy's rescue could be ensured only through a collective assault on the slave regime itself.

Robert Smith had little inkling that his own slaves were mobilizing against him. He would later insist that he had always treated Biddy and his other Black bondspeople like members of his own family, "subjecting them to no greater control" than his "own children."[46] Although his words smack of both self-delusion and self-inflation, Robert's sense of confidence wasn't entirely misplaced. The prospect of Biddy or Hannah escaping from him with their large families was inconceivable. Fortified in the Santa Monica Mountains and reinforced by a new team of trailhands, Robert had stacked the odds in his favor.

Smith's claims of benevolence echo a common refrain among the Mississippi Saints and their descendants. Another Mormon settler, Louisa Barnes Pratt, wrote that the Black people of San Bernardino "though free, still remained with their masters"—a rather counterintuitive description of freedom.[47] Bishop William Crosby made an almost identical argument about his own bondspeople. Many of the historical accounts written by descendants of San Bernardino slaveholders tend toward hagiography and simply parrot descriptions of Black devotion.[48] A descendent of Agnes Flake wrote that Elizabeth Flake Rowan "could not control her grief" upon the death of her mistress, eulogizing her as "the best woman what ever lived" who "never hit me when I didn't deserve it." According to this account, she even begged to remain bound to Agnes's children after they decided to return to Utah.[49]

San Bernardino had essentially developed its own variant on the "loyal slave" myth that permeated the plantation South and, later, metastasized into the Lost Cause legend of Confederate innocence. Time and again, slaveholders assured themselves that their bondspeople, content with their place in the natural hierarchy, couldn't possibly covet freedom. Such fictions, while soothing the conscience of slaveholders, created a false sense of security. Convinced of their own beneficence, they were unable to see the rebellion brewing in front of their eyes.[50]

Unbeknownst to Smith, the Black community of San Bernardino had been preparing for their moment. As within most enslaved communities, their progress was incremental. Biddy's was a rebellion in slow motion. She and her Black compatriots chipped away slowly at the absolute authority that slaveholders expected to wield over them.

Rande landed an early blow. His escape—one of the rare Black success stories in frontier Utah—exposed the limits of Smith's control. It may have even been a critical factor in Smith's decision to relocate to Southern California. Even if Biddy couldn't replicate Rande's feat with small children in tow, the façade of Smith's mastery had been cracked. Rande had demonstrated how Biddy could, under the right conditions, transform herself from the basis of Smith's wealth into the source of his undoing.[51]

Green Flake and Hark Wales, enslaved members of the original pioneer company to the Great Basin, set another important precedent. They personally visited Brigham Young on the eve of the Mississippi Saints' departure for San Bernardino in 1851. The expedition would break up several enslaved families, they informed Young, as certain husbands and wives were owned by different Mormon patriarchs, some of whom planned to move to California and some of whom intended to stay in Utah. They urged Young to prevent separation by reallocating some Black people to new Mormon households.

William Crosby wrote in a muddled fury to Young when he heard of this intervention. The independence exhibited by Green was especially provoking to him. Green was "a mean dirty I sarvace [savage] lying disafected Saucy to Brother Flake's wife Disobediant," Crosby wrote. He claimed that Green talked of freedom (the gall!) and of wishing to marry a white woman (the horror!). In Crosby's eyes this was a request for property redistribution, made at the behest of the property itself.[52]

Crosby's objections fell flat. Young ultimately sided with the enslaved over the once and future Mormon bishop. To avoid the breakup of at least a few families, Young shuffled several Black people between households. Although Hark Wales was ultimately separated from his wife, Green Flake fared better. Young's intervention eventually resulted in freedom for Flake as well as a woman named Rose (perhaps Flake's wife) and her mother, Violet. The ailing Agnes Flake later attempted to reacquire Green and have him brought to California. But she died of tuberculosis while Green Flake settled into a prosperous life of farming in Utah and later Idaho.[53]

Although Biddy wasn't party to these negotiations, she would have witnessed the effects and could therefore draw several important conclusions. First, a degree of negotiation within the bonds of slavery, even if heavily circumscribed, was possible. Second, powerful patrons could, with the right incentives, override the iron will of enslavers. Third, independent action, while fraught with peril, could yield dramatic results. Green Flake's so-called disobedience won him an audience with Brigham Young, a moral victory over William Crosby, and ultimately freedom from Agnes Flake.

The rebellion against Robert Smith began with Biddy and Hannah. They knew that if Smith broke trail before they got word to any ally in San Bernardino, there could be no rescue operation. Numerous obstacles stood in their way, not least among them the problem of distance. Bound to Smith's Jumuba ranch, they lived at least three miles from any other enslaved people, who all resided in the town of San Bernardino. The litany of jobs on the ranch probably kept them south of the Santa Ana River most days. Yet some tasks—errands for Rebecca or perhaps the delivery of a baby in town—would have provided the opportunity they needed to inform an ally of Smith's plans. Given their long history of enslavement within the same communities, Elizabeth Flake Rowan would have been one of their first points of contact. Rather than a devoted slave, as she's portrayed in Flake family reminiscences, Elizabeth was a shrewd and ambitious woman, who likely relished the opportunity to conspire for her friends' freedom.[54]

Another ally was Hannah's husband, Toby Embers. As the property of Bishop William Crosby, Toby wasn't permitted to live with his wife. Nonetheless, he saw Hannah with some regularity. They had at least two children together, Charlie and Martha. Sometime in 1855, Toby brought Charlie into his care, suggesting that he knew of the impending departure and was already taking steps to combat the separation of his family. He may have also suspected that Hannah was the target of sexual assault by Robert Smith. He therefore had plenty of motives for retribution against his wife's owner and predator.[55]

Toby's probable brother, Grief Embers, may have also assisted. Recall that Grief served as bugler to the settlement and was regarded as a favorite by many of the white colonists.[56] Grief and Toby were both included in a list of Mormon loyalists drawn up by the colony's cofounders. They were identified as those "connected with us in our Mission," a distinction that probably earned them a degree of confidence among their fellow Mormons. Had either one of them informed against Robert Smith, by this point a well-known member of the opposition camp, they probably would have found a receptive audience.[57]

Biddy eventually won white allies as well. A man named Dr. A. H. Cooper would later face threats on his life for his alleged role in Biddy's case. Little is known about Cooper, but the surviving evidence suggests that he had involved himself in the case from an early stage. Perhaps Biddy or Hannah had met Dr. Cooper in their capacities as midwives. It may have been Cooper, acting on their instructions, who first took the petition to Judge Hayes. A white man, especially a doctor, was more likely to win an audience with the judge than any Black petitioner. But even if he was the intermediary to Hayes, Cooper didn't act alone. Only the coordinated efforts of the Black community could ensure that Biddy's case received a hearing.[58] Freedom suits in other states like New York relied on such mixed-race coalitions, and there's no reason to think that Biddy and Hannah didn't employ a similar strategy.[59]

The fact that we've never learned the identity of the informant is a source of frustration to some historians, seen as another handicap to knowledge imposed by the poor record-keeping of frontier Los Angeles. Yet there's another way to view the mystery: as a testament to Biddy's tactical acumen. She and her allies deliberately covered their tracks to protect those involved in such a risky undertaking. Judge Hayes himself later speculated that Biddy and Hannah operated in secrecy, given the precarity of their situation, "and very cautiously communicated to those who might assist them."[60] Smith's methods of control, honed over decades of slaveholding, proved incapable of containing the ingenuity of the enslaved. Neither he nor Hayes nor anyone else in Southern California was able to uncover the full extent of their operation. It confounds historians still. We should celebrate, not lament, that fact.

Whoever the petitioner may have been, he or she persuaded Hayes to act. The judge issued a writ of habeas corpus and dispatched a team of men to seek out Smith before he could make his getaway. Latin for "produce the body," habeas corpus is a powerful legal tool, which has been used to challenge illegal enslavement for hundreds of years. The writ itself didn't confer freedom. But it did require Smith to answer to the court—if he could be apprehended in time.[61]

. . .

January 1856. Hidden away in one of the many canyons of the Santa Monica Mountains, Robert Smith could finally celebrate the passing of his annus horribilis. Although he had been forced to abandon his land, he retained much of his capital in the form of thirteen enslaved laborers, with the fourteenth on the way. Soon they would be on the trail to Texas and a fresh start for Robert, far from the prying eyes of Mormon elders and Black abolitionists. For Biddy, however, the path ahead was more of the same, yet another road to slave country.

They never broke trail.

The sound of his world shattering came to Smith faintly at first: just the distant echo of hoofbeats against the hard earth of the canyon floor on an unusually cold winter night. Smith probably thought nothing of the commotion, initially. It was surely just another mounted party passing through the canyon. Biddy, however, would have jumped to attention at the sound of hoofbeats. If she listened closely, she could make out the sound of multiple riders, closing in on their position. The rumbling of the horses' approach would have grown in volume until suddenly a posse of armed men charged into the Smith camp.

Smith had been caught flat-footed. He and his men—including his three sons and a handful of hired hands—may have drawn their guns on the troopers. But they held their fire. They soon learned that these riders weren't there for Smith's cattle or his goods. They were agents of the law, and they had come for the women and children that Smith claimed as property.

They carried with them a writ of habeas corpus, signed by the district judge, ordering Smith to deliver Biddy and the others. He would have the opportunity to answer the writ in the district court of Los Angeles.[62]

In the meantime the lawmen separated the Black women and children from Robert Smith. Biddy and her daughters would be taken to Los Angeles. They were joined by at least four of Hannah's children: Marion (four), Jane (eight), Nathaniel (ten), and Ann (seventeen), along with Ann's daughter, Mary (two). Hannah would be sent to San Bernardino to deliver her child, a boy she named Henry. Some of Hannah's other children—Lawrence (twelve) and Martha (two)—were eventually allowed to join her there. All minors, whether in Los Angeles or San Bernardino, would be placed in the custody of local law enforcement. For Biddy the whole process would have unfolded in a blur. Separation from Hannah, her closest confidant, only heightened the uncertainty and disquiet of the moment.[63]

Robert Smith, now stripped of his enslaved laborers, was left to fume in his Santa Monica hideout and plot his next move. So began the last stand of California's largest slaveholder.

8 The Trial

Biddy entered Los Angeles at the dawn of a new year and, she hoped, the birth of a new era for her family. But no one was celebrating yet. The crude wooden wagon that likely carried Biddy and her children from the Santa Monica Mountains more closely resembled a refugee's caravan than a triumphal procession. A greeting party of feral dogs, "barking and howling as if mad," would have followed in the party's wake, as they always did when wagons rolled into town. Strangers' faces may have peered out, mutely, from half-closed doors as the cacophonous parade passed by. Although the journey to Los Angeles had finally put some distance between Biddy and her enslaver, it otherwise didn't feel much different than previous ruptures in her life. She had been seized and transported by strangers on multiple occasions. And none of those dislocations ever brought her any closer to freedom.[1]

Los Angeles from a distance in January 1856 presented an unremarkable sight for a woman who had crossed the continent and spent the past half decade near a settlement of similar size. Like San Bernardino, Los Angeles numbered no more than a few thousand residents. Most of them referred to it as the "pueblo." Approaching from the west, as Biddy did, Los Angeles would have appeared as a low line of flat-roofed adobes and

The Los Angeles Plaza and the surrounding streets largely as they would have appeared to Biddy when she entered the pueblo in January 1856. Huntington Digital Library, Huntington Library, San Marino, California.

single-story timber structures, punctuated by the cupola of the old Spanish church and the occasional two-story brick building. Native women with their washing likely assembled along one of the irrigation canals, known as *zanjas*, that latticed the pueblo and its outskirts.[2]

After crossing a short plain, the wagon party entered the pueblo itself. Biddy and the others now wound through a tangle of narrow, ungraded streets. They rumbled past saloons, gambling houses, various shops, and more saloons.[3] Streaks of black bitumen, used as waterproofing for the flat roofs, dripped down the adobe façades and suffused the pueblo with the sharp smell of tar in hotter months.[4] Several hundred yards to the north lay the central plaza, a treeless square ringed by the whitewashed town homes of the *californio* elite. Crowds gathered on Sundays to watch bullfights and cockfights, ignoring the recent prohibition on those pastimes.[5] In the summertime the horse-beaten dirt roads kicked up clouds of stifling dust. In the winter the streets became muddy quagmires, slowing traffic and coating pedestrians' boots in a thick brown cake.[6]

Still, the pueblo usually teamed with activity, on foot and on horseback: Indian laborers trudging to their next worksite; Yankee miners in search of their next drink; senoritas in their Sunday best; German shopkeepers, reassembling the items in their storefronts; Chinese vendors, pushing vegetable carts; and splendidly attired *caballeros*, galloping by "with a rattle of spurs" and a rumble of hoofs. As one early visitor commented, "All the odds and ends of humanity seemed here brought in contact, and, chattering and jabbering in their many tongues, made up strange scenes, rarely witnessed in so small a place."[7] The pueblo that Biddy's wagon rolled through was a polyglot border town at the crossroads of Indigenous, Mexican, European, Chinese, and American cultures.[8]

Biddy didn't have time to take it all in. After just a few blocks the wagon would have pulled onto Spring Street, then stopped in front of a long, worn structure of sun-dried brick. Formerly known as the Rocha Adobe, it now served as a multipurpose municipal building, housing many of the city and county government offices. It also functioned as the district courthouse, where Biddy would soon make her bid for freedom.[9]

She and the children, however, were bound for the enclosure to the rear of the old adobe, where two years earlier, an imposing new structure had been erected. It was a square, two-story building, the lower level made of adobe and the upper story of brick, situated within a treeless yard of swept dirt. A large plank fence surrounded the complex. Although they had committed no crimes, Biddy and the children were now inmates of the Los Angeles county jail.[10]

The jail, regarded as one of the most secure in the American Southwest, consisted of two main areas. The second floor housed the county inmates, each one confined to a small cell and "secured by strong shackles on each leg," according to a contemporary report. A lack of light and ventilation made each cell an inferno in the summer months. "To be confined in one of these dungeons in hot weather must itself be a torture," the report concluded. A veritable caldron of disease, the jail lacked medical facilities and even a change of clothes for its inmates.[11]

Biddy and the others—her three daughters and at least four of Hannah's children—were likely confined on the lower floor, in the lockup used for the city's prisoners. Rather than individual cells, the ground-floor prison contained two large apartments, one for men and the other for women. California Indians, rounded up on flimsy vagrancy charges, often filled this part of the jail. All prisoners probably defecated in a common pot. There were no beds or cots. Unless the jailer made special arrangements for Biddy and the others, they would have spent sleepless nights huddled

This panorama of Los Angeles, ca. late 1860s, was taken about a decade after Biddy won her emancipation but still contains many of the key sites in that trial. The jail that held Biddy and her daughters is the square, two-story building, sitting in a large yard enclosed by a tall wooden fence (right). In front of the jail is the whitewashed, single-story adobe building where Biddy made her historic bid for freedom. C. C. Pierce Collection of Photographs, Huntington Library, San Marino, California.

together on the earthen floor.[12] Still, conditions in the new jail were a considerable improvement over the old one, a crude adobe dungeon in which all prisoners were shackled to a heavy pine log "like a string of fresh fish."[13]

Biddy and the children were among the earliest inmates in a prison system that would eventually become one of the most infamous in the country. Today, Los Angeles imprisons more people than any other city in the United States—which is the most heavily incarcerated nation in the world. A disproportionate number of them are Black.[14]

Judge Benjamin Hayes had ordered the confinement of Biddy and the others for their own protection, yet the decision ate at him. Their imprisonment left them "isolated from even the kindly glance of sympathy," he wrote. Because "they could not comprehend the reason," their confinement "might well have inspired them with distrust" for the upcoming trial and its presiding authorities. But to house Biddy and the others in private residences in Los Angeles would be too costly, Hayes reasoned.[15]

Despite her dismal surroundings, Biddy may not have looked upon her situation as entirely unwelcome. Ironically, her confinement in prison was as free as she had ever been. For perhaps the first time in her life, she was miles away from anyone who claimed her as property. And her suit for freedom—the largest such case ever tried west of Texas—was about to begin.[16]

. . .

Biddy did not, however, have the law on her side. Although California banned slavery and involuntary servitude in its 1849 constitution, most major legal decisions since then had gone in favor of slaveholders. In more than a dozen cases like Biddy's, California courts returned freedom-seeking African Americans to bondage. According to one scholar, "The California court offered more protection to slave property than the court of any other free state."[17] The outlook for Biddy and the others was dim.

California did possess some prominent antislavery jurists and lawyers, but they were outnumbered by antagonists and frequently assaulted, verbally and physically. "It is enough to bring down upon the man all the indignation of all the idlers and vagabonds in the country to dare express a free Northern sentiment," lamented the *Daily Alta California*.[18] When the question of Black freedom arose in the courtroom, it was often accompanied by "menace, and threats of violence," according to Cornelius Cole, one of the state's most distinguished antislavery lawyers. Upon the conclusion of one such case, the opposing attorney drew a pistol on Cole to demonstrate "his fidelity to the cause of the South."[19] As the future US senator John Conness recalled: "If any man could be found who had temerity enough to believe it [slavery] was a bad system, and his opinions became known, he was proscribed, clubbed, or shot, according to the pleasure of the ruffians who dominated public opinion" in California.[20]

Conness spoke from experience. In 1853 the chief justice of the California Supreme Court, Hugh C. Murray, chased him around a San Francisco barroom, bowie knife in hand. Murray, a native of Missouri, was known for his hair-trigger temper and a violent attachment to slaveholding rights. Three years after his confrontation with Conness, Murray accosted an abolitionist merchant in his Sacramento store and bludgeoned him with a heavy stick.[21] Murray may have drawn his inspiration from Preston Brooks, a US representative from South Carolina, who savagely caned the antislavery firebrand Charles Sumner on the Senate floor in the spring of that same year.[22]

Murray presided over a decidedly proslavery court. All but two of the seven justices who sat on the California Supreme Court between 1852 and 1857 came from the slave states. One of those Northerners was Southern by political inclination and a supporter of the state-rights' extremist John C. Calhoun. California voters could have ensured otherwise, as judicial aspirants prior to the Civil War were directly elected rather than appointed. But, as with the state's political offices, most seats on the court went to proslavery partisans.[23]

In 1852, California slaveholders gained yet another advantage: the state's fugitive slave law. The statute allowed slaveholders who arrived prior to 1850 to retain their human property, unaffected by California's constitutional ban on human bondage, so long as they eventually returned to the South. In effect, the measure ensured that residence on free soil didn't automatically confer freedom on African Americans, as some argued it should. Like the national Fugitive Slave Act of 1850, the California law also provided monetary aid for the recapture of those deemed "fugitives" from slavery. And it stipulated harsh punishments for anyone aiding Black freedom-seekers or obstructing their recapture.[24] Extended until 1855, the state's fugitive slave law amounted to what historian Stacey Smith called "a three-year suspension of the antislavery constitution."[25]

A test case, challenging the statute, made its way through California's courts in 1852. It involved three kidnapped African Americans: Robert Perkins, Carter Perkins, and Sandy Jones, all with seemingly indisputable claims to freedom. The three men had been taken from Mississippi to California during the gold rush. Planning to leave the state, their owner agreed to free them. He returned to Mississippi alone in 1851. As freedmen, they worked as teamsters in California and accrued an astounding $3,200 in property. But in the spring of 1852 a posse of white vigilantes stormed their cabin, loaded them into a wagon, and dragged them before a Sacramento justice of the peace, who declared them fugitives from slavery and approved their removal to Mississippi.[26]

The Republican lawyer Cornelius Cole took the case to the state Supreme Court, where it came before Hugh Murray and Justice Alexander Anderson of Tennessee. Predictably, the court ruled against the three Black men. The antislavery clause in the state constitution was a mere "declaration of principle," Murray wrote in his opinion. Any slave brought into the state, he elaborated, "does not become ipso facto free, [nor is] his status changed." According to Murray, the main purpose of the fugitive slave clause was to rid the state of free people of color by encouraging white men to reclaim former slaves and remove them to the South. Free Blacks, he wrote, were a "pernicious" group that became "festering sores upon the body politic."[27]

Here was a powerful legal precedent from California's highest court, which could be deployed against freedom-seeking African Americans like Biddy. Perhaps as many as fifteen hundred enslaved Black people had been transported to California before the Civil War. Many of them were taken back to the slave states in the early 1850s. But those who remained, even those who had attained freedom, were subject to seizure under the state's fugitive slave law.[28] Although the law was allowed to lapse in 1855, it remained unchallenged within the state Supreme Court. In the eyes of California's highest court, therefore, Biddy and other Black Americans still resided on quasi-unfree soil.[29]

Robert Smith may have reasonably expected a similar ruling from Judge Benjamin Hayes of the District Court of Los Angeles. Although Hayes had signed the writ of habeas corpus that initiated the trial, he didn't fit the description of a free-soil crusader or even a sympathetic interlocutor for someone like Biddy. Before coming to California, Hayes had spent his professional career in the slave state of Missouri. Through marriage his fortunes were linked to a prominent slaveholding family from Maryland. One of his family's slaves, a man named Lewis, accompanied Hayes briefly on his overland journey to California.[30] Several years later, Hayes wrote to his wife about the possibility of bringing one of their family's enslaved children to Los Angeles.[31]

Hayes had been steeped in the proslavery paternalism of the antebellum South—a fact reflected in his initial judgments on the case. He claimed to "appreciate the kindly attachment that grows up between master and slave." And he saw no evidence that Robert Smith had mistreated Biddy and the others at the trial's outset. On the contrary, he wrote, "the two parties have doubtless been of mutual advantage here, and their labor, which he has enjoyed, probably remunerated him for their 'support.'"[32] Smith would employ similar logic in his own defense.

Hayes had another reason to tow the proslavery line in his handling of the case: his constituents. The men who voted him into office as district judge were on the whole firmly antiabolitionist. Like Hayes himself, the majority of Los Angeles's American-born settlers came by way of the slave states—a "manly population," he wrote, "such as you find on the frontiers of Missouri."[33] Although Latino men comprised the majority of the county's voters, they too, especially the ranchero elite, aligned themselves with the Southern Democrats who controlled the region. In short, the Los Angeles electorate was sympathetic to the property claims of slaveholders and hostile to the freedom claims of people like Biddy. And Hayes knew it.[34]

Thus, when Robert Smith prepared his defense in early 1856, he had legal precedent and much of Los Angeles at his back.

. . .

Smith's case rested on a curious strategy: He defended his right to transport people as property while simultaneously insisting that they exercised free will. He claimed that the women and children in question had *voluntarily* elected to travel with him across the country, beginning nearly ten years earlier. They had "left Mississippi with their own consent, rather than remain there," he informed Judge Hayes in his sworn defense. During their years together in Utah and California, Smith had "supported them," he continued, "subjecting them to no greater control than his own children." The planned trip to Texas was just another consensual move for his family, Black and white.[35]

All this would have been news to Biddy, who had by now endured more than a decade under Smith's ownership, steered by his whims and wanderlust. There had been nothing voluntary in any of her forced relocations. But did Hayes know that? Would he be convinced by Smith's claims of patriarchal benevolence? And even if not, could Biddy's lawyer plainly disprove Smith? Those were the questions upon which the fate of fourteen women and children hung.

Until this point Hayes had demonstrated little concern over the presence of human bondage in California. Not only had he considered importing an enslaved child himself, he also saw slavery firsthand when riding circuit in San Bernardino, which was part of his jurisdiction. During one of his recent visits Hayes stayed with Bishop William Crosby, whose "Negro servants" attended to the guests. The presence of Black slaves in an ostensibly free state elicited no comment from Hayes, an assiduous diarist, beyond a quick line of praise for the "good table" they prepared.[36] He was personally fond of Crosby, his "excellent host," overlooking the fact that much of that excellence depended on the forced labor of others.[37] The only San Bernardino resident who held more people in bondage than Crosby was Robert Smith.

And yet Hayes had to concede that there was something suspicious about Smith's defense. Although the judge found much to admire in the institution of slavery, he knew coercion when he saw it. Biddy, Hannah, and the children weren't bound for Texas as voluntary migrants. Much of Smith's argument was built on an obvious lie.[38] To warrant a ruling against Smith, however, the lie would have to be proved. And there was the rub. For the only people who could controvert Smith's claims were prohibited from testifying in any California court. Smith's deceit was as shrewd as it was transparent.

Biddy, Hannah, and the others were legally muzzled in California, the result of one of the first major laws enacted by the state legislature. Passed in 1850, the statute prohibited African Americans and Native Americans from giving evidence "in favor of or against any white person" in criminal cases. Anyone with "one eighth part or more of Negro blood" was deemed a "mulatto" and thus barred from testifying, as was anyone with "one half of Indian blood." The legislature extended the prohibition to civil cases in 1851. By mid-decade the testimony ban was applied to Chinese immigrants as well.[39]

California slaveholders employed the testimony ban to sinister effect. In numerous cases they abducted African Americans as "fugitives," hauled them before justices of the peace, and claimed them as property. Barred from giving evidence, Black Californians—including those who had been emancipated or never enslaved—couldn't defend themselves against false charges. They lost nearly every case before 1856.[40] Legally prohibited from testifying against their enslaver, Biddy, Hannah, and their children faced a similar fate.

. . .

The trial was scheduled for mid-January. In the meantime Smith returned to San Bernardino. Rebecca, the Smith boys, and a few of his hired hands joined him there, scheming over ways to burnish their defense and reclaim Robert's human property. While the court claimed temporary custody over most of his enslaved laborers, Smith managed to retain several of them. Hannah, who had recently given birth to her eighth child, was released into Smith's custody in San Bernardino. Her son Lawrence joined her. With the birth of Hannah's baby, a boy named Henry, Smith gained ownership (albeit now disputed) over his fourteenth person. No one in the American Far West laid claim to a greater number of enslaved people. And no one had more to lose in the impending trial.[41]

At some point during the trial, Biddy and the remaining children were temporarily relocated from the city jail to the home of Robert and Winnie Owens. The Owens family must have requested the move. Judge Hayes, uneasy about confining so many women and children in the town's notorious lockup, obliged. Located a few short blocks east of the courthouse, the Owens home was an adobe structure situated on "a narrow and sandy driveway" on San Pedro Street.[42] Although spacious by the standards of frontier Los Angeles, the adobe itself couldn't accommodate eight or more new arrivals. So Owens probably converted his adjoining stable into a makeshift hostel. The home and its outlying buildings became a hub where Biddy's friends and allies gathered as the trial unfolded.[43]

Robert Owens, familiarly known as Bob, was a good friend to have. Although his family had relocated to Los Angeles just a few years earlier, they had already established themselves as the preeminent household in the pueblo's Black community. A natural entrepreneur, Bob Owens would profit from investments in horses, horticulture, real estate, government contracts, and mining.[44] The livery stable that may have temporarily housed Biddy generated much of his wealth. According to his grandson, Owens stocked the stable with wild horses and mules purchased from as far away as San Diego. A team of vaqueros broke the animals and sold them to a steady stream of travelers. Whenever a steamer unloaded passengers in Los Angeles, "it seemed that every body headed for old Bob's stable," his grandson recalled.[45] Judge Hayes later memorialized Owens as "a shrewd man of business, energetic, and honorable in his dealings."[46] No one who knew "Uncle Bob" would ever disagree.[47]

His wife, Winnie, ascended Los Angeles's social ladder alongside her husband. She began her career in Los Angeles as a washerwoman and domestic worker in other women's homes, but would soon be regarded as one of the finest hosts in the city. Her dinner parties became news items, her cooking the stuff of legend. She applied those skills to various fund-raisers and philanthropic ventures for the early Black community of Los Angeles. Even members of the white elite eagerly sought invitations to her events.[48] More than just an organizer of people, Winnie would also become the manager of the family's many properties. That real estate portfolio would make her the wealthiest Black woman in the pueblo by the late 1860s.[49] The only surviving photo of Winnie Owens captures her at the peak of her prosperity (see chapter 13). She sits on her front porch, straight as a rod, elegantly dressed and radiating a palpable sense of pride and dignity that comes from hard-won success.

Bob and Winnie Owens understood the stakes of the trial as well as anyone. Before coming to California, the Owens family had been enslaved in Texas and therefore knew firsthand the horrors that awaited Biddy there. They managed to escape only after Bob accrued enough capital from hiring himself out. First he bought his own freedom, then Winnie's freedom, then freedom for their son and two daughters. Emancipation cost the Owens household roughly $3,000, a small fortune for any family, white or Black.[50]

By the time Biddy and the others arrived, the Owens home was already a well-known refuge for Black freedom-seekers. "Many slave owners have claimed that their property was kept in hiding" at the San Pedro Street adobe, recalled an old resident of Los Angeles. In one instance, Bob and Winnie harbored a fugitive woman from her owner, "a drunken brute" from Rancho Cucamonga.[51] Several sources suggest that Bob Owens had been a key player in securing the writ of habeas corpus, apprehending Robert Smith, and initiating Biddy's trial.[52] In other words, the Owens family had become key conductors on the nascent (and little-known) Pacific Coast spur of the Underground Railroad. The case against Smith was their greatest mission yet.[53]

Deliverance—this is what Biddy must have felt as she crossed the threshold into the Owens home. She had gone from slavery to prison and now into warmth and security of the San Pedro Street adobe, surrounded by friends and cloistered from enemies. The battle wasn't won, not by a long shot. But at least Biddy had a community behind her. And dinners that Robert Smith could only dream of.

Perhaps no one was as pleased with their new accommodations as

Biddy's daughter Ellen. According to a family memoir, the romance between Ellen and Charles Owens began sometime before the trial. If so, it was a painfully constrained courtship. Any encounters while Ellen lived and labored under the control of Robert Smith would have been fleeting, stolen only at great personal risk. With the trial under way a lovesick Charles may have persuaded his parents to open their home to Ellen and her family. Now, under the protective umbrella of the Owens home, the romance between Charles and Ellen finally blossomed. Would that fragile bloom survive? That depended on what came next.[54]

. . .

The trial began amid a city divided against itself. For Los Angeles's many proslavery partisans, here was a chance to vindicate the right to hold others as property. For the town's small Black population and their white allies, the trial might serve as a long-overdue affirmation of the state's free-soil constitution. Rarely did the fates of so many enslaved people rest in the hands of a single judge. Hayes felt the pressure keenly. The weight of "public opinion" prompted him to write a lengthy report on the case, published in newspapers in Los Angeles, Sacramento, and Philadelphia. Even the *New York Daily Times* would cover the proceedings.[55]

The space where the trial unfolded hardly matched the gravity of the occasion, however. The Los Angeles courtroom was almost comically proportioned and arranged. According to a contemporary report, the courtroom was a jurisprudential "hog-pen," squeezing together judge, lawyers, defendants, petitioners, court officers, observers, and sometimes jurors (though not in this case). These "victims" of architectural folly all jockeyed for space within "a sort of compressed parallelogram, having length, with the smallest possible modicum of breadth," the report continued. Hayes was "condemned to ruminate" in a "crib" at the far end of the gallery, straining to see over the high railing of his bench. Before him, the two lawyers were crammed together, with space for a chair or two but not a table. If they wished to take notes, they could use their hats. Robert Smith, Biddy, and several of the enslaved children probably sat directly behind their respective lawyers, in the front row of the gallery. In addition to the "cribbed, cabined, and confined dimensions of the room," there was also dust and filth to contend with, "which no amount of sweeping or cleansing can keep away."[56] When it rained, torrents of water poured down the walls and on either side of Hayes's bench, leading the local paper to condemn the building as "altogether unfit for the purpose of a Court Room."[57] Like the town that surrounded it, the Los Angeles courthouse was a creature of the frontier.

Scandal erupted almost as soon as the trial began. On the second day of the proceedings, Judge Hayes peered down from his bench at the two assembled parties. On one side sat Robert Smith and his attorney, Alonzo Thomas; on the other, Biddy and several of the children. The day before, Biddy's lawyer had been present. Now he was gone.

A note, delivered that morning, explained his absence: "I, as attorney on the opposite side, being no longer authorized to prosecute the writ [of habeas corpus], and being discharged by the same parties who are responsible to me, decline further to prosecute the matter." Smith's lawyer immediately filed a motion for dismissal. He argued that without legal representation, Biddy and the others had no case.[58]

Hayes could have ended the trial then and there. Instead, he sought an explanation for the sudden and mysterious absence. He may have asked Biddy or someone else in the courtroom for clarification. Had any of them discharged their attorney? No, they could truthfully answer. Had their attorney spoken to them before he quit? Again, no. Hayes was clearly troubled. "Any citizen can understand how disastrous it might be to his rights and interests, in our Courts, if such a precedent in an attorney were approved," he later wrote. "No attorney can desert his clients at his own pleasure, without good reason . . . and fair notice to them."[59]

Hayes denied the motion for dismissal and instead issued a subpoena for the missing lawyer. Several days later, Sheriff David Alexander tracked down Biddy's lawyer and brought him to the courtroom to testify. His story was one of intimidation, bribery, and ultimately capitulation.

The trouble started when one of Smith's cronies, or perhaps even Smith himself, accosted one of Biddy's main allies. This was the person (still unnamed in the court records) who first petitioned Hayes for the writ of habeas corpus and had subsequently funded Biddy's legal case. There would be blood, Smith's man threatened, unless the case was dropped. The petitioner had displayed tremendous courage to bring the suit in the first place. But his or her nerve finally gave out. The threat of violence from Smith's armed henchmen was all too real. In a panic the petitioner urged the lawyer to drop the case, offering him $100 in addition to the $100 he had already been paid. The lawyer, knowing he was next on Smith's hit list, took the money and disappeared.[60]

Until this point Hayes viewed Smith as a benevolent master, perhaps disingenuous in his defense but not wanton or cruel. The lawyer's disappearance and subsequent testimony, however, had cast Smith in a new light. Although Smith denied any knowledge of the scheme, Hayes was unconvinced. "It is possible—yet strange, if possible—that the defendant had nothing to do with (to say the least) of an ill-advised stratagem to frustrate the writ of habeas corpus," he wrote.[61] "It gives room for a painful suspicion—It has too much the air of force."[62]

The trial, just a few days old, had already taken a devious turn. There was no telling what other stratagems Smith might employ to win his case and reclaim his human property. With a new sense of urgency Hayes decided to test the central pillar of Smith's defense: that Biddy and Hannah had voluntarily agreed to move to Texas. To do so, Judge Hayes would employ a series of unconventional—some might even say illegal—measures that soon embroiled the trial in another layer of controversy.

. . .

Biddy was the fulcrum on which Robert Smith's case would stand or fall. Hayes realized this almost immediately upon receiving Smith's defense. Smith had insisted that all women and children in question had migrated with him voluntarily, yet he mentioned only Hannah by name as being "well disposed to remain with him." Why had he failed to name Biddy and her daughters? "It is remarkable, that the defendant does not pretend that Biddy and her three children are 'well-disposed' to remain with him," Hayes wrote. "His own oath expressly excludes them from the (so-called) 'voluntary' arrangement."[63]

What Hayes did next transformed Biddy from passive observer to star witness.

He invited Biddy into his chambers, along with two community leaders, to witness her private testimony. Neither Abel Stearns nor Dr. James B. Winston had any formal role in the case, but their stature lent gravitas and greater legitimacy to the proceedings. Stearns, a rancher and businessman originally from Massachusetts, was one of Southern California's wealthiest residents. Winston was a native of Virginia and the future owner of the Bella Union Hotel, a popular gathering place for white Southern transplants in Los Angeles. Hayes likely hoped that the presence of a Virginian and a Yankee would demonstrate his balance on the slavery question.[64]

For perhaps the first time in her life, Biddy could speak openly to white men about her enslavement. The record does not include the questions Hayes asked, only the answers she gave. They were clear, concise, and damning to Smith's case.

"I have always done what I was told to do," Biddy began. But, she continued, "[I] always feared this trip to Texas, since I first heard of it." Biddy's central concern, as always, were her three daughters. "I do not wish to be separated from my children, and do not in such case wish to go." These words, albeit mediated through a reporter, are among the very few from Biddy that survive.[65]

They express singular courage. Biddy was keenly aware of the potential repercussions of her testimony. If Smith prevailed in the trial and retained control over Biddy and her daughters, the consequences would have been severe. Nothing in her past—including a decade of labor exploitation, multiple forced relocations, and likely rape—suggested that Smith was a man to abide such a challenge to his authority. Furthermore, Biddy hardly knew the men who oversaw her interview and had scant reason to trust white authorities of any sort. Two of them were Southern by birth, a fact probably not lost on Biddy. Her testimony was a calculated gamble taken by a woman willing to risk everything for a fleeting chance at freedom.

Hayes was deeply moved by Biddy's courage and acumen, which confirmed his suspicions about the case. Smith had assured her that she and her children would be free in Texas, yet Biddy saw through the ruse. "On Biddy, it is clear, the artful promise made no impression," Hayes wrote. Her "glorious instinct of freedom" had lifted a "bright torch" to expose the subterfuge.[66] Abandoned by her lawyer, Biddy took her fate, and the fate of thirteen others, into her own hands.

Next, Hayes interviewed Biddy's eldest daughter, Ellen, and Hannah's eldest, Ann. Ellen's prime concern was her mother. According to the record of her testimony, "Whithersoever her mother goes," she too would go. Ann too insisted that she wouldn't be separated from her family. She would stay with her own young child and with her mother, who "would rather die than go and leave her children."[67] Again, familial love prevailed over the fear that Smith inspired.

If Hayes's intentions were noble, his understanding of California law was shaky at best. The state legislature, with the state Supreme Court concurring, had legally prohibited any African American from testifying against a white person. Therefore in most California freedom suits Black people looked on in forlorn silence. Yet Hayes actively sought out the Black plaintiffs' views to contradict Smith's defense. True, he conducted private interviews rather than open courtroom testimony. But because he introduced their views from the bench, the effect was the same: the word of three Black women—those held in bondage no less—had swayed the entire case.

The only adult witness outstanding was Hannah herself. But Hayes had already heard enough. He adjourned the court for the day and asked both parties to reassemble the next morning, Saturday, January 19, 1856. He was ready to render a decision.

PART II Freedom

9 The Decision

Slavery or freedom. Texas or California. These were the starkly diverging paths that Biddy confronted as she entered the courtroom on the morning of Saturday, January 19, 1856, to learn her fate. Her three daughters likely sat close beside her. A few seats away was the man who claimed them as his property, who had hauled them across the country, and who was now planning to steal them away once again. The only person standing in the way of this cataclysmic rupture for Biddy and her family was Judge Benjamin Hayes, perched on his bench at the end of the long, cramped courtroom. He had called them all into court this day to hear his decision in the largest freedom suit California would ever witness.

It was unequivocal. All persons in question—Biddy, Ellen, Ann (Biddy's daughter), Harriet, Hannah, Ann (Hannah's daughter), Lawrence, Nathaniel, Jane, Charles, Marion, Martha, Mary, and newborn Henry—"are entitled to their freedom and are free forever," Hayes ruled. The record doesn't state whether shouts of glee or outrage accompanied his words.[1]

For Hayes it was a simple matter of constitutionality. Biddy and the others were free as soon as they set foot in California, he argued. He quoted the state constitution in a later report, which declares, "*Neither slavery no involuntary servitude, unless for the punishment of crimes, shall ever be tolerated in this State.*"[2] To rule against their freedom, as Hayes saw it, would be to rule against the state's founding document. (He made no comment on the earlier decisions from California jurists which did precisely that.)

The events of the previous week had only reinforced Hayes's conviction that Biddy and the others required the protection of the court. Robert Smith or one of his accomplices had terrorized Biddy's lawyer in a ploy to have the entire case dismissed. Before that, Smith deliberately misled Biddy and Hannah in an attempt to remove them to Texas against their best interests. Biddy's private testimony exposed the ruse and helped convince Hayes that justice lay on the side of the enslaved.

Hayes was now determined to separate the women and children from their enslaver. He placed the minors in the temporary custody of the Los Angeles and San Bernardino sheriffs. Because Hannah and several of her children were in San Bernardino that day, Hayes ordered them to come to court on Monday to receive news of their freedom in person.[3] Robert Smith's mastery had finally been thwarted. Or so it seemed.

. . .

Biddy, however, couldn't celebrate her family's deliverance just yet. Although Hayes had attempted to choreograph the trial and render an indisputable ruling, events again spiraled beyond his control. Smith wasn't prepared to capitulate so easily. After all, a vast sum of money resided in those fourteen women and children. Without them he had only $500 to his name; with his human property, he might net thousands of dollars on the Texas slave market. So long as Smith and his cronies remained nearby, the newly-proclaimed freedom of Biddy, Hannah, and their children was in jeopardy.[4]

Hayes detected something amiss on the Monday after his ruling. Hannah was supposed to be there that morning to receive the news of her emancipation. But she never appeared. Nor did Smith. The evidence for their disappearance is written at the bottom of the same document in which Hayes proclaimed freedom for the fourteen women and children. He wrote it as an addendum: "On this Monday January 21st 1856 the said Smith and the said parties so ordered to appear as aforesaid do not appear."[5]

Hayes had to wonder: Did Smith kidnap Hannah, along with Lawrence and newborn Henry in an attempt to salvage at least some of his human assets? The judge adjourned the court until the following morning. He probably then ordered his sheriff to ride to San Bernardino to investigate.

The next day, both Hannah and Smith appeared in court. She had not been kidnapped after all. But to what extent was she still being coerced by Smith? This was the question at the crux of a rapidly evolving trial.

Ironically, Hannah's court-ordered freedom was now a potential liability. As a freedwoman, she could "voluntarily" return to Smith and travel with him to Texas. And because Texas outlawed the immigration of free people of color, Hannah would be reenslaved as soon as she crossed into the state. "No man of any experience in life will believe, that it was ever *true, or ever intended* to be realized—this pleasant prospect of freedom in Texas," Hayes wrote. But unless it could be proved that Hannah was being taken against her will, she couldn't be prevented from choosing this path. She could, in other words, return herself to slavery.[6]

To ascertain Hannah's true wishes, Hayes again stretched (one might say, violated) California law. He called her to speak in open court, despite the prohibition on Black testimony that had been in place since 1850. A bewildered Hannah rose from her seat and probably passed her newborn son to Biddy or one of her other children as she approached the stand.

If Hayes expected another exposure of Smith's nefarious scheme, he was to be disappointed. The testimony was a "humiliating spectacle," Hayes wrote. Hannah, visibly shaken and uneasy, responded to the questions with "cold replies" and long silences. She never denied her wish to go to Texas. Instead, she stated for the record her intention as a freedwoman: to remain with Smith.[7]

Hannah left the courtroom that day alongside her once and, most likely, future enslaver.

. . .

Hayes wasn't finished, however. He knew Hannah's testimony had been coerced. "Nothing else—*except force*—can account rationally" for her responses, he wrote. He wouldn't let that be the final word. Hayes ordered Sheriff David Alexander to ride sixty miles east to San Bernardino to seek out Hannah. There the sheriff would interview her privately, away from the menacing influence of her enslaver. Like the interview with Biddy a week earlier, Hayes hoped this would confirm the truth and finally clinch the case against Smith.[8]

Hannah faced not only reenslavement but also continued sexual abuse. The evidence, as Hayes himself intimated, was written on her children's skin. Hayes noted that Hannah was "a woman nearly white, whose children are all nearly so, one of whose daughters [Jane] . . . cannot easily be distinguished from the white race."[9] Hayes didn't elaborate. But the mere mention of skin tone suggested that he knew that a male member of the Smith household had fathered Jane, and perhaps other children as well. Indeed, it became well-known in the Black community of San Bernardino and Los Angeles that Henry, born during the trial, was Robert Smith's son.[10] Hannah was the survivor of rape, which may explain her pained testimony. Her reticence and extreme discomfort bore the hallmarks of a victim of abuse.[11]

When Sheriff Alexander located Hannah on Thursday, January 24, he found a markedly different woman from the one who had appeared in court two days earlier. In private she could finally speak her mind. Hannah now confessed that Rebecca Smith had "compelled" her to take an oath that "she would state in Court that it was her desire to return to Texas." What methods Rebecca employed to force such self-destructive testimony from Hannah we can only imagine. Robert Smith's cronies may have done much of the dirty work, but Rebecca was a crucial coconspirator in her husband's schemes to reclaim his laborers by whatever means necessary. Decades of slave-ownership had honed her powers of coercion. Now that Hannah was "breathing freer," in the words of Hayes, she announced her true desire: "to stay in California and be protected by the law and the Courts."[12]

But she wouldn't repeat this statement in open court. Hannah made that clear to Sheriff Alexander during the interview. To do so would risk retribution from Rebecca and perhaps other members of the family as well. It would also violate the oath that Hannah had taken before the Smiths. Rather than break that oath, she was willing to risk reenslavement. Discretion being the better part of valor, Hayes decided not to request that Hannah speak again in court. Her private testimony was enough, he hoped, to finally close the case.[13]

. . .

The evidence against Robert Smith was mounting. But he still had several options. There were enough holes in the case against him and enough legal measures still available to reclaim some of his former slaves.

The most conclusive, though perhaps most costly option, was an appeal. If Smith gained a hearing before the California Supreme Court, he may have won the case. Chief Justice Hugh Murray, unapologetically proslavery and anti-Black, would have given Smith a sympathetic hearing, to say the least. Simply by repeating the logic from his 1852 Perkins decision—which remanded to slavery three previously emancipated African Americans—Murray could have dealt a similar fate to Biddy and the thirteen others. Much of the evidence against Smith from the Los Angeles trial would have been deemed inadmissible. The crucial testimony of Biddy and Hannah, after all, was prohibited by California law.[14]

Smith didn't need to take his case to Sacramento, however. He could have simply appeared before a Los Angeles probate court, over which a judge from Kentucky presided, to exploit the state's flexible wardship law. That law, part of the 1850 Act for the Government and Protection of Indians, allowed white householders to seize Indigenous minors from their families and bind them as unpaid servants. The statute also applied to Black minors. A petitioner merely had to bring the child's "friend" before the court, state that the parents were unfit, and claim legal guardianship for themselves. Who qualified as a "friend" was left to the discretion of the court.[15] States like Mississippi would later adopt similar laws, part of their notorious Black Codes, to retain control over emancipated Black workers in the post–Civil War era.[16]

Black and Native wards could be found in the homes of some of Southern California's most eminent residents, including Judge Hayes's friends and acquaintances. A Tennessee transplant named Cave Couts, for instance, put the guardianship law to lucrative effect on his sprawling San Diego ranch, where he held more than a dozen Indigenous children as his wards. Couts attempted to acquire an Indian ward for Hayes's sister but apparently without success.[17] In Los Angeles the former mayor and wealthy landholder Benjamin Davis Wilson helped his mother-in-law claim the labor of two Black girls, Emily and Maria.[18] The county clerk who issued the wardship papers, John W. Shore, was himself the guardian of an enslaved boy named Tom.[19] In total, Los Angeles judges ruled on the guardianship status of seventeen enslaved children between 1852 and 1858. In every case they decided in favor of their enslavers-cum-guardians. Guardians discovered a winning strategy by invoking a familiar proslavery trope: that Black women lacked the moral grounding and means to adequately care for their own children.[20]

Robert Smith could have made the same argument about Biddy and Hannah—however palpably untrue such a statement would have been—and petitioned for guardianship of their children. And he almost certainly would have won. "It may be admitted that he has the ordinary qualifications, and, under other circumstances than the present, might be the guardian of those under 21 years of age," Hayes wrote. If Smith continued to live in California, "he might retain the care of them, and, perhaps, received unmolested the fruits of their labor, as others are doing with Indians and, occasionally, with persons of color," Hayes continued.[21] As minors under the age of twenty-one, twelve of the fourteen former slaves would have become Smith's legal wards. To avoid separation from their children, Biddy and Hannah would have been forced to remain as well. They then would have been right back where they started: under the control of Robert Smith.

. . .

Smith, however, had other plans. Instead of pursuing his various legal options, he sought more direct ways of reclaiming his labor force. Smith's hired hands alongside one of his sons did most of the dirty work. They may have acted on Robert's behalf, or they may have taken the initiative themselves. Regardless of whose orders they followed, they made their intentions clear: to override Judge Hayes's decision and bring as many enslaved people to Texas as possible. As one of the conspirators thundered, "It was right Smith should have the Negroes."[22] The freedom suit was on the verge of becoming a kidnapping trial.

Smith's cronies first targeted the home of Robert Owens. On Friday evening two of Smith's teamsters, Hartwell Cottrell and another man named Meredith, pounded on the door and demanded an audience with some of the women inside. Both men were visibly drunk and agitated.

They spoke first to Ellen, Biddy's eldest, and to Ann, Hannah's eldest, attempting to lure them back with a series of implausible appeals. The judge had perjured himself. Smith wouldn't force them into bondage in Texas. He wanted them "well situated." None of it worked. Ellen and Ann weren't going anywhere.

Cottrell and Meredith stormed off, but not before making several more threats. Smith had plenty of money, Cottrell shouted. And "by God he will see them out with it," Meredith added. "Tell old Bob [Owens], if he has not anything to do with it, not to have," Meredith continued, "or he will be sorry for it."[23]

Cottrell returned later that night, probably with a few more drinks in him, for another round of appeals and threats. One of Smith's sons joined him. The younger Smith—who is unnamed in the record, though it was probably Willy, the second-born—pulled Ann outside the home for a "long conversation." No witness heard what they discussed (or, rather, what the white men threatened). The nature of their encounter therefore can only be surmised.

One scholar has imagined the meeting as a lover's rendezvous. More likely, it was a confrontation between assailant and victim. Willy and Ann had grown up together from the ages of eight and ten, respectively. At fourteen or fifteen Ann became pregnant with Mary while living on the Smiths' Jumuba ranch. Because there were few possible romantic partners in the enslaved community in San Bernardino, it's likely that one of the Smith men fathered Mary—and the most likely among them was Willy.[24] If so, Willy would have assumed an additional claim on Ann's future in this final desperate conversation. And his attempts to lure her back to the Smith encampment would have had an added layer of menace. Not only was he the son of the man who once owned her; he may have also been her rapist.[25]

By remaining in the Owens family home, Biddy and the others risked assault or abduction. Bob Owens himself was also in danger. His affluence wouldn't shield him or any of his guests from violence, especially not from drunk and seasoned trailhands like Cottrell and Meredith. Because none of the Black people in the Owens home could legally testify in court—despite what Hayes had allowed so far—any white assailant would likely avoid legal consequences.

Dr. A. H. Cooper, one of the rare white allies to Los Angeles's Black community, alerted the authorities to the nocturnal visits of the Smith gang. Biddy and the others were moved from the Owens home back to the jail, where they could be guarded more securely. Hannah too was placed in protective custody. Authorities rescued her from the Smith camp, which had since relocated from San Bernardino to Santa Monica. Cottrell and Meredith were arrested and deposed. They were instructed to appear in court on Monday, most likely to face kidnapping charges. The message from Los Angeles law enforcement was clear: Smith could no longer command the movement of the women and children he once claimed as property.[26]

Yet members of the Smith gang were undeterred. Cottrell, who Hayes regarded as "the most unscrupulous" of all the perpetrators, was released soon after his arrest. On Sunday evening, he and one of the Smith sons—likely Willy once more—appeared at the county jail where Biddy and most of the others were now held. They again targeted Ann. With a bottle of brandy they attempted to coax her back to their camp. According to the jailer, their intention was "to carry off some of the children." Again, none followed them. Nevertheless, the encounter deeply unsettled Biddy, Hannah, and their children. No place, it seemed, was safe from the machinations of Smith's men. Despite what Hayes had proclaimed a week earlier, they weren't free yet.[27]

. . .

Robert Smith viewed the trial as a contest over private property; many Angelenos saw it as a matter of public welfare. The emancipation of Biddy and thirteen others would have amounted to a significant increase in the pueblo's free Black population, which at that point numbered only a few dozen. For a certain class of Angeleno, this was an alarming, some would say intolerable, development. To prevent it, a handful of vigilantes volunteered to help Smith reclaim his former slaves. Policing the Los Angeles color line was in their view a community endeavor.[28]

Los Angeles had long been a dangerous place for Black people, especially those who dared to defy their alleged owners. The most infamous antecedent to Biddy's case took place in the winter of 1851. It began when a passerby heard cries of agony emanating from the courtyard of an adobe in town. He discovered a man named Thomas Thorn whipping two Black men. Thorn had led a company of miners and roughly a dozen enslaved people overland from Texas. They would soon be bound for the gold fields of Northern California. But when two of the enslaved men refused to go any further, Thorn brought out his whip. No Black man would defy his authority, he vowed, regardless of what California's laws had to say in the matter.[29]

When Los Angeles marshal John H. Purdy attempted to intervene on behalf of the Black men, he was confronted by a delegation of his fellow citizens. Purdy, who once operated an abolitionist newspaper in his home state of Ohio, had survived plenty of dustups over his antislavery views. But he met his match in the rowdies of Los Angeles. "They told me that I was required to leave the city within the space of 24 hours, at my peril," he later reported, "which I distinctly understood to mean the peril of my life." Purdy departed the next morning for San Francisco. "Mob Law," lamented the Los Angeles mayor, "is triumphant as respects the existence of negro slavery in this district." It would take years for some of the Black men under Thorn's control to win their freedom.[30]

Los Angeles was in danger of devolving into a similarly chaotic spectacle in January 1856, as white vigilantes rallied to Robert Smith's defense. Several Angelenos had offered to help Smith "get the petitioners by force." Although Smith never admitted to enlisting their aid, he undoubtedly viewed their involvement as an asset in his case.[31]

Dr. A. H. Cooper, who had befriended Biddy and the others, became a target that weekend. An armed former constable named Joseph Clark approached him on horseback on Saturday evening, insisting that the case "must be settled that night on Southern principles, or I would suffer for it," Cooper recalled. Clark became increasingly agitated, dismounted, and reached for his pistol. "You are a d---d abolitionist," he bellowed, "and I would as soon blow your brains out as not." Cooper dashed into a nearby building to avoid a showdown in the streets. Mounting his horse, Clark vowed to "settle it with you before morning." Cooper had witnessed the confrontation at Bob Owens's home the previous evening, and as a white man he was legally permitted to testify against Smith and his cronies. The purpose of the former constable's threats, Cooper reasoned, "was to intimidate me from appearing as a witness."[32]

Such threats carried weight in frontier Los Angeles. The town witnessed two hundred homicides between 1850 and 1859, at a time when

Los Angeles only housed between five thousand to ten thousand residents. It was a per capita murder rate fifty times higher than New York City's, which made it one of the bloodiest places anywhere in America. A more comparable homicide rate could be found in the Mexican border towns at the height of the cartel wars in the early 2000s.[33] The pueblo's transient population of gamblers, drunks, cattle thieves, luckless miners, and cut-throats from both sides of the border made for a potent demographic brew, seasoned with a strong dose of racial animus.

Even a brief stroll through Los Angeles after sunset necessitated a small arsenal. "Almost every night pistols were fired in the street under my windows, in consequence of disputes originating in gambling-houses and other places of ill repute," wrote one traveler.[34] When the sun rose the next morning, "it was not an infrequent thing to find a dead Indian on the street," a shell-shocked Methodist minister recalled.[35] The mounting body count inspired a macabre sense of humor in the local press. "The week past has been comparatively quiet; four persons have been killed it is true, but it has been considered a poor week for killing," quipped the editor of the *Southern Californian*.[36] As one of the town's early residents recalled, Los Angeles "was barbarism gone to seed."[37]

Local law enforcement could do little to staunch the bloodletting. Los Angeles possessed an anemic police force consisting of a single sheriff and undersheriff for the county, and a marshal and two constables for the city.[38] Although the city council attempted to outlaw firearms within town limits in 1850, the proposal failed. By 1855 the district court had executed just one person for the crime of murder. In the absence of effective policing, a vigilante subculture flourished. Over the next quarter century, vigilantes lynched thirty-seven people, mostly Mexican men. Rather than an activity limited to the so-called rabble, vigilantism attracted some of the town's most eminent residents. It was a former constable after all who accosted Biddy's ally, Dr. Cooper. The previous year, the mayor of Los Angeles resigned his office to lead the lynching of a desperado from Texas. After stringing up the condemned criminal, he was reelected without opposition.[39] The presence of armed vigilantes patrolling the pueblo's streets and byways may have been comforting to some Angelenos—but certainly not to Biddy.

Hayes thus had to act quickly to prevent the courtroom proceedings from devolving into street violence. He knew as well as anyone that even the city's jail, where Biddy and the others were held, wasn't safe from a committed Los Angeles mob or from Smith's entourage. On Monday morning he issued a contempt charge for Cottrell for attempting to carry off some of the Black children. He also contemplated issuing kidnapping charges for members of Smith's party.[40]

In his report on the trial Hayes quoted extensively from the California statutes on kidnapping. The language described Smith's actions almost exactly. Section 55 of the law read: "Every person who shall hire, *persuade*, entice, decoy, or seduce *by false promises, misrepresentations, and the like*, any *negro, mulatto, or colored person, to go out of this State*, or to be taken or removed therefrom, for the purpose, and *with the intent* to sell such negro, etc. into slavery or involuntary servitude, or *otherwise employ him or her to his own use, or to the use of another, without the free will and consent of such negro*, etc. shall be deemed to have committed the crime of kidnapping and punished." In his ruling, Hayes had tellingly used the term "seducing" to describe Smith's attempts to carry Biddy and the others to Texas.[41] The punishment for such an act, Hayes noted, was confinement for one to ten years in the state prison.[42]

Smith had squandered whatever influence he once enjoyed with the Southern-born judge. Whether he would have ultimately served time for kidnapping, we'll never know. The mere threat of a prison sentence sufficiently spooked California's largest slaveholder. He never again appeared in the Los Angeles courtroom. As Hayes prepared for the next phase in an increasingly chaotic trial, Smith was already on his way to Texas—without Biddy or any of the other people he once held as property.

· · ·

Did Biddy bother to watch as Robert Smith's now-diminished company passed through the pueblo and on to the far horizon? Probably not. She had seen far too much of him and his wagons and his cattle over the past fifteen years. As had her daughters. Two of them, Ann and Harriet, had known nothing but life under his control, while Ellen was just a small child by the time he purchased them in the early 1840s. Many of Hannah's children were born under his roof as well. Life beyond the bounds of Smith's command had been, for as far back as most of them could remember, inconceivable.

As the faint outline of Smith's wagon company faded into the distance, the full import of their victory may have been hard to fathom. After all, they had already heard their freedom declared in court only to endure multiple kidnapping attempts by Smith's cronies and imprisonment, once more, in the city jail. Biddy could be forgiven for doubting the power of Los Angeles's feeble judicial system over the insidious methods of her enslaver. For years, freedom was a fantasy that could only be whispered among themselves.

But eventually it became clear that Smith wasn't coming back. Their enslaver was gone for good. Perhaps tentatively at first but then with growing conviction, the whispers of freedom grew into a chorus. At last they could proclaim their liberty for all to hear.

Word reached their enslaved compatriots in San Bernardino. Inspired by Biddy and Hannah's success, the Black community there launched a parallel movement for freedom. One former slaveholder, Daniel M. Thomas, documented their self-emancipations, which began that same month. Thomas's own bondsman, Philemon, was one of the first to flee. Then several of Bishop William Crosby's enslaved workers—including Grief Embers, the colony's much-loved bugler; Hannah's husband, Toby Embers; and Hark Wales, a famous member of the first Mormon party to reach the Salt Lake Valley in 1847—left their owner.[43] By the end of the year Black slavery in San Bernardino ceased to exist. Biddy and Hannah's courtroom victory had freed more than just the fourteen members of their families; it emancipated an entire colony.

Those self-emancipations nearly killed the colony's bishop. Although William Crosby claimed that he was eager "to get rid of them, as they had little to do, and ate a good deal more than they worked," he felt the absence of his Black laborers almost immediately.[44] According to a neighbor, "The Bishop has been quite sick, from over exertion and exposure while at work on the Mill."[45] That mill is where several of his enslaved people once worked, doubtlessly saving Crosby from the most taxing tasks. The illness of the bishop, finally stripped of his workforce, marked a poetic end to what had been the most prosperous and durable slaveholding settlement in California.

No one of course lost more than Robert Smith. By the mid-1850s he was the proprietor of a flourishing cattle ranch, a respected patriarch in the Mormon community, and the owner of one of the largest groups of enslaved Black people ever assembled in the Far West. But within just six months his entire dominion withered before his eyes. His ranch had been seized, his standing within his community ruined, and fourteen enslaved people removed from his control. Then, on the long road to Texas, his trailhands revolted. They nearly succeeded in robbing the company before Smith discovered their plot and forced them from the wagon party.[46] The final humiliation came in March 1856, when Smith was cut off from the LDS Church by a unanimous vote of his former brethren in San Bernardino.[47]

As Biddy or any of her Black peers could attest, California wasn't born free with its antislavery constitution. It only became free after a prolonged, collective struggle by the enslaved themselves. Biddy herself played the decisive role in that struggle, when she provided the testimony to expose her enslaver's ruse, thereby unraveling his case and subsequently the labor regime upon which many Southern California landowners had come to depend. Finally, the long trail that she traveled in slavery—which spanned thousands of miles of terrain and consumed the first thirty-eight years of her life—had come to an end. She and her children were truly "free forever." Yet as Biddy learned already, where one trail ended, another had just begun.

10 Freedwoman

Less than a month after the trial ended, Benjamin Hayes saw his nightmare spring to life on the streets of Los Angeles. His day in mid-February 1856 began promisingly enough. He and his three-year-old-son, Chauncey, were out for a carriage ride, a favorite activity of theirs. Chauncey was devoted to horses and Hayes devoted—some might say anxious and overprotective—to his son.[1] As they merrily bumped along the ungraded streets of the pueblo, Chauncey slipped from the buggy. Before Hayes could extend a hand to catch him, Chauncey tumbled to the earth. Hayes looked on helplessly as his only child hit the dirt, directly under "the heels of the horse."

Hayes would always regard what happened next as "one of the most singular [events]" of his life.

Moments before impact with an oncoming carriage, a woman leapt from the side of the road, "rushed under the very wheels, and snatched him from death!" Hayes recognized her as "one of these same poor Negro women," whom he had emancipated just weeks before.[2]

Although Hayes never named the Black woman in any surviving document, the evidence points to Biddy. Of the fourteen people Hayes freed, all were minors except for two: Biddy and Hannah. True, Ellen and Ann could rightfully be considered women, but that's a term few white writers at the time would have applied to seventeen-year-old African Americans. To most white Americans, especially a Southerner like Hayes, they would have been "girls." Because Hannah had permanently settled in San Bernardino by this point, that leaves only Biddy who fits Hayes's description. As a cattle driver on the overland trail, Biddy would have witnessed the killing power of wagon wheels—and perhaps had even saved others before Chauncey.

Hayes saw the hand of God upon Biddy that day. "Providence" had guided her toward his son, he claimed, perhaps as some sort of divine compensation for his role in her emancipation. Years later, he wrote to a friend to wonder "if a Judge could be repaid for any duty performed by him—what do you think can be the measure of my reward, in such circumstances?" He continued, "If dear Jack, you had a boy—and one only—you would feel as I do; and yet your kindness of heart easily will teach you what must be the lively gratitude of a father who has escaped from such danger."[3]

How did Hayes express that gratitude? What would be Biddy's reward for her act of split-second heroism? Hayes never said. But later developments suggest that he found ways to demonstrate his thankfulness. The event marked a pattern in Biddy's subsequent years, in which moments of profound courage or kindness or insight won her the esteem, and sometimes the patronage, of Los Angeles's most influential citizens.

Biddy also won admirers from further afield. Newspapers from the abolitionist press of the Northeast, identifying Biddy by name, celebrated her emancipation as an unexpected victory in the national crusade against slavery. According to the *Liberator*, the trial raised the crucial question of whether the laws of free states like California "lose their validity when they come into collision with the interests of slavery." Past experience indicated that "the great influence of the Slave Power" would once again trump California's flimsy constitutional protections for people like Biddy. And yet in this instance California's constitution withstood the assault. "This was a triumphant victory over the Slave Power," the *Liberator* concluded, "which indicates that California will not always be counted on its side."[4] The *National Antislavery Standard* expressed similar surprise over the ruling: "It was not to be expected that in that remote and benighted region much good law was to be found."[5] As a rare rebuke to slaveholding expansionists, the case "should attract much attention" from freedom-lovers everywhere, according to the *New York Daily Times*. The ruling would prove a legal precedent "of the highest value" in the ongoing struggle against slavery, the *Times* predicted.[6]

Within the space of several months Biddy had challenged her enslaver in court, delivered her family from bondage, rescued the son of the city's most powerful legal figure, and seemingly turned the tide against slavery in the West. She had gone from property to prisoner to freedwoman to savior. American history offers few comparable examples of such dramatic turnabouts in status. This was Biddy's moment.

But moments pass. And for a Black woman in frontier Los Angeles, surrounded by many people who still saw her as a nuisance if not a menace, they pass quickly.

. . .

Those who cheered Hayes's ruling and Biddy's emancipation did so from thousands of miles away, from their printing presses in New York, Boston, and Philadelphia. The mood back home was decidedly different. Hayes had rendered his verdict; now the people of Los Angeles would render theirs.

The backlash came almost immediately. Hayes was denounced as an "abolitionist," a term tantamount to a four-letter word in antebellum Los Angeles. "Even at Sacramento," Hayes recalled, "I was 'Damned' (so Gov. [John] Downey informed me)." Years later, Hayes still had difficulty comprehending how he had provoked such outrage "for declaring a simple proposition of *law*—for granting a clear constitutional right!" But there was nothing self-evident in the ruling, according to many of Hayes's fellow Angelenos. People like Biddy, they insisted, didn't deserve any constitutional rights.[7]

Hayes wrote voluminously, often feverishly, to justify his decision and turn the tide of public opinion in his favor. After all, he was an elected official, with plans to run again in 1858. He went to James S. Waite, editor of the *Los Angeles Star*, "to satisfy the public mind here." Hayes dashed off a five-thousand-word account of the trial that consumed nearly a full broadsheet, rendered in densely packed text.[8] *The Star* dubbed it the "celebrated Slave Case."[9] Still, that wasn't enough for Hayes. He wanted to add the transcriptions from the trial's witnesses, including Biddy's testimony in his chambers. But Waite refused to allocate more space in his "little Star," Hayes sniffed.[10]

Next the judge appealed to one of the most influential men in Los Angeles, the former mayor and powerbroker Benjamin Davis Wilson, a native of Tennessee. Hayes pleaded with Wilson to "see if your influence can get [the account] printed" in one of the state's major newspapers in Sacramento or San Francisco.[11] The judge's public relations campaign had grown from a local effort to a statewide mission. Wilson succeeded in securing a place for the full account in the *Daily Democratic Journal,* one of the leading papers in California.[12] But not all press was good press. Six weeks later, Hayes's account also appeared in the *National Anti-Slavery Standard,* published simultaneously in New York and Philadelphia.[13] Hayes must have blanched when he saw his words reprinted in a preeminent abolitionist outlet. "Abolitionist," after all, was the slander he was trying to shed.

Not only were Hayes's electoral prospects in doubt, his personal safety was also at risk. His anxieties stemmed from personal experience. As a young lawyer and new arrival in Los Angeles in 1850, Hayes had taken on the case of a Black man named Stephen Cribbs. Cribbs's father had recently died, leaving him in the possession of a mule. As a free man, Cribbs was entitled to this inheritance, Hayes argued. A mob of white Angelenos thought otherwise. Before Hayes had the opportunity to vindicate Cribbs's rights in court, they improvised their own proceedings by trapping Cribbs alone in a room. They intended to abduct him and sell him into slavery or, failing in that, to kill him. Witnesses to the altercation heard the report of pistol shots, then saw a wounded Cribbs scramble from the home and vault an adjoining adobe wall. Cribbs was never seen in Los Angeles again. Hayes began to arm himself in fear that the mob would come for him next.[14]

He wouldn't have long to wait. Shortly after the Cribbs case, Hayes made the dangerous decision to prosecute two sons of José Maria Lugo for murder. The Lugo family, a ranching dynasty whose property became the Mormon colony of San Bernardino, had friends in high (and low) places.[15] Despite Hayes's best efforts, the two young men were acquitted. But the Lugos apparently weren't satisfied yet. One night after the trial Hayes heard the sound of approaching hoofbeats outside his office. Thinking it was a friend come to visit him, he opened the door to find a mounted rider, his face covered in shadow. When Hayes inquired what the visitor wanted, the response was "an instantaneous flare of light" and a thundering blast. The rider wheeled his horse and dashed off into the night as a dazed Hayes gradually regained his senses to discover that a bullet had passed through his hat and smashed into the adobe wall behind him. He had escaped death by mere inches. The would-be assassin was never apprehended, but it was rumored that he had come to exact revenge on Hayes for daring to prosecute members of the Lugo family.[16] Hayes considered himself fortunate; several officers of the peace would be gunned down in the line of duty that decade.[17]

Death may have eluded Hayes for the moment, but it clung to his wife, Emily. She had joined her husband in Los Angeles several years earlier, hoping that the temperate climate might sooth her wracking cough. Warm winters, however, hardly offset the strain induced by crude living conditions and her husband's long absences as he shuttled between court duties in Los Angeles, San Bernardino, and San Diego. Their second child, a baby girl born in April 1855, lived only a few hours.[18]

In the aftermath of the Biddy trial and the run-up to another election, anxiety suffused the household. Emily pleaded with her husband to return to private practice and a more settled life. "If you should [run for reelection]," she warned in September 1857, "I will start off for another country!"[19] Hayes preferred to see the "jest" in her threat, but he couldn't overlook his wife's deteriorating condition, which rendered her bedridden for days at a time. The same night that she issued her ultimatum, Emily, at the age of thirty-six, suffered a catastrophic hemorrhage of the lungs. She died within minutes.[20]

Shattered by grief, Hayes groped for ways to survive. Visits to the gravesite of his wife and infant daughter provided one source of solace. Alcohol provided another. Despite his multiple attempts at sobriety, drink was a demon he simply couldn't shake. Hayes "was known as a jurist of high standing," one of his admiring contemporaries wrote, "though on account of his love for strong drink, court on more than one occasion had to be adjourned."[21] In later years "his habits of intemperance" would become so pronounced, "as to entirely unfit [him] for his profession," according to another Angeleno.[22] Hayes grew ever more attached to his one remaining child, Chauncey, who often accompanied him by carriage on his long legal circuit through Southern California.[23] As Hayes dwelt on mortality and the fickle hand of fate, as he often did, his thoughts may have turned to Biddy and her miraculous rescue of his son, his last remaining tether to happiness.[24]

Despite decreeing the largest legal emancipation in the American West, Benjamin Hayes has been largely lost to history. The most complete compendium of American freedom suits, an indispensable two-volume study, makes no mention of his ruling.[25] Other freedom-seekers who challenged their status in court—Dred Scott foremost among them—would become household names in antebellum America, but not Biddy or Hannah. Sheer distance from the nerve centers of the antislavery struggle may partly explain the neglect. Hayes rendered his decision from a crumbling adobe room in a frontier town better known for mob executions than legal emancipations. The trial's thin paper trail also helps explain its light imprint on legal history. Because Robert Smith didn't appeal the ruling, the case never came before higher courts, whose formal decisions were more likely to find their way into legal textbooks.[26] Furthermore, the original courtroom reports from the trial were either lost or destroyed. Our best surviving sources are the retrospective newspaper accounts written by Hayes—elaborate attempts at self-justification, muddled by occasionally convoluted prose—as he struggled to dispel some of the outrage that his ruling had unleashed.[27]

. . .

As Hayes battled over his reputation, Biddy battled for survival. The euphoria of emancipation faded all-too-fast. Indeed, her postliberation experiences in Los Angeles anticipated some of the struggles that African Americans would encounter roughly a decade later in the Reconstruction-era South. Freedom, as Biddy discovered, was not merely the absence of a master; it was a state of being that required active maintenance, especially within a society that still saw her as a prisoner, a ward, or a servant rather than a neighbor. To transcend those labels, Biddy would have to perform a sort of social alchemy and help transform the very nature of Los Angeles itself. Freedom had to be won, then defined, then defended.[28]

Although slavery had been synonymous with dislocation, freedom did not necessarily bring union. Ironically, one of Biddy's first experiences as a freedwoman was separation from many of those she knew, loved, and helped raise. Hannah had remained in San Bernardino for much of the trial, and in its aftermath she decided to settle there with her husband, Toby Embers. Most of her children joined her. So ended a partnership of more than a decade, which had sustained two families across thousands of miles and through countless traumas. Biddy and Hannah would continue to aid one another in future years, but they would do so from separate households and increasingly from different worlds.[29]

As one extended family separated, however, another reunited. After being relocated from the Owens household to the prison during the trial, Biddy and her daughters returned to the home on San Pedro Street as newly freed people. It must have been a rapturous reunion for Charles Owens and Ellen in particular, whose love had flowered during the tumultuous weeks of the trial. They married on October 16, 1856. For Biddy as well, the move to the Owens household would have been a homecoming of sorts. Those adobe walls would provide sanctuary from an otherwise unforgiving and sometimes perilous environment during her unsteady early years in freedom.[30]

Biddy could be excused for harboring misgivings about her new community. Some of the thugs who threatened her family during the trial were now her neighbors. The major overland trail from the slave states terminated in Los Angeles, hence why Southern transplants accounted for a majority of the town's American-born population. For years to come, Los Angeles remained "a stronghold of Southern men," populated by a class of migratory backwoodsmen known pejoratively as "Pikes" for Pike County, Missouri, from which some of them hailed. As visitors noted, these Pikes weren't the sort of people prone to critical self-reflection or the reevaluation of their prejudices.[31] They certainly didn't have a monopoly on racism, however. Angelenos from all backgrounds contributed to a rash of racial violence that roiled the pueblo in the months and years after Biddy's emancipation.

Much of that violence was directed against the region's Hispanic population, amounting to what some historians have described as a "race war."[32] In 1857, Biddy would have witnessed gangs of would-be conquistadors—they called themselves "filibusterers"—swelling the streets of the pueblo, stockpiling munitions, and "strutt[ing] about . . . [with] rifles and revolvers" in preparation for an invasion of the Mexican state of Sonora. Their leader, a former California state senator named Henry Crabb, planned to carve out a slaveholding colony from California's neighbor to the southeast. From their base at Los Angeles about one hundred soldiers-of-fortune marched south that spring toward what they hoped would be slavery's newest frontier.[33]

They had more bluster than ability. Mexican soldiers captured or executed most of the invaders, including Crabb, whose decapitated head they stuffed into a jar of embalming fluid as a macabre warning to future filibusterers. That grim display, however, did little to diminish the appetites of proslavery imperialists, including those from Los Angeles, who would continue to launch (unsuccessful) forays into various parts of Latin America for the rest of the decade.[34] Biddy may have escaped Robert Smith, but she remained within rifle range of aspiring slaveholders.

Armed men stampeded through the pueblo and its outlying hamlets again the next year, rounding up and executing more than a dozen Mexican victims. The vigilantes mustered after receiving news that the county sheriff and several of his constables had been gunned down by a roving band of outlaws, led by Juan Flores. Flores had orchestrated an improbable breakout from San Quentin the previous October, hijacking a brig from the prison's dock and steering it, while still in handcuffs, toward safe harbor in San Francisco Bay. His subsequent crime spree in the Southern California countryside set off rumors—unfounded but impactful—that he planned to align with local Indians to wage a biracial war of extermination against white American settlers. Dr. John S. Griffin, the brother-in-law of Benjamin Hayes, took command of a "Committee of Safety" in Los Angeles, cramming the jail with scores of poor Mexican men accused of all manner of crimes. Others took more drastic action. They seized suspected Mexican conspirators, hanging some and beheading others.[35] Those scenes would have triggered nightmarish flashbacks for Biddy, who had survived a not dissimilar splurge of racial violence while a young enslaved woman in Mississippi in 1835.

Even setting aside the violence, Biddy had entered multiethnic Los Angeles as color lines were hardening and opportunities shrinking. True, plenty of upwardly mobile white migrants still sought unions with the *californio* ranching elite. And skin tone didn't dictate social worth or legal rights to the extent that it did in Biddy's native Georgia or Mississippi. Still, Angelenos were well on their way to a clearly articulated racial hierarchy, with working-class Mexicans, Native Americans, and Black people firmly embedded in the lowest social strata.[36]

The sharpest blow for Biddy and her Black neighbors came not from the mobs of Los Angeles, but from the pen of Chief Justice Roger Taney in Washington, DC. In March 1857 he issued his now infamous decision in the case *Dred Scott v. Sanford.* The contours of Scott's case followed the rough outline of Biddy's own suit for freedom the previous year. Scott, an enslaved man, had been taken by his owner into free territory—in his case, Wisconsin and Illinois. Scott argued that residence on free soil made him a free man. Taney saw things differently. With a single ruling, the chief justice struck down Scott's freedom claims, barred all African Americans from the rights of citizenship, and extended the dominion of slavery. The historical record had made clear, Taney argued, that African Americans were "so far inferior, that they had no rights which the white man was bound to respect." Slaveholders in turn had the right to sojourn with their human property wherever they pleased.[37]

Scott was remanded to slavery and the nation lurched one step closer to disunion. Abraham Lincoln, a former congressmen from Illinois, drew a dispiriting conclusion from the ruling. The Supreme Court had decreed that what a "master might lawfully do with Dred Scott, in the free state of Illinois, every master might lawfully do with any other one, or one thousand slaves, in Illinois, or in any other free state," he wrote.[38] It didn't take a legal mind as sharp as Lincoln's to see the upshot of Taney's decision: Slavery, momentarily in retreat after Biddy's victory, was again extending its national reach.

. . .

What's in a name? True, a rose by any other word would smell as sweet. But for Black people like Biddy, names carried powerful possibilities. In bondage, African Americans "often had to bear appellations imposed by enslavers and were typically denied the use of surnames that would identify them as members of families," according to historian Tiya Miles.[39] In freedom, then, a carefully selected name could restore a sense of familial belonging and even conjure lost worlds.

From here on, she would be known as Biddy Mason.

Biddy Mason's full name appears on a probate document with her signature marked with an X. Probate Court, Second Series, Case Number: 14493, Los Angeles Area Court Records, Huntington Library, San Marino, California.

Few facets of Biddy's biography are as misunderstood as the surname she selected for herself in freedom. Numerous sources implausibly suggest that she took the name in honor of Amasa Mason Lyman, the cofounder of the Mormon colony of San Bernardino in which she labored for nearly half a decade. The theory raises several questions. First, why choose the name of a Mormon religious leader when she had never converted to the LDS faith and would identify consistently as a Methodist for the rest of her life? Second, why honor the very same leader who had sanctioned, or at least didn't disturb, her own enslavement? And finally, even if there was a degree of affinity for Lyman—which seems unlikely—why adopt his middle rather than his last name?[40]

Biddy selected the name Mason, not because it had significance to a white Mormon's lineage, but because it held deep meaning for her own family. In doing so, she followed the practices of newly freed people across the country. Many of them, like Biddy, rejected the surname of their latest enslaver to distance themselves from a condition and set of relationships that they had finally transcended. Biddy would never let the name Smith sully her proud family line. She broke from Robert Smith twice over, first legally and now symbolically by jettisoning any nominal connection to his household.[41]

Instead, she reached deeper into the past. Mason may have been the surname of a former husband or lover, perhaps the father of Ann. There was indeed a Black man named Mason near the Mississippi homestead where Ann was raised. He comes into the historical record as one of the few African Americans to convert to Mormonism during the LDS mission to the slave states.[42] Biddy's decision therefore may have been a tribute to a man she loved, then lost. In official documents, including her last will, Biddy was identified as a "widow," despite never marrying in the eyes of the law.[43] She may have listed her marital status in such a way to deflect the aspersions that often fell on single mothers, even if she had never taken a husband. Or, as seems likely, she identified as a widow because that's precisely how she saw herself. And his name may have been Mason.

Or perhaps Biddy reached back further still, all the way to her earliest days in Hancock County, Georgia. Census records reveal a man named Thomas Mason, a slaveholder living in Hancock County around the time of Biddy's birth. Thomas Mason's plantation may have been the site of her family's labor, as well as the place they once called home.[44] Biddy only lived in Hancock Country for about five years before she was either sold or forcibly relocated.[45] That early dislocation undoubtedly ripped her from some, maybe most, of her family. Her chosen surname therefore may have been a tribute—and more than that, a symbolic bond—to those she lost long ago. Other freedpeople made similar naming decisions as they attempted to reconnect with family or at least acknowledge the links that had been shattered by slavery. "Mason," therefore, was far more than just a name on a census or tax assessment record. It was an appeal, a thread of memory, reaching across time and space to stitch together a sundered past.[46]

Biddy Mason also selected a birthdate for herself. Formerly enslaved people rarely knew the exact day or even the year of their births, as slaveholders didn't make calendars available to those they held as chattel. The enslaved marked Sundays, usually a day of rest, and Christmas, a day of festivity. Otherwise, they worked according to seasons, not to specific points on the calendar. Biddy may have known she was born in the summer, and later, she could have used a knowledge of historical events, say presidential administrations, to triangulate the approximate year of her birth. But beyond that the facts were hazy. Nonetheless, she would hereafter give a precise date for her birth: August 15, 1818. That date was later inscribed in the family's Bible and etched onto her headstone.[47]

What might have drawn her to that particular date? Perhaps it was a celebration. Each year, on August 15, the pueblo honored its patron saint, La Nuestra Senora de los Angeles (or more familiarly, the Virgin Mary). The festival served as something of a birthday party for the pueblo itself, with Angelenos, in all their finery, flocking to the central plaza to celebrate the heavenly namesake of their city.[48] Although Biddy wasn't Catholic, she was certainly devout, and she likely felt a special affinity for Mary—her faith, her suffering, her mother's love, her transcendence. By celebrating her own birthday on August 15, Biddy Mason could simultaneously commemorate two of the great forces in her life: her Christian faith and the city she now called home.

. . .

Celebrations, however, were in short supply during Mason's early years in freedom. Survival required employment, and the only role available to someone like Mason was a taxing, poorly paid job as a domestic servant.[49] One employer described the demands of the job, which probably didn't pay more than twenty-five cents per day: "My servant is hired to do whatever she is told to do and to be at anytime subject to my command."[50] Under such conditions freedom was only a short remove from slavery. Nevertheless, Mason had to take whatever meager opportunities she could find. Her daughters were all expected to contribute to the family's income stream as well. By 1860, if not earlier, even twelve-year-old Harriet would be living under another roof, likely as a domestic laborer, as the family struggled to make ends meet.[51]

Mason's primary task was to keep the grit and grime of other households at bay. Even some of the pueblo's most prominent citizens lived in humble, one might say crude, conditions. Emily Hayes complained of her "*mud* house, with a mud floor. The walls are whitewashed, but the ceiling looks like an old smoke-house, and leaks finely when it rains."[52] Dirt and dust proliferated. "By pouring water on the floors of our rooms we could ally the dust enough to sweep," one resident of nearby San Gabriel recalled. "To tell of the fleas would take one entire chapter."[53]

The filth of the homes emulated the muck of the pueblo as a whole. "After heavy winter rains mud was from six inches to two feet deep," recalled Harris Newmark, one of the city's most famous memoirists. "During the summer, dust piled up to about the same extent."[54] One morning after a particularly heavy rain, a local wag planted a series of signs in the impassable streets: "Beware of quicksand! Fare for ferrying across, 25 cents. No duck-hunting allowed in this pond! Boats leave this landing every half-hour."[55]

Mud wasn't the worst of it, though. Angelenos tossed food, rubbish, unwanted tools, even animal carcasses into the streets. The corpses were left to fester "for days at a time," Newmark wrote. He recalled "one instance of a horse dying on Alameda Street and lying there until a party of Indians cut up the carcass for food." Packs of feral dogs roamed the streets, scavenging for such throwaways. Tormenting these dogs became a "classical pastime" in the pueblo, according to one account, with Angelenos "appending tin kettles and fire works to the tails of the canine race."[56] Others took more lethal action by lacing the streets with poison. As a result, Mason would have occasionally navigated the cadavers of dead dogs on her way to work in the morning.[57]

Whatever path Mason picked, she almost certainly avoided one street in particular. Spanish-speakers called it Calle de los Negros, but Mason would have known it as Negro Alley (others typically used a nastier slur). Radiating southeast from the plaza for a single city block, the alley was a "malodorous thoroughfare" flanked on both sides by crumbling, low-slung adobe buildings, in which saloons, gambling parlors, and later opium dens proliferated.[58] On any given day, pleasure-seekers crammed into these buildings and spilled out onto the dirt road, jostling, swearing, and brawling. Gunshots and the groans of stabbing victims occasionally rang out, but "an officer would not have had the temerity to attempt an arrest in Nigger Alley," wrote Horace Bell.[59] No one dared to intervene when a mob stripped and whipped a Black man on the alley in 1854 for the apparent sin of using "expressive language" about African American rights. The local press gleefully reported that after "about one hundred stripes, his African blood cooled down," and he conceded that his earlier declaration of rights "was a humbug."[60]

The etymology of the alley reveals a great deal about the assumptions that Mason faced in early Los Angeles. Calle de los Negros had been named originally for the dark-skinned Mexicans who purportedly frequented its establishments and resided nearby.[61] But Anglos, ignorant or oblivious to this early history, linked the alley firmly to African Americans by rechristening it with a common racist slur. No matter that few Black people could be found near the alley on most days. Vice and Blackness—the two paired naturally in the minds of many of Mason's neighbors.

Like the pueblo's manure-strewn streets, the Los Angeles River served as a dumping ground for all manner of waste. Along its banks could be found "not only the daily refuse of the living" but also the bloated bodies of "countless dead horses and dogs, picked up off the streets and thrown

Mason would have steered a wide course around Calle de los Negros, known as the vice district of early Los Angeles. C. C. Pierce Collection of Photographs, Huntington Library, San Marino, California.

unceremoniously into the riverbed to await decomposition and enough current to travel downstream," historian Bill Deverell wrote.[62] Eighty dead horses, killed in a stable fire in 1887, were dumped into the riverbed in a single go. The Los Angeles River also became a favored depository for murder victims.[63]

Yet the river also gave life. As the city's only source of water, it was the very reason that Los Angeles existed. On any given day, women lined the banks of the river, fetching water, washing clothing, and splashing in its shallows. Such sights may be hard to picture. Today the Los Angeles river is a "grey channel" of concrete, with little more than an anemic trickle running through it. But when Mason lived near its banks, the river was a bona fide waterway that wound for fifty miles across Southern California to the Pacific, hugging some of the more populous parts of Los Angeles and giving sustenance to the city.[64]

Radiating from the river were a series of tributary canals called *zanjas* (or "sankeys" in the parlance of phonetically-challenged Anglo settlers). A web of these open-air waterways crisscrossed the pueblo—fifty miles of them by 1870—giving Los Angeles a distinctive, not unlovely character that drew comment from virtually every visitor. The zanjas were the life-

A zanja runs in front of the San Pedro Street home (right) of Robert and Winnie Owens, where Mason lived during her early years in freedom. C. C. Pierce Collection of Photographs, Huntington Library, San Marino, California.

blood of the pueblo, reflected in the fact that the city official responsible for maintaining them collected a salary 50 percent higher than the mayor's. Those living near a zanja, as did Mason in the 1850s, simply helped themselves to its contents, while those living further afield paid carriers like "Bill the Waterman" for personal deliveries.[65]

Like the river that fed them, though, the open-air zanjas were also vectors of filth. In the absence of bridges, livestock splashed through the earthen canals, often leaving bodily waste in their wake. Dead animals, and even the odd dead person, had to be plucked occasionally from the public water supply. Laws against bathing, washing clothes, and dumping refuse into the zanjas were honored in the breach.[66] "A stranger would be very apt to suppose that our water canals were built for the purpose of carrying off the garbage and foul matter that is continually accumulating within the precincts of a city," lamented the *Los Angeles Star*, "instead of being the source from which a large portion of the inhabitants are supplied with water for domestic purposes."[67]

Under such conditions disease constantly stalked the pueblo. Biddy's first summer in Los Angeles was a time of sickness. "A sort of influenza is prevailing in the city, so common on this coast and so severe often at Los Angeles," wrote Benjamin Hayes, who would become all-too-familiar with illness in California.[68] Dysentery, easily carried along the pueblo's waterways, and smallpox, which erupted in epidemics roughly once a decade, were two of the major killers. Disease typically preyed on the poorest, most vulnerable families.

In the summer of 1857 it came for the Masons. Ann's symptoms may have been mild at first. And she was in safe hands with her mother, a veteran healer, by her bedside. Surely she had survived worse as a small child along the overland trail and in her years of slavery in Utah and Southern California. Yet the disease progressed steadily, and on August 1 it finally overwhelmed Mason's middle child. There is no record of what killed her. Whatever it was, it likely came through the water. A zanja ran in front of the Owens home, where the Masons still lived.[69]

Here was the cruelest irony of emancipation. Biddy had done the impossible—keep her family together across three thousand miles of slavery—only to have her daughter snatched from her in freedom. As is the case with so much of Mason's life, no words survive from Biddy or her other daughters about what the family suffered that summer. Then again, no words could possibly convey the despair into which they had been plunged just eighteen months after their liberation. We have only this, a single line in the family Bible: "Died, Miss Ann Mason, August 1, 1857." She was fourteen years old.[70]

11 Healer

Every Monday two groups assembled near the decaying adobe that served as the Los Angeles County courthouse. One group came willingly; the other by force. One came to buy; the other to be bought. Once the bidding began, the site of Biddy Mason's emancipation became the backdrop to a "slave mart," a weekly auction of Indigenous convicts that enriched the city as it drove its Native American population to the brink of collapse.[1]

The auction fueled a vicious cycle that pumped a continuous supply of cheap labor into Southern California's agricultural and urban economies. Once purchased, Indigenous convicts were carried off to the pueblo's outlying ranchos and vineyards or else forced onto a chain gang and marched toward the latest public works project. Compensation, if any, came in the form of aguardiente, a stomach-turning local brandy. As soon as these once-and-future convicts consumed their "wages," the city marshal pounced. Armed with a heavy cane and flanked by his Native deputies, the marshal seized any inebriated Indian he could find and hauled them to an open-air corral near the courthouse or tossed them into the county jail. The inmates awoke the next morning to an all-too-familiar sight: a crowd of eager bidders who would drag them off for another week of hard labor. And repeat.[2]

Frontier Los Angeles was not known for its vigilant police force, but when it came to regulating Indigenous people, the pueblo made an exception. And no wonder. The weekly sale of Native convicts was Los Angeles's second-largest source of municipal revenue, behind only the license fees imposed on the town's proliferating saloons and gambling dens. Meanwhile, the land barons made out like bandits, securing five days of labor for as little as one dollar. Southern California's budding wine industry, in particular, thrived off Indigenous exploitation.[3]

Although Angelenos had grown accustomed to the sight of labor abuse, at least some of them lamented the crude commodification of Native workers. Horace Bell compared the Los Angeles auction to the slave marts of New Orleans and Constantinople. The only difference, according to Bell, was that "the slave at Los Angeles was sold fifty-two times a year as long as he lived, which did not generally exceed one, two, or three years, under the new dispensation."[4] Another early resident suggested that "it would have been a righteous retribution on the white wretches who supplied the Indians with intoxicants if they could have been sold into perpetual slavery" themselves.[5] In 1853, Judge Benjamin Hayes had attempted to outlaw the auction. But his decision was either ignored or overruled.[6] Not until 1937 would California legislators finally abolish Indian convict leasing.[7]

Rather than ban or curtail the auction, Los Angeles decided to address conditions on the front end of the process. On any given weekend, California Indians overflowed the county jail. The city marshal arrested forty-one Indians on one particularly busy night, amounting to nearly 20 percent of the city's entire Indigenous population.[8] The inmates were left to fester in the prison's ground-floor lockup, deprived of even rudimentary medical attention. When a non-Native inmate died of "bilious fever" in 1856, the conditions of the prison became a subject of public concern. "It is quite certain that our jail is not a suitable place for a man who is very sick," the *Los Angeles Star* reported.[9] Two years later, some basic improvements had been made to the jail, but medical care remained in a deplorable state.[10] "We do not wish to have prisoners pampered with high living," the *Star* began, in case anyone worried that the editor had gone soft. The sickly conditions of the prison, however, had become an embarrassment. Clearly something had to be done.[11]

That's where Biddy Mason came in—right back to the jail that once confined her.

. . .

By the time she won her freedom, Mason was a veteran medical practitioner. Her training probably began as a child in Georgia or Mississippi. Because enslaved people couldn't trust white medical authorities—who were just as likely to experiment on their loved ones' cadavers as address their ailments—African Americans turned to their own communities for healing.[12] From a young age, therefore, many enslaved children undertook what one historian calls "an extended process of apprenticeship" and what one Black practitioner dubbed "fireside trainin'."[13] That training took place at the feet of enslaved elders, mostly women, who transferred their vast medical knowledge to the younger generations. From such an elder, young Biddy likely learned the essentials of plantation medicine: how to concoct remedies to soothe flesh flayed by whipping, to reduce the aches of field labor, and to ease the pain of childbirth.[14]

Her training continued into adulthood alongside Hannah. To serve effectively as midwives to the colony at San Bernardino, Biddy and Hannah had to hone remarkably diverse skill sets. They required botanical knowledge—how to select the right plants (and avoid poisonous ones), and produce the correct tea, ointment, or poultice to address specific complaints. They required anatomical knowledge—how to intervene to secure the speediest and safest delivery. And they required vast stores of empathy and a sixth sense for their patients' needs—how to encourage and console in just the right way, how to maintain their composure in moments of crisis, how to get women back on their feet after complicated deliveries. Thus, when Biddy arrived in Los Angeles in 1856, she brought with her a skill set that few medical authorities in the pueblo could match.[15]

Yet her skills counted for little if she couldn't practice. Simply put, Black women in antebellum America were not supposed to possess expertise, medical or otherwise. Their expected place in society was to fill the unskilled, backbreaking jobs that others refused—namely as washerwomen and domestic servants. Drudgery, that's what Black women were built for, in the eyes of their employers. Despite her storehouse of lifesaving knowledge, Mason could only find roles as a domestic servant during her early years in the pueblo. She and her daughters were seemingly condemned to a hand-to-mouth existence under other people's roofs.

But then, finally, Mason caught a break. Sometime around 1859, her reputation had made its way to someone willing to give her a chance in his medical practice. This prospective employer, however, wasn't exactly a boss she would have chosen for herself. In fact, he was just about the unlikeliest ally imaginable: a former slaveholder from Virginia named John S. Griffin.

. . .

For most of his life John S. Griffin had treated people like Mason as property. The bows of his family tree hung heavy with slaveholding patriarchs, including his uncle William Clark, a Kentucky planter-cum-overland explorer whose name is now indelibly linked with Meriwether Lewis and their famous expedition. Although orphaned at an early age, Griffin's family wealth insulated him from material discomfort. He moved to Kentucky, where another uncle provided him with a classical education. Griffin continued his schooling at the University of Pennsylvania, earning a medical degree in 1837. That training springboarded him to the officer corps in the US military. When war broke out with Mexico in 1846, Griffin marched west with General Stephen Watts Kearney as that army's ranking surgeon. Accompanying him overland was his enslaved attendant Caswell Wade—though Griffin barely made mention of him in any surviving papers.[16]

Griffin's pedigree, his education, and his military reputation cemented him in the upper echelons of Los Angeles society when he settled there in 1854. Just the second professionally trained doctor to arrive in the pueblo, Griffin was also, by many accounts, the best (even if patients like Benjamin Hayes expressed some consternation about the doctor's dependence on cod liver oil as a catchall curative).[17] Griffin would later cofound the Los Angeles County Medical Association and serve as its first president.[18]

Griffin plowed his wealth into Southern California real estate and other business ventures. Only rarely did his judgment lapse. After the Civil War he sold his stake in the Rancho San Pasqual for $7.50 an acre to a group of migrants from Indiana, gloating, "This is once where I got the best of those damned Yankees."[19] Twenty years later that same land was selling for $1,000 an acre and had given rise to Pasadena, a city of "palatial homes,

John S. Griffin, a former slaveholder from Virginia, hired Biddy Mason into his Los Angeles medical practice in 1859. Security Pacific National Bank Collection, Los Angeles Public Library Special Collections.

paved streets and massive business blocks, the wonder of the tourist and the paradise of the health-seeker," in the words of one Angeleno.[20] It also became home to three surviving children of the abolitionist martyr John Brown. Their presence helped transform the land of former slaveholders into a pilgrimage site for racial justice.[21] By the 1920s, Pasadena was the the richest city, per capita, in the nation.[22]

That real estate misadventure aside, Griffin would distinguish himself as one of the leading developers of early Los Angeles. In 1863 he snapped up two thousand acres of sheep pasture in the northeast section of the town, converting the grassland into a thriving suburb, first called East Los Angeles and now known as Lincoln Heights. Griffin capitalized on city property as well with large commercial buildings in his portfolio, including the new county courthouse.[23] After the Civil War, Griffin cofounded the Los Angeles City Water Company, one of the most ambitious enterprises the city had ever seen. That company and its employees (including a self-taught Irish engineer named William Mulholland) built much of Los Angeles's modern water infrastructure: reservoirs, canals, and iron pipes running for miles beneath the city streets.[24]

In short, Griffin had a nose for opportunity. And he sensed a rare chance in Biddy Mason.

Mason, however, didn't look anything like Griffin's other partners or business ventures. And she certainly didn't share his politics, which remained staunchly proslavery, and later pro-Confederate. So what drew Griffin to Mason? Were her obvious abilities enough to overcome his inborn prejudices?

According to most everyone who met her, Mason coupled consummate skill with personal charm. Radiating from contemporary sources, even those composed by her white neighbors, is awe for Mason's charisma. "I knew her very well," recalled Joseph Mesmer, one of the city's early civic leaders. "She was a woman so tender-hearted and sympathetic that she never failed to endear herself to all with whom she came in contact."[25] Others were equally lavish in their praise. Mason was "great-hearted," "charitable," "kindly," "lovable," "cheerful," "sterling," "an inspiration." The mere recollection of Mason's kindness brought grown men to tears.[26] Her later successes testified to an uncanny ability to neutralize prejudice and win friends in unlikely places.

But to display her charm and her skills, Mason would first have to win an audience with Griffin, which likely required a formal introduction. Such an introduction could have come from one of several sources, including from Robert Owens, in whose home Mason still lived. Bob Owens "became very popular with all classes," and he counted Griffin among "his most intimate friends," according to Owens's grandson and namesake.[27] Owens and Griffin would become neighbors. As both men expanded their real estate holdings, they came to own adjoining properties.[28] The era of de jure residential segregation in Los Angeles was still decades in the future, and proximity appears to have bred familiarity between Owens and Griffin, despite the racial prejudices of the latter.

Or the introduction may have come from an even closer source: Griffin's brother-in-law, Benjamin Hayes. The doctor had married the judge's sister, Louisa Hayes, the same year that Mason won her freedom. The newlyweds moved into a home purchased from none other than David Alexander, the sheriff in that trial.[29] Although Griffin would later complain that "Hayes is no especial favorite of mine," a sense of family loyalty kept the two men on cordial terms. That fidelity—a "matter of conscience," in Griffin's words—may have also facilitated the introduction to Mason.[30]

Hayes had come to admire, even to revere as heaven-sent, the woman who entered his courtroom only a few years earlier as a slave. Mason challenged his paternalistic assumptions that bondage presented "mutual advantage" for enslavers and enslaved alike. Her testimony lifted a "bright torch" to expose the hollow claims of her owner and compelled Hayes to see her as a woman and a mother rather than as chattel. It was most likely Mason who, just one month later, leapt in front of a moving carriage to rescue the judge's son from oblivion. Such heroism would not go unrewarded, especially not by a man known to be fiercely attached to his friends.[31] An introduction to his brother-in-law was the least he could do.

The result for Mason was an end to domestic servitude and a job as a nurse in Griffin's medical practice. With a salary of $2.50 a day—as opposed to little more than 25 cents as a domestic laborer—Mason could finally start building for the future.[32]

. . .

Beyond her talents and her human touch, Mason had something else that Griffin valued: a willingness to go where he wouldn't. In 1859 the city appointed Griffin to the role of physician to the County Hospital and Jail.[33] He now counted among his patients the scores of inebriated Indians that filled the prison every weekend. What was the patrician doctor to do? Surely, that pestilential chamber was no place for the Ivy League–educated scion of a planter family and budding real estate tycoon, with a long list of well-heeled clients who required his attention. Griffin wouldn't avoid the prison altogether. But for some of the grubbier work, he now had a suitable substitute at his disposal.[34]

Griffin's nuisance was Mason's opportunity. Here was her chance to escape the relentless grind of domestic service and showcase the medical skills that she had honed over the preceding decades. By all accounts, Mason threw herself into the work. She became, in the words of one Black Angeleno, "a frequent visitor to the jail, speaking a word of cheer and leaving some token and a prayerful hope with every prisoner."[35] Most of the Indigenous inmates—accustomed to the cruel carousel of arrest, abuse, and forced labor—had probably never received such care from anyone outside their own community. At last, here was someone who saw them as people, rather than mere fuel for the maintenance of Southern California's vineyards and ranches.

Local authorities noted the improved conditions of the prisoners in the months after Mason arrived—though they generally credited the jailor rather than the Black nurse. When members of a grand jury toured the jailhouse in November 1859, they found "the prison and all the cells in a clean and healthy condition."[36] Later reports confirmed a decided improvement in sanitation and prisoner health.[37] Not all Angelenos cheered the results, however. Henry Hamilton, the proslavery editor of the *Los Angeles Star*, offered a cheaper solution to the so-called Indian problem: "We say, whip the Indians at once, and stop the expense of their keeping in the County Jail."[38]

Mason's work in the prison was more than just a means to a living. It was an act of solidarity, of Christian charity, of community-building, and of resistance. Every Monday the Indian auction performed a grotesque inversion of space, converting the site of her emancipation—the Los Angeles courthouse and its environs—into a staging ground for slavery. It was a weekly reminder that although she had escaped from bondage, her community had not. Mason's mission was to muster her vast medical knowledge and protect these people as best she could. It was an undertaking motivated by her profound faith, heading Christ's call to uplift the "least of these brothers and sisters."[39] It was also a deeply personal endeavor. Mason had been imprisoned within those very walls. And she herself had once labored in Southern California's agricultural economy under a seemingly unbreakable yoke. Her personal emancipation marked only the beginning of her broader, multiethnic fight for freedom, survival, and dignity for all Angelenos.[40]

There was only so much she could do, however. The Native population that built the pueblo from its early days had been whittled down by decades of disease, violence, and overwork.[41] Los Angeles barely noticed. The sight of a dead Indian decomposing in the city streets "was scarcely thought of sufficient importance to constitute a case for serious investigation," according to an appalled visitor.[42] One employer hauled a dying Native servant from his home and discarded her on the street. Had she expired under his roof, he may have been liable for burial expenses.[43] With

Indigenous life treated like a disposable good, the body count piled up. In 1850 the Native population of Los Angeles stood at 3,693. By 1870 that figure had withered to a mere 219—a 94 percent decline in the space of two decades.[44]

Shortly thereafter, Los Angeles discontinued its Indian slave mart. The decision wasn't prompted by humanitarian scruples or even by the passage of the Thirteenth Amendment, which abolished slavery and involuntary servitude across the United States (albeit with a loophole for forced convict labor). Rather, the Indigenous auction had consumed itself. By the 1870s there simply wasn't enough human fodder remaining to feed a system that had enriched the city and its landholders for more than two decades.[45]

· · ·

Amid all the death came new life. Charles Owens and Ellen Mason married in October 1856, nine months after the trial and a day after Ellen's eighteenth birthday. Two years later, Ellen gave birth to the family's first child, a baby boy. She named him Robert, after her father-in-law, who had done so much to secure her family's freedom. Then in 1860 came their second child, Henry. For Biddy, still grieving the loss of her daughter Ann, these two grandsons were not only emotional balms, they were miniature miracles. Against all odds and in spite of multiple dislocations, her family had survived. Here was the next generation, born free in a place they could finally call home.

Little Robert and Henry had joined a Black lineage in California that reached back into the mythical past. A sixteenth-century Spanish epic novel described a rich island off the coast of Asia, populated by a tribe of powerful Black women. Ruling over these Amazonian warriors, her body dusted with gold, was the mighty Queen Calafia. The legend spurred several voyages of would-be conquistadors. Even Hernán Cortés, the conqueror of the Aztecs, went in search of Calafia's golden land. But no one ever found it. Even so, Queen Calafia lent her name to the northwestern rim of Spain's New World empire, part of which became the US state of California in 1850. In other words, Biddy Mason lived in a place named for a Black woman.[46]

Los Angeles also boasted a Black origin story. In 1781 twelve families

Biddy Mason's grandson, Robert Curry Owens, was one of the first free-born Black children in Los Angeles. Miriam Matthews Photograph Collection, UCLA Special Collections.

from the Mexican provinces of Sinaloa and Sonora set off on a seven-month march to Alta California to found a settlement between Mission San Gabriel and the Presidio of Santa Barbara. They called their new home El Pueblo de la Reina de los Ángeles—or Los Angeles for short.[47] More than half of the pueblo's founding settlers were of African descent. For them the distant frontier of Alta California provided a welcome escape from the strict *casta* system of colonial Mexico.[48]

In the absence of rigid racial hierarchies, many of these African-descended residents flourished. One of them, Maria Rita Valdez Villa, won a grant to the 4,500-acre Rancho Rodeo de Las Aquas. Today it's more commonly known as Beverly Hills.[49] Another mixed-race family, the Pico dynasty, supplied California with much of its leadership during the US–Mexico War. Andres Pico successfully led the Mexican troops against the American invaders at the Battle of San Pasqual in 1846, while his brother Pio served as the last Mexican governor of California.[50]

By that time, however, the Picos and other mixed-race families in California had distanced themselves from their African roots. Although the color line in Mexican California was indistinctly drawn—especially by US standards—Blackness was still a liability. Cultural cachet, political power, and land grants followed Spanish bloodlines. When Mason arrived in Los Angeles, the pueblo only contained a few dozen residents who identified as Black. It fell to her and her African American neighbors to recover the city's proud heritage.[51]

. . .

Of all the titles that Mason would eventually garner for herself—freedwoman, nurse, midwife, entrepreneur, developer—the role of community-builder probably ranked among her most cherished. That work began before she set foot in Los Angeles. The court case against her enslaver in early 1856 was a multiethnic, transregional effort, utilizing an extended information network and uniting Black and white allies across Southern California. Their shared ordeal forged a community of freedom-seekers, who would draw strength from the knowledge that, as they had triumphed once, they could surely do so again.

That community employed a time-tested survival strategy honed by the experiences of enslavement. Because slave families were so often ruptured by sale, Black people turned to those beyond their bloodline to create more durable bonds. These extended families became "the central units of slave life," according to historian Ira Berlin. They defined a community's values, met its needs, and created networks of trust in a world frequently disordered by the whims of their owners.[52] Those networks didn't dissolve upon emancipation. Rather, extended families like Biddy's and Hannah's constituted the building blocks of Black communities in freedom, when the trust and mutual support they provided remained as important as ever.[53]

At the heart of that community was the joint Mason-Owens family, living together on San Pedro Street, just southeast of the plaza. "As my mind runs back through the misty past, I have many fond recollections of the happiest home in all California," wrote Biddy's grandson, Robert Curry Owens, in his later years. That happiness came in the form of "a Grandfather two Grandmothers mother and Father, and Brother all living in the same Block."[54] Mason counted other prominent Black Angelenos as neighbors, including the minister Jesse Hamilton, who solemnized several African American marriages that decade. Another neighbor was the barber and future political leader, Lewis Green, in whose home Harriet Mason lived and worked.[55]

Other Black Angelenos lived just a few doors down, notably John and Amanda Ballard, along with their children. Like most of the pueblo's Black leaders, Ballard was born into slavery but won his freedom sometime in the late 1840s or early 1850s. Less than two decades later, Ballard ranked as one of the community's largest landholders, with the means to pay $1,000 in gold coin for a choice piece of property in central Los Angeles.[56] The doors of the Owens, Mason, Ballard, and Green households would have been open to one another, as residents intermixed and sometimes intermarried. "In those pastoral, pueblo days," recalled Harris Newmark, "it was no indiscretion for a friend to walk into another friend's house without knocking."[57]

Although many Black families settled together, they did so by choice rather than municipal fiat. "There were no special districts then, as there are now," recalled John Ballard's son, William, in a 1933 interview.[58] African Americans could be found in most corners of the pueblo, sometimes comingled with prominent white and *californio* residents. Take, for instance, Peter Biggs. One of the first Black homeowners of his generation, Biggs lived next to one of the wealthiest men in Southern California, Jonathan Temple. Biggs's popular barber shop catered to a primarily white Southern clientele.[59]

Early residents recalled this small Black community with deep fondness. Joseph Mesmer counted himself a friend to Biddy Mason, Robert Owens, and several other Black Angelenos. "The first groups of colored people who came to Los Angeles just after the Mexican pueblo became and [*sic*] American town were a fine lot," he wrote. "Scrupulously honest, good Christians, devoted church members, good citizens and neighbors, [they were] always ready and willing to do a kindly act."[60] Harris Newmark recalled the "good" Winnie Owens, whom he once employed.[61] Benjamin Hayes would later comment on the prosperity of Black Angelenos. "They are farmers, mechanics, or of some one or other useful occupation," he wrote, "and remarkable for good habits."[62]

While Hannah had settled in San Bernardino, several of her children relocated to Los Angeles, beginning with her eldest daughter Ann. Like Ellen Mason, Ann followed her heart. She married a Black Angeleno named Manuel Pepper, who, according to family lore, had played an instrumental role in triggering the 1856 freedom suit. Their union eventually produced seven children.[63] Two of Hannah's teenage sons, Charles and Nathanial, lived with the Pepper family for a time. In 1862, Hannah would bring another son, Henry, to Los Angeles to apprentice with the barber Lewis Green.[64] Perhaps it was Green's role in employing and housing Biddy's daughter Harriet that won him the trust of Hannah. Although separated by sixty miles, Biddy and Hannah would continue to see one another as they guided their children through the next stages of their lives. Their joint family, forged in slavery, formed the nucleus of Black Southern California in freedom.[65]

. . .

Even though they belonged to the same extended network, Biddy and Hannah traveled increasingly divergent paths. After the trial Hannah settled into a life of freedom in San Bernardino with Toby Embers, the father of at least two of her children. They could finally live as husband and wife. Yet the shadow of Robert Smith hung over their marriage. Hannah was the survivor of rape, and the proof lay in the light skin of several of her children and the name that at least one of them carried. Hannah's youngest child went by Henry Smith.[66] Although doubtlessly a joy to Hannah, these children may have been a source of some distress to Embers, a reminder of what little power he had to protect his wife. Despite his stature within the community, a sense of powerlessness stalked Embers to his dying days.

There was still plenty to celebrate, though. In November 1857, Embers became one of the first homeowners among the freed population of Southern California, paying $150 for a property on lot 7, block 5 within the city limits of San Bernardino. The next year, perhaps to commemorate the accomplishment, he hosted a party for the local Black community. The guest list would have included many of the central players in the freedom suit, including Hannah, her children, Grief Embers and his wife Harriet, and Elizabeth Flake (later Rowan).[67]

Although most of them had recently faced down powerful men, they were unprepared for what happened next. It began with a commotion at the front door. A group of local roughs, led by a man named Joseph McFeely, forced their way into the home. Drunk and foul-mouthed, they began harassing the guests. Toby Embers, not one to abide hooliganism in his own home, attempted to eject the intruders. But he was outnumbered and overpowered. McFeely's thugs savagely beat him and tossed him into the street.[68]

The next morning, Embers went to the office of a local justice of the peace to report the assault. Before he could finish swearing out the complaint, however, McFeely barged into the office. He snatched the complaint, then shoved it back at Embers. Eat it, McFeely demanded, as he placed the barrel of his pistol against Toby's temple. Forced to pick between death and humiliation, Embers chose the latter. He swallowed the document.[69]

Despite the repeated threats to his life, Embers refused to cave. Perhaps the experiences of his wife's freedom suit inspired him with faith in the legal system of Southern California. In February 1859 a grand jury indicted McFeely for "assault with intent to inflict bodily harm." He was arrested several months later and brought to trial.[70]

This time, however, the justice system failed the Black people of Southern California. The ban on African American testimony remained in place, and, unlike Benjamin Hayes, the judge in Embers's case didn't seek any way around the law. According to Judge A. D. Boren, "The court is of the opinion that a colored person may file a complaint but not testify in open court."[71] Without testimony from Embers or any of the other Black partygoers, the jury was deadlocked. After two days of deliberations the jurors finally returned a verdict of not guilty.[72]

The triumph of emancipation had shaded into the tragedy of incomplete freedom. Embers was sixty at the time of the assault, an old man by the standards of his day. He never recovered.[73]

. . .

The news was bad and only getting worse. Seemingly every report brought word of Black communities in crisis across the state. The proslavery wing of California's Democratic machine, known as the Chivalry, had further tightened its grip on state politics in the years since Biddy and Hannah's emancipation. In the 1859 gubernatorial contest, the Chivs tallied 62 percent of the statewide vote and proceeded to install a throng of Southern-born loyalists in California's plum posts.[74] In Los Angeles the Chivalry stalwart and future Confederate general Joseph Lancaster Brent exercised a near monopoly on local politics. "No one could be elected whom I did not support, and no one defeated whom I befriended," he boasted.[75]

California's Republican Party, meanwhile, floundered. Across every other free state, legions of antislavery Republicans had stormed into office, riding a wave of outrage over the machinations of the so-called Slave Power. But in California, outrage was reserved for African Americans and their supposed allies. Antiabolitionist thugs regularly stampeded Republican meetings, hounding speakers and pelting attendees with rotten food. "The name of 'black Republicans' stunk in their nostrils worse than that of a horse-thief," wrote one Californian.[76] California Republicans responded to the onslaught by abandoning many of their party's progressive policies and nominating a slaveholding North Carolinian for governor—a humiliating concession for a political organization that purported to be antislavery.[77] And that candidate still lost in a landslide. California was the only free state that failed to elect a Republican to Congress before the Civil War.[78]

Black Californians were on their own. Despite the obvious perils, they organized conventions in 1855, 1856, and again in 1857, drawing African American leaders from across the state in a campaign for civil rights. Their main target was the ban on Black testimony in California's courtrooms, a law that had nearly scuttled Biddy Mason's bid for freedom and allowed Toby Embers's assailant to walk free.[79] The collective efforts of the state's African Americans made California "a civil rights frontier," home to the first major Black political movement in the West.[80] And yet their appeals fell on deaf ears. The testimony ban remained on the books, and the specter of slavery continued to haunt the state.

That became clear in January 1858 with the sensational trial of Archy Lee. The case shared much in common with Mason's from two years earlier. Both Archy and Biddy had been enslaved in Mississippi; both had been forcibly transported to California; both were rescued with a writ of habeas corpus then imprisoned during their trials; and both argued that the state's free-soil constitution entitled them to freedom. Unlike Biddy's case, however, Lee's came before the state Supreme Court, a bastion of proslavery jurisprudence. Although the justices—both Southerners by birth and political inclination—didn't deny that California's constitution had technically outlawed slavery, they made an exception in this instance. Lee's enslaver suffered from poor health and even poorer knowledge of California's laws, they argued. He was entitled to his human property, the justices ruled, and permitted to return to Mississippi with Lee. Chief Justice David Terry had himself hauled several enslaved men into California roughly a decade earlier, an experience that doubtlessly influenced his decision.[81]

Even for those accustomed to California's proslavery prejudices, the ruling stretched credulity. The press rightly dubbed the case "California's Dred Scott." In fact, the California court's contorted logic would have made even Roger Taney blush. Fueled by outrage, the Black community of San Francisco sprang to action. They lined the wharves of the city, scanning for any sign of Lee and his enslaver. When the two men were finally spotted boarding a steamer, the city police intervened. Officers boarded the ship and wrestled Lee from his would-be owner. Lee secured a new trial in the US District Court. This time he had Edward Baker, an electrifying orator and personal friend to Abraham Lincoln, as his attorney. And this time, Archy Lee got justice. He was finally freed in April 1858.[82]

The celebrations were short-lived, however. In September 1859, California's antislavery advocates suffered one of their worst reversals yet. The blow was dealt by the same man, Chief Justice Terry, who nearly condemned Lee to a lifetime of slavery. Terry goaded the antislavery Democratic senator David Broderick into a feud by branding him an ally of the "Black [Frederick] Douglass."[83] Those were fighting words in antebellum California, even for a professed opponent of the Slave Power like Senator Broderick. The two men agreed to settle their differences on a remote field near Lake Merced with French dueling pistols at ten paces. (Terry resigned his seat on the Supreme Court to take part.) As they readied themselves, Broderick's hair-trigger pistol prematurely discharged, leaving Terry, a former Texas Ranger, with a clean shot. He leveled his weapon, took aim, and fired.[84] Broderick died three days later, the most famous dueling fatality since Alexander Hamilton. Allegedly, his dying words were: "They have killed me because I was opposed to the extension of slavery and a corrupt Administration."[85]

Barred from the polls, Black Californians voted with their feet. As many as eight hundred African Americans fled California that decade for the Canadian province of British Columbia, where gold had been discovered.

More so than riches, though, the lure was freedom. Whereas the recent *Dred Scott* decision had denied citizenship rights to all Black people in the United States, the British colonial government imposed no such race-based restrictions. For the first time in their lives, many of these Black expatriates became voting citizens. Some of the leading Black Californians joined the exodus, including Archy Lee, who had apparently already had enough of "freedom" in California. "I cannot describe with what joy we hailed the opportunity to enjoy that liberty under the 'British lion' denied us beneath the pinions of the American Eagle," one prominent migrant wrote.[86]

The decade closed on a lonely note for Biddy Mason and her fellow Black Angelenos. Their leaders had fled the state; their elected representatives had ignored their pleas; their most powerful ally had been gunned down; and their enemies now pressed their advantage. The Colored Executive Committee concluded that the "political prospects" of African Americans in California were "never more discouraging" and resolved to suspend efforts to overturn the testimony ban until they won a change of administration.[87] And that wasn't even the worst of it. War was coming for Los Angeles.

12 Unionist

Biddy Mason didn't need to read the words to know that they held power. Seven pages in neat, sloping longhand would hereafter serve as proof, for any who challenged the fact, that she was a free woman. The county clerk had produced the document, likely at Mason's request. First, he copied out the ruling of Judge Benjamin Hayes from January 19, 1856, which declared Biddy, Hannah, and their children "free forever." Then he wrote an addendum to certify that this was a "full, true and correct copy of the original order . . . as the same appears on file in my office." He added the date: January 9, 1860.[1]

Four years after securing her release from Robert Smith, Mason was still fighting for her freedom. The delay in obtaining proof of her emancipation reflects not any apathy on Mason's part or even the usual bureaucratic logjams within the county clerk's office, but rather a heightened sense of insecurity by the turn of the new decade. Mason's struggle for survival and self-determination had entered a perilous new phase.

The warning signs were everywhere. First came the barrage of bad news from elsewhere in the state, including the death of Senator Broderick and the exodus of hundreds of African Americans to British Canada. Then came word that the Colored Executive Committee had suspended its major operations, worn down by unremitting Democratic resistance to virtually every element of their agenda. After years of struggle, even some of the most tenacious Black Californians were losing hope.[2]

Then came the movement to reenslave Southern California. On an almost annual basis since 1849, prominent residents had petitioned to split California's southern counties, including Los Angeles, into a separate territory. Proponents of an independent Southern California cited a litany of complaints: not enough seats within the legislature, disproportionate levies on their ranching economy, the ungovernable size of the state. Concerns over taxation and representation were largely a smokescreen, however, for a more sinister objective. Political observers across the country—from Abraham Lincoln to the local press—knew that the true purpose of state division was the reintroduction of slavery into Southern California.[3] An independent territory would no longer be bound by California's antislavery constitution. Sometimes advocates of the measure said the quiet part aloud. If California were to be split, "the southern division will become a slave State," one proslavery miner exulted. "It is settled almost entirely by Southerners, and they will exert themselves to the utmost extent to carry the day."[4]

A bill to divide the state south of San Luis Obispo made its way through the legislative process in 1859.[5] With a vital push from the Chivalry lawmakers of Los Angeles, the bill cleared the state assembly and senate, then came before a popular referendum in Southern California, where voters approved state division by a three-to-one margin. The only thing now standing between proslavery schemers and their dream of a separate Southern California—which they provisionally named Colorado—were members of the US Congress.[6] It was at this exact moment, as the bill traveled to Washington, DC, for final approval in early 1860, that Mason requested a copy of her freedom papers. She would take no chances in the would-be slave territory of Southern California.

What ultimately prevented the division of California was an even greater schism. By the time the bill reached Washington, the national crisis over slavery had cleaved the Capitol into two warring camps. Sectional strife had reached such a fevered pitch that "the only persons [in Congress] who do not have a revolver and a knife are those who have two revolvers," quipped Senator James Henry Hammond of South Carolina.[7] In such a charged atmosphere, there would be no debate on the California bill. It died quietly in committee. Black Angelenos could breathe a sigh of relief, for the time being at least.

But soon they turned their attention to an even graver threat. The upcoming presidential election pitted the one-term congressman Abraham Lincoln against a Democratic Party that had fractured over how aggressively to push the slavery issue: to the hilt, or a little less so. California's entire congressional delegation threw its support behind John C. Breckinridge of Kentucky, the most ardently proslavery candidate in the four-man field. So, too, did the voters of Los Angeles. Every Tuesday the Breckinridge Club held mass rallies outside the Montgomery Saloon, followed by torchlit processions to the plaza. Supporters punctuated one rally with a hundred-gun salute in honor of Breckinridge.[8]

And if the "Black Republican" Lincoln was to prevail over their candidate? Well, they would turn those guns to other purposes. Biddy Mason had lived long enough in Los Angeles to know these weren't idle threats. As she anxiously awaited the election returns, those threats only grew in volume, until the ranking US military officer in Los Angeles, Winfield Scott Hancock, decided that something had to be done to protect the city's loyal minority. He began fortifying the pueblo, even arming his wife with an arsenal of derringers. "Rebellion," he concluded, "was imminent."[9]

. . .

The Breckinridge supporters were as good as their word. Although Lincoln didn't appear on the ballot in ten Southern states, he ran up huge margins in the Northeast. Thanks to the divided Democratic ticket, he even eked out a victory in California, albeit by a mere 700 ballots out of 120,000 votes cast. It the lowest tally he received in any free state, and what Lincoln called "the closest political bookkeeping that I know of."[10] In Los Angeles County he finished third behind Breckinridge and the other Democratic candidate, Stephen A. Douglas. Nevertheless, Lincoln ultimately netted 180 electoral votes from 18 states, enough to carry him into the White House. One month later, South Carolina adopted secessionist ordinances and broke from the Union.[11]

From there, the rebellion swept west. It reached as far as the Confederate Territory of Arizona, just about 240 miles from Los Angeles. Many predicted that California would be next. "They deceive themselves who suppose that California could stand aloof from the contest," Benjamin Hayes wrote. "A firebrand of the flimsiest material might soon enkindle a blaze that would sweep the State."[12] That spark flew from Charleston harbor when, on April 12, secessionists opened fire on Fort Sumter and ignited the Civil War. When news of Fort Sumter reached Los Angeles by Pony Express twelve days later, secessionists swept into the streets to celebrate.[13]

Mason confronted the menace of rebellion nearly everywhere she went. She would have seen secessionists charging through the streets, hurrahing for the rebel president Jefferson Davis; she would have heard the strains of a popular new ditty, "We'll Hang Abe Lincoln to a Tree," echoing from saloons; and she likely would have been harassed by impromptu orators, hurling epithets at any "Black Republican" they could find. She probably also bandaged bloodied Unionists, the victims of local rebels looking to express their Confederate sympathies more concretely.[14]

It wasn't just the ruffians and thugs that Mason had to fear. "The leading men of the county were for the Jeff Davis government first, last and all the time," wrote Horace Bell, a rare Los Angeles Unionist.[15] The list of Confederate-sympathizing Angelenos included political powerbroker Joseph Lancaster Brent, former California attorney general E.J.C Kewen, Los Angeles undersheriff Andrew Jackson King, the premier newspaper editor Henry Hamilton, and even Mason's employer, Dr. John S. Griffin.[16] Some expressed those sympathies quietly, others more flamboyantly.

And some clandestinely. Two Confederate secret societies—the Knights of the Golden Circle and the Knights of the Columbian Star—operated in California, each with their own baroque oaths, signs, symbols, grips, and key words. A federal detective infiltrated a secret cell in Los Angeles, where he uncovered a membership of more than 250. Those members had selected a secluded rendezvous point in the Southern California countryside and prepared to "commence a guerrilla warfare," according to the detective.[17] In neighboring San Bernardino, the rump of the old Mormon colony where Mason once labored and Hannah continued to live, rebels also mustered in secret. One federal officer concluded that "if troops do not come here this town will be in the hands of secessionists."[18] US officials calculated that thousands of Californians belonged to these clandestine organizations, and only awaited an opportune moment to throw off the cloak of secrecy and strike at the government.[19] Mason was surrounded by the hostile, often spectral, presence of rebellion.

Plenty of Confederate sympathizers, though, felt no need to hide. The epithets flew at Mason from the streets and from the newssheets—none with as much spleen as Henry Hamilton's *Los Angeles Star*. Born in Ireland, Hamilton migrated to America as a young man. As he made a "leisurely course westward to California, he sojourned long enough in New Orleans to become imbued with Southern sentiments," according to one of his contemporaries. Hamilton purchased the ailing *Star* from its previous editor, James S. Waite, who had been the first to report Mason's emancipation just five years earlier. Hamilton "injected new life into the sheet" by giving the people of Los Angeles what they wanted: literary polish, blistering editorials, and full-throated Southern partisanship.[20]

Hamilton made his weekly *Star* into the anti-Black, pro-Confederate mouthpiece of Southern California. He celebrated Confederate victories, blasted Union policies, and kept up a steady drip of racist vitriol for years. This was an "abolition war," Hamilton thundered, "instigated, carried on, and to be consummated, by the degradation of the white race, and the elevation of the African family over them."[21] He sneered at Northern outrage over the massacre at Fort Pillow, where Confederate soldiers butchered hundreds of Black soldiers as they attempted to surrender (little more than a "band of runaway negroes," he shrugged).[22] Although Mason couldn't read these editorials herself, others in the Black community could. And all of them would have felt the ominous spell cast by Los Angeles's leading newspaper.

As rebels rallied and the pueblo convulsed, Mason likely kept her freedom papers close at hand. By this point she had been a freedwoman for only five years, a brief stretch compared to nearly four decades of enslavement. Freedom could be won, as she herself proved; but it could also be lost, especially in a war-torn frontier town that contemporaries called the "South" of the West.[23] Her distance from the main theaters of the conflict wouldn't insulate her from its tragic consequences.

She and her family were prepared to flee, if necessary. Robert Owens made friends with the two telegraph operators in Los Angeles for precisely that purpose. Because news from the East traveled slowly by steamship or overland express, newly installed telegraph lines provided the only sure means of communication with the outside world. "These boys kept old

Bob posted as to telegraphic news before it appeared in print," Owens's grandson recalled. Should they receive word that the war had turned decisively in the Confederacy's favor, Owens had a plan. "My grandfather kept himself [and his] Family always prepared to leave the United States."[24] Mexico, a beacon for many Black freedom-seekers during the Civil War era, was probably their intended destination.[25]

. . .

The Mason-Owens family never fled, however. Instead, they stayed and they fought, forming a thin blue wedge of Unionism in a town overrun by their enemies. Many of the local Unionists rallied around Captain Winfield Scott Hancock, Los Angeles's quartermaster and ranking officer. To prevent US military supplies from falling into rebel hands, Hancock buried all arms and ammunition under bags of grain, then prepared to "contest every foot of ground, aided by the few loyal friends who promised their support," recalled his wife, Almira, who had herself been enlisted in the pueblo's defense. "I was at the time a pretty good shot," she wrote.[26] Whether male or female, Black or white, "Unionist" was a dangerous badge to wear in Civil War–era Los Angeles.

Fortunately for the beleaguered loyalists, backup was on the way. The commander of the US Department of the Pacific deemed it "indispensably necessary to throw reenforcements into [Southern California] immediately" as "there is more danger of disaffection at this place than any other in the State."[27] First came a company of dragoons, led by Major James Henry Carleton, a former slaveholder though a committed Unionist.[28] They established camp on the southern outskirts of town. Ignoring death threats from local secessionists, they raised the US flag over the courthouse for the first time since the war began. Rebels countered by defenestrating a Unionist from an upstairs window at the Bella Union Hotel. His offense was the public reading of a patriotic poem.[29]

Threats of violence didn't deter Robert Owens. In the summer of 1861 the commander of the Pacific Department authorized the formation of a local militia of loyal citizens, along with the shipment of 150 firearms and 6,000 rounds of ammunition. Owens was among the earliest enlistees in this unit, the Los Angeles Home Guard, making him one of the first Black men anywhere in the country to take up arms against the Confederate rebellion.[30] African Americans wouldn't be allowed in most US military units for another seventeen months.[31]

No amount of military drilling, however, could have prepared Robert Owens for what, or rather who, appeared that same year. General Albert Sidney Johnston, the former commander of the US Department of the Pacific, arrived in Los Angeles in May 1861. A committed secessionist, Johnston had resigned his commission and fled his headquarters in the Unionist enclave of San Francisco for the rebel hotbed of Southern California. From there he planned to make an overland march to his home state of Texas, where he would offer his services to the Confederacy. In the meantime, Los Angeles could furnish him with men, rations, wagons—and a family reunion. His brother-in-law was none other than Dr. John S. Griffin, Mason's employer. Johnston moved into the Griffin home along with his wife, children, and an enslaved man named Rand.[32]

For weeks to come, members of the Mason-Owens family were thrown together with the man who would become the second-highest ranking officer in the Confederacy. While taking orders from her employer, Mason likely looked after the needs of Johnston and his pregnant wife. Mason may have even delivered the Johnstons' fifth child, born several months later. Robert Owens, meanwhile, outfitted Johnston and members of his rebel retinue from his livery stable on San Pedro Street.[33] The irony of simultaneously equipping himself for the Union and these men for the Confederacy would've been painfully apparent to Owens. He had little choice in the matter, however. To refuse service to someone of Johnston's stature, not to mention the brother-in-law of Mason's employer, simply wasn't an option.

That summer, Johnston slipped out of the state to join the Confederate war effort in the East. An armed guard of about eighty men, calling themselves the Los Angeles Mounted Rifles, escorted him on the overland journey. In doing so, the Mounted Rifles became the only militia from a free state to march under a Confederate banner.[34] The coming years would witness a veritable parade of rebel soldiers, officers, and dignitaries streaming east from California: William Gwin, the former US senator; Joseph Lancaster Brent, the Los Angeles powerbroker and future Confederate general; David S. Terry, the former chief justice and killer of Senator Broderick; Cameron Thom, the future mayor of Los Angeles; several congressmen; at least three state senators; a cluster of assemblymen; and a small army of US military officers, including Confederate generals Lewis Armistead, Richard Garnett, and George Pickett (whose name would become forever linked with the calamitous final charge at Gettysburg). Los Angeles was the launching point of their rebellious careers.[35]

Some of those eastbound rebels joined a Confederate army marching west. Since the first summer of the war, an invasion force from Texas had been rampaging across the Southwest, gobbling up territory and scattering Union forces from the Rio Grande to the Colorado River. "The Texas rebels and Arizona cut-throats, like the ancient Goths and Vandals, are at the very gates," groaned a US soldier stationed in New Mexico.[36] In March 1862 the rebel invaders captured Santa Fe, becoming the first and only rebel army to seize a capital city in Union territory. By that point the invaders had blazed a one-thousand-mile path of destruction from San Antonio. And they were hungry for more.[37] "*The objective aim and design of the campaign*," wrote one of its officers, "*was the conquest of California.*"[38]

Unionists on the Pacific Coast trembled at the thought.[39] Southern California, in particular, could be easily overrun by the Confederate Army of New Mexico, about three thousand strong by this point. Those numbers might swell further as disaffected Angelenos rallied to the advancing Confederate ranks. A rebel reconnaissance force made it within fifty miles of the California border in March 1862, where they clashed with US troops in the westernmost skirmish of the war. Biddy Mason's freedom papers would be of little use if the rebel invaders finally broke through.[40]

. . .

If necessity is the mother of invention, crisis was, for Robert Owens, the wellspring of opportunity. Obliged to equip rebel leaders like Albert Sidney Johnston during the early months of the war, Owens increasingly aligned profits with patriotism by meeting the swelling demands of the US military in Los Angeles.

The approaching rebel army had finally roused California from its torpor and galvanized the loyal population. Nearly seventeen thousand Californians would volunteer for service in the US military over the course of the conflict. For reference the entire prewar US Army numbered little more than fifteen thousand troops. The overwhelming majority of California's Civil War volunteers hailed from the more populous and loyal

The military installation at Drum Barracks was the key node in the Unionist effort to reclaim Los Angeles County from its Confederate-sympathizing majority. Note the camel. Title Insurance and Trust and C.C. Pierce Photography Collection 1860–1960, California Historical Society Collection, USC Digital Library.

northern counties.[41] Nevertheless, Los Angeles's Unionists benefited, as they welcomed thousands of these troops to counter the secessionist presence in the region. They also greeted more peculiar defenders. A caravan of thirty-one camels, employed by the US Army, created a minor sensation in the pueblo, as throngs of curious onlookers came to gawk at the animals in their corrals on Main and, later, Spring Streets.[42]

While US troops had bivouacked within the pueblo in the first phase of the conflict, their growing numbers necessitated a more permanent headquarters. They eventually got one in Wilmington, about twenty miles south of Los Angeles. Constructed in 1862, Camp Drum was a sprawling complex of five barracks, a two-story hospital, and a sixteen-room house for officers, as well as buildings for the commissary, quartermaster, granary, store room, blacksmith shop, guard house, powder magazine, stables, and corrals. Construction costs totaled $1 million, a hefty sum at the time. Later renamed Drum Barracks, the compound housed nearly eight thousand troops over the course of the war, one of the largest concentrations of manpower that the American Southwest had ever seen. Drum Barracks also became the headquarters of a new US military department, covering Southern California and Arizona. Los Angeles had been garrisoned against itself.[43]

The military buildup created opportunities for those with the right connections. "Competition for Government trade was keen," according to Harris Newmark, "and energetic efforts were made by merchants to secure their share of the crumbs, as well as the loaves, that might fall from Uncle Sam's table."[44] Before his departure for the military theaters of the East, quartermaster Winfield Scott Hancock dispensed many of those contracts himself. He would have rewarded the loyalists who rallied around him during the frenzied early days of the war. Owens, a member of the Home Guard, had distinguished himself as a Unionist before it paid to be one. Perhaps as a result, he won several coveted government contracts for both Drum Barracks and the city of Los Angeles. One of those contracts made him the procurer of hay for Southern California's cavalry. Another turned his livery business into a military operation. "His Main Street Stable was known as "Government Corral," recalled his grandson, "as his contract called for the care of all animals belonging to the government while in the city."[45]

Before the war Owens had been successful; by the end of it he was rich. His real estate alone was valued at $2,850, with a large tract of land encompassing his stables on San Pedro Street and a nearby property at First and Main Streets, purchased in 1864. He needed plenty of space, after all, for his thirty pigs, three horses, and a cow. He also owned a small fortune in animal feed, including $400 in barley alone, to cover his government contracts. As his wealth grew, he diversified his assets. He held shares in at least five different mining companies as well as land claims in another two mining districts.[46]

That wealth would have been a thin shield, however, if Confederate forces in the Southwest broke through to Los Angeles. Fortunately for the Mason-Owens family, the once rapid advance of the Confederate Army of New Mexico came to an abrupt halt in the spring of 1862 when a detachment of Union troops destroyed the rebels' supplies at the Battle of Glorieta Pass in New Mexico (sometimes called, rather grandiosely, the

"Gettysburg of the West"). Without the resources to fuel their forward march across an unforgiving landscape, the rebels reversed course. Their tactical withdrawal soon devolved into a madcap retreat, as Confederates ditched clothing, weapons, ammunition, even sick and dehydrated comrades. By the time they made it back to Texas, they had suffered a 30 percent casualty rate, one of the highest of any Confederate army over the course of the war.[47]

The same month that the broken remnants of the rebel army limped into Texas, Hannah arrived in Los Angeles. She had come to apprentice her youngest son, Henry, to the successful Black barber Lewis Green.[48] Hannah could see that the locus of Black wealth and opportunity had shifted decisively to Los Angeles. The proof was in Biddy Mason's nursing practice, Robert Owens's government contracts, and Green's barbering business. As Mason's neighbor, Green was probably already familiar to Hannah. Meanwhile, a formidable secessionist element still menaced San Bernardino, which lacked the military protection that Los Angeles enjoyed in the form of Drum Barracks.[49] Parting from her youngest child was doubtlessly agonizing for Hannah. But she did it for her son's safety, security, and future. It was one more sacrifice in a lifetime full of them.

. . .

The deadliest wartime assault on California wasn't struck by the Confederacy; it was made by nature. In a relentless procession beginning in the winter of 1861–62, Los Angeles County fell victim to floods, then disease, then drought, and finally a heavy sprinkling of locusts to round out the quartet of biblical plagues. No resident could ever recall such a cursed time. Biddy Mason found herself in the thick of it.

First came the rains. "Morning, noon, and night—day in and day out—it has been rain, rain, rain," Henry Hamilton complained in January 1862.[50] Within a month Los Angeles received more than three times its annual average rainfall. No mail could be delivered for five consecutive weeks. And when it finally did arrive, the rains reduced all papers to a pulp. A local wit put a "To Let" sign on the post office.[51] Rivers ran through the streets, pulverizing adobe homes and destroying the city's new water system, the largest municipal project ever undertaken in Los Angeles to that point.[52]

Sunshine became statewide news, with headlines like "A Phenomenon" announcing a momentary break in the clouds.[53]

Hannah fared even worse. The rains swelled the Santa Ana River until it rivaled the Mississippi in size, according to an early local historian.[54] The river overran its banks and washed away much of San Bernardino. The neighboring settlement of Agua Mansa, once a "miniature Eden," was wiped off the map, "leaving nothing save a hideous plain of black boulders and cobbles-stones," Horace Bell wrote.[55] Flooding "absolutely tore Southern California to pieces," reported a Union soldier stationed in the region.[56]

Elsewhere in the state, the damage was even greater. California's central basin became a vast inland sea, 250 to 300 miles long and 20 to 60 miles wide. The water covered the tops of telegraph poles at places and severed communication across the state. The capital at Sacramento was submerged for months. Leland Stanford, the state's first Republican governor, traveled to his inauguration by rowboat. When he floated back to his mansion later that day, the floodwaters had risen so high that he had to reenter his home by a second-story window. The waters churned with all matter of debris—household furniture, fragments of ruined homes, tree trunks, branches, and scores of dead animals—which were then littered across the state.[57] As always, the poorest were the hardest hit. When the Yuba River escaped its banks, it drowned an entire community of Chinese miners.[58]

The total damage was catastrophic: one-third of the state's property destroyed; one-quarter of California's eight hundred thousand cattle drowned; and one-eighth of all homes damaged or carried away. Never before, or since, has California suffered more destructive flooding.[59]

Then came the plague. Beginning in late 1862, smallpox swept through Los Angeles. Soon the disease was claiming as many as fourteen lives in a single day. Deaths became so frequent that local authorities discontinued the customary tolling of the church bells in honor of the deceased.[60] Residents sealed themselves inside their homes like tombs. An eery stillness pervaded the whole city, aside from the rumbling of the smallpox wagon, known as the "Black Maria," as it made its way, laden with stricken patients, for the city hospital or pesthouse in Chavez Ravine.[61] "Not a soul in the streets, except the funeral procession," Benjamin Hayes wrote. "Every window shut: not a person at the doors."[62] Harris Newmark recalled that "fatalities were so frequent and the nature of the contagion so feared that it was difficult to persuade undertakers to bury the dead."[63]

Dr. John S. Griffin helped spearhead the response, with Mason at his side. Having proven herself a skilled healer within the pestilential confines of the county prison, her reward was an even more dangerous job: to halt the fast-spreading epidemic. She likely forged into the most contagious parts of the city, perhaps to places Griffin dared not venture himself. She may have been responsible for inoculating residents after shipments of the smallpox vaccine arrived from San Francisco early in 1863.[64]

She may have also assisted the operations of the Board of Health, formed in January that year. The Board divided Los Angeles into five districts. Commissioners—and perhaps Mason as well—were to inspect each residence in their district, and to affix a yellow flag on every afflicted home, which would be quarantined. By that point the school commissioners had closed all schools in the city.[65] A city ordinance mandated that those who refused inoculation would be arrested and carried "by force, if necessary, before such city Surgeon or Physician, for the purpose of being vaccinated."[66] By some metrics Civil War–era Los Angeles marshaled a more aggressive response to the smallpox outbreak than any municipality at the height of the COVID-19 pandemic 160 years later.

The crisis was a deeply personal one for Mason. Not only did it summon all her skills as a nurse, it also threw her two main responsibilities—mother and healer—into tension. Just seven years earlier her daughter Ann had been taken by one of the pueblo's periodic outbreaks. Could she keep her family safe during this far deadlier epidemic, when her role forced her into close contact with the contagion? As with her previous work for Dr. Griffin, Mason would have been sent into the pueblo's poorest communities, where smallpox proved most virulent. No community needed her more than Sonoratown, a cramped working-class neighborhood festooned with yellow quarantine flags. She must have worried constantly that the Black Maria would come for her daughters or grandsons as it had come for so many of her patients.[67]

Meanwhile, Mason continued in her role as midwife. In July 1862, Henry Dwight Barrows, the US marshal for Southern California and arguably the most powerful Unionist in Los Angeles, hired "Aunt Biddy" to deliver his baby daughter and look after his postpartum wife. Mason stayed on to care for mother and child for an additional two weeks.[68] Given the importance of the task as well as his controversial position—the US marshal was responsible for policing Confederate activity in the region—Barrows needed someone he could trust, professionally *and* politically. For that he paid Mason a handsome fee of twenty-seven dollars.[69] She must have done well that year, because she was assessed for the same amount in a federal license tax (ten dollars) as her wealthy host Robert Owens. Her occupation was listed as "physician" in the tax rolls, a reflection of her growing professional stature.[70]

Then came the drought. The deluge of 1862 gave way to the desiccation of 1863. For the next two years only an occasional drizzle fell on Southern California. Vineyards wilted, ranches withered, and the dust swept in, carried by scorching Santa Ana winds. "From the dense clouds of stifling dust that filled the air, and dimmed the light of the sun, and blinded and choked people . . . it might have been imagined we had been transported from the once green plains and hills of California, to the deserts of Arabia," reported the *Star*.[71] As fodder gave out, animals were left to scrounge desperately for survival, falling by the hundreds and then the thousands. The plains around the city became a "veritable Golgotha" of bleached animal bones. As many as fifty thousand cattle, amounting to 70 percent of the region's total bovine population, perished within two years.[72]

Southern California's economy withered almost as quickly as its once-verdant hills. In 1863 and again in 1864, Los Angeles collected no taxes. Currency disappeared from circulation. The county's assessed valuation fell by more than half. The names of prominent rancheros, until recently the baronial overlords of the region's agricultural economy, appeared on an ever-growing delinquent tax list. Squatters, lawyers, and loan sharks moved in for the kill. For the landed elite that had dominated California since the Spanish colonial period, it was the end of an era.[73] "Southern California's reputation among Yankees as a natural desert and a cultural backwash," one historian wrote, "could scarcely improve after this."[74]

Unlike so many of her neighbors, Mason weathered the natural disasters of the war years. Despite the crippling economic conditions in the city and its surroundings, she somehow managed to save. And despite her proximity to the epidemic, she and her family managed to survive. By some measures she even thrived. The Civil War marks the emergence of Biddy Mason as a recognizable figure in the civic life of Los Angeles.

Evidence of her success can be seen in a monumental work of art,

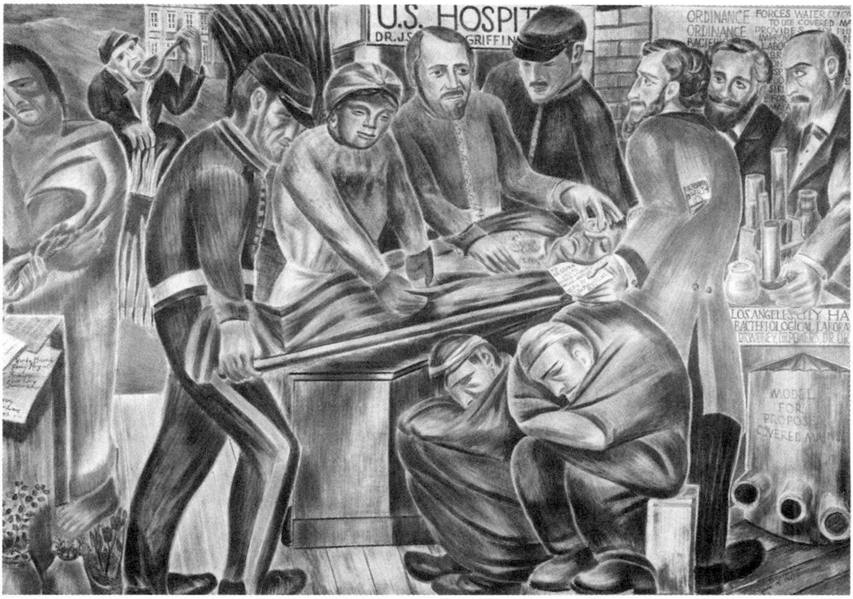

Biddy Mason occupies a central position in Bernard Zakheim's "History of Medicine in California" mural series. This is the first known artistic representation of Mason and a tribute to her pioneering medical work during the Civil War. Courtesy of UCSF Archives and Special Collections; Adam Gottstein, on behalf of the estate of Bernard Zakheim.

produced well after her death. "The History of Medicine in California," a series of murals by the famed New Deal artist Bernard Zakheim, features Mason in one of its ten panels. She works alongside Dr. Griffin and several Union soldiers as they examine a stricken patient. Although white doctors populate much of the panel, Mason nevertheless occupies the center of the frame. Zakheim depicts her not as subordinate to white medical authorities but as she was: a medical authority in her own right. The first known artistic representation of Mason, the work is a remarkable tribute to an otherwise overlooked figure in the history of medicine in California.[75]

By saving lives in a time of crisis, Mason challenged deeply embedded presumptions about Black people's capacities and their broader place in society. Most white Americans in the antebellum era couldn't conceive of Black people as useful contributors to the body politic. American political rhetoric bristled with claims of Black "dependence" and "indolence." Even free people of color existed outside the political community, according to statesmen like Henry Clay and jurists like Roger Taney. In 1857, during Mason's first full year of freedom, the US Supreme Court declared Africans Americans ineligible for citizenship.[76]

The war years presented an opportunity to change all that. Men like Robert Owens, and eventually two hundred thousand African American soldiers and sailors across the country, asserted their citizenship by force of arms. As Frederick Douglass famously declared, "He who fights [for] America may claim America as his own country—and have that claim respected."[77] Mason wasn't given the opportunity to shoulder arms for her country, but she, like countless other Black women, found ways to contribute nonetheless. By supporting the Union when Unionism brought insults and threats of violence, and by leaping to action at the height of a health crisis, Mason made herself both vulnerable and indispensable. Her appearance in a monumental work of public art, roughly seventy years later, speaks to the lasting resonance of her sacrifice.[78]

. . .

The blast could be heard for miles. By the time the panicked crowds arrived from Los Angeles on the night of April 27, 1863, the full magnitude of the calamity was coming into view. Sometime around five o'clock that evening, while on a routine trip from the port of San Pedro, the sixty-ton steamer *Ada Hancock* had suddenly exploded, apparently due to a fault in its boiler. Soldiers from nearby Drum Barracks crammed into rescue boats and plunged into the water to retrieve whoever or whatever they could from the smoldering wreckage. "Bodies were brought ashore without heads, or arms or legs," the *Star* reported, while stray parts were found bobbing in the water "at great distance from the wreck." A majority of the fifty-six passengers were feared dead.[79]

In the middle of the carnage, the single deadliest event in Los Angeles's history to that point, was Harriet Mason. Earlier that day she had boarded the *Ada Hancock* with her employer's family.

Her mother likely arrived with Dr. Griffin that evening, as part of an emergency medical operation. Biddy would have searched frantically for her daughter amid the dead and mutilated passengers brought to shore. So far, the body count included the captain of the steamship, a pair of

Mormon missionaries, two Black men, the oldest son of the slain Confederate general Albert Sidney Johnston, and others. Harriet, however, was not among them.[80]

Instead, she was busy with a rescue operation of her own. According to news reports that circulated locally, nationally, and internationally, Harriet saved the lives of multiple passengers in the chaotic moments after the explosion, all while displaying "the most undaunted courage and indomitable perseverance and calmness."[81] After rescuing the two young children of her employer, Phineas Banning (who also happened to own the ruined ship), Harriet turned her attention to several women frantically treading water around the wreckage. Somehow Harriet managed to keep their "heads above water for some time after the vessel had gone down," enabling others to bring them safely to shore.[82] When she finally came ashore herself, Harriet would have been reunited with her frantic mother, who had agonized over the likely loss of a second child.

Harriet, only fifteen or sixteen years old at the time, was interviewed. The press marveled at how she "retained her presence of mind to such an extent that she has been able to describe, in minutia, the whole occurrence; give the location—upon the vessel—of nearly every one who was within her view at the time of the explosion." According to one admiring editor, "She will long be remembered by many of those who were spared with their lives." However, the press never bothered to identify her by name—only by the epithet "Darkness."[83] Nor did the reports include any of Harriet's own words, or state whether she herself had been wounded in the blast. Later in life, Harriet identified as an "invalid" and "unable physically to attend to business matters."[84] She didn't specify the cause of her disabilities. Perhaps she suffered from the aftereffects of the *Ada Hancock* blast and from putting the lives of others before her own.

• • •

For years to come, Biddy Mason and her Black neighbors would celebrate the day, January 1, 1863, with a ball and banquet. The annual gala commemorated the moment that the United States government finally linked the Union war effort and the Black freedom struggle with the passage of the Emancipation Proclamation. The itinerary varied from year to year, but almost always included eulogies to Abraham Lincoln and a reading of the document that, on paper at least, dealt a death blow to slavery in America.[85]

Celebrations during the war years, however, would need to be much more discreet. The Emancipation Proclamation unleashed a fresh wave of grievance-mongering and race-baiting that put Mason and her peers back in the cross hairs of their secessionist neighbors. Whereas the Owens family had hosted a large Fourth of July celebration for the Black residents of Los Angeles and San Bernardino in 1860, the holiday passed without note in 1863 and 1864.[86] Patriotism, after all, often invited violence. When several dozen Unionists attempted to celebrate the US victory at the battle of Gettysburg in July 1863, they were met by a mob of armed men, who shot two of the loyalists.[87]

Henry Hamilton led the charge against the Emancipation Proclamation from the pages of the *Los Angeles Star*. "By the stroke of his pen, Mr. Lincoln frees every slave in rebeldom—robs every master of his servant, every household of its property," he spat. "Was ever such an outrage perpetrated in the name of law, or such foul perjury committed, as by this man, sworn to maintain the Constitution and govern by the laws[?]"[88] The question was rhetorical.

E.J.C. Kewen, a state legislator and former attorney general of California, was even angrier. Widely regarded as the finest orator in Los Angeles, Kewen had fashioned himself into a silver-tongued auxiliary to the Confederacy and a friend to slaveholders everywhere.[89] He outdid himself with his flame-throwing outrage over the Emancipation Proclamation. In a three-hour speech, punctuated by cheers, applause, and even bouquets of flowers, Kewen castigated the "the treasonable heresies of the Abolition creed." He blamed the "saturnalia of blood" of the war not on the rebels who fired first but on "the negro, with all his distinguished characteristics of inferiority." Republicans were "Union destroyers and ebony idolaters," while slavery "was as innocent of offence to the Government as the humblest species of animate or inanimate property."[90] Mason and Black Angelenos would have multiple run-ins with Kewen in the years to come.

By this point in the war, however, they finally had a degree of protection from such rebels. "Treason's hideous crest shall not pollute the fair land of California," resolved the US Department of the Pacific.[91] As the US military presence around Los Angeles grew, so too did the campaign against the Confederate sympathizers who Lincoln called "the fire in the rear." By war's end civil and military authorities would arrest nearly two hundred pro-secessionist Californians. Many of them were imprisoned, albeit briefly, at a new island penal complex in San Francisco Bay known as Alcatraz.[92]

US marshal and Mason's onetime employer Henry Dwight Barrows led the clampdown in Los Angeles. He wrote weekly reports on secessionist activity in Los Angeles for the *San Francisco Bulletin* and eventually rounded up some of the pueblo's most prominent citizens on charges of treason, including Andrew Jackson King, Henry Hamilton, and E.J.C. Kewen.[93] The instigators were quickly released, and Kewen and Hamilton soon won seats in the state legislature on unapologetically pro-Southern platforms. Nevertheless, the arrests served notice to would-be rebels that treason came with consequences. Mason's employer, Dr. Griffin, grew increasingly paranoid over the repercussions of his own pro-Confederate politics. "I know every movement I make is noticed," he wrote to fellow Southerner Benjamin D. Wilson in July 1863.[94]

Suspicion fell even on Benjamin Hayes, who faced a hotly contested bid for reelection that fall. He had already antagonized the town's formidable proslavery faction by emancipating Mason and thirteen other Black women and children in 1856. Now, a growing number of Unionists distrusted him as well. Although he publicly supported the US war effort, he had privately conceded that "the North I consider to be wrong *on the vital issue*, and the South is right."[95] Running as an independent, Hayes lost to the Unionist Pablo de la Guerra by a mere fifty-nine votes. He attributed the defeat to the US soldiers stationed at Fort Yuma, who voted "solid, against me."[96] Out of office for the first time in a decade, Hayes returned to private practice and retreated increasingly into his historical manuscripts.[97]

Rising Unionism enabled California to confront what had been the *bête noire* of the state's Black community since the 1850s: the ban on African American testimony. The law had almost scuttled Mason's bid for freedom in 1856. By mid-war Black Californians finally had enough support to do something about it. Determined to reverse a decade of electoral embarrassment, Republicans fused with loyal Democrats under the banner of the new Union Party.[98] With a firm majority in the statehouse, Unionists introduced a bill to overturn the ban on Black testimony. It passed comfortably, despite the objections of old guard Democrats. Governor Stanford signed it into law in the spring of 1863—although the prohibition on Chinese and Indian testimony remained in force.[99]

Other victories followed from there. In November 1864, Abraham Lincoln faced former Union general George B. McClellan in his bid for reelection. McClellan opposed emancipation and flirted with the possibility of a negotiated peace for the Confederacy. In Los Angeles, Southerners like Griffin, Wilson, and Kewen campaigned frantically for him. "If some steps are not taken to raise [money] we shall be badly beaten," Griffin complained.[100] Sure enough, they were. Lincoln carried California with 58 percent of the vote, a margin of victory previously unimaginable for the state's long-suffering Republicans. He even competed in Los Angeles County, thanks to the US soldiers stationed there, though the county board of canvassers later threw out the Republican ballots of hundreds of troops in four precincts.[101]

As the election results came in, Union armies continued their advance into the heart of the plantation South. Even corners of Georgia, previously unscarred by the war, now fell in the path of General Sherman's March to the Sea. By year's end, cavalry from Sherman's army cut across Hancock County, where Biddy had been born roughly forty-five years earlier and where members of her long-lost family likely still labored in bondage. Not for long, however. Like Mason, they too would be "free forever."

. . .

Dr. John S. Griffin was visiting with his friend Harris Newmark, a prominent German-Jewish merchant, when he got the news. President Abraham Lincoln had been shot. Griffin "was on his feet instantly, cheering for Jeff Davis," according to Newmark. Mason's employer then "seized his hat and rushed for the door, hurrahing for the Confederacy." He would have dashed into the street had Newmark not seized him and "held him back," preventing Griffin from a vulgar display over the president's death in his "unbalanced condition."[102]

Had Griffin made it into the street, he would have found the unlikeliest reveller of them all, Peter Biggs. Like many members of the pueblo's Black community, Biggs had spent much of his life in slavery before migrating to Los Angeles. An entrepreneur par excellence, Biggs allegedly made a small fortune by rounding up stray cats in Los Angeles, then shipping them to

San Francisco for a handsome fee to remedy the city's rat infestation.[103] Biggs became one of the first Black property-owners of his generation in Los Angeles.[104] "A tonsorial celebrity," Biggs was best known as the owner of a popular barber shop next to the Bella Union Hotel.[105] With a nose for opportunity, he named his shop the "New Orleans Shaving Saloon" and catered to the pueblo's large Southern clientele. He molded his politics accordingly.[106]

When Biggs, the so-called Black Democrat, got word of Lincoln's death, he joined other Confederate sympathizers in their celebrations. "The Southern 'patriots' got on a bust," wrote Horace Bell. "They howled and they hurrahed until they fell in the streets, dead drunk."[107] In response, the Department of the Pacific issued General Orders No. 27, which considered such displays as "virtually accessory after the fact."[108]

Biggs and seven other revelers were rounded up in the coming days, then marched more than twenty miles to Drum Barracks the next month. Biggs hobbled along with a ball and chain around his ankle. "Not in the least discouraged," he "threw his hat up into the air as he passed some acquaintances on the road, and gave three hearty cheers for Jeff Davis," according to Newmark.[109] The "Black Democrat" was finally released in July, but only after he, a former slave himself, agreed to acknowledge the legality of emancipation.[110] Civil War–era Los Angeles was not without its ironies.

Were Biggs's celebrations merely the performance of a practiced opportunist, designed to curry favor from his Southern patrons? Or were they the sincere displays of a political convert? No one could quite tell. Regardless, the image of Biggs hurrahing for Jefferson Davis enroute to Drum Barracks provides a useful corrective to overly tidy narratives about the African American freedom struggle. Black Angelenos charted various, sometimes conflicting, paths to survival during the war.[111] There was no single way to "be" Black in Los Angeles, and the precarity of existence there summoned a range of adaptative measures from the town's residents. Despite his politics, Biggs remained a central figure in the multiethnic pueblo. His daughter Juana later married Hannah's son Nelson.[112]

While Biggs awaited his sentencing, Mason and much of Los Angeles mourned the martyred president. On April 19 all businesses in the city closed and citizens draped the pueblo with "symbols of mourning." A funeral procession lined up on the Arcadia Block, just south of the plaza. They marched to the beat of muffled drums, with a company of dismounted cavalry leading the procession. Civic leaders and various associations followed. “Citizens generally” brought up the rear in a long, mournful loop around the city.[113]

Mason likely marched at the tail end of the procession, alongside her Black neighbors in silent tribute to the “Great Emancipator.” Lincoln’s death was a heavy blow for a community that had at last begun to carve out some tangible political gains. Yet Mason understood as well as anyone that the freedom of her people never depended on the actions of a single man. Her own liberation, after all, had been a community effort. That community, tempered in the crucible of war and a decade of collective struggle, was poised to carry the fight forward.

13 Reconstructing Los Angeles

Major Horace Bell thought he was leaving the war behind when he rode from battle-scarred Louisiana for Los Angeles in the summer of 1866. Bell had spent the previous five years in the service of the US Army, much of that time behind enemy lines. His latest deployment as chief of scouts in western Louisiana had him spying on a Confederate cavalry force led General Joseph Lancaster Brent, a fellow Angeleno. Now, Bell, along with his wife and child, was finally coming home.[1]

If Bell expected a hero's welcome, however, he was to be bitterly disappointed. He found Los Angeles "the most vindictive, uncompromising community in the United States... eager to go on vociferating its bitterness long after regions which the conflict had laid waste were willing to quit." His old friends "turned their backs on me." He wound up in dozens of brawls, by his own count, and narrowly escaped an assassination attempt on the road between El Monte and Los Angeles. His crime? He had dared to wear Union blue. "The idea," his old acquaintances huffed, "of a Los Angeles man of your stamp fighting on the side of the blacks!"[2] Although Bell had a penchant for exaggeration and a flair for the dramatic, no one could deny that postwar Los Angeles seethed with hostility toward African Americans and their alleged allies.

Biddy Mason confronted that hostility daily. Unlike Bell, who could simply remove his Union uniform and all that its blue fabric signified, Mason couldn't alter the color of her skin. Her presence and her prominence reminded many Angelenos of what they increasingly came to believe: that even if slavery was lamentable, emancipation had gone too far. And so, in the decade after the Civil War, they sought to turn back the tide of history and unwind the gains that Mason and her Black neighbors had so tenaciously made. In the words of Horace Bell, "the Civil War continued to rage" in Reconstruction-era Los Angeles.[3]

Reconstruction and Los Angeles are terms rarely paired together in historical accounts of this period. Histories of Reconstruction generally center on the American South, where the two major struggles of the era—preserving freedom for four million African Americans and unifying a shattered nation—reached their most dramatic heights. But what of the West? The struggles over freedom and reunion often generated as much friction there as they did in the East. And in few western locales were the central issues of Reconstruction debated with as much furor and urgency as in Los Angeles. There white revanchists positioned themselves on the bleeding edge of a national rebellion against Reconstruction. Only by embarking on an unprecedented period of institution-building and political organizing could Mason and her neighbors hope to stem the anti-Black current that threatened to engulf them.[4]

They would be forced to do so without their most influential and affluent leader. While visiting his half-brother in Stockton, California, in the first months after the war, Robert Owens suddenly fell ill. He died on August 18, 1865, leaving a wife, three children, two grandchildren, and a grieving community.[5] Who now would guide that community forward? And how could Black Los Angeles muster the political, social, financial, and, crucially, the spiritual resources to meet the challenges of a fractured postwar order?

. . .

"I have never seen Los Angeles so sad," Benjamin Davis Wilson sighed in the summer of 1865.[6] Flooding, smallpox, and two years of drought had sapped the region of its vitality and leeched the color from the land. Cattle, dropping by the thousands, took with them the wealth of Southern

California's ranching elite. Plunged into debt, rancheros swapped their "rich velvets, broadcloth and gold embroidery" for "old soldiers' cast off clothes."[7] The depression didn't discriminate, however. Property values everywhere tumbled, as financial panic shot down the social ladder. "The war-stricken towns of Mississippi, Louisiana and western Texas through which I had ridden on my way back to the Pacific Coast" were, according to Horace Bell, "prosperous in comparison" to Los Angeles, "the most God-forsaken country I had ever seen."[8]

Where her neighbors saw decay, Biddy Mason saw opportunity. By this point she had been husbanding her earnings for nearly a decade. Because Los Angeles still lacked a bank, Mason had only a few options for her savings: deposit her money in the local post office; ship it to San Francisco; or transform it into something else.[9] A slumping economic outlook and declining land values gave her the opening she needed. It seems she had been waiting for this moment.

Although unlettered, Mason was a quick study. From her first days in the pueblo, she had been surrounded by entrepreneurs. Her former hosts, Robert and Winnie Owens, had assembled a lucrative portfolio in Los Angeles real estate. They probably directed her attention to various opportunities in town as a means of elevating their friend and building the Black community. Her employer, John S. Griffin, invested in land on an even grander scale, and he too may have shared some real estate tips with his trusted nurse. Furthermore, Mason attended the same small, multiracial Methodist church as Robert M. Widney, who would become the city's first real estate agent. She wasn't one to let lessons go unheeded.

Mason herself credited a different kind of inspiration, albeit one dismissed by writers and historians ever since: her faith. According to a later report, the idea to invest in real estate came to her through divine visitation. "The Good Lord appeared before me and told me to buy some property and keep it as long as I lived," she would tell others. Condescension drips from the pen of the writer who recounted the story of Mason's vision. Although impressed with her business acumen, the reporter belittled the "old mammy's story" as "only a dream." Nevertheless, she deserved credit for "some sort of premonition," he continued, "for it is surely not characteristic of her race to possess such wonderful insight."[10]

Mason's Christian peers would have interpreted her vision differently, to say the least. Such experiences were nothing to scoff at. They were celebrated by her coreligionists—"noteworthy but by no means unheard-of or controversial," according to historians Anthony Kaye and Gregory Downs.[11] In fact, Mason's divine visit placed her in a distinguished lineage of visionaries, from biblical forebears to more contemporary Black prophets like Nat Turner and Harriet Tubman. The religious memoirs of African American women in particular abound with accounts of heavenly visitations, which serve as signposts on the path to a holy life.[12] "Like the very breath of God," is how the Methodist preacher Charles Grandison Finney described similar encounters.[13] What Mason actually saw that day only she could know. But many at the time, especially her fellow Methodists, would have perceived a providential purpose in Mason's decision to invest. Her faith had already carried her to freedom. Was it unreasonable to expect that it could guide her to prosperity?

But where exactly to invest? Mason couldn't afford land on popular residential streets, like San Pedro and Main, so she turned to more obscure corners of the pueblo. The southern reaches of Spring Street, just below the old courthouse, were an attainable alternative. She was already familiar with that part of town. It was onto the dirt road of Spring Street that ten years earlier she had stepped as a freedwoman for the first time after hearing Judge Hayes's ruling. The street's name allegedly came from the city's famous surveyor, Edward O. C. Ord, who, when courting a young Spanish woman in the late 1840s, called her his *primavera.* That Spring Street was underdeveloped and rather unloved, with some lots serving as the backyard stables for the abutting homes along Main, meant that Mason might find something within reach.[14]

On November 28, 1866, Biddy Mason became a homeowner. For $250 she gained title to two adjoining lots on Spring Street and Fort Street (now Broadway), between Third and Fourth. Enclosed by a long willow fence, the lots each measured 165 feet deep and 120 feet wide (about 40,000 square feet of Los Angeles real estate in total). The land contained a ditch for water and plenty of space to grow any healing herbs she might need for her medical practice. The deed lists William M. Buffum and James F. Burns as sellers.[15] Mason may have known Burns personally. He had been named a justice of the peace just two months after her freedom suit. According to a later report, Burns thought Mason "may be deranged" for wishing to part with her hard-earned money in exchange for such an unpromising piece of property.[16]

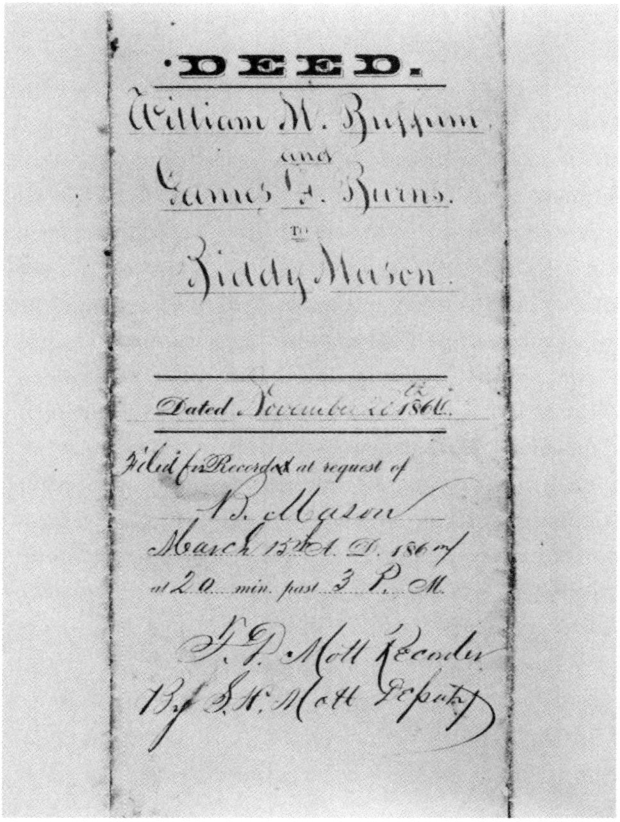

DEED.

William M. Buffum

and

James F. Burns.

To

Biddy Mason.

Dated November 1866.

Filed for Record at request of

B. Mason

March 15th A. D. 1867

at 20 min. past 3 P. M.

J. P. Mott Recorder

By S. H. Mott Deputy

The front page of the deed to Mason's first property purchase, 1866. Miriam Matthews Photograph Collection, UCLA Special Collections.

Mason, however, understood the value of property in a way no white seller possibly could. After all, she had once been considered a piece of property herself. Treated as another man's possession and denied the rights of ownership—including ownership of her own person—Mason no doubt relished the opportunity to acquire something lasting for herself and for her family. As historian Tiya Miles writes, "Having possession was a salve that reinforced a sense of self-worth in a society that demeaned Black people by equating them with objects."[17] Although Mason wouldn't move to her Spring Street property for years to come, it retained enormous value for her. She vowed never to sell the property and insisted that her children keep the vow as well. Never again would they suffer another dislocation or forced removal. The chain had been broken. This was their home.[18]

With a prescience that would become a pattern, Mason struck the market at just the right time. The depression of the war years gave way to an unprecedented boom across Southern California, beginning at roughly the moment that Mason secured title to her new homestead. While the collapse of the ranching economy bankrupted the ancestral elite, it eventually created a windfall for aspiring landowners. Developers subdivided the region's cattle estates as land-hungry settlers rushed in. "Every steamer was crowded with immigrants seeking cheap lands for homes," recalled one early resident.[19] "Our county is very promising," a once-despondent Benjamin D. Wilson wrote. "Lands are doubling up every few months."[20]

Urban properties like Mason's likewise skyrocketed in value. The assessed value of real estate in Los Angeles roughly quadrupled between 1866 and 1870.[21] Labor and building supplies could hardly keep pace. "The city and the country are covered with the skeleton frames of buildings which for a long time have remained unfinished for the want of material," reported the *Alta California* in 1868.[22] To capitalize on the soaring demand, Robert M. Widney began publishing the monthly *Real Estate Advertiser*, birthing an industry that would come to define the image of Los Angeles.[23] According to one expert on the subject, this was the beginning of "perhaps the most extraordinary expansion in American urban history."[24] Through the booms (and busts) that would follow, Mason continued to invest, entwining her fortune with the fate of the city she called home.

• • •

Biddy Mason's decision to invest may have been motivated by another consideration as well: the death of Robert Owens and the leadership vacuum he left in his wake. For more than a decade, Owens had been the de facto head of Black Los Angeles. A conductor of California's Underground Railroad, a veteran of the Union Home Guard, a government contractor during the Civil War, and an increasingly successful real estate investor, Owens had distinguished himself in multiple ventures, often at great personal risk. His achievements won him admirers across the city, while his stature provided something of a protective umbrella for the broader Afri-

The women of the Mason-Owens family in front of the Owens home, ca. 1865–70. Mason sits at the left, while Winnie Owens occupies the center of the frame. Their three daughters are seated to the right. Miriam Matthews Photograph Collection, UCLA Special Collections.

can American community. But now he was gone. Without its patriarch what was Black Los Angeles to do?

Turn to its matriarchs. Mason's property purchase was not just a personal investment; it was an act of community building. Land provided a collective hedge against the perils of the post-emancipation era. Only through property ownership would African Americans have the security and autonomy to realize the promise of freedom. Mason's Spring Street homestead did that and more, expanding the real estate footprint of the Black community and creating a node for future organizing. Her investment, in short, cemented her place at the center of Black Los Angeles.[25]

The twin power of property and Black matriarchy radiates from one of the most remarkable images of early Los Angeles: a group portrait of the women and children of the Mason-Owens family. They sit on the front porch of the Owens home, arrayed in their Sunday best. Winnie Owens occupies the center of the frame in a collared and elegantly embroidered dress. On the left-hand side sits Biddy Mason. The child next to her is most likely her eldest grandson, Robert Curry Owens. Nestled on her lap and clothed in an infant's white dress, a baby (identity unknown) peeks out between the planks of the picket fence. The other three young women—perhaps Ellen and Harriet Mason and Winnie's daughter Martha Hall—are similarly well-dressed. The home itself bears the hallmarks of middle-class comfort: a wooden gate, ornamental trim, and shuttered windows with lace curtains.[26]

If photographs of Black homeowners for this period and place are rare, photographs of women homeowners, aside from this one, are practically nonexistent. The image was probably taken in the years after the Civil War, perhaps to mark the passing of Robert Owens. The Black dress that Winnie Owens wears may be a symbol of mourning. But the photograph is also a celebration—a keepsake to showcase the prosperity of the Mason-Owens women in his absence. Photographic portraits, usually the preserve of Southern California's high society, didn't come cheap in Reconstruction-era Los Angeles. But the Mason-Owens women had the means to capture this moment in time, a visual record of their remarkable rise. All of the subjects in this photo, except for the two children, had spent most of their lives in slavery. Now they were a houseproud family at the heart of Black Los Angeles.[27]

As the portrait reveals, leadership in Black Los Angeles was a joint family affair. Like her mother, Ellen Owens prospered in the postwar years, alongside her husband, Charles. "Charles was much like his father, a man of fine physique and appearance, similar in size and a man of fine character and manhood," recalled Joseph Mesmer, a white friend to the early Black community.[28] Charles inherited his father's livery stable on San Pedro Street, which he ran profitably for several years before moving the business to the junction of Main and First Streets. Meanwhile, he and Ellen continued to invest in real estate. They owned a block of twelve lots on Olive Street between Sixth and Seventh, from which the Mason-Owens family profited for generations.[29] In 1868, Mason purchased some of these lots, abutting what is now Pershing Square.[30]

The widowed Winnie Owens remained a pillar of Black Los Angeles long after her husband's death. Her legendary dinner parties brought together diverse guest lists and drew awestruck commentary from as far away as Stockton. Observers marveled at how Winnie charmed the unlikeliest of her guests, including dyed-in-the-wool Democrats. *The Los Angeles News*, normally a viciously anti-Black rag, had only praise for her gatherings: "The viands were everything that could be wished for, and wit and pleasant humor ruled the hour, the health of Mrs. Owens was proposed and responded to by the guests present, and after a toast to the memory of the late Robert Owens... the guests took their departure well satisfied with having been entertained by aunt Winnie."[31] Among those toasting Winnie and her late husband at this particular gathering in 1867 were the notorious Confederate sympathizers E.J.C. Kewen and John S. Griffin.[32]

Biddy Mason had already demonstrated a similar ability to unite the seemingly incompatible for mutual benefit. To succeed as a nurse, midwife, and budding real estate investor, she had to cross barriers that others would have deemed insurmountable. Her warmth and her skill tended to deactivate at least some of the prejudices of at least some of her neighbors. As she understood, Black Los Angeles was never a community unto itself. It was a bridge. And she and her extended family were its architects.

. . .

Those bridges, however, could only reach so far. Postbellum Los Angeles remained "a stronghold of Southern men," as one local writer put it.[33] In the immediate postwar years the city welcomed back some of its rebel defectors as well as newcomers from the South, like George S. Patton, the son of a Confederate colonel killed in action. (Patton would marry one of Benjamin D. Wilson's daughters and give his name to his son, the future World War II general.)[34] Cameron Thom, a cavalry officer wounded at Gettysburg in the service of the Confederacy, returned to Los Angeles in 1865. He regained his seat as district attorney and was later elected mayor of Los Angeles.[35] Although Confederate general Joseph Lancaster Brent never returned, his friends repeatedly reassured him that "you will be welcome by all your neighbors," as "the animosities... of the war are dying away fast."[36]

That spirit of reconciliation generally didn't cross racial lines, however, despite the best efforts of Biddy Mason and Winnie Owens. Wartime animosities, when directed toward the region's African American population, continued to fester and even grow in the postbellum period. Former undersheriff Andrew Jackson King made sure of it. During the war King had been briefly jailed for treasonous activity, including an "ostentatious display" of a life-size portrait of Confederate general P.G.T. Beauregard in the Bella Union Hotel.[37] He made no apologies. "We have been, and are yet a secessionist," he exulted more than six months after the Confederate surrender. If it was treason to oppose "Black Republicanism," King proclaimed, we "here declare our intension [*sic*] to remain traitors to the end of our lives."[38]

King did so through the pages of the *Los Angeles News*, a former Unionist newspaper he purchased in 1865 and operated alongside Charles Beane, a Confederate officer.[39] Nearly every column crackled with white hot rage and, even by the standards of the time, breathtaking racism. King yearned for a return to what he imagined as an Edenic state of nature between humane masters and happy slaves. Once Black people tasted the forbidden fruit of "unfortunate freedom," King wrote, they "lost whatever of honesty and faithfulness there was in their simple nature" and became forever corrupted.[40] Now, he wrote, African Americans were nothing but "depraved and besotted blackamoors, whose physical odors pollute the atmosphere" with a "soul . . . as black and as putrid as his body." He summoned a menagerie of vicious animal metaphors—hyenas, crocodiles, and "rapacious beasts"—to convey his disgust for a people who had the gall to desire freedom.[41] King's paper became the standard of California's unreconstructed rebels, unfurled in all its fury.

The anti-Black and anti-Republican diatribes emanating from Los Angeles should dispel a common misconception about this period in American history: that the political project of Reconstruction was somehow confined to the American South. Slave emancipation stirred a deep sense of racial resentment among white voters across the country, even in places with relatively small Black populations. Many Californians feared that the progressive policies of the Republican Party, deployed first in the former Confederate states of the South, might soon find their way west and unsettle their carefully constructed racial hierarchy. California's multiethnic population—including Black, Indigenous, and Chinese communities—made it especially vulnerable to a racial reordering, they reasoned. To keep that from happening, white Californians mounted what can only be described as a rebellion against Reconstruction.[42]

That rebellion began in earnest in the fall of 1867 with a series of critical elections. The gubernatorial contest pitted the Unionist George Gorham against the Democrat Henry Haight. Whereas Gorham appealed to the "universal brotherhood of man," Haight appealed to division.[43] He repeatedly invoked the specter of Black and Chinese suffrage—neither of which was legal in California—to enflame his white voter base. "The people of California love their free institutions too well to surrender them to the control of Chinese and Negroes," Haight told a voter in Los Angeles before the election.[44] He even made a pledge: African Americans "will never, with the consent of the people of this State, either vote or hold office."[45]

Voters chose division over unity, bigotry over brotherhood. Republicans lost seats in most state elections that fall, but nowhere did they suffer greater embarrassment than in California. Only in California did Republicans lose the statehouse, their congressional majority, and the governorship, which Haight carried by ten points, a wider margin of victory than any gubernatorial candidate in any other state.[46] "I could scarcely credit the tidings of the complete democratic victory in California," exulted David S. Terry, the former state chief justice and killer of Senator Broderick. "The knell of the radical black republican party has been sounded."[47] According to one historian, the Democratic victory was nothing short of a "political revolution" by "a party that only a year earlier had seemed so blackened by the stain of rebellion that few thought it would ever rise again."[48]

Governor Haight was true to his pledge. California would not, under his watch, endorse any national measures for Black or Chinese rights. He began his term by stonewalling the Fourteenth Amendment. As framed by Republicans in Congress, the Fourteenth Amendment granted citizenship rights and equal protection under the law to Black Americans. The amendment came to California during a legislative recess in the summer of 1866. Once in office, Haight could have summoned the legislature to vote on the measure, but, to no one's surprise, he simply sat on it. California thus became the only free state that refused to ratify the Fourteenth Amendment before the turn of the decade.[49]

The proposed Fifteenth Amendment, which would have enfranchised Black men across the country, faced even longer odds in California. By the time the amendment came west for ratification in late 1869, Democrats had extended their legislative majority. (In a sign of the political mood in the state, Andrew Jackson King had been made county judge of Los Angeles that same year.)[50] The debate in the statehouse ended before it began. William Gwin Jr., a Confederate cavalry officer and son of California's former slaveholding senator of the same name, struck the first blow. "The negroes, too indolent and improvident, ever to become property holders, are ruining the South" and they would ruin the West as well, Gwin fumed. California's lawmakers rejected the Fifteenth Amendment by a margin of five-to-one.[51]

California's resistance was largely symbolic. Because more than two-thirds of the states ultimately ratified the Fourteenth and Fifteenth Amendments, both measures became national law. Still, California withheld its token ratification of the amendments until 1959 and 1962, respectively. For context, the United States would launch astronauts into outer space before California deigned to endorse the two major civil rights laws of the Reconstruction era.[52]

Meanwhile, the Ku Klux Klan gathered force. By 1870 self-identified members of the KKK were operating in every former Confederate state—and in California. Although almost entirely overlooked by historians, Klansmen menaced the Reconstruction-era West, primarily by targeting Chinese immigrants. The California press reported on a wide range of outrages attributed to local Klansmen: threatening letters sent through the mail, brutal attacks on Chinese agricultural workers, and even the burning of a church that served Chinese parishioners.[53] To be sure, these attacks never approached the level of violence witnessed in the former Confederate states. The Western Klan was not a formal organization so much as a loose band of vigilantes who periodically borrowed the name and some of the aesthetics of their Southern counterparts to instil greater terror. Hair-splitting over the vigilantes' affiliations, however, would not have comforted any of their victims.[54]

Klansmen left their mark in Los Angeles as well. In June 1871 a threatening note was posted, reading: "Notice is hereby given by the undersigned persons that you have to leave and quit this place of order of Government Laws!" The identity of the victim is unknown, though he or she was likely active in Republican politics, a common target of the Klan. The notice insisted that the evacuation must take place "Within 48 ours [*sic*] Peacibly [*sic*], we will hold and protecte [*sic*] this section . . . undter [*sic*] all circumstances." It was decorated with "the usual skull and cross-bones accompaniments," supposedly a common Klan signature.[55] When that same month a Black man was bludgeoned on the streets of neighboring El Monte for "putting on airs," Andrew Jackson King's paper celebrated the assault. He reminded readers that "the Monte isn't a good place yet for saucy negroes" and called for more "Ku Klux legislation."[56]

From Mason's perspective the distance separating California from Mississippi had never been as wide as the maps suggested. That became even more apparent when the bane of her early years in plantation slavery made a surprise appearance in Los Angeles. California farmers had been experimenting with cotton since the Civil War, if not earlier, in an attempt to capitalize on the disruptions to the Southern market. In the postwar years eighty acres of white cotton bolls sprouted in Los Angeles, not far from Mason's new homestead. She couldn't of course be forced to pick the stuff anymore. But the mere existence of cotton in Los Angeles would have been a visceral reminder of a past that, even after all these years, she could never quite escape.[57]

. . .

Black Angelenos needed a social refuge, somewhere to take shelter from the storm winds of racist hysteria howling around them. They needed a political hub, somewhere to gather strength even as the Black leadership in San Francisco conceded that "all our energy has left us."[58] And they needed a spiritual center, somewhere to draw inspiration and summon the faith that, however bleak the moment, they would once again overcome. In short, they needed a church. That was the conclusion drawn by Biddy Mason and her neighbors by the late 1860s.

Black Los Angeles was not without its places of worship. Beginning as early as 1854, African Americans assembled in the Owens home for weekly prayer, as Robert "conducted [services] and read selections from the Bible," according to Joseph Mesmer, a friend of the family.[59] Later sources credit Mason with hosting services as well.[60] She and Winnie may have shared those responsibilities after the death of Robert, ensuring that the faithful still had a space to gather. But Mason and others yearned for something more permanent, a place to call their own, large enough to accommodate rising numbers of Black Christians in Los Angeles.

They drew inspiration from a national movement of Black church-building in the Reconstruction era. As soon as they had the resources to do so, African Americans erected places of worship, which doubled as meeting halls, schools, social service bureaus, charities, and employment centers. Polyglot communities of men and women, young and old, literate and nonliterate, formerly enslaved and freeborn came together as one within their houses of worship. That is, the church became the very heart of the Black public sphere.[61] Not coincidentally, it was from the Black church that generations of African American political leaders would spring, including Hiram Revels, the first Black senator, and later, Martin Luther King Jr.[62]

Black Angelenos hailed from various faith traditions, but one denomination held special meaning for many of them: the African Methodist Episcopal (AME) Church. Founded by Richard Allen and Absalom Jones after they were forcibly removed from a whites-only seating area in their Philadelphia congregation in 1789, the AME Church became a leader in the struggle for freedom and civil rights, growing into the first interstate Black organization in America. W.E.B. DuBois considered it "the greatest Negro organization in the world."[63] By 1869 the AME Church counted a membership in the hundreds of thousands.[64] Still, it didn't extend as far as Los Angeles. Mason was determined to change that.

Church-building in Los Angeles, however, presented unique challenges. James Woods, a Wesleyan-educated Presbyterian minister from Massachusetts, learned that the hard way when he attempted to organize the first Protestant congregation in the pueblo the mid-1850s.[65] "The name of this city is in Spanish the city of angels, but with much more truth might it be called at present the city of Demons," he gasped upon his arrival in 1854.[66] When Woods tried to visit a condemned man in jail, the prisoner refused his company, saying he would sooner have a bear turned on him than a minister.[67] Lacking a sacred space, Woods preached to a congregation of twelve from the adobe courthouse where Mason would win her freedom the next year. He found his surroundings dispiriting, to say the least.[68] For one of his sermons Woods drew from the story of Sodom and Gomorrah, only to realize that he didn't need to reach into the biblical past for examples of urban depravity and decay; "I could have found them in the very scenes now transpiring around me."[69] He fled "this retreat of Satan" for greener pastures the next year.[70]

In setting out a church of their own, the African American community had one distinct advantage that even an experienced minister like Woods lacked: Black women. Church-building in frontier Los Angeles required not only faith but tenacity and an instinct for survival, the very traits that carried Mason across the continent and out of bondage. Men may have done most of the preaching within the Black church—and generally with an air of patriarchal condescension that characterized much of the sermonizing of the era—but women often wielded the power behind the pulpit. Women, after all, generally made up the majority of Black congregations, and they compensated for a lack of formal leadership by carving out key positions for themselves. Known variously as "gospel mothers," "church mothers," and "old shepherds," some women exercised genuine authority within their congregations. As one male Black Baptist griped, "Woe to that disciple who is so unfortunate as to be out of their favor."[71] Years later, W.E.B. DuBois wrote that "Black women [are] . . . the main pillars of those social settlements which we call churches; and they have with small doubt raised three-fourths of our church property."[72]

Mason had already distinguished herself as one of the city's few church founders. Sometime after the war she joined a predominantly white Methodist congregation. By 1868 she was one of approximately fifteen charter members who raised funds to erect a meetinghouse on Fort Street, directly across the road from her homestead. It was only the third Protestant church to be built in Los Angeles.[73] Mason would retain her membership in the Fort Street Methodist Church for the rest of her life, even as she turned much of her energy toward the spiritual needs of her Black brethren.[74] Mason's Christianity was ecumenical and interracial.

A year after establishing the Fort Street Methodist meetinghouse, Mason joined with fellow Black Angelenos to begin organizing for a sanctuary of their own. The challenges were threefold. First, they would need to find a suitable site. Then they would need to raise funds for the construction of a permanent structure. And finally, they would need enough cash leftover to cover the annual taxes and the costs of upkeep. Together, those expenses would run well north of $1,000 and perhaps closer to $2,000, a daunting sum for a community that, despite some individual successes, was still struggling to find its footing.[75]

Black Los Angeles compensated for a lack of resources with an abundance of willpower and organizational know-how. The same people who now led the church-building campaign—Mason's family, Hannah's family, Elizabeth Rowan's family, and members of the Owens family—were those who had spearheaded the freedom suit of 1856. Many of them, including Hannah, Biddy, Elizabeth Rowan, and Oscar Smith, had known one another since the 1840s, when they lived together in the Mormon colony at Cottonwood, Utah.[76] They also had new allies to call upon. T.M.D. Ward, the bishop of Bethel AME Church in Sacramento and one of the state's leading Black clergymen, came to Los Angeles in 1869 to assist in the campaign. Meanwhile, Mason's brethren at Fort Street Methodist Church lent their chapel to their Black coreligionists—perhaps an arrangement that she herself negotiated—as a space to gather and rally support.[77] That many of the church-builders had, like Mason, "worn the iron-yoke of oppression" only deepened their faith and determination, according to Ward. "They appreciate the goodness of that Power who has broken their bonds, and invested them with the Aegis of liberty."[78]

By spring 1869 the Black Christians of Los Angeles had taken their first major strides toward perpetuity. They had a name, the African Methodist Episcopal Church of Los Angeles. They had a board of trustees, consisting of Charles Owens, John Ballard, Jeremiah M. Redding, Lewis Green, George Smith, John Hall, and Samuel Johns (sometimes spelled Jones). And they even had a plot of land. On March 13, 1869, they purchased a lot from a well-known doctor on the western fringes of the city at Fourth and Charity (now Grand) for seventy-five dollars.[79] (The site is roughly where the headquarters of the multinational law firm Latham and Watkins stands today.)[80]

The land purchase was the easy part, however. Now the real work began. Although the deed had been registered in the names of seven men, it was the Black women of Los Angeles who "commenced this glorious work" of church-building, according to Bishop Ward.[81] "In point of liberality they excel any people I ever sojourned among," Ward marveled. "Every dwelling opened its doors; every house spread its sumptuous board." An early history of the city gives three names as "the first members" of the church: Biddy Mason, Winnie Owens, and Alice Coleman.[82]

The women of the Mason-Owens family formed the axis around which the critical fundraising efforts spun. In September they organized a "Grand Festival" to help finance the construction costs of their church. Tickets could be purchased from Winnie, Biddy, Ellen, and Hannah's daughter Ann, among others, for two dollars each.[83] The event was well-attended and well-reviewed.[84] By the end of the month Black Los Angeles had raised more than $1,500. Most of those contributions came from the parishioners themselves, including fifty-dollar donations each from Mason, Charles Owens, Amanda Ballard, and Hannah's son Nelson.[85]

The African Methodist Episcopal Church of Los Angeles, the first Black house of worship constructed in Southern California, opened its doors in the fall of 1870. "A neat and substantial" building, the two-story brick church rose up on Bunker Hill on the western rim of the city.[86] The church should be "very gratifying to those true Christians who know no prejudice as to color or caste in the matter of souls to be saved," reported the *Los Angeles Star*. After only several months in operation, the "Little Church on the Hill" was already "in a flourishing condition," according to the *Star*, "and constantly enrolling new members in the 'Army of the Lord.'"[87] From a mustard seed of faith, nurtured by Biddy Mason since her years in bondage, sprang a community with the power to move mountains.[88] Today, First African Methodist Church of Los Angeles boasts a membership of roughly twenty thousand.[89]

. . .

The church-building campaign provided Black Los Angeles not only with a space for worship but also a template for collective action. Those organizational capacities would be sorely tested in the months and years to come as Los Angeles divided over the issue of Black suffrage. Despite staunch opposition in the California state legislature, the Fifteenth Amendment was now national law, meaning that Black men everywhere had the right to vote. Biddy Mason knew as well as anyone, however, that what the law said and what local authorities allowed were two very different things.

This next phase of the Black freedom struggle began with a celebration. In the early hours of April 12, 1870, a group of about fifty people assembled on the AME Church property to commemorate the ratification of the Fifteenth Amendment and the beginning of a new era in Black political rights, or so they hoped.[90] They followed this gathering with an even grander affair that night at Stearns Hall. Dancing continued until midnight, at which point guests descended on a late-night banquet, prepared by Winnie Owens. Alongside numerous members of the Black community were some conspicuous white guests, including the onetime rebel E.J.C. Kewen.[91]

The backlash from the Democratic press was as swift as it was predictable. "The 15th Amendment, whether adopted legally or illegally, or whether adopted at all, can make no change in the views of the Democracy as to the iniquity of that measure," huffed Andrew Jackson King's *Los*

Angeles News.[92] Faced with a firestorm of criticism for his presence at the ball, Kewen clarified his position and distanced himself from his Black neighbors. "That the negro has been elevated into citizenship is a fault not imputable to any co-operation of mine," he wrote. He "accepted" the Fifteenth Amendment "as I would the Providential affliction of the cholera or small-pox" or any other similarly "unavoidable" calamity.[93]

The controversy over the ball served as the prelude to a broader struggle over Black suffrage. The source of the troubles this time was ironically the same man who had recently signed his name to some of the major acquisitions of the city's Black community, including Biddy Mason's first land purchase and the deed to the property upon which the AME Church was built. Thomas D. Mott had certified those documents in his capacity as county clerk of Los Angeles. Black property purchases were one thing, however; African American voting rights quite another for Mott. He flatly refused to register any Black voter in Los Angeles, a veto power he claimed as clerk.[94]

Lewis Green wasn't about to let a single clerk stand in the way of his constitutional rights. A veteran of the Navy, Green arrived in Los Angeles during the US–Mexico War and soon established himself as one of the leading members of the Black community with "the best appointed barber-shop and baths in the city," according to Joseph Mesmer. "Fine-looking" and "well liked," Green was "the very pink of courtesy," Mesmer wrote.[95] He was also prosperous, with $1,500 in real estate and personal property by 1870.[96] In other words, Green wasn't someone to be pushed around. He filed a writ of mandamus in April 1870, trusting the local courts to enforce national law.

It's easy to overlook the imprint of women like Mason in the struggle for Black men's suffrage. Her name doesn't appear on any voter registry or on any lawsuit to defend those rights. But it would fly in the face of everything we know about Mason and the women around her to assume that they simply stayed silent during such a consequential struggle, with implications for the entire community. As historian Elsa Barkley Brown writes, Black politics was born from the belief that freedom "would accrue to each of them individually only when it was acquired by all of them collectively."[97] Across the country Black women participated in the key public forums—parades, rallies, mass meetings—which fueled the struggle for Black male suffrage. In Los Angeles "the ladies are also moving," a Black correspondent to the *San Francisco Elevator* proudly reported.[98]

Mason had already demonstrated a keen political sensibility and an ability to defy traditional gender roles. As the cofounder of her community's church, she had navigated the snares that sunk numerous ecclesiastical efforts before hers. The result was an institution as much political as it was spiritual. It was on the grounds of the AME Church, after all, that the Black community first celebrated the ratification of the Fifteenth Amendment. And it was likely from the AME Church that they rallied when that amendment came under attack by the county clerk. That politics was traditionally defined as a man's dominion would not have dissuaded someone of Mason's mettle or faith. In testing such boundaries, Mason followed the example set by other Black churchwomen of her generation. "You will not let what man may say or do, keep you from doing the will of the Lord or using the gifts you have for the good of others," the Black preacher Julia A. J. Foote wrote.[99] As a long-standing community leader and medical authority, Mason wielded immense influence over her peers, including her neighbor, Lewis Green. She wasn't one to sit idle while such a campaign was under way.[100]

When Lewis Green walked into the Los Angeles County Courthouse on April 28, he did so with the collective energy of the city's Black women behind him. He had other champions as well, including his lawyer, Robert M. Widney, the city's pioneering realtor and Mason's fellow parishioner at the Fort Street Methodist Church. Perhaps it was Mason who secured his legal services. In addition, Green could draw on the support of the Lincoln Club, the newly formed social and benevolent organization of Black Los Angeles.[101] And of course, he also had the law of the land on his side—or so he thought.

Judge Ygnacio Sepúlveda ruled otherwise. True, the Fifteenth Amendment had been enshrined in the Constitution, Sepúlveda conceded. But that alone was insufficient to secure Black male suffrage. "The wording and spirit of the Amendment is so general in its meaning that it cannot be operative," he continued. Until additional legislation was passed to protect the amendment and punish its violation, clerks like Thomas Mott could simply ignore the amendment, Sepúlveda concluded. Green left the court as he had come in: disfranchised.[102] Clerks in Sacramento, San Joaquin,

Santa Clara, and San Francisco, in addition to Los Angeles, refused to register Black voters.[103]

Only with intervention from the national government were the voting rights of Black Californians restored. Congress passed an "An Act to Enforce the Fifteenth Amendment to the Constitution," which President Ulysses S. Grant signed into law in May 1870. The new act levied fines and imposed other penalties on those who obstructed anyone's suffrage rights. Mott, finally compelled by a law he couldn't dodge, begrudgingly added Green's name to the voter registry on June 21, 1870. Several weeks later, Charles Owens registered to vote for the first time, marking the birth of what would become a Black family dynasty in Republican politics.[104]

For years to come, Black Los Angeles hosted gala events to commemorate emancipation and suffrage, the two signal victories of the era. Members of the Mason-Owens family could be expected at such gatherings, sometimes in central roles. They joined large crowds of their fellow Black Angelenos and a smattering of white attendees over music, speeches, literary readings, dancing, and dining, often well into the night. In other words, Black Los Angeles celebrated their political triumphs in the same way that they had won them: as a community.[105]

. . .

For Hannah, in San Bernardino, the Reconstruction period was similarly one of hard-earned victories. She became a homeowner in 1866—the same year as Biddy—when she inherited Toby Embers's property on First Street. The plot was a large one, roughly 300 feet by 150 feet, situated at the core of the original Mormon settlement. As one of the first Black-owned properties in California's Inland Empire, the home became a gathering place for the local community. Hard memories hung over the house, however, as it was here that Embers had been brutally beaten by a crowd of white thugs roughly eight years earlier. Nevertheless, it was Hannah's home, a lifeline to stability after a lifetime of dislocation.[106]

Two years later, Hannah gave it away. She gifted the home to Charles and Martha, her two children by Embers, "in consideration of the natural love and affection she has for [them]."[107]

Why bequeath her home only two years after she herself had inherited it? Although the property deed makes no mention of Hannah's mortality, it likely doubled as her last will and testament. She was roughly forty-five years old when she put her X to this document, well beyond the life expectancy of the average Black woman of the era. She had spent most of those years in bondage, dragged from one plantation and farmstead to the next, as she fought to keep her children alive and her family together. This was her final gift.

Hannah's sacrifices would have a multigenerational impact, down to the present. Although some of her children struggled—including Marion, who spent ten years in prison for arson on the perjured testimony of a dubious witness—others thrived. Her oldest daughter, Ann, worked alongside Biddy Mason and other Black women of Los Angeles as one of the founding members of the AME Church there. Hannah's son Nelson, who had married Peter Biggs's daughter, also contributed to the founding of the church. Altogether, members of Hannah's family donated as much toward the establishment of Los Angeles's first Black church as the Mason-Owens family, though they rarely receive mention in histories of First AME.[108] Another daughter, Jane, was active in the AME Church of Sacramento after moving there with her husband, George Goins.[109]

Two of Hannah's most successful children were those who inherited her homestead, Charles and Martha. Charles Embers became one of the first Black settlers of Tucson, Arizona, where he moved shortly after the Civil War. He worked as a cook, a freighter, and a surveyor in the mining boomtown, becoming a homeowner four times over and something of a local celebrity. He remained in Tucson until his death in 1935 at the age of eighty-six, by which point he had outlived every other petitioner from the 1856 freedom suit, including his siblings and Mason's children.[110]

Martha Embers married Israel Beal in 1870. Born into slavery in Virginia, Beal won his freedom during the Civil War, then enlisted in the Union Army in time to accompany Sherman's forces on the March to the Sea in 1864. Detachments of that army raided Biddy Mason's birthplace of Hancock County, Georgia, and likely freed members of her long-lost family. After the war the Beals bought land—a purchase made possible in part by Martha's inheritance from Hannah—roughly twelve miles east of her mother's former home. Their property eventually grew to fifty-seven acres on which the Beals erected a spacious two-story home. Israel Beal is remembered today as a founder of Redlands, California, having hauled freight, graded tracts, and provided the materials with which to build the city. The Beals also cofounded the first house of worship in the area, Terrace Congregational Church, alongside a small group of white congregants.

Subsequent generations carried forward the family's pioneering legacy. Martha and Israel's grandson, Charlie, won fame as a jazz pianist, playing alongside Louis Armstrong and touring across Europe. Today many of Hannah's descendants remain in San Bernardino and Redlands, the cities that their family built.[111]

According to her descendants, Hannah is buried in Pioneer Cemetery in San Bernardino, although her headstone has since been displaced, lost, or destroyed.[112] We can therefore only imagine what might be inscribed on her tomb. To do justice to her many roles and accomplishments would require a substantial slab of marble. Pioneer. Survivor. Midwife. Freedwoman. Homeowner. Community-builder. These are just some of the titles that a fitting tribute could contain. Or perhaps something even simpler. Founding Mother of Southern California.

14 Philanthropist

Angelenos were no strangers to mob violence, but even by their perverse standards, what erupted on October 24, 1871, was "barbarism [at] full tide."[1] It started around nightfall. Responding to news that a Chinese gang member had gunned down a white citizen, five hundred frenzied residents of all backgrounds pushed their way onto Calle de los Negros, where most of the city's Chinese immigrants lived in a cluster of moldering adobe buildings. None of the Chinese residents hiding inside had been involved in the gunfight that summoned the mob. But the vigilantes either didn't know or didn't care. They climbed onto the roof of the main adobe and fired on the petrified people huddled within. After someone tossed a flaming torch into the building, the mob charged "like a tiger maddened by the taste of blood."[2]

And then the killing began. Chinese residents, including a respected doctor and an adolescent boy, were dragged from their rooms. The mob shot some, stabbed others, and hauled the remainder to makeshift gallows in the city streets. When the lynchers ran out of rope, a woman from a nearby boardinghouse donated her clothesline. The city's race-baiting publisher, Andrew Jackson King, rushed to join the fray. In his excitement one of his pistols prematurely discharged and blew off the top of his

Bodies of the victims of the Los Angeles Chinese Massacre of 1871, one of the largest mass lynchings in American history. Security Pacific National Bank Collection, Los Angeles Public Library Special Collections.

finger, "putting him *hors de combat*," according to Harris Newmark.[3] Some Angelenos, like Robert Widney, an advocate for Black voting rights, attempted to halt the slaughter. But there was little he or anyone else could do against the blind rage of hundreds.

By daybreak at least eighteen immigrants lay dead, amounting to roughly 10 percent of the city's entire Chinese population. The Los Angeles Chinese Massacre remains one of the largest mass lynchings in American history.[4]

Where was Biddy Mason amid the carnage? Perhaps she treated the wounds of those lucky enough to escape the mob. Or she may have even harbored a fugitive from the violence as they dashed past her home, located just a few blocks south of the Chinese district.[5] Such acts of colorblind bravery would have been consistent with her character. Unfortunately we have only our imaginations and informed speculation to guide us here. The eyewitnesses to the massacre fixed their attention on the main theater of the slaughter around Calle de los Negros, while those on the fringes of the violence, like Mason, went unnoticed. We don't therefore know exactly what she did that night.[6]

But we do know how she acted in the days and years to come. The Chinese Massacre was a tipping point for the city as a whole. Outraged commentary from newspapers across the country branded Los Angeles a sinkhole of race hatred and a source of shame for its residents.[7] Over the next two decades Mason would channel her land, her wealth, and her expertise into a range of egalitarian enterprises to combat that reputation. For instance, she rented some of her properties to Chinese businesses at reasonable rates, in contrast to many landlords who continued to blacklist Asian renters to confine them to the poorest neighborhoods.[8] Through philanthropy and fair-minded business practices, Mason joined a cadre of citizens determined to turn the page on the city's violent past and build a better Los Angeles, a place where residents, regardless of race or background, might one day live free of fear.

. . .

"If you hold your hand closed . . . nothing good can come in," Biddy Mason told her family. "The open hand is blessed, for it gives in abundance, even as it receives." This was Mason's "beatitude," in the words of the civil rights leader Sue Bailey Thurman, who first recorded the now famous quotation.[9] In two simple sentences Mason articulated an enduring theory of faith-driven philanthropy, which informed a lifetime of good works and forever transformed her city. To give is to receive. Acts of charity bring their own rewards. Although such sentiments have become well-worn adages, Mason's philosophy of cheerful giving marked her as something of a radical by the standards of her times. In philanthropy as in so many other things, Mason was a pioneer.[10]

Gilded Age philanthropist—the term conjures a very specific image. The archetype is a titan of industry endowing libraries, universities, museums, and performance spaces, with names like Vanderbilt, Carnegie, and Rockefeller emblazoned above soaring, neoclassical façades. These men (and occasionally their wealthy wives, widows, and heiresses) dispensed immense resources to burnish legacies and leave lasting monuments. Their philanthropy emerged from a sense of duty and often from egos as mammoth as the buildings that bore their names. Joy is an emotion that rarely creeps into their treatises on giving. Nor do Black people, except as recipients, feature prominently in the literature on philanthropy. The history of philanthropy is coded white.[11]

The view from Biddy Mason's Los Angeles enables us to see the history of giving in new ways. As the scholar Tyrone McKinley Freeman argues, African Americans articulated a more capacious understanding of philanthropy than their wealthier white counterparts. For Black people philanthropy was far more than just the act of funding charities or endowing institutions. It was a way of life. They gave constantly—their resources, their time, their expertise, their faith—not only "out of necessity for survival" but also "as an expression of their identity," according to Freeman. This was the Black "gospel of giving." And women like Mason were its early evangelists.[12]

Biddy Mason gave much of what she had: her money, her medical expertise, her spiritual gifts, and her knowledge from a storehouse of worldly experience. Unlike most white philanthropists, she gave even when she had few resources of her own, as someone only recently freed from slavery. By 1870, Mason's total net worth amounted to $3,000, a sizable sum but hardly an inexhaustible fortune, especially when the specter of financial collapse haunted Los Angeles for much of this period.[13] And yet she never stopped giving.

Mason's "gospel of giving" was molded by personal experience. She understood the power of philanthropy because she had once been a recipient. She first arrived in Southern California as an enslaved woman, with few sources of support aside from her children and Hannah's family. Then, when she needed them most, the Black community rallied to her defense. The Owens family provided her not only with housing and assistance but also with a model of philanthropic giving that aimed to elevate the lowest among them. Mason, in turn, dedicated herself to vulnerable populations like the Indigenous inmates of the county jail, where she herself had been imprisoned.[14]

Giving begat giving. The Black community of Los Angeles had provided for Mason, and Mason provided for the Black community of Los Angeles. She directed much of her philanthropic activity toward her fellow Christians. Before Black Angelenos had a church, she contributed her home. And once they erected a church, she contributed more and more of her resources. What started with a fifty-dollar donation in 1869 grew to a recurring commitment of hundreds of dollars.[15] A Black pastor later estimated that she gave as much as $500 to help launch the congregation.[16] For years thereafter Mason almost single-handedly floated the operations of the AME Church.[17]

Several sources also credit Mason with founding the first day nursery in the city. Although we have few details of this establishment, it aligns with what we know about Mason and her commitments. The nursery may have emerged naturally from her work as a midwife. Many postpartum women, especially Black domestics, would have required childcare as they adjusted to the dual demands of paid labor and motherhood. Mason understood these strains as well as anyone. So it seems that she devised a system to relieve working mothers of some of their burdens by looking after the same children that she had brought into this world.[18]

If historians have overlooked evidence of Black women's philanthropy, Mason's contemporaries and near-contemporaries certainly didn't. "Biddy Mason was well known throughout Los Angeles county for her charitable work," wrote Kate Bradley Stovall. "In the slums of the city, she was known as 'Grandma Mason,' and did much active service toward uplifting the worst element in Los Angeles."[19] According to the Black journalist Charlotta Bass, "destitute families who had drifted into Los Angeles found refuge in the home of Mrs. Mason."[20] Her friend Joseph Mesmer recalled that while Mason had won fame and fortune as an investor in real estate, her greatest legacy was "the life of a splendid, God-fearing, Christian woman, doing His work in deeds of relieving and aiding the poor, particularly those of her own color."[21] What was written in 1912 of Madam C. J. Walker, a self-made Black millionaire and philanthropist, could have equally been said of Mason roughly half a century earlier: "The habit of giving long since became a part of her."[22]

. . .

Inextricable from her identity as a philanthropist was Mason's work as a nurse and midwife. For midwifery, like philanthropy, was a means of building healthier, safer, better communities. Although white male doctors often belittled the expertise of female practitioners, especially Black ones like Mason, their patients knew better.[23] The very future of Los Angeles, after all, depended on the skills of the city's small cadre of midwives. "We who have such praise for the rapid growth of the population in Los Angeles must not forget the faithful midwives of early days," Harris Newmark insisted.[24] Their labor was all the more essential for its scarcity. "It was then almost impossible to obtain nurses," Newmark recalled of Los Angeles in 1870.[25]

Mason was thus in constant demand. Her former employer, Dr. John S. Griffin, retired from his practice in 1873, leaving his nurse to manage her own business by this point, if not earlier.[26] Her routine was never routine. She hurried from home to home, the wealthy and the humble alike, and from one end of the city to the other. Long days and sleepless nights took their toll on even the hardiest nurses, leaving them "look[ing] like you've come out of the sewer pipe," according to one Black midwife.[27] Mason often stayed on for weeks after a successful delivery, caring for mother and child alike.[28] She attested to the taxing variability of the job. "I have been a midwife for thirty-seven years and never saw five women who were affected alike by confinement," she reported at the end of her long career in 1887.[29]

The demands of midwifery required a diverse skill set. Black midwives often doubled as religious leaders, using prayer and spirituals to ease the anxieties of childbirth and to bless mother and child. African American midwives in the South described "some kind of feeling knowing they are always blessed" or that they would "take the Lord into their insides" to guide their actions.[30] Mason's status as a church leader within both white and Black congregations doubtlessly burnished her credentials as a midwife. So too did her natural intuition, an undefinable expertise that her admirers often called "mother-wit," and which no professional doctor, no matter how much medical training they undertook, could match. "Altho [*sic*] unlettered, [Biddy] Mason was amply fortified with that heaven-sent 'mother-wit' that has been the guiding spirit for those who were in bondage," according to the *California Eagle*.[31]

Mason needed all these skills and more to overcome deep-rooted prejudices about women's capacity for medical work. One of the earliest published birth manuals urged women to "submit to their station" and steer clear of any medical profession, including midwifery. Victorian conventions deepened the mistrust of female practitioners, who were seen as inherently unsuited to the demands of such a strenuous profession. Worse yet, they might be "unsexed" by the bloody work of medicine, which would rile women's natural sensibilities with nervous excitement. In large parts of the country, middle-class Americans simply refused the services of midwives.[32]

If female practitioners were suspect in the eyes of many, Black women were doubly so. They thus rarely received the credit due to them. For instance, the first women's hospital in the United States, which opened in Alabama in 1844, was run by a group of about twelve skilled enslaved women. Yet most of their names have been lost to history. Their manager Dr. James Marion Sims, however, is known as the "father of American gynecology," with scant reference to the surgical nurses who did most of the work within the hospital.[33]

Yet no amount of inborn prejudice could dispel an increasingly obvious fact: Mason was a master at her craft. By most counts she delivered hundreds of babies across roughly three decades of work in Los Angeles.[34] Mason was "a midwife of reputation," according to her onetime employer Horace Bell.[35] "She was particularly adept," recalled Joseph Mesmer. "She served in many of the best families and babies who became noted citizens were brought into the world by her skillful ministrations."[36] Mason, in fact, delivered some of Mesmer's siblings.[37] To have been delivered by Mason was an honor that bestowed lifelong bragging rights. The famous musician Lauretta Green Butler, who opened the first Black professional dance studio in Los Angeles and later starred in a radio play about Biddy Mason, boasted of "the distinction of being the last child . . . Mason helped into the world," though others likely came after her.[38]

. . .

Biddy Mason's stunning success is often celebrated but rarely explained. To say the odds were stacked against her would be a profound understatement. So how did someone who arrived in Los Angeles as a slave so adroitly ascend the socioeconomic ladder, despite the region's deep history of violent discrimination, and sometimes murderous rage, directed against people like her? Mason's rise required an act of social alchemy—indeed, nothing short of a fundamental transformation of the city itself—with few parallels in the history of the American West.

Recall that shortly before Mason arrived, Angelenos had forcibly ousted Black people and their allies from the pueblo, leading the mayor to conclude that "Mob Law is triumphant as respects the existence of negro slavery in this district."[39] After Mason's emancipation Judge Benjamin Hayes was "damned" by white Californians for daring to uphold the state's antislavery constitution.[40] The mob lost little of its fury or power in the intervening years. The racial violence that erupted in Los Angeles's Chinese district in October 1871 rivaled the carnage seen in the most unreconstructed recesses of the South. Although the victims this time were Chinese rather than Black, neither Mason nor any of her African American neighbors would take comfort in that fact. The color line of Los Angeles was often drawn in blood.

And yet Mason crossed that line again and again. As we've seen, she did so with a collection of traits—medical skills, personal charm, and profound courage—that softened the ingrained prejudices of those around her, including prominent white Southerners. Even John S. Griffin, a former a Virginia slaveholder who cheered the death of Abraham Lincoln, couldn't overlook Mason's unique gifts. These were the traits that led Joseph Mesmer's family, who owned a bakery near Mason's home, to shower her with "cakes and delicacies" every time she visited the shop. Her "tender-hearted" warmth, according to Mesmer, was simply irresistible.[41]

Breaking down barriers required sustained, often thankless work. And in this Mason had a model in Robert and Winnie Owens, who went so far as to host anti-abolitionist firebrands like E.J.C. Kewen in their home. With unconditional hospitality they challenged the caricatures that animated their neighbors' racism. Kewen once thundered that "the Negro . . . [carried] the black brand of Heaven's condemnation on his person." Yet thanks to these interventions, he would eventually attend a Fifteenth Amendment celebration with his Black neighbors.[42] And while he retained many of his prejudices, he had at least been forced to see his neighbors as something more than mere abstractions.[43]

Midwifery enabled Mason to infiltrate the affections, or at least to counter the ignorance of Angelenos in much the same way. Her work brought her into the most intimate sanctums of her neighbors' homes and under the most stressful conditions. Many of her patients would have been Southern-born whites, those previously conditioned to view someone like Mason as property rather than a person, and certainly not as a life-saving medical expert. It would require an especially firm sort of bigotry to sustain those views after Mason safely delivered one's child or saved the life of one's wife. Surely, some Angelenos still clung to their prejudices despite Mason's skilful service. Yet gradually—year by year, patient by patient, new life by new life—she transformed Los Angeles.

. . .

Mason must have boarded the steamer from Los Angeles in 1872 with some trepidation. She would have set out from the very same port and in a similar ship that nearly killed her daughter Harriet in the tragic *Ada Hancock* explosion a decade earlier. Her destination, Stockton, was tinged with as much misfortune as her point of embarkation. Stockton was where Robert Owens had gone seven years earlier on a similar visit. He never returned. The perils of the journey were warranted, however. Biddy Mason was on a mission to educate her family.

Mason wanted for her family in freedom what had long been denied her in slavery. The same reason that Robert Smith had prevented Biddy from attaining literacy was why she now coveted it for her children and grandchildren: Education was the key to Black advancement. Literacy enabled African Americans to negotiate contracts, to decipher accounts, to negotiate mortgages, to read the Bible, and ultimately to transcend their enslaved past. The African American schoolhouse, like the Black church, became a potent symbol of freedom in the post-emancipation period as well as a hub for community organizing.[44] Precisely because of education's liberatory potential, white supremacist mobs burned hundreds of Black schools in the Reconstruction South.[45]

In Los Angeles, Black education similarly became a fighting matter. The mere mention of school integration sent Andrew Jackson King into fits. Desegregation would "degrade the entire youth of the country," making "our public schools . . . the receptacle of a recently enslaved race," he fumed.[46] With a logic that prefigured some of the twenty-first-century debates over American education, King warned that a teacher "is as much a politician as a member of the Legislature," wielding the power "to corrupt the minds of the youth with their damnable doctrines of social equality."[47] To King's relief, Black students remained segregated by California law and underfunded by local practice.[48]

Although violence against Black schools in California never reached the epidemic levels seen in the South, schoolhouses were frequent targets. Los

Angeles opened its first Black school in 1865, and for years to come, students suffered frequent disruptions. The school moved locations no fewer than four times between 1865 and 1875 and occasionally closed altogether for lack of funds.[49] It was also vandalized. "The young Hoodlums of this city are in the habit of going on the hill west of Hill street, and stoning the house used by the colored school," the *Star* reported. "They have already broken sixty-six panes of glass in that building."[50] Another juvenile criminal robbed the schoolhouse, making off with the possessions of some of the students. Although arrested, he was soon released "with no worse punishment than a little good advice."[51]

Mason sought something better for her own family. Northern California had the finest Black schools in the state, so to Northern California her grandchildren would go. The decision must have been a wrenching one for Mason. Although mobility and freedom were synonymous for many African Americans in the South—movement meant the opportunity to finally escape the plantations to which they'd been bound as slaves—for Mason the opposite held true. After traversing the continent in slavery, she sought rootedness for herself and her family in freedom. Nevertheless, her grandchildren's future trumped her personal desires in this instance. Sometime around 1870, Robert and Henry Owens left Los Angeles along with their mother, Ellen.

Robert and Henry first attended the segregated public school in Oakland, where Ellen also received some instruction.[52] In 1871 the Oakland school board abruptly closed the Black schoolhouse, forcing the family to relocate. Stockton, where the Black educator and activist Jeremiah Sanderson had recently opened a school, was the logical destination. Sanderson's reputation was such that African Americans from all over the state sent their children to his Stockton school.[53] According to Delilah Beasley, the boys boarded with Sanderson until they finished their courses.[54] Unable to bear the separation, and perhaps eager to inspect the progress of their education for herself, Mason joined them in 1872 for a long stay.[55]

For years thereafter, Robert C. Owens credited his grandmother with his professional "salvation." Charles Owens had initially insisted on a more practical education for his son. "He took me to Jack Goodwin's horse shoeing shop to learn the trade," Robert recalled. After all, the livery business had supported the Owens family for the past two generations. But Robert rebelled: "I frankly told him that a man who worked all his life with his head down and the wrong end of his body in the air could not succeed, he only knew to stop work when the whistle blew."[56] Charles could have easily overruled his headstrong son—if not for the intervention of Mason. "She told my Father that he could not make a Farmer or a Blacksmith out of a boy who wanted to be a politician, and she was right," Robert recalled.[57] Robert Owens went on to a leading role in the Republican Party of Los Angeles and by 1905 had become one of the richest Black men in America.[58] In more ways than one, his path to prosperity had been laid by his grandmother.

Even as she sent her grandchildren north for their schooling, Mason continued to support Black education in Los Angeles. She did so primarily through regular contributions to the AME Church, which by 1875 was doing double duty as the city's Black schoolhouse.[59] She could take personal satisfaction in the progress of the school. The list of students who passed their examinations in any given year included the names of her friends and allies—the children of John Ballard, Lewis Green, and several of Hannah's grandchildren.[60] Mason's work followed a rich tradition of Black women's educational activism. Black mothers, in particular, viewed education as "nothing less than a sacred, a spiritual duty" for which their familial roles had ideally suited them.[61]

Despite limited resources and the apathy, if not hostility, of communities outside their own, Black students in California made remarkable progress through the 1870s and beyond. Rates of Black literacy surged in postbellum California, while school attendance for Black girls surpassed their white counterparts.[62] Even the Los Angeles press, rarely inclined to credit Black successes, took note. The *Evening Express* praised the "painstaking teacher" of the local Black school as well as her ambitious students. "The recitations of the class in geography would have done credit to any class in any school. They were prompt and correct also in their answers in arithmetic," according to an 1874 report.[63] Results only improved from there. The next year, the *Evening Express* noted that "the class passed a very creditable examination, and the school is steadily increasing in numbers."[64] The next generation of Black Los Angeles was rising to meet the lofty expectations of elders like Mason, who had sacrificed so much for their children's advancement.

. . .

Advances in education paralleled other developments across the city. By the mid-1870s, Los Angeles bore little resemblance to the tumble-down frontier outpost that Mason first encountered two decades earlier. The city now boasted streetlights, banks, a sewage system, asphalt sidewalks, tree-lined streets, and the beginnings of a railroad hub.[65] In addition to horse-drawn carriages, streetcars could now be seen trundling down the road in front of Mason's Spring Street property.[66] A grand, three-story Italianate building known as the Pico House supplanted the grimy old Confederate hangout, the Bella Union, as the premier hotel in Los Angeles.[67] Even the name Calle de los Negros would soon give way. It was rechristened Los Angeles Street, though the alley hadn't yet shed its reputation for vice.[68] While zanjas still crisscrossed the city, pipes carried water directly to many residents. Some homes now featured what would eventually become the emerald symbol of residential opportunity in Southern California: ever-green lawns, no matter the season or how severe the latest drought.[69] The changes had been so rapid that the writer J. Ross Browne "scarcely knew the town" after an absence of just four years.[70]

Paeans to the city's growth doubled as obituaries for its Mexican past. A burgeoning industry of Southern California tourist literature celebrated Los Angeles's "Americanization"—a synonym for progress, prosperity, and most of all, whiteness. With withering condescension, writers bid farewell to many of the characteristics that they associated with the city's Mexican and mestizo heritage. "Crooked, ungraded, unpaved streets; low, lean, ricket, adobe houses, with flat asphaltum roofs, and here and there an indolent native, hugging the inside of a blanket, or burying his head in a gigantic watermelon, were then the most notable features of this quondam Mexican town," one writer remarked of Los Angeles after the Civil War. "But what a wonderful change has come over [the city]," he marveled just a few years later.[71] Brick had supplanted adobe, Protestant churches outnumbered Catholic chapels, and American-born citizens filled the city's streets.[72] Brown was the shade of the past; white the color of the future.[73]

Biddy Mason, however, muddied the monochrome presumptions of Los Angeles's boosters. Here was a successful resident who conformed to elements of this narrative—she was Protestant, English-speaking, and financially successful—without the crucial feature: whiteness. What to do with such a troublesome contradiction to the color-coded story of Los Angeles's development?

Boosters formulated a simple solution: ignore her. The proliferating tourism literature of this era, which would fundamentally shape the mythos of the city to the present, rarely commented on the city's prosperous African American community. Indeed, Black Angelenos were largely invisible to the city's most vocal promoters. Even Harris Newmark—an assiduous, some might say Proustian, chronicler of Los Angeles's early history—misremembered key details about his Black neighbors. He correctly identified the Mason-Owens descendants as "among the most prosperous negroes in America" but conflated the accomplishments of Biddy Mason and Winnie Owens.[74] Like Newmark, a visiting Austrian archduke briefly noted the unprecedented successes of some Black Angelenos. He had been told that "several . . . are very rich," though the otherwise inquisitive noblemen didn't bother to investigate further. He concluded with a dismissive shrug: "They are not much in evidence."[75] His indifference notwithstanding, the mere mention of Black Angelenos distinguishes the archduke's account from the vast majority of travel accounts of the era.

African Americans refused to be written out of the history of their city—a city they themselves continued to shape. The Owens family, for instance, helped lead a successful petition campaign to redevelop and widen San Pedro Street, where they owned substantial amounts of property.[76] Jeremiah Redding, a trustee of the AME Church and business associate of Charles Owens, opened the Barnum Restaurant and Chop House in 1875, one of the few fine dining establishments in Los Angeles.[77] And businesswoman Caroline Burton operated an independent hairdressing salon for some two decades beginning around 1870. Meanwhile, Black men wielded their hard-won Fifteenth Amendment rights to build a substantial Republican voting bloc.[78] Although most Black Angelenos still worked as laborers and domestics, several had accumulated significant amounts of property that soared in value as the city expanded.[79]

Biddy Mason's Spring Street homestead, once considered on the outskirts of town, now sat squarely within a rapidly growing commercial district.[80] Mason herself shaped that district by erecting a complex of four wooden commercial buildings on her property, which she rented to local businesses, including a Chinese laundry and a Chinese haberdashery.[81] According to Los Angeles tax assessment records, Mason's net assets approached $4,000 by the mid-1870s, thanks in large part to the improvements that she had made to her land. Her Spring Street property alone cemented her place as the wealthiest African American in the city by a comfortable margin.[82]

Mason made her presence known in other ways as well. Sometime in the 1870s—the precise date is unknown—she sat for a photograph.

That act alone distinguished her. Photographic portraits of Black women from the Reconstruction-era West are exceptionally rare. No comparable image exists for any other African American in Los Angeles during this period, and few from anywhere else across the state.[83] The cost was prohibitive for most Black people at the time, and photographers didn't generally seek out African American subjects on their own. Aside from the expense, there was also time and discomfort to consider. Harris Newmark recalled the "inconvenience, almost tantamount to torture, to which the patron was subjected in sitting out an exposure" in the studio of Valentin Wolfenstein, who operated the Sunbeam Gallery in Los Angeles in the 1870s.[84] It was most likely Wolfenstein who photographed Mason. As a Union veteran of the Civil War and the city's preeminent photographer, Wolfenstein would have been the natural choice for her portrait.[85]

The result was the clearest likeness of Mason that survives, and her only other photograph aside from the Civil War–era group portrait, in which she appears with other members of the Mason-Owens family. (Wolfenstein purchased the Sunbeam Gallery from William Godfrey, the likely photographer of that earlier image, suggesting that Mason had established some sort of relationship with the studio).[86] Like that earlier image, this portrait served as both a family keepsake and as a monument to personal success. Prominent Black women in the East, including Sojourner Truth and Harriet Tubman, had their photographs taken for similar reasons. Perhaps better than any other object, a photograph captured their likeness and signaled their triumph over the degrading anonymity of slavery. For Black women like Truth, Tubman, and Mason, sitting for a photograph was a political act.[87]

Many of Mason's distinguishing characteristics radiate from this portrait: her stature, her dignity, her resilience. She sits upright, emanating the prowess that had carried her across the continent and which drew praise from later commentators.[88] Her posture and bearing defy the years she must have spent stooped low in Southern cotton fields and cramped slave quarters. Her clothing, too, erases the traces of her enslaved past. She wears a dark dress, buttoned up to her neck, where it meets a large satin

Biddy Mason, ca. late 1870s. Miriam Matthews Photograph Collection, UCLA Special Collections.

bow fastened with a square pin of silver or bone. The pin bears a cross, a fitting emblem for a church founder. Her hair, perhaps just beginning to grey, is pulled back in a tight bun behind her head. She is professional, pious, accomplished. Most of all, she is irrepressible. If her eyes betray a trace of sorrow, the lasting impression of the portrait is of a woman unbroken by misfortune and steeled by adversity, who had yet to meet a challenge she couldn't surmount.[89]

. . .

Mason knew from experience that all booms eventually run their course. And when they do, the economic hangover could be severe. From the Panic of 1837 that resulted in her sale to Robert Smith to the depression of the Civil War years, Mason bore deep scars from previous crashes. Perhaps this experience is what led her to do something she previously refused to consider: to sell some of her land. In January 1875 she parted with a strip of her Spring Street property for $1,500 in gold coin. Although she retained a majority of her original homestead, the sale was a dramatic decision for someone who invested divine significance in that land.[90]

It was also an uncannily savvy transaction. Unlettered though she may have been, Mason knew how to read market forces as well as anyone in Los Angeles. When she first bought the land in 1866, Mason had caught the market at its trough. Now, she sold at its apex, just as warning signs from elsewhere in the country signaled that the recent real estate boom teetered on the brink of a bust. $1,500 was a substantial sum, and hopefully enough to help her weather the gathering financial storm.[91]

While the depression hit most parts of the country in 1873, it took until mid-1875 to reach Los Angeles. When it did, the crash struck with crippling force. The first major casualty was the Temple and Workman Bank, one of only two financial institutions in Los Angeles, which collapsed in early 1876. William Workman, until then one of the richest men in Southern California, took his own life several months later.[92] His depositors and creditors didn't fare much better. "Times became dreadfully bad," Harris Newmark wrote. "From greatest prosperity, we dropped to the depths of despair."[93] Years of financial hardship followed, known then as the "Great Depression," until the crash of 1929 usurped the name.

Because calamities generally came to Los Angeles in pairs, a smallpox epidemic erupted that same year and lingered for the next twenty-three months. "One could not go out on the street, at any time of the day or night, without a hearse rushing by with a smallpox corpse in it," one resident recalled.[94] As one of the few nurses in the city, Mason would have formed the advance guard of the city's epidemic response, once again placing her life on the line for the welfare of her neighbors, while Los Angeles withdrew into itself. According to Horace Bell, the "visitations of smallpox, and the breaking of Temple & Workman's bank almost shattered the faith of our people in the future of Los Angeles."[95]

The crash exacted a toll on the rich and poor alike. Hannah's eldest daughter, Ann, was widowed around the same time the depression set in. Like Ellen Owens, Ann had married one of their allies from the historic 1856 freedom suit.[96] But unlike Ellen, she didn't enjoy a happy, prosperous, or even safe marriage to her husband Manuel Pepper. Pepper had spent the proceeding years on a series of drunken sprees, which spawned knife fights, gunfights, and an attempt on his own life.[97] Ann prevented her husband from slitting his throat after one particularly violent episode. In return she endured years of physical abuse. On one occasion Pepper "set fire to his house and tried to burn it over [the] heads" of his wife and children, according to a report.[98] So common were his arrests for battery that the local press made him the butt of savage jokes, referring to domestic abuse as "his favorite pastime."[99] He was imprisoned on multiple occasions, sometimes for months at a time. Pepper died around 1875, likely from the effects of chronic alcohol abuse.[100]

Even the most prosperous Black Angelenos suffered during the depression. Amanda and John Ballard, a man with "a very kind face and a soft voice with a southern drawl," had formed the nucleus of early Black Los Angeles, alongside neighbors like Mason and the Owens family.[101] Ballard was a founding member of the AME Church as well as an ambitious investor in Los Angeles real estate. By 1871 the Ballards had accumulated a portfolio worth more than $1,000. But that same year, Amanda died in childbirth, marking the beginning of a steep reversal for John and his now motherless seven children.[102] When the depression hit, Ballard sold the last of his once sizable real estate holdings, and with a mere $270 in personal property, relocated his family to a homestead in a remote corner of the Santa Monica Mountains, where Biddy and Hannah had been rescued roughly two decades earlier.[103]

Ballard carved out a hardscrabble livelihood for his family, enduring derision, assaults, and even attempted arson by white squatters. "People would cheer and jeer and joke," recalled an acquaintance, but Ballard remained as imperturbable and "as serious as if he were driving up to Abraham Lincoln's front door."[104] The squatters failed to dislodge him. Ballard continued to homestead and to vote into the 1890s. He is now rightly remembered as a pioneer of coastal Southern California. Thanks to the efforts of a small group of activists—including Ballard's descendants, local residents, and historian Patty Colman—the peak overlooking his homestead was officially renamed Ballard Mountain in 2010.[105]

The depression years brought a curious new addition to the Black community of Los Angeles: a white baby. One morning in January 1878, John Hall opened his front door to discover a basket at his feet. Bundled inside was a newborn infant with a note pinned to its clothes "asking Hall to keep the child and raise it," according to local reports.[106] The decision to leave their baby with the Halls was no accident. John Hall was a founding trustee of the AME Church, a substantial landholder, and a respected leader in the community.[107] That Hall's community happened to be African American evidently mattered little to the white birthparents of this fostered child.

As time would show, they chose wisely. Failing to uncover the identity of the child's parents, the Halls took the baby into their home and fittingly named him Moses. "Mr. Hall seems to be very proud of his charge and promises that it shall receive just as good care as it could were it to be reared in the house of Congress," a local paper reported.[108] He was true to his word. Moses Hall would go on to a long and successful career, with a prosperous stint in real estate like his adoptive father before him.[109]

Black institutions, like the people who ran them, struggled to stay afloat during the depression years. At the time, the total Black population in the city numbered fewer than 150, and the burdens of maintaining their community's church fell heavily on just a few households like Mason's. She and her neighbors managed to hold on to the church property through the depression—an impressive feat in a period of panicked liquidations—though they struggled to pay the annual taxes and insurance. Despite the best efforts of its parishioners, the AME Church closed its doors for several years in the late 1870s.[110]

Black Americans' troubles ran deep and wide during those years. Even before the depression hit, the Republican Party's Reconstruction program rested on shaky foundations. A Democratic resurgence, beginning in California as early as 1867, had eroded national support for Black rights. One by one, the former Confederate states were "redeemed"—that is, the Republican leadership was overthrown, often violently. The depression completed the work that white terrorist organizations like the Ku Klux Klan began. By 1876 the federal government withdrew the last US troops from the South as national support for Black rights collapsed. Reconstruction was dead. And so began what historians call the "nadir" of American race relations.[111]

. . .

Although its population continued to grow, Los Angeles had become an increasingly lonely place for Biddy Mason during the panic and in the years thereafter. She had already lost a daughter, her oldest friend in Hannah, and her greatest patron in Robert Owens. Subsequent years would witness the death of the man who first proclaimed her free as well as other members of her extended family.

Benjamin Hayes spent his final years in a struggle to recover the past. Voted from office during the Civil War, he had returned to private practice and to his true passion: the history of Southern California. Perhaps now he could finally complete his long-deferred account of the region. Who else, after all, could possibly realize such a monumental project? Hayes had himself born witness—and indeed helped mold—much of the history he hoped to capture. And what he didn't observe firsthand he could find in his enormous collection of historical documents, one of the finest private archives in the state. The story of Los Angeles, from frontier backwater to emerging metropolis, awaited its bard.

Yet by 1876, after years of careful study and compulsive collecting, that history was still unwritten.[112] Hayes confronted the painful fact that "time has slipped away." When the famous bibliophile and California historian Hubert Howe Bancroft visited the judge's home on a treasure-hunting expedition, Hayes reluctantly agreed to part with his collection. "It is the delivering, stillborn, of my last and largest hope," Hayes said as he handed over his archive of dozens of heavy scrapbooks, made from hollowed-out legislative journals.[113]

Hayes couldn't quit the past, however. His scrapbooks were his "companion-creations," Bancroft wrote. "Every paper, every page, was to him a hundred memories of a hundred breathing realities."[114] Hayes thus enlisted himself as a researcher for Bancroft, as he took up residence in the Hotel Lafayette in Los Angeles. And that's how he left this world: in the process of research in 1877, lovingly pouring over the history that he himself shaped yet could never bring himself to write.[115]

Charles Owens was the next to go. Little is known about his final years, except that he continued to invest in Los Angeles real estate and to enlarge his family's fortune, despite the financial setbacks of the late 1870s. When he died on September 12, 1882, he was likely the wealthiest African American in Los Angeles next to his mother-in-law, Biddy Mason. He left his estate, valued at $4,200, to his widow, Ellen, and his two sons, Robert and Henry.[116] Robert would eventually reach heights of economic prosperity undreamed of by his father and grandfather.

Winnie Owens followed her son the next year. She spent her final days in the same San Pedro Street home in which she had raised her family and once housed the newly emancipated Biddy Mason.[117] When Winnie passed on April 17, 1883, the tributes poured in. No public events, whether "church festivals, firemen's entertainments" or "weddings," were "complete without the cheerful face and kindly voice of Aunt Winnie," read her obituary in the *Los Angeles Herald*. Like Mason, "she was a devout believer in the Christian religion" and a supporter of both the Fort Street Methodist Church and the AME Church. She led a "life of kindness and usefulness," the obituary concluded.[118] Most of her estate passed to her daughter, Martha Tingle, with the remainder going to her grandsons, Robert and Henry.[119]

By the early 1880s, Mason had buried about half of her family and witnessed friends like John Ballard move away. She grew increasingly weary and occasionally forgetful, worn down by personal loss and the inescapable passage of time.[120] At this point she likely began suffering from what doctors would later diagnose as "chronic nephritis," a degenerative kidney disease. Common symptoms include fatigue and painful swelling of the feet and ankles. On especially bad days, even a few steps could be shattering.[121] But she couldn't rest yet. There was still work to do.

15 City-Builder

Los Angeles is a city on the edge—the edge of a continent and, perpetually, the brink of the next disaster.[1] That was as true in Biddy Mason's time as it is today. Mason was now in her upper sixties, having survived a series of natural disasters and catastrophes of various kinds. The Civil War brought a deluge, a drought, and a plague. The Reconstruction era brought financial panic and yet another smallpox epidemic. The latest round of calamity felt more personal though. The disasters of the 1880s came for her home, the Spring Street property she had purchased some twenty years earlier and which she had hoped would sustain her family for generations to come.

Rain lashed Southern California from January to May 1884, converting creeks to rivers, streets to canals, and farms to swamps. The Los Angeles River leapt its banks and, with "ungovernable fury," carved a thick vein of destruction across the city and surrounding areas.[2] As many as fifty houses and "large sections of vineyards and orchards in the low-lying portions of the city were carried away by the mad waters," according to Harris Newmark. Several people were killed.[3] A crowd of some two hundred onlookers pushed their way onto the East Los Angeles bridge to witness the devastation, only to become part of it. The bridge collapsed, bringing with it a tumbling mass of humanity into the roiling waters below.[4]

As with most natural disasters, the poor suffered disproportionately. Many of them lived in cheaply constructed homes along the riverbed. They stood no chance against surging floodwaters. At a time of rising housing costs and limited supply, homeless flood victims had nowhere to go.[5] When the clouds finally parted in the spring of 1884, Angelenos faced a ravaged city and an even more daunting recovery process than they did after the record-breaking deluge of the Civil War.[6]

Mason felt she had to do something. The timber buildings on her Spring Street land may have been sodden, but they were still standing, unlike so many people's homes. Food and supplies were what people needed most, she decided. Mason instructed her local grocery store, located just down the street at Fourth and Spring, to open its doors to those made homeless by the flood. They should be supplied with whatever they needed, free of charge. She would cover their bills herself.[7]

No good deed went unpunished, apparently. On July 31, 1885, a billowing plume of smoke could be seen rising into the night sky above Spring Street. "The fire department responded at once," only to find that two wooden buildings at the site were already "burning like an oil tank," according to the *Los Angeles Times*. An "immense crowd of people" swarmed onto Spring Street to witness "the progress of the fire," as the firemen attempted to battle the blaze. Amid the tumult the chief engineer was "disabled" by an unspecified "painful accident." There was nothing to be done for the two structures at the heart of the fire, except to watch the flames finish their work. Firefighters did manage to save the two adjacent buildings, but they were badly "scorched" and soon deemed beyond repair.[8]

What was once Biddy Mason's homestead was now little more than the skeletal husk of charred timber beams and abandoned structures.

That property had been the repository of most of her wealth as well as the source of much of her income. To maximize the value of her real estate, Mason had leased her four Spring Street buildings to various businesses, while she herself lived in a rented home elsewhere in the city.[9] At the time of the fire her property housed the Los Angeles Stencil Works as well as a carpenter's shop, a painter's studio, a baby carriage shop, a Chinese laundry, and a Chinese haberdashery.[10] They were either destroyed entirely or irreparably damaged. The total losses came to an estimated $3,500, a crippling sum for Mason and the ruined businesses on her land. She had no insurance.[11]

. . .

Mason now faced a painful decision: abandon her homestead or find a way to rebuild. She could have cut her losses, sold the land, and used her remaining funds to buy a more durable home in which to spend the remainder of her days. She was, after all, approaching seventy years old. Retirement must have been a tempting proposition. Instead, she embarked on a major new business enterprise—the most ambitious and, as it turned out, the wisest of her long career.

The embers on her burnt property were still warm when Mason began planning a grand redevelopment project. She cleared away the rubble, hired an architect and a contractor, and on the ashes of the old structures, erected a two-story commercial complex that would become known throughout the city as the Mason Block.[12] Brick was then considered the most fashionable and forward-looking material (not to mention fireproof), so in brick Mason built.[13] She reserved the upper story of her block as private residences. The ground floor she rented to businesses.

As always, Mason kept her loved ones close. After years of living in rented accommodations, she finally moved into a home of her own at 237 S. Spring Street. Her widowed daughter Ellen also relocated to the spacious rooms above Mason's business block.[14] So, too, did Mason's grandsons, Robert and Henry. They would open a livery stable from one of the downstairs storerooms, thus continuing the family business into its third generation, though the enterprising brothers still pursued other ventures on the side.[15] Mason had thus transformed the ashes of her homestead into a residential and business compound for a family dynasty. The heart of Black Los Angeles had been forged in fire.

New businesses began moving into the Mason Block almost immediately, bringing in hundreds of dollars, if not more, in rental income every month.[16] One of her earliest and most celebrated tenants was a candy factory. Two "experienced candy manufactures of San Jose, Cal. are just opening an extensive candy factory and store in the new Mason block, No. 239 South Spring Street, where they are prepared to cater to the family or wholesale trade in everything appertaining to the candy trade," the

Biddy Mason's business block on Spring Street, with commercial space on the ground floor and private apartments above, ca. 1907–1908. Miriam Matthews Photograph Collection, UCLA Special Collections.

Los Angeles Herald reported in January 1886. "These gentlemen come to this city highly endorsed as reliable business men," the *Herald* enthused, "and are perfect in the art of doing up confections, of every description, with nothing but the purest ingredients and a disposition to please their patrons."[17]

The Mason-candy partnership was more than just a business venture; it was a union of genuine affinity. Mason had a sweet tooth. Recall that whenever she visited her local bakery, run by the Mesmer family, she would leave with an armful of "cakes and delicacies." The Mesmers later sold the bakery and opened the United States Hotel, from which they continued to supply their "tender-hearted and sympathetic" friend with a regular stock of "editables [*sic*]."[18] Mason now had a literal factory full of

Mason's grandsons operated a livery stable from her Spring Street property, ca. 1890. Also pictured: the candy factory that rented space from Mason. Miriam Matthews Photograph Collection, UCLA Special Collections.

temptations at her doorstep. The candy business brought with it another one of Mason's great pleasures in life: happy children. We can imagine her dispensing sweets to the delighted children of her neighborhood, or on warm days, opening her upstairs windows to let in the squeals of glee from those gathering around the candy factory below.

The list of businesses at 235–241 S. Spring Street reveals the ways in which Mason joined her commercial interests, her personal interests, and her ethics—what we might call her entrepreneurial credo. While unseemly businesses proliferated at neighboring addresses—Los Angeles hadn't quenched its bottomless thirst for liquor, after all—Mason simply refused to rent to anyone or any trade remotely associated with vice. No tobacco wholesalers or retailers; no breweries, distilleries, or saloons; no

EARLY BLACK LOS ANGELES

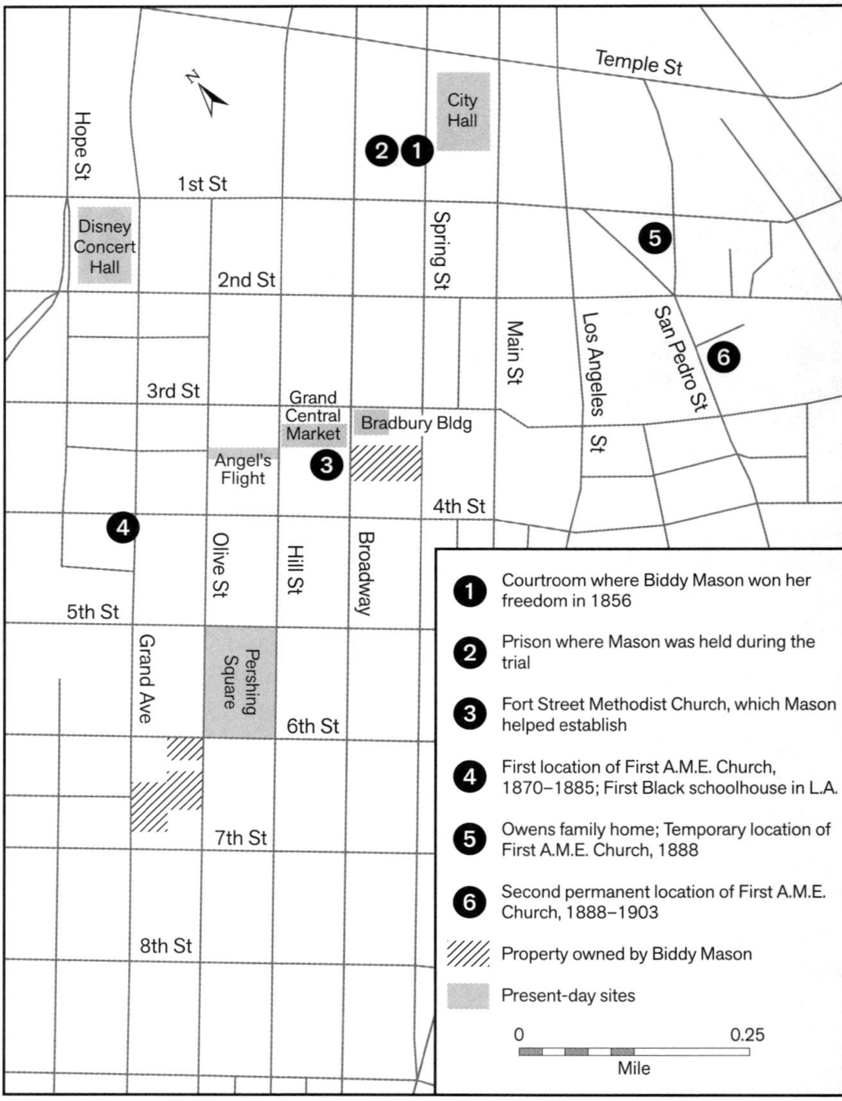

Map by Erin Greb.

gunsmiths or shooting galleries; no cigar shops; and not even a single lawyer or insurance agent could be found in her block.[19]

Instead, the businesses of the Mason Block reflected her lifelong commitments to family, faith, healing—and sweets. In addition to her grandsons' stables and the candy factory, Mason housed a bakery, an artist's studio, and a prosthetic limb retailer. Her Christian faith was represented by a clergyman's office. And her dedication to public health could be seen in the space she provided for an apothecary, a dentist's office, and a homeopathic pharmacy. The Mason Block also contained one of the largest medical practices in the city, with no fewer than six doctors operating out of her property.[20] Although Mason had retired from nursing and midwifery by the late 1880s, she continued to serve the health and welfare of Los Angeles.

Mason's redevelopment project coincided with, and indeed helped precipitate, a fundamental reorientation of the commercial geography of Los Angeles. When she purchased the property in 1866, her section of Spring Street lay at the fringes of the city, containing little more than a cluster of dilapidated timber structures. By redeveloping her land, she helped transform the neighborhood into a bustling, downtown commercial district, with sturdy and stylish Victorian structures rising on every side of her block.[21] Mason's "storerooms . . . became some of the most desirable business properties in the city," according to Joseph Mesmer.[22] By the early twentieth century, Spring Street would be known as the "Wall Street of the West." Biddy Mason's property, from humble homestead to business emporium, was the story of metropolitan Los Angeles in microcosm.

. . .

Biddy Mason built in more ways than one. While simultaneously managing her Spring Street property, she resurrected the first Black church of Los Angeles and ushered it into a new era. She therefore merits the dual distinction of being the church's founder, thanks to her efforts in the late 1860s, as well as its refounder. Those titles, however, came at a price. Her efforts to keep the AME Church afloat would bring Mason into conflict with litigious white neighbors and even her fellow parishioners.

After the church was forced to temporarily close during the "Great Depression" of the 1870s, Mason single-handedly provided the funds to cover the congregation's taxes and insurance. The AME Church reopened its doors in late 1882. Her gift enabled the hiring of Rev. H. L. Harris, who began his tenure with weekly sermons on Friday evenings, according to the *Los Angeles Times*. He also opened a Sunday school, which catered to a mixed-race group of twenty-two Black and white students.[23] The church elected a new slate of trustees—all-male, of course—including Lewis Green (the city's first Black voter) and John Hall (the adoptive father of the white infant, Moses).[24]

And then, just two years after refounding the congregation, Mason closed the church's doors. The decision rattled her fellow parishioners. A group of them published a letter in the *Los Angeles Herald*, which doubled as a plea for funds and an effort to publicly shame Mason. "We have a church in this city on the corner of Fourth and Charity streets," the letter began. "The colored people are not allowed by Mrs. Biddy Mason (colored) to hold divine services in it, because she has paid the taxes and insurance on it for the last two or three years." According to the letter, Mason demanded repayment to the tune of $300. "We have to call upon the citizens of Los Angeles to donate all they can," the letter concluded, "so we can worship God in our dedicated church and not in a dance hall."[25]

The letter may, at first glance, trouble the image of Mason as a selfless philanthropist. That was likely the intention of her aggrieved coreligionists in publishing the plea, at least. How could their patroness bar them from their house of worship and relegate their sacred gatherings to some profane public space? Mason merely mimed the role of gracious benefactor, they seemed to suggest. Upon reading the letter, some may have been tempted to imagine base designs from Mason.

Biddy Mason may have been a cheerful giver, but she wasn't a pushover. And she certainly hadn't risen to the socioeconomic pinnacle of her community by being manipulated. She temporarily closed the church, not to punish her fellow parishioners but to encourage a more equitable division of their collective expenses. The trustees of the AME Church included some of the wealthiest Black men in the city. And yet, until this point, she continued to shoulder the costs for the entirety of the congregation. Mason remained a generous philanthropist, but it was high time that others shared some of the burden.

If Mason took offense to the letter, she didn't let that dampen her giving spirit. She continued to funnel her resources into the congregation in

Ellen Mason Owens Huddleston remarried after the death of her first husband, Charles Owens, and played a key role in the continued growth of the First AME Church of Los Angeles. Miriam Matthews Photograph Collection, UCLA Special Collections.

the aftermath of the dispute. In November 1885 she purchased a second property for the church, a plot of land located in the Bennet Tract (now the historic West Adams neighborhood of Los Angeles). Her grandson, Robert Owens, and her son-in-law, Granville Huddleston, who had recently married the widowed Ellen, were listed alongside Mason as trustees on the property. Church-building remained a family affair.[26]

Yet why purchase a second property when sustaining the first had already proved costly enough? Mason did so because the church's original location was under threat. In early 1886 a white Angeleno named Lucy Gillmore sued most of the members of the Mason-Owens family. Her lawyer claimed that Gillmore "for a long time hitherto has been, and is now in the possession of that certain lot" on Fourth and Charity—that is, the property on which the AME Church stood. Gillmore named as defendants Mason's two grandsons, her daughter Ellen, and Ellen's husband,

Granville Huddleston, as well as several other Black parishioners. Because some of those defendants, including John Ballard, no longer lived in Los Angeles and never received notice of the lawsuit, they weren't able to contest Gillmore's claims. The Mason-Owens family was on its own. They appeared in the superior court of Los Angeles in February, only to concede that "they sold to the African M.E. Church of Los Angeles City all right title or interest that they ever had." In other words, it wasn't their case to contest.[27]

Mason's long-serving lawyer, Christopher North Wilson, attempted to craft a case nonetheless. He argued that Gillmore "does not state facts sufficient" to justify her claim on the property. Indeed, there is no surviving document in the case file to prove that Gillmore had legal title to that land, although contemporary newspaper reports suggest that she was gifted the property by Judge Anson Brunson, who had himself purchased it from the AME trustees in 1885.[28] Curiously, Brunson was the judge who now presided over Gillmore's lawsuit. He found that the defense, having no identifiable *defendants*, lacked a case. Brunson ruled in favor of Gillmore in May 1886. The first Black church in Southern California now belonged to a white litigant. She probably demolished the building shortly thereafter.[29]

If anyone knew how to handle setbacks, it was Mason and her family. Thanks again to their efforts, the church moved onward and eventually upward. The parishioners opted not to erect a new church building on the plot that Mason had recently purchased for them, perhaps due to a lack of funds.[30] Instead, they found other accommodations. By 1888, Ellen and her husband, Granville Huddleston, had moved back to San Pedro Street, along with a special guest: a minister named Jordan Allen. He preached from Ellen's parlor at 31 San Pedro Street. The first Black church of Los Angeles had come full circle. The church began in one home of the Mason-Owens family; and now it reemerged in another.[31]

Ellen's home-cum-chapel, however, was only a temporary solution. The congregation again turned to Mason, by now a veteran church-builder with the scars to prove it, in search of a permanent home. Reprising her role from two decades earlier, she coordinated fundraising efforts to secure a property for the congregation.[32] They found one for $7,000 on Old Second Street (later renamed Azusa Street) and San Pedro, just down the road from Ellen's home.[33] By September 1888 the cornerstone of the new church had been laid, and one month later Rev. Allen delivered the dedi-

The members of the First African Methodist Church of Los Angeles after relocating from Ellen's parlor to this substantial house of worship on Azusa Street, ca. 1900, Miriam Matthews Photograph Collection, UCLA Special Collections.

catory sermon in the new building.[34] By the turn of the new decade, the AME Church had a membership of 121.[35]

Its numbers climbed steadily, often exponentially, from there. Never again would the church struggle to find space to worship or souls to fill its pews. Despite some frictions with their brethren over their forty-year stewardship of First AME, Mason and her family had ensured a lasting future for what would become one of the largest, most powerful Black churches in the nation.[36]

. . .

Mason had developed a distaste for courtrooms and nearly everything that came with them. "I thought the courts that were to keep peace made as much trouble as anybody," she concluded in 1887.[37] By this point she had participated in several bruising legal battles, including the one that stripped First AME of its land. Of course, she had won her freedom through the district court of Los Angeles some thirty years earlier. Even so, the experience didn't exactly endear her to the legal system. Her lawyer had abandoned her case mid-trial; she was thrown into the county jail; and her children were nearly kidnapped and carried to Texas. With the death of Judge Benjamin Hayes in 1877, there were few left in Los Angeles's sprawling court system she could truly trust.

Mason's wealth and her extensive business operations—not to mention the immutable liabilities of her race and gender—had made her a target. In January 1886 a courier knocked on her door with a court summons. She had been served.[38] Mason probably turned to her two most trusted counselors, her daughter Ellen and grandson Robert, in search of a plan. She summoned her lawyer, Christopher North Wilson, an amateur beekeeper and successful attorney with an affinity for underrepresented clients. He was known to take cases that other lawyers wouldn't—namely those of Native tribes and Chinese immigrants, which earned him the nickname "Chinese" Wilson. Wilson represented the Mason-Owens family in the lawsuit over the AME Church property, and he would continue to serve as Biddy's most trusted legal adviser for years to come.[39]

The case against Mason in this instance was seemingly straightforward. She had hired a man named David Mulrein to pave the sidewalk in front of her Spring Street property. Mulrein claimed he was never paid for the work. Mason had apparently violated the contract, for which Mulrein claimed fifty dollars in damages.[40]

The stakes of the case may seem trivial, especially compared with Mason's 1856 court appearance, which resulted in the largest legal emancipation in California history. While fifty dollars amounted to a significant payday for Mulrein, it was an inconsequential sum for one of the city's richest women. Perhaps she should just pay the man and be done with it. But Mason wasn't thinking about her pocketbook; she was worried about her reputation. She had made a name for herself as a businesswomen and philanthropist of scrupulous integrity, a reputation upon which her growing commercial empire depended. She hadn't battled decades of prejudice and dispelled innumerable stereotypes only to concede now.

Mason walked into court on February 17, 1886, to face Mulrein and a jury of eight. Unlike her previous courtroom appearance three decades earlier, she could now testify in her own defense. She took the stand, anxious to vindicate her character. Unfortunately, none of her responses were logged in the court records. Based on the surviving transcriptions of her lawyer's arguments, it appears Wilson prosecuted a vigorous case in her defense. He argued that the contract was obtained by fraud, perhaps by exploiting Mason's illiteracy. Another worker, it seems, already had a contract to lay the pavement in front of her property before Mulrein entered the picture. Robert Owens, who often acted as his grandmother's agent, was sworn in to clarify the nature of these transactions.[41]

The jury adjourned to deliberate. Was Mason right? Had Mulrein exploited her lack of literacy to force a contract on her, even though she had already paid someone else for the same job? Or was Mulrein right? Had Mason, the wealthy owner of a new business block, stiffed one of her workers for as little as fifty dollars? If that was the case, could anyone trust her in future dealings?

It took the jurors all of ten minutes to settle those questions and reach a verdict: "We the jury in the above entitled action find for the defendant." Mason had carried the day with her standing intact.[42]

The next year she was back in court—this time as a key witness in a sensational libel suit that consumed entire broadsheets in the Los Angeles press. Major Horace Bell, the hot-blooded Unionist, had settled most of his feuds from the Civil War era. But he'd made plenty of new enemies since then. He skewered scores of political opponents in his "prickly and dreaded little paper," *The Porcupine*, among other writings.[43] "Excepting the mayor and one or two allies," he wrote in a typical barb, "the city government of Los Angeles was a corrupt, drunken, lawless, vagabond crowd."[44] His enemies exacted their revenge with a scurrilous pamphlet, published in 1886, which among other alleged crimes accused Bell of such "violent" domestic abuse that his wife had to be "committed to the Stockton Insane Asylum" in 1870.[45]

That's where Mason came in. She and her daughter Harriet had served as nurses in the Bell household during the time in question, at which point Mrs. Bell was suffering from the aftereffects of a particularly difficult childbirth. Mrs. Bell was eventually sent to Northern California to recover. If anyone knew the reasoning behind her relocation—whether from domestic abuse or some other cause—it would have been her nurses. Confident that Mason would vindicate him, Bell sued the pamphleteers for libel. The court called Mason to testify.[46]

The courtroom was packed with curious onlookers when Mason entered on June 21, 1887. She took the stand and Bell's attorney approached.

"A pin might have been heard to drop in the room while waiting for her answers," according to the *Los Angeles Times*.[47] The transcript of her testimony is the longest surviving document in Mason's own words (or at least her words as mediated through a courtroom reporter).

"I know Maj. Horace Bell and his wife," Mason began. "I went there as a midwife" in 1870 for "about ten days." Mrs. Bell had been "very sick at one time" with what Mason identified as "some fever," though she "was not out of her mind." Mason claimed to have never seen "any straight jacket put on" Mrs. Bell. In fact, not much was out of the ordinary, aside from the pain and illness brought on by an especially difficult delivery. Then Mason gave the crucial testimony: "Maj. Bell treated his wife very well all the time that I was there." Not content to let the matter rest, the defense wanted further exculpatory details to paint the prosecution as slanderous and therefore clinch the libel suit for Bell.

That's when Mason became decidedly less cooperative. "She would sit still without answering for some time, and it seemed almost impossible to get anything out of her," the *Los Angeles Times* reported. Mason ducked and weaved, blaming her "poor" memory for the vagueness in her responses. "I can't tell it the way I want to," she insisted. "It is better to leave it with God." When later pressed in cross-examination, she again dodged. "Of course I did not want to testify—an old woman like me," she proclaimed.[48]

It might be tempting to chalk up Mason's testimony to the muddled misremembrances of a forgetful witness, attempting to recollect events nearly two decades past. That's how the *Los Angeles Times* characterized her—as "a most unwilling witness," overwhelmed by the onslaught of questions from both the prosecution and the defense. She comes across as an object of pity, if not annoyance, in this telling.

But there's another way to view Mason's testimony. Rather than an episode of elderly befuddlement, her testimony can be seen as a master class in dissemblance from someone long practiced in the art and too shrewd to be drawn into open conflict with powerful white patrons.[49] The libel suit had placed Mason in an impossible position. Bell was her former employer and a like-minded Unionist during the Civil War, while the defendants were, in Mason's own words, "friends of mine."[50] One of those friends was her fellow parishioner at the mixed-race Fort Street Methodist Church. Another, G. Wiley Wells, was a courageous defender of Black rights, having prosecuted more than one thousand suspected Klansmen as US attorney for northern Mississippi during Reconstruction.[51] It was Wells who sold Mason the property in the Bennet Tract for the use of the Black church. Mason's evasive answers weren't senselessly obstructionist, as the court reporting might have us believe. They were tactical. She gave just enough information to avoid perjuring herself, incriminating her employer, or impugning the reputation of her friends—a delicate line to tow.

It was a line that tripped other Black women of the era. Before Biddy Mason rose to fame and fortune in Los Angeles, Mary Ellen Pleasant of San Francisco was indisputably the most successful Black businesswoman in California, with at least $30,000 to her name by 1870.[52] But all that changed after a series of ruinous court cases. Those trials exposed the most intimate recesses of her life to public scrutiny and triggered a feeding frenzy in the San Francisco press. Indifferent to evidence, newspapers branded Pleasant a madam, a voodoo queen, a baby-stealer, and even a murderer. Call it media profiteering. Call it yellow journalism. Or call it what it most likely was: the insecurity of those perched atop the racial order, eager to topple a Black woman who had dared to surpass her white neighbors. Pleasant would not be the first prominent Black woman to be impugned, with little substantiation, by the white press. And she would not be the last. She never recovered from the defamation.[53]

And yet Mason somehow managed to avert the savage public glare that often fell on prominent Black women. Her canny court performance deflected the sort of media scrutiny that ultimately consumed Pleasant. Mason may not have liked the law. But she was awfully good at it.

. . .

Biddy Mason had now lived long enough in Los Angeles to witness several economic swings and dips. But never anything like this. Nobody had. What became known simply as "the Boom" began roughly around the time Mason was developing her Spring Street property and fending off David Mulrein's lawsuit. Within a matter of months Southern California had been gripped by a real estate mania with few parallels anywhere in the nation's history. Roughly $100 million in property (equivalent to about $3.4 billion today) changed hands in 1887 alone.[54] Within three years 130,000 settlers had permanently relocated to Southern California, as Los Angeles ballooned in population by 500 percent. Writers ran out of superlatives and metaphors to describe the changes that swept over their city. The only comparable reference point was the California Gold Rush about four decades earlier.[55]

Los Angeles lived in a constant state of frenzy during the boom years. An army of two thousand real estate agents stalked the city's streets, buttonholing any pedestrian within arm's reach and packing would-be customers onto trains bound for the latest subdivision.[56] To trumpet the newest opportunities, realtors staged parades through the city with bands and block-long processions. "Elephants and other animals of jungle and forest, as well as human freaks—the remnants of a stranded circus or two—were gathered into shows and used as magnets," Harris Newmark recalled.[57] Buyers stood in line through the night to be first to bid on a newly advertised piece of property. A plot of land might be bought and sold three times in a single day.[58]

Two factors more than any other drove the mania: transportation and weather. In 1885, Los Angeles gained its second transcontinental railroad line, which broke the decade-long monopoly of the Southern Pacific over California's rail network. A furious rate war followed. The price of a ticket plummeted from $125 to as low as $1 for the fare between Kansas City and Los Angeles.[59] Suddenly transportation from the wintry doldrums of the Midwest to the perennial sunshine of Southern California had come within reach of the common laborer. The city of Pasadena threw its first Tournament of Roses Parade on January 1, 1890, to celebrate and advertise (and perhaps gloat over) the pleasures of relocation. Southern California bloomed while most of the country remained huddled inside.[60]

Pasadena was one of several outlying towns to reap the rewards of the boom. Dozens of new developments—including Claremont, Monrovia, Covina, Whittier, Fullerton, Burbank, Glendale—sprang up during the boom years. The old ranchlands of E.J.C Kewen, Benjamin D. Wilson, and John S. Griffin now hosted some of the stateliest mansions in California. Santa Monica, once a sleepy summer retreat for wealthy Angelenos, grew into a city in its own right.[61] And in Azusa—"a town which had nothing to recommend it save publicity," according to one of the foremost historians of the subject—the price of lots soared.[62]

The boom birthed the now famous advertising industry of Los Angeles. Or perhaps it was the other way around. Chambers of commerce, boards of trade, realty syndicates, and the California Immigrant Union all got into the business of selling Southern California. Writers, often on the payroll of railroad corporations, published reams of firsthand travel accounts to extol the glories of the West.[63] Some of their claims rang true. Others were colorfully outlandish. According to one booster, plants grew so fast in the fertile Southern California soil that "if you want to pick a melon in this country, you have to get on horseback."[64] Much of the mythos of Los Angeles—land of sunshine, city of the future, magnet of opportunity, playground for the rich—is traceable to this moment in time, when fortunes rose like smoke and anything seemed possible.[65]

The difference between sincere booster and unscrupulous shark could be difficult to discern. The latter predominated as the boom wore on. Swindlers, charlatans, and confidence men of all varieties slunk into Los Angeles to prey on the hordes of new migrants. Speculators hawked worthless plots by the hectare. As Harris Newmark wrote, "Land advertised as having 'water privileges' proved to be land *under water* or in dry creeks; land described as possessing scenic attractions consisted of—mountains and chasms!"[66] According to Horace Bell, the speculators of Widneyville attempted to disguise scores of Joshua Trees, a common desert succulent that dotted their bone-dry development. They shipped in cartloads of oranges and impaled the fruits on the spines of the cacti. "Suddenly the desert fruited like the orange grove . . . [as] Easterners stood agape at the Elysian sight," Bell wrote, albeit with his typical penchant for hyperbole.[67] "Did ever such a flock of such luscious goslings so insist on flying into the mouth of the fox," lamented another observer.[68]

At least one Angeleno, however, proved impossible to swindle. Biddy Mason, with her "splendid sense of the financial value of property," refused to be drawn into the maelstrom of speculation.[69] While the rest of the city staked fortunes on dubious futures, Mason invested in what she already had. It was during the boom years that she transformed her Spring Street plot into one of the most lucrative business blocks in the city. The residential and commercial spaces within the Mason Block only became more desirable as the population multiplied and migrants competed over the slim housing stock.[70] Commercial property on Spring Street, in particular, soared in value in the late 1880s. For instance, a two-story building on a sixty-one-foot lot, smaller than Mason's, fetched $87,000 in 1887.[71]

When the inevitable bust came, Mason emerged unscathed. She could look on the vacant lots, abandoned townsites, and now penniless "millionaires of a day" as cautionary tales, the foreseeable casualties of a desire to grow too rich too fast. She, like much of the Black community in the late 1880s, had taken a far more conservative approach. They husbanded rather than gambled their resources.[72] As a result, Mason entered the new decade at the peak of her prosperity, with nearly $40,000 in assessed property.[73] The full value of her assets was undoubtedly even higher than that. Only 160 people in Los Angeles, of a population of more than 50,000, owned as much as she did.[74]

Mason had become far more than just a wealthy property-holder though. She was an exemplar, living proof of the promise of the West, as hundreds and then thousands of African Americans streamed toward Los Angeles in search of a new beginning.

. . .

People of all backgrounds relocated to Los Angeles during the boom years, but few demographics moved with as much urgency or in such volume as African Americans. The Black population of Los Angeles jumped twelvefold between 1880 and 1890, from just over one hundred residents to upwards of twelve hundred. Most of that migration came in the back half of the decade.[75] African Americans now accounted for 2.5 percent of the city's population, up from 0.9 percent a decade earlier. Los Angeles would soon surpass San Francisco as the most populous Black community anywhere in the Far West.[76]

The rise of Black Los Angeles was largely attributable to the collapse of Reconstruction. Stripped of their rights in the South, African Americans voted with their feet and headed West. More than six thousand so-called Exodusters moved to Kansas in the late 1870s.[77] Even more extensive was settlement in Oklahoma, where a total of thirty-two all-Black towns sprung up.[78] Many of the California-bound Black migrants came by way of Texas, just as the apartheid Jim Crow regime descended over the state.[79] Their movements were, in the words of historian Steven Hahn, the "early rumblings" of the Great Migration, a seismic shift in the nation's demography that ultimately witnessed the relocation of 1.5 million African Americans from the former slave states by 1930.[80]

Push factors alone can't account for the rapid growth of Black Los Angeles. The West exerted a strong pull on African Americans. Not least of their considerations was the prospect of good wages. A janitor in Los Angeles, for instance, took home three to four times what a Black agricultural laborer might earn in the South.[81] And whereas most African Americans worked for shares on rented land in the former slave states, they could reasonably aspire to purchase a home of their own in Los Angeles.[82] Some might even dare to dream of attaining wealth. They could read in the local press how "among the negro population some have become more than financially independent." One example stood out among the rest: "Mrs. Biddy Mason."[83]

Mass migration required organization and facilitation. That's where Mason's African Methodist Episcopal Church came in. The church had already distinguished itself as a spiritual home, a political hub, and an educational center. Now it would also serve as an employment agency. In 1887 the church's pastor began recruiting Black Southerners for jobs throughout the city, having "already received numerous applications," according to the *Los Angeles Times*. "He believes that this is a good place for his people, and that they will be good people for this place," the *Times* continued.[84] Other labor recruiters fanned out across Los Angeles to capitalize on the Black tide surging from the South.[85]

Upon arrival, migrants could turn to multiple Black institutions for aid, support, and community. Los Angeles now boasted three Black congregations in addition to the AME Church that Mason cofounded. Aspiring property-owners could seek assistance from the California Land, Loan, and Building Association, founded in the home of Mason's eldest daughter, Ellen, in 1888. The Association lent money to Black Angelenos "to aid them in the matter of securing homes of their own."[86] African Americans also grouped themselves into numerous voluntary organizations, including a temperance order, two literary societies, and a thirty-two-piece brass band.[87] Neighboring Pasadena formed a popular "Colored Athletic Club." None other than Robert Owens, evidently an accomplished sportsman in addition to an entrepreneur, won the hundred-yard dash at the Club's gathering in summer 1890. He took home a diamond-studded shirt as his trophy.[88]

One of the most popular outlets for new arrivals was the local Republican Party, over which Owens held considerable sway. "A big factor in Politics" by his own account, Owens served on several powerful com-

Robert Curry Owens, ca. 1880–90, played a leading role in the Republican Party of Los Angeles, though internal power struggles occasionally brought him into conflict with other Black Angelenos. Miriam Matthews Photograph Collection, UCLA Special Collections.

mittees, dispensed patronage jobs, and represented the party at statewide conventions. He also organized the first "colored Republican club" in Los Angeles.[89] The arrival of hundreds of new Black voters in the late 1880s further strengthened the party operation that Owens had set in motion. By 1890 he was hailed as "a really fine specimen of our colored citizens" by the *Los Angeles Herald*, having fulfilled many of the political ambitions that his grandmother Biddy had nurtured in him.[90]

Such a rapid spike in population generated electoral power, but it also produced frictions, especially within the rough-and-tumble world of ward politics. Owens found himself in the thick of it, as Black Republicans divided along lines of regional origin. Owens headed the California bloc while most of the newcomers formed the Texas faction. Owens and his allies would not allow themselves to be "bossed," as they put it, by any old Johnny-come-lately from the South. In July 1888 the two factions met in a church in an attempt to reconcile their differences—only to enflame them. "Anybody passing within a block of Rev. Brown's chapel would certainly wager that no worshipping of the Deity was going on there," the *Herald* reported.[91]

Owens was back in the trenches a few months later. His grievance this time was a Black lawyer named R.C.O. Benjamin and his weekly newspaper, the *Observer*, which routinely relitigated the spats within the African American wing of the Republican Party. Benjamin pulled no punches. When he rounded on Owens, Owens struck back—literally. Accompanied by several allies, Owens tracked down the offending editor outside the Los Angeles courthouse. They had him outflanked and outnumbered. The first blow struck Benjamin "fair and square" on his nose. Then "Owens swung out his right mauler, which settled with a dull thud on Benjamin's upper lip," according to the *Evening Express*.

Fortunately for the battered editor, a small army of cops—three constables, five deputy sheriffs, and two policemen—rushed to the scene before Owens and his allies could do even more damage. Owens proceeded to the township court, where he offered to pay a "double fine" if he could "be allowed the pleasure of once more interviewing the colored publisher."[92] Owens may have inherited his grandmother's ambition, but certainly not her gentleness or restraint.

. . .

Despite the bad blood between them, Robert Owens and the hundreds of new arrivals from Texas had at least one thing in common: They all followed the trail that Biddy Mason had blazed decades earlier. Owens owed much of his wealth as well as his political opportunities to his grandmother, while scores of migrants found employment through the church she founded and funded. For all of them, Mason modeled how the previously unimaginable could enter the realm of the possible. In the space of thirty-five years she had grown from head of a family, to leader of a community, to standard-bearer for a city.

Mason's impact extended far beyond the Black community. Indeed, that was part of her power—her ability to connect disparate elements of the city in all its size, sprawl, diversity, and history. She bridged eras: from frontier past to metropolitan future. She moved between worlds: South-

Los Angeles from Biddy Mason's Spring Street in the 1890s. Title Insurance and Trust and C.C. Pierce Photography Collection 1860–1960, California Historical Society Collection, USC Digital Library.

ern, Western, enslaved, free, poor, rich. And she transcended color lines: Black, white, Mexican, Indigenous, and Chinese. Everyone, it seemed, saw a little of themselves in this former slave from Georgia. She embodied the dynamism of their ever-changing, ever-growing city. Therein lies one of the pieces to the puzzle of Mason's unprecedented success.

The city she built bore almost no resemblance to the pueblo she first encountered less than four decades earlier. By 1890 most of the zanjas had been filled in, the dirt roads had been paved, and the adobes had been leveled. In their place towering business blocks "sprang up like toadstools" and hundreds of miles of concrete, stone, and asphalt latticed the city.[93] The telephone made its appearance. So too did electricity. Despite the protests of the gas company that electric light "attracted bugs, contributed to blindness and had a bad effect on ladies' complexions," Angelenos were growing increasingly dependent on the technology.[94] They could now be ferried down the bustling commercial district on Spring Street via electric cable cars. Mason's candy factory, bakery, or doctor's office was just a short ride away from most corners of the city.[95] Meanwhile, the unofficial mascot of frontier Los Angeles, the elaborately ornamented *caballero*, was fading into the mists of time. Mason's grandsons closed their Spring Street stables after three generations in the livery business.[96]

Visitors could scarcely comprehend the changes. Rev. James Woods had attempted to organize the first Protestant church in Los Angeles in the mid-1850s, only to flee what he called "this retreat of Satan" and "the city of Demons" within a year.[97] He returned decades later, like Rip Van Winkle awakening to a world transformed. "Then there were not over a dozen wood and brick buildings," he wrote of his time there in the 1850s. "Now grand and massive structures of granite and brick, neat and attractive cottages, stately and beautiful mansions stretch along the streets and spread over the hills and across the plains in architectural beauty in the midst of orange forests and floral loveliness."[98] Los Angeles in 1890 boasted forty churches, fifteen banks, and six daily and twenty weekly newspapers. Four universities were founded during the boom years alone. Whereas most patients once received their care from a small handful of mobile doctors and nurses like Mason, they now had six hospitals to choose from.[99] This was a brave new world for an elderly woman like Mason. But it was a world she continued to shape.

As Los Angeles grew wealthier, however, it also became more unequal. Despite Mason's best efforts, the poorest residents continued to suffer. Predominantly Chinese and Latino, they concentrated in overcrowded neighborhoods known as Sonoratown and Chinatown.[100] Anglos looked upon those districts, with their decaying homes, dirt streets, and open gutters as a "counter-space, everything their city was not"—and what they had so proudly left behind.[101] The *Los Angeles Times* devoted broadsheets to lurid descriptions of Chinatown: "Hell's half acre," "a physical and moral blot," a "plague-spot of corruption," and "where humanity stands on a level that is scarcely human."[102] In 1887 arsonists reduced the east side of Chinatown's Calle de los Negros to ash. The city bulldozed the rest of it and relocated the Chinese residents further north.[103]

The pearl-clutching disgust of the Anglo press belied the ugly truth that these neighborhoods were slums by design. City officials could have invested municipal funds to improve the predominantly Chinese and Latino districts north of the plaza. But they chose not to. Instead, investment flowed to street works and water projects that fed the whiter, more affluent neighborhoods to the south. In a vicious feedback loop, deliberate underdevelopment reinforced stereotypes of Mexican and Chinese residents "as dirty, diseased, backward, and unable to change with changing times."[104] The end result was a self-fashioned tale of two cities, an early chapter in Los Angeles's long history of extreme inequality.

Parts of Black Los Angeles benefited, albeit unintentionally, from the city's inegalitarian development. As a landlord in a predominantly Anglo and particularly desirable southern district, Mason saw her property values increase with each municipal project aimed at Spring Street and its environs. There were social benefits as well. As was the case elsewhere in the West, the presence of a more despised minority put a floor on how far Black residents could fall in the eyes of their white neighbors.[105] Compared to the so-called alien Chinese and impoverished Mexicans, middle-class African Americans conformed to the city's self-image as a place on the make. Mason herself never asked for these benefits—indeed she dedicated her entire life to lessening the distinctions of color and caste—and yet she nevertheless found herself on the privileged side of an increasingly segregated city.

With that privilege came responsibility. According to a near contemporary, Mason's properties became "a refuge for stranded and needy settlers."[106] New arrivals to Los Angeles, regardless of their color or background, routinely sought the assistance of "Grandma Mason." Having come to the city from North Carolina, a white laborer named Meredith P. Snyder was immediately sent by his employer to Mason's home. "The kindly, cheerful greeting of this good soul made me feel almost that I was again at my old home," Snyder recalled. For him, Mason's whole life was a lesson in virtue and a model for how to "strive against selfishness" in "effort for others."[107] Snyder would go on to become one of the most prominent public servants in early twentieth-century Los Angeles, serving as mayor from 1900 to 1904 and again from 1919 to 1921. Mason had provided the introduction to the city he would one day lead.

Mason increasingly took on ambassadorial roles in her twilight years. When the African Methodist Episcopal Church made preparations for its twenty-first annual California Conference in October 1888, Los Angeles presented itself as a fitting venue and Mason an appropriate host. She was one of the few women allowed to play a prominent role—and one of only two women named in the official report—in an event otherwise orchestrated by the senior ministers of the major congregations across the state. On the closing afternoon of the conference, the attendees marched to Mason's Spring Street property for a final celebration. After saying grace and singing "Praise God from whom all blessings flow," attendees sat down to "a most excellent repast."[108] It was only right to conclude the conference where the Black church of Los Angeles had begun: with Biddy Mason.

Mason's popularity, however, was creating problems for her family. For years she had worked a "triple day," consisting of full-time paid employment, another long shift within the household, and a third stint of community activism and public service.[109] As she entered her seventies, her legendary vigor was visibly fading. Her chronic nephritis probably now manifested in extreme fatigue and painful swelling of her hands and feet. Her relentless work regimen had become unsustainable. But try telling that to Biddy Mason. There were still so many who needed her help. According to an early Black Angeleno, "As [Mason] grew more feeble, it became necessary for her grandson to stand at the gate each morning and turn away the line which had formed waiting for her assistance."[110]

. . .

Mason had spent a lifetime in the service of others, but now she needed help herself. As her condition deteriorated, she called on the care of a doctor. Her name was Elizabeth Follansbee. The first female professor in a medical school in California as well as the first woman admitted to the Los Angeles County Medical Association, Follansbee was, like Mason before her, a barrier-breaker. Mason could have, of course, called on the services of any one of the six male doctors who operated their large practice just one floor below in the Mason Block. But she sought a kindred spirit. One pioneering health worker required the expertise of another.[111]

Mason, now seventy-two years old, was fading as Christmas approached in 1890. There was still time, though, to recall some of the words that had guided her through life's long journey. Because it was Advent season, her family and her fellow parishioners likely turned to the book of Isaiah. Chapter 9, verse 2 of that book holds a favorite Christmastime passage, traditionally read in anticipation of the birth of Christ: "The people that walked in darkness have seen a great light: they that dwell in the land of the shadow of death, upon them hath the light shined."[112]

For Mason, drifting toward her final rest, those words would have had a special resonance. She too had walked in darkness, stumbling onward for three thousand miles and through nearly four decades in slavery. She too had finally seen a great light, as she stepped out of the cramped Los Angeles courthouse and into the clear air of Spring Street as a free woman for the first time. And she too had carried that brightness forward to illuminate the lives of those around her.

As her loved ones gathered close beside her in those final weeks, they could see it clearly: Upon Biddy Mason, the light shined.

16 Matriarch

Biddy Mason spent years preparing her final gift. By 1891 she had amassed a fortune in real estate that one of her lawyers estimated at $100,000, making her the nineteenth-century equivalent of a multimillionaire.[1] Although members of her extended family, notably Robert and Winnie Owens, had accrued significant wealth in their lifetimes, none of them had to contemplate the disbursement of such a vast sum. In fact, no African American in Los Angeles—and very few anywhere in the West—ever had. Mason summoned her lawyers and began drafting a document that was considered so rare for a Black woman as to warrant a headline in the *Los Angeles Times*: her last will.[2]

A will was far more than just an itemized list of assets and disbursements. Estate planning, especially for someone as forward-looking as Mason, was "the confrontation of one's mortality, assessment of one's life, and contemplation of one's legacy," in the words of a leading scholar on the subject.[3] Wills are among the oldest documents in existence, dating to the time of the Egyptian Pharaohs. Although generally written in dry legal language, a will is a deeply personal document, a chance to speak beyond the grave to ensure the security of one's family and to articulate values that will transcend one's death.[4]

Freighted with meaning no matter the circumstances, a will had even greater significance for someone like Mason. Historically, African Americans had been the subjects, not the authors, of estate plans. Black people routinely appeared in nineteenth-century wills as property to be distributed, their families shattered with the stroke of a lawyer's pen.[5] Hannah and three of her children, for instance, had been torn from their home and sold to Robert Smith per the conditions of her deceased owner's estate. Members of Mason's family in Georgia almost certainly fell victim to similar arrangements. Mason's will, first drafted in 1888, thus transformed what had been the hacksaw of the Black family into an instrument for its survival.

"In the name of God, Amen." So began Mason's will, thereby proclaiming her Christian faith and binding her heirs to the provisions of the document by an even higher power than the lawyers who signed it. Such invocations of the almighty were common preambles for Christian testators dating back to the Middle Ages. William Shakespeare's will, for instance, began with those same words.[6] The document continued: "I Biddy Mason, of the city and county of Los Angeles, State of California . . . being of sound and disposing mind and memory, and not acting under duress, menace, fraud, or under influence of any person whatsoever, do make, publish and declare this my last Will and Testament, in manner following."[7]

She then laid out the provisions of her will. First she directed "that my body be decently buried with proper regard to my station in life and the condition and circumstances of my estate." Then she instructed her heirs to pay off the remaining mortgage on her property and settle any outstanding debts, drawing on the rental income from the Mason Block. The remainder of the document described and distributed her assets. Most of her wealth was stored in her land along Spring Street and Broadway, which she divided between her daughters, Ellen and Harriet, and her grandsons, Robert and Henry. Not included in her will, though eventually passed down to Robert, was another precious inheritance: a copy of her freedom papers.[8] Mason signed the bottom of her will with an X. It was the last time she would put her mark to anything.[9]

Mason could finally rest in the knowledge that her descendants would be secure for generations to come. By endowing her family line, she had exorcised the most hateful demon of her enslaved past. Since childhood, the specter of family separation had haunted her. The forced journey to

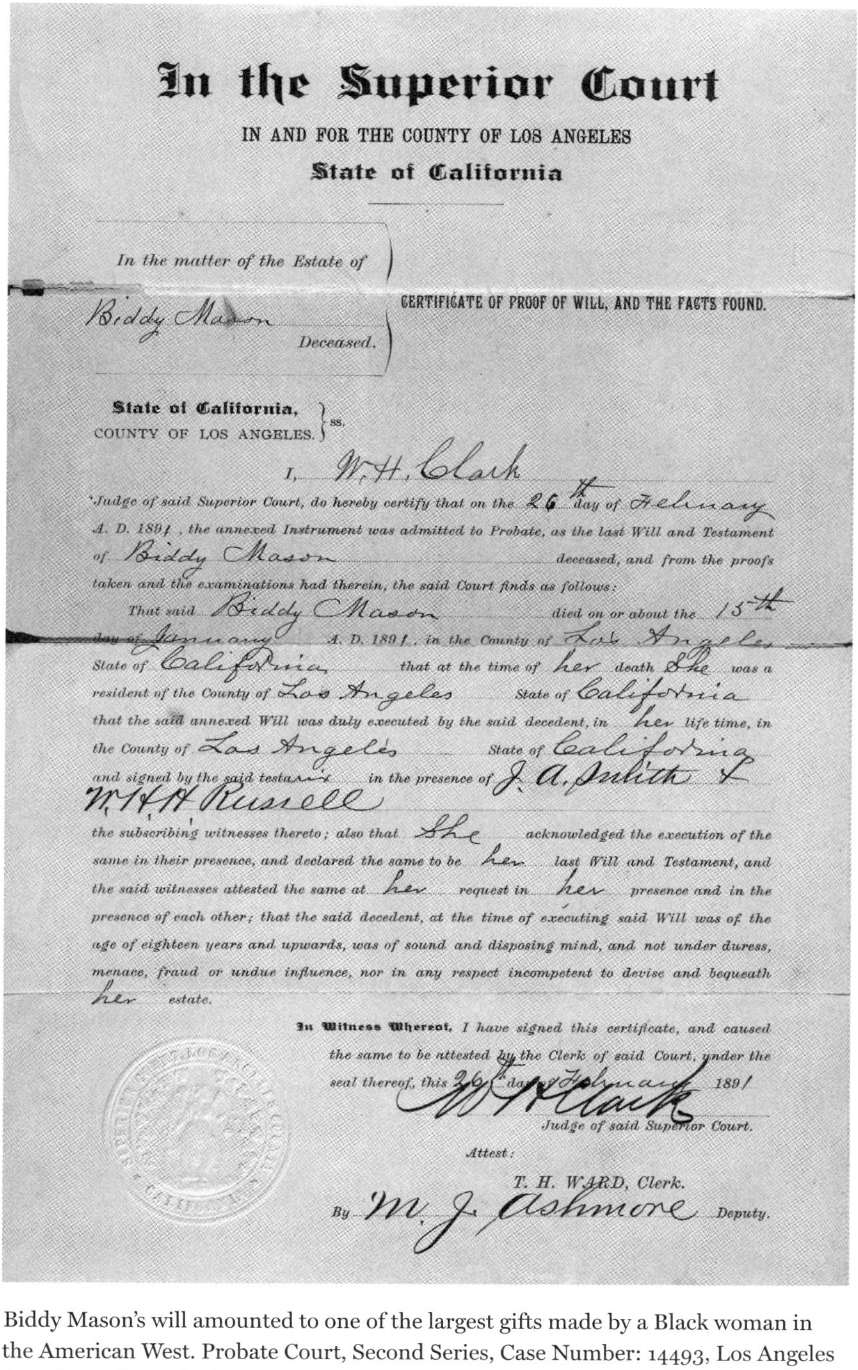

In the Superior Court

IN AND FOR THE COUNTY OF LOS ANGELES

State of California

In the matter of the Estate of

Biddy Mason

Deceased.

CERTIFICATE OF PROOF OF WILL, AND THE FACTS FOUND.

State of California,
COUNTY OF LOS ANGELES. } ss.

I, W. H. Clark

Judge of said Superior Court, do hereby certify that on the 26th *day of* February *A. D. 1891, the annexed Instrument was admitted to Probate, as the last Will and Testament of* Biddy Mason *deceased, and from the proofs taken and the examinations had therein, the said Court finds as follows:*

That said Biddy Mason *died on or about the* 15th *day of* January *A. D. 1891, in the County of* Los Angeles *State of* California *that at the time of* her *death* She *was a resident of the County of* Los Angeles *State of* California *that the said annexed Will was duly executed by the said decedent, in* her *life time, in the County of* Los Angeles *State of* California *and signed by the said testatrix in the presence of* J. A. Smith & W. H. H. Russell *the subscribing witnesses thereto; also that* She *acknowledged the execution of the same in their presence, and declared the same to be* her *last Will and Testament, and the said witnesses attested the same at* her *request in* her *presence and in the presence of each other; that the said decedent, at the time of executing said Will was of the age of eighteen years and upwards, was of sound and disposing mind, and not under duress, menace, fraud or undue influence, nor in any respect incompetent to devise and bequeath* her *estate.*

In Witness Whereof, *I have signed this certificate, and caused the same to be attested by the Clerk of said Court, under the seal thereof, this* 26th *day of* February *1891*

W. H. Clark

Judge of said Superior Court.

Attest:

T. H. WARD, Clerk.

By M. J. Ashmore *Deputy.*

Biddy Mason's will amounted to one of the largest gifts made by a Black woman in the American West. Probate Court, Second Series, Case Number: 14493, Los Angeles Area Court Records, Huntington Library, San Marino, California.

Mississippi, the overland march to Utah, the freedom trial in Los Angeles, the scramble to find her footing in a hostile city—each chapter of Mason's odyssey was a battle to preserve her family. Her will was her final triumph.

Biddy Mason died at her Spring Street home on January 15, 1891, just four days shy of the thirty-fifth anniversary of her emancipation.

. . .

On Sunday, January 18 at 2 p.m., a "large concourse of people" gathered on Broadway outside the mixed-race Methodist Church. They were there to pay their final respects to a woman who had done so much for so many. Biddy Mason had been a charter member of the church and remained a pillar of that congregation for decades, though her influence extended far beyond any one community of faith. The multiracial congregation who grieved Mason in death reflected the diversity and breadth of her mission in life.[10] Fittingly, the church stood directly across the street from a large property that Mason had willed to her descendants. After most of the mourners made their way home, Mason was interred in the family plot in Evergreen Cemetery in East Los Angeles.[11]

Although not large enough to host the funeral, the African Methodist Episcopal Church probably held an additional service in Mason's honor. This was a hallowed moment for the city's Black community. Many of them had survived enslavement, a regime that discarded Black life without ceremony. The relentless rhythms of plantation labor afforded them little time to properly mourn the passing of loved ones. And even if they managed to establish family burial grounds, they could be torn from those sacred sites at a moment's notice through sale or forced migration. It should be little wonder why Mason's family spent $571 on her funeral expenses, a princely sum at the time, and several hundred more on the upkeep on their family plot in Evergreen Cemetery.[12] This was no extravagance; it was a declaration: Black life is precious.[13]

The tributes to Mason poured in immediately after her death and continued for generations to come. The decades that she spent in Los Angeles "have been filled with good works," read her obituary in the *Los Angeles Times*, "and we are sure she has been welcomed into the better land with the plaudit 'well done.'"[14] The *Los Angeles Evening Express* remembered her as a "good old soul."[15] In the years to come, she would be eulogized by businessmen, politicians, journalists, historians, civil rights pioneers, and masses of ordinary people too numerous to mention.[16] "The name of Biddy Mason is reverenced in the City of Los Angeles where her kindness to the poor is fresh in the minds of the public," wrote Delilah Beasley in her pathbreaking book *Negro Trail Blazers*, published in 1919.[17] When conducting doctoral research in Los Angeles in the 1930s, the sociologist J. Max Bond discovered that Mason's "philanthropic endeavors are still referred to by old citizens."[18]

One of the loveliest tributes to Mason was rendered in glass. When First AME erected a new house of worship, a grand neogothic chapel at Eighth and Towne Streets, it was only right that Mason should have a place of honor within the church. After all, no one had done more for that congregation, dating back to the antebellum era. In 1904 the church commissioned a stained-glass window of its founding mother and filled its pews with "many who had known Biddy Mason" for a special service in her memory. Mason's portrait was placed on a draped easel at the front of the congregation, while Harriet installed the window of her mother.[19]

Then a distinguished lineup of speakers paid tribute to Mason's many virtues. In its coverage of the service, the *Los Angeles Times* reckoned that Mason had been "the richest colored woman west of the Mississippi Valley," though few speakers fixated on her wealth. Instead, the focus was on her essential, unshakable goodness. In a sign of Mason's far-reaching influence, Los Angeles mayor Meredith Snyder kicked off the commemorations. Snyder had met Mason when he first arrived in Los Angeles as a common laborer roughly a quarter-century earlier. She left an enduring imprint on the future mayor. As Snyder recited the "lessons" learned from Mason's lifetime of philanthropy, he elicited shouts of "Amen!" and "Yes, indeed, Brother Mayor" from the teary-eyed congregation. "Her life," he proclaimed, "was an effort for others."[20]

Subsequent speakers added luster to the verbal monument the mayor had begun. "Pioneers all praise her life of good deeds, raising the fallen and helping her race by practical aid and sterling example," recalled one eulogist. Toward the end of the service, Rev. Peter Green, "a presiding elder in the [Black] church as far back as anyone can remember," rose to speak. "Bent with the weight of years" and "with tears streaming down his face," Green "detailed the struggles of the early days, and the love of Biddy Mason for the church of Christ, not only her own denomination, but the great body of those who served the Lord," the *Los Angeles Times* reported. The "white haired patriarch" bowed in homage to the church's founding matriarch.[21]

. . .

There would be no stained-glass windows or glowing tributes to Mason's former enslaver, Robert Smith. As mourners in Los Angeles lined up to honor the woman he once owned, an ailing Smith confronted his own mortality and the weight of history from his ranch in Texas.

Trouble had followed Smith east after the 1856 trial that stripped him of his most valuable assets. On the route from California, Smith's trail-hands turned on their boss. They had planned to rob his family of their livestock and leave the Smiths for dead. Robert, however, caught wind of the plan before it could be put into action and forced roughly a dozen men from his wagon company. The family continued on to Texas, where Smith established a ranch outside San Antonio. Although he managed to acquire a few enslaved people to help work his land, Smith never regained such a considerable store of human property as he once controlled in California. Biddy Mason's wealth made her former owner look like a dirt farmer in comparison.[22]

Smith's sons inherited his commitment to slavery and at least some of his fierce restlessness. All four fought for the Confederacy, while one of them, Willy "Seco" Smith, would become a minor frontier legend. Seco claimed to have killed a Comanche chief, skinned him, and made saddle strings from his hide.[23] There seems to have been little affection between father and sons. One of Smith's grandchildren recalled that his father "always talked about his sweet mother [Rebecca], but he never did say anything about his father [Robert]. We never did know why."[24]

Smith's later years were marked by loneliness and often soaked in liquor. His alcohol abuse drove away his wife Rebecca for a period of years, though she returned to him as his health declined. Smith died in Atascosa County, Texas, while visiting his daughter. Rebecca requested that he be buried in his Mormon temple robes, which she had carried from California and kept boxed up in Texas for the past three and a half decades. That Smith had long since been cut off from the LDS Church apparently didn't trouble Rebecca.[25] He was laid to rest in October 1891, just nine months after the passing of Biddy Mason, who, in her thirty-five years of freedom, had eclipsed her former owner in every conceivable way.[26]

. . .

Mason's Spring Street homestead and the adjacent property on Broadway continued to rise in value in the years after her death. Most of the land passed first to Ellen and Harriet, per the terms of their mother's will. Robert Owens managed the tenants of the Mason Block for both of them. A dispute over Robert's custodianship of the properties in the 1890s, however, drew the family into court and the headlines of the Los Angeles press. It was hard to avoid scrutiny, after all, as the descendants of Biddy Mason. Few articles failed to mention Mason's philanthropy, as if to shame her descendants, whose feud had become "a matter of public knowledge to many Angelenos," according to the *Los Angeles Times*.[27]

The family came to a resolution in 1900, clearing the way for the next phase in their historic rise.[28] By this point their Spring Street property alone was worth an estimated $200,000 to $250,000. But that estimate didn't fully account for the immense value of the land itself, which sat squarely within Los Angeles's most lucrative commercial district, surrounded by some of the premier buildings in Southern California. Their neighbors included the new million-dollar Hellman Block, the twelve-story headquarters of the Southern California Bank, as well as the Angelus Hotel, one of the finest in the state.[29]

Like his grandmother before him, Robert had an eye for opportunity. In 1905 he laid out his vision for the land. He planned to pull down the old two-story brick building and erect a six-story block in its place. The top five floors would be rented to businesses, according to Robert. The ground floor, though, was to be reserved for something special: the Biddy Mason Memorial Institute. Honoring Mason's love of children, the charity would support Black education in Los Angeles. As one of the leading patrons of Booker T. Washington's Tuskegee Institute, Robert hoped to eventually establish its analogue on the West Coast. It was to be a fitting tribute to Mason "on the basis of whose frugality and keen business acumen have been founded the fortunes of her descendants," according to the *Los Angeles Times*.[30]

The Biddy Mason Memorial Institute never came to be—at least not in the form that Owens had originally envisioned.[31] His Spring Street redevelopment project called for an outlay of $250,000, a staggering sum, even for someone of his means. Harriet, however, did successfully establish a memorial to Mason. In 1913 she endowed a college scholarship, known as the Biddy Mason Memorial Scholarship Fund, "to keep alive the memory of her mother."[32] Meanwhile, Owens continued drawing up plans for the Mason Block, as the property grew from six to eight to ten stories in his mind's eye.[33] His ambition wouldn't rest.

Owens directed most of his time and assets toward other initiatives. Real estate, politics, philanthropy, activism—there were few ventures in Black Los Angeles that eluded him. The *Colored American Magazine* hailed Owens in 1905 as "the most conspicuous colored man in this city or on the coast."[34] He met with President Teddy Roosevelt, drew praise from W.E.B. DuBois, dined with the Los Angeles mayor, and hosted Booker T. Washington on several occasions. Washington, perhaps the most influential African American anywhere in the country, referred to Owens as his "Western man."[35] Still, Robert attempted to keep a low profile among some of his neighbors. As one journalist noted, Owens "keeps secret, that he, a negro, is landlord to white tenants."[36] Even the richest Black Angeleno had to tow the color line.

Owens continued to build on his family's extensive real estate holdings, purchasing (and inheriting) new properties at a rapid clip. His brother Henry died prematurely in 1894, followed by his aunt Harriet in 1914 and his mother Ellen in 1921. Because Harriet had no children, generations of wealth became concentrated in his branch of the family tree. His real estate portfolio included a grand home at Tenth and Albany, the Waldorf Hotel at Fourth and Ruth, a large estate at Figueroa and Twenty-Third, and several other properties dotted throughout the city.[37] The crown jewel in his portfolio, the Mason Block, made him the "wealthiest negro west of Chicago," according to the *Colored American Magazine*.[38] Several years later, another newspaper dubbed him the "richest negro in America, if not the world."[39] Even if others might have disputed that title, there was no gainsaying the fact that the Mason-Owens family had achieved in just a few generations something beyond all imagining for their enslaved ancestors.[40]

. . .

The most enduring tributes to Biddy Mason weren't built in brick, or carved in stone, or rendered in glass. They populated the city in flesh and blood. Thousands of Black migrants moved west in the years after Mason's death, seeking a life that she, more than any other single person, had made possible. Black Los Angeles itself was a living monument to Mason's pathbreaking influence.

Conditions for Black people in the South had deteriorated further since the last major wave of westward migration in the late 1880s. Mason's death coincided with the dawn of the Jim Crow era. Across the South, African Americans were stripped of the right to vote and in many cases the right to life. By 1900 lynch mobs had murdered more than twenty-five hundred Black people, mostly young men. When anti-lynching activist Ida B. Wells published an editorial decrying the violence, vigilantes destroyed her printing press and drove her from her home state of Tennessee. Even African Americans who escaped the mob were trapped in inescapable cycles of landless poverty or else arrested on trumped-up charges and pressed into backbreaking convict labor.[41]

Amid dwindling opportunities and rising violence in the South, thousands of African Americans sought refuge in the West. The Black population of Los Angeles rocketed from just 100 in 1880 to more than 2,000 in 1900 to 15,500 in 1920 to nearly 40,000 a decade later.[42] "We always had the impression that going to California was like going to heaven," one Black Southerner recalled.[43] "God's country," others called it.[44] Even if they hadn't heard of Biddy Mason or Robert Owens by name, prospective migrants nonetheless knew that Los Angeles produced success stories without parallel in the Jim Crow South.

The Black press of Los Angeles made sure of it. In touting the opportunities of their hometown, African American journalists often out-boosted the boosters of the city's boom years, while giving it their own spin. Much of their writing was animated by a central thesis: Los Angeles was the anti-South, a haven for aspirational African Americans. "Southern California is more adapted for the colored man than any other part of the United States," enthused the *Colored American Magazine*. The Mason-Owens properties at the heart of Spring Street, "the central thoroughfare of Los Angeles," were landmarks to the opportunities that Los Angeles offered.[45]

Black Angelenos, and Biddy Mason's descendants in particular, had become so conspicuous in their success that they drew favorable attention from the white press as well. In February 1909, on the one-hundredth anniversary of Abraham Lincoln's birth, the *Los Angeles Times* dedicated a long section of a special issue to the city's African American population. "If the negroes of Los Angeles and Southern California can be taken as examples of the race," the future congressman and famed playwright John S. McGroarty wrote in the introductory article, "it would seem from their own showing of indisputable facts that the 'negro problem' is a thing that has no existence."[46] The articles that followed, written by local Black leaders, laid out a narrative of steady forward progress, with Mason cast in the leading role. In fact, some of the key information on her life story comes from that issue.[47] The *Los Angeles Times* would prove a rare, if imperfect, ally to the city's Black residents in the years to come.[48]

"One never forgets Los Angeles and Pasadena," wrote W.E.B. DuBois in a long article on the charms of the region and the progress of its Black residents in 1913. The civil rights pioneer wasn't known for pollyannish sensibilities, but Southern California brought out the cheerful warrior in him. "These colored people are pushing and energetic... and used to working together," DuBois enthused. Robert Owens featured prominently in the piece. "Of the business life of Los Angeles one may get some idea from... the business block owned by R. C. Owens, the wealthiest colored resident of the city," according to DuBois. In addition to numerous Black businesses, there were "above all, homes—beautiful homes." Black Angelenos "are without doubt the most beautifully housed group of colored people in the United States," DuBois proclaimed. To illustrate the point, he included multiple photos of Mason-Owens properties.[49]

He wasn't wrong about the homes. It was the prospect of homeownership that drew many African Americans to Los Angeles in the first place. The city's major Black publications, the *Eagle* and the *Liberator*, practically overflowed with real estate advertisements. By 1910, Los Angeles boasted the highest rate of Black homeownership of any American city. More than a third of all African Americans in Los Angeles owned their own home, compared to just 2.4 percent in New York City, 11 percent in New Orleans, and 14 percent in Dallas.[50] Like Biddy Mason before them, thousands of Black migrants finally had a place to call their own.

Homeownership was only possible with gainful employment, and that too Los Angeles offered. The city's stratospheric growth generated a constant demand for labor. By the early twentieth century, a professional class

The luxurious interior of one of Robert C. Owens's properties, photographed in 1909, attracted the attention of W.E.B. DuBois, who wrote a rapturous review of his trip to Southern California. Miriam Matthews Photograph Collection, UCLA Special Collections.

of Black ministers, physicians, photographers, architects, police officers, and schoolteachers was emerging.[51] There were, to be sure, numerous barriers to entry in the labor market. Newspaper ads often specified race as a qualification and Black job-seekers were frequently turned away at the door. The jobs available to most migrants were generally unskilled and low-paying. Black men filled blue-collar positions as janitors, porters, waiters, chauffeurs, or in construction. Most Black women worked in the same role that Mason performed when she first arrived a half-century earlier, as domestic laborers.[52] And yet Black Angelenos learned to aspire for more. Such work was a starting point, not the end game. According to historian Douglas Flamming, the city's African Americans formed "a blue-collar bourgeoisie, earning working-class wages but holding middle-class aspirations." Forebears like Mason had showed them the way.[53]

When the First AME Church of Los Angeles erected this neogothic sanctuary at Eighth and Towne in 1903, it was regarded as the grandest Black-owned property in the city. Miriam Matthews Photograph Collection, UCLA Special Collections.

Black migrants came for jobs and homes; they stayed for the institutions and sense of community. By 1910, Los Angeles boasted three Black newspapers, twelve churches, seven fraternal clubs, a literary society, a debating society, and numerous women's organizations. Indeed, it was women who powered the associational life of Black Los Angeles. They ran the Women's Civil League, the Sojourner Truth Industrial Club, and the Women's Day Nursery, a successor to Mason's early efforts to assist working mothers. Mason and Winnie Owens had provided a template for mutual aid, social welfare, and entrepreneurship, which their successors formalized into twenty different women's clubs by 1920.[54]

Few, if any, institutions did more to foster Black Los Angeles than the church that Mason cofounded decades earlier. First AME was a spiritual and social anchor for a migratory people who might otherwise be cast adrift in a city of transplants. In 1903 the congregation moved from its location on Azusa Street to a new site at Eighth and Towne. There, they erected the most magnificent Black-owned building the city had ever seen—a four-story neogothic sanctuary capped by a bell tower and four soaring spires. At the front of the building, a bank of stained-glass windows, including the one featuring Mason, greeted congregants as they entered. Construction costs exceeded $20,000. First AME now had a membership of nine hundred, including many of the wealthiest African Americans in the city. They worshipped to the melodies of a fifty-person choir, accompanied by piano, organ, strings, and bass.[55] Gone were the days of a single working woman bankrolling the church's operating costs.

Some things didn't change, though. First AME continued its mission of social welfare and racial uplift to which Mason and her fellow congregants had devoted themselves since the mid-nineteenth century. Members of First AME could now pursue many of their philanthropic activities through the Los Angeles Forum, which they founded in 1903. In addition to a weekly town hall meeting for the city's Black community, the Forum also offered scholarships, charitable relief, and a venue for mass politics. It was through the Forum that Dr. Ruth Temple, the first professionally credentialed Black female physician in Los Angeles, was able to finance her medical training.[56] Countless others benefited from the philanthropy and community of the Forum in its four decades of operation.

The view from Spring Street in the early twentieth century presents a radically different perspective on African American history in the Jim Crow era. Traditionally, the period is seen as one of relentless decline in Black life, as an apartheid political regime descended across much of the country. But as the South was "redeemed" by white Democrats, Black Americans sought a redemption of a different sort in the West.[57] There they found a city of hope, a place built and sustained by a migrant from even leaner circumstances than their own. She had risen from enslavement to become one of the wealthiest Black entrepreneurs anywhere in the country. If they could replicate even a fraction of Biddy Mason's success, Los Angeles would match the descriptions of its most vigorous boosters. Not all Black Angelenos, of course, would find what they were looking for. And all of them, the rich and the poor alike, discovered that some dark forces were impossible to escape.

. . .

In 1914 the white-hooded knights of the Ku Klux Klan stormed across Southern California. Illuminated by a flaming wooden cross in the hills outside Los Angeles, they staged a mock trial for a condemned Black man. A speedy execution followed. They tied his lifeless body to one of their horses and rode out as a posse, white robes fluttering in the wind. When they reached the lieutenant governor's home, they dumped the Black body on the front porch. Affixed to the corpse was a white flag, with the letters "KKK" etched beneath the image of a skull and crossbones—a warning of the reign of terror to come.

Audiences cheered.

This was the climactic scene to the epic *Birth of a Nation*, filmed in locations across Los Angeles County. The Klansmen in this case may have been actors, but none of what they portrayed was make-believe. They depicted scenes that had been enacted countless times, with vicious regularity, across the Reconstruction-era South. Within a decade of the film's screening, the Klan would register thousands of new members in Southern California as well.[58]

Black Angelenos saw D. W. Griffith's blockbuster film for the terror that it was. Viewed by twenty-five million Americans, the movie did more to shape the memory of the Civil War and Reconstruction than any single historian could. Griffith narrated a sweeping epic in which the white South is laid low by the ravages of war and the caprice of its former slaves. He portrayed African Americans as riotous, barefooted, drunken politicians and the rapists of white women. Only through the interventions of chivalric Klansmen is order finally restored by film's end. In case anyone missed the message, the author of the book upon which the film was based spelled it out: "I believe that Almighty God anointed the white men of the south by their suffering during that time . . . to demonstrate to the world that the white man must and shall be supreme."[59]

Birth of a Nation sparked what historian Quintard Taylor called "the most extensive organized protest ever conducted against a feature film."[60] Black Angelenos led the way. The city's Black press, the Forum of First AME, and the newly chartered Los Angeles chapter of the NAACP staged a lengthy pressure campaign to prevent the film from screening. Although they failed to block *Birth of a Nation* outright, they did successfully pressure Griffith "to cut some of the most vicious attacks against the morals of the Negro people," according to editor Charlotta Bass.[61]

Despite vigorous protest, the Klan leapt from the silver screen into the neighborhoods of Los Angeles. Grand Goblin William S. Coburn organized the first chapters in Los Angeles in 1921, with a downtown office just a few streets north of the Mason Block. Chapters soon popped up in neighboring Santa Monica, Huntington Park, Redondo Beach, Hermosa Beach, Long Beach, and Glendale. By mid-decade, Los Angeles had become the "the epicenter of Klan strength" in California, which ranked eleventh of the forty-eight states, measured by total number of KKK events.[62] In 1922 a mob of more than one hundred Klansmen abducted a Spanish couple accused of bootlegging, which resulted in a deadly shootout with the Inglewood police. A subsequent raid turned up membership lists, featuring the names of thousands of Klansmen across the West, including three thousand in Los Angeles County alone. The Los Angeles chief of police and the LA County sheriff were among those on the list. As the *California Eagle* put it: "In speaking to the police, you are frequently talking to the Klan."[63]

The *Eagle*'s editor, Charlotta Bass, knew the Klan all too well. "From early morning until far into the night," anonymous callers rang Bass at her office with savage, threatening messages. One night, she looked out her office window to discover "eight of the hooded boys" trying to force their way in. She reached into her desk, pulled out a gun, and gestured toward the Klansmen outside. Despite never having handled a gun before, Bass maintained a preternatural calm. The Klansmen, however, dashed from the scene at the sight of an armed Black woman. Bass had been confirmed in her belief that "those gentlemen who cover their heads and faces with sheets and hoods, are cowards of an indiscriminate and blasphemous type."[64]

Black Angelenos brought that same fighting spirit to the battle over housing. Although their homes drew praise from as far as W.E.B. DuBois's editorial office in New York, African Americans in Los Angeles faced some of the same obstacles to property ownership as their counterparts elsewhere in the country. The principal barrier was the restrictive covenant, what one Black Angeleno called "invisible walls of steel."[65]

A restrictive covenant was a legally binding agreement among homeowners in a given neighborhood not to sell to particular ethnic groups. Most often, these covenants excluded African Americans, but restrictions were routinely extended to Mexicans, Asians, and Jews as well. Hence one of the great ironies of Los Angeles's post-emancipation history: a former slave, in a frontier town full of Confederates, could live anywhere she could afford; her wealthy great-grandchildren, in a forward-looking city populated by self-styled progressives, were excluded from most of it. Black Los Angeles became more segregated even as it grew more prosperous.[66]

Yet Black homeowners found ingenious ways to elude restrictions and even to exploit racism to their own advantage. They knew, after all, that "the white people would pay any price to keep the colored folks out of their communities," as one Black entrepreneur put it. Armed with this knowledge, he would buy property through a white friend, then make a point of conspicuously examining his new purchase. "Whenever a white person seemed curious, I would inform him that I was planning to build soon. On the next day the whites would be after me to sell. I would buy the property sometimes for $200 and sell it for $800 or $900."[67] Another entrepreneur bought a piece of land in the Adams Street district. "The next day I filled a wagon full of Negro children and took them out to my property," he explained. "The whites wanted to know what I was doing there. I told them that I was going to build an orphan's home for Negro children." He made a profit of $2,000 from frantic white buyers.[68]

Restrictive covenants nevertheless had a lasting impact on the racial geography of Los Angeles. During Biddy Mason's lifetime the Black community often clustered in certain parts of the city, such as San Pedro Street or around her Spring Street properties. But African Americans could generally be found in every corner of Los Angeles through the nineteenth century.[69] By the 1920s, however, they were effectively excluded from the affluent west side of the city. They therefore moved east, gathering along Central Avenue, the spine of "quite possibly the most ethnically and racially diverse urban area in America," according to historian Douglas Flamming.[70] Central Avenue, also called South Central or simply "the Avenue," housed more than six thousand Black Americans by 1920, alongside large communities of Japanese, Jews, and ethnic Mexicans.[71]

Central Avenue would grow into one of the most vibrant Black communities west of Harlem. Year by year, it expanded upward and stretched southward, through Watts, Willowbrook, Compton, and Carson. Some of the finest Black buildings and largest Black businesses in the West took root on the Avenue. Opened in 1928 and constructed entirely by African American workers, the Hotel Somerville hosted high-end Black visitors who were denied access to less luxurious white-owned hotels. Down the street was the Golden State Mutual Life Insurance Company, which grew into the largest Black business in the state by midcentury. Its headquarters housed two magnificent murals to Black pioneers of California. The image of Biddy Mason still greets visitors as they enter the building on West Adams. The Avenue is also where Charlotta Bass built the *California Eagle* into a leading voice for Black rights and a tireless critic of those who would deny them. Conspicuous, prosperous, proud, resilient—this was Black Los Angeles in the wake of Biddy Mason.[72]

. . .

W.E.B. DuBois may have been intoxicated by the "sensuous beauty" of Los Angeles, but he wasn't blinded to its shortcomings. Even as he celebrated the well-housed residents—Biddy Mason's descendants foremost among them—he blanched at the omnipresent racism in the so-called City of Angels. "Los Angeles is not Paradise, much as the sight of its lilies and roses might lead one at first to believe," he wrote. "The color line is there and sharply drawn. Women have had difficulty in having gloves and shoes fitted at the stores, the hotels do not welcome colored people, the restaurants are not for all that hunger."[73] Much of the city's glimmer was a mirage.

What gave DuBois hope, more so than even the stately homes sprouting across African American neighborhoods, was the spirit of Black Los Angeles. "The black folk are fighters and not followers of the doctrine of surrender," he proclaimed.[74] They challenged Klansmen, foiled restrictive covenants, lobbied city councilors, built businesses, and invested in their collective future. This—the relentless struggle for their community's rights—was as much a part of their inheritance as the properties that their forebears had left them. Black Angelenos belonged to a glorious lineage of fighters, dating back to their city's antebellum roots, when an enslaved woman named Biddy walked into a decaying adobe courtroom and insisted that she, at last, was free.

Epilogue

IN SEARCH OF BIDDY MASON

The story goes something like this. Nearly a century after her death, Biddy Mason "finally receive[d] her due" with a headstone to mark her final resting place in Evergreen Cemetery in Boyle Heights. About three thousand people, led by the city's first Black mayor, Tom Bradley, gathered on Palm Sunday in 1988 for a commemorative service at First AME, the church that Mason herself cofounded. A smaller delegation of church members later decamped for the cemetery to unveil the new tombstone. Under the shade of a magnolia tree, they sang "Amazing Grace" and spoke of Mason's enduring yet neglected legacy. "Our young people need to know about her," Mayor Bradley insisted. The new headstone was a long overdue act of historical restitution. Until then, Mason lay in an unmarked grave.[1]

Most all of that is true. Members of First AME funded the new tombstone and turned out by the thousands to honor their founding mother in March of 1988. Mayor Bradley spoke powerfully of Mason's legacy and the need for remembrance. And Mason's contributions to Los Angeles had indeed gone unrecognized, at least outside of the city's Black community, for far too long.

But one key detail is off: the part about Mason lying in an unmarked grave for nearly one hundred years. The very first provision of Mason's

Members of First AME Church erected a headstone at Biddy Mason's burial site at Evergreen Cemetery in 1988. Photo by author.

last will and testament directed that "my body be decently buried with proper regard to my station in life and the condition and circumstances of my estate."[2] Mason's family honored that provision by spending nearly $1,000 between the expenses of her funeral and the upkeep of their family plot in Evergreen Cemetery.[3] Later sources suggest that they did indeed erect a physical monument on Mason's gravesite. "Out in Evergreen Cemetery there stands a white marble shaft pointing up to heaven," wrote the Black columnist John Fowler in the *California Eagle* in 1937. "Under the shadow of this mute testimony," Fowler continued, lay the remains of Biddy Mason.[4]

What, then, became of this monument? Decay? Removal? Vandalism? And what explains the persistence of the myth that one of Los Angeles's wealthiest, most beloved residents was tossed into an unmarked grave? Despite the generous assistance of Evergreen Cemetery staff and local historians, I've been unable to locate more than a passing reference to the original monument.[5] However magnificent it may have been, nothing remains. In life as in death, mystery clings to Biddy Mason's story.

. . .

Erasures often reveal as much as they obscure. In fact, the monument probably has more to teach us in its absence than it would if it were still standing watch over Mason's gravesite—however unpleasant that lesson may be. Its disappearance is an allegory for the tenuous place of Black women in the history and memory of the American West. The common narrative about Mason's 1988 headstone may have been wrong about her previously unmarked grave, but that misconception speaks to an underlying truth: Even the wealthiest Black women, with tributes carved in stone and endowments to last for generations, struggle for their due.[6]

Compounding the intrinsic challenges of Black history is the problem of place. Los Angeles has long advertised itself as the city of the future, and as such, leaves little room for contemplation of its often-troubled past. The tourist literature that drew migrants westward by the tens of thousands in the late nineteenth century touted the promise of tomorrow, the prospect of a fresh start under perennial sunshine. Few remnants from Biddy Mason's Los Angeles survive. Much of the old urban core has been emptied, leveled, paved over, and redesigned. Unless the homeless are included, the population of downtown Los Angeles is smaller in the twenty-first century than it was at the time of Mason's death.[7]

Historical traces of nonwhite communities are especially scarce. As historian Bill Deverell reminds us, "Los Angeles matured, at least in part, by covering up places, people, and histories that those in power found unsettling."[8] That meant most all ethnic communities were eventually forced from their original downtown locations. And most landmarks to the city's diverse past have been bulldozed.[9] A once flourishing corridor of Black churches that had graced Paloma Street is now a historical graveyard of concrete and asphalt.[10]

Biddy Mason's family attempted to curb this urban amnesia with a lasting tribute to their matriarch. At the turn of the twentieth century, Robert Curry Owens planned to commemorate his grandmother through the real estate that he inherited from her. His grand vision for the family's Spring Street property included a ground floor dedicated exclusively to the Biddy Mason Memorial Institute, intended as a western analogue to Booker T. Washington's charitable work in the East.[11] Yet the Biddy Mason Institute never advanced beyond the planning stage. Funding proved elusive, and the family eventually sold the land. Parking structures now occupy much of Mason's original homestead, which once sat at the heart of the "Wall Street of the West."

That didn't deter Mason's spiritual descendants from pressing forward, decades later, with plans for a permanent memorial. By the early 1970s, First AME had outgrown its neogothic sanctuary on Eighth and Towne Streets. Loathe to leave vacant such a magnificent structure with such a glorious history, local leaders formed the Federation of Black History and Arts. They won support from the Los Angeles mayor and their local congressman, and secured recognition for the church as Historic-Cultural Monument No. 71.[12] They also applied for the National Register of Historic Places. In October 1971 the Federation launched "Dime for Biddy Mason Day" to raise funds to convert the historic church into a multipurpose public space, which would house a museum, a research library, a day care, and a culinary arts department. They called it the Biddy Mason Center. Nearly everything was in place. Then, in July 1972, a fire broke out at the church, sweeping through the proposed Biddy Mason Center and destroying an estimated $220,000 in property. Damaged beyond repair, the church where Martin Luther King Jr. once preached was demolished soon thereafter.[13]

When not otherwise burned or bulldozed, traces of Biddy Mason have been physically removed. The oldest artistic representation of Mason, a splendid 1930s mural by the artist Bernard Zakheim (see chapter 12), is now collecting dust in a Bay Area storage facility, inaccessible to the general public. Along with nine other murals depicting "The History of Medicine in California," Mason's panel once graced the walls of a central building on the University of California–San Francisco's campus. Despite a spirited public protest, all ten murals were removed in 2021 while the building was razed as part of a billion-dollar campus redevelopment project. As of now, there is no plan to ever redisplay the artworks. Perhaps with the right leverage or enough public pressure, Mason's mural will eventually see the light of day.[14]

. . .

Despite the setbacks, the work of remembering Biddy Mason and the roots of Black Los Angeles never ceased. Monuments disappeared, buildings caught fire, artwork has been removed. And yet Mason's spirit still moves among us. We just need to look closely.[15]

Some of the most enduring tributes are rendered in ink, not stone. Delilah Beasley, more than any other single figure, deserves credit for launching the history of the Black West. Like Mason, Beasley began her professional career as a nurse, which gave her access to the libraries of her white patients. There she schooled herself in American history. Her education continued when she relocated from Ohio to Berkeley, California, in 1910. For the next eight-and-a-half years, she scoured the state for sources and recorded oral testimony from an aging generation of Black pioneers, including Mason's daughter Ellen. The end result was her magisterial *Negro Trail Blazers of California* (1919), which introduced a new generation of readers to the life of Biddy Mason, among other Black leaders. *Negro Trail Blazers* remains a landmark in the field.[16]

Los Angeles–based editor Charlotta Bass continued that tradition through the pages of the *California Eagle*, one of the West's preeminent and longest-running Black newspapers. She regularly celebrated the life of Biddy Mason, both in her own words and by publishing the contributions of others, despite chronic harassment from the Ku Klux Klan.[17] Bass would make history in 1952, when she became the first woman as well as the first African American to run for vice president of the United States, appearing on the ticket for the Progressive Party. She is buried several hundred yards from the final resting place of Biddy Mason in Evergreen Cemetery.[18]

Miriam Matthews is rightly regarded as the "dean of Los Angeles black history."[19] The Matthews family moved to Pasadena from Pensacola, Florida, in 1907, part of the wave of westbound Black migrants seeking refuge from the Jim Crow South. In 1927, Miriam graduated from UC Berkeley and soon thereafter became the first African American librarian in the Los Angeles library system. She dedicated much of her time and expertise to the history of the Black West. By the 1980s she had assembled the most extensive collection of archival materials on Black Los Angeles in existence, including numerous documents and photographs related to the life story of Biddy Mason.[20] Everything that has been written on Mason, including this book, rests on the foundations laid by Beasley, Bass, and Matthews.

Although the first artistic representation of Mason remains in storage, other works can still be seen. None is grander than a set of murals

Top: A magnificent mural by Charles Alston hangs in the old Golden State Mutual Life Insurance Company lobby. Biddy Mason can be seen toward the top left with her three daughters. "The Negro in California History—Exploration and Colonization, 1527–1850" by Charles Alston, courtesy of Community Impact Development, II, LLC.

Bottom: The mural overlooking the altar at First African Methodist Church of Los Angeles. Biddy Mason leads a flock of sheep in the bottom right. "God and Us" mural, image courtesy of First African Methodist Episcopal Church of Los Angeles.

This commemorative wall, designed by Sheila Levrant de Bretteville, celebrates the life of Biddy Mason. It sits at the site of her Spring Street homestead. Photo by author.

executed in 1948 by the African American artists Charles Alston and Hale Woodruff. Two monumental panels soar above the lobby entrance at the Los Angeles headquarters of the Golden State Mutual Life Insurance headquarters, the largest Black business in California in its day. One of the two panels features Mason among a panoply of Black pioneers.[21] Another large mural to Mason rises above the pulpit at First AME. Like the Golden State Mutual Life Insurance building, the church was designed by the famed Black architect Paul Williams. The congregation relocated there in 1969. A beatific Mason, from her place in the mural, continues to watch over the church she cofounded.

From the 1990s on, several major initiatives have sought to recover the history of early Black Los Angeles. *The Power of Place*, a project directed by scholar Dolores Hayden with funding from the National Endowment for the Humanities, established one of the most moving and significant monuments to Mason. Designed by Sheila Levrant de Bretteville and sitting at the site of Mason's Spring Street homestead, the monument tells Mason's life story through objects and prose embedded in an eighty-two-foot-long concrete wall.[22] The complex is now known as Biddy Mason Memorial Park. Other initiatives, including the African American Historic Places Project and the Los Angeles Civic Memory Working Group, aim to rectify the long history of forgetting in LA.[23] Similarly, ongoing work through the National Park Service's National Underground Railroad Network to Freedom seeks to identify, register, and commemorate historic sites in Southern California with significance to Biddy Mason's story.[24] With funding from the NEH, a collaborative research project, *The Long Road to Freedom*, resulted in scholarly work and a digital map of early Black Los Angeles.[25] Aspects of Mason's life have been reimagined in several theatrical performances as well as in the award-winning young reader's book, *Biddy Mason Speaks Up* (2019).[26]

Mason's presence is often felt through acts of charity as much as it is seen through works of art. Her living descendants—their very existence a testament to Mason's astounding fortitude and love—continue to manage the Biddy Mason Foundation in her honor.[27] Not to be confused with the family's organization is the Biddy Mason Charitable Foundation, which has been supporting foster youth in Los Angeles since 2013. That Foundation has already contributed hundreds of thousands of dollars to youth in need, thus keeping alight Mason's philanthropic legacy and the memory of her good works. If you bought this book, you made a contribution to the Biddy Mason Charitable Foundation.[28]

. . .

Upon Biddy Mason, the light shined. Nearly everyone who met her could testify to that fact. That's why countless Angelenos entrusted her with the sacred task of bringing their children into the world. That's why newcomers to the city were sent to her door to seek her counsel, regardless of their station, race, or background. That's why well-wishers and guidance-seekers continued to crowd around her Spring Street home, despite the pleas of her family to let their aging grandmother rest. And that's why eulogies and tributes came tumbling forth from every corner of the city after her death, and continued to do so for generations to come, even as fire and decay and misfortune stymied so many of their efforts.

Although most tributes focused on her prosperity and philanthropy later in life, the light had been with her all along. It was there in the dark belly of the slave regime, where a young Biddy worked through the day and into the night, praying that her daughters might escape some of the traumas she had already endured. It was there as she struggled through a moving screen of dust at the rear of her owner's westbound wagon company toward some distant point on the horizon. It was there when she raised her voice in a crumbling Los Angeles courthouse to challenge the once unassailable will of her enslaver and win a historic victory for her family. And it was there as she took her first tenuous steps out of bondage, surrounded by hostile neighbors still willfully unaccustomed to the concept of Black freedom.

Try to imagine her in that moment, a newly freed woman at the far edge of a yet-unfree nation. She is still struggling to survive, and within a year, mourning the loss of her second-born daughter. For comfort and guidance she turns to her hosts, who hold worship services in their San Pedro Street home. There, in a small adobe dwelling within their forlorn frontier town, they gather as one. Little about this humble congregation suggests the twenty-thousand-member megachurch it will eventually become. No soaring altarpiece, no elevated choir, no rich vestments, not even a proper clergyman among them. Just these freedpeople, migrants all, who, whether through force or free will, now find themselves together in Los Angeles. To unify them, they draw from a shared hymnal of sorts, a set of well-loved songs passed through the generations and mingled here, in this self-made sacred space. Biddy joins them now. As she does, their voices rise together, reaching higher and higher, echoing, filling the hollow of this makeshift church, and, by some holy alchemy of sound and spirit, guiding her to which she had been striving these long, weary years: the way home.[29]

Acknowledgments

At its core this is a book about the making of a community. And, fittingly, it took a community to make this book. Scholarship can be a solitary endeavor, but I was never alone in the decade of research, writing, outreach, coffee dates, breakfasts, lunches, dinners, workshops, conferences, tours, lectures, public events, and collaborations of all kinds that ultimately resulted in this book. In the process I accrued intellectual debts and gained dear friends in equal measure.

Five stalwarts have been at the heart of this project from the very beginning. It was my many conversations with Sarah Barringer Gordon, starting when I was still in grad school, that launched this project and numerous collaborations along the way. Thank you, Sally, for years of friendship. Jackie Broxton, the executive director of the Biddy Mason Charitable Foundation, is like family. The giving spirt of Biddy Mason burns brightly through Jackie's stewardship of the Foundation and her personal example. Patty Colman is an inspiration to us all, not only as the author of one of the most important works on early Black Los Angeles but as a friend and scholar of consummate generosity. No one knows more about the history of early Los Angeles than Paul Spitzzeri, who shared a vast archive of sources upon which much of this book rests. I'm humbled by his knowledge and his kindness. Bill Deverell has been a true friend and untiring mentor ever since I first stumbled into his office as an over-eager high school student.

At a time of deep unease for humanists and the pursuit of knowledge in general, a simple fact bears repeating: publicly funded research benefits us all. I'm deeply grateful to three institutions, without whom this book simply wouldn't have been possible. A Collaborative Research Grant from the National Endowment for the Humanities seeded early research and deepened my understanding of Black Los Angeles. Support from the National Park Service enabled us to bring Biddy Mason's story to a much wider audience. Perhaps most critically, a Research, Development and Engagement Fellowship from Britain's Arts and Humanities Research Council provided the time and resources I needed to complete the book. The NEH, the NPS, and the AHRC are treasures—and long may they continue.

Biddy Mason's legacy, and the legacy of California's other Black founders, lives on through their families. Robynn and Cheryl Cox, direct descendants of Mason, shared their knowledge and graciously endured years of eager questions from me. Ryan Ballard, direct descendent of John Ballard, is as good as they come, and I hope we'll continue our collaboration well into the future. How can I ever properly thank Angela Wilkinson? Angie is the direct descendent of Hannah Embers Smiley and a tireless champion of California's Black history. Since 2022, we've been crisscrossing Southern California together in search of her family's story. What started as a research collaboration blossomed into a lifetime friendship.

Speaking of legacies, First African Methodist Church of Los Angeles, which Mason cofounded more than 150 years ago, carries her vision forward in that same giving spirit. The good people of First AME opened their doors and their arms to me as I pursued the history of their founding mother. A special thanks to Reverend J. L. Armstrong, Wanda M. Kwomo, and Linda Smith in the office of Reverend Dr. Timothy Tyler. With equal warmth, Reverend Dr. Mandy Sloan McDow welcomed me into the community of Los Angeles First United Methodist Church, of which Mason was a charter member. No mention of LA's faith community would be complete without thanks to Dr. Lorn Foster, a leading scholar of the Black church of Los Angeles, who shared innumerable insights and resources.

I had the fortune to begin my career at one excellent research university and to continue it at another. I spent nine happy years at Durham University, where I benefited immeasurably from the wisdom and friendship of Richard Huzzey, Ara Keys, Sarah Davies, Stephen Taylor, Eleanor Barraclough, John Henry Clay, Elizabeth Archibald, Ted Gup, Jacob Wiebel, David Schley, Tom Stammers, and Matt Johnson, among so many others. Now at the University of Texas at Dallas, I'm already accruing intellectual debts to Natalie Ring, Eric Schlereth, Annie Gray Fischer, Ben Wright, and Nils Roemer.

Several long-suffering colleagues read the manuscript in full, when it was even longer than the book you now hold. My deepest thanks (and apologies) to Jackie Broxton, Paul Spitzzeri, Patty Colman, Bill Deverell, Will Myers, and three anonymous readers from the University of California Press.

Piecing together Biddy Mason's story from fragmentary evidence required research assistance from numerous talented historians and genealogists: Alexandra Montgomery, Laura Voisin George, Som-Mai Nguyen, Liv Smith, Arielle Alterwaite, Francis Russo, Sian Winship, Kenyatta Berry, Emily Alley, Louisa Brandt, Maria Brandt, and the education team for the San Manuel Mission Indians. This book benefited profoundly from a long research collaboration with the National Park Service Underground Railroad Network to Freedom—namely, Dan Ott, Gabrielle Harlan, and our all-star research duo of Christella Maldonado and Isaiah Martin.

Archivists, librarians, and curators rescued me from error and ignorance at every turn. A special thanks to Genevieve Preston at San Bernardino County Historical Archives, Kenny Law at Evergreen Cemetery, Jenny Watts at the Huntington Library, and Nathan Gonzalez at the A. K. Smiley Library, in addition to the many other wise folks at the Huntington, the Bancroft Library, the Seaver Center, UCLA Library Special Collections, and the Church History Library in Salt Lake City. Much of the book was written in the literary sanctum that is the London Library.

As any writer knows, books are made through conversations, ideas, and inspiration shared by others. That is especially true for this one. An extra special thanks, as ever, to Steve Hahn, who helped me think through the questions at the core of this book. My deep gratitude also to Amy Tanner Thiriot, Brian McGinty, Tyrone McKinley Freeman, Charles Dew, Michele Zack, Gay Yuen, Marne Campbell, Brenda Stevenson, Stacey Smith, Andy Graybill, Mary Ann Irwin, Paul Pasa, Michael Boyette, Amanda Bellows,

Alison Rose Jefferson, Laura Brodie, Paul Reeve, Dan Lynch, Al Broussard, Kelly Lytle Hernandez, Dana Weiner, Nathaniel Philbrick, Rita Colfield, Dana Johnson, DeEtta Demaratus, Will Thomas, Ada Pinkston, Nick Cataldo, Dawn Dennis, Rea Berg, Rev. Dylan Littlefield, Kim Cooper, Richard Schave, Megan Kate Nelson, Donna Graves, Brian Brown, Lyndon Dodds, Elizabeth Caldwell, Nora Slonimsky, Alice Baumgartner, Chantal Eyong, Sabaah Folayan, John Smallcombe, Priscilla Daniels Mark, Michael Lamb, and everyone else in the Southwood Hall Book Club. I'm especially grateful to Adam Gottstein, Lope Yap, Temi Washington, Laura Voisin George, and Jackie Broxton, my comradees in the campaign to preserve Bernard Zakheim's beautiful mural of Biddy Mason. I wasn't kidding when I said this project was a community effort.

This book benefited from the greatest support team any author has ever had, starting with my agent Sandy Dijkstra, who fought, in her inimitable style, to make it happen. Others at SDLA, especially Elise Capron and Andrea Cavallaro, were there for me every step of the way, as was Jonathan Kirsch. My editor Niels Hooper and everyone else at the University of California Press believed in the power of Biddy Mason's story and ushered it into the world with utmost care. Thanks also to Erin Greb for her beautiful maps and to Laura Voisin George for tracking down the images that populate this book.

My family is the bedrock upon which everything else rests. Thanks to my in-laws Raman and Monolita Mitra, my brother-in-law Rono, and grandmother-in-law Khama. Lindsay would be my favorite sister and Gigi would be my favorite niece, even if they had competition. My parents, Nancy and Les, have always been there for me, with bottomless love and unflagging support, and that was especially true with this project. They inspired me to pursue Biddy Mason's story well before I knew it would become a book. And then they buoyed me when I needed it most.

My wife Rumi. Through thick and thin and thin and thick, you've been my muse, my editor, my cheerleader, my heart. Your imprint is on every page of this book, which you read with your usual care and insight. But your true impact on this project goes so far beyond words on the page. And I, in turn, have no adequate words to sufficiently convey my thankfulness or my love.

The last word belongs to our son, Indra. You'll probably be crawling by the time this book is published. And already, your mother and I are coming to understand a few things. That love is not a finite resource. That our hearts grow bigger each day with you. And although we'll never have to endure what Biddy Mason did as a parent, thank God, we can now comprehend the all-powerful force that sustained her. This, and all that comes after, is for you.

Notes

ABBREVIATIONS

Bancroft	Bancroft Library, University of California–Berkeley
CHL	Church History Library, Salt Lake City, Utah
HEHL	Henry E. Huntington Library, San Marino, California
LAR	Los Angeles County Recorder's Office, Norwalk, California
LOC	Library of Congress, Washington, DC
MHS	Massachusetts Historical Society, Boston
Seaver	Seaver Center for Western History Research, Los Angeles, California
SBCHA	San Bernardino County Historical Archives, San Bernardino, California
UCLA	Charles E. Young Research Library, Special Collections, University of California–Los Angeles
UNC	Southern Historical Collection, Wilson Library, University of North Carolina–Chapel Hill
VHS	Virginia Historical Society, Richmond

INTRODUCTION

1. For a description of the jail, see "The County Jail," *Los Angeles Star*, January 30, 1858. For Biddy's presence there, see "Suit for Freedom," *Los Angeles Star*, February 2, 1856. On the winter weather in Southern California, see San Bernardino Branch *Journal*, entries for December 1855 and January 1856, CHL. December 25 was recorded as the "coldest night we have ever experienced in this country."

2. Kelly Lytle Hernandez, *City of Inmates: Conquest, Rebellion, and the Rise of Human Caging in Los Angeles, 1771–1965* (University of North Carolina Press, 2017), 1.

3. Stacey L. Smith, *Freedom's Frontier: California and the Struggle over Unfree Labor, Emancipation, and Reconstruction* (University of North Carolina Press, 2013); Kevin Waite, *West of Slavery: The Southern Dream of a Transcontinental Empire* (University of North Carolina Press, 2021).

4. "Suit for Freedom."

5. "Suit for Freedom."

6. There is one other photograph of Biddy Mason, an ensemble rather than a portrait (see chapter 12).

7. Kate Bradley Stovall, "The Negro Woman in Los Angeles and Vicinity—Some Notable Characters," *Los Angeles Times*, February 9, 1909.

8. For the conversion of three thousand miles to six million steps, see Richard Bell, *Stolen: Five Free Boys Kidnapped into Slavery and Their Astonishing Odyssey Home* (Simon and Schuster, 2019), 92.

9. Only a small number of cases freed more people than the fourteen individuals, who won their emancipation in Los Angeles in 1856. See, for instance, the legal actions of the Queen family of Maryland (1796) and *Jerry et al. v. Jeremiah Townsend* (1856). For other points of comparison, see the Digital Library on American Slavery, https://dlas.uncg.edu/); and Helen T. Catterall, ed., *Judicial Cases Concerning American Slavery and the Negro*, 5 vols. (Carnegie Institution, 1926–37); Loren Schweninger, *Appealing for Liberty: Freedom Suits in the South* (Oxford University Press, 2019); William G. Thomas, *A Question of Liberty: The Families Who Challenged Slavery from the Nation's Founding to the Civil War* (Yale University Press, 2020). Thanks to Som-Mai Nguyen for her careful research into the matter and to Will Thomas for helping me better understand the legal terrain.

10. Judge Benjamin Hayes, "In re Hannah . . . ," January 19, 1856, MSS, Golden State Mutual Life Insurance Company records, box 41, Young Research Library, UCLA.

11. John Mack Faragher, *Eternity Street: Violence and Justice in Frontier Los Angeles* (W. W. Norton, 2016), 2.

12. Daniel Brendan Lynch, "Southern California Chivalry: The Convergence of

Southerners and Californios in the Far Southwest, 1846–1866" (PhD dissertation, UCLA, 2015), 12–15.

13. See, for instance, Narcissa P. Saunders to Henry Haight, June 10, 1868, Haight Papers, HEHL; Waite, *West of Slavery*, 221–26.

14. The estimate comes from John W. Kemp, an attorney for the legal affairs of the Mason estate, in "A Memorial Window Dedicated to Mrs. Biddy Mason," *LA Times*, March 7, 1904. Although other estimates were lower, they still placed her wealth among the top 0.3 percent of all Angelenos; *Los Angeles Herald*, July 19, 1889. She gifted part of her property to her grandsons prior to her death in 1891, at which point her estate was appraised at more than $41,000; "In the matter of the estate of Biddy Mason, deceased, Inventory and Appraisement, March 5, 1891," Los Angeles Area Court Records, Probate Court, second series, case #14493, HEHL.

15. "The Washington and Huddleston Block," *The Liberator* (Los Angeles) 5 (March 1904); "Negro Will Build Block," *LA Times*, August 12, 1905; Stovall, "Negro Woman."

16. The phrase comes from Tyrone McKinley Freeman, *Madam C. J. Walker's Gospel of Giving: Black Women's Philanthropy During Jim Crow* (University of Illinois Press, 2020).

17. Delilah L. Beasley, *The Negro Trail Blazers of California* (n.p., 1919), 109.

18. Lonnie G. Bunch, *Black Angelenos: The Afro-American in Los Angeles, 1850–1950* (California Afro-American Museum, 1989), 21; Douglas Flamming, *Bound for Freedom: Black Los Angeles in Jim Crow America* (University of California Press, 2005), 51.

19. For example, no fewer than ten major factual errors appear in the space of two pages in Jean Pfaelzer, *California, A Slave State* (Yale University Press, 2023), 157–58. See also Katie Hickman, *Brave Hearted: The Dramatic Story of Women of the American West* (Virago, 2022), 296–304, and recent reporting, notably "Kevin de Leon Seeks to Rename Pershing Square for Biddy Mason, Ex-slave and Unsung L.A. Hero," *Los Angeles Times*, June 19, 2024.

20. Tiya Miles, *All That She Carried: The Journey of Ashley's Sack, a Black Family Keepsake* (Random House, 2021), 223.

21. It was a private record, kept by her owner's overland wagon company to Utah; Robert Smith wagon roster, 1848, CHL. See also Amy Tanner Thiriot, *Slavery in Zion: A Documentary and Genealogical History of Black Lives and Black Servitude in Utah Territory, 1847–1862* (University of Utah Press, 2022), 78. Biddy appeared in a public record for the first time two years later, in "Utah Territory Slave Schedule, 1850," draft, Utah Territorial Census, MS 2672, box 1, folder 6, CHL.

22. On the silences of the archive, see Evelyn Brooks Higginbotham, "Beyond the Sound of Silence: Afro-American Women in History," *Gender and History* (Spring 1989); Darlene Clark Hine, "Lifting the Veil, Shattering the Silence," in *The State of Afro-American History: Past, Present, and Future*, ed. Darlene Clark Hine

(Louisiana State University Press, 1986); Saidiya Hartman, *Lose Your Mother: A Journey Along the Atlantic Slave Route* (Farrar, Straus and Giroux, 2007); Saidiya Hartman, *Wayward Lives, Beautiful Experiments: Intimate Histories of Social Upheaval* (W. W. Norton, 2019); Marisa J. Fuentes, *Dispossessed Lives: Enslaved Women, Violence, and the Archive* (University of Pennsylvania Press, 2016); Brian Connelly and Marisa Fuentes, eds., "From Archives of Slavery to Liberated Futures?," *History of the Present* 6 (Fall 2016): 105–215; Maria R. Montalvo, *Enslaved Archives: Slavery, Law, and the Production of the Past* (Johns Hopkins University Press, 2024).

23. On silence and dissemblance as a survival strategy, see Darlene Clark Hine, "Rape and the Inner Lives of Black Women in the Middle West: Preliminary Thoughts on the Culture of Dissemblance," *Signs: Journal of Women in Culture and Society* 14, no. 4 (Summer 1989).

24. Each has been the subject of important biographies. See David Waldstreicher, *The Odyssey of Phillis Wheatley: A Poet's Journeys Through American Slavery and Independence* (Farrar, Straus and Giroux, 2023); Nell Irvin Painter, *Sojourner Truth: A Life, a Symbol* (W .W. Norton, 1997); Tiya Miles, *Night Flyer: Harriet Tubman and the Faith Dreams of a Free People* (Penguin, 2024); Catherine Clinton, *Harriet Tubman: The Road to Freedom* (Back Bay, 2004).

25. Walter Prescott Webb, "The American West: Perpetual Mirage," *Harper's Magazine* (May 1957), 30.

26. Beasley, *Negro Trail Blazers*; Charlotta A. Bass, *Forty Years: Memoirs from the Pages of a Newspaper* (Charlotta A. Bass, 1960); Miriam Matthews Photograph Collection and box 41, Golden State Mutual Life Insurance Company records, both in UCLA.

27. Early seminal studies include Kenneth Wiggins Porter, *The Negro on the American Frontier* (Arno Press, 1971); W. Sherman Savage, *Blacks in the West* (Greenwood Press, 1976); Lawrence B. de Graaf, "Recognition, Racism, and Reflections on the Writings of Western Black History," *Pacific Historical Review* 44 (February 1975): 22–51; Quintard Taylor, *In Search of the Racial Frontier: African Americans in the American West, 1528–1990* (W. W. Norton, 1998); Lawrence B. de Graaf, Kevin Mulroy, and Quintard Taylor, eds., *Seeking El Dorado: African Americans in California* (Autry Museum, 2001); Quintard Taylor and Shirley Ann Wilson Moore, *African American Women Confront the West, 1600–2000* (University of Oklahoma Press, 2003). For excellent local studies, see Albert Broussard, *Black San Francisco: The Struggle for Racial Equality in the West, 1900–1954* (University Press of Kansas, 1993); Quintard Taylor, *The Forging of a Black Community: Seattle's Central District from 1870 Through the Civil Rights Era* (University of Washington Press, 1994); Tyina L. Steptoe, *Houston Bound: Culture and Color in a Jim Crow City* (University of California Press, 2015). For key biographies, see Quincy D. Newell, *Your Sister in the Gospel: The Life of Jane Manning James, a Nineteenth-Century Black Mormon* (Oxford University Press, 2019); Lynn M.

Hudson, *The Making of "Mammy Pleasant": A Black Entrepreneur in Nineteenth-Century San Francisco* (University of Illinois Press, 2003); and the forthcoming biography of William Alexander Leidesdorff (University of Nebraska Press) by Dana Elizabeth Weiner.

28. Flamming, *Bound for Freedom*; Josh Sides, *L.A. City Limits: African American Los Angeles from the Great Depression to the Present* (University of California Press, 2004); Brenda Stevenson, *The Contested Murder of Latasha Harlins: Justice, Gender, and the Origins of the L.A. Riots* (Oxford University Press, 2013).

29. Patty R. Colman, "John Ballard and the African American Community of Los Angeles, 1850–1905," *Southern California Quarterly* 94, no. 2 (Summer 2012); Marne L. Campbell, *Making Black Los Angeles: Class, Gender, and Community, 1850–1917* (University of North Carolina Press, 2016).

30. Dolores Hayden, "Biddy Mason's Los Angeles, 1856–1891," *California History* 68, no. 3 (1989): 86–99; DeEtta Demaratus, *The Force of a Feather: The Search for a Lost Story of Slavery and Freedom* (University of Utah Press, 2002); Thiriot, *Slavery in Zion*; Sarah Barringer Gordon, "A 'Free' State: A Story of Law an Slavery in Antebellum California," *Journal of the Early Republic* 4, no. 2 (Summer 2025): 213–49.

31. In addition to the sources cited in note 22, my models include Saidiya Hartman, "Venus in Two Acts," *Small Axe* 26 (June 2008): 1–14; LaKisha Michelle Simmons, "Black Feminist Theories of Motherhood and Generation: Histories of Black Infant and Child Loss in the United States," *Signs: Journal of Women in Culture and Society* 46, no. 2 (2021): 311–35; Miles, *All That She Carried*; Paula Fass, "Cultural History/Social History: Some Reflections on a Continuing Dialogue," *Journal of Social History* 37 (Fall 2003): 39–46; and the entire December 2015 issue of *Social Text* dedicated to "The Question of Recovery: Slavery, Freedom, and the Archive."

32. The estimates come from Smith, *Freedom's Frontier*, 40.

33. On the "nadir," see Steven Hahn, *A Nation Under Our Feet: Black Political Struggles in the Rural South from Slavery to the Great Migration* (Belknap, 2003), 440; Rayford W. Logan, *The Negro in American Life and Thought: The Nadir, 1877–1901* (New York, 1954); Leon F. Litwack, *Trouble in Mind: Black Southerners in the Age of Jim Crow* (New York, 1998).

34. "Lifting as We Climb" was the motto for the National Association of Colored Women, founded in 1896.

CHAPTER 1: MISSISSIPPI BOUND

1. Jacob Stroyer, *My Life in the South* (Salem Observer, 1885), 42–44; Frederick Law Olmsted, *A Journey in the Seaboard Slave States* (Sampson Low, Son & Co., 1856), 55; Charles Dickens, *American Notes for General Circulation*, fourth edition (Chapman and Hall, 1842), vol. 2, 17; Basil Hall, *Travels in North America*

in the Years 1827 and 1828, third edition (Robert Cadell, 1830), vol. 3, 197; William Wells Brown, *Narrative of William W. Brown, a Fugitive Slave* (Anti-Slavery Office, 1847), 33–34; Steven Deyle, *Carry Me Back: The Domestic Slave Trade in American Life* (Oxford University Press, 2005), 98, 146–47; William G. Thomas, *The Iron Way: Railroads, the Civil War, and the Making of Modern America* (Yale University Press, 2011), 35–37; Waite, *West of Slavery*, 58–59.

2. G. W. Featherstonaugh, *Excursion Through the Slave States* (John Murray, 1844), vol. 2, 317.

3. Henry Box Brown, *Narrative of the Life of Henry Box Brown* (Lee and Glynn, 1851), 45–47; Louis Hughes, *Thirty Years a Slave* (South Side Printing Company, 1897), 12–13. See also Bell, *Stolen*, 89–92, 97.

4. We do, however, know that her mother was born in Louisiana, according to a later census record; Biddy Mason, Census of 1880.

5. Numerous contemporary articles and news stories refer to Biddy as "Bridget." But she rarely, if ever, used this name herself. Only one census record, that of 1860, lists her as Bridget. Even her will, a formal document prepared by lawyers, states her official name as "Biddy Mason."

6. Ira Berlin, *Generations of Captivity: A History of African-American Slaves* (Harvard University Press, 2003), chap. 4; Joshua D. Rothman, *The Ledger and the Chain: How Domestic Slave Traders Shaped America* (Basic Books, 2023), 3.

7. On Biddy's early years, see her testimony in *LA Times*, June 22, 1887.

8. James Redpath, *The Roving Editor: Or, Talks with Slaves* (A. B. Burdick, 1859), 247.

9. John Brown, *Slave Life in Georgia: A Narrative of the Life, Sufferings, and Escape of John Brown, a Fugitive Slave, Now in England*, ed. L.A. Chamerovzow (New Broad Street, 1855), 110–19.

10. Frederick Douglass, "What to the Slave Is the Fourth of July?" in *Selected Speeches and Writings*, ed. Philip S. Foner (Lawrence Hill, 1999).

11. Daina Ramey Berry, *The Price for Their Pound of Flesh: The Value of the Enslaved, from Womb to Grave, in the Building of a Nation* (Beacon Press, 2017), 68, 70.

12. W. Brown, *Narrative of William W. Brown*, 43–46. See also Hughes, *Thirty Years a Slave*, 8–12.

13. Walter Johnson, *Soul by Soul: Life Inside the Antebellum Slave Market* (Harvard University Press, 1999).

14. Charles Ball, *Slavery in the United States: A Narrative of the Life and Adventures of Charles Ball* (John S. Taylor, 1837), 124–25; See also Hall, *Travels in North America*, vol. 3, 34–40; Adam Hodgson, *Remarks During a Journey Through North America in the Years 1819, 1820, and 1821* (Samuel Whiting, 1823), 125–26; Harriet Martineau, *Retrospect of Western Travel* (William Clownes and Sons, 1838), vol. 2, 83–85. See also, Deyle, *Carry Me Back*, 143–44, 157.

15. Frederick Douglass, *My Bondage and My Freedom* (Miller, Orton & Mulligan, 1855), 51–52, 60.

16. Deyle, *Carry Me Back*, 246. Kenneth M. Stampp, *The Peculiar Institution: Slavery in the Ante-bellum South* (Vintage, 1956), 199–200; Michael Tadman, *Speculators and Slaves: Masters, Traders, and Slaves in the Old South* (University of Wisconsin Press, 1996), 146–54.

17. Miles, *All That She Carried*, 183; Hartman, *Lose Your Mother*.

18. Elizabeth Keckley, *Behind the Scenes, or Thirty Years a Slave, and Four Years in the White House* (G. W. Carleton & Co., 1868), 23.

19. J. Brown, *Slave Life in Georgia*, 117–18.

20. H. Brown, *Narrative of the Life of Henry Box Brown*, 16–17. On the psychological trauma of slavery, see Nell Irvin Painter, *Soul Murder and Slavery* (Markham Press, 1995).

21. Solomon Northup, *Twelve Years a Slave* (Derby and Miller, 1853), 88.

22. Bell, *Stolen*, 138.

23. Deyle, *Carry Me Back*, 253–56.

24. Quoted in Eugene D. Genovese, *Roll, Jordan, Roll: The World the Slaves Made* (Vintage, 1974), 456.

25. James Scott, *Weapons of the Weak: Everyday Forms of Peasant Resistance* (Yale University Press, 1987).

26. Herbert G. Gutman, *Slavery and the Numbers Game: A Critique of Time on the Cross* (University of Illinois Press, 1975), 124; Deyle, *Carry Me Back*, 4, 42–44, 172; Tadman, *Speculators and Slaves*, chap. 2; Rothman, *Ledger and Chain*, 7.

27. Some historians have suggested that these estimates might be too low, and that the total value of all enslaved property could have been as high as $4 billion. Deyle, *Carry Me Back*, 4, 42–44, 59, 172; Stuart Bruchey, ed., *Cotton and the Growth of the American Economy: 1790–1860: Sources and Readings* (Harcourt Brace, 1967), table 3-A; Calvin Schermerhorn, *The Business of Slavery and the Rise of American Capitalism, 1815–1860* (Yale University Press, 2015).

28. Brian Schoen, *The Fragile Fabric of Union: Cotton, Federal Politics, and the Global Origins of the Civil War* (Johns Hopkins University Press, 2009); Sven Beckert, *Empire of Cotton: A Global History* (Knopf, 2014).

29. Joshua D. Rothman, *Flush Times and Fever Dreams: A Story of Capitalism and Slavery in the Age of Jackson* (University of Georgia Press, 2012), 4; John Hebron Moore, *The Emergence of the Cotton Kingdom in the Old Southwest: Mississippi, 1770–1860* (Louisiana State University Pres, 1988), 16.

30. David J. Libby, *Slavery and Frontier Mississippi, 1720–1835* (University Press of Mississippi, 2004), 75; Rothman, *Flush Times*, 10–12. See also Joseph G. Baldwin, *The Flush Times of Alabama and Mississippi: A Series of Sketches* (D. Appleton and Co., 1854).

31. Claudio Saunt, *Unworthy Republic: The Dispossession of Native Americans*

and the Road to Indian Territory (W. W. Norton, 2020), 208, see also 110, 124–35, 203–207; Libby, *Slavery and Frontier Mississippi*, 101–103.

32. Rothman, *Flush Times*, 3–4.

33. Libby, *Slavery and Frontier Mississippi*, 101–103.

34. Rothman, *Flush Times*, 216–17; Eron Rowland, *History of Hinds County, Mississippi, 1821–1922* (Andesite Press, 2017).

35. Baldwin, *Flush Times of Alabama and Mississippi*, 81–83.

36. Rothman, *Flush Times*, 6, see also 7–9.

37. Baldwin, *Flush Times of Alabama and Mississippi*, 81. See also Johnson Jones Hooper, *Adventures of Captain Simon Suggs, Late of the Tallapoosa Volunteers* (T. B. Peterson, 1848), 12.

38. Alexis de Tocqueville, *Democracy in America*, trans. Henry Reeve (George Adlard, 1838), vol. 1, 83, 211, 376.

39. Moses Grandy, *Narrative of the Life of Moses Grandy; Late a Slave in the United States of America* (C. Gilpin, 1843), 56.

40. Hughes, *Thirty Years a Slave*, 36.

41. Kate Bradley Stovall, "The Negro Woman in Los Angeles," *LA Times*, February 12, 1909.

42. Libby, *Slavery and Frontier Mississippi*, 70–71; Moore, *Emergence of the Cotton Kingdom*, 86–90, 98.

43. See Grandy, *Narrative of the Life of Moses Grandy*, 56. Edward E. Baptist, *The Half Has Never Been Told: Slavery and the Making of American Capitalism* (Basic Books, 2014).

44. J. Brown, *Slave Life in Georgia*, 127–29.

45. J. Brown, *Slave Life in Georgia*, 172. The description comes from Brown's experiences on a Georgia plantation, but it's equally applicable to Biddy's in Mississippi.

46. *Vicksburg Register*, quoted in Libby, *Slavery in Frontier Mississippi*, 96.

47. Richard Hofstadter, "The Paranoid Style in American Politics," *Harper's Magazine*, November 1964. See also Walter Johnson, *River of Dark Dreams: Slavery and Empire in the Cotton Kingdom* (Harvard University Press, 2013), chap. 8; Rothman, *Flush Times*, 98–100.

48. Virgil Stewart and Augustus Q. Walton, *A History of the Detection, Conviction, Life, and Designs of John A. Murel, the Great Western Land Pirate* (pamphlet, 1835). The Murel story circulated for decades thereafter, even making its way into Mark Twain's *Life on the Mississippi* (Harper, 1883), 215–17. Rothman, *Flush Times*, 75–87.

49. Rothman, *Flush Times*, 91–113.

50. "A Tale of Horror," *Liberator*, December 10, 1836.

51. Henry S. Foote, *Casket of Reminiscences* (Chronicle Publishing Company, 1874), 251, 252.

52. Abraham Lincoln, "The Perpetuation of Our Political Institutions," January

27, 1838, in *The Collected Works of Abraham Lincoln*, ed. Roy P. Basler (Rutgers University Press, 1953), vol. 1, 108–15.

53. Rothman, *Flush Times*, 249.

54. According to Marie Jenkins Schwartz, a majority of slave children lived in two-parent households; Schwartz, *Born in Bondage: Growing Up Enslaved in the Antebellum South* (Harvard University Press, 2000), 50.

55. For a brief discussion of the legend of Biddy's time among the Cherokee, see Demaratus, *Force of a Feather*, 19, 218n6; and Bass, *Forty Years*, 7–8.

56. Utah Slave Schedule, 1850, CHL. On racial categorization, see Carole Emberton, *To Walk About in Freedom: The Long Emancipation of Priscilla Joyner* (Norton, 2022), 3.

57. H. Brown, *Narrative of the Life of Henry Box Brown*, 9.

58. Quoted in Stephanie M. H. Camp, *Closer to Freedom: Enslaved Women and Everyday Resistance in the Plantation South* (University of North Carolina Press, 2004), 72–73. See also Sally E. Hadden, *Slave Patrols: Law and Violence in Virginia and the Carolinas* (Harvard University Press, 2001).

59. Harriet Jacobs, *Incidents in the Life of a Slave Girl, Written by Herself*, ed. Lydia Maria Child (n.p., 1861), 29, 119.

60. Mary Chesnut, *Mary Chesnut's Civil War*, ed. C. Vann Woodward (Yale University Press, 1981), 29.

61. Northup, *Twelve Years a Slave*, 188–89, 199–200, 229, 254–60; Deborah Gray White, *Ar'n't I a Woman? Female Slaves in the Plantation South* (W. W. Norton, 1985), 29–30, 41.

62. Quoted in Schwartz, *Born in Bondage*, 45.

63. Keckley, *Behind the Scenes*, 38–39. The literature on sexual violence and the trauma it produced is extensive. See, for example, Thelma Jennings, "Us Colored Women Had to Go Through a Plenty: Sexual Exploitation of African-American Slave Women," *Journal of Women's History* 1, no. 3 (Winter 1990); Nikki Marie Taylor, *Driven Toward Madness: The Fugitive Slave Margaret Garner and Tragedy on the Ohio* (Ohio University Press, 2016), 92–109; Brenda Stevenson, *Life in Black and White: Family and Community in the Slave South* (Oxford University Press, 1996), 236–37; Brenda Stevenson, "What's Love Got to Do with It? Concubinage and Enslaved Women and Girls in the Antebellum South," *Journal of African American History* 98, no. 1 (Winter 2013); Saidiya Hartman, *Scenes of Subjection: Terror, Slavery, and Self-Making in Nineteenth-Century America* (Oxford University Press, 1997), chap. 2; Fuentes, *Dispossessed Lives*; Wendy Warren, "The Cause of Her Grief: The Rape of a Slave in Early New England," *Journal of American History* 93, no. 4 (March 2007): 1031–49.

64. See the testimony of both Ellen and Ann during their family's freedom suit in 1856, in "Suit for Freedom," *Sacramento Daily Democratic State Journal*, February 19, 1856; Robert Curry Owens, "My Grandfather," MSS, UCLA.

65. Quoted in White, *Ar'n't I a Woman?*, 120. See also Carroll Smith-Rosenberg,

Disorderly Conduct: Visions of Gender in Victorian America (Oxford University Press, 1986).

66. Quoted in Camp, *Closer to Freedom*, 79.

67. Grandy, *Narrative of the Life of Moses Grandy*, 28. See also J. Brown, *Slave Life in Georgia*, 132. See also Thavolia Glymph, *Out of the House of Bondage: The Transformation of the Plantation Household* (Cambridge University Press, 2003).

68. Hughes, *Thirty Years a Slave*, 43–44; Schwartz, *Born in Bondage*, 56.

69. Quoted in Schwartz, *Born in Bondage*, 1.

70. Douglass, *My Bondage and My Freedom*, 54.

71. Hughes, *Thirty Years a Slave*, 43–44. See also Grandy, *Narrative of the Life of Moses Grandy*, 27–28.

72. Statistics on infant mortality comes from studies of Alabama in 1850, in Schwartz, *Born in Bondage*, 73. See also John Campbell, "Work, Pregnancy, and Infant Mortality Among Southern Slaves," *Journal of Interdisciplinary History* 14, no. 4 (Spring 1984): 793–812.

73. White, *Ar'n't I a Woman?*, 122–23; Camp, *Closer to Freedom*, 32.

74. White, *Ar'n't I a Woman?*, 105–15, 126, 131.

75. Moore, *Emergence of the Cotton Kingdom*, 16–19; Deyle, *Carry Me Back*, 64; Rothman, *Flush Times*, 294–98.

CHAPTER 2: MAKING A PATRIARCH

1. For the Dean estate, see "South Carolina Probate Records, Files and Loose Papers, 1732–1964," Images, http://FamilySearch.org, accessed June 14, 2016. County courthouses, South Carolina, and South Carolina Department of Archives and History, Columbia. For more on Edgefield District, see Orville Vernon Burton, *In My Father's House Are Many Mansions: Family and Community in Edgefield, South Carolina* (University of North Carolina Press, 1985). Thanks to Alexandra Montgomery for her research into Smith and his family.

2. Demaratus, *Force of a Feather*, 14–15.

3. E. Wooley and Vivian Wooley, eds., *Edgefield County, South Carolina, Wills, 1787–1836* (Southern Historical Press, 1991), 206–207; "South Carolina Probate Records, Files and Loose Papers" and "South Carolina Probate Records, Bound Volumes, 1671–1977," Images, http://FamilySearch.org, accessed June 14, 2016; County courthouses, South Carolina, and South Carolina Department of Archives and History, Columbia; Smith's obituary in *San Antonio Express*, October 31, 1891. Smith inherited again from his family on his mother's side, when his aunt, Margaret (Dean) Holloway, left him part of her estate in her 1888 will.

4. On plantation romances, see David W. Blight, *Race and Reunion: The Civil War in American Memory* (Harvard University Press, 2001), 211–54.

5. James Oakes, *The Ruling Race: A History of American Slaveholders* (Norton,

1982), 76–92, 76. James David Miller, *South by Southwest: Planter Emigration and Identity in the Slave South* (University of Virginia Press, 2002).

6. Ethel Uhl Klemcke and Bob Weed, *Robert Mays Smith from South Carolina to Texas (The Long Way)* (Henington Publishing Company, 1988), 1–2.

7. Steven Hahn, *The Roots of Southern Populism: Yeoman Farmers and the Transformation of the Georgia Upcountry, 1850–1890* (Oxford University Press, 1983); Stephanie McCurry, *Masters of Small Worlds: Yeoman Households, Gender Relations, and the Political Culture of the Antebellum South Carolina Low Country* (Oxford University Press, 1995).

8. United States Census, 1840; "Mississippi, State Archives, Various Records, 1820–1951," Database with images, http://FamilySearch.org, accessed November 2, 2020. Mississippi Department of Archives and History, Jackson; Gordon, "A 'Free' State," 222.

9. The only evidence for their purchase comes from the Mississippi tax lists of this period, and because the year 1843 is missing from the records, a more precise date is impossible to determine.

10. On Ann's age, see J.D.B. De Bow, *Statistical View of the United States . . . Being a Compendium of the Seventh Census* (Washington, DC: Beverley Tucker, 1854), 332; "Suit for Freedom," *Los Angeles Star*, February 2, 1856. On slave marriage, see Tyler D. Parry, *Jumping the Broom: The Surprising Multicultural Origins of a Black Wedding Ritual* (University of North Carolina Press, 2020); Tera W. Hunter, *Bound in Wedlock: Slave and Free Black Marriage in the Nineteenth Century* (Harvard University Press, 2017). If Biddy arrived on the Smith farm as early as 1842, there's a chance that Ann's father was an enslaved man owned by Smith himself. Tax records point to Robert owning one other adult slave by 1844, in addition to Biddy. The timeline, however, suggests that Biddy likely gave birth to Ann prior to her forced relocation to Smith's farm. In which case, the father was likely an enslaved person on or near her previous plantation. Perhaps this was the man whose name she took in freedom: "Mason."

11. Frederick Law Olmsted, *A Journey in the Back Country* (New York: Mason Brothers, 1860), 141; Deborah Gray White, *Ar'n't I a Woman?*, 49.

12. Glymph, *Out of the House of Bondage*; Jones-Rogers, *They Were Her Property*, 2–16.

13. Richard H. Steckel, "Slave Mortality: Analysis of Evidence from Plantation Records," *Social Science History* 3, nos. 3 and 4 (October 1979): 86–114; Richard H. Steckel, "A Dreadful Childhood: The Excess Mortality of American Slaves," *Social Science History* 10 (Winter 1986): 428.

14. Schwartz, *Born in Bondage*, 92–93, 107–108; Keckley, *Behind the Scenes*, 19.

15. Libby, *Slavery and Frontier Mississippi*, 70–71; Moore, *Emergence of the Cotton Kingdom*, 86–90, 98.

16. Olmsted, *Journey in the Back Country*, 140–41.

17. Campbell, *Making Black Los Angeles*, 39.

18. Demaratus, *Force of a Feather*, 21–24.

19. For the racial categorization of Hannah, see Utah Slave Schedule, 1850, CHL; *Los Angeles Star*, February 2, 1856. On incest on slave plantations, see Alexis Broderick Neumann, "American Incest: Kinship, Sex, and Commerce in Slavery and Reconstruction" (PhD dissertation, University of Pennsylvania, 2018). See also Demaratus, *Force of a Feather*, 22.

20. Annette Gordon-Reed, *The Hemingses of Monticello: An American Family* (Norton, 2008).

21. Demaratus, *Force of a Feather*, 21–22; Campbell, *Making Black Los Angeles*, 39, 47.

22. For more on Rande, see chapter 4.

23. George W. Beattie and Helen Pruit Beattie, *Heritage of the Valley: San Bernardino's First Century* (1939), 186 n13; Sharla M. Fett, *Working Cures: Healing, Health, and Power on Southern Slave Plantations* (University of North Carolina Press, 2002), 75–76.

24. Quoted in Fett, *Working Cures*, 27.

25. Deyle, *Carry Me Back*, 215. See also Katherine Paugh, *The Politics of Reproduction: Race, Medicine, and Fertility in the Age of Abolition* (Oxford University Press, 2017); Johnson, *Soul by Soul*; White, *Ar'n't I a Woman?*, 32; Richard Holcombe Kilbourne, *Debt, Investment, Slaves: Credit Relations in East Feliciana Parish, Louisiana, 1825–1885* (University of Alabama Press, 2014), 49–50; Robert Colby, "Negroes Will Bear Fabulous Prices: The Economics of Wartime Slave Commerce and Visions of the Confederate Future," *Journal of the Civil War Era* 10, no. 4 (December 2020): 453–55; Berry, *Price for Their Pound of Flesh*, 11.

26. Olmsted, *Journey in the Seaboard Slave States*, 55. See also Olmsted, *Journey in the Back Country*, 283–86.

27. Quoted in White, *Ar'n't I a Woman?*, 31.

28. Deyle, *Carry Me Back*, 215; Berry, *Price for Their Pound of Flesh*, 12–13; Jacqueline Jones, *Labor of Love, Labor of Sorrow: Black Women, Work, and the Family, from Slavery to the Present* (Basic Books, 2009), 9–42.

29. White, *Ar'n't I a Woman?*, 87; Camp, *Closer to Freedom*, 18; Berry, *Price for Their Pound of Flesh*, 13; Olmsted, *Journey in the Back Country*, 153.

30. For more on "unnatural increase," see Jennifer L. Morgan, *Laboring Women: Reproduction and Gender in New World Slavery* (University of Pennsylvania Press, 2011); Paugh, *Politics of Reproduction*.

31. Quoted in Schwartz, *Born in Bondage*, 20.

32. W. Brown, *Narrative of William W. Brown*, 46–48, 89–90. See also Northup, *Twelve Years a Slave*, 188–89, 199–200, 229, 254–60.

33. Berry, *Price for Their Pound of Flesh*, 78–79; Aisha Djelid, "'The Master Whished to Reproduce': Slavery, Forced Intimacy, and Enslavers' Interference in Sexual Relationships in the Antebellum South, 1808–1861," *American Nineteenth Century History* 25, no. 1 (April 2024): 21–43.

34. "Indenture of Apprenticeship, Hannah Smiley to Lewis G. Green, April 7, 1862," Los Angeles County Miscellaneous Records, 1859–1870, Seaver.

35. R. Isabela Morales, *Happy Dreams of Liberty: An American Family in Slavery and Freedom* (Oxford University Press, 2022), 28–29.

36. For Hannah's "yellow" skin, see De Bow, *Being a Compendium of the Seventh Census*, 332. See also Sharon Block, *Colonial Complexions: Race and Bodies in Eighteenth-Century America* (University of Pennsylvania Press, 2018). For the description of Hannah's whiteness, see *Los Angeles Star*, February 2, 1856.

37. Utah Slave Schedule, 1850, CHL.

38. Quoted in White, *Ar'n't I a Woman?*, 102–103.

39. On the significance of female-headed households and extended kin networks like Biddy's and Hannah's, see Stevenson, *Life in Black and White*. On Biddy and Hannah's families in Los Angeles, see Campbell, *Making Black Los Angeles*, 54–56; Colman, "John Ballard."

40. Albert J. Raboteau, *Slave Religion: The "Invisible Institution" in the Antebellum South* (Oxford University Press, 1978, 2004), 149–55, 175, 209, 212; Christine Leigh Heyrman, *Southern Cross: The Beginnings of the Bible Belt* (University of North Carolina Press, 1997); W.E.B. Du Bois, *The Negro Church* (1903; reprint, Cascade Books, 2011), 9–46.

41. Thornton Stringellow, *A Brief Examination of Scripture Testimony on the Institution of Slavery* (Washington, DC: Congressional Globe Office, 1850), 16.

42. Ephesians 6:5. See also Luke E. Harlow, *Religion, Race, and the Making of Confederate Kentucky, 1830–1880* (Cambridge University Press, 2014); John Patrick Daly, *When Slavery Was Called Freedom: Evangelicalism, Proslavery, and the Causes of the Civil War* (University of Kentucky Press, 2002); Drew Gilpin Faust, ed., *The Ideology of Slavery: Proslavery Thought in the Antebellum South, 1830–1860* (Louisiana State University Press, 1981); Heyrman, *Southern Cross*.

43. H. Brown, *Narrative of the Life of Henry Box Brown*, 29.

44. Raboteau, *Slave Religion*, 177, 295, 299, 333. See also Laurie F. Maffly-Kipp, *Setting Down the Sacred Past: African American Race Histories* (Harvard University Press, 2010); Anthony E. Kaye, with Gregory P. Downs, *Nat Turner, Black Prophet: A Visionary History* (Farrar, Straus and Giroux, 2024), xx–xxi, 64.

45. Grandy, *Narrative of the Life of Moses Grandy*, 56–57; H. Brown, *Narrative of the Life of Henry Box Brown*, 10; Libby, *Slavery and Frontier Mississippi*, 86–87.

46. Ball, *Slavery in the United States*, 221.

47. Hughes, *Thirty Years a Slave*, 51–52.

48. John Brown, *Autobiography of Pioneer John Brown* (Publisher's Press, 1941), 36, 41–42; William E. Parrish, "The Mississippi Saints," *The Historian* 50, no. 4 (August 1988): 490–91.

49. J. Brown, *Autobiography of Pioneer John Brown*, 36–55.

50. Joseph Smith Jr., *The Book of Mormon* (Palmyra, NY: E. B. Grandin, 1830);

Terryl L. Givens, *By the Hand of Mormon: The American Scripture That Launched a New World Religion* (Oxford University Press, 2003); Grant Hardy, *Understanding the Book of Mormon: A Reader's Guide* (Oxford University Press, 2010).

51. Max Perry Mueller, *Race and the Making of the Mormon People* (University of North Carolina Press, 2017), 31–59.

52. J. Brown, *Autobiography of Pioneer John Brown*, 44.

53. J. Brown, *Autobiography of Pioneer John Brown*, 39.

54. J. Brown, *Autobiography of Pioneer John Brown*, 43.

55. Quoted in Richard Lyman Bushman, *Joseph Smith: Rough Stone Rolling* (Vintage, 2005), 80–83. See also Givens, *By the Hand of Mormon*, 60. See also Alexander Campbell, *Delusions: An Analysis of the Book of Mormon* (Boston: Benjamin H. Greene, 1832).

56. Mark Twain, *Roughing It* (Hartford, CT: American Publishing, 1873), 127–35.

57. J. Brown, *Autobiography of Pioneer John Brown*, 43, 46.

58. Leonard J. Arrington, "Mormon beginnings in the South," CHL.

59. The description of LDS baptism comes from *Doctrine and Covenants* 20:73; and Newell, *Your Sister in the Gospel*, 21.

60. Osmer D. Flake, *William J. Flake, Pioneer-Colonizer* (printed by author, 1948), 4.

61. "To His Excellency, Daniel Dunklin, Governor of the State of Missouri," reprinted in *Evening and the Morning Star* 2, no. 15 (December 1833): 226–31.

62. J. Brown, *Autobiography of Pioneer John Brown*, 36–55.

63. Parrish, "Mississippi Saints"; Leonard J. Arrington, "Mississippi Mormons," *The Ensign* (June 1977); Kate B. Carter, "Mississippi Saints," in *Our Pioneer Heritage* (1958–77), vol. 2, 421–76; Charmaine Lay Kohler, *Southern Grace: A Story of the Mississippi Saints* (Beagle Creek Press, 1995).

64. Thiriot, *Slavery in Zion*, l–li, 6–7; Dennis Drake, *William Crosby: Through the Needle's Eye* (n.d., copy in CHL).

65. Quoted in Benjamin E. Park, *Kingdom of Nauvoo: The Rise and Fall of a Religious Empire on the American Frontier* (Liveright, 2020), 50–51.

66. John L. Brooke, *The Refiner's Fire: The Making of Mormon Cosmology, 1644–1844* (Cambridge University Press, 1996); Stephen A. Marini, *Radical Sects of Revolutionary New England* (Harvard University Press, 1982); John H. Wigger, *Taking Heaven by Storm: Methodism and the Rise of Popular Christianity in America* (Oxford University Press, 1998); Paul E. Johnson, *A Shopkeeper's Millennium: Society and Revivals in Rochester, New York, 1815–1837* (Hill and Wang, 1978).

67. Book of Mormon, Ether 13:2.

68. H. Dean Garrett, "The Coming Forth of the Doctrine and Covenants," in *Regional Studies in Latter-day Saint Church History: Ohio*, ed. Milton V. Backman (Brigham Young University, 1995), 89–103; Bushman, *Rough Stone Rolling*,

128–31, 172–73; Peter Crawley, *A Descriptive Bibliography of the Mormon Church* (Brigham Young University), vol. 1, 37–42; Jared Farmer, *On Zion's Mount: Mormons, Indians, and the American Landscape* (Harvard University Press, 2008), 36–37.

69. B. Carmon Hardy, "Lords of Creation: Polygamy, the Abrahamic Household, and Mormon Patriarchy," *Journal of Mormon History* 20, no. 1 (Spring 1994): 126.

70. Quoted in Hardy, "Lords of Creation," 128.

71. The Tenth Commandment, Exodus 20:17. Udney Hay Jacob, *An Extract: From a Manuscript Entitled the Peace Maker* (Nauvoo, IL: Joseph Smith 1842), 16.

72. Stringfellow, *Brief Examination of Scripture Testimony*, 4; on the relationship between Mormonism and slaveholding patriarchy, see Waite, *West of Slavery*, 125–30.

73. J. Brown, *Autobiography of Pioneer John Brown*, 46.

74. Alex Beam, *American Crucifixion: The Murder of Joseph Smith and the Fate of the Mormon Church* (PublicAffairs, 2014). Bushman, *Rough Stone Rolling*, 549–50.

75. J. Brown, *Autobiography of Pioneer John Brown*, 47, 56.

CHAPTER 3: OVERLAND

1. Park, *Kingdom of Nauvoo*, 8, 21–22, 55, 57, 248–60; Thomas Richards Jr., Breakaway Americas: The Unmanifest Future of the Jacksonian United States (Johns Hopkins University Press, 2020), 81; Richard E. Bennett, *We'll Find the Place: The Mormon Exodus, 1846–1848* (1997; reprint, University of Oklahoma Press, 2009), 24; Thomas L. Kane, *The Mormons: A Discourse Delivered Before the Historical Society of Pennsylvania* (Philadelphia: King & Baird, 1850), 3–10.

2. Esteban, an enslaved man in the company of the would-be conquistador Cabeza de Vaca in the early sixteenth century, was one of the few African-descended people to have made a longer overland journey. See Andres Resendez, *A Land So Strange: The Epic Journey of Cabeza de Vaca* (Basic Books, 2007).

3. Quoted in John G. Turner, *Brigham Young: Pioneer Prophet* (Harvard University Press, 2012), 176.

4. Turner, *Brigham Young*, 3.

5. Turner, *Brigham Young*, 88, 91, 111–13, 132–41.

6. Bennett, *We'll Find the Place*, 31–40; Wallace Stegner, *Gathering of Zion: The Story of the Mormon Trail* (University of Nebraska Press, 1992), 43–44, 58.

7. Bennett, *We'll Find the Place*, 58.

8. Thiriot, *Slavery in Zion*, 23.

9. John Brown, *Autobiography of Pioneer John Brown*, 71.

10. J. Brown, *Autobiography of Pioneer John Brown*, 72; Shirley Ann Wilson Moore, *Sweet Freedom's Plains: African Americans on the Overland Trails, 1841–1869* (University of Oklahoma Press, 2016), 55–57.

11. Thiriot, *Slavery in Zion*, 73.

12. Scholars are working to recover the stories of Black pioneers at last. See Thiriot, *Slavery in Zion*; Moore, *Sweet Freedom's Plains*; Paul Reeve, *Century of Black Mormons* (https://exhibits.lib.utah.edu/s/century-of-black-mormons/page/about) ; W. Paul Reeve, Christopher B. Rich Jr., and LaJean Purcell Carruth, *This Abominable Slavery: Race, Religion, and the Battle over Human Bondage in Antebellum Utah* (Oxford University Press, 2024).

13. Seco Smith quoted in the family memoir, Klemcke and Weed, *Robert Mays Smith*, 3.

14. Andrew Torget, *Seeds of Empire: Cotton, Slavery, and the Transformation of the Texas Borderlands, 1800–1850* (University of North Carolina Press, 2015); Alice Baumgartner, *South to Freedom: Runaway Slaves to Mexico and the Road to the Civil War* (Basic Books, 2020).

15. Klemcke and Weed, *Robert Mays Smith*, 2–3; Demaratus, *Force of a Feather*, 32–33.

16. From the report of Seco Smith, in Klemcke and Weed, *Robert Mays Smith*, 3.

17. Waite, *West of Slavery*, 30–32; Charles Ralph Desmond Hart, "Congressmen and the Expansion of Slavery into the Territories: A Study in Attitudes, 1846–1861" (PhD dissertation, University of Washington, 1965).

18. J. Brown, *Autobiography of Pioneer John Brown*, 88–93; on the mud, see Stegner, *Gathering of Zion*, 56–58.

19. On Biddy's role along the journey, see the account of her daughter, Ellen, conducted by Delilah Beasley, in *The Negro Trail Blazers of California* (n.p., 1919), 90. See also Demaratus, *Force of a Feather*, 32–35.

20. J. Brown, *Autobiography of Pioneer John Brown*, 96.

21. On the settlement patterns of slaveholders in the Far West, see Stacey L. Smith, "Remaking Slavery in a Free State: Masters and Slaves in Gold Rush California," *Pacific Historical Review* 80 (February 2011).

22. Robert Smith wagon roster, 1848, CHL; Thiriot, *Slavery in Zion*, 78.

23. Thiriot, *Slavery in Zion*, 8; Drake, *William Crosby*, 54.

24. J. Brown, *Autobiography of Pioneer John Brown*, 97–98.

25. Robert Smith wagon roster, 1848, CHL.

26. Merrill J. Mattes, *Platte River Road Narratives* (University of Illinois Press, 1988), 5; Moore, *Sweet Freedom's Plains*, 1.

27. Mattes, *Platte River Road Narratives*, 1–5.

28. Stegner, *Gathering of Zion*, 6.

29. Smith, *Freedom's Frontier*; Waite, *West of Slavery*; Moore, *Sweet Freedom's Plains*.

30. Newell, *Your Sister in the Gospel*, 65. On the use of liberty poles in early American political culture, see Arthur M. Schlesinger, "Liberty Tree: A Genealogy," *New England Quarterly* 25, no. 4 (December 1952): 435–58; Simon New-

man, *Parades and the Politics of the Street: Festive Culture in the Early American Republic* (Penn Press, 2010), 25, 130.

31. Quoted in *Frontier Guardian*, August 8, 1849. See also Bennett, *We'll Find the Place*, 243–44; Stegner, *Gathering of Zion*, 1–6; Thiriot, *Slavery in Zion*, 31; Farmer, *On Zion's Mount*, 48.

32. Turner, *Brigham Young*, 146–48, 163. See also Armand L. Mauss, *All Abraham's Children: Changing Mormon Conceptions of Race and Lineage* (University of Illinois Press, 2003), chap. 2; Jan Shipps, *Mormonism: The Story of a New Religious Tradition* (University of Illinois Press, 1985), 61–63.

33. Quoted in Raboteau, *Slave Religion*, 311.

34. On the significance of Exodus to the enslaved, see Kaye with Downs, *Nat Turner, Black Prophet*, xx–xxi, 64.

35. Thiriot, *Slavery in Zion*, 21–22.

36. Rather than traveling west, Black freedom-seekers often went south to Mexico. See Baumgartner, *South to Freedom.*

37. Recapture was the fate of Marinda Redd, when she attempted to escape while traveling with her owner through Kansas. See her interview in the *Broad Axe*, March 25, 1899, and Tonya Reiter, "Redd Slave Histories: Family, Race, and Sex in Pioneer Utah," *Utah Historical Quarterly* 85, no. 2 (Spring 2017): 108–26.

38. Camp, *Closer to Freedom*. See also White, *Ar'n't I a Woman?*, 70–71.

39. J. Brown, *Autobiography of Pioneer John Brown*, 100; Beasley, *Negro Trail Blazers*, 90.

40. Stegner, *Gathering of Zion*, 121–27.

41. Quoted in Bennett, *We'll Find the Place*, 127.

42. Stegner, *Gathering of Zion*, 129–33; J. Brown, *Autobiography of Pioneer John Brown*, 84.

43. J. Goldsborough Bruff, *Gold Rush: The Journals, Drawings, and Other Papers of J. Goldsborough Bruff*, ed. Georgia Willis Read and Ruth Gaines (Columbia University Press, 1949), 34, 56, 60, 86, 173. See also William Clayton, *William Clayton's Journal*, ed. Lawrence Clayton (Lawrence Clayton, 1921), entries for April 28 and 29, 1847.

44. Unsurprisingly, Black laborers often brought up the rear of wagon companies, while white overlanders claimed the more favorable positions in the procession. See, for example, Madison Berryman Moorman, *The Journal of Madison Berryman Moorman, 1850–1851*, ed. Irene D. Paden (California Historical Society, 1948), 30.

45. *Congressional Globe*, 31st Congress, 1st session, 480.

46. James K. Polk, January 5, 1847, in *Polk: The Diary of a President, 1845–1849*, ed. Allan Nevins (Longmans, Green and Co., 1952), 183.

47. On the morning routine of overland companies, see Jesse Applegate, "A Day with the Cow Column in 1843," *Overland Monthly* 1, no. 2 (August 1868): 127–33.

48. Quoted in Moore, *Sweet Freedom's Plains*, 77.

49. Applegate, "Day with the Cow Column in 1843," 127, 128, 129.

50. Flake, *William J. Flake*, 11.

51. Anna Maria Goodell, "Diary," in Kenneth L. Holmes, ed., *Covered Wagon Women: Diaries & Letters from the Western Trails, 1840–1890* (Arthur H. Clark Company, 1998), vol. 7, 98.

52. On enslaved motherhood, see Schwartz, *Born in in Bondage*, 53; Fett, *Working Cures*, 127; Miles, *All That She Carried*, 3.

53. John D. Unruh Jr., *The Plains Across: The Overland Emigrants and the Trans-Mississippi West, 1840–60* (University of Illinois Press, 1979), 408–13.

54. Alvin A. Coffey, "The Autobiography of Alvin A. Coffey," *Overland Journal* 20, no. 2 (Summer 2002), 69.

55. Unruh, *Plains Across*, 408–409; Moore, *Sweet Freedom's Plains*, 143–45; Merrill J. Mattes, "The Council Bluffs Road: A New Perspective on the Northern Branch of the Great Platte River Road," *Nebraska History* 65, no. 2 (Summer 1984), 193; Sarah Keyes, *American Burial Ground: A New History of the Overland Trail* (Penn Press, 2023).

56. Unruh, *Plains Across*, 408.

57. J. Brown, *Autobiography of Pioneer John Brown*, 100–101.

58. Moore, *Sweet Freedom's Plains*, 131–33.

59. Quoted in Thiriot, *Slavery in Zion*, 44.

60. Quoted in James Belich, *Replenishing the Earth: The Settler Revolution and the Rise of the Anglo-World, 1783–1939* (Oxford University Press, 2009), 336.

61. On Fort Laramie, see Stegner, *Gathering of Zion*, 138–45.

62. J. Brown, *Autobiography of Pioneer John Brown*, 101.

63. Coffey, "Autobiography of Alvin A. Coffey," 70.

64. Bennett, *We'll Find the Place*, 186–96; Stegner, *Gathering of Zion*, 145–60.

65. Ethan Rarick, *Desperate Passage: The Donner Party Perilous Journey West* (Oxford University Press, 2009).

66. Bennett, *We'll Find the Place*, 208–15; Stegner, *Gathering of Zion*, 158–67.

67. J. Brown, *Autobiography of Pioneer John Brown*, 101.

68. J. Brown, *Autobiography of Pioneer John Brown*, 101; "The Locality History of South Cottonwood Camp," MSS typescript, no author, no date, CHL.

69. J. Brown, *Autobiography of Pioneer John Brown*, 101.

70. Howard R. Egan, *Pioneering the West: Major Howard Egan's Diary*, ed. William M. Egan (Howard R. Egan Estate, 1917), 105.

CHAPTER 4: CHILDREN OF ZION, SEED OF CAIN

1. On the late spring, see J. Brown, *Autobiography of Pioneer John Brown*, 102.

2. Although Black women fled less frequently than their male counterparts, they often played crucial roles in coordinating escapes. See Camp, *Closer to Freedom*, 28, 36–54; Stephanie Camp, "'I Could Not Stay There': Enslaved Women,

Truancy and the Geopolitics of Everyday Forms of Resistance in the Antebellum Plantation South," *Slavery and Abolition* 23, no. 3 (2002): 1–20.

3. Benjamin Mathews to Brigham Young, March 31, 1849, Brigham Young Office Files, CR 1234 1, box 21, folder 16, CHL. A report of Jim's escape can be found in *Frontier Guardian*, August 8, 1849, although he isn't identified by name in the article.

4. Carter, "Mississippi Saints," 456.

5. Mathews to Young, March 31, 1849, CHL; Hadden, *Slave Patrols*; and Camp, *Closer to Freedom*, 25.

6. For more on Rande's flight, see Thiriot, *Slavery in Zion*, 10, 87. For Mathews, see Carter, "Mississippi Saints," 456.

7. Francis McKown to Brigham Young, March 31, 1849, Brigham Young Office Files, CR 1234 1, box 21, folder 16, CHL.

8. McKown later returned to Mississippi. A woman matching the description of the onetime runaway appears in an 1860 record of his household; Thiriot, *Slavery in Zion*, 37; McKown to Young, March 31, 1849, CHL. Young maintained his position on returning freedom-seekers to bondage in the coming years; see Turner, *Brigham Young*, 227.

9. Newell G. Bringhurst, *Saints, Slaves, and Blacks: The Changing Place of Black People within Mormonism*, second edition (Greg Kofford Books, 2018), 40–42.

10. Bankhead interviewed in the *Broad Ax*, March 25, 1899.

11. Jared Farmer, *On Zion's Mount: Mormons, Indians, and the American Landscape* (Harvard University Press, 2008), 17, 23.

12. Bennett, *We'll Find the Place*, 346–49.

13. "The Locality History of South Cottonwood Camp," MSS typescript, no author, no date, CHL; Elizabeth Newman Hutchinson, *Holladay, Salt Lake County, Utah* (published by the author, 1971), 2; Stephen L. Carr, ed., *Holladay-Cottonwood: Places and Faces* (Holladay-Cottonwood Heritage Committee, 1987), 10–14; Farmer, *On Zion's Mount*, 43–45.

14. Quoted in Newell, *Your Sister in the Gospel*, 73. On the work regimen for enslaved women in Utah, see Thiriot, *Slavery in Zion*, 40. On the Smith children, see Klemcke and Weed, *Robert Mays Smith*, 1.

15. Seventh Census of the United States, Schedule 3, Productions of Agriculture in the State of Deseret, June 1850, CHL; Hutchinson, *Holladay, Salt Lake County, Utah*, 8. On white Americans' assumptions about Black capacities for labor, see Kathryn Olivarius, *Necropolis: Disease, Power, and Capitalism in the Cotton Kingdom* (Harvard University Press, 2022).

16. Alex Bankhead interview in the *Broad Ax*, March 25, 1899.

17. Thiriot, *Slavery in Zion*, 36 and 368n26. Robert M. Smith, Agnes Flake, William Crosby, Daniel M. Thomas, William Lay, Utah County; John Brown, Abraham Smoot, John H. Bankhead, Great Salt Lake County; Joseph Robinson,

Iron County; Records of the Bureau of the Census, *1850 Census: Seventh Census of the United States*; National Archives Microfilm Publication M432, 1009 rolls, Utah Territory Productions of Agriculture, MS 2672, Record Group 29, CHL.

18. Seventh Census of the United States, Schedule 3, Productions of Agriculture in the State of Deseret, June 1850, CHL.

19. David M. Potter, *The Impending Crisis, 1848–1861*, ed. Don E. Fehrenbacher (Harper & Row, 1976); Michael A. Morrison, *Slavery and the American West: The Eclipse of Manifest Destiny and the Coming of the Civil War* (University of North Carolina, 1997), chap. 4.

20. Joanne Freeman, *The Field of Blood: Congressional Violence and the Road to Civil War* (Picador, 2018).

21. *Congressional Globe*, 31st Congress, 1st session, August 29, 1850, pp. 1702.

22. *Congressional Globe*, 31st Congress, 1st session, March 4, 1850, pp. 451–55

23. Robert Toombs speech, November 13, 1860, in William W. Freehling and Craig M. Simpson, eds., *Secession Debated: Georgia's Showdown in 1860* (Oxford University Press, 1992), 31–50.

24. For more on the transcontinental expansion of slavery, see Waite, *West of Slavery*.

25. "Vexed" was precisely the term they used. See *Frontier Guardian*, August 8, 1849; and Bringhurst, *Saints, Slaves, and Blacks*, 63–64.

26. Kane to Young, February 19, 1851, in Matthew J. Grow and Ronald W. Walker, eds., *The Prophet and the Reformer: The Letters of Brigham Young and Thomas L. Kane* (Oxford University Press, 2015), 95–96.

27. Waite, *West of Slavery*, 125–34.

28. Book of Mormon, Alma 27:9, 43:29; Mosiah 7:15.

29. 2 Nephi 26:33. See also *Doctrine and Covenants* 58:64, 68:8, 84:62, 101:79, 112:28; E. S. Abdy, *Journal of a Residence and Tour in the United States* (John Murray, 1835), III:58; Mueller, *Race and the Making of the Mormon People*, 31–118; and Bringhurst, *Saints, Slaves, and Blacks*, 6–9; Reeve, Rich, Carruth, *This Abominable Slavery*, 44–45.

30. Joanna Brooks, *Mormonism and White Supremacy: American Religion and the Problem of Racial Innocence* (Oxford University Press, 2020), 25.

31. "To His Excellency, Daniel Dunklin, Governor of the State of Missouri," reprinted in *Evening and the Morning Star* 2, no. 15 (December 1833): 226–31. See also Lester E. Bush, "Mormonism's Negro Doctrine: An Historical Overview," *Dialogue: A Journal of Mormon Thought* 8, no. 1 (1973): 11–13.

32. Joseph Smith to Brother Oliver Cowdery, n.d., in *Latter Day Saints' Messenger and Advocate* 2, no. 7 (April 1836): 289–91; see also "The Abolitionists," and W. Parrish letter, also in *Latter Day Saints' Messenger and Advocate* 2, no. 7 (April 1836): 295–96 and 299–301.

33. Joseph Smith, *General Smith's Views of the Powers and Policy of the Government of the United States* (Pontiac, MI: Jackson Print, 1844), 1, 6–7; Park, *King-*

dom of Nauvoo, 183–90, 212–14; Spencer W. McBride, *Joseph Smith for President: The Prophet, the Assassins, and the Fight for American Religious Freedom* (Oxford University Press, 2021).

34. Given that Mormon missionaries in the South, like Abraham Smoot, actively suppressed news of Joseph's campaign manifesto, there's reason to believe Robert Smith never saw it. Brooks, *Mormonism and White Supremacy*, 41.

35. Quoted in Bringhurst, *Saints, Slaves, and Blacks*, 68–69.

36. Turner, *Brigham Young*, 195–98. Dale L. Morgan, *The State of Deseret* (Utah State University Press, 1987), 7–66.

37. Howard R. Lamar, *The Far Southwest: A Territorial History* (University of New Mexico Press, 2000).

38. Morrison, *Slavery and the American West*, chap. 4.

39. Parley P. Pratt, *The Autobiography of Parley Parker Pratt* (New York: Russell Brothers, 1874), 408–12; Demaratus, *Force of a Feather*, 41–42.

40. Glymph, *Out of the House of Bondage*, 36, 39, 51; Jones-Rogers, *They Were Her Property*, 2–5, 16, 70–73.

41. See chapter 9.

42. The first settlers of Cottonwood included the largest slaveholders in Utah: Robert Smith, William Crosby, William Lay, James M. Flake, John H. Bankhead, and John Brown. "Locality History of South Cottonwood Camp," CHL.

43. For biographies see "A Century of Black Mormons," http://centuryofblackmormons.org; Thiriot, *Slavery in Zion*, 203–205, 220–29.

44. Thiriot, *Slavery in Zion*, 196–200. On other marriages within the Black community, see Daniel M. Thomas to Lyman, February 4, 1856, Lyman Collection, CHL.

45. Farmer, *On Zion's Mount*, 49.

46. Quoted in Turner, *Brigham Young*, 222.

47. March 8, 1863, *Journal of Discourses*, 10:110.

48. See Genesis 9:24–25. Bringhurst, *Saints, Slaves, and Blacks*, 40–42. See also Turner, *Brigham Young*, 208–20; W. W. Phelps's Fourth of July speech in *Deseret News*, July 26, 1851.

49. Reeve, Rich, Carruth, *This Abominable Slavery*, 45–46, 166–67; "A Century of Black Mormons," http://centuryofblackmormons.org; Newell, *Your Sister in the Gospel*; W. Paul Reeve, *Religion of a Different Color: Race and the Mormon Struggle for Whiteness* (Oxford University Press, 2015), 128–48.

50. The quote is impossible to verify, but even if apocryphal, it accurately conveys the despair that Black Mormons would have felt; Reiter, "Redd Slave Histories," 115; Newell, *Your Sister in the Gospel*, 91, 102–104; Mueller, *Race and the Making of the Mormon People*, 189–92.

51. Brooks, *Mormonism and White Supremacy*, 11, 36–37, 49.

52. J. Brown, *Autobiography of Pioneer John Brown*, 120; Mueller, *Race and the Making of the Mormon People*, 181–83.

53. Reeve, Rich, Carruth, *This Abominable Slavery*, 139–41; Reeve, *Religion of a Different Color*, 150.

54. Quoted in Turner, *Brigham Young*, 225.

55. "Governor's Message," *Deseret News*, January 10, 1852.

56. "An Act in Relation to Service," in *Acts, Resolutions and Memorials, Passed at the Several Annual Sessions of the Legislative Assembly of the Territory of Utah* (Salt Lake City: Joseph Cain, 1855), 160–62. The best treatment of the law is Reeve, Rich, and Carruth, *This Abominable Slavery*, 120–56.

57. Thiriot, *Slavery in Zion*, xi.

58. Reiter, "Redd Slave Histories," 114.

59. Bringhurst, *Saints, Slaves, and Blacks*, 70–73.

60. Brooks, *Mormonism and White Supremacy*, 39.

61. Horace Greeley, *An Overland Journey from New York to San Francisco, in the Summer of 1859* (New York: M. Saxton, Barker & Co., 1860), 211–12. See also Young to Kane, April 14, 1856, in Grow and Walker, *Prophet and the Reformer*, 195–96.

62. M. Guy Bishop, "Politics, Land, Apostasy: The Last Days of the San Bernardino Mormon Colony, 1855–1857," *Pacific Historian* 30, no. 4 (Winter 1986): 19–22.

63. Utah Slave Schedule, Utah Territory, 1851, CHL; Thiriot, *Slavery in Zion*, xxxi–xxxiv.

CHAPTER 5: CALIFORNIA BOUND

1. The title of this chapter appeared first as the title to Stacey L. Smith's dissertation, "California Bound: Unfree Labor, Race, and the Reconstruction of the Far West, 1848–1870" (PhD dissertation, University of Wisconsin–Madison, 2008).

2. Kristen Phipps, "Desert Slavery: How the Old Spanish Trail Sustained Captivity and Coerced Labor in the North American West" (PhD dissertation, University of Nevada–Las Vegas, 2025); Stephen P. Van Hoak, "And Who Shall Have the Children? The Indian Slave Trade in the Southern Great Basin, 1800–1865," *Nevada Historical Society Quarterly* 41, no. 1 (Spring 1998), 6–7; James F. Brooks, *Captives and Cousins: Slavery, Kinship, and Community in the Southwest Borderlands* (University of North Carolina Press, 2002); Farmer, *On Zion's Mount*, 33.

3. Thiriot, *Slavery in Zion*, 98; Leonard J. Arrington, *Charles C. Rich: Mormon General and Western Frontiersman* (BYU Press, 1974), 159; Beattie and Beattie, *Heritage of the Valley*, 171–72.

4. Turner, *Brigham Young*, 181–82; Edward Leo Lyman, *San Bernardino: The Rise and Fall of a California Community* (Salt Lake City, 1996), 19, 23, 38–39, 243, 379; Milton R. Hunter, "Brigham Young, Colonizer," *Pacific Historical Review* 6, no. 4 (December 1937): 341–60.

5. Brigham Young, Heber Kimball, and Willard Richards to Amasa Lyman and Charles Rich, March 17, 1851, in Amasa Mason Lyman Collection, CHL.

6. Parley Parker Pratt, "A Mormon Mission to California in 1851: From the Diary of Parley Parker Pratt," ed. Reva Holdaway Stanley and Charles L. Camp, *California Historical Society Quarterly* 14, no. 1 (March 1935): 68.

7. William Chandless, *A Visit to Salt Lake* (London: Smith, Elder, & Co., 1857), 295.

8. Pratt, "Mormon Mission to California," 66.

9. Chandless, *Visit to Salt Lake*, 296.

10. Pratt, "Mormon Mission to California," 67–68.

11. Chandless, *Visit to Salt Lake*, 295–96, 298.

12. Pratt, "Mormon Mission to California," 67–68.

13. *Congressional Globe*, 31st Congress, 1st session (March 4, 1850), 451–55.

14. Silas Richards diary, March 16, 1851, MS 16402, CHL. It continued to snow into April; see entries for April 17 and 26, 1851.

15. On San Bernardino's natural advantages, see *Alta California*, October 13, 1851, and July 3, 1853; *Southern Californian*, February 8, 1855.

16. Lyman, *San Bernardino*, 35.

17. Smith, *Freedom's Frontier*, 42–44; on the remoteness of some slaveholding communities, see *Daily Republican Banner and Nashville Whig*, March 28, 1850, Ralph Bieber Collection, HEHL.

18. John Carr, *Pioneer Days in California* (Eureka, CA: Times Publishing Company, 1891), 346.

19. John Batchelder Peirce to Hitty Perice, January 13, 1851, Peirce Papers, MHS.

20. Waite, *West of Slavery*, 5, 91–122 ; Leonard Richards, *The California Gold Rush and the Coming of the Civil War* (Vintage, 2007); Arthur Quinn, *The Rivals: William Gwin, David Broderick, and the Birth of California* (Crown, 1994).

21. *The Mississippian* (Jackson), October 26, 1849, Bieber collection, HEHL. See also Robert M. Dickson to Father and Mother, January 24, 1853; Robert M. Dickson to Margaret Dickson, December 10, 1852, both in William G. Dickson Papers, series 1.1, folder 7, UNC.

22. *The Mississippian* (Jackson), October 26, 1849, Bieber collection, HEHL.

23. Smith, *Freedom's Frontier*, 60; Horace Bell, *On the Old West Coast* (Grosset & Dunlap, 1930), 21.

24. Robert R. Givens to his father, September 10, 1852, Robert R. Givens letters, Bancroft. See also Carr, *Pioneer Days in California*, 346; Anna Lee Marston, ed., *Records of a California Family: Journals and Letters of Lewis C. Gunn and Elizabeth LeBreton Gunn* (n.p., 1928), 171.

25. "Slavery and California," *National Era*, February 19, 1852, 30.

26. See also Augusta Joyce Crocheron, "California Memories," *The Contribu-*

tor 7, no. 1 (October 1885): 20–22; *The Journals of Addison Pratt*, ed. S. George Ellsworth, p. 409, in Marilyn Warne Mills Collection, CHL.

27. Edward Leo Lyman, *Amasa Mason Lyman: Mormon Apostle and Apostate* (University of Utah Press, 2009); Hutchinson, *Holladay, Salt Lake County, Utah* (published by the author, 1971), 4.

28. Arrington, *Charles C. Rich*, xv–xvi; Stegner, *Gathering of Zion*, 47, 183. For a firsthand account, see Edward O .C. Ord, *The City of the Angels and the City of the Saints*, ed. Neal Harlow (Huntington Library, 1978), 20.

29. Lyman, *San Bernardino*, 55; Beattie and Beattie, *Heritage of the Valley*, 180; "Locality History of South Cottonwood Camp," CHL.

30. "Deed from Lugo, et als. to Lyman & Rich," February 26, 1852, in Abstract of Title, 1905, CHL; Jose Del Carmen Lugo, Vida en un Rancho, A. K. Smiley Library Special Collections, Redlands, CA.

31. "Deed from Lugo, et als." CHL; Lyman, *San Bernardino*, viii, 55, 58, 100, 125; Beattie and Beattie, *Heritage of the Valley*, 182–84; Bishop, "Politics, Land, and Apostasy," 22.

32. *Southern Californian*, October 19, 1854. See also *Los Angeles Star*, October 22, 1853.

33. Lyman, *San Bernardino*, 52; Beattie and Beattie, *Heritage of the Valley*, 16, 179, 308.

34. Lyman, *San Bernardino*, 59–60.

35. Byron R. Skinner, *Black Origins in the Inland Empire* (Book Attic Press, 1983), 25.

36. Lyman, *San Bernardino*, 59.

37. San Bernardino Branch Journal, November 24, 25, 26, and December 15, 1851, CHL; H. C. Rolfe, "Story of the Old Fort," in Rolfe scrapbooks, vol. 2, San Bernardino County Historical Archives.

38. Rolfe, "Story of the Old Fort."

39. Skinner, *Black Origins in the Inland Empire*, 29–30. Beattie and Beattie, *Heritage of the Valley*, 62, 201; Luther A. Ingersoll, *Century Annals of San Bernardino* (L. A. Ingersoll, 1904), 133–35; Thiriot, *Slavery in Zion*, 209–11.

40. Flake, *William J. Flake*), 20.

41. Beattie and Beattie, *Heritage of the Valley*, 193; Lyman, *San Bernardino*, 70.

42. Demaratus, *Force of a Feather*, 45.

43. They were later called Serranos by the Spanish. Today they belong to the San Manuel Nation. For more, see "Tribal History, From Then to Now," https://sanmanuel-nsn.gov/culture/history.

44. Beattie and Beattie, *Heritage of the Valley*, 12, 16, 51, 67, 68, 91; George Harwood Phillips, *Vineyards and Vaqueros: Indian Labor and the Economic Expansion of Southern California, 1771–1877* (Arthur H. Clark, 2010), 2016. My thanks to Christella Maldonado and to the education team for the San Manuel Mission Indians for their help in locating Smith's Jumuba ranch.

45. Beattie and Beattie, *Heritage of the Valley*, 12, 16, 51, 67, 68, 91; Ord, *City of the Angels and City of the Saints*, 8–9.

46. Ord, *City of the Angels and City of the Saints*, 16.

47. On the current location of Jumuba, see Demaratus, *Force of a Feather*, 220n64; Beattie and Beattie, *Heritage of the Valley*, 91.

48. San Bernardino Branch tithing accounts, 1851–1857 LR 1594 21; San Bernardino Branch tithing record, 1853 October to 1857 March LR 1594 23. See also San Bernardino Branch tithing papers LR 1594 24, all in CHL. See also Thiriot, *Slavery in Zion*, 50.

49. Daniel M. Thomas to Amasa Lyman, February 4, 1856, Lyman Collection, CHL.

50. Assessment Roll Book 1, pp. 12 and 13, 1853 –1857, A1979.2.1, box 1, folder 1 and Assessment Roll Book 2 p. 36, 1855–1857, A1979.2.2, box 1, folder 2, both in Assessor Records, SBCHA. Thanks to Genevieve Preston for bringing my attention to these files. Thanks also to Fitz Brundage for this insight about untaxable human property.

51. "Deed from Lugo, et. als. to Lyman & Rich," in Abstract of Title, 1905, CHL.

52. Benjamin Hayes, *Pioneer Notes from the Diaries of Judge Benjamin Hayes, 1849–1875*, ed. Marjorie Tisdale Wolcott (Marjorie Tisdale Wolcott, 1929), 104–105, entry for February 16, 1854

53. On the communitarian spirit of early San Bernardino, see Lyman, *Amasa Mason Lyman*, 197.

CHAPTER 6: HIDING IN PLAIN SIGHT

1. *Southern Californian*, February 8, 1855.

2. Bell, *On the Old West Coast*, 298.

3. *Alta California* quoted in Lyman, *San Bernardino*, 49.

4. *Alta California*, December 1, 1853, and "The Mormons in San Bernardino," *Millennial Star* 16, no. 27, July 8, 1854.

5. *Alta California*, February 7, 1854.

6. Bernardino Branch tithing accounts, 1851–1857 LR 1594 21; San Bernardino Branch tithing record, 1853 October–1857 March, LR 1594 23, both in CHL.

7. Demaratus, *Force of a Feather*, 45. For firsthand observations from a nearby cattle estate, see Ord, *City of the Angels and the City of the Saints*, 12.

8. Harris Newmark, *Sixty Years in Southern California, 1853–1913*, 4th edition (Zeitlin & Ver Brugge, 1970), 88.

9. Lyman, *San Bernardino*, 230–31.

10. San Bernardino Branch tithing accounts, 1851–1857 LR 1594 21; San Bernardino Branch tithing record, 1853 October to 1857 March, LR 1594 23, both in CHL.

11. Klemcke and Weed, *Robert Mays Smith*, 1. On enslaved wet nurses, see Jones-Rogers, *They Were Her Property*, 102–106.

12. John J. Zaborney, *Slaves for Hire: Renting Enslaved Laborers in Antebellum Virginia* (Louisiana State University Press, 2012). On slave hiring in California gold country, see George McKinley Murrell to Elisebeth Murrell, October 15–17, 1849; Murrell to John Grider, August 24, 1850; Murrell to Samuel Murrell, January 29–February 1, 1851, all in Murrell Correspondence, HEHL. On the labor shortage in San Bernardino, see Beattie and Beattie, *Heritage of the Valley*, 215.

13. Lyman Journal, Vol. 14, April 26, 1854, Lyman Collection, CHL.

14. Lyman, *San Bernardino*, 289. Lyman's cofounder, Charles Rich, also came to rely on Black labor in the form of a man named Dick. See David Seely to Lyman, February 8, 1853, Correspondence, 1841–1877, box 3, folder 11, Lyman Collection, MS 829, CHL; Bond for the delivery of Richard, no date, Charles C. Rich Collection, CHL. Thiriot, *Slavery in Zion*, 50–52; Arrington, *Charles C. Rich*, 185.

15. Beattie and Beattie, *Heritage of the Valley*, 186n13.

16. *LA Times*, June 22, 1887.

17. Lyman, *San Bernardino*, 71.

18. Sylvia D. Hoffert, "Childbearing on the Trans-Mississippi Frontier, 1830–1900," *Western Historical Quarterly* 22, no. 3 (August 1991): 278–283; Christ Rigby Arrington, "Pioneer Midwives," in *Mormon Sisters: Women in Early Utah*, ed. Claudia Bushman (Salt Lake City, 1976).

19. Berry, *Price for Their Pound of Flesh*, 95, 130–31.

20. Indenture of Apprenticeship, Hannah Smiley to Lewis G. Green, April 7, 1862, Los Angeles County Miscellaneous Records, 1859–1870, Seaver.

21. A complete index of Biddy and Hannah's children, including their ages, comes from the judicial ruling that freed them, Benjamin Hayes, January 19, 1856, *In re Hannah*, MSS, UCLA.

22. *Alta California*, October 25, 1852; "The Mormons at San Bernardino—their politics," reprinted in *Millennial Star* 15, no.4 (January 22, 1853): 61–62; Lyman, *San Bernardino*, 215.

23. San Bernardino Branch *Journal*, December 24, 1851, CHL.

24. San Bernardino Branch *Journal*, September 4, 1852, CHL; Lyman, *San Bernardino*, 77.

25. Lyman, *San Bernardino*, 64–66, 100, 210; Beattie and Beattie, *Heritage of the Valley*, 202, 204; H. C. Rolfe, "Centennial History of San Bernardino County," in Rolfe Scrapbooks, vol. 1, pp. 53–54, SBCHA; *Deseret News*, March 19, 1853.

26. *Southern Californian*, July 27 and August 24, 1854. See also *Southern Californian*, October 19, 1854.

27. Lyman, *San Bernardino*, 227. See also Arrington, *Charles C. Rich*, 187.

28. Newmark, *Sixty Years in Southern California*, 88; Bell, *On the Old West Coast*, 299; Rolfe, "Centennial History of San Bernardino County," 53–54; Ingersoll, *Century Annals of San Bernardino*, 136; Beattie and Beattie, *Heritage of the*

Valley, 196–97; Arrington, *Charles C. Rich*, 174; Lyman, *San Bernardino*, 74, 114, 235, 251.

29. *Southern Californian*, February 8 and March 28, 1855; *Alta California*, November 6, 1854, and May 6, 1855; "Deed from Lugo, et. al. to Lyman & Rich," in Abstract of Title, 1905, CHL; Lyman, *San Bernardino*, 129–131; Ingersoll, *Century Annals of San Bernardino*, 142; Arrington, *Charles C. Rich*, 171–73.

30. Lyman, *Amasa Mason Lyman*, 214; Beattie and Beattie, *Heritage of the Valley*, 217.

31. Thiriot, *Slavery in Zion*, 6–7; Dennis Drake, *William Crosby: Through the Needle's Eye* (published by the author, n.d., copy in CHL), 26, 32–34, 52; Amasa Lyman journal, March 19, 1848, Lyman Collection, CHL; Bennett, *We'll Find the Place*, 308–309.

32. Hayes, *Pioneer Notes*, 104–105, entry for February 16, 1854.

33. Chandless, *Visit to Salt Lake*, 306. Another visitor praised the "ample and varied provision" of the hotel; *L.A. Star*, October 22, 1853. See also *Southern Californian*, October 19, 1854; Lyman Journal, vol. 14, March 31, 1854, Lyman Collection, CHL; Drake, *William Crosby*, 70, 81–82; Thiriot, *Slavery in Zion*, 56.

34. Caroline Barnes Crosby's diary, November 29, 1855, typescript, in Marilyn Warne Mills Collection, CHL; Rolfe, "Story of the Old Fort"; Lyman, *San Bernardino*, 131–32; Flake, *William J. Flake*, 21–25; Demaratus, *Force of a Feather*, 46–50; diary of Louisa Barnes Pratt, in Carter, *Our Pioneer Heritage*, vol. 4, 500; "The Mormons" reprinted in *Millennial Star* 17, no. 4 (January 27, 1855): 62–63.

35. *LA Star*, April 2, 1853; *Southern Californian*, September 21, 1854; Lyman, *San Bernardino*, 90, 135; Beattie and Beattie, *Heritage of the Valley*, 205; Ingersoll, *Century Annals of San Bernardino*, 137, 149.

36. *Alta California*, November 6, 1854.

37. *Southern California*, March 1, 1855. See also *Alta California*, October 19, 1855; *Millennial Star*, no. 44, November 3, 1855.

38. See, for instance, *LA Star*, October 22, 1853, and December 20, 1856; Bell, *On the Old West Coast*, 298.

39. *La Estrella*, August 14, 1852.

40. Court of Sessions, San Bernardino Minutes, 1853–1855, MS 5163, CHL. Only rarely did criminal proceedings come before the court. See, for example, entries for August 6 and 8, 1855. For the private boarding of prisoners, see October 4, 1853. See also H. C. Rolfe, "Pen Sketches of Pioneer Bench and Bar of the County of San Bernardino," vol. 2, in Rolfe scrapbooks, SBCHA; Lyman, *San Bernardino*, 196, 288, 330; Beattie and Beattie, *Heritage of the Valley*, 256–58.

41. Article I, Section 18, *Constitution of the State of California* (San Francisco: Alta California, 1849), 4.

42. See, again, John Taylor's commentary on slavery in San Bernardino in "The Mormons," *Millennial Star*, 62–63. For slavery in California generally, see Smith, *Freedom's Frontier*, and Waite, *West of Slavery*.

43. Edwin A. Sherman, "Sherman Was There: The Recollections of Major Edwin A. Sherman," ed. Allen B. Sherman, *California Historical Society Quarterly* 23, nos. 3–4 (September–December 1944), 351–52; On Green, see M.H.D. Kerr, "Thomas Jefferson Green," *Dictionary of North Carolina Biography*; and Waite, *West of Slavery*, 38–39.

44. Nevada County Historical Landmarks Commission Application for Registration of Historical Landmark: Kentucky Ridge Mine Slave Colony. My thanks to Linda Jack for sharing this document and her research on William F. English.

45. Stacey L. Smith, "Slavery in a Free State: Masters and Slaves in Gold Rush California," *Pacific Historical Review* 80, no. 1 (February 2011): 37.

46. James Gadsden to M. Estes, December 10, 1851, in Charleston *Courier*, February 7, 1852; Gadsden to Thomas Jefferson Green, December 7, 1851, William Alexander Leidesdorff Papers, HEHL; Gadsden to Green, January 29, 1849, Green Papers, box 3, folder 30, UNC; *California State Assembly Journal* (1852): 159–60.

47. Lyman, *Amasa Mason Lyman*, 212.

48. Rolfe, "Pen Sketches," Rolfe scrapbooks, SBCHA.

49. Court of Sessions, San Bernardino Minutes, December 4, 1854, CHL.

50. Hunt supported the division of California to make way for an independent territory in the southern half of the state, which many anticipated would legalize slavery; *LA Star*, April 2, 1853. See also Waite, *West of Slavery*, 155–59.

51. Quoted in Skinner, *Black Origins in the Inland Empire*, 27–28.

52. The brief interview with Martha is included in Beattie and Beattie, *Heritage of the Valley*, 186n13.

53. Quoted in Thiriot, *Slavery in Zion*, 100.

54. Lyman, *San Bernardino*, 35; Beattie and Beattie, *Heritage of the Valley*, 186; Drake, *William Crosby*, 75, 86. For the ways in which Mormon slaveholders denied their slaveholding, see Thiriot, *Slavery in Zion*, 31–41; Reiter, "Redd Slave Histories," 111.

55. Chandless, *Visit to Salt Lake*, 306; "Suit for Freedom," *Los Angeles Star*, February 2, 1856. See also Carter, *Our Pioneer Heritage*, vol. 4, 500.

56. Flake, *William J. Flake*, 21–25; Skinner, *Black Origins in the Inland Empire*, 30–31; Thiriot, *Slavery in Zion*, 226–29.

57. Andrés Resendez, *The Other Slavery: The Uncovered Story of Indian Enslavement in America* (Houghton Mifflin Harcourt, 2016). See also Native Bound Unbound, https://nativeboundunbound.org/.

58. Benjamin Madley, "'Unholy Traffic in Human Blood and Souls': Systems of California Indian Servitude Under U.S. Rule," *Pacific Historical Review* 83, no. 4 (November 2014): 627.

59. J. Ross Browne, *Crusoe's Island: A Ramble in the Footsteps of Alexander Selkirk* (New York: Harper & Brothers, 1864), 284–88; Albert Hurtado, *Indian Survival on the California Frontier* (Yale University Press, 1988); George Harwood Phillips, *Vineyards and Vaqueros: Indian Labor and the Economic Expansion*

of Southern California, 1771–1877 (University of Oklahoma Press, 2010); George Harwood Phillips, "Indians in Los Angeles, 1781–1875: Economic Integration, Social Disintegration," *Pacific Historical Review* 49, no. 3 (August 1980); Madley, "Unholy Traffic," 645; Robert Glass Cleland, *Cattle on a Thousand Hills: Southern California, 1850–1880* (Huntington Library, 1954), 30.

60. Brendan C. Lindsay, *Murder State: California's Native American Genocide, 1846–1873* (University of Nebraska Press, 2015); Benjamin Madley, *An American Genocide: The United States and the California Indian Catastrophe* (Yale University Press, 2016), 67–102.

61. Quoted in Madley, "Unholy Traffic," 627; and *Congressional Globe*, 36th Congress, 1st session (May 26, 1860), 2366–69.

62. Ord, *City of Angels and the City of the Saints*, 13–16.

63. Thaddeus S. Kenderdine, *A California Tramp and Later Footprints* (Newtown, PA, n.p., 1888), 190–91.

64. Bancroft, "Personal Observations during a tour through the Line of Missions of Upper California," MSS, 22–23, Bancroft Library. See also Hayes, *Pioneer Notes*, 224–25.

65. Howard Lamar, "From Bondage to Contract: Ethnic Labor in the American West, 1600–1890," in Steven Hahn and Jonathan Prude, eds., *The Countryside in the Age of Capitalist Transformation: Essays in the Social History of Rural America* (University of North Carolina Press, 1985); Michael Magliari, "'A Species of Slavery': The Compromise of 1850, Popular Sovereignty, and the Expansion of Unfree Indian Labor in the American West," *Journal of American History* 109, no. 3 (December 2022): 521–47.

CHAPTER 7: UNMAKING A PATRIARCH

1. San Bernardino Branch *Journal*, August 17, 1855, CHL. See also entries for August 6, November 29, and December 5, 1855, and May 14, 1856.

2. San Bernardino Branch *Journal*, August 17, 1855, CHL.

3. On rumor and politics in enslaved communities, see Steven Hahn, *A Nation Under Our Feet: Black Political Struggles in the Rural South from Slavery to the Great Migration* (Belknap, 2003), 57–60, 129–37.

4. "Patent for Rancho San Bernardino," in Abstract of Title, 1905, CHL.

5. Beattie and Beattie, *Heritage of the Valley*, 182–84; Arrington, *Charles C. Rich*, 196; Lyman, *San Bernardino*, 55, 58, 100, 125.

6. Beattie and Beattie, *Heritage of the Valley*, 238–45.

7. Assessment Roll Book 1, pp. 12 and 13, 1853 –1857, A1979.2.1, box 1, folder 1 and Assessment Roll Book 2 p. 36, 1855–1857, A1979.2.2, box 1, folder 2, both in Assessor Records, SBCHA; Bishop, "Politics, Land, and Apostasy."

8. H. C. Rolfe, "The Early Political History of San Bernardino County," Rolfe scrapbooks, vol. 2, SBCHA.

9. See also Stegner, *Gathering of Zion*, 4; Turner, *Brigham Young*, 243.

10. Bishop, "Politics, Land, Apostasy," 24–27; Lyman, *San Bernardino*, 145, 152–54. For the election results, see *Southern California*, April 25, 1855.

11. San Bernardino Branch *Journal*, December 5, 1855, CHL.

12. Arrington, *Charles C. Rich*, 189–192; Beattie and Beattie, *Heritage of the Valley*, 230–37.

13. Chandless, *Visit to Salt Lake*, 305.

14. Ord, *City of the Angels and City of the Saints*, 35.

15. First quote from Young to Lyman, January 29, 1855, Lyman Collection, CHL; second quoted in Lyman, *San Bernardino*, 169.

16. Lyman, *San Bernardino*, 151. See also Lyman, *Amasa Mason Lyman*, 220–21.

17. *Alta California*, June 11, 1855. See also *Southern Californian*, May 30, 1855; *Alta California*, May 28, 1855.

18. *Southern Californian*, October 5, 1854.

19. *Alta California*, October 19, 1855; *LA Star*, August 4, 1855. See also *LA Star*, June 23, 1855; *Alta California*, August 17, 1855.

20. The lower estimate comes from *LA Star*, December 22, 1855; the higher estimate comes from San Bernardino Branch *Journal*, December 10, 1855, CHL.

21. *Southern Californian*, May 30, 1855.

22. San Bernardino Branch *Journal*, December 31, 1855, CHL.

23. *LA Star*, January 25, 1855.

24. *Southern Californian*, October 12, 1854.

25. *LA Star*, January 25, 1855.

26. San Bernardino Branch *Journal*, August 17 and 18, 1855, CHL.

27. Klemcke and Weed, *Robert Mays Smith*, 3.

28. "Constitution of Republic of Texas," *Laws of the Republic of Texas* (Houston: Office of the Telegraph, 1838), vol. 1, 9–25.

29. Andrew J. Torget, *Seeds of Empire: Cotton, Slavery, and the Transformation of the Texas Borderlands, 1800–1850* (University of North Carolina Press, 2015).

30. "Suit for Freedom," appendix B, *Daily Democratic Journal*, February 19, 1856.

31. Kenderdine, *California Tramp*, 186–95. See also Newmark, *Sixty Years in Southern California*, 88; and Ord, *City of Angels and City of the Saints*, 12.

32. Lyman, *San Bernardino*, 291; Susan Straight, "Biddy Mason and Hannah Embers Were Here," *Alta Journal*, August 2, 2021.

33. On San Pedro, see Ord, *City of Angels and City of the Saints*, 7.

34. Demaratus comes to a similar conclusion in *Force of a Feather*, 49.

35. Owens, "My Grandfather," MSS, UCLA.

36. Gordon, "A 'Free' State," 227.

37. "Judge Benjamin Ignatius Hayes," MSS typescript, Joseph Mesmer Papers, box 6, folder 2, UCLA Special Collections; Hayes, *Pioneer Notes*, foreword, 13,

75, 90, 93; Faragher, *Eternity Street*, ix, 277–279; Demaratus, *Force of a Feather*, 65–70; Ronald C. Woolsey, "Pioneer Views and Frontier Themes: Benjamin Hayes, Horace Bell, and the Southern California Experience," *Southern California Quarterly* 72, no. 3 (1990): 258.

38. Hayes mentions some of these details in "Suit for Freedom," *Los Angeles Star*, February 2, 1856, and "Suit for Freedom," *Daily Democratic State Journal*, February 19, 1856. The petitioner is mentioned, but again not by name, in Chandless, *Visit to Salt Lake*, 306.

39. *LA Star*, February 2, 1856.

40. Owens, "My Grandfather," MSS, UCLA, and a brief interview with Ellen in Beasley, *Negro Trail Blazers*, 90.

41. Flake, *William J. Flake*, 226–29.

42. Beasley, *Negro Trail Blazers*, 90

43. On Hayes's visit to San Bernardino, see San Bernardino Branch *Journal*, October 15, 1855, CHL.

44. Owens, "My Grandfather," MSS, UCLA.

45. For more on Robert Owens, see Lonnie G. Bunch, *Black Angelenos: The Afro-American in Los Angeles, 1850–1950* (California Afro-American Museum, 1989), 14–15; Campbell, *Making Black Los Angeles*, 52–56; Owens, "My Grandfather," MSS, UCLA.

46. *LA Star*, February 2, 1856.

47. Skinner, *Black Origins in the Inland Empire*, 30; Carter, *Our Pioneer Heritage*, vol. 4, 500.

48. See, for instance, Charmaine Lay Kohler, *Southern Grace: A Story of the Mississippi Saints* (Beagle Creek Press, 1995); Drake, *William Crosby*.

49. Flake, *William J. Flake*, 23–24, 27–28.

50. Blight, *Race and Reunion*; Kevin Levin, *Searching for Black Confederates: The Civil War's Most Persistent Myth* (University of North Carolina Press, 2019); Stephanie McCurry, *Confederate Reckoning: Power and Politics in the Civil War South* (Harvard University Press, 2010).

51. Benjamin Mathews to Brigham Young, March 31, 1849, Brigham Young Office Files, CR 1234 1, box 21, folder 16, CHL.

52. William Crosby to Brigham Young, March 12, 1851, Brigham Young Office Files, CR 1234 1, box 22, folder 6, CHL.

53. Brigham Young to William Crosby, March 12, 1851, Brigham Young Office Files, CR 1234 1, box 22, folder 6, CHL; Reeve, Rich, and Carruth, *This Abominable Slavery*; Thiriot, *Slavery in Zion*, 356–57; Turner, *Brigham Young*, 228; Skinner, *Black Origins*, 12–13; "Hark Wales," in "A Century of Black Mormons," https://exhibits.lib.utah.edu/s/century-of-black-mormons/page/wales-hark#?c=&m=&s=&cv=&xywh=-1502%2C-17%2C3787%2C1257.

54. Thiriot, *Slavery in Zion*, 226–29.

55. Demaratus, *Force of a Feather*, 49; "Suit for Freedom," *Daily Democratic State Journal*, February 19, 1856.

56. Rolfe, "Story of the Fort," Rolfe scrapbooks, SBCHA; Thiriot, *Slavery in Zion*, 197–99.

57. List of Loyalists in San Bernardino, circa April 1851, Charles C. Rich Collection, CHL.

58. Testimony of A. H. Cooper, in "Suit for Freedom," *Daily Democratic State Journal*, February 19, 1856.

59. Sarah L.H. Gronningsater, "'On Behalf of His Race and the Lemmon Slaves': Louis Napoleon, Northern Black Legal Culture, and the Politics of Sectional Crisis," *Journal of the Civil War Era* 7, no. 2 (June 2017).

60. *Daily Democratic Journal*, February 19, 1856.

61. Demaratus, *Force of a Feather*, 77–79; Gordon, "A 'Free' State," 217–18. On the extensive and overlooked history of habeas activism in the nineteenth-century West, see Katrina Jagodinsky, "'The Last Rose of Summer': A Century of Women's Habeas Petitions and Gendered Violence," and Cory James Young, "'A Slave in Nebraska' and Other Black Habeas Activism on the Gilded Age Plains," both in *Western Historical Quarterly* 56, no. 2 (Summer 2025); and "Petitioning for Freedom: Habeas Corpus in the American West, 1812–1914," https://petitioningforfreedom.unl.edu/.

62. On the rescue, see Owens, "My Grandfather," MSS, UCLA; Hayden, "Biddy Mason's Los Angeles," 90; Demaratus, *Force of a Feather*, 77–79. On the cold weather that season, see San Bernardino Branch *Journal*, entries for December 25, 26, 27, 29, 1855, CHL.

63. Hayes, *In re Hannah*, UCLA; "Suit for Freedom," *Daily Democratic Journal*, February 19, 1856; Owens, "My Grandfather," MSS, UCLA, 5; Beasley, *Negro Trail Blazers*, 90; Demaratus, *Force of a Feather*, 77–80.

CHAPTER 8: THE TRIAL

1. On the wagons of antebellum Los Angeles and the dogs that trailed them, see James L. Woods, *Recollections of Pioneer Work in California* (San Francisco: Joseph Winterburn, 1878), 198–99; Horace Bell, *Reminiscences of a Ranger* (Wallace Hebberd, 1927), 5. Quote from Newmark, *Sixty Years in Southern California*, 85.

2. William H. Brewer, *Up and Down California* (Yale University Press, 1930), 13.

3. On liquor in early Los Angeles, see Hayes, *Pioneer Notes*, 90; John S. Griffin, *Los Angeles in 1849: A Letter from John S. Griffin to Col J.D. Stevenson, March 11, 1849* (privately printed, 1949), 9.

4. Socrates Hyacinth, "On Foot in Southern California," *Overland Monthly* 2, no. 1 (January 1869), 23; Ord, *City of the Angels and the City of the Saints*, 8–9.

5. David Samuel Torres-Rouff, *Before L.A.: Race Space, and Municipal Power in Los Angeles, 1781–1894* (Yale University Press, 2013), 27, 141, 204.

6. Robert M. Fogelson, *The Fragmented Metropolis: Los Angeles, 1850–1930* (1967; reprint, University of California Press, 1993), 25; Newmark, *Sixty Years in Southern California*, 34, 584.

7. Kenderdine, *California Tramp*, 198. See also Bell, *Reminiscences of a Ranger*, 10; Charles Loring Brace, *The New West: Or, California in 1867–1868* (New York: Putnam, 1869), 278.

8. Greg Hise, "Border City: Race and Social Distance in Los Angeles," *American Quarterly* 56, no. 3 (September 2004), 546.

9. On the Rocha House, see Paul Spitzzeri, "Crime and Justice in Los Angeles, 1850–1875," *Trembling on the Brink*, September 28, 2016, http://tremblingontheb rink.blogspot.com/2016/09/this-pictures-thousand-words-los.html?m=1.

10. Hernandez, *City of Inmates*, 1–44; Faragher, *Eternity Street*, 2.

11. "The County Jail," *Los Angeles Star*, January 30, 1858. For more on conditions in the jail, see *Los Angeles Star*, May 17, 1856; and Henry Winfred Splitter, "Los Angeles in the 1850's As Told by Early Newspapers," *Historical Society of Southern California Quarterly* 31, nos. 1–2 (March–June 1949), 116–17.

12. This description of the ground floor prison also from "The County Jail," *Los Angeles Star*, January 30, 1858.

13. Bell, *Reminiscences of a Ranger*, 38; Newmark, *Sixty Years in Southern California*, 115.

14. Hernandez, *City of Inmates*, 1.

15. "Suit for Freedom," *Daily Democratic State Journal*, February 19, 1856.

16. See introduction, note 9. Also see Som-Mai Nguyen, "Which Is Something Unusual," September 5, 2020, www.biddymasoncollaborative.com.

17. Paul Finkelman, "The Law of Slavery and Freedom in California 1848–1860," *California Western Law Review* 17, no. 3 (1980–81), 452. See also Smith, *Freedom's Frontier*, 62–75; Gordon, "A 'Free' State," 214.

18. *Daily Alta California*, March 10, 1855.

19. Cornelius Cole, *Memoirs of Cornelius Cole, Ex-Senator of the United States from California* (McLoughlin Brothers, 1908), 114–15.

20. John Conness, *Some of the Men and Measures of the War and Reconstruction Period* (Boston: Nathan Sawyer & Son, 1882), 5.

21. Charles W. McCurdy, "Prelude to Civil War: A Snapshot of the California Supreme Court at Work in 1858," *California Supreme Court Historical Society Yearbook* (1994), 4; Cole, *Memoirs of Cornelius Cole*, 117–18. For a brief biography of Murray, see Oscar Tully Shuck, ed., *History of the Bench and Bar of California* (Commercial Printing House, 1901), 86–87.

22. Michael E. Woods, *Emotional and Sectional Conflict in the Antebellum United States* (Cambridge University Press, 2014), chap. 6.

23. McCurdy, "Prelude to Civil War," 4; see also Shuck, *History of the Bench and Bar of California*, 86–87.

24. "An Act Respecting Fugitives from Labor, and Slaves brought to this State prior to her admission into the Union," in Hayes Scrapbooks, vol. 43, Bancroft.

25. Smith, *Freedom's Frontier*, 64.

26. Ray R. Albin, "The Perkins Case: The Ordeal of Three Slaves in Gold Rush California," *California History* 67, no. 4 (1988): 215–27; Jason Gillmer, "Black, White, and Gold: Litigating Slavery in the American West," Gonzaga University School of Law Research Paper, February 8, 2021; Brian McGinty, *Archy Lee's Struggle for Freedom: The True Story of California Gold. the Nation's Tragic March Toward Civil War, and a Young Black Man's Fight for Liberty* (Lyons Press, 2020), 29–30.

27. *In re Perkins*, 2 Cal. 424 (1852), 438, 441.

28. Smith, *Freedom's Frontier*, appendix, 237–45.

29. Gordon, "A 'Free' State," 214; McGinty, *Archy Lee's Struggle for Freedom*, 25–27.

30. Hayes, *Pioneer Notes*, 13.

31. Hayes to Mrs. Emily Hayes, June 28, 1851, in Hayes, *Pioneer Notes*, 75.

32. "Suit for Freedom," *Los Angeles Star*, February 2, 1856.

33. Benjamin Hayes to B. M. Hughes, January 24, 1853, in Hayes, *Pioneer Notes*, 90–93.

34. Waite, *West of Slavery*, 100–107; Daniel Brendan Lynch, "Southern California Chivalry: The Convergence of Southerners and Californios in the Far Southwest, 1846–1866" (PhD dissertation, UCLA, 2015); Douglas Monroy, *Thrown Among Strangers: The Making of Mexican Culture in Frontier California* (University of California Press, 1990), 50, 75, 115, 136.

35. "Suit for Freedom," *Los Angeles Star*, February 2, 1856.

36. Hayes, *Pioneer Notes*, 104–105.

37. *Southern Californian*, October 19, 1854. Although unsigned, the article has been attributed to Hayes.

38. "Suit for Freedom," *Los Angeles Star*, February 2, 1856.

39. "An Act Concerning Crimes and Punishments," April 16, 1850, ch. 99, sec. 14, and "An Act to Regulate Proceedings in Civil Cases, in the Courts of This State," April 20, 1851, ch. 5, se. 394, both in State of California, *Statutes of California*, 1850, 1851; Smith, *Freedom's Frontier*, 56; Waite, *West of Slavery*, 94; McGinty, *Archy Lee's Struggle for Freedom*, 6, 29.

40. Smith, *Freedom's Frontier*, 72; Gordon, "A 'Free' State," 214.

41. Benjamin Hayes, *In re Hannah*, January 19, 1856, MSS, Golden State Mutual Life Insurance Company records, box 41, UCLA.

42. Paul Barrows, "A Relic of Old Pueblo Days," *Los Angeles Herald*, May 12, 1901.

43. "Suit for Freedom," appendix, *Daily Democratic Journal*, February 19, 1856.

44. *Henry Cardwell vs. Robert Owens*, filed March 8, 1856, Los Angeles County Court, Los Angeles Area Court Records, Case No. 59, HEHL; In the matter of the estate of Robert Owens, Los Angeles Area Court Records, Probate Court, Case No. 316, September 25, 1865.

45. Owens, "My Grandfather," MSS, UCLA.

46. J. J. Warner, Benjamin Hayes, and Joseph P. Widney, *An Historical Sketch of Los Angeles County, California* (Los Angeles: Mirror Printing, 1876), 44.

47. For more tributes to Owens, see "Negro Settlers," MSS typescript, box 4, folder 4, Joseph Mesmer Papers, UCLA; Newmark, *Sixty Years in Southern California*, 138. See also Bunch, *Black Angelenos*, 14–15; Campbell, *Making Black Los Angeles*, 52–56; Lynn Hudson, *West of Jim Crow: The Fight Against California's Color Line* (University of Illinois Press, 2020), 210; Quintard Taylor, *In Search of the Racial Frontier: African Americans in the American West, 1528–1990* (W. W. Norton, 1998), 90.

48. *Los Angeles Semi-Weekly News*, October 1, 1867; *Daily Evening Herald* (Stockton, CA), October 11, 1867; *Los Angeles Daily Star*, March 11, 1872; *Los Angeles Herald*, April 19, 1883.

49. Los Angeles Census, 1870; In the matter of the estate of Winnie Owens, deceased, 1893, Los Angeles Superior Court, Los Angeles Area Court Records, case no 2272, HEHL.

50. Estimates differ slightly between two sources but equate to roughly $3,000; *Los Angeles Herald*, April 19, 1883; *LA Times*, April 19, 1883.

51. Barrows, "Relic of Old Pueblo Days," *Los Angeles Herald*, May 12, 1901.

52. Owens, "My Grandfather," MSS, UCLA; Hayden, "Biddy Mason's Los Angeles, 1856–18891," 89–90.

53. On the Underground Railroad in the Far West, see the terrific work of the National Park Service's Network to Freedom, https://www.nps.gov/orgs/1205/index.htm.

54. Owens, "My Grandfather," MSS, UCLA.

55. See Judge Benjamin Hayes's report on the trial, both titled "Suit for Freedom." The first was published in the *Los Angeles Star*, February 2, 1856. The second, an altered and slightly longer version, appeared in *Daily Democratic State Journal* (Sacramento), February 19, 1856. It was also republished in *National Anti-Slavery Standard*, April 5, 1856. For more national coverage, see *New York Daily Times*, March 27, 1856; *National Anti-Slavery Standard*, March 22, 1856; "Important Judicial Decision in California," *The Liberator*, March 28, 1856. On the excitement surrounding the trial, see the letter of Joseph Mesmer, March 23, 1939, in Bass, *Forty Years*, 114–17.

56. "The County Courthouse Buildings," *Los Angeles Star*, November 29, 1856. See also *Los Angeles Star*, November 4, 1857; *Los Angeles Star*, March 10, 1860. Thanks to Paul Spitzzeri for guiding me to these sources.

57. *Los Angeles Star*, December 31, 1859, in Hayes, *Pioneers Notes*, 183; Newmark, *Sixty Years in Southern California*, 256.

58. "Suit for Freedom," *Los Angeles Star*, February 2, 1856.

59. "Suit for Freedom," *Los Angeles Star*, February 2, 1856; Demaratus, *Force of a Feather*, 88.

60. Suit for Freedom," *Daily Democratic State Journal*, February 19, 1856.

61. "Suit for Freedom," *Los Angeles Star*, February 2, 1856.

62. "Suit for Freedom," *Daily Democratic State Journal*, February 19, 1856.

63. "Suit for Freedom," *Los Angeles Star*, February 2, 1856.

64. For Stearns, see *Los Angeles Star*, August 14, 1852.

65. "Suit for Freedom," appendix B, *Daily Democratic Journal*, February 19, 1856.

66. "Suit for Freedom," appendix B, *Daily Democratic Journal*, February 19, 1856.

67. "Suit for Freedom," appendix B, *Daily Democratic Journal*, February 19, 1856.

CHAPTER 9: THE DECISION

1. Benjamin Hayes, *In re Hannah*, January 19, 1856, MSS, Golden State Mutual Life Insurance Company records, box 41, UCLA.

2. "Suit for Freedom," *Los Angeles Star,* February 2, 1856 (italics in original).

3. Hayes, *In re Hannah*, MSS, UCLA.

4. "Suit for Freedom," *Daily Democratic State Journal*, February 19, 1856.

5. Hayes, *In re Hannah*, MSS, UCLA.

6. "Suit for Freedom," *Los Angeles Star*, February 2, 1856 (emphasis in the original).

7. For more on Hannah's testimony and the events leading to it, see Demaratus, *Force of a Feather*, 117–20.

8. "Suit for Freedom," *Los Angeles Star*, February 2, 1856 (emphasis in the original). See also Demaratus, *Force of a Feather*, 139.

9. "Suit for Freedom," *Los Angeles Star*, February 2, 1856.

10. Again, see "Indenture of Apprenticeship," Seaver.

11. On the rape and sexual abuse of Hannah and Biddy, see chapter 2.

12. "Breathing freer" from "Suit for Freedom," *Los Angeles Star*, February 2, 1856; all other quotes come from the testimony of the sheriff, given in court on January 24 and 25, printed in "Suit for Freedom," *Daily Democratic State Journal*, February 19, 1856.

13. "Suit for Freedom," *Daily Democratic State Journal*, February 19, 1856.

14. For Murray, see Cole, *Memoirs of Cornelius Cole*, 117–18; McCurdy, "Prelude to Civil War," 4; Waite, *West of Slavery*, 99.

15. "An Act for the Government and Protection of Indians," *Statutes of Califor-*

nia, 1850, pp. 408–10; see also Smith, *Freedom's Frontier*, 110–25; Resendez, *The Other Slavery*, 264–73; Sarah Barringer Gordon and Jan Shipps, "Fatal Convergence in the Kingdom of God: The Mountain Meadows Massacre in American History," *Journal of the Early Republic* 37 (Summer 2017):335–38; Madley, *American Genocide*, 157–60; Waite, *West of Slavery*, 103–105.

16. See "An Act to Confer Civil Rights on Freedmen, and for other Purposes," in *Laws of the State of Mississippi* (Jackson, MS: J. J. Shannon & Sons, 1866), 82–91.

17. Michael Magliari, "Free Soil, Unfree Labor: Cave Johnson Couts and the Binding of Indian Workers in California, 1850–1867," *Pacific Historical Review* 73 (August 2004): 349–90. Hayes himself had a Cahuilla Indian servant named Benito; Hayes, *Pioneer Notes*, 96, 224–25.

18. In the matter of the guardianship of Emily and Maria (negroes), April 18, 1857, Probate Court, #66, Los Angeles Area Court Records, HEHL. On the Hereford's slave-ownership, see Margaret Hereford Wilson to Benjamin D. Wilson, September 14, 1856, and Benjamin D. Wilson to Margaret Hereford Wilson, October 23, 1856, Benjamin D. Wilson Collection, box 10, HEHL.

19. Charnan Williams, "The History of Slavery and Race in California from the Gold Rush to the United States Civil War, 1848–1865" (PhD dissertation, University of Michigan, 2022), 71–72. Ironically, Shore would later reissue Biddy's freedom papers.

20. In the matter of the guardianship of guardianship of Rose, a minor child, Los Angeles Area Court Records, Probate Court, No. 45, HEHL; Smith, *Freedom's Frontier*, 109–10.

21. "Suit for Freedom," *Los Angeles Star*, February 2, 1856.

22. Testimony of James M. Barnes, in "Suit for Freedom," *Daily Democratic State Journal*, February 19, 1856.

23. Testimony of Dr. A. H. Cooper in "Suit for Freedom," *Daily Democratic State Journal*, February 19, 1856.

24. Later in life Willy went by the name "Seco" and became a minor frontier legend in Texas. He was a notorious drunk, with fifteen children (not including Mary) among three wives. See Klemcke and Weed, *Robert Mays Smith*.

25. Testimony of Dr. A. H. Cooper in "Suit for Freedom," *Daily Democratic State Journal*, February 19, 1856. For more speculation on the paternity of Ann's child, see Demaratus, *Force of a Feather*, 141–46.

26. "Suit for Freedom," *Daily Democratic State Journal*, February 19, 1856; Demaratus, *Force of a Feather*, 141–46.

27. Testimony of the jailer, F. J. Carpenter in "Suit for Freedom," *Daily Democratic State Journal*, February 19, 1856.

28. My thanks to Sally Gordon for these insights.

29. Declaration of John Edwards, February 28, 1850; Police Report, February and March, 1850; Declaration of J. H. Purdy, March 5, 1850, all in Alcalde/Los Angeles County Court Records, vol. 6: Criminal, Seaver; Faragher, *Eternity Street*,

210–11; John Albert Wilson, *History of Los Angeles County, with Illustrations Descriptive of Its Scenery, Residences, Fine Blocks, and Manufactories* (Oakland, CA: Thompson & West, 1880), 90.

30. Stephen C. Foster to Governor Peter H. Burnett, March 12, 1850, Los Angeles Prefecture Records, vol. 2, 840–43, HEHL; Declaration of Purdy, March 5, 1850, Seaver; Smith, *Freedom's Frontier*, 55.

31. Testimony of A. J. Henderson, in "Suit for Freedom," *Daily Democratic State Journal*, February 19, 1856.

32. Testimony of A. H. Cooper, in "Suit for Freedom," *Daily Democratic State Journal*, February 19, 1856.

33. Faragher, *Eternity Street*, 2, 263.

34. Julius Froebel, *Seven Years' Travel in Central America, Northern Mexico, and the Far West of the United States* (London: Richard Bentley, 1859), 568. See also Brewer, *Up and Down California*, 14; Newmark, *Sixty Years in Southern California*, 59, 224.

35. Woods, *Recollections of Pioneer Work*, 203. See also Joseph Lancaster Brent, *The Lugo Case: A Personal Experience* (Searcy & Pfaff, 1926), 7; William F. Deverell, *Whitewashed Adobe: The Rise of Los Angeles and the Remaking of Its Mexican Past* (University of California Press, 2004), 25.

36. *Southern Californian*, November 16, 1854. See also *Daily Alta California*, October 19 1854; *Southern Californian*, August 31, 1854, and October 26, 1854.

37. Bell, *On the Old West Coast*, 165.

38. Paul R. Spitzzeri, "Judge Lynch in Session: Popular Justice in Los Angeles, 1850–1875," *Southern California Quarterly* 87 (Summer 2005): 83.

39. Richard Griswold del Castillo, *The Los Angeles Barrio, 1850–1890: A Social History* (University of California Press, 1982), 106; Spitzzeri, "Judge Lynch in Session," 83–86, 114–15; Faragher, *Eternity Street*, 7–17, 263, 299–313; Torres-Rouff, *Before L.A.*, 9–10, 99, 194; Woods, *Recollections of Pioneer Work*, 201–202; Newmark, *Sixty Years in Southern California*, 139–40; Bell, *On the Old West Coast*, 240–44; see also Ken Gonzalez-Day, *Lynching in the West, 1850–1935* (Duke University Press, 2006); William D. Carrigan and Clive Webb, *Forgotten Dead: Mob Violence Against Mexicans in the United States, 1848–1928* (Oxford University Press, 2013).

40. "Suit for Freedom," *Los Angeles Star*, February 2, 1856; Demaratus, *Force of a Feather*, 147.

41. Hayes, *In re Hannah*, MSS, UCLA (emphasis in the original).

42. "Suit for Freedom," *Los Angeles Star*, February 2, 1856.

43. Thomas to Lyman, February 4, 1856, Lyman Collection, CHL. See also Thiriot, *Slavery in Zion*, 105–107; and "Negro Settlers," Joseph Mesmer Papers, MSS typescript, Box 4, folder 4, UCLA.

44. Chandless, *Visit to Salt Lak*e, 306.

45. William S. Warren to Lyman, April 3, 1856, Lyman Collection, CHL.

46. Klemcke and Weed, *Robert Mays Smith*, 14

47. Richard Hopkins, "Minutes of Special Conference," March 15, 1856, in *Deseret News*, July 2, 1856. My thanks to Christella Maldonado for locating this source for me.

CHAPTER 10: FREEDWOMAN

1. "Judge John Chauncey Hayes," MSS typescript, Joseph Mesmer Papers, box 6, folder 2, UCLA.

2. Benjamin Hayes to Jack Hinton, September 20, 1863, Benjamin Hayes Scrapbooks, vol. 14, Bancroft. For an excellent discussion of the letter and how she discovered it, see Demaratus, *Force of a Feather*, 185–92.

3. Hayes to Hinton, September 20, 1863, Bancroft.

4. "Important Judicial Decision in California," *The Liberator*, March 28, 1856.

5. *National Anti-Slavery Standard*, March 22, 1856.

6. *New York Daily Times*, March 27, 1856. A reprinted version of the article appears in Hayes Scrapbooks, vol. 43, Bancroft.

7. Hayes to Hinton, September 20, 1863, Bancroft.

8. "Suit for Freedom," *Los Angeles Star*, February 2, 1856.

9. News clipping in Hayes Scrapbooks, vol. 43, Bancroft.

10. Benjamin Hayes to Benjamin D. Wilson, February 12, 1856, Benjamin D. Wilson Collection, box 9, HEHL. Hayes also collected news items related to the 1856 ruling in his scrapbooks, under a separate section he titled "The Slave Case." "The Slave Case," Hayes Scrapbooks, vol. 43, Bancroft.

11. Hayes to Wilson, February 12, 1856, Wilson Collection, box 9, HEHL.

12. "Suit for Freedom," *Daily Democratic Journal*, February 19, 1856. See also Hayes Scrapbooks, vol. 43, Bancroft.

13. *National Anti-Slavery Standard*, 5 April 1856.

14. "In the matter of the estate of Alexander Cribbs, deceased," February and March 1850, Alcalde/Los Angeles County Court Records, vol. 6: Criminal, Seaver. Faragher, *Eternity Street*, 209–210; Williams, "Slavery and Race in California," 87–90; On the judge's personal arsenal, see Hayes, *Pioneer Notes*, 110.

15. Part of Jose Maria's property became the Jumuba ranch on which Biddy labored.

16. Hayes, *Pioneer Notes*, 75–79; Bell, *Reminiscences of a Ranger*, 184, 195. On the trial, see Brent, *Lugo Case.*

17. Newmark, *Sixty Years in Southern California*, 52–53, 56.

18. Benjamin D. Wilson to Margaret Hereford Wilson, Benjamin D. Wilson Collection, July 13, 1856, box 10, HEHL; Hayes, *Pioneer Notes*, 123.

19. Hayes, *Pioneer Notes*, 169.

20. Hayes, *Pioneer Notes*, 166–67, 169, 172; Demaratus, *Force of a Feather*, 156–57; Faragher, *Eternity Street*, 369–70.

21. Newmark, *Sixty Years in Southern California*, 46–47.

22. John W. Shore to Joseph Lancaster Brent, July 9, 1865, Joseph Lancaster Brent Papers, box 2, HEHL.

23. "Judge Benjamin Ignatius Hayes," MSS typescript, Joseph Mesmer Papers, box 6, folder 2, UCLA.

24. On Hayes's fears of losing his son, see Hayes, *Pioneer Notes*, 197.

25. Helen T. Catterall, ed., *Judicial Cases Concerning American Slavery and the Negro*, 5 vols. (Carnegie Institution of Washington, 1926–37).

26. On the challenges of locating freedom suits from the lower courts, see Paul Finkelman, *An Imperfect Union: Slavery, Federalism, and Comity* (University of North Carolina Press, 1981), 17.

27. Hayes's ruling was preserved when a court clerk made a copy of the case in 1860, now held in facsimile at UCLA.

28. On emancipation as a process, rather than an event, see Emberton, *To Walk About in Freedom*, 55–59, 71.

29. Hayes, *In re Hannah*, January 19, 1856, MS, UCLA, for the list of children who remained in San Bernardino.

30. Beasley, *Negro Trail Blazers*, 109–10; Patty R. Colman, "John Ballard and the African American Community of Los Angeles, 1850–1905," *Southern California Quarterly* 94, no. 2 (Summer 2012): 200.

31. Charles Nordhoff, *California: Fore Health, Pleasure, and Residence* (New York: Harper & Brothers, 1873), 137; Ludwig Louis Salvator, *Los Angeles in the Sunny Seventies: A Flower from the Golden Land*, trans. Marguerite Eyer Wilbur (McCallister and Zeitlin, 1929), 30.

32. Deverell, *Whitewashed Adobe*, 15; Leonard Pitt, *Decline of the Californios: A Social History of the Spanish-Speaking Californians, 1846–1890* (University of California Press, 1966), 148–66.

33. Newmark, *Sixty Years in Southern California*, 205; Hayes, *Pioneer Notes*, 170.

34. Robert E. May, *The Southern Dream of a Caribbean Empire* (University Press of Florida, 1973), 2002; William S. Kiser, *Illusions of Empire: The Civil War and Reconstruction in the U.S.-Mexico Borderlands* (Penn Press, 2021), 26; Barney Hagan, "Matamoros: Exploring the Relationship Between the Civil War and North American Borderlands in the American Southwest" (PhD dissertation, University of Oxford, 2024); Deverell, *Whitewashed Adobe*, 18–20; Bell, *Reminiscences of a Ranger*, 214.

35. Newmark, *Sixty Years in Southern California*, 205–209; Bell, *Reminiscences of a Ranger*, 402–10; Bell, *On the Old West Coast*, 74; *Daily Alta California*, February 15, 1857; Deverell, *Whitewashed Adobe*, 21–23; Faragher, *Eternity Street*, 337–72. For other incidents of racial hysteria, see Benjamin D. Wilson to Margaret Hereford Wilson, July 20 and August 3, 1856, Wilson Collection, box 10, HEHL; Brent, *Lugo Case*, 4–5. Elite Latino men also took part in the violence

against mostly lower-class Mexicans. For a counterargument to the claim that racism drove much of that decade's vigilante violence, see Spitzzeri, "Judge Lynch in Session."

36. Torres-Rouff, *Before L.A.*, 57–65, 95, 107–109, 136–38; Pitt, *Decline of the Californios*, 148–66.

37. *Dred Scot v. Sanford*, 60 U.S. (19 How.) 393 (1857); Don E. Fehrenbacher, *The Dred Scott Case: Its Significance in American Law and Politics.* (Oxford University Press, 1978), 323, 372, 384.

38. Quoted in Finkelman, *Imperfect Union*, 317.

39. Tiya Miles, *Night Flyer: Harriet Tubman and the Faith Dreams of a Free People* (Penguin, 2024), 104–105. See also Miles, *All That She Carried*, 175.

40. My thanks to Amy Tanner Thiriot for helping me think through these questions.

41. Elizabeth Regosin, *Freedom's Promise: Ex-Slave Families and Citizenship in the Age of Emancipation* (University Press of Virginia, 2002), 55–58; Herbert G. Gutman, *The Black Family in Slavery and Freedom, 1750–1925* (Basil Blackwell, 1976), 230.

42. J. Brown, *Autobiography of Pioneer John Brown*, 46; Demaratus, *Force of a Feather*, 218n8.

43. In the matter of the estate of Biddy Mason, Last Will and Testament, Los Angeles Area Court Records, Probate Court, second series, case #14493, HEHL.

44. Thiriot, *Slavery in Zion*, 275; Whitney Nell Stewart, *This Is Our Home: Slavery and Struggle on Southern Plantations* (University of North Carolina Press, 2023).

45. *Los Angeles Times*, June 22, 1887.

46. On freedpeople's naming practices, see Regosin, *Freedom's Promise*, 55–77; Gutman, *Black Family* 230–31, 245–52; Eric Foner, *Reconstruction: America's Unfinished Revolution, 1863–1877* (Harper & Row, 1988), 79; Eugene D. Genovese, *Roll, Jordan, Roll: The World the Slaves Made* (Vintage, 1974), 446; Johnson, *Soul by Soul*, 195–96. On the search for family after emancipation, see Heather Andrea Williams, *Help Me to Find My People: The African American Search for Family Lost in Slavery* (University of North Carolina Press, 2012), 140–68; and Judith Giesberg, *Last Seen: The Enduring Search by Formerly Enslaved People to Find Their Lost Families* (Simon and Schuster, 2025).

47. Beasley, *Negro Trail Blazers*, 110.

48. Wilson, *History of Los Angeles County*, 91.

49. On domestic roles for Black women in the West, see *The Elevator*, March 16, 1866; Newmark, *Sixty Years in Southern California*, 123; Mesmer, "Negro Settlers," MSS typescript, Joseph Mesmer Papers, box 4, folder 4, UCLA; Shirley Ann Wilson Moore and Quintard Taylor, "The West of African American Women," in *African American Women Confront the West, 1600–2000* (University of Oklahoma Press, 2003), 10; Willi Coleman, "African American Women and Community

Development in California, 1848–1900," in *Seeking El Dorado: African Americans in California*, ed. Lawrence B. de Graaf, Kevin Mulroy, and Quintard Taylor (Autry Museum, 200), 1113; Lynn M. Hudson, *The Making of "Mammy Pleasant": A Black Entrepreneur in Nineteenth-Century San Francisco* (University of Illinois Press, 2003), 33.

50. Quoted in Lawrence B. de Graaf, "Race, Sex, and Region: Black Women in the American West, 1850–1920," in *History of Women in the United States*, vol. 14 (K. G. Saur, 1993), 76; Phillips, "Indians in Los Angeles," 443.

51. Census of 1860 lists Harriet under the roof of another Black family, Lewis and Maria Green. As members of the same tightknit African American community, the Greens were likely more forgiving employers than many other Angelenos.

52. Emily Hayes to her sister, February 28, 1852, in Hayes, *Pioneer Notes*, 87–88.

53. Laura King, "Reminiscences of Mission San Gabriel," *Annual Publications, Historical Society of Southern California* 11 (1920): 59.

54. Newmark, *Sixty Years in Southern California*, 34; see also Fogelson, *Fragmented Metropolis*, 25.

55. Newmark, *Sixty Years in Southern California*, 584.

56. *Southern Californian*, November 16, 1854.

57. Newmark, *Sixty Years in Southern California*, 57.

58. J. M. Guinn, "Los Angeles in the Later Sixties and Early Seventies," *Annual Publication of the Historical Society of Southern California* 3, no. 1 (1893): 66.

59. Bell, *Reminiscences of a Ranger*, 12–13. See also Newmark, *Sixty Years in Southern California*, 30; James L. Woods, *California Pioneer Decade of 1849: The Presbyterian Church* (Hansen Co., 1922), 69.

60. *Southern Californian*, December 14, 1854. Thanks to Paul Spitzzeri for directing me to this source. For another case of a Black man nearly murdered on the Alley, see *L.A. Star*, May 7, 1853, clipping in Hayes Scrapbooks, vol. 49, Bancroft.

61. Paul Spitzzeri, "The Black Pioneers of Los Angeles County: The Counting of African Americans in the 1850 Federal and 1852 State Censuses," Homestead Blog, January 18, 2021.

62. Deverell, *Whitewashed Adobe*, 108.

63. Deverell, *Whitewashed Adobe*, 107–108.

64. Deverell, *Whitewashed Adobe*, 94–98, 124; Blake Gumprecht, *The Los Angeles River: Its Life, Death, and Possible Rebirth* (Johns Hopkins University Press, 1999).

65. Newmark, *Sixty Years in Southern California*, 116–18, 302; Salvator, *Los Angeles in the Sunny Seventies*, 54; Gumprecht, *Los Angeles River*, 44, 58–60.

66. Gumprecht, *Los Angeles River*, 61–62; Torres-Rouff, *Before L.A.*, 80; Hise, "Border City," 551; Fogelson, *Fragmented Metropolis*, 24, 28; Cleland, *Cattle on a Thousand Hills*, 78; Newmark, *Sixty Years in Southern California*, 116–18.

67. *Los Angeles Star*, June 16, 1855.

68. Hayes, *Pioneer Notes*, 121.

69. On the Owens family zanja, see Paul Barrows, "A Relic of Old Pueblo Days," *Los Angeles Herald*, May 12, 1901.

70. Beasley, *Negro Trail Blazers*, 110; Mesmer, "Negro Settlers," Joseph Mesmer Papers, MSS typescript, box 4, folder 4, UCLA.

CHAPTER 11: HEALER

1. The term "slave mart" was applied by Bell in *Reminiscences of a Ranger*, 34–36.

2. This description is adapted from Kevin Waite, "The Slave Labor That Built Los Angeles," in *Alta Journal* 29, September 23, 2024. See also Bell, *Reminiscences of a Ranger*, 34–36; Browne, *Crusoe's Island*, 284; Newmark, *Sixty Years in Southern California*, 286; *Los Angeles Star*, October 30, 1852; Benjamin Davis Wilson, *The Indians of Southern California in 1852*, ed. Walton Caughey (Huntington Library, 1952), 52; Faragher, *Eternity Street*, 246–47; Phillips, "Indians in Los Angeles," 444–51.

3. Faragher, *Eternity Street*, 247; Bell, *Reminiscences of a Ranger*, 35; Newmark, *Sixty Years in Southern California*, 202; Phillips, *Vineyards and Vaqueros*, 278–84.

4. Bell, *Reminiscences of a Ranger*, 34–36. See also Browne, *Crusoe's Island*, 284.

5. J. M. Guinn, *Historical and Biographical Record of Southern California* (Chapman Publishing Company, 1902), 148.

6. *Los Angeles Star*, December 3, 1853; Faragher, *Eternity Street*, 248.

7. Madley, "Unholy Traffic," 660.

8. *Los Angeles Star*, June 30, 1860; Hernandez, *City of Inmates*, 39.

9. *Los Angeles Star*, May 17, 1856.

10. On improvements to the prison, including an asphalt floor to replace the earthen surface that Biddy once slept on, see *Los Angeles Star*, June 14, 1856; May 9, 1857; November 14, 1857; November 13, 1858.

11. *Los Angeles Star*, January 30, 1858.

12. Berry, *Price for Their Pound of Flesh*, 148–93.

13. Both quotes from Fett, *Working Cures*, 75–76.

14. Fett, *Working Cures*, 60–70, 129.

15. Hayden, "Biddy Mason's Los Angeles," 88–94.

16. John S. Griffin, *A Doctor Comes to California: The Diary of John S. Griffin*, ed. George Walcott Ames Jr. (California Historical Society, 1943), 44; Lynch, "Southern California Chivalry," 25–32; H. D. Barrows, "Memorial Sketch of Dr. John S. Griffin," *Annual Publication of the Historical Society of Southern California and Pioneer Register* 4, no. 2 (1898): 183–85. See also Robert E. May, "Invis-

ible Men: Blacks and the U.S. Army in the Mexican War," *The Historian* 49, no. 4 (August 1987): 463–77.

17. Hayes, *Pioneer Notes*, 121. See also Barrows, "Memorial Sketch," 183.

18. Marco R. Newmark, "Medical Profession in the Early Days of Los Angeles," *Historical Society of Southern California* 34, no. 1 (March 1952), 75; Newmark, *Sixty Years in Southern California*, 422–23; Wilson, *History of Los Angeles County*, 237.

19. Quoted in Albert Lucian Lewis, "Los Angeles in the Civil War Decades, 1850–1868" (PhD dissertation, University of Southern California, 1970), 293–94; Salvator, *Los Angeles in the Sunny Seventies*, 155–58.

20. Glenn S. Dumke, *The Boom of the Eighties in Southern California* (1944; reprint, Huntington Library, 1991), 89; Guinn, "Los Angeles in Later Sixties and Early Seventies," 65.

21. My thanks to Michele Zack for sharing her knowledge and passion for this story.

22. Hudson, *West of Jim Crow*, 1, 216.

23. Joseph Mesmer, "Sonoratown," MSS typescript, Joseph Mesmer Papers, box 4, folder 5, UCLA; Rafaela Cota de Temple to John S. Griffin and J. S. Griffin and Supervisors of L.A. County, May 18, 1867, both in Los Angeles County Miscellaneous Records, 1859–1870, Seaver; Salvator, *Los Angeles in the Sunny Seventies*, 135; John S. Griffin, Assessment Book, Los Angeles City for the Year 1881, Seaver.

24. Gumprecht, *Los Angeles River*, 63–71; William L. Kahrl, *Water and Power: The Conflict over Los Angeles' Water Supply in the Owens Valley* (University of California Press, 1982), 9–25; Torres-Rouff, *Before L.A.*, 175–78; John S. Griffin, Prudent Beaudry and Solomon Lazard, Common Council of Los Angeles, Los Angeles County Miscellaneous Records, 1859–1870, p. 444–45, Seaver.

25. Joseph Mesmer, "Negro Settlers," MSS typescript, Joseph Mesmer Papers, box 4, folder 4, UCLA.

26. All quotes come from various speakers at a tribute service to Mason, in "A Memorial Window Dedicated to Mrs. Biddy Mason," *The Liberator* (Los Angeles) (March 1904).

27. Owens, "My Grandfather," MSS, UCLA.

28. Deed, M. Whistler to Robert Owens, April 9, 1864, Los Angeles Area Court Records, Los Angeles District Court, No. 1279, HEHL.

29. Benjamin D. Wilson to Margaret Hereford Wilson, October 20, 1856, Wilson Collection, box 10, HEHL.

30. John S. Griffin to Benjamin D. Wilson, July 29 [1863?], Wilson Collection, box 14, HEHL.

31. Hayes, *Pioneer Notes*, xi.

32. Beasley, *Negro Trail Blazers*, 90, 109; Demaratus, *Force of a Feather*, 174. Hayden, "Biddy Mason's Los Angeles," 93.

33. *Los Angeles Star*, May 14, 1859.

34. Hayes, *Pioneer Notes*, 185.

35. Kate Bradley Stovall, "The Negro Woman in Los Angeles and Vicinity—Some Notable Characters," *Los Angeles Times*, February 9, 1909.

36. *Los Angeles Star*, November 26, 1859.

37. *Los Angeles Star*, March 10 and September 8, 1860. The costs for such care amounted to $3,803 for "support of indigent sick, medicines, etc." and $375 for Griffin's salary; *Los Angeles Star*, December 22, 1860.

38. *Los Angeles Star*, March 9, 1861.

39. Matthew 25:40.

40. Hernandez, *City of Inmates*, 41–42.

41. Wilson, "Indians of Southern California," 22; Louise Pubols, "Born Global: From Pueblo to Statehood," in *Companion to Los Angeles*, ed. William Deverall and Greg Hise (Blackwell, 2010); Michael J. Gonzalez, *This Small City Will Be a Mexican Paradise: Exploring the Origins of Mexican Culture in Los Angeles, 1821–1846* (University of New Mexico Press, 2005), 125–27.

42. Froebel, *Seven Years' Travel*, 568. See also John Russell Bartlett, *Personal Narrative of Explorations and Incidents in Texas, New Mexico, California, Sonora, and Chihuahua* (London: D. Appleton & Company, 1854), vol. 2, 82.

43. Lindley Bynum, ed., "Los Angeles in 1854–5: The Diary of Rev. James Woods," *The Quarterly: Historical Society of Southern California* 23, no. 2 (June 1941), entry for January 13, 1855.

44. Phillips, "Indians in Los Angeles," 448. See also, Hernandez, *City of Inmates*, 43–44.

45. Reports of the Indigenous auction could be found in the local press until 1869; *Los Angeles Daily News*, February 11, 1869; Phillips, "Indians in Los Angeles," 451.

46. Jack D. Forbes, "The Early African Heritage of California," in *Seeking El Dorado*, 73–77; Hernandez, *City of Inmates*, 22.

47. There's some disagreement over the official full name of Los Angeles, with others suggesting longer variations.

48. Forbes, "Early African Heritage of California," 74–89; Taylor, *In Search of the Racial Frontier*, 32–34; Monroy, *Thrown Among Strangers*, 103–106.

49. My thanks to Priscilla Daniels Mark, a descendent of Maria Rita Valdez Villa, for sharing her family's incredible story with me.

50. J. Max Bond, "The Negro in Los Angeles" (PhD dissertation, University of Southern California, 1936), 2–4, 10–12; Taylor, *In Search of the Racial Frontier*, 45–47; Bunch, *Black Angelenos*, 10–12; Torres-Rouff, *Before L.A.*, 23–25, 32–33.

51. Campbell, *Making Black Los Angeles*, 15–19; Forbes, "Early African Heritage of California," 82–85.

52. Ira Berlin, *Generations of Captivity: A History of African-American Slaves* (Harvard University Press, 2003), 192; Dylan C. Penningroth, *The Claims of Kinfolk: African American Property and Community in the Nineteenth-Century*

South (University of North Carolina Press, 2003), 171; Brenda Stevenson, *Life in Black and White: Family and Community in the Slave South* (Oxford University Press, 1996).

53. Gutman, *Black Family*, 185, 200, 204, 212–14, 220–26; Elsa Barkley Brown, "To Catch the Vision of Freedom: Reconstructing Southern Black Women's Political History, 1865–1880," in *African American Women and the Vote, 1837–1965*, ed. Ann D. Gordon (University of Massachusetts Press, 1997), 66.

54. Owens, "Robert C. Owens," MSS, UCLA.

55. 1860 Census; see also Colman, "John Ballard," 206.

56. Colman, "John Ballard," 201–19.

57. Newmark, *Sixty Years in Southern California*, 185.

58. Interview with William Ballard in Bond, "Negro in Los Angeles," 12.

59. Kendra Field and Daniel Lynch, "'Master of Ceremonies': The World of Peter Biggs in Civil War–Era Los Angeles," *Western Historical Quarterly* 47 (Winter 2016): 379–405; Colman, "John Ballard," 206–207. For one of Biggs's early land purchases, see Deed, Henry Dalton to Peter Biggs, October 28, 1859, Los Angeles County Miscellaneous Records, 1859–1870, Seaver.

60. Joseph Mesmer, "Negro Settlers," MSS typescript, Joseph Mesmer Papers, box 4, folder 4, UCLA;

61. Newmark, *Sixty Years in Southern California*, 138.

62. Warner, Hayes, and Widney, *Historical Sketch*, 44.

63. Owens, "My Grandfather," MSS, UCLA; Douglas Flamming, *Bound for Freedom: Black Los Angeles in Jim Crow America* (University of California Press, 2005), 23.

64. "Indenture of Apprenticeship, Hannah Smiley to Lewis G. Green," April 7, 1862, Los Angeles County Miscellaneous Records, 1859–1870, Seaver; Colman, "John Ballard," 207.

65. Campbell, *Making Black Los Angeles*, 51–56.

66. Robert Owens testified "that he knows the aforesaid minor Henry Smith and knows that his Father Robert Smith has deserted his child and has never provided for him since the time of his birth"; "Indenture of Apprenticeship," April 7, 1862, Seaver.

67. Demaratus, *Force of a Feather*, 180–81.

68. Demaratus, *Force of a Feather*, 180–81

69. Testimony of James W. Wilson, November 12, 1858, in *People v. McFeely*, Court Case 42, SBCHA.

70. Warrant, Joseph McFeely, June 7, 1859; arrest notice, June 9, 1859, both in *People v. McFeely*, SBCHA.

71. *People v. McFeely*, SBCHA.

72. Verdict, *People v. McFeely*, SBCHA.

73. Demaratus, *Force of a Feather*, 182.

74. Waite, *West of Slavery*, 119–20; Richards, *Californian Gold Rush*, 183; Ger-

ald Stanley, "The Politics of the Antebellum Far West: The Impact of the Slavery and Race Issues in California," *Journal of the West* 16 (1977): 22–24; David Alan Johnson, *Founding the Far West: California, Oregon, and Nevada, 1840–1890* (University of California Press, 1992), 245–48.

75. Joseph Lancaster Brent, *Memoirs of the War Between the States* (Nanine B. Sloo, 1940), 22.

76. Carr, *Pioneer Days in California*, 342. See also Incidents in California, Statement by Judge John Currey for Bancroft Library, MSS, 1878, Bancroft; Stephen J. Field, *Personal Reminiscences of Early Days in California* (Stephen J. Field, 1893), 114.

77. Edward Stanly, Speech of the Hon. Edward Stanly, delivered at Sacramento, July 17, 1857; *Congressional Globe*, 25th Congress, 2nd session, appendix, 87; and *Sacramento Daily Union*, August 27, 1857.

78. Gerald Stanley, "The Republican Party in California, 1856–1868" (PhD dissertation, University of Arizona, 1973), 59–60; Stanley, "Politics of the Antebellum Far West," 19–20; Carr, *Pioneer Days in California*, 328, 342; Cole, *Memoirs of Cornelius Cole*, 113–14.

79. For reports on these Colored Conventions, see Stokes, *Proceedings of the First State Convention of the Colored Citizens of the State of California*, November, 1855; Booth, *Proceedings of the Second Annual Convention of Colored Citizens of the State of California*, December 9–13, 1856; and *Frederick Douglass' Paper*, July 17, 1857. See also Rudolph M. Lapp, *Blacks in Gold Rush California* (Yale University Press, 1977), 187–230; Shirley Ann Wilson Moore, "'We Feel the Want of Protection': The Politics of Law and Race in California, 1848–1878," in *Taming the Elephant: Politics, Government, and Law in Pioneer California*, ed. John F. Burns and Richard J. Orsi (University of California Press, 2003), 116–17; Taylor, *In Search of the Racial Frontier*, 91–94.

80. Taylor, *In Search of the Racial Frontier*, 83–92; Hudson, *West of Jim Crow*, 3–4.

81. *Stovall v. Archy, a Slave*, Case Files of the US Commissioner, Record Group 21, Records of the District Courts of the United States, 1685–2009; McGinty, *Archy Lee's Struggle for Freedom*, 1–12, 42–45, 54–60; Waite, *West of Slavery*, 188, 120.

82. McGinty, *Archy Lee's Struggle for Freedom.*

83. *Daily Columbus Enquirer* (Columbus, GA), October 14, 1859.

84. Waite, *West of Slavery*, 120–21; Richards, *California Gold Rush*, 3–7, 219–21.

85. Edward D. Baker, *Oration of Colonel Edward D. Baker over the Dead Body of David C. Broderick, a Senator of the United States, 18th September, 1859* (n.p., n.d.), 7–13.

86. Mifflin Wistar Gibbs, *Shadow and Light: An Autobiography* (n.p., 1902), 63; see also Stacey L. Smith, "*Dred Scott* on the Pacific: African Americans, Citizenship, and Subjecthood in the North American West," *Southern California Quarterly* 100, no. 1 (Spring 2018): 46–57.

87. Quoted in Robert J. Chandler, "Friends in Time of Need: Republicans and Black Civil Rights in California During the Civil War," *Arizona and the West* 24, no. 4 (Winter 1982): 322.

CHAPTER 12: UNIONIST

1. John W. Shore, January 9, 1860, addendum to Benjamin Hayes, *In re Hannah*, January 19, 1856, MS, Golden State Mutual Life Insurance Records, box 41, UCLA. Ironically, John W. Shore, the county clerk who issued Mason's freedom papers, himself held an enslaved boy named Tom as his ward. See chapter 9.

2. Chandler, "Friends in Time of Need," 322.

3. Abraham Lincoln, Draft of Resolutions for presentation in the US House of Representatives, January 1855, in Roy P. Basler, ed., *The Collected Works of Abraham Lincoln* (Rutgers University Press, 1953), vol. 2, 301; Stephen C. Foster to Governor Peter H. Burnett, March 12, 1850, Los Angeles Prefecture Records, vol. 2, 840–43, HEHL; John Bachelder Peirce to Hitty Peirce, September 17, 1851, John Bachelder Peirce Papers, MHS; Carr, *Pioneer Days in California*, 346; *Sacramento Daily Union*, March 3, 1859, March 26, 1859, August 13, 1859.

4. Robert R. Givens to his father, September 10, 1852, Robert R. Givens letters to family, Bancroft. See also Hinton Rowan Helper, *The Land of Gold: Reality Versus Fiction* (Baltimore, MD: Henry Taylor, 1855), 278–79; "The Southern Convention at Vicksburg, Part 2," *De Bow's Review* 27 (August 1859), 216; Unsigned extract of a letter to James Gadsden, August 22, 1852, in Thomas Jefferson Green Papers, box 3, folder 33, UNC; *Texas State Gazette*, July 29, 1854.

5. "An Act granting the consent of the Legislature to the Formation of a different Government for the Southern Counties of this State," *Statutes of California, 1859*, 310–11.

6. Ward M. McAfee, "California's House Divided," *Civil War History* 33, no. 2 (1987): 115–30; Lynch, "Southern California Chivalry," 110–13; Waite, *West of Slavery*, 106–10; Richards, *California Gold Rush*, 222–25.

7. Quoted in David M. Potter, *The Impending Crisis, 1848–1861*, ed. Don E. Fehrenbacher (Harper & Row, 1976), 389.

8. Newmark, *Sixty Years in Southern California*, 282; John W. Robinson, Los Angeles in Civil War Days, 1860–1865 (University of Oklahoma Press, 1977, 2013), 36–42. See also Winfield J. Davis, *History of Political Conventions in California, 1849–1892* (Sacramento: California State Library, 1893), 169–70; Richards, *California Gold Rush*, 228.

9. Almira Hancock, *Reminiscences of Winfield Scott Hancock by His Wife* (New York: Charles L. Webster, 1887), 58.

10. Quoted in Milton H. Shutes, *Lincoln and California* (Stanford University Press, 1943), 46.

11. Brian McGinty, *Lincoln and California: The President, the War, and the*

Golden State (Potomac Books, 2023), 34–36; Kevin Waite, "Lincoln Looks West: California and the Fate of the Nation in the Civil War Era," *Ohio Valley History* (Spring 2026); Faragher, *Eternity Street*, 384; Glenna Matthews, *The Golden State in the Civil War: Thomas Starr King, the Republican Party, and the Birth of Modern California* (Cambridge University Press, 2012), 81–82.

12. Hayes, *Pioneer Notes*, 251.

13. Newmark, *Sixty Years in Southern California*, 294; Robinson, *Los Angeles in Civil War Days*, 50–51.

14. Maymie R. Krythe, "First Hotel of Old Los Angeles: The Romantic Bella Union," part 2, *Historical Society of Southern California Quarterly* 33, no. 1 (June 1951): 162; Waite, *West of Slavery*, 183–90.

15. Bell, *On the Old West Coast*, 72.

16. Sumner to Col. E. D. Townsend, April 28, 1861; Sumner to Col. George Wright, September 30, 1861, OR, Series I, Vol. L, Part 1, p. 472, 643; Hayes, *Pioneer Notes*, 256; Newmark, *Sixty Years in Southern California*, 306. Robinson, *Los Angeles in Civil War Days*, 46.

17. Gustav Brown to A. Jones Jackson, October 16, 1864, OR, Series I, Vol. L, Part 2, pp. 1018–19.

18. Clarence Bennett to Sumner, August 6, 1861, OR, Series I, Vol. L, Part 1, pp. 556–58.

19. Robert Robinson to Brigadier General John S. Mason, August 10, 1864, OR, Series I, Vol. L, Part 2, pp. 938–40; Robinson, *Los Angeles in Civil War Days*, 77.

20. Joseph Mesmer, "Henry Hamilton," MSS typescript, Joseph Mesmer Papers, box 6, folder 2, UCLA. See also John W. Robinson, "A California Copperhead: Henry Hamilton and the Los Angeles Star," *Arizona and the West* 23 (Fall 1981): 213–18.

21. *Los Angeles Star*, January 11, 1862.

22. *Los Angeles Star*, April 23, 1864.

23. Brace, *New West*, 277.

24. Owens, "My Grandfather," MSS, UCLA.

25. James David Nichols, *The Limits of Liberty: Mobility and the Making of the Eastern U.S.-Mexico Border* (University of Nebraska Press, 2018); Sarah Cornell, "Citizens of Nowhere: Fugitive Slaves and African Americans in Mexico, 1833–1857," *Journal of American History* 100, no. 2 (2013): 351–74; Alice Baumgartner, *South to Freedom: Runaway Slaves to Mexico and the Road to the Civil War* (Basic Books, 2020). On Mexico as a place of opportunity and reinvention for African Americans, see Karl Jacoby, *The Strange Career of William Ellis: The Texas Slave Who Became a Mexican Millionaire* (W. W. Norton, 2016).

26. Hancock, *Reminiscences of Winfield Scott Hancock*, 59–60.

27. General E. V. Sumner, to Col. E.D. Townsend, April 30, 1861, OR, Series I, Vol. L, Part 1, p. 474; Sumner to Col. E. D. Townsend, September 17, 1861, OR, Series I, Vol. L, Part 1, p. 623.

28. Hancock, *Reminiscences of Winfield Scott Hancock*, 62; Andrew E. Masich, *Civil War in the Southwest Borderlands, 1861–1867* (University of Oklahoma Press, 2017), 276.

29. Robinson, *Los Angeles in Civil War Days*, 53–58.

30. Captain Jonathan W. Davidson to Major D. C. Buell, August 10, 1861, OR, Series I, Vol. L, Part 1, p. 562–563; Captain Jonathan W. Davidson to Major D.C. Buell, August 13, 1861, OR, Series I, Vol. L, Part 1, pp. 567–68; *Los Angeles Star*, August 31, 1861; Robinson, *Los Angeles in Civil War Days*, 68–69.

31. Douglas R. Egerton, *Thunder at the Gates: The Black Civil War Regiments that Redeemed America* (Basic Books, 2016).

32. Ashbury Harpending, *The Great Diamond Hoax and Other Stirring Incidents in the Life of Ashbury Harpending*, ed. James H. Wilkins (James H. Barry, 1913), 28–36, 43; Robinson, *Los Angeles in Civil War Days*, 51–52, 62–64; Owens, "My Grandfather," MSS, UCLA; Hancock, *Reminiscences of Winfield Scott Hancock*, 67–68.

33. Owens, "My Grandfather," MSS, UCLA.

34. Faragher, *Eternity Street*, 385–86; Robinson, *Los Angeles in Civil War Days*, 62–64.

35. Cameron Thom to Pembroke Thom, January 5, 1863 and September 27, 1863, Thom Family Papers, section 3, folder 5, VHS; *Los Angeles Star*, November 29, 1862, December 12, 1863; Bell, *On the Old West Coast*, 74; Robinson, *Los Angeles in Civil War Days*, 83–85; Alvin M. Josephy Jr., *The Civil War in the American West* (Vintage, 1991), 235–36.

36. William Need to Simon Cameron, September 27, 1861, OR, Series I, Vol. L, Part 1, pp. 635–37.

37. Megan Kate Nelson, *The Three-Cornered War: The Union, the Confederacy, and Native Peoples in the Fight for the West* (Scribner, 2020), 100; Masich, *Civil War in the Southwest Borderlands*, 84–92; Kevin Waite, "The Brittle West: Secession and Separatism in the Southwest Borderlands during the Civil War Era," *Southwestern Historical Quarterly* 127, no. 1 (July 2023): 8–9.

38. T. T. Teel, "Sibley's New Mexican Campaign—Its Objects and the Causes of Its Failure," in *Battles and Leaders of the Civil War*, ed. Robert Underwood Johnson and Clarence Clough Buel (Castle, 1995), vol. 2, p. 700 (italics in original); see also Baylor to Earl Van Dorn, August 14, 1861, OR, Series I, Vol. 4, p. 23.

39. Gurden Chapin to Henry Halleck, February 28, 1862, OR, Series I, Vol. 9, pp. 634–35; Robinson, *Los Angeles in Civil War Days*, 66, 73.

40. W. H. Watford, "The Far-Western Wing of the Rebellion, 1861–1865," *California Historical Society Quarterly* 34 (June 1955): 132, 139; W. H. Watford, "Confederate Western Ambitions," *Southwestern Historical Quarterly* 44 (October 1940): 161–68.

41. Matthews, *Golden State in the Civil War*, 3, 115; Masich, *Civil War in the Southwest Borderlands*, 39, 48. Cecily N. Zander, *The Army Under Fire: The Pol-*

itics of Antimilitarism in the Civil War Era (Louisiana State University Press, 2024), 26–29.

42. *Los Angeles Star*, June 22, 1861; Newmark, *Sixty Years in Southern California*, 297. On the proslavery origins of the US camel corps, see Kevin Waite, "The Sinister Reason Camels Were Brought to the American West," *National Geographic*, October 26, 2021.

43. Robinson, *Los Angeles in Civil War Days*, 90–94; Aurora Hunt, *The Army of the Pacific* (Arthur H. Clark, 1951), 40–46; Matthews, *Golden State in the Civil War*, 117–19.

44. Newmark, *Sixty Years in Southern California*, 246–47.

45. Owens, "My Grandfather," MSS, UCLA. For an advertisement of Owens's livery stable, see *Semi-Weekly Southern News*, August 30, 1861.

46. In the matter of the estate of Robert Owens, September 25, 1865, and November 8, 1865, Los Angeles Area Court Records, Probate Court, Case No. 316, HEHL; Deed, M. Whistler, Trustee of the Methodist Episcopal Church to Robert Owens, April 9, 1864, Los Angeles Area Court Records, case number 1279, HEHL. See also notices in *Los Angeles Tri-Weekly News*, June 25, 1864, and March 25, 1865.

47. Henry Hopkins Sibley to General S. Cooper, May 4, 1862, OR, Series I, Vol. 9, pp. 506–12; Donald S. Frazier, *Blood and Treasure: Confederate Empire in the Southwest* (Texas A&M University Press, 1995), 238–77; Nelson, *Three-Cornered War*, 109–21; Waite, "Brittle West," 9–10.

48. Indenture of Apprenticeship, Hannah Smiley to Lewis G. Green, April 7, 1862, Los Angeles County Miscellaneous Records, 1859–1870, Seaver, pp. 53–54.

49. See, for example, Hayes, *Pioneer Notes*, 257; K. H. Dimmick to General E. V. Sumner, August 8, 1861, OR, Series I, Vol. L, Part 1, p. 559; Clarence Bennett to Sumner, August 6, 1861, ORs, Series I, Vol. L, Part 1, pp. 556–58; Benjamin Franklin Gilbert, "The Confederate Minority in California," *California Historical Society Quarterly* 20 (June 1941): 168.

50. *Los Angeles Star*, January 4, 1862.

51. Newmark, *Sixty Years in Southern California*, 291; *Los Angeles Star*, January 11 and 25, 1862; Pitt, *Decline of the Californios*, 245.

52. Torres-Rouff, *Before L.A.*, 168–70.

53. *Los Angeles Star*, January 25, 1862.

54. Guinn, *Historical and Biographical Record of Southern California*, 138

55. Bell, *Reminiscences of a Ranger*, 62. Benjamin Hayes made similar observations; see Hayes, *Pioneer Notes*, 270.

56. Edward E. Ayer, "Reminiscences of Edward Ayer's First Trip from Home in 1860," MSS typescript, 1924, HEHL, 20.

57. Brewer, *Up and Down California*, 249.

58. B. Lynn Ingram and Frances Malamud-Roam, *The West Without Water:*

What Past Floods, Droughts, and Other Climatic Clues Tell Us About Tomorrow (University of California Press, 2013), 29.

59. Ingram and Malamud-Roam, *West Without Water*, 28–39; Brewer, *Up and Down California*, 243; Cleland, *Cattle on a Thousand Hills*, 126–30.

60. Cleland, *Cattle on a Thousand Hills*, 132.

61. Robinson, *Los Angeles in Civil War Days*, 113.

62. Hayes, *Pioneer Notes*, 284.

63. Newmark, *Sixty Years in Southern California*, 322.

64. *Los Angeles Star*, January 31, 1863.

65. *Los Angeles Star*, November 22, 1862.

66. *Los Angeles Star*, January 31, 1863. See also *Los Angeles Star*, February 7, 1863; February 14, 1863; and March 7, 1863.

67. Robinson, *Los Angeles in Civil War Days*, 113.

68. Diary of Henry Dwight Barrows, July 16 and July 30, 1862, Barrows and Weyse Family Papers, box 2, HEHL. My thanks to Louisa Brandt for drawing my attention to this source.

69. Diary of Barrows, Cash Account, July, Barrows and Weyse Family Papers, box 2, HEHL.

70. United States tax assessments for the year 1862, entries for Biddy Mason and Robert Owens, National Archives.

71. *Los Angeles Star*, April 9, 1864.

72. Guinn, *Historical and Biographical Record of Southern California*, 138. Newmark, *Sixty Years in Southern California*, 328–29; Pitt, *Decline of the Californios*, 244–46; Wilson, *History of LA County*, 54; Robinson, *Los Angeles in Civil War Days*, 133–34.

73. Cleland, *Cattle on a Thousand Hills*, 130–37; Griswold del Castillo, *Los Angeles Barrio*, 41–46; Brace, *New West*, 284–85; Torres-Rouff, *Before L.A.*, 170–71; See also Henry Hamilton to Benjamin D. Wilson, February 2, 1864, box 15, Wilson Collection, HEHL.

74. Pitt, *Decline of the Californios*, 247.

75. Jackie Broxton and Kevin Waite, "A Monument to California's Black History—and a Great Work of Art—May Soon Be Destroyed," *Los Angeles Times*, July 10, 2020. My thanks to Laura Voisin George for drawing my attention to these panels.

76. Chandra Manning, "Working for Citizenship in Civil War Contraband Camps," *Journal of the Civil War Era* 4, no. 2 (June 2014): 176. See also Amy Murrell Taylor, *Embattled Freedom: Journeys Through the Civil War's Slave Refugee Camps* (University of North Carolina Press, 2018).

77. Frederick Douglass, "Men of Color, To Arms!" *Douglass' Monthly* (March 1863).

78. On Black women's struggles for freedom and citizenship during the Civil War, see Hahn, *Nation Under Our Feet*, 62–115; Thavolia Glymph, *The Women's*

Fight: The Civil War's Battles for Home, Freedom, and Nation (University of North Carolina Press, 2022), 87–124, 221–49; Taylor, *Embattled Freedom*; McCurry, *Confederate Reckoning*; Manning, "Working for Citizenship in Contraband Camps."

79. *Los Angeles Star*, May 2, 1863. See also *Los Angeles Daily News*, May 22, 1863; *Marysville Appeal*, May 1 and 3, 1863; *Freeman's Journal and Daily Commercial Advertiser* (Dublin), May 20, 1863; *Strathearn Herald* (Crieff, Scotland), May 23, 1863; Mary Boardman to Margaret Hereford Wilson, July 11, 1863, box 14, Wilson Collection, HEHL. The steamer was named for the daughter of Winfield Scott Hancock, in tribute to the service he rendered to the war-torn pueblo.

80. *New York Times*, May 31, 1863; Newmark, *Sixty Years in Southern California*, 320.

81. *Los Angeles Daily News*, May 1, 1863.

82. *New York Times*, May 31, 1863. See also *Otago Daily Times* (Otago, New Zealand), July 15, 1863; *The New-Zealander* (Auckland), July 14, 1863; *Sydney Morning Herald* (Sydney, Australia), June 29, 1863.

83. We can identify "Darkness" as Harriet because she was the only "colored servant" of Phineas Banning at the time, as noted in her description in the papers; *Los Angeles Daily News*, May 1, 1863.

84. Harriet Washington and W. H. Washington vs. Robert C. Owens and Ellen Huddleston, complaint, filed March 8, 1898, Superior Court of Los Angeles, Los Angeles Area Court Records, case no. 30301, HEHL.

85. See, for instance, *Los Angeles Daily News*, April 26, 1870; *Evening Express*, January 4, 1875; *Los Angeles Times*, November 14, 1885; *Los Angeles Times*, December 23, 1885; *Los Angeles Herald*, January 3, 1886. Celebrations were sometimes linked with the anniversary of the passage of the Fifteenth Amendment.

86. Joseph Mesmer, "Negro Settlers," MSS typescript, Mesmer Papers, box 4, folder 4, UCLA; Newmark, *Sixty Years in Southern California*, 321, 330.

87. Faragher, *Eternity Street*, 392.

88. *Los Angeles Star*, January 3, 1863.

89. Faragher, *Eternity Street*, 376–78.

90. E.J.C. Kewen, *Speech of Hon. E.J.C. Kewen, on The State of the Union; Delivered before the Democracy of Sacramento in Assembly Hall, April 27, 1863*, copy in HEHL, 5–8.

91. General Orders No. 17, Department of the Pacific, April 23, 1862, OR, Series I, Vol. L, Part 1, p. 1021–1022.

92. Matthews, *Golden State in the Civil War*, 179, 185.

93. Robinson, *Los Angeles in Civil War Days*, 78, 101–104, 110–11.

94. John S. Griffin to BD Wilson, July 29, [1863?], Wilson Collection, box 14, HEHL. See also Griffin to Wilson, [n.d. but assumed August 1863], Wilson Collection, box 14, HEHL; and Hayes, *Pioneer Notes*, 261–63.

95. Hayes, *Pioneer Notes*, 254 (emphasis in the original).

96. Hayes, *Pioneer Notes*, 189.

97. John W. Shore to Joseph Lancaster Brent, July 9, 1865, Brent Papers, box 2, HEHL; Demaratus, *Force of a Feather*, 158–161.

98. Cole, *Memoirs of Cornelius Cole*, 157–58.

99. Matthews, *Golden State in the Civil War*, 174–77.

100. Griffin to Wilson, October 27, 1864, Wilson Collection, box 15, HEHL; Wilson, Draft notes supporting George McClellan, 1864, Wilson Collection, box 15, HEHL.

101. Shore to Brent, July 9, 1865, Brent Papers, box 2, HEHL; Robinson, *Los Angeles in Civil War Days*, 148–51; Matthews, *Golden State in the Civil War*, 190.

102. Newmark, *Sixty Years in Southern California*, 337.

103. Bell, *Reminiscences of a Ranger*, 22.

104. Deed, Henry Dalton to Peter Biggs, October 28, 1859, Los Angeles County Miscellaneous Records, 1859–1870, Seaver.

105. Newmark, *Sixty Years in Southern California*, 60, 137–38.

106. Benjamin Hayes knew Biggs previously in Missouri, as his friend had owned Biggs. Upon Hayes's arrival in Los Angeles, Biggs was one of the first to greet Hayes at the Bella Union. Hayes, *Pioneer Notes*, 71.

107. Bell, *On the Old West Coast*, 75.

108. Field and Lynch, "'Master of Ceremonies,'" 399–400; *Los Angeles Tri-Weekly News*, April 22, 1865. See also OR, Series I, Vol. L, Part 2, pp. 1198–1202; D. Michael Bottoms, *An Aristocracy of Color: Race and Reconstruction in California and the West, 1850–1890* (University of Oklahoma Press, 2013), 62–63.

109. Newmark, *Sixty Years in Southern California*, 330. See also Mesmer, "A White Pioneer Reminisces," in Bass, *Forty Years*, 114–17; Mesmer, "Negro Settlers," MSS typescript, Mesmer Papers, box 4, folder 4, UCLA.

110. Field and Lynch, "Master of Ceremonies," 400.

111. Field and Lynch, "Master of Ceremonies," 380–82.

112. Field and Lynch, "Master of Ceremonies," 403.

113. *Los Angeles Tri-Weekly News*, April 22, 1865.

CHAPTER 13: RECONSTRUCTING LOS ANGELES

1. Faragher, *Eternity Street*, 440–41; Woolsey, "Pioneer Views and Frontier Themes," 257.

2. All quotes from Bell, *On the Old West Coast*, 76–78.

3. Bell, *On the Old West Coast*, 78.

4. On Reconstruction in the West, see Elliott West, *Continental Reckoning: The American West in the Age of Expansion* (University of Nebraska Press, 2023); Elliott West, "Reconstructing Race," *Western Historical Quarterly* 34, no. 1 (Spring 2003): 6–26; Eugene H. Berwanger, *The West and Reconstruction* (University of Illinois Press, 1981); Joshua Paddison, *American Heathens: Religion, Race, and Reconstruction in California* (University of California Press and the Huntington

Library, 2012); Bottoms, *Aristocracy of Color*; Kevin Waite, "The West and Reconstruction after the American Civil War," in *The Oxford Handbook on Reconstruction*, ed. Andrew L. Slap (Oxford University Press, forthcoming); Smith, *Freedom's Frontier*; Waite, *West of Slavery*, chap. 8.

5. Owens, "My Grandfather," MSS, UCLA; "In the matter of the estate of Robert Owens," September 25, 1865 and November 8, 1865, Los Angeles Area Court Records, Probate Court, Case No. 316, HEHL.

6. Benjamin Davis Wilson to Joseph Lancaster Brent, July 10, 1865, Brent Papers, box 2, HEHL. See also Wilson to Brent, September 21, 1865, Brent Papers, box 2, HEHL.

7. Bell, *On the Old West Coast*, 82.

8. Bell, *On the Old West Coast*, 82.

9. Newmark, *Sixty Years in Southern California*, 260.

10. *Pomona Daily Review*, November 17, 1908. I've standardized some of the dialect used in the article. See also Joseph Mesmer, "Negro Settlers," MSS typescript, Joseph Mesmer Papers, box 4, folder 4, UCLA.

11. Kaye and Downs, *Nat Turner, Black Prophet*, 40.

12. All in William L. Andrews, *Sisters of the Spirit: Three Black Women's Autobiographies of the Nineteenth Century* (Indiana University Press, 1986): "The Life and Religious Experience of Jarena Lee," 37–39; "Memoirs of the Life, Religions Experience, Ministerial Travels and Labours of Mrs. Zilpha Elaw," 56, 137; Julia A .J. Foote, "A Brand Plucked from the Fire," 202. See also Miles, *Night Flyer*, 17, 76, 112, 169.

13. Quoted in Kaye and Downs, *Nat Turner, Black Prophet*, 40.

14. Newmark, *Sixty Years in Southern California*, 335–36; Guinn, "Los Angeles in the Later Sixties and Early Seventies," 64.

15. Deed, William M. Buffum and James F. Burns to Biddy Mason, November 28, 1866, photostat copy, Golden State Mutual Life Insurance Records, box 41, UCLA; Stovall, "Negro Woman in Los Angeles," *Los Angeles Times*, February 9, 1909; Beasley, *Negro Trail Blazers*, 90, 109; Demaratus, *Force of a Feather*, 175; Hayden, "Biddy Mason's Los Angeles," 96–97.

16. *Pomona Daily Review*, November 17, 1908.

17. Miles, *All That She Carried*, 129, 268. See also Emberton, *To Walk About in Freedom*, 136–39; Dylan C. Penningroth, *Before the Movement: The Hidden History of Black Civil Rights* (Liveright, 2024), 79.

18. Beasley, *Negro Trail Blazers*, 90, 109.

19. Guinn, "LA in Later Sixties and Early Seventies," 64. See also Brace, *New West*, 293; Salvator, *Los Angeles in the Sunny Seventies*, 47.

20. Benjamin D. Wilson to Joseph Lancaster Brent, June 1, 1869; and Wilson to Brent, January 17, 1869, both in Brent Papers, box 3, HEHL.

21. Cleland, *Cattle on a Thousand Hills*, 166–73, 182; Newmark, *Sixty Years in*

Southern California, 353, 376; Meyer Joseph Newmark to Joseph Lancaster Brent, January 5, 1869, Brent Papers, box 3, HEHL.

22. *Alta California*, December 3, 1868.

23. Newmark, *Sixty Years in Southern California*, 401; Faragher, *Eternity Street*, 443–44.

24. Fogelson, *Fragmented Metropolis*, 1.

25. "Minutes of an interview between the Colored Ministers and Church Officers at Savannah with the Secretary of War and Major-Gen. Sherman," February 13, 1865, Freedmen and Southern Society Project, https://www.freedmen.umd.edu/savmtg.htm.

26. Miriam Matthews Photograph Collection, UCLA Special Collections.

27. The photographer was most likely William Godfrey, operating out of his Sunbeam Gallery; Carl Mautz, *Biographies of Western Photographers* (Carl Mautz Publishing, 1997), 104. My thanks to Jenny Watts for helping me decipher the photograph.

28. Mesmer, "Negro Settlers," Mesmer Papers, UCLA.

29. Beasley, *Negro Trail Blazers*, 110; Mesmer, "Negro Settlers," Mesmer Papers, UCLA; entries for Charles Owens in Assessment Book, Los Angeles City for the Years 1887–1882, Seaver.

30. Deed, Charles Owens and Martha Hall to Biddy Mason, July 7, 1868, LAR. Several months later, the family sold some of these lots; Deed, Charles Owens, Martha Hall, Biddy Mason to John Schumacker, November 7, 1868, LAR.

31. *LA Semi-Weekly News*, October 1, 1867.

32. *Daily Evening Herald* (Stockton, CA), October 11, 1867. See also *Los Angeles Star*, March 11, 1872; *Los Angeles Herald*, April 19, 1883; *Los Angeles Times*, April 19, 1883.

33. Nordhoff, *California*, 137.

34. Newmark, *Sixty Years in Southern California*, 363.

35. Jackson Graves, *My Seventy Years in California, 1857–1927* (Times-Mirror Press, 1927), 122–24; Lewis, "Los Angeles in the Civil War Decades," 281–82; Faragher, *Eternity Street*, 440. On the redemptive promise of California for the Civil War's wounded veterans, see William Deverell, "Convalescence and California: The Civil War Comes West," *Southern California Quarterly* 90, no. 1 (Spring 2008).

36. Matthew Keller to Brent, August 17, 1865, Brent Papers box 2, HEHL. The Unionist Phineas Banning even named one of his sons after Brent. See Phineas Banning to Brent, August 3, 1865, and Joseph Brent Banning to Brent, October 11, 1865, both in Brent Papers, box 2, HEHL.

37. Henry D. Barrows to James Henry Carleton, April 9, 1862, OR, Series I, Vol. L, Part 1, pp. 993–94.

38. *LA Semi-Weekly News*, November 24, 1865.

39. "Assignment of bond and personal property, Thomas A. Sanchez to A.J.

King," March 8, 1865, Los Angeles County Miscellaneous Records, 1859–1870, pp. 353–54, Seaver.

40. *Los Angeles Semi-Weekly News*, January 4, 1867.

41. *Los Angeles Semi-Weekly News*, January 25, 1867; see also *Los Angeles Semi-Weekly News*, December 21, 1866.

42. Berwanger, *West and Reconstruction*; Paddison, *American Heathens*; Bottoms, *Aristocracy of Color*; Smith, *Freedom's Frontier*; Waite, *West of Slavery*, chap. 8.

43. George C. Gorham, *Speech Delivered by George C. Gorham of San Francisco* (San Francisco: Union State Central Committee, 1867), 13; Stanley, "Republican Party in California," 203–204.

44. Haight to A. A. Boyle, September 18, 1867, in *LA News*, October 1, 1867.

45. Henry H. Haight, *Inaugural Address of H.H. Haight* (New York: Douglas Taylor's Democratic Book and Job Printing Office, 1868), 13. See also William S. Burns to Haight, October 28, 1867, and Haight to John Bigler, May 7, 1868, both in Haight Papers, HEHL; Berwanger, *West and Reconstruction*, 107–108.

46. *Tribune Almanac and Political Register for 1868* (New York, 1868), 43–65. See also Stanley, "Republican Party," 207–210; Berwanger, *West and Reconstruction*, 202–208; Thomas E. Malone, "The Democratic Party in California, 1865–1868" (MA thesis, Stanford University, 1949), 62–63; and Waite, "West and Reconstruction."

47. David S. Terry to Cornelia (Runnels) Terry, October 11, 1867, Terry Papers, box 1, HEHL.

48. Bottoms, *Aristocracy of Color*, 55.

49. Three other free states—Oregon, New Jersey, and Ohio—ratified the Fourteenth Amendment but later rescinded their ratifications under Democratic majorities. Smith, *Freedom's Frontier*, 210.

50. Newmark, *Sixty Years in Southern California*, 397.

51. Gwin quoted in Bottoms, *Aristocracy of Color*, 87–90. See also John S. Hager, *Speech of Hon. John S. Hager, of San Francisco, in the Senate of California, January 28th, 1870*, (n.p., n.d.), 3–5, 11.

52. Smith, *Freedom's Frontier*, 210–13; Bottoms, *Aristocracy of Color*, 87–93; Stanley, "Republican Party in California," 236; Paddison, *American Heathens*, 27; Waite, "West and Reconstruction."

53. (Sacramento) *Daily Union*, April 16 and May 1, 1868; *Marysville Daily Appeal*, July 25, 1868, March 3, March 17, May 13, May 19, and June 13, 1869; *Alta California*, April 22, 1869, and January 6, 1871.

54. Kevin Waite, "The Forgotten History of the Western Klan," *The Atlantic*, April 6, 2021. On the diffuse, unstructured nature of the Reconstruction-era Klan, see Elaine Frantz Parsons, "Midnight Rangers: Costume and Performance in the Reconstruction-Era Ku Klux Klan," *Journal of American History* 92, no. 3 (December 2005): 815–16; and Hahn, *Nation Under Our Feet*, 267.

55. Wilson, *History of Los Angeles County*, 101; Colman, "John Ballard," 217–18.

56. *Los Angeles Daily News*, June 29, 1871.

57. Matthew Keller to Joseph Lancaster Brent, August 17, 1865, Brent Papers, box 2, HEHL; Cleland, *Cattle on a Thousand Hills*, 178–80; On cotton experiments in California see, John L. Strong, "Cotton Experiments in California" *Overland Monthly* 6, no. 4 (April 1871): 326–35; John Strong, "Labor in Cotton Culture," *Overland Monthly* 13, no. 1 (July 1874): 18–25; *San Francisco Bulletin*, October 18, 1870; *Pacific Rural Press*, November 28, 1874.

58. Quoted in Chandler, "Friends in Time of Need," 338.

59. Mesmer, "Negro Settlers," MSS typescript, Joseph Mesmer Papers box 4, folder 4, UCLA. See also *Los Angeles Tribune*, January 2, 1887. Wilson, *History of Los Angeles County*, 120; Michael E. Engh, *Frontier Faiths: Church, Temple, and Synagogue in Los Angeles, 1846–1888* (University of New Mexico Press, 1992), 43; Colman, "John Ballard," 210.

60. Bass, *Forty Years*, 21. Fred M. Baker and Jesse H. Sterling, "History," (n.p., n.d.); "History of the First African Methodist Episcopal Church of Los Angeles" (n.p., n.d.). My thanks to Lorn Foster for sharing these sources, as well as his insights on the early Black church of Los Angeles.

61. Elsa Barkley Brown, "Negotiating and Transforming the Public Sphere: African American Political Life in the Transition from Slavery to Freedom," in *Jumpin' Jim Crow: Southern Politics from Civil War to Civil Rights*, ed. Jane Dailey, Glenda Gilmore, Bryant Simon (Princeton University Press, 2000), 29–30. See also Brown, "To Catch the Vision of Freedom," 67–68; Evelyn Brooks Higginbotham, *Righteous Discontent: The Women's Movement in the Black Baptist Church, 1880–1920* (Harvard University Press, 1993).

62. Hahn, *Nation Under Our Feet*, 232–33.

63. W.E.B. Du Bois, *The Souls of Black Folk* (reprint, Simon and Schuster, 2005), 191.

64. Bettye Collier-Thomas, *Jesus, Jobs, and Justice: African American Women and Religion* (Knopf, 2010); James T. Campbell, *Songs of Zion: The African Methodist Episcopal Church in the United States and South Africa* (Oxford University Press, 1995), 5–14; Tyrone McKinley Freeman, *Madam C. J. Walker's Gospel of Giving: Black Women's Philanthropy During Jim Crow* (University of Illinois Press, 2020), 40–48.

65. Engh, *Frontier Faiths*, 12–17.

66. Both quotes from entry for November 12, 1854, in Bynum, "Los Angeles in 1854–5: The Diary of Rev. James Woods," 70–72.

67. Entry for December 3, 1854, in Bynum, "Los Angeles in 1854–5: The Diary of Rev. James Woods," 76.

68. In Bynum, "Los Angeles in 1854–5: The Diary of Rev. James Woods," 79; Woods, *Recollections of Pioneer Work in California*, 197.

69. Entry for April 29, 1855, in James L. Woods, *California Pioneer Decade of 1849: The Presbyterian Church* (Hansen Co., 1922), 68.

70. Entry for April 29, 1855, in Bynum, "Los Angeles in 1854–5: The Diary of Rev. James Woods," 83.

71. Quoted in Hahn, *Nation Under Our Feet*, 233. Still, many of these positions were mere auxiliary roles. On patriarchy in the AME Church, see Freeman, *Madam C. J. Walker's Gospel of Giving*, 48; Collier-Thomas, *Jesus, Jobs, and Justice*; Andrews, *Sisters of the Spirit*, 13, 19.

72. Quoted in Higginbotham, *Righteous Discontent*, 1.

73. Engh, *Frontier Faiths*, 43, 189–90.

74. "The Last of Aunt Biddy," *Los Angeles Evening Express*, January 19, 1891; *Los Angeles Times*, January 16 and 18, 1891.

75. The sum comes from T.M.D. Ward's observation that Black Angelenos had already raised $1,400 by the end of that summer; *Elevator*, September 3, 1869.

76. For a list of that leadership, see *Elevator*, September 3, 1869; *Los Angeles Star*, September 25, 1869.

77. *Elevator*, September 3, 1869; *Los Angeles Daily News*, August 24, 1869.

78. *Elevator*, September 3, 1869.

79. Deed, Joseph Kurtz to Jeremiah Redding, et al. March 13, 1869, LAR. My thanks to Patty Colman for providing me with a copy of this deed. See also *Los Angeles Daily News*, March 11, 1869.

80. The seller of that land, Dr. Joseph Kurtz, happened to be John Hall's neighbor; Colman, "John Ballard," 210–11.

81. *Elevator*, September 3, 1869.

82. Wilson, *History of Los Angeles County*, 120.

83. *Los Angeles Star*, September 25, 1869.

84. *Los Angeles Star*, October 2, 1869. Further fundraising came from a lecture series titled "The Future of the Colored Race"; *Los Angeles Star*, April 9 and April 16, 1870. The next year, Black Los Angeles hosted another grand festival; *Los Angeles Star*, October 19, 1870; *Los Angeles Daily News*, October 26, 1870.

85. *Elevator*, September 3, 1869. See also Paul Spitzzeri, "Resiliency, Resolve and Risk: Explorations of Black History in Los Angeles, 1860–1885," *Homestead Blog*, April 24, 2020, https://homesteadmuseum.blog/2020/04/24/in-fitting-fashion-explorations-of-black-history-in-los-angeles-1870-1886/.

86. *Los Angeles Star,* September 7, 1870. *Elevator*, September 3, 1869, gives some sense of the building's proposed dimensions: two stories and nearly 1,500 square feet.

87. *Los Angeles Star*, April 11, 1871.

88. Matthew 17:20.

89. "About First AME Church," accessed April 23 2025, https://www.famechurchla.org/ministries/about-fame-church/.

90. Colman, "John Ballard," 212–13.

91. *Los Angeles Daily News,* April 14, 1870; *Los Angeles Star,* April 9 and 16, 1870; *San Francisco Elevator,* April 22, 1870; Paul Spitzzeri, "The Black Pioneers of Los Angeles County, 1850–1900, Presentation Postview," *Homestead Blog,* June 17, 2023, https://homesteadmuseum.blog/2023/06/17/the-black-pioneers-of-los-angeles-county-1850-1900-presentation-postview-implementing-the-15th-amendment-in-los-angeles-1870/. My deep thanks to Paul for providing many of these newspaper sources.

92. *Los Angeles Daily News,* April 26, 1870. See also *Los Angeles Daily News,* May 24, 1870.

93. Kewen's letter in *Los Angeles Daily News,* April 29, 1870.

94. Colman, "John Ballard," 215.

95. Mesmer, "Negro Settlers," MSS typescript, Mesmer Papers box 4, folder 4, UCLA. See also Warner, Hayes, and Widney, *Historical Sketch of Los Angeles County,* 44.

96. 1870 Census.

97. Brown, "To Catch the Vision of Freedom," 86–87.

98. *Elevator,* March 11, 1870.

99. Foote, "Brand Plucked from the Fire," in Andrews, *Sisters of the Spirit,* 227.

100. For more on Black women's strategies to make themselves heard, despite their exclusion from certain political channels, see Rosalyn Terborg-Penn, *African American Women in the Struggle for the Vote, 1850–1920* (Indiana University Press, 1998); Elsa Barkley Brown, "Womanist Consciousness: Maggie Lena Walker and the Independent Order of Saint Luke," *Signs* 14, no. 3 (Spring 1989): 611–14; Brown, "Negotiating and Transforming the Public Sphere"; Brown, "To Catch the Vision of Freedom"; Carla L. Peterson, *"Doers of the Word": African-American Women Speakers and Writers in the North, 1830–1880* (Oxford University Press, 1995); Martha S. Jones, *All Bound Up Together: The Woman Question in African American Public Culture, 1830–1900* (University of North Carolina Press, 2007), 140–52; Mary Ryan, *Women in Public: Between Banners and Ballots, 1825–1880* (Johns Hopkins University Press, 1992); Glenda Gilmore, *Gender and Jim Crow: Women and the Politics of White Supremacy in North Carolina, 1896–1920* (University of North Carolina Press, 1996), 18; Hahn, *Nation Under Our Feet,* 227–28.

101. *Elevator,* March 11, 1870.

102. The full ruling is reprinted in the *Los Angeles Star,* May 7, 1870. See also *Los Angeles Star,* April 30, 1870; *Los Angeles Daily News,* April 21 and 30, 1870; Hayes Scrapbooks, vol. 58, Bancroft.

103. Berwanger, *West and Reconstruction,* 180–81.

104. Colman, "John Ballard," 214–16.

105. *Los Angeles Star,* December 18, 1871; *Evening Express,* March 26, 1874; *Los Angeles Herald,* April 1, 1874; *Evening Express,* January 4, 1875; *Evening Express,* April 9, 1875; *Evening Express,* April 14, 1875; *Los Angeles Herald,* April 14, 1875; *Evening Express,* April 4, 1876; *Los Angeles Times,* October 9, 1885; *Los Angeles*

Times, December 23, 1885; *Los Angeles Herald*, January 3, 1886; *Evening Express*, June 20, 1895; *Los Angeles Herald*, January 2, 1896; *Los Angeles Times*, December 27, 1896; *Los Angeles Times*, January 2, 1898; *Los Angeles Times*, January 2, 1900. My thanks to Paul Spitzzeri for directing me to these sources.

106. Deed of Hannah Embers to Martha Embers and Charles Embers, June 26, 1868, Book of Deeds, San Bernardino, SBCHA; Hannah Embers, United States Internal Revenue, tax assessment records, California, 1866, National Archives; Demaratus, *Force of a Feather*, 179. For the location of Hannah's property, lot 5 in San Bernardino, see Original Map of the Ranch San Bernardino Survey, Plan of the City of San Bernardino, p. 6, SBCHA.

107. Deed of Hannah Embers, SBCHA. See also Charles Embers, tax assessment records, San Bernardino, 1874–1875, SBCHA.

108. Between Nelson, Ann, and Jane Embers (the wife of Charles Embers), Hannah's family contributed $100 toward the building of First AME; *Elevator*, September 3, 1869.

109. For well-sourced biographies of Hannah's children, see Thiriot, *Slavery in Zion*, 281–89.

110. James Walter Yancy, "The Negro of Tucson: Past and Present" (MA thesis, University of Arizona, 1933), 15–17.

111. My deepest thanks to Angela Wilkinson, descendent of Hannah and Martha and Israel Beal, who shared her family's scrapbooks with me and accompanied me on numerous historical tours through the area.

112. Interview with Angela Wilkinson, July 15, 2024. Angela and I have been searching for any sign of Hannah's headstone for years, with no success to date.

CHAPTER 14: PHILANTHROPIST

1. Bell, *On the Old West Coast*, 166.

2. Wilson, *History of Los Angeles County*, 84.

3. Newmark, *Sixty Years in Southern California*, 433. King had railed against Chinese immigration for years through the pages of the *Los Angeles Daily News*, even as he himself employed a Chinese cook in his home; Scott Zesch, "Chinese Los Angeles in 1870–71: The Makings of a Massacre," *Southern California Quarterly* 90 (Summer 2008): 127.

4. Scott Zesch, *The Chinatown War: Chinese Los Angeles and the Massacre of 1871* (Oxford University Press, 2012), 122–50; Faragher, *Eternity Street*, 459–80; Bell, *On the Old West Coast*, 166–75; *Los Angeles Star*, October 25, 1871; *Los Angeles Star*, October 26, 1871; *Los Angeles Daily News*, October 26 and 28, 1871; Torres-Rouff, *Before L.A.*, 181–95; Spitzzeri, "Judge Lynch in Session," 105–11.

5. Mason's residence was listed at "1st street below Main" in *The First Los Angeles City and County Directory, 1872* (Ward Ritchie Press, 1963), 8.

6. For eyewitness accounts, see Joseph Mesmer, "Chinese Massacre," Joseph

Mesmer Papers, box 2, folder 6, UCLA; Bell, *On the Old West Coast*, 166–75; Newmark, *Sixty Years in Southern California*, 433.

7. "The Los Angeles Massacre," *New York Times*, November 10, 1871.

8. Her Spring Street properties housed a Chinese laundry and a Chinese haberdashery; *Los Angeles Times*, August 1, 1885.

9. The famous quote comes from an interview that Thurman conducted with Mason's great-granddaughter, Gladys Owens; Sue Bailey Thurman, *Pioneers of Negro Origin in California* (Acme, 1952), 46–47.

10. Freeman, *Madam C. J. Walker's Gospel of Giving*, 194.

11. Tyrone McKinley Freeman, "7 Ways to Read Around the History of Philanthropy's Diversity Problem This Black History Month," *Histphil* (blog), February 25, 2019.

12. Freeman, *Madam C. J. Walker's Gospel of Giving*, 187.

13. Census of 1870.

14. Freeman, *Madam C. J. Walker's Gospel of Giving*, 21.

15. *Elevator*, September 3, 1869.

16. "A Memorial Window Dedicated to Mrs. Biddy Mason," *Los Angeles Times*, March 7, 1904, and *The Liberator* (Los Angeles), March 1904.

17. *Los Angeles Herald*, July 19, 1884. See also Kate Bradley Stovall, "The Negro Woman in Los Angeles and Vicinity—Some Notable Characters," *Los Angeles Times*, February 9, 1909.

18. Thurman, *Pioneers of Negro Origin*, 46; Taylor, *In Search of the Racial Frontier*, 206.

19. Stovall, "The Negro Woman," *Los Angeles Times*, February 9, 1909.

20. Bass, *Forty Years*, 8.

21. Mesmer, "A White Pioneer Reminisces," in Bass, *Forty Years*, 116.

22. Quoted in Freeman, *Madam C. J. Walker's Gospel of Giving*, 25. See also A'Lelia Bundles, *On Her Own Ground: The Life and Times of Madam C. J. Walker* (Simon & Schuster, 2001).

23. Deirdre Cooper Owens, *Medical Bondage: Race, Gender, and the Origins of American Gynecology* (University of Georgia Press, 2017), 54; Richard W. Wertz and Dorothy C. Wertz, *Lying-In: A History of Childbirth in America* (The Free Press, 1977), 55–58.

24. Newmark, *Sixty Years in Southern California*, 250.

25. Newmark, *Sixty Years in Southern California*, 409.

26. Newmark, *Sixty Years in Southern California*, 648–49.

27. Quoted in Jenny M. Luke, *Delivered by Midwives: African American Midwifery in the Twentieth-Century South* (University Press of Mississippi), 28.

28. See, for instance, her work in the home of Henry Dwight Barrows, Diary of Henry Dwight Barrows, July 16 and July 30, 1862, Barrows and Weyse Family Papers, box 2, HEHL.

29. *Los Angeles Times*, June 22, 1887.

30. Quoted in Luke, *Delivered by Midwives*, 28.

31. *California Eagle*, July 23, 1937; Luke, *Delivered by Midwives*, 24.

32. Wertz and Wertz, *Lying-In*, 55.

33. Sims was known to perform experimental surgeries on enslaved women, without anesthesia. Owens, *Medical Bondage*, 1–2. See also Luke, *Delivered by Midwives*, 14–18.

34. Hayden, "Biddy Mason's Los Angeles," 92.

35. *Los Angeles Times*, June 22, 1887.

36. Mesmer, "Negro Settlers," MSS typescript, Joseph Mesmer Papers, box 4, folder 4, UCLA.

37. Mesmer, "A White Pioneer Reminisces," in Bass, *Forty Years*, 116.

38. *California Eagle*, July 23, 1937. For the radio play, see *California Eagle*, June 23, 1938.

39. Stephen C. Foster to Governor Peter H. Burnett, March 12, 1850, Los Angeles Prefecture Records, vol. 2, pp. 840–43, HEHL.

40. Benjamin Hayes to Jack Hinton, September 20, 1863, Benjamin Hayes Scrapbooks, vol. 14, Bancroft.

41. Mesmer, "Negro Settlers," MSS typescript, Joseph Mesmer Papers, box 4, folder 4, UCLA.

42. Kewen, *State of the Union. Speech of Hon. E.J.C. Kewen. on The State of the Union; Delivered before the Democracy of Sacramento in Assembly Hall, April 27, 1863* (n.p., n.d), 7.

43. *Los Angeles Daily News*, April 14, 1870; *Los Angeles Star*, April 9, 16, and 29, 1870; *San Francisco Elevator*, April 22, 1870.

44. Hilary Green, *Educational Reconstruction: African-American Schools in the Urban South, 1865–1890* (Oxford University Press, 2016); Hahn, *Nation Under Our Feet*, 276.

45. Campbell F. Scribner, "Surveying the Destruction of African American Schoolhouses in the South, 1864–1876," *Journal of the Civil War Era* 10, no. 4 (December 2020): 469–94.

46. *LA Semi-Weekly News*, March 20, 1866.

47. *LA Semi-Weekly News*, July 17, 1866.

48. See "An Act to Establish, Support and Regulate Common Schools, and to Repeal Former Acts Concerning Same," May 3, 1855, *The Statutes of California, Passed at the Sixth Session of the Legislature* (Sacramento: B.B. Redding, State Printer, 1855), 229–37; "An Act to Establish, Support, and Regulate, Common Schools, and to Repeal Former Acts Concerning the Same," April 28, 1860, *The Statutes of California, Passed at the Eleventh Session of the Legislature, 1860* (Sacramento: Charles T. Botts, State Printer, 1860), 321–26.

49. Paul Spitzzeri, "The Black Pioneers of Los Angeles County: The 'Colored School' of Los Angeles, 1865–1875," *Homestead Blog*, February 6, 2024; *Los Angeles*

Daily News, October 5, 1870. On the separate and unequal conditions in the Black school, see *Los Angeles Star*, July 15 and 16, 1872.

50. *Los Angeles Star*, August 29, 1871.

51. *Los Angeles Herald*, August 12, 1874.

52. F. H. Crumbly, "A Los Angeles Citizen," *Colored American Magazine* 9, no. 3 (September 1905), 484; Beasley, *Negro Trail Blazers*, 109–110.

53. Charles Wollenberg, *All Deliberate Speed: Segregation and Exclusion in California Schools, 1855–1975* (University of California Press, 1976), 11–12, 17.

54. Beasley, *Negro Trail Blazers*, 109–110.

55. "Letter List," *Daily Stockton Independent*, July 19, 1872.

56. Owens, "Robert C. Owens," MSS, UCLA.

57. Owens, "Robert C. Owens," MSS, UCLA.

58. Crumbly, "Los Angeles Citizen," *Colored American Magazine*, 484; *Pomona Daily Review*, November 17, 1908.

59. *Los Angeles Herald*, July 25, 1875. See also Collier-Thomas, *Jesus, Jobs, and Justice*, 45–49.

60. See, for instance, *Los Angeles Star*, May 29, 1875.

61. Gilmore, *Gender and Jim Crow*, 14; Susan Bragg, "Anxious Foot Soldiers: Sacramento's Black Women and Education in Nineteenth-Century California," in *African American Women Confront the West*, ed. Taylor and Moore, 98–107.

62. Willi Coleman, "African American Women and Community Development in California, 1848–1900," in *Seeking El Dorado*, ed. de Graaf, Mulroy, and Taylor, 102; Matthews, *Golden State in the Civil War*, 207.

63. *Los Angeles Evening Express*, June 10, 1874. See also, *Los Angeles Star*, June 21, 1871, and June 25, 1872.

64. *Los Angeles Evening Express*, May 27, 1875. See also Campbell, *Making Black Los Angeles*, 67.

65. Cleland, *Cattle on a Thousand Hills*, 220–21; *New York Times*, April 23, 1868.

66. Newmark, *Sixty Years in Southern California*, 460–61; Graves, *My Seventy Years in California*, 97.

67. Salvator, *Los Angeles in the Sunny Seventies*, 134–35; Torres-Rouff, *Before L.A.*, 204–205.

68. Newmark, *Sixty Years in Southern California*, 510.

69. Salvator, *Los Angeles in the Sunny Seventies*, 125–26. See also Mesmer, "Early Homes," MSS typescript, Joseph Mesmer Papers, Box 4, folder 5, UCLA; and Carey McWilliams, *Southern California: An Island on the Land* (Peregrine Smith, 1973), ix.

70. Extract of a letter from Browne in *Los Angeles Daily Star*, December 20, 1874. See also Benjamin C. Truman, *Semi-Tropical California* (San Francisco: Bancroft, 1874), 18.

71. Truman, *Semi-Tropical California*, 27; *New York Times*, April 23, 1868. See also Brace, *New West*, 279–280.

72. Deverell, *Whitewashed Adobe*, 133–38.

73. Alexander Finkelstein, "Los Angeles's 1863–1876 Boom," *Southern California Quarterly* 99, no. 2 (Summer 2017): 142–48.

74. Newmark, *Sixty Years in Southern California*, 138.

75. Salvator, *Los Angeles in the Sunny Seventies*, 30.

76. "Petitions for the widening of San Pedro Street," Los Angeles Area Court Records, Los Angeles County, Case #988, HEHL.

77. See advertisement in *Evening Express*, August 19, 1875, and *Los Angeles Herald*, October 6, 1875.

78. Warner, Hayes, and Widney, *Historical Sketch of Los Angeles County*, 44.

79. See, for instance, the entries for Lewis Green, John Hall, Biddy Mason, Charles Owens, Winnie Owens, and Robert C. Owens in Assessment Book, Los Angeles City for the Year 1875, Seaver.

80. Salvator, *Los Angeles in the Sunny Seventies*, 124–26; Warner, Hayes, and Widney, *Historical Sketch of Los Angeles County*, 77.

81. *Los Angeles Times*, August 1, 1885.

82. Biddy Mason, Assessment Book, Los Angeles City for the Year 1876, Seaver.

83. John W. Ravage, *Black Pioneers: Images of the Black Experience on the North American Frontier*, second edition (University of Utah Press, 2008); Peter E. Palmquist and Thomas R. Kailbourn, *Pioneer Photographers of the Far West: A Biographical Dictionary, 1840–1865* (Stanford University Press, 2000), 673.

84. Newmark, *Sixty Years in Southern California*, 365.

85. My thanks to Jenny Watts of the Huntington Library, who helped me read this photograph and identity Wolfenstein as the likely photographer. See *Los Angeles Star*, January 7, 1877, for an advertisement for Wolfenstein's gallery around the time Mason had her portrait done. See Mautz, *Biographies of Western Photographers*, 156.

86. Mautz, *Biographies of Western Photographers*, 104.

87. Laura Wexler, *Tender Violence: Domestic Visions in an Age of US Imperialism* (University of North Carolina Press, 2000), 2; Teresa Zackodnik, "The Green-Backs of Civilization: Sojourner Truth and Portrait Photography," *American Studies* 46, no. 2 (Summer 2005).

88. Stovall, "Negro Woman in Los Angeles," *Los Angeles Times*, February 9, 1909.

89. Demaratus, *Force of a Feather*, 177; Arielle Xena Alterwaite, "Biddy Mason in Images: A Monumental Life in Monumental Forms," *Los Angeles Review of Books*, December 17, 2021.

90. Deed, Biddie [*sic*] Mason to J. H. Jones and Charles M. Wright, January 2, 1875, LAR.

91. Cleland, *Cattle on a Thousand Hills*, 222–23.

92. Paul R. Spitzzeri, *The Workman and Temple Families of Southern California* (Seligson Publishing, 2007); Newmark, *Sixty Years in Southern California*, 479.

93. Newmark, *Sixty Years in Southern California*, 478. See also Edward Lancaster Watkins to Joseph Lancaster Brent, August 28, 1875, and Watkins to Brent, March 21, 1876, both in Brent Papers, box 3, HEHL.

94. Graves, *My Seventy Years in California*, 99. See also, Benjamin D. Wilson to Brent, March 5, 1877, Brent Papers, box 3, HEHL.

95. Bell, "Los Angeles 1882," p. 10, typewritten MSS, Bell Papers, HEHL.

96. Owens, "My Grandfather," MSS, UCLA.

97. *Semi-Weekly Southern News*, June 19, 1861; *Los Angeles Daily News*, February 26, 1871, and November 2, 1872; *Evening Express*, July 24, 1875.

98. *Evening Express*, July 24, 1874.

99. *Los Angeles Herald*, March 23, 1875.

100. *Los Angeles Star*, October 9 and 10, 1871; *Los Angeles Herald*, March 23, 1875.

101. Wendell P. Daily, *An Album of Memories* (Schauer Printing Press, 1946), 162.

102. Colman, "John Ballard," 219–23.

103. John Ballard, Assessment Book, Los Angeles City for the Year 1875, Seaver.

104. Frederick Hastings Ringe, *Happy Days in Southern California* (Cambridge, MA: n.p., 1898), 136; Daily, *Album of Memories*, 162; Colman, "John Ballard," 219–23.

105. My thanks especially to Ryan Ballard and to Patty Colman for sharing this story with me. See also the film *To Right a Wrong: The Story of Ballard Mountain* (2022) and Coleman, "John Ballard," 229.

106. *Los Angeles Herald*, January 11, 1878.

107. For Hall's substantial property transactions, see *Evening Express*, October 3, 1874; *Los Angeles Herald*, March 26, 1874; *Los Angeles Herald*, October 7, 1875; *Evening Express*, December 18, 1876; *Los Angeles Herald*, July 8, 1883; *Los Angeles Times*, July 21, 1883; *Los Angeles Times*, November 19, 1884. And for his wealth invested in real estate, see Assessment Book, Los Angeles City for the Years 1875, 1876, 1877, Seaver.

108. *Evening Express*, January 14, 1878. See also Newmark, *Sixty Years in Southern California*, 527–28.

109. Paul Spitzzeri, "Resiliency, Resolve, and Risk: Explorations of Black History in Los Angeles, 1860–1885," *Homestead Blog*, April 24, 2024, https://homesteadmuseum.blog/2020/04/24/in-fitting-fashion-explorations-of-black-history-in-los-angeles-1870-1886/.

110. *Los Angeles Times*, December 2, 1882. Although some historians claim that the trustees of First AME were forced to sell the church property during this

period, I've uncovered nothing in the primary source record to suggest they relinquished the building or the land until a lawsuit in 1885.

111. The term was coined by Rayford Logan, *The Negro in American Life and Thought: The Nadir, 1877–1901* (Dial Press, 1954). On the collapse of Reconstruction, see Hahn, *Nation Under Our Feet*, 413; Foner, *Reconstruction*, chaps. 11 and 12; and Manisha Sinha, *The Rise and Fall of the Second American Republic: Reconstruction, 1860–1920* (Liveright, 2024), chap. 8.

112. Hayes did contribute a long section to a centennial history of Los Angeles County, published that year, though the volume didn't measure up to his ambition for a magnum opus of Southern California. See Warner, Hayes, and Widney, *Historical Sketch of Los Angeles County*.

113. All quotes from Hubert Howe Bancroft, "Historic Researches in the South," in *Literary Industries: A Memoir* (San Francisco: History Company, 1890), 481, 482.

114. Bancroft, "Historic Researches in the South," 484.

115. Wilson, *History of Los Angeles County*, 102; Demaratus, *Force of a Feather*, 164–70; Mesmer, "Judge Benjamin Ignatius Hayes," MSS typescript, Joseph Mesmer Papers, box 6, folder 2, UCLA.

116. In the matter of the estate of Charles Owens, October 14, 1882, Los Angeles Superior Court, Los Angeles Area Court Records, case #1825, HEHL.

117. *Los Angeles Times*, April 19, 1883.

118. *Los Angeles Herald*, April 19, 1883. See also Mesmer, "Negro Settlers," Mesmer Papers, box 4, folder 4, UCLA.

119. In the matter of the estate of Winnie Owens, deceased, 1883, Los Angeles Superior Court, Los Angeles Area Court Records, case #2272, HEHL.

120. This is a common refrain of hers in her courtroom testimony from 1887; *Los Angeles Times*, June 22, 1887.

121. "Biddy Mason," Internment Book #3, November1890–December 1900, Evergreen Cemetery archives.

CHAPTER 15: CITY-BUILDER

1. Mike Davis, *The Ecology of Fear: Los Angeles and the Imagination of Disaster* (Verso, 1998).

2. Bascom A. Stephens, ed., *Resources of Los Angeles* (Los Angeles: Sprague and Rodehaver, 1887), 4.

3. Newmark, *Sixty Years in Southern California*, 541.

4. Deverell, *Whitewashed Adobe*, 103–105; Brian Andrew Ebiner, "Disaster in Los Angeles, 1884," *Los Angeles Corral of the Westerners* 286 (Spring 2017): 1–8.

5. On the housing shortage, see *Los Angeles Daily Times*, January 3, 1882.

6. Deverell, *Whitewashed Adobe*, 103–104.

7. Stovall, "Negro Woman in Los Angeles," *Los Angeles Times*, February 9, 1909; Thurman, *Pioneers of Negro Origin*, 46.

8. *Los Angeles Times*, August 1, 1885.

9. Mason previously lived at 155 Spring Street, at 108 Fort Street, and at First and Main. *The First Los Angeles City and County Directory, 1872* (Ward Ritchie Press, 1963), 8; *Los Angeles City Directory, 1878* (Los Angeles: Mirror Printing, 1878), 73; *Los Angeles City and County Directory, 1883–84* (San Francisco: Southern California Publishing Co., n.d.), 189. See also, Hayden, "Biddy Mason's Los Angeles," 97.

10. *Los Angeles Times*, August 1, 1885.

11. *Los Angeles Times*, August 1, 1885.

12. *Los Angeles Times*, September 17 and 19, 1885.

13. Deverell, *Whitewashed Adobe*, 133–35.

14. *Los Angeles City and County Directory, 1884–85* (Los Angeles, Burton-Taney, 1885), 241, 284.

15. *Los Angeles City Directory, 1887–8* (Los Angeles: Smith & McPhee, 1888), 322; *Los Angeles City Directory, 1888* (Los Angeles: W.H.L. Corran, 1888), 545–46; F. H. Crumbly, "A Los Angeles Citizen," *Colored American Magazine* 9, no. 3 (September 1905): 482–85.

16. *Los Angeles Times*, December 17, 1885; *Los Angeles Herald*, November 23, 1886.

17. *Los Angeles Herald*, January 26, 1886.

18. Joseph Mesmer, "Negro Settlers," MSS typescript, Mesmer Papers, box 4, folder 4, UCLA.

19. *City Directory, 1888*, pp. 760–860.

20. *City Directory, 1888*, pp. 769, 770, 771, 775, 789, 793, 799, 801, 814, 841–43, 860.

21. Newmark, *Sixty Years in Southern California*, 518; Fogelson, *Fragmented Metropolis*, 148.

22. Mesmer, "A White Pioneer Reminisces," in Bass, *Forty Years*, 116; and Mesmer, "Negro Settlers," MSS typescript, Joseph Mesmer Papers, box 4, folder 4, UCLA.

23. *Los Angeles Times*, December 2, 1882; *City Directory, 1881–82*, p. 23.

24. *Los Angeles Herald*, July 9, 1884.

25. *Los Angeles Herald*, July 19, 1884.

26. Deed, November 30, 1885, between G. Wiley Wells and William Comer, Robert C. Owens, William Ballard, Biddy Mason, and Granville Huddleston, Lot 25, Block I, Bennet tract, LAR. See also *Los Angeles Times*, February 28, 1886.

27. *Lucy Gillmore vs. Jeremiah M. Redding, et al.*, May 17, 1886, Los Angeles Superior Court, Los Angeles Area Court Records, case #4722, HEHL.

28. *Los Angeles Times*, June 20, 1885, and August 12, 1885. My thanks to Patty

Colman, Sally Gordon, and Paul Spitzzeri, who helped untangle the complexities of the case.

29. *Gillmore v. Redding, et al.*, HEHL.

30. *Los Angeles Evening Post Record*, May 21, 1898.

31. *City Directory, 1888*, pp. 86, 375, 789.

32. *Los Angeles Tribune*, July 7, 1888. Robert C. Owens and others assisted Mason in the fundraising campaign. See also *Los Angeles Tribune*, August 31, 1888.

33. *Los Angeles Herald*, August 14, 1888; *Los Angeles Tribune*, July 7, 1888.

34. *Los Angeles Times*, August 23 and September 23, 1888; *Los Angeles Evening Express*, September 24, 1888; *Los Angeles Tribune*, October 22, 1888.

35. *Los Angeles Evening Express*, October 23, 1900; Engh, *Frontier Faiths*, 189.

36. The Azusa Street property was sold in 1907 for $15,000, at which point the congregation had already relocated to a grander building on Eighth and Towne; *Los Angeles Times*, January 11, 1907.

37. *Los Angeles Times*, June 22, 1887.

38. *David Mulrein (plaintiff) vs. Biddy Mason (defendant)*, filed November 18, 1887, recorded April 30, 1889, Los Angeles Superior Court, Los Angeles Area Court Records, case #5235, HEHL.

39. In the matter of the estate of Biddy Mason, Los Angeles Area Court Records, Probate Court, second series, case #14493, HEHL; Merry Ovnick, "Looking for the Founders of the Historical Society of Southern California," *Southern California Quarterly* 97, no. 2 (Summer 2015): 169–70; "John T. Wilson and the Lopez Family," The Lopez Adobe Blog, August 8, 2015. Thanks to Paul Spitzzeri for additional biographical material on Wilson.

40. *Mulrein v. Mason*, HEHL.

41. *Mulrein v. Mason*, HEHL.

42. *Mulrein v. Mason*, HEHL. From later newspaper coverage it appears Mulrein appealed the decision and was able to collect some money for his efforts, although there was no evidence of his appeals in the official court records. See *Los Angeles Times*, November 18, 1887.

43. Lanier Bartlett, introduction, Bell, *On the Old West Coast*, xiii.

44. Bell, "Los Angeles 1882" typewritten MSS, pp. 2–3, Horace Bell Papers, HEHL.

45. *Los Angeles Times*, March 17, 1887.

46. *Los Angeles Times*, March 17, 1887, and June 22, 1887.

47. *Los Angeles Times*, June 22, 1887.

48. *Los Angeles Times*, June 22, 1887.

49. On the "culture of dissemblance" practiced by Black women across the country, see Darlene Clark Hine, "Rape and the Inner Lives of Black Women in the Middle West: Preliminary Thoughts on the Culture of Dissemblance," *Signs: Journal of Women in Culture and Society* 14, no. 4 (Summer 1989).

50. *Los Angeles Times*, June 22, 1887.

51. David M. Hargrove, "Guilford Wiley Wells," *Mississippi Encyclopedia*, https://mississippiencyclopedia.org/entries/wells-guilford-wiley/.

52. Hudson, *Making of "Mammy Pleasant,"* 8.

53. Hudson, *Making of "Mammy Pleasant,"* 64, 77–78, 82–97.

54. CPI Inflation Calculator, https://www.officialdata.org/us/inflation.

55. Dumke, *Boom of the Eighties*, 5, 9; Stephens, *Resources of Los Angeles*, 23, 27.

56. Dumke, *Boom of the Eighties*, 4–5, 47.

57. Newmark, *Sixty Years in Southern California*, 571.

58. Mesmer, "Real Estate Booms," MSS, Joseph Mesmer Papers, box 4, folder 5, UCLA.

59. Dumke, *Boom of the Eighties*, 17–24; Torres-Rouff, *Before L.A.*, 220.

60. Yvette J. Saavedra, *Pasadena Before the Roses: Race, Identity, and Land Use in Southern California, 1771–1890* (University of Arizona Press, 2018), 182–85.

61. Newmark, *Sixty Years in Southern California*, 570.

62. Dumke, *Boom of the Eighties*, 82–83.

63. See the works of John Hittell, Charles Dudley Warner, Charles Nordhoff, and Benjamin Truman.

64. Quoted in Dumke, *Boom of the Eighties*, 31.

65. Fogelson, *Fragmented Metropolis*, 63–64; Dumke, *Boom of the Eighties*, 28–39.

66. Newmark, *Sixty Years in Southern California*, 573.

67. Bell, *On the Old West Coast*, 269.

68. T. S. Van Dyke, *Millionaires of a Day: An Inside History of the Great Southern California "Boom"* (New York: Fords, Howard & Hulbert, 1890), 105.

69. Beasley, *Negro Trail Blazers*, 109

70. Newmark, *Sixty Years in Southern California*, 581.

71. Dumke, *Boom of the Eighties*, 47.

72. Flamming, *Bound for Freedom*, 78.

73. *Los Angeles Herald*, July 19, 1889.

74. My thanks to Liv Smith for these calculations, based on the assessed real estate valuations of Los Angeles as published in *Los Angeles Herald*, July 19, 1889.

75. The demographic flood began in earnest in 1886. See *Los Angeles Herald*, August 26, 1886.

76. Bunch, *Black Angelenos*, 19–20; Campbell, *Making Black Los Angeles*, 31–37.

77. Nell Irvin Painter, *Exodusters: Black Migration to Kansas After Reconstruction* (Knopf, 1976).

78. Taylor, *In Search of the Racial Frontier*, 137, 148. See also Anthony W. Wood, "Forty Years Within the Veil: The Black West and Counternarratives of Race and Place in the Rocky Mountains" (PhD dissertation, University of Michigan, 2024).

79. Flamming, *Bound for Freedom*, 50.

80. Hahn, *Nation Under Our Feet*, 455–57, 465.

81. Alison Rose Jefferson et al., *Survey LA: Los Angeles Citywide Historic Context Statement: African American History of Los Angeles* (City of Los Angeles Department of City Planning, Office of Historic Resources, 2018), 20.

82. Bunch, *Black Angelenos*, 19–20.

83. *Los Angeles Evening Express*, December 31, 1887.

84. *Los Angeles Times*, March 10, 1887.

85. *Los Angeles Herald*, February 4, 1886; *Los Angeles Times*, July 25, 1886.

86. *Los Angeles Tribune*, May 29, 1888. See also *Los Angeles Herald*, May 30, 1888.

87. *Los Angeles Evening Express*, December 31, 1887.

88. *Pasadena Evening Express*, August 5, 1890.

89. Owens, "Robert C. Owens," MSS, Golden State Mutual Life Insurance Records, box 41, UCLA. For his numerous positions, see also *Los Angeles Times*, April 21, 1888; *Los Angeles Times*, April 25, 1888; *Los Angeles Evening Express*, May 16, 1888; *Los Angeles Evening Express*, June 19, 1888; *Los Angeles Evening Express*, November 22, 1888; *Los Angeles Herald*, February 19, 1889; *Los Angeles Times*, July 3, 1890.

90. *Los Angeles Herald*, October 30, 1890; Owens, "Robert C. Owens," MSS, UCLA.

91. *Los Angeles Herald*, July 4, 1888.

92. *Los Angeles Evening Express*, September 8, 1888.

93. Dumke, *Boom of the Eighties*, 4; Newmark, *Sixty Years in Southern California*, 519; Clarence Pullen, "Los Angeles," *Harper's Weekly*, October 18, 1890, p. 807; Torres-Rouff, *Before L.A.*, 256.

94. Newmark, *Sixty Years in Southern California*, 535. Josh Lappen, "Cultures of Power: Electrification, Politics, and Visibility in Greater Los Angeles" (PhD dissertation, University of Oxford, 2024), 3.

95. For a listing of street railway companies, see *City Directory, 1887–8*, pp. 15–16.

96. There is a listing for the Owens Bros. stable in 1888 but none by 1890; *Los Angeles City Directory, 1890* (Los Angeles: W.H.L. Corran, 1890).

97. Entries for November 12, 1854, and April 29, 1855, "Diary of Rev. James Woods," in Bynum, "Los Angeles in 1854–5," 70–72, 83.

98. Woods, *California Pioneer Decade of 1849*, 124.

99. Pullen, "Los Angeles," 807.

100. "Sonoratown," MSS typescript, Joseph Mesmer Papers, box 4, folder 5, UCLA; Albert Camarillo, *Chicanos in a Changing Society: From Mexican Pueblos to American Barrios in Santa Barbara and Southern California, 1848–1930* (Southern Methodist University Press, 1979, 2005), 105, 109, 113, 119.

101. Hise, "Border City," 548. See also Deverell, *Whitewashed Adobe*, 16; Natalia Molina, *Fit to Be Citizens? Public Health and Race in Los Angeles, 1879–1939*

(University of California Press, 2006), 15–45; Thaddeus S. Kenderdine, *California Revisited, 1858–1897* (Newtown, PA: Doylestown Publishing, 1898), 170–72.

102. *Los Angeles Times*, April 8, 14, 15, 1882; February 5, 1886.

103. Torres-Rouff, *Before L.A.*, 233.

104. Torres-Rouff, *Before L.A.*, 226–27, 240.

105. Lawrence B. de Graaf, "The City of Black Angels: Emergence of the Los Angeles Ghetto, 1890–1930," *Pacific Historical Review* 39, no. 3 (August 1970): 329; Morales, *Happy Dreams of Liberty*, 143; Wood, "Forty Years Within the Veil," introduction.

106. Stovall, "Negro Woman in Los Angeles," *Los Angeles Times*, February 9, 1909.

107. Snyder's tribute to Mason in "A Memorial Window Dedicated to Mrs. Biddy Mason," *The Liberator* (Los Angeles), 5 (March 1904); and *Los Angeles Times*, March 7, 1904.

108. *Christian Recorder* (Philadelphia), December 20, 1888.

109. Freeman, *Madam C. J. Walker's Gospel of Giving*, 65.

110. Stovall, "Negro Woman in Los Angeles," *Los Angeles Times*, February 9, 1909.

111. "In the matter of the estate of Biddy Mason, deceased, annual and final account," filed March 3, 1892, Los Angeles Area Court Records, Probate Court, second series, case #14493, HEHL; "Biddy Mason," Internment Book #3, November 1890–December 1900, Evergreen Cemetery archives.

112. Isaiah 9:2.

CHAPTER 16: MATRIARCH

1. The estimate comes from John W. Kemp, an attorney for the legal affairs of the Mason estate, in "A Memorial Window Dedicated to Mrs. Biddy Mason," *Los Angeles Times*, March 7, 1904.

2. "An Old Colored Woman's Will," *Los Angeles Times*, January 21, 1891. See also *Los Angeles Times*, January 23 and March 5, 1891. On the rarity of wills during this period, see Karen Sneddon, "Speaking for the Dead: Voice in Last Wills and Testaments," *St. Johns Law Review* 85, no. 2 (Spring 2011): 686; Lawrence M. Friedman, "Patterns of Testation in the 19th Century: A Study of Essex County (New Jersey) Wills," *American Journal of Legal History* 8, no. 1 (January 1964): 34–35.

3. Karen Sneddon, "In the Name of God, Amen: Language in Last Wills and Testaments," *Quinnipiac Law Review* 29, no. 3 (2011): 666.

4. Freeman, *Madam C. J. Walker's Gospel of Giving*, 168–71.

5. Sneddon, "In the Name of God, Amen," 715–16.

6. Sneddon, "In the Name of God, Amen," 688–96.

7. "In the matter of the estate of Biddy Mason," Los Angeles Area Court Records, Probate Court, second series, case #14493, HEHL.

8. Kate Bradley Stovall, "The Negro Woman in Los Angeles and Vicinity—Some Notable Characters," *Los Angeles Times*, February 9, 1909.

9. "In the matter of the Estate of Biddy Mason," HEHL.

10. "The Last of Aunt Biddy," *LA Evening Express*, January 19, 1891; *Los Angeles Times*, January 16 and 18, 1891.

11. "Biddy Mason," Internment Book #3, November 1890–December 1900, Evergreen Cemetery archives.

12. "In the matter of the estate of Biddy Mason, deceased, annual and final account," filed March 3, 1892, and "final account of executor, report and petition for discharge," filed April 19, 1898, both in Los Angeles Area Court Records, Probate Court, second series, case #14493, HEHL.

13. Emberton, *To Walk About in Freedom*, 153; Suzanne E. Smith, *To Serve the Living: Funeral Directors and the African American Way of Death* (Harvard University Press, 2010).

14. *Los Angeles Times*, January 16, 1891. See also, *Los Angeles Herald*, January 16, 1891; "AME Conference," *Sacramento Daily Union*, August 10, 1891.

15. "The Last of Aunt Biddy," *Los Angeles Evening Express*, January 19, 1891.

16. Joseph Mesmer, Mayor Meredith Snyder, Charlotta Bass, Delilah Beasley, and Sue Bailey Thurman were among her most prominent eulogists.

17. Beasley, *Negro Trail Blazers*, 109.

18. Bond, "Negro in Los Angeles," 12.

19. "A Memorial Window Dedicated to Mrs. Biddy Mason," *Los Angeles Times*, March 7, 1904, reprinted in *Liberator* (Los Angeles), (March 1904).

20. *Los Angeles Times*, March 7, 1904.

21. *Los Angeles Times*, March 7, 1904.

22. Klemcke and Weed, *Robert Mays Smith*, 14.

23. Demaratus, *Force of a Feather*, 152–56.

24. Klemcke and Weed, *Robert Mays Smith*, 221.

25. Richard Hopkins, "Minutes of Special Conference," March 15, 1856, in *Deseret News*, July 2, 1856.

26. Demaratus, *Force of a Feather*, 153–55; Klemcke and Weed, *Robert Mays Smith*, 15–16. My thanks to Michael Boyette, a direct descendent of Robert Smith, for sharing his family's history with me.

27. "Negro Will Build Block," *Los Angeles Times*, August 12, 1905. See also *Los Angeles Times*, November 5, 1897; *Los Angeles Herald*, March 9, 1898; *Evening Express*, March 25, 1898; *Los Angeles Herald*, March 26, 1898; *Evening Express*, October 12, 1898; *Los Angeles Times*, October, 13, 1898; *Los Angeles Herald*, October 13, 1898; *Evening Express*, October 14, 1898; *Los Angeles Times*, October 14, 1898, May 5, 1899, January 27, 1900; *Evening Express*, March 31, 1900; *Los Angeles Times*, April 1, 12 and 28, 1900. See also "In Re Estate of Biddy Mason, petition of Harriet Washington," filed April 5, 1898, Los Angeles Area Court Records, Probate Court, second series, case #14493, HEHL; and *Harriet Washington and W.H.*

Washington vs. Robert C. Owens and Ellen Huddleston, complaint, filed March 8, 1898, Superior Court of Los Angeles, Los Angeles Area Court Records, case #30301, HEHL.

28. Robert agreed to pay Harriet $3,200 in settlement. "*Harriet Washington vs. Robert C. Owens*, in the matter of the estate of Biddy Mason, deceased," Los Angeles Superior Court, October 1898, Los Angeles Area Court Records, case #29464, HEHL. A second case was settled several years later, after Ellen sued Harriet over failure to pay taxes on the property, which they jointly owned. See *Los Angeles Times*, June 22, 1900.

29. "The Washington and Huddleston Block," *The Liberator* (Los Angeles) (March 1904).

30. "Negro Will Build Block," *Los Angeles Times*, August 12, 1905.

31. That vision lives on through the Biddy Mason Charitable Foundation, which supports foster youth in Los Angeles.

32. "The Negro and California History," typescript, p. 26, HEHL. My thanks to Patty Colman for directing my attention to this source.

33. *Pomona Daily Review*, November 17, 1908.

34. Crumbly, "Los Angeles Citizen," 482.

35. Owens, "Robert C. Owens," MSS, UCLA; *The Liberator* (Los Angeles) (December 1902), 5; "The Owens Banquet," *The Liberator* (Los Angeles) (January 1903), 10; "Colored California," *Crisis* 6, no. 4 (August 1913); *California Eagle*, June 26, 1941; Campbell, *Making Black Los Angeles*, 177–78.

36. *Pomona Daily Review*, November 17, 1908.

37. *Los Angeles Times*, August 12, 1905; "Negroes Who Have Won Place or Fortune in Los Angeles and Pasadena," *Los Angeles Times*, February 9, 1909; *Pomona Daily Review*, November 17, 1908; Bond, "Negro in Los Angeles," 13.

38. Crumbly, "Los Angeles Citizen," 484.

39. *Pomona Daily Review*, November 17, 1908.

40. Although Mason's descendants continue to thrive in Los Angeles, Owens himself came to a tragic end. Amid a dispute with some family members, he shot his wife, Anna, and his son-in-law before turning the gun on himself. "Triple Tragedy at Long Beach," *Imperial Valley Press*, February 15, 1932; "Negro Amuck, Murders 2," *San Pedro News Pilot*, February 15, 1932.

41. Hahn, *Nation Under Our Feet*, 425–30, 440–51; Higginbotham, *Righteous Discontent*, 1–5; Ida B. Wells, *Southern Horrors: Lynch Law in All Its Phases* (New York, 1892); W. Fitzhugh Brundage, *Lynching in the New South: Georgia and Virginia, 1880–1930* (University of Illinois Press, 1993); Leon F. Litwack, *Trouble in Mind: Black Southerners in the Age of Jim Crow* (Knopf, 1998), 280–312; Edward L. Ayers, *The Promise of the New South: Life After Reconstruction* (Oxford University Press, 2007), 156–58.

42. Flamming, *Bound for Freedom*, 24–25; Fogelson, *Fragmented Metropolis*, 77–78; Lawrence B. de Graaf and Quintard Taylor, introduction to *Seeking El*

Dorado, ed. de Graaf, Mulroy, and Taylor, 19; Taylor, *In Search of the Racial Frontier*, 206.

43. Quoted in Bunch, *Black Angelenos*, 10.

44. Flamming, *Bound for Freedom*, 50.

45. E. H. Rydall, "California for Colored Folks," *Colored American Magazine* 12 (May 1907): 386.

46. John S. McGroarty, "The Emancipated," *Los Angeles Times*, February 9, 1909. On the mutual affection between McGroarty and the city's Black residents, see Deverell, *Whitewashed Adobe*, 228–30.

47. Stovall, "Negro Woman in Los Angeles," *Los Angeles Times*, February 9, 1909

48. Flamming, *Bound for Freedom*, 52–54.

49. W.E.B. DuBois, "Colored California," *Crisis* 6, no. 4 (August 1913): 192–95.

50. Bunch, *Black Angelenos*, 21. See also Campbell, *Making Black Los Angeles*, 83–86; Bond, "Negro in Los Angeles," 22, 56, 81; Taylor, *In Search of the Racial Frontier*, 233–34.

51. Garrot, "Negro Professional Men in the City"; and Stovall, "The Negro Woman in Los Angeles," both in *Los Angeles Times*, February 9, 1909.

52. Flamming, *Bound for Freedom*, 70–77.

53. Flamming, *Bound for Freedom*, 78.

54. *California Eagle*, June 20, 1914; Jefferson et al., *Survey LA*, 133–37; Flamming, *Bound for Freedom*, 138–40; de Graaf, "Race, Sex, and Region," 83; Bond, "Negro in Los Angeles,"115; Moore and Taylor, "West of African American Women," in *African American Women Confront the West*, ed. Taylor and Moore, 11–12; Campbell, *Making Black Los Angeles*, 76–81; Willi Coleman, "African American Women and Community Development in California, 1848–1900, in *Seeking El Dorado*, 112; Taylor, *In Search of the Racial Frontier*, 207–208.

55. Rev. G. R. Bryant, "Religious Life of Los Angeles Negroes," *Los Angeles Times*, February 9, 1909; Flamming, *Bound for Freedom*, 112–13.

56. Theodore W. Troy, "The Forum," *Los Angeles Times*, February 9, 1909; Flamming, *Bound for Freedom*, 25–26; Jefferson et al., *Survey LA*, 18, 77.

57. William Deverell, "Redemptive California? Re-thinking the Post-Civil War," *Rethinking History* 11, no. 1 (March 2007): 74–75.

58. Hudson, *West of Jim Crow*, 179.

59. Thomas Cripps, *Slow Fade to Black: The Negro in American Film, 1900–1942* (Oxford University Press, 1977), 44.

60. Taylor, *In Search of the Racial Frontier*, 238–39. See also W.E.B DuBois, "The Slanderous Film," *Crisis* (December 1915): 76–77.

61. Bass, *Forty Years*, 35.

62. Hudson, *West of Jim Crow*, 172.

63. Quoted in Hudson, *West of Jim Crow*, 178–80.

64. Bass, *Forty Years*, 54–59.

65. Quoted in Bond, "Negro in Los Angeles," 35n24.

66. Bond, "Negro in Los Angeles," 33; Flamming, *Bound for Freedom*, 69, 153–56; de Graaf, "City of Black Angels," 336; Fogelson, *Fragmented Metropolis*, 147, 195–204; Jefferson, et al., *Survey LA*, 41.

67. Interview with unnamed subject in Bond, "Negro in Los Angeles," 34.

68. Interview with unnamed subject in Bond, "Negro in Los Angeles," 34. See also de Graaf, "City of Black Angels," 337–40.

69. de Graaf, "City of Black Angels," 333.

70. Flamming, *Bound for Freedom*, 99.

71. Flamming, *Bound for Freedom*, 92–99.

72. Hudson, *West of Jim Crow*, 2; Josh Sides, *L.A. City Limits: African American Los Angeles from the Great Depression to the Present* (University of California Press, 2004), chap. 1.

73. Du Bois, "Colored California," 193–94.

74. Du Bois, "Colored California," 194.

EPILOGUE

1. Gregory Crouch, "Early Black Heroine of L.A. Finally Receives Her Due," *Los Angeles Times*, March 28, 1988.

2. "In the matter of the estate of Biddy Mason," Los Angeles Area Court Records, Probate Court, second series, case #14493, HEHL.

3. "In the matter of the estate of Biddy Mason, deceased, annual and final account," filed March 3, 1892, and "final account of executor, report and petition for discharge," filed April 19, 1898, both in Los Angeles Area Court Records, Probate Court, second series, case #14493, HEHL.

4. John Fowler, "Spreading Joy, *California Eagle*, July 23, 1937. See also the reference to Mason's "tomb" in Fowler, "Spreading Joy," *California Eagle*, June 26, 1941. Winnie Owens, Biddy Mason, Charles Owens, Ellen Huddleston, and Harriet Washington are all buried in the plot. My thanks to Isaiah Martin for his research on Evergreen Cemetery.

5. My deep thanks to Kenny Law, Rev. Dylan Littlefield, Kim Cooper, and Richard Schave.

6. Trouillot, *Silencing the Past*; David Glassberg, *Sense of History: The Place of the Past in American Life* (University of Massachusetts Press, 2001).

7. Norman M. Klein, *The History of Forgetting: Los Angeles and the Erasure of Memory* (1997; reprint, Verso, 2008), 1.

8. Deverell, *Whitewashed Adobe*, 7–8. See also Laura Dominguez, "Memory Makers: Tracing Race, Heritage, and Repair in Los Angeles, 1781–2012" (PhD dissertation, University of Southern California, 2023).

9. Klein, *History of Forgetting*, 1; William Alexander McClung, *Landscapes of Desire: Anglo Mythologies of Los Angeles* (University of California Press, 2000), xv.

10. Flamming, *Bound for Freedom*, 376.

11. "Negro Will Build Block," *Los Angeles Times*, August 12, 1905.

12. Materials from the Federation of Black History and Arts in Los Angeles, a campaign for Biddy Mason Day in 1971; and press release, Los Angles Municipal Arts Department, January 6, 1971, all in Golden State Mutual Life Insurance Records, box 41, UCLA.

13. *Los Angeles Times*, July 4, 1972, late final edition.

14. Jackie Broxton and Kevin Waite, "A Monument To California's Black History—and a Great Work of Art—May Soon Be Destroyed," *Los Angeles Times*, July 10, 2020; Karishma Patadia, "Supporters Rally Around New Deal Mural Threatened by UCSF Construction," KQED, August 3, 2020; Luara Paull, "New Hope for Jewish Muralist's Historic Work at UCSF," *Jewish News of Northern California*, August 12, 2020; Kevin Waite, "UCSF Should Save This California Monument to Black History," *San Francisco Examiner*, October 7, 2020.

15. See Lauret Savoy, *Trace: Memory, History, Race and the American Landscape* (Counterpoint, 2015), 30

16. Ana Cecelia Alvarez, biographical essay, in *Trailblazer: Delilah Beasley's California* (Clockshop, 2019), 28–36.

17. *California Eagle*, July 23, 1937; March 23, 1939; December 5, 1940; June 26, 1941; Bass, *Forty Years*, 7–8, 20–21, 114–17; Bass, *Forty Years*, 54–59.

18. Flamming, *Bound for Freedom*, 17–19, 26–27, 32–33, 365–68.

19. Flamming, *Bound for Freedom*, 108.

20. Miriam Matthews, request for materials, handwritten, March 16, 1971, Golden State Mutual Life Insurance Records, box 41, UCLA; Miriam Matthews Photograph Collection, UCLA; Miriam Matthews Papers, UCLA. See also Claudia Maureen Horning, "Trailblazing Librarian in the Golden State: A Look at the life and Career of Miriam Matthews" (MA thesis, University of California Los Angeles, 2012).

21. Laura Dominguez, "How Two African American Artists Explored the Roots of Racism on the West Coast," *PBS SoCal*, May 25, 2021.

22. Dolores Hayden, *The Power of Place: Urban Landscapes as Public History* (MIT Press, 1995). For another remarkable work of art featuring Biddy Mason, see Ada Pinkston's alternate reality installation, "The Open Hand Is Blessed." My thanks to Ada for sharing her vision with me. See Arielle Alterwaite, "Biddy Mason in Images," *Los Angeles Review of Books*, December 17, 2021.

23. Christopher Hawthorne, ed., *Past Due: Report and Recommendations of the Los Angeles Mayor's Office Civic Memory Working Group* (Huntington–USC Institute on California & the West, 2021); for the African American Historic Places Project, see https://www.getty.edu/projects/african-american-historic-places-los-angeles/.

24. For the National Park Service National Underground Railroad Network to Freedom, see https://www.nps.gov/orgs/1205/index.htm. For two new listings related to Biddy Mason, see "National Park Service adds 31 new listings in 13 states

to the National Underground Railroad Network to Freedom Program," National Park Service, May 1, 2025.

25. "The Long Road to Freedom," National Endowment for the Humanities Collaborative Research Grant, codirected by Sarah Barringer Gordon and Kevin Waite; see https://biddymasoncollaborative.com/.

26. Arisa White, Laura Atkins, and Laura Freeman, *Biddy Mason Speaks Up* (Heydey, 2019). For an early radio play on her life story, see *California Eagle*, June 23, 1938; for a stage play, see *California Eagle*, December 5, 1940. More recent work includes "The Story of Biddy Mason," written by Dana Johnson and Annie Loui, and short plays by Jackie Broxton, performed at the Biddy Mason Charitable Foundation.

27. Biddy Mason Foundation, https://biddymason.info/foundation.

28. Biddy Mason Charitable Foundation, https://biddymason.com/.

29. The language here is inspired by a description of evensong in Thomas Pynchon, *Gravity's Rainbow* (1973; reprint, Penguin, 1995), 136. For this, I have my beloved professor, the dearly missed Steven Fix, to thank.

Bibliography

ARCHIVAL MATERIALS

A. K. Smiley Library, Redlands, CA

Jose Del Carmen Lugo, Vida en un rancho

Bancroft Library, University of California, Berkeley

Hubert Howe Bancroft, "Personal Observations during a tour through the Line of Missions of Upper California," MSS, typescript, 187–?

John Currey, "Incidents in California," Statement by Judge John Currey for Bancroft Library, MSS, 1878

Robert R. Givens Letters to Family, 1849–1859

William McKendree Gwin, "Memoirs on the History of the United States, Mexico, and California, 1850–1860"

Benjamin Hayes Scrapbooks

Edward Stanly, Speech of the Hon. Edward Stanly, delivered at Sacramento, July 17, 1857

California State Library, Sacramento

Jeremiah Burke Sanderson Collection

Church History Library, Salt Lake City, UT

Abstract of Title, 1905
Charles C. Rich Collection
David H. Holladay Diary, July–August 1855
Amasa M. Lyman Collection
Marilyn Warne Mills Collection
Silas Richards Diaries
San Bernardino Branch *Journal*
San Bernardino Branch tithing accounts, 1851–1857
San Bernardino Branch tithing record, 1853 October–1857 March
San Bernardino Branch tithing papers, 1856–1857
Utah Territorial Census, Schedule 3, MS
Court of Session, San Bernardino Minutes, 1853–1855
"Old Fort Site - Big Cottonwood - now Holladay," typescript MS by Arthur J. Wagstaff
"The Locality History of South Cottonwood Camp," MSS typescript, no author, no date, CHL

Evergreen Memorial Cemetery, Los Angeles, CA

Internment Book #3, November 1890–December 1900

Henry E. Huntington Library, San Marino, CA

Edward E. Ayer Reminiscences
Barrows and Weyse Family Papers
Horace Bell Papers
Ralph Bieber Collection (uncatalogued)
Joseph Lancaster Brent Papers
Franklin Augustus Buck Papers
Judson-Fairbanks Correspondence
Matthew Keller Collection
William Alexander Leidesdorff Collection
Los Angeles Area Court Records
Los Angeles Prefecture Records
The Negro and California History, typescript
William G. Ritch Collection
David Smith Terry Papers
Benjamin Davis Wilson Collection

Los Angeles County Recorder's Office, Norwalk, CA

Deed, William M. Buffum and James F. Burns to Biddy Mason, November 28, 1866

Deed, Charles Owens and Martha Hall to Biddy Mason, July 7, 1868
Deed, Charles Owens, Martha Hall, and Biddy Mason to John Schumacker, November 7, 1868
Deed, Joseph Kurtz to Jeremiah Redding et al. March 13, 1869
Deed, Biddie [*sic*] Mason to J. H. Jones and Charles M. Wright, January 2, 1875
Deed, Biddy Mason to M. Shannon, April 7, 1884
Deed, G. Wiley Wells to William Comer, Robert C. Owens, William Ballard, Biddy Mason, and Granville Huddleston, November 30, 1885

Massachusetts Historical Society, Boston

John Bachelder Peirce Papers, 1839–1881

Missouri State Archives

Mormon War Papers, 1837–1841

National Archives, Washington, DC

United States tax assessments, California, 1862
United States Internal Revenue, tax assessment records, California, 1866

Private Collections

Angela Wilkinson, family scrapbooks

San Bernardino County Historical Archives, San Bernardino, CA

Assessment Roll, Assessor Records, San Bernardino County
Brand Book, Recorder Records, San Bernardino County
Deed of Hannah Embers, June 26, 1868, Book of Deeds, San Bernardino
Horace C. Rolfe Scrapbook
Map of the Rancho San Bernardino Survey, Plan of the City of San Bernardino
Tax assessment records, San Bernardino, 1874–1875
People v. McFeely, Court Case 42, 1858

Seaver Center for Western History Research, Los Angeles, CA

Alcalde/Los Angeles County Court Records, Vol. 6: Criminal
Los Angeles Miscellaneous Records, 1859–1870
Tax Assessments Records, Los Angeles, 1875–1884, 1885–1888

Southern Historical Collection, Wilson Library, University of North Carolina at Chapel Hill

William G. Dickson Papers

Thomas Jefferson Green Papers
Nicholas Washington Woodfin Papers

UCLA Library Special Collections, Charles E. Young Research Library

Golden State Mutual Life Insurance Company Records
Robert Curry Owens, "My Grandfather," MS
Robert Curry Owens, "Autobiography," MS
Benjamin Hayes, January 19, 1856, *In re Hannah*, MS
Federation of Black History and Arts in Los Angeles, Campaign for Biddy Mason Day, 1971
Miriam Matthews Papers
Miriam Matthews Photograph Collection
Joseph Mesmer Papers

Virginia Historical Society, Richmond

Thom Family Papers

NEWSPAPERS AND PERIODICALS

The Atlantic
Baltimore Sun
Broad Ax
California Eagle
Charleston Courier
The Crisis
Colored American Magazine
Daily Alta California
Daily Democratic State Journal (Sacramento, CA)
De Bow's Review
Deseret News
Douglass' Monthly
Evening and the Morning Star
Freeman's Journal and Daily Commercial Advertiser (Dublin)
Harper's Weekly
Imperial Valley Press
Latter Day Saints' Messenger and Advocate
The Liberator
Los Angeles Daily News
Los Angeles Evening Express
Los Angeles Herald
Los Angeles Review of Books

Los Angeles Star
Los Angeles Times
Millennial Star
National Anti-Slavery Standard
New York Daily Times
New York Tribune
Otago Daily Times (New Zealand)
Overland Monthly
Pomona Daily Review
Sacramento Daily Union
San Antonio Express
San Francisco Bulletin
San Francisco Elevator
San Francisco Examiner
San Pedro News Pilot
Southern Californian
Sydney Morning Herald
Texas State Gazette

GOVERNMENT DOCUMENTS AND COURT RULINGS

"An Act to Confer Civil Rights on Freedmen, and for other Purposes." In *Laws of the State of Mississippi*. Jackson, MS: J. J. Shannon & Sons, 1866.

Acts, Resolutions and Memorials, Passed at the Several Annual Sessions of the Legislative Assembly of the Territory of Utah. Salt Lake City: Joseph Cain, 1855.

Communication of Governor Latham to the President of the United States in Relation to the Division of the State of California. Sacramento, CA: C. T. Botts, State Printer, 1860.

Congressional Globe, 1843–1861.

"Constitution of Republic of Texas." *Laws of the Republic of Texas*. Houston: Office of the Telegraph, 1838.

Constitution of the State of California. San Francisco: Alta California, 1849.

De Bow, J.D.B. *Statistical View of the United States, Embracing its Territory, Population—White, Free Colored, and Slave—Moral and Social Condition, Industry Property, and Revenue; the Detailed Statistics of Cities, Towns, and Counties; Being a Compendium of the Seventh Census*. Washington, DC: Beverley Tucker, 1854.

Dred Scot v. Sanford, 60 U.S. (19 How.) 393 (1857).

Execution of Colonel Crabb and Associates. Message from the President of the United States. February 16, 1858. House Executive Doc. No. 64, 35th Congress, 1st Session. State of California, Statutes of California. 1850–.

In re Archy, 9 Cal. 147 (Cal. 1858).
In re Perkins, 2 Cal. 424 (October 1, 1852).
The Statutes of California, Passed at the Sixth Session of the Legislature. Sacramento, CA: B.B. Redding, State Printer, 1855.
The Statutes of California, Passed at the Eleventh Session of the Legislature. Sacramento, CA: Charles T. Botts, State Printer, 1860.
The War of the Rebellion: A Compilation of the Official Records of the Union and Confederate Armies. 128 vols. Washington, DC: Government Printing Office, 1880–1901.

LOS ANGELES CITY DIRECTORIES

The First Los Angeles City and County Directory, 1872. Reproduced in facsimile. Ward Ritchie Press, 1963.
Directory of Los Angeles for 1875. Los Angeles: Mirror Book and Job Printing Office, 1875.
Los Angeles City Directory, 1878. Compiled by Aaron Smith. Los Angeles: Mirror Printing, 1878.
Los Angeles City and County Directory for 1881–2. San Francisco: Southern California Directory, Co.. n.d.
Los Angeles City and County Directory, 1883–84. San Francisco: Southern California Publishing Co.. n.d.
Los Angeles City and Santa Ana Valley Directory for 1883–84. Los Angeles: Nonpareil Press, 1883.
Los Angeles City and County Directory, 1884–85. Los Angeles. Burton-Taney, 1885.
Los Angeles City and County Directory, 1886–7. Los Angeles: Times-Mirror, 1886.
Los Angeles City Directory, 1887–8. Los Angeles: Smith & McPhee, 1888.
Los Angeles City Directory, 1888. Los Angeles: W.H.L. Corran, 1888.
Los Angeles City Directory, 1890. Los Angeles: W.H.L. Corran, 1890.

PRIMARY SOURCES

Abdy, E. S. *Journal of a Residence and Tour in the United States*. 3 vols. John Murray, 1835.
Adams, John Quincy. *The Diary of John Quincy Adams, 1794–1845*. Edited by Allan Nevins. Scribner, 1951.
Aitken, W. *A Journey up the Mississippi River from Its Mouth to Nauvoo*. Ashton-Under-Lyne: John Williamson, 1845.
Andrews, William L. *Sisters of the Spirit: Three Black Women's Autobiographies of the Nineteenth Century*. Indiana University Press, 1986.

Applegate, Jesse. "A Day with the Cow Column in 1843." *Overland Monthly* 1, no. 2 (August 1868): 127–33.

Baldwin, Joseph G. *The Flush Times of Alabama and Mississippi: A Series of Sketches*. New York: D. Appleton and Co., 1854.

Baker, Edward D. *Oration of Colonel Edward D. Baker over the Dead Body of David C. Broderick, a Senator of the United States, 18th September, 1859*. N.p., n.d.

Ball, Charles. *Slavery in the United States: A Narrative of the Life and Adventures of Charles Ball*. New York: John S. Taylor, 1837.

Bancroft, Hubert Howe. "Historic Researches in the South." In *Literary Industries: A Memoir*. San Francisco: History Company, 1890.

Barrows, H. D. "Memorial Sketch of Dr. John S. Griffin." *Annual Publication of the Historical Society of Southern California and Pioneer Register* 4, no. 2 (1898): 183–85.

Bartlett, John Russell. *Personal Narrative of Explorations and Incidents in Texas, New Mexico, California, Sonora, and Chihuahua*. 2 vols. London: D. Appleton & Company, 1854.

Basler, Roy P., ed. *The Collected Works of Abraham Lincoln*. 8 vols. Rutgers University Press, 1953.

Bass, Charlotta A. *Forty Years: Memoirs from the Pages of a Newspaper*. Charlotta A. Bass, 1960.

Bell, Horace. *Reminiscences of a Ranger*. Wallace Hebberd, 1927.

Bell, Horace. *On the Old West Coast*. Grosset & Dunlap, 1930.

Bennett, John C. *The History of the Saints; or an Expose of Joe Smith and Mormonism*. Boston: Leland & Whiting, 1842.

Brace, Charles Loring. *The New West: Or, California in 1867–1868*. New York: Putnam, 1869.

Brent, Joseph Lancaster. *The Lugo Case: A Personal Experience*. Searcy & Pfaff, 1926.

Brent, Joseph Lancaster. *Memoirs of the War Between the States*. Nanine B. Sloo, 1940.

Brewer, William H. *Up and Down California*. Yale University Press, 1930.

Brown, Henry Box. *Narrative of the Life of Henry Box Brown*. Manchester, England: Lee and Glynn, 1851.

Brown, John. *Autobiography of Pioneer John Brown*. Edited by John Zimmerman Brown. Publisher's Press, 1941.

Brown, John. *Slave Life in Georgia: A Narrative of the Life, Sufferings, and Escape of John Brown, a Fugitive Slave, Now in England*. Edited by L. A. Chamerovzow. London: No. 27, New Broad Street, 1855.

Brown, William Wells. *Narrative of William W. Brown, a Fugitive Slave*. Boston: Anti-Slavery Office, 1847.

Browne, J. Ross. "The Coast Rangers: A Chronicle of Adventures in California, Part I." *Harpers Weekly* 23, no. 133 (June 1861).

Browne, J. Ross. "The Coast Rangers: A Chronicle of Adventures in California. Part II." *Harper's Weekly* 23, no. 135 (August 1861).

Browne, J. Ross. *Crusoe's Island: A Ramble in the Footsteps of Alexander Selkirk.* New York: Harper & Brothers. 1864.

Bruff, J. Goldsborough. *Gold Rush: The Journals, Drawings, and Other Papers of J. Goldsborough Bruff.* Edited by Georgia Willis Read and Ruth Gaines. Columbia University Press, 1949.

Burnett, Peter H. *Recollections and Opinions of an Old Pioneer.* New York: D. Appleton and Company, 1880.

Bynum, Lindley, ed. "Los Angeles in 1854–5: The Diary of Rev. James Woods." *The Quarterly: Historical Society of Southern California* 23, no. 2 (June 1941): 65–86.

Campbell, Alexander. *Delusions: An Analysis of the Book of Mormon.* Boston: Benjamin H. Greene, 1832.

Carr, John. *Pioneer Days in California.* Eureka, CA: Times Publishing Company, 1891.

Casserly, Eugene. *The Issues of the Contest: Speech of Hon. Eugene Casserly in San Francisco, August 19, 1868.* San Francisco: Independent Dispatch Print, 1868.

Casserly, Eugene. *Speech of Hon. Eugene Casserly on the Fifteenth Amendment, and the Labor Question, Delivered in San Francisco, California, July 28, 1869.* San Francisco, 1869.

Catterall, Helen T., ed. *Judicial Cases Concerning American Slavery and the Negro.* 5 vols. Carnegie Institution, 1926–37.

Chandless, William. *A Visit to Salt Lake.* London: Smith. Elder, & Co., 1857.

Chesnut, Mary. *Mary Chesnut's Civil War.* Edited by C. Vann Woodward. Yale University Press, 1981.

Chevalier, Michael. *Society, Manners, and Politics in the United States.* Boston: Weeks, Jordan and Company, 1839.

Church of Jesus Christ of Latter-day Saints. *Doctrine and Covenants.* Church of Jesus Christ of Latter-day Saints, 2013.

Clark, Bennett C. "Diary of a Journey from Missouri to California in 1849." Edited by Ralph P. Bieber. *Missouri Historical Review* 23 (1928): 3–43.

Clayton, William. *William Clayton's Journal.* Edited by Lawrence Clayton. Lawrence Clayton, 1921.

Cleveland, Henry, ed. *Alexander H. Stephens in Public and Private with Letters and Speeches Before, During, and Since the War.* Philadelphia, 1886.

Coffey, Alvin A. "The Autobiography of Alvin A. Coffey." *Overland Journal* 20, no. 2 (Summer 2002): 64–73.

Cole, Cornelius. *Memoirs of Cornelius Cole, Ex-Senator of the United States from California.* McLoughlin Brothers, 1908.

Conness, John. *Some of the Men and Measures of the War and Reconstruction Period.* Boston: Nathan Sawyer & Son, 1882.

Crocheron, Augusta Joyce. "California Memories." *The Contributor* 7, no. 1 (October 1885): 20–22.

Crosby, Elisha Oscar. *Memoirs of Elisha Oscar Crosby: Reminiscences of California and Guatemala from 1849 to 1864*. Edited by Charles Albro Barker. Huntington Library, 1945.

Daily, Wendell P. *An Album of Memories*. Schauer Printing Press, 1946.

Davis, Winfield J. *History of Political Conventions in California, 1849–1892*. Sacramento: California State Library, 1893.

Dickens, Charles. *American Notes for General Circulation*. Fourth edition. 2 vols. London: Chapman and Hall, 1842.

Douglass, Frederick. "What to the Slave Is the Fourth of July?" In *Selected Speeches and Writings*. Edited by Philip S. Foner. Lawrence Hill, 1999.

Douglass, Frederick. *My Bondage and My Freedom*. New York: Miller, Orton & Mulligan, 1855.

Du Bois, W.E.B.. *The Souls of Black Folk*. Reprint, Simon and Schuster, 2005.

Egan, Howard R. *Pioneering the West: Major Howard Egan's Diary*. Edited by William M. Egan. Howard R. Egan Estate, 1917.

Farnham, Eliza W. *California. In-Doors and Out*. New York: Dix, Edwards & Co. 1856.

Faust, Drew Gilpin, ed. *The Ideology of Slavery: Proslavery Thought in the Antebellum South, 1830–1860*. Louisiana State University Press, 1981.

Featherstonaugh, G. W. *Excursion Through the Slave States*. 2 vols. London: John Murray, 1844.

Field, Stephen J. *Personal Reminiscences of Early Days in California, with Other Sketches*. Stephen J. Field, 1893.

Flake, Osmer D. *William J. Flake, Pioneer-Colonizer*. Printed by author, 1948.

Foote, Henry S. *The Bench and Bar of the South and Southwest*. St. Louis, MO: Soule. Thomas & Wentworth, 1876.

Foote, Henry S. *Casket of Reminiscences*. Washington, DC: Chronicle Publishing Company, 1874.

Freehling, William W. and Craig M. Simpson, eds., *Secession Debated: Georgia's Showdown in 1860* Oxford University Press, 1992.Froebel, Julius. *Seven Years' Travel in Central America, Northern Mexico, and the Far West of the United States*. London: Richard Bentley, 1859.

Gibbs, Mifflin Wistar. *Shadow and Light: An Autobiography*. Washington, DC, 1902.

Goodell, Anna Maria. "Diary." In *Covered Wagon Women: Diaries & Letters from the Western Trails, 1840–1890*. Vol. 7. Edited by Kenneth L. Holmes. Arthur H. Clark Company, 1998.

Goodman, Jessie H., ed. *Overland in 1849: From Missouri to California by the Platte River and the Salt Lake Trail, an Account from the Letters of G.C. Pearson*. Cole Holmquist Press, 1961.

Gorham, George C. *Speech Delivered by George C. Gorham of San Francisco,*

Union Nominee for Governor, at Platt's Hall, San Francisco, July 10, 1867. San Francisco: Union State Central Committee, 1867

Grandy, Moses. *Narrative of the Life of Moses Grandy; Late a Slave in the United States of America*. London: C. Gilpin, 1843.

Grant, Ulysses S. *Personal Memoirs of U.S. Grant*. New York: Charles L. Webster & Co., 1885–86.

Graves, Jackson A. *My Seventy Years in California, 1857–1927*. Times-Mirror Press, 1927.

Greeley, Horace. *An Overland Journey from New York to San Francisco in the Summer of 1859*. New York: M. Saxton, Barker & Co., 1860.

Griffin, John S. *A Doctor Comes to California: The Diary of John S. Griffin*. Edited by George Walcott Ames Jr. California Historical Society, 1943.

Griffin, John S. *Los Angeles in 1849: A Letter from John S. Griffin to Col J.D. Stevenson. March 11, 1849*. Privately printed, 1949.

Grow, Matthew J., and Ronald W. Walker, eds. *The Prophet and the Reformer: The Letters of Brigham Young and Thomas L. Kane*. Oxford University Press, 2015.

Guinn, J. M. *Historical and Biographical Record of Southern California*. Chapman Publishing Company, 1902.

Guinn, J. M. *A History of California and an Extended History of Los Angeles and Environs*. Historic Record Company, 1915.

Guinn, J. M. "Los Angeles in the Later Sixties and Early Seventies." *Annual Publication of the Historical Society of Southern California* 3, no. 1 (1893): 63–68.

Hager, John S. *Speech of Hon. John S. Hager, of San Francisco, in the Senate of California, January 28th, 1870*. n.p., n.d.

Haight, Henry H. *Inaugural Address of H.H. Haight*. New York: Douglas Taylor's Democratic Book and Job Printing Office, 1868.

Haight, Henry H. *Message of H.H. Haight. Governor of the State of California, Transmitting the Proposed Fifteenth Amendment to the Federal Constitution*. Sacramento, CA: D.W. Gelwicks, 1870.

Haight, Henry H. *Speech of H.H. Haight. Esq. Democratic Candidate for Governor, Delivered at the Great Democratic Mass Meeting at Union Hall, July 9, 1867*. N.p, n.d.

Hall, Basil. *Travels in North America in the Years 1827 and 1828*. 3 vols. Third edition. Edinburgh: Robert Cadell, 1830.

Hancock, Almira. *Reminiscences of Winfield Scott Hancock by His Wife*. New York: Charles L. Webster, 1887.

Harpending, Ashbury. *The Great Diamond Hoax and Other Stirring Incidents in the Life of Ashbury Harpending*. Edited by James H. Wilkins. James H. Barry, 1913.

Hastings, Lansford Warren. *The Emigrants Guide to Oregon and California*. Cincinnati, OH: G. Conclin, 1845.

Hayes, Benjamin. *Pioneer Notes from the Diaries of Judge Benjamin Hayes*,

1849–1875. Edited by Marjorie Tisdale Wolcott. Marjorie Tisdale Wolcott, 1929.

Heiskell, Hugh Brown. *A Forty-Niner from Tennessee: The Diary of Hugh Brown Heiskell*. Edited by Edward M. Steel. University of Tennessee Press, 1998.

Helper, Hinton Rowan. *The Land of Gold: Reality Versus Fiction*. Baltimore, MD: Henry Taylor, 1855.

Hodgson, Adam. *Remarks during a Journey Through North America in the Years 1819, 1820, and 1821*. New York: Samuel Whiting, 1823.

Hooper, Johnson Jones. *Adventures of Captain Simon Suggs, Late of the Tallapoosa Volunteers*. Philadelphia: T. B. Peterson, 1848.

Howard, Volney E., and A. Hutchinson, eds. *Statutes of the State of Mississippi*. New Orleans: E. Johns & Co., 1840.

Hughes, Louis. *Thirty Years a Slave*. Milwaukee: South Side Printing Company, 1897.

Jacob, Udney Hay. *An Extract: From a Manuscript Entitled the Peace Maker*. Nauvoo, IL: Joseph Smith, 1842.

Jacobs, Harriet. *Incidents in the Life of a Slave Girl, Written by Herself*. Edited by Lydia Maria Child. Boston, 1861.

Jones, Daniel Webster. *Forty Years Among the Indians*. Salt Lake City, UT: Juvenile Instructor Office, 1890.

Kane, Thomas L. *The Mormons: A Discourse Delivered Before the Historical Society of Pennsylvania*. Philadelphia: King & Baird, 1850.

Keckley, Elizabeth. *Behind the Scenes. Or Thirty Years a Slave, and Four Years in the White House*. G.W. Carleton & Co., 1968.

Kenderdine, Thaddeus S. *A California Tramp and Later Footprints*. Newtown, PA: n.p., 1888.

Kenderdine, Thaddeus S. *California Revisited, 1858–1897*. Newtown, PA: Doylestown Publishing, 1898.

Kewen, E.J.C. *Speech of Col. E.J.C. Kewen at the American Mass Meeting Orleans Hotel, Sacramento, August 8, 1855*. N.p., n.d. Copy in HEHL.

Kewen, E.J.C. *State of the Union. Speech of Hon. E.J.C. Kewen. on The State of the Union; Delivered before the Democracy of Sacramento in Assembly Hall, April 27, 1863*. N.p., n.d.

King, Laura. "Reminiscences of Mission San Gabriel." *Annual Publications, Historical Society of Southern California* 11 (1920): 58–62.

Lee, John D. *The Writings of John D. Lee*. Edited by Samuel Nyal Henrie. Fenestra Books, 2002.

Marston, Anna Lee, ed. *Records of a California Family: Journals and Letters of Lewis C. Gunn and Elizabeth LeBreton Gunn*. N.p., 1928.

Martineau, Harriet. *Retrospect of Western Travel*. 3 vols. London: William Clownes and Sons, 1838.

Marryat, Frederick. *A Diary in America, with Remarks on Its Institutions*. 3 vols. London: Longman, Orme, Brown, Green & Longmans, 1839.

Moorman, Madison Berryman. *The Journal of Madison Berryman Moorman, 1850–1851*. Edited by Irene D. Paden. California Historical Society, 1948.
Nevins, Allan, ed. *Polk: The Diary of a President, 1845–1849*. Longmans, Green and Co., 1952.
Newmark, Harris. *Sixty Years in Southern California, 1853–1913*. Fourth edition. Zeitlin & Ver Brugge, 1970.
Nordhoff, Charles. *California: Fore Health, Pleasure, and Residence*. New York: Harper & Brothers, 1873.
Northup, Solomon. *Twelve Years a Slave*. Auburn, NY: Derby and Miller, 1853.
Olmsted, Frederick Law. *A Journey in the Back Country*. New York: Mason Brothers, 1860.
Olmsted, Frederick Law. *A Journey in the Seaboard Slave States*. London: Sampson Low, Son & Co., 1856.
Ord, Edward O. C. *The City of the Angels and the City of the Saints*. Edited by Neal Harlow. Huntington Library, 1978.
Pennington, J.W.C. *A Narrative of Events of the Life of J.H. Banks, an Escaped Slave*. Liverpool: M. Rourke, 1861.
Pratt, Parley P. *The Autobiography of Parley Parker Pratt*. New York: Russell Brothers, 1874.
Pratt, Parley Parker. "A Mormon Mission to California in 1851: From the Diary of Parley Parker Pratt." Edited by Reva Holdaway Stanley and Charles L. Camp. *California Historical Society Quarterly* 14, no. 1 (March 1935): 59–73.
Quincy, Josiah. *Figures of the Past, from the Leaves of Old Journals*. Boston: Robert Brothers, 1884.
Redpath, James. *The Roving Editor: Or Talks with Slaves*. New York: A. B. Burdick, 1859.
Richardson, James D., ed. *A Compilation of the Messages and Papers of the Confederacy*. United States Publishing Company, 1905.
Rigdon, Sidney. *Oration Delivered by Mr. S. Rigdon. on the 4th of July 1838*. Far West, MO: Journal Office, 1838.
Ringe, Frederick Hastings. *Happy Days in Southern California*. Cambridge, MA: n.p., 1898.
Salvator, Ludwig Louis. *Los Angeles in the Sunny Seventies: A Flower from the Golden Land*. Translated by Marguerite Eyer Wilbur. McCallister and Zeitlin, 1929.
Shafter, Oscar Lovell. *Life, Diary, and Letters of Oscar Lovell Shafter*. Edited by Flora Haines Loughead. Blair-Murdock Company, 1915.
Smith, Joseph Jr. *The Book of Mormon*. Palmyra, NY: E. B. Grandin, 1830.
Smith, Lucy. *Biographical Sketches of Joseph Smith, the Prophet*. Liverpool: Orson Pratt, 1853.
Stephens, Bascom A., ed. *Resources of Los Angeles*. Los Angeles: Sprague and Rodehaver, 1887.
Stewart, Virgil, and Augustus Q. Walton. *A History of the Detection, Conviction,*

Life and Designs of John A. Murel, the Great Western Land Pirate. Pamphlet. Cincinnati, 1835.
Stringellow, Thornton. *A Brief Examination of Scripture Testimony on the Institution of Slavery*. Washington, DC: Congressional Globe Office, 1850.
Strong, John L. "Cotton Experiments in California." *Overland Monthly* 6, no. 4 (April 1871): 326–35.
Strong, John L. "Labor in Cotton Culture." *Overland Monthly* 13, no. 1 (July 1874): 18–25.
Stroyer, Jacob. *My Life in the South*. Salem, MA: Salem Observer, 1885.
Stuart, James. *Three Years in North America*. 2 vols. Edinburgh: Robert Cadell, 1833.
Taylor, Benjamin F. *Between the Gates*. Chicago: S. C. Griggs, 1878.
Teel, T. T. "Sibley's New Mexican Campaign—Its Objects and the Causes of Its Failure." In *Battles and Leaders of the Civil War*. Vol. 2, edited by Robert Underwood Johnson and Clarence Clough Buel. Castle, 1995.
Tocqueville, Alexis de. *Democracy in America*. 2 vols. Translated by Henry Reeve. New York: George Adlard, 1838.
Tribune Almanac and Political Register for 1868. New York, 1868.
Truman, Benjamin C. *Semi-Tropical California*. San Francisco: Bancroft, 1874.
Twain, Mark. *Life on the Mississippi*. New York: Harper, 1883.
Twain, Mark. *Roughing It*. Hartford, CT: American Publishing Company, 1873.
Van Dyke, T. S. *Millionaires of a Day: An Inside History of the Great Southern California "Boom."* New York: Fords, Howard & Hulbert, 1890.
Walker, David. *An Appeal to the Colored Citizens of the World*. Boston: David Walker, 1830.
Warner, J. J. Benjamin Hayes, and Joseph P. Widney. *An Historical Sketch of Los Angeles County, California*. Los Angeles: Mirror Printing, 1876.
Wells, Ida B. *Southern Horrors: Lynch Law in All Its Phases*. New York, 1892.
Wilson, Benjamin Davis. *The Indians of Southern California in 1852*. Edited by John Walton Caughey. Huntington Library, 1952.
Wilson, John Albert. *History of Los Angeles County, with Illustrations Descriptive of Its Scenery, Residences, Fine Blocks, and Manufactories*. Oakland, CA: Thompson & West, 1880.
Woods, James L. *California Pioneer Decade of 1849: The Presbyterian Church*. Hansen Co., 1922.
Woods, James L. *Recollections of Pioneer Work in California*. San Francisco: Joseph Winterburn, 1878.
Wooley, James E., and Vivian Wooley, eds. *Edgefield County, South Carolina, Wills, 1787–1836*. Southern Historical Press, 1991.
Yoseloff, Thomas, ed. *Voyage to America: The Journals of Thomas Cather*. Thomas Yoseloff, 1961.

SECONDARY SOURCES

Aird, Polly. "'You Nasty Apostates. Clear Out': Reasons for Disaffection in the Late 1850s." *Journal of Mormon History* 30, no. 2 (Fall 2004): 129–207.

Albin, Ray R. "The Perkins Case: The Ordeal of Three Slaves in Gold Rush California." *California History* 67, no. 4 (1988): 215–27.

Arrington, Leonard J. *Charles C. Rich: Mormon General and Western Frontiersman*. BYU Press, 1974.

Arrington, Leonard J. "Mississippi Mormons." *The Ensign* (June 1977).

Arrington, Christ Rigby. "Pioneer Midwives." In *Mormon Sisters: Women in Early Utah*, ed. Claudia Bushman. Salt Lake City, 1976.

Ayers, Edward L. *The Promise of the New South: Life After Reconstruction*. Oxford University Press, 2007.

Backman, Milton V. *Heavens Resound: A History of the Latter-day Saints in Ohio*. Deseret Book Company, 1983.

Baptist, Edward E. *The Half Has Never Been Told: Slavery and the Making of American Capitalism*. Basic Books, 2014.

Baumgartner, Alice. *South to Freedom: Runaway Slaves to Mexico and the Road to the Civil War*. Basic Books, 2020.

Beam, Alex. *American Crucifixion: The Murder of Joseph Smith and the Fate of the Mormon Church*. PublicAffairs, 2014.

Beasley, Delilah L. *The Negro Trail Blazers of California*. Los Angeles, 1919.

Beattie, George W., and Helen Pruit Beattie. *Heritage of the Valley: San Bernardino's First Century*. San Pasqual Press, 1939.

Beckert, Sven. *Empire of Cotton: A Global History*. Knopf, 2014.

Beckert, Sven, and Seth Rockman, eds. *Slavery's Capitalism: A New History of American Economic Development*. University of Pennsylvania Press, 2016.

Belich, James. *Replenishing the Earth: The Settler Revolution and the Rise of the Anglo-World, 1783–1939*. Oxford University Press, 2009.

Bell, Richard. *Stolen: Five Free Boys Kidnapped into Slavery and Their Astonishing Odyssey Home*. Simon and Schuster, 2019.

Benedict, Michael Les. "The Rout of Radicalism: Republicans and the Elections of 1867." *Civil War History* 18 (December 1972): 334–44.

Bennett, Richard E. *We'll Find the Place: The Mormon Exodus, 1846–1848*. 1997. Reprint, University of Oklahoma Press, 2009.

Bennett, Richard E., Susan Easton Black, and Donald Q. Cannon. *The Nauvoo Legion in Illinois: A History of the Mormon Militia, 1841–1846*. University of Oklahoma Press, 2010.

Berlin, Ira. *Generations of Captivity: A History of African-American Slaves*. Harvard University Press, 2003.

Berry, Daina Ramey. *The Price for Their Pound of Flesh: The Value of the Enslaved, from Womb to Grave, in the Building of a Nation*. Beacon Press, 2017.

Berry, Daina Ramey, and Deleso A. Alford, eds. *Enslaved Women in America: An Encyclopedia*. ABC-Clio, 2012.

Berwanger, Eugene H. *The West and Reconstruction*. University of Illinois Press, 1981.

Bestor, Arthur Eugene. *Backwoods Utopias: The Sectarian and Owenite Phases of Communitarian Socialism in America, 1663–1829*. University of Pennsylvania Press, 1950.

Bishop, M. Guy. "Politics. Land, and Apostasy: The Last Days of the San Bernardino Mormon Colony, 1855–57." *Pacific Historian* 30, no. 4 (Winter 1986): 18–31.

Blackhawk, Ned. *Violence over the Land: Indians and Empires in the Early American West*. Harvard University Press, 2006.

Blair, William A. *With Malice Toward Some: Treason and Loyalty in the Civil War Era*. University of North Carolina Press, 2014.

Blight, David W. *Race and Reunion: The Civil War in American Memory*. Harvard University Press, 2001.

Block, Sharon. *Colonial Complexions: Race and Bodies in Eighteenth-Century America*. University of Pennsylvania Press, 2018.

Bottoms, D. Michael. *An Aristocracy of Color: Race and Reconstruction in California and the West, 1850–1890*. University of Oklahoma Press, 2013.

Bringhurst, Newell G. *Saints, Slaves, and Blacks: The Changing Place of Black People within Mormonism*. Second edition. Greg Kofford Books, 2018.

Brooke, John L. *The Refiner's Fire: The Making of Mormon Cosmology*. Cambridge University Press, 1996.

Brooks, James F. *Captives and Cousins: Slavery, Kinship, and Community in the Southwest Borderlands*. University of North Carolina Press, 2002.

Brooks, Joanna. *Mormonism and White Supremacy: American Religion and the Problem of Racial Innocence*. Oxford University Press, 2020.

Broussard, Albert. *Black San Francisco: The Struggle for Racial Equality in the West, 1900–1954*. University Press of Kansas, 1993.

Brown, Elsa Barkley. "To Catch the Vision of Freedom: Reconstructing Southern Black Women's Political History, 1865–1880." In *African American Women and the Vote, 1837–1965*. Edited by Ann D. Gordon. University of Massachusetts Press, 1997.

Brown, Elsa Barkley. "Negotiating and Transforming the Public Sphere: African American Political Life in the Transition from Slavery to Freedom." In *Jumpin' Jim Crow: Southern Politics from Civil War to Civil Rights*. Edited by Jane Dailey, Glenda Gilmore, and Bryant Simon. Princeton University Press, 2000.

Brown, Elsa Barkley. "Womanist Consciousness: Maggie Lena Walker and the Independent Order of Saint Luke." *Signs* 14, no. 3 (Spring 1989): 611–33.

Bruchey, Stuart, ed. *Cotton and the Growth of the American Economy, 1790–1860: Sources and Readings*. Harcourt Brace, 1967.

Brundage, W. Fitzhugh. *Lynching in the New South: Georgia and Virginia, 1880–1930*. University of Illinois Press, 1993.

Bunch, Lonnie G. *Black Angelenos: The Afro-American in Los Angeles, 1850–1950*. California Afro-American Museum, 1989.

Bundles, A'Lelia. *On Her Own Ground: The Life and Times of Madam C. J. Walker*. Simon & Schuster, 2001.

Burton, Orville Vernon. *In My Father's House Are Many Mansions: Family and Community in Edgefield, South Carolina*. University of North Carolina Press, 1985.

Bush, Lester E. "Mormonism's Negro Doctrine: An Historical Overview." *Dialogue: A Journal of Mormon Thought* 8, no. 1 (1973): 11–68.

Bushman, Richard Lyman. *Joseph Smith: Rough Stone Rolling*. Vintage, 2005.

Butler, Anthea. *White Evangelical Racism: The Politics of Morality in America*. University of North Carolina Press, 2021.

Camarillo, Albert. *Chicanos in a Changing Society: From Mexican Pueblos to American Barrios in Santa Barbara and Southern California, 1848–1930*. 1979; reprint, Southern Methodist University Press, 2005.

Camp, Stephanie M. H. *Closer to Freedom: Enslaved Women and Everyday Resistance in the Plantation South*. University of North Carolina Press, 2004.

Camp, Stephanie M. H. "'I Could Not Stay There': Enslaved Women, Truancy and the Geopolitics of Everyday Forms of Resistance in the Antebellum Plantation South," *Slavery and Abolition* 23, no. 3 (2002): 1–20.

Campbell, Craig S. *Images of the New Jerusalem: Latter Day Saint Faction Interpretations of Independence*. University of Tennessee Press, 2004.

Campbell, James T. *Songs of Zion: The African Methodist Episcopal Church in the United States and South Africa*. Oxford University Press, 1995.

Campbell, John. "Work, Pregnancy, and Infant Mortality among Southern Slaves." *Journal of Interdisciplinary History* 14, no. 4 (Spring 1984): 793–812.

Campbell, Marne L. "African American Women. Wealth Accumulation, and Social Welfare Activism in 19th-century Los Angeles." *Journal of African American History* 97, no. 4 (Fall 2012): 376–400.

Campbell, Marne L. *Making Black Los Angeles: Class, Gender, and Community, 1850–1917*. University of North Carolina Press, 2016.

Carlson, Shirley J. "Black Ideals of Womanhood in the Late Victorian Era." *Journal of Negro History* 77, no. 2 (Spring 1992): 61–73.

Carlton-LaNey, Iris, Jill Hamilton, Dorothy Ruiz, and Sandra Carlton Alexander. "Sitting with the Sick: African American Women's Philanthropy." *Affilia* 16 (Winter 2001): 447–66.

Carr, Stephen L., ed. *Holladay-Cottonwood: Places and Faces*. Holladay-Cottonwood Heritage Committee, 1987.

Carrigan, William D., and Clive Webb. *Forgotten Dead: Mob Violence Against Mexicans in the United States, 1848–1928*. Oxford University Press, 2013.

Carter, Kate B. "Mississippi Saints." In *Our Pioneer Heritage. Salt Lake City, 1958–77.* 20 vols. Vol. 2, 421–76.
Catterall, Helen. *Judicial Cases Concerning American Slavery and the Negro.* 5 vols. Carnegie Institute of Washington, 1926–37.
Chandler, Robert J. "Friends in Time of Need: Republicans and Black Civil Rights in California During the Civil War." *Arizona and the West* 24, no. 4 (Winter 1982): 319–40.
Clark, Christopher. *The Communitarian Moment: The Radical Challenge of the Northampton Association.* Cornell University Press, 1995.
Cleland, Robert Glass. *The Cattle on a Thousand Hills: Southern California, 1850–1880.* Huntington Library, 1954.
Clendenen, Clarence C. "A Confederate Spy in California: A Curious Incident of the Civil War." *Southern California Quarterly* 45 (September 1963): 219–234.
Clendennen, Clarence C. "Dan Showalter—California Secessionist." *California Historical Society Quarterly* 40 (December 1961): 309–25.
Clinton, Catherine. *Harriet Tubman: The Road to Freedom.* Back Bay, 2004.
Colby, Robert. "Negroes Will Bear Fabulous Prices: The Economics of Wartime Slave Commerce and Visions of the Confederate Future." *Journal of the Civil War Era* 10, no. 4 (December 2020): 453–55.
Colman, Patty R. "John Ballard and the African American Community of Los Angeles. 1850–1905." *Southern California Quarterly* 94, no. 2 (Summer 2012).
Collier-Thomas, Bettye. *Jesus, Jobs, and Justice: African American Women and Religion.* Knopf, 2010.
Collier-Thomas, Bettye. "'Sister Laborers': African American Women, Cultural Capital, and Educational Philanthropy, 1865–1970." In *Cultural Capital and Black Education: African American Communities and the Funding of Black Schooling, 1865 to the Present.* Edited by V. P. Franklin and Carter Julian Savage. Information Age Publishing, 2004.
Cornell, Sarah. "Citizens of Nowhere: Fugitive Slaves and African Americans in Mexico. 1833–1857." Journal of American History 100, no. 2 (2013): 351–74.
Cripps, Thomas. *Slow Fade to Black: The Negro in American Film, 1900–1942.* Oxford University Press, 1977.
Daly, John Patrick. *When Slavery Was Called Freedom: Evangelicalism, Proslavery, and the Causes of the Civil War.* University of Kentucky Press, 2002.
Davis, Mike. *The Ecology of Fear: Los Angeles and the Imagination of Disaster.* Verso, 1998.
Demaratus, DeEtta. *The Force of a Feather: The Search for a Lost Story of Slavery and Freedom.* University of Utah Press, 2002.
Deverell, William. "Convalescence and California: The Civil War Comes West." *Southern California Quarterly* 90, no. 1 (Spring 2008): 1–26.
Deverell, William. "Redemptive California? Re-thinking the Post–Civil War." *Rethinking History* 11, no. 1 (March 2007): 61–78.

Deverell, William F. *Whitewashed Adobe: The Rise of Los Angeles and the Remaking of Its Mexican Past*. University of California Press, 2004.
Deyle, Steven. *Carry Me Back: The Domestic Slave Trade in American Life*. Oxford University Press, 2005.
Djelid, Aisha "'The Master Whished to Reproduce': Slavery, Forced Intimacy, and Enslavers' Interference in Sexual Relationships in the Antebellum South, 1808–1861." *American Nineteenth Century History* 25, no. 1 (April 2024): 21–43.
Drake, Dennis. *William Crosby: Through the Needle's Eye*. Copy in Church History Library. Published by the author, n.d.
Du Bois, W.E.B. *The Negro Church*. 1903; reprint, Cascade Books, 2011.
Dumke, Glenn S. *The Boom of the Eighties in Southern California*. 1944; reprint, Huntington Library, 1991.
Ebiner, Brian Andrew. "Disaster in Los Angeles. 1884." *Los Angeles Corral of the Westerners* 286 (Spring 2017): 1–8.
Egerton, Douglas R. *Thunder at the Gates: The Black Civil War Regiments That Redeemed America*. Basic Books, 2016.
Emberton, Carole. *To Walk About in Freedom: The Long Emancipation of Priscilla Joyner*. Norton, 2022.
Engh, Michael E. *Frontier Faiths: Church, Temple, and Synagogue in Los Angeles, 1846–1888*. University of New Mexico Press, 1992.
Faragher, John Mack. *Eternity Street: Violence and Justice in Frontier Los Angeles*. Norton & Company, 2016.
Farmer, Jared. *On Zion's Mount: Mormons. Indians, and the American Landscape*. Harvard University Press, 2008.
Fass, Paula. "Cultural History/Social History: Some Reflections on a Continuing Dialogue." *Journal of Social History* 37 (Fall 2003): 39–46.
Fehrenbacher, Don E. *The Dred Scott Case: Its Significance in American Law and Politics*. Oxford University Press, 1978.
Fett, Sharla M. *Working Cures: Healing, Health, and Power on Southern Slave Plantations*. University of North Carolina Press, 2002.
Field, Kendra, and Daniel Lynch. "'Master of Ceremonies': The World of Peter Biggs in Civil War–Era Los Angeles." *Western Historical Quarterly* 47 (Winter 2016): 379–405.
Finkelman, Paul. *An Imperfect Union: Slavery. Federalism, and Comity*. University of North Carolina Press, 1981.
Finkelman, Paul. "The Law of Slavery and Freedom in California 1848–1860." *California Western Law Review* 17, no. 3 (1980–1981): 437–64.
Finkelstein, Alexander. "Los Angeles's 1863–1876 Boom." *Southern California Quarterly* 99, no. 2 (Summer 2017): 140–83.
Flamming, Douglas. *Bound for Freedom: Black Los Angeles in Jim Crow America*. University of California Press, 2005.

Fogelson, Robert M. *The Fragmented Metropolis: Los Angeles, 1850–1930*. 1967; reprint, University of California Press, 1993.

Foner, Eric. *Reconstruction: America's Unfinished Revolution, 1863–1877*. Harper & Row, 1988.

Frazier, Donald S. *Blood and Treasure: Confederate Empire in the Southwest*. Texas A&M University Press, 1995.

Freehling, William W. *The Road to Disunion: Secessionists at Bay, 1776–1854*. Oxford University Press, 1990.

Freeman, Joanne. *The Field of Blood: Congressional Violence and the Road to Civil War*. Picador, 2018.

Freeman, Tyrone McKinley. *Madam C. J. Walker's Gospel of Giving: Black Women's Philanthropy During Jim Crow*. University of Illinois Press, 2020.

Friedman, Lawrence M. *Dead Hands: A Social History of Wills, Trusts, and Inheritance Law*. Stanford Law Books, 2009.

Friedman, Lawrence M. "Patterns of Testation in the 19th Century: A Study of Essex County (New Jersey) Wills." *American Journal of Legal History* 8, no. 1 (January 1964): 34–53.

Fuentes, Marisa J. *Dispossessed Lives: Enslaved Women, Violence, and the Archive*. University of Pennsylvania Press, 2016.

Garrett, H. Dean. "The Coming Forth of the Doctrine and Covenants." *Regional Studies in Latter-day Saint Church History: Ohio*. Edited by Milton V. Backman Brigham Young University, 1995.

Genovese, Eugene D. *Roll, Jordan, Roll: The World the Slaves Made*. Vintage, 1974.

Giesberg, Judith. *Last Seen: The Enduring Search by Formerly Enslaved People to Find Their Lost Families*. Simon and Schuster, 2025.

Gilbert, Benjamin Franklin. "The Confederate Minority in California." *California Historical Society Quarterly* 20 (June 1941): 154–70.

Gilmore, Glenda. *Gender and Jim Crow: Women and the Politics of White Supremacy in North Carolina, 1896–1920*. University of North Carolina Press, 1996.

Givens, Terryl L. *By the Hand of Mormon: The American Scripture That Launched a New World Religion*. Oxford University Press, 2003.

Glassberg, David. *Sense of History: The Place of the Past in American Life*. University of Massachusetts Press, 2001.

Glymph, Thavolia. *Out of the House of Bondage: The Transformation of the Plantation Household*. Cambridge University Press, 2003.

Glymph, Thavolia. *The Women's Fight: The Civil War's Battles for Home, Freedom, and Nation*. University of North Carolina Press, 2022.

Gonzalez, Michael J. *This Small City Will Be a Mexican Paradise: Exploring the Origins of Mexican Culture in Los Angeles, 1821–1846*. University of New Mexico Press, 2005.

Gonzalez-Day, Ken. *Lynching in the West, 1850–1935*. Duke University Press, 2006.

Gordon, Ann D., ed. *African American Women and the Vote, 1837–1965*. University of Massachusetts Press, 1997.

Gordon, Sarah Barringer. "A 'Free' State: A Story of Law and Slavery in Antebellum California." *Journal of the Early Republic* 4, no. 2 (Summer 2025): 213–49.

Gordon, Sarah Barringer. *The Mormon Question: Polygamy and Constitutional Conflict in Nineteenth-Century America*. University of North Carolina Press, 2002.

Gordon, Sarah Barringer, and Jan Shipps. "Fatal Convergence in the Kingdom of God: The Mountain Meadows Massacre in American History." *Journal of the Early Republic* 37 (Summer 2017): 307–47.

Gordon-Reed, Annette. *The Hemingses of Monticello: An American Family*. Norton, 2008.

Graaf, Lawrence B., de. "The City of Black Angels: Emergence of the Los Angeles Ghetto, 1890–1930." *Pacific Historical Review* 39, no. 3 (August 1970): 323–52.

Graaf, Lawrence B., de. "Race, Sex, and Region: Black Women in the American West, 1850–1920." In *History of Women in the United States*. Vol. 14, *Intercultural and Interracial Relations*. K. G. Saur, 1993.

Graaf, Lawrence B. de. "Recognition, Racism, and Reflections on the Writings of Western Black History," *Pacific Historical Review* 44 (February 1975): 22–51.

Graaf, Lawrence B., de, Kevin Mulroy, and Quintard Taylor, eds. *Seeking El Dorado: African Americans in California*. Autry Museum, 2001.

Green, Hilary. *Educational Reconstruction: African-American Schools in the Urban South, 1865–1890*. Oxford University Press, 2016.

Greenberg, Kenneth S., ed. *Nat Turner: A Slave Rebellion in History and Memory*. Oxford University Press, 2004.

Griswold del Castillo, Richard. *The Los Angeles Barrio, 1850–1890: A Social History*. University of California Press, 1982.

Gronningsater, Sarah L. H. "'On Behalf of His Race and the Lemmon Slaves': Louis Napoleon. Northern Black Legal Culture, and the Politics of Sectional Crisis." *Journal of the Civil War Era* 7, no . 2 (June 2017): 206–41.

Guenther, Todd. "Could These Bones Be from a Negro? Some African American Experiences on the Oregon-California Trail." *Overland Journal* 19, no. 2 (Summer 2001): 45–53.

Gumprecht, Blake. *The Los Angeles River: Its Life, Death, and Possible Rebirth*. Johns Hopkins University Press, 1999.

Gumprecht, Blake. "Who Killed the Los Angeles River?" In *Land of Sunshine: An Environmental History of Metropolitan Los Angeles*. Edited by William Deverell and Greg Hise. University of Pittsburg Press, 2005.

Gutman, Herbert G. *The Black Family in Slavery and Freedom, 1750–1925*. Basil Blackwell, 1976.

Gutman, Herbert G. *Slavery and the Numbers Game: A Critique of Time on the Cross*. University of Illinois Press, 1975.
Hackel, Steve W. *Children of Coyote, Missionaries of Saint Francis: Indian-Spanish Relations in Colonial California, 1769–1850*. University of North Carolina Press, 2005.
Hadden, Sally E. *Slave Patrols: Law and Violence in Virginia and the Carolinas*. Harvard University Press, 2001.
Hahn, Steven. *A Nation Under Our Feet: Black Political Struggles in the Rural South from Slavery to the Great Migration*. Belknap, 2003.
Hahn, Steven. *The Roots of Southern Populism: Yeoman Farmers and the Transformation of the Georgia Upcountry, 1850–1890*. Oxford University Press, 1983.
Hardy, B. Carmon. "Lords of Creation: Polygamy, the Abrahamic Household, and Mormon Patriarchy." *Journal of Mormon History* 20, no. 1 (Spring 1994): 119–52.
Hardy, Grant. *Understanding the Book of Mormon: A Reader's Guide*. Oxford University Press, 2010.
Harlow, Luke E. *Religion. Race, and the Making of Confederate Kentucky, 1830–1880*. Cambridge University Press, 2014.
Hartman, Saidiya. *Lose Your Mother: A Journey Along the Atlantic Slave Route*. Farrar, Straus and Giroux, 2007.
Hartman, Saidiya. *Scenes of Subjection: Terror, Slavery, and Self-Making in Nineteenth-Century America*. Oxford University Press, 1997.
Hartman, Saidiya. *Wayward Lives, Beautiful Experiments: Intimate Histories of Social Upheaval*. W. W. Norton, 2019.
Hartman, Saidiya. "Venus in Two Acts," *Small Axe* 26 (June 2008): 1–14.
Hawthorne, Christopher, ed. *Past Due: Report and Recommendations of the Los Angeles Mayor's Office Civic Memory Working Group*. Huntington-USC Institute on California & the West, 2021.
Hayden, Dolores. "Biddy Mason's Los Angeles, 1856–1891." *California History* 68, no. 3 (1989): 86–99.
Hayden, Dolores. *The Power of Place: Urban Landscapes as Public History*. MIT Press, 1995.
Heerman, M. Scott. *The Alchemy of Slavery: Human Bondage and Emancipation in the Illinois Country. 1730–1865*. University of Pennsylvania Press, 2018.
Hernandez, Kelly Lytle. *City of Inmates: Conquest, Rebellion, and the Rise of Human Caging in Los Angeles, 1771–1965*. University of North Carolina Press, 2017.
Heyrman, Christine Leigh. *Southern Cross: The Beginnings of the Bible Belt*. University of North Carolina Press, 1997.
Hickman, Katie. *Brave Hearted: The Dramatic Story of Women of the American West* Virago, 2022.

Higginbotham, Evelyn Brooks. "Beyond the Sound of Silence: Afro-American Women in History." *Gender and History* (Spring 1989): 50–67.
Higginbotham, Evelyn Brooks. *Righteous Discontent: The Women's Movement in the Black Baptist Church, 1880–1920*. Harvard University Press, 1993.
Hine, Darlene Clark. "Lifting the Veil, Shattering the Silence." In *The State of Afro-American History: Past, Present, and Future.* Edited by Darlene Clark Hine. Louisiana State University Press, 1986.
Hine, Darlene Clark. "Rape and the Inner Lives of Black Women in the Middle West: Preliminary Thoughts on the Culture of Dissemblance." *Signs: Journal of Women in Culture and Society* 14, no. 4 (Summer 1989): 912–20.
Hine, Darlene Clark. "'We Specialize in the Wholly Impossible': The Philanthropic Work of Black Women." In *Lady Bountiful Revisited: Women, Philanthropy, and Power*. Edited by Kathleen D. McCarthy. Rutgers University Press, 1990.
Hine, Robert V. *Community on the American Frontier: Separate but Not Alone.* University of Oklahoma Press, 1980
Hine, Robert V. *California's Utopian Colonies.* 1953; reprint, University of California Press, 1983.
Hise, Greg. "Border City: Race and Social Distance in Los Angeles." *American Quarterly* 56, no. 3 (September 2004): 545–58.
Hoffert, Sylvia D. "Childbearing on the Trans-Mississippi Frontier, 1830–1900." *Western Historical Quarterly* 22, no. 3 (August 1991): 272–88.
Hofstadter, Richard. "The Paranoid Style in American Politics." *Harper's Magazine,* November 1964.
Hudson, Lynn. *West of Jim Crow: The Fight Against California's Color Line.* University of Illinois Press, 2020.
Hudson, Lynn M. *The Making of "Mammy Pleasant": A Black Entrepreneur in Nineteenth-Century San Francisco*. University of Illinois Press, 2003.
Hunt, Aurora. *The Army of the Pacific*. Arthur H. Clark, 1951.
Hunt, Rockwell D. "History of the California State Division Controversy." *Annual Publication of the Historical Society of Southern California* 13 (1924): 37–53.
Hunter, Milton R. "Brigham Young. Colonizer." *Pacific Historical Review* 6, no. 4 (December 1937): 341–60.
Hunter, Tera W. *Bound in Wedlock: Slave and Free Black Marriage in the Nineteenth Century*. Harvard University Press, 2017.
Hurtado, Albert. *Indian Survival on the California Frontier*. Yale University Press. 1988.
Huston James L. *Calculating the Value of the Union: Slavery, Property Rights. and the Economic Origins of the Civil War*. University of North Carolina Press, 2003.
Hutchinson, Elizabeth Newman. *Holladay, Salt Lake County, Utah*. Published by the author, 1971.

Ingram, B. Lynn. "California Megaflood: Lessons from a Forgotten Catastrophe." *Scientific American*. January 1, 2013.

Ingram, B. Lynn, and Frances Malamud-Roam. *The West Without Water: What Past Floods, Droughts, and Other Climatic Clues Tell Us About Tomorrow*. University of California Press, 2013.

Ingersoll, Luther A. *Century Annals of San Bernardino County*. L. A. Ingersoll, 1904.

Jacoby, Karl. *The Strange Career of William Ellis: The Texas Slave Who Became a Mexican Millionaire*. W. W. Norton, 2016.

Jagodinsky, Katrina. "'The Last Rose of Summer': A Century of Women's Habeas Petitions and Gendered Violence." *Western Historical Quarterly* 56, no. 2 (Summer 2025): 133–51.

Jefferson, Alison Rose, et al. *Survey LA: Los Angeles Citywide Historic Context Statement: African American History of Los Angeles*. City of Los Angeles Department of City Planning, Office of Historic Resources, 2018.

Jennings, Thelma. "Us Colored Women Had to Go Through a Plenty: Sexual Exploitation of African-American Slave Women." *Journal of Women's History* 1, no. 3 (Winter 1990): 45–74.

Johnson, Dana, et al. *Trailblazer: Delilah Beasley's California*. Clockshop, 2019.

Johnson, David Alan. *Founding the Far West: California, Oregon, and Nevada, 1840–1890*. University of California Press, 1992.

Johnson, Paul E. *A Shopkeeper's Millennium: Society and Revivals in Rochester, New York, 1815–1837*. Hill and Wang, 1978.

Johnson, Walter. *River of Dark Dreams: Slavery and Empire in the Cotton Kingdom*. Harvard University Press, 2013.

Johnson, Walter. *Soul by Soul: Life Inside the Antebellum Slave Market*. Harvard University Press, 1999.

Jones, Jacqueline. *Labor of Love, Labor of Sorrow: Black Women, Work, and the Family, from Slavery to the Present* (Basic Books, 2009).

Jones, Martha S. *All Bound Up Together: The Woman Question in African American Public Culture, 1830–1900*. University of North Carolina Press, 2007.

Jones-Rogers, Stephanie E. *They Were Her Property: White Women as Slave Owners in the American South*. Yale University Press, 2019.

Josephy, Alvin M., Jr. *The Civil War in the American West*. Vintage, 1991.

Kahrl, William L. *Water and Power: The Conflict over Los Angeles' Water Supply in the Owens Valley*. University of California Press, 1982.

Karp, Matthew J. *This Vast Southern Empire: Slaveholders at the Helm of American Foreign Policy*. Harvard University Press, 2016.

Kaye, Anthony E., with Gregory P. Downs. *Nat Turner, Black Prophet: A Visionary History*. Farrar, Straus and Giroux, 2024.

Keyes, Sarah. *American Burial Ground: A New History of the Overland Trail*. Penn Press, 2023.

Kilbourne, Richard Holcombe. *Debt, Investment, Slaves: Credit Relations in East Feliciana Parish, Louisiana, 1825–1885*. University of Alabama Press, 2014.

King, Wilma. *Stolen Childhood: Slave Youth in Nineteenth-Century America*. Indiana University Press, 1995.

Kiser, William S. *The Borderlands of Slavery: The Struggle over Captivity and Peonage in the American Southwest*. Penn Press, 2017.

Kiser, William S. *Illusions of Empire: The Civil War and Reconstruction in the U.S.–Mexico Borderlands*. Penn Press, 2021.

Klein, Norman M. *The History of Forgetting: Los Angeles and the Erasure of Memory*. 1997. Reprint, Verso, 2008.

Klemcke, Ethel Uhl, and Bob Weed. *Robert Mays Smith from South Carolina to Texas (The Long Way)*. Henington Publishing Company, 1988.

Kohler, Charmaine Lay. *Southern Grace: A Story of the Mississippi Saints*. Beagle Creek Press, 1995.

Krauthamer, Barbara. *Black Slaves, Indian Masters: Slavery, Emancipation, and Citizenship in the Native American South*. University of North Carolina Press, 2013.

Krythe, Maymie R. "First Hotel of Old Los Angeles: The Romantic Bella Union," part 1. *Historical Society of Southern California Quarterly* 33, no. 1 (March 1951).

Krythe, Maymie R. "First Hotel of Old Los Angeles: The Romantic Bella Union," part 2. *Historical Society of Southern California Quarterly* 33, no. 2 (June 1951): 141–79.

Lamar, Howard R. *The Far Southwest: A Territorial History*. University of New Mexico Press, 2000.

Lamar, Howard R. "From Bondage to Contract: Ethnic Labor in the American West. 1600–1890." In *The Countryside in the Age of Capitalist Transformation: Essays in the Social History of Rural America*. Edited by Steven Hahn and Jonathan Prude. University of North Carolina Press, 1985.

Lapp, Rudolph M. *Archy Lee: A California Fugitive Slave Case*. Heyday, 1969.

Lapp, Rudolph M. *Blacks in Gold Rush California*. Yale University Press, 1977.

Leavitt, Judith Walzer. *Brought to Bed: Childbearing in American, 1750–1950*. Oxford University Press, 1986.

LeSueur, Stephen C. *The 1838 Mormon War in Missouri*. University of Missouri Press, 1987.

Levin, Kevin. *Searching for Black Confederates: The Civil War's Most Persistent Myth*. University of North Carolina Press, 2019.

Libby, David J. *Slavery and Frontier Mississippi, 1720–1835*. University Press of Mississippi, 2004.

Licht, Walter. *Industrializing America: The Nineteenth Century*. Johns Hopkins University Press, 1995.

Lindsay, Brendan C. *Murder State: California's Native American Genocide, 1846–1873*. University of Nebraska Press, 2015.

Litwack, Leon F. *Trouble in Mind: Black Southerners in the Age of Jim Crow*. Knopf, 1998.

Logan, Rayford W. *The Negro in American Life and Thought: The Nadir, 1877–1901*. Dial Press, 1954.

Loveland, Anne C. *Southern Evangelicals and the Social Order, 1800–1860*. Louisiana State University Press, 1980.

Luke, Jenny M. *Delivered by Midwives: African American Midwifery in the Twentieth-Century South*. University Press of Mississippi, 2018.

Lyman, Edward Leo. *Amasa Mason Lyman: Mormon Apostle and Apostate*. University of Utah Press, 2009.

Lyman, Edward Leo. *San Bernardino: The Rise and Fall of a California Community*. Signature Books, 1996.

Lynch, Daniel B. *Dancing with Manifest Destiny: Elite Men of Color and the Making of American Los Angeles*. University of Oklahoma Press, 2026.

Madley, Benjamin. *An American Genocide: The United States and the California Indian Catastrophe*. Yale University Press, 2016.

Madley, Benjamin. "'Unholy Traffic in Human Blood and Souls': Systems of California Indian Servitude under U.S. Rule." *Pacific Historical Review* 83, no. 4 (November 2014): 626–67.

Madoff, Ray D. *Immortality and the Law: The Rising Power of the American Dead*. Yale University Press, 2010.

Maffly-Kipp, Laurie F. *Setting Down the Sacred Past: African American Race Histories*. Harvard University Press, 2010.

Magliari, Michael. "Free Soil, Unfree Labor: Cave Johnson Couts and the Binding of Indian Workers in California, 1850–1867." *Pacific Historical Review* 73 (August 2004): 349–90.

Magliari, Michael. "Free State Slavery: Bound Indian Labor and Slave Trafficking in California's Sacramento Valley, 1850–1864." *Pacific Historical Review* 81 (2012): 155–92.

Magliari, Michael. "'A Species of Slavery': The Compromise of 1850, Popular Sovereignty, and the Expansion of Unfree Indian Labor in the American West." *Journal of American History* 109, no. 3 (December 2022): 521–47.

Manning, Chandra. "Working for Citizenship in Civil War Contraband Camps." *Journal of the Civil War Era* 4, no. 2 (June 2014): 172–204.

Marini, Stephen A. *Radical Sects of Revolutionary New England*. Harvard University Press, 1982.

Masich, Andrew E. *Civil War in the Southwest Borderlands, 1861–1867*. University of Oklahoma Press, 2017.

Mattes, Merrill J. "The Council Bluffs Road: A New Perspective on the Northern Branch of the Great Platte River Road." *Nebraska History* 65, no. 2 (Summer 1984).

Mattes, Merrill J. *Platte River Road Narratives*. University of Illinois Press, 1988.

Matthews, Glenna. *The Golden State in the Civil War: Thomas Starr King, the*

Republican Party, and the Birth of Modern California. Cambridge University Press, 2012.
Mauss, Armand L. *All Abraham's Children: Changing Mormon Conceptions of Race and Lineage.* University of Illinois Press, 2003
Mautz, Carl. *Biographies of Western Photographers: A Reference Guide to Photographers Working in the 19th Century American West.* Carl Mautz Publishing, 1997.
May, Robert E. "Invisible Men: Blacks and the U.S. Army in the Mexican War." *The Historian* 49 no. 4 (August 1987): 463–77.
May, Robert E. *Manifest Destiny's Underworld: Filibustering in Antebellum America.* University of North Carolina Press, 2004.
May, Robert E. *Slavery. Race, and Conquest in the Tropics: Lincoln, Douglas, and the Future of Latin America.* Cambridge University Press, 2013.
May, Robert E. *The Southern Dream of a Caribbean Empire.* University Press of Florida, 1973.
Mayer, Henry. *All on Fire: William Lloyd Garrison and the Abolition of Slavery.* St. Martins, 1998.
McAfee, Ward M. "California's House Divided." *Civil War History* 33, no. 2 (1987): 115–30.
McBride, Spencer W. *Joseph Smith for President: The Prophet. the Assassins, and the Fight for American Religious Freedom.* Oxford University Press, 2021.
McClung, William Alexander. *Landscapes of Desire: Anglo Mythologies of Los Angeles.* University of California Press, 2000.
McCurdy, Charles W. "Prelude to Civil War: A Snapshot of the California Supreme Court at Work in 1858." *California Supreme Court Historical Society Yearbook* (1994).
McCurry, Stephanie. *Confederate Reckoning: Power and Politics in the Civil War South.* Harvard University Press, 2010.
McCurry, Stephanie. *Masters of Small Worlds: Yeoman Households, Gender Relations, and the Political Culture of the Antebellum South Carolina Low Country.* Oxford University Press, 1995.
McDaniel, W. Caleb. *Sweet Taste of Liberty: A True Story of Slavery and Restitution in America.* Oxford University Press, 2019.
McGinty, Brian. *Archy Lee's Struggle for Freedom: The True Story of California Gold. the Nation's Tragic March Toward Civil War, and a Young Black Man's Fight for Liberty.* Lyons Press, 2020.
McGinty, Brian. *Lincoln and California: The President. the War, and the Golden State* Potomac Books, 2023.
McWilliams, Carey. *Southern California: An Island on the Land.* Peregrine Smith, 1973.
Miles, Tiya. *All That She Carried: The Journey of Ashley's Sack, a Black Family Keepsake.* Random House, 2021.

Miles, Tiya. *Night Flyer: Harriet Tubman and the Faith Dreams of a Free People.* Penguin, 2024.

Miller, David. *South by Southwest: Planter Emigration and Identity in the Slave South.* University of Virginia Press, 2002.

Molina, Natalia. *Fit To Be Citizens? Public Health and Race in Los Angeles, 1879–1939.* University of California Press, 2006.

Monroy, Douglas. *Thrown Among Strangers: The Making of Mexican Culture in Frontier California.* University of California Press, 1990.

Montalvo, Maria R. *Enslaved Archives: Slavery, Law, and the Production of the Past.* Johns Hopkins University Press, 2024.

Moore, John Hebron. *The Emergence of the Cotton Kingdom in the Old Southwest: Mississippi, 1770–1860.* Louisiana State University Pres, 1988.

Moore, Shirley Ann Wilson. *Sweet Freedom's Plains: African Americans on the Overland Trails, 1841–1869.* University of Oklahoma Press, 2016.

Moore, Shirley Ann Wilson. "'We Feel the Want of Protection': The Politics of Law and Race in California, 1848-1878." In *Taming the Elephant: Politics, Government, and Law in Pioneer California.* Edited by John F. Burns and Richard J. Orsi. University of California Press, 2003.

Morales, R. Isabela. *Happy Dreams of Liberty: An American Family in Slavery and Freedom.* Oxford University Press, 2022.

Morgan, Jennifer L. *Laboring Women: Reproduction and Gender in New World Slavery.* University of Pennsylvania Press, 2011.

Morgan, Philip D. *Slave Counterpoint: Black Culture in the Eighteenth-Century Chesapeake Lowcountry.* University of North Carolina Press, 2012.

Morrell, Joseph R. "Medicine of the Pioneer Period in Utah." *Utah Historical Quarterly* 23, no. 2 (April 1955): 127–44.

Morris, Christopher. "An Event in Community Organization: The Mississippi Slave Insurrection Scare of 1835." *Journal of Social History* 22, no. 1 (Autumn 1988): 93–111.

Morrison, Michael A. *Slavery and the American West: The Eclipse of Manifest Destiny and the Coming of the Civil War.* University of North Carolina, 1997.

Moss, Kay K. *Southern Folk Medicine, 1750–1820.* University of South Carolina Press, 2010.

Mueller, Max Perry. *Race and the Making of the Mormon People.* University of North Carolina Press, 2017.

Nelson, Megan Kate. "The Civil War from Apache Pass." *Journal of the Civil War Era* 6, no. 4 (December 2016): 510–35.

Nelson, Megan Kate. *The Three-Cornered War: The Union, the Confederacy, and Native Peoples in the Fight for the West.* Scribner, 2020.

Newell, Quincy D. *Your Sister in the Gospel: The Life of Jane Manning James, a Nineteenth-Century Black Mormon.* Oxford University Press, 2019.

Newman, Simon. *Parades and the Politics of the Street: Festive Culture in the Early American Republic.* Penn Press, 2010.

Newmark, Marco R. "Early Los Angeles Bench and Bar." *Historical Society of Southern California Quarterly* 34, no. 4 (December 1952): 327–46.

Newmark, Marco R. "Medical Profession in the Early Days of Los Angeles." *Historical Society of Southern California* 34, no. 1 (March 1952): 71–80.

Nichols, James David. *The Limits of Liberty: Mobility and the Making of the Eastern U.S.-Mexico Border*. University of Nebraska Press, 2018.

Oakes, James. *The Ruling Race: A History of American Slaveholders*. Norton, 1982.

Olivarius, Kathryn. *Necropolis: Disease, Power, and Capitalism in the Cotton Kingdom*. Harvard University Press, 2022.

Ovnick, Merry. "Looking for the Founders of the Historical Society of Southern California." *Southern California Quarterly* 97, no. 2 (Summer 2015): 156–77.

Owens, Deirdre Cooper. *Medical Bondage: Race, Gender, and the Origins of American Gynecology*. University of Georgia Press, 2017.

Paddison, Joshua. *American Heathens: Religion, Race, and Reconstruction in California*. University of California Press and the Huntington Library, 2012.

Painter, Nell Irvin. *Exodusters: Black Migration to Kansas after Reconstruction*. Knopf. 1976.

Painter, Nell Irvin. *Sojourner Truth: A Life, a Symbol*. Norton, 1997.

Painter, Nell Irvin. *Soul Murder and Slavery*. Markham Press, 1995.

Palmquist, Peter E., and Thomas R. Kailbourn. *Pioneer Photographers of the Far West: A Biographical Dictionary, 1840–1865*. Stanford University Press, 2000.

Park, Benjamin E. *Kingdom of Nauvoo: The Rise and Fall of a Religious Empire on the American Frontier*. Liveright, 2020.

Parrish, William E. "The Mississippi Saints." *The Historian* 50, no. 4 (August 1988): 489–506.

Parry, Tyler D. *Jumping the Broom: The Surprising Multicultural Origins of a Black Wedding Ritual*. University of North Carolina Press, 2020.

Parsons, Elaine Frantz. "Midnight Rangers: Costume and Performance in the Reconstruction-Era Ku Klux Klan," *Journal of American History* 92, no. 3 (December 2005): 811-836.

Patton, Annaleone D. *California Mormons by Sail and Trail*. Deseret Book Company, 1961.

Paugh, Katherine. *The Politics of Reproduction: Race, Medicine, and Fertility in the Age of Abolition*. Oxford University Press, 2017.

Penningroth, Dylan C. *Before the Movement: The Hidden History of Black Civil Rights* Liveright, 2024.

Penningroth, Dylan C. *The Claims of Kinfolk: African American Property and Community in the Nineteenth-Century South*. University of North Carolina Press, 2003.

Peterson, Carla L. *"Doers of the Word": African-American Women Speakers and Writers in the North, 1830–1880*. Oxford University Press, 1995.

Pfaelzer, Jean. *California, A Slave State*. Yale University Press, 2023.

Phillips, George Harwood. *Chiefs and Challengers: Indian Resistance and Cooperation in Southern California*. University of California Press, 1975.
Phillips, George Harwood. "Indians in Los Angeles. 1781–1875: Economic Integration, Social Disintegration." *Pacific Historical Review* 49, no. 3 (August 1980): 427–51.
Phillips, George Harwood. *Vineyards and Vaqueros: Indian Labor and the Economic Expansion of Southern California, 1771–1877*. Arthur H. Clark, 2010.
Pitt, Leonard. *Decline of the Californios: A Social History of the Spanish-Speaking Californians, 1846–1890*. University of California Press, 1966.
Pitzer, Donald E,. ed. *America's Communal Utopias*. University of North Carolina Press, 1997.
Porter, Kenneth Wiggins. *The Negro on the American Frontier*. Arno Press, 1971.
Potter, David M. *The Impending Crisis, 1848–1861*. Completed and edited by Don E. Fehrenbacher. Harper & Row, 1976.
Prince, Gregory A. *Power from on High: The Development of Mormon Priesthood*. Signature, 1995.
Pubols, Louise. "Born Global: From Pueblo to Statehood." In *A Companion to Los Angeles*. Edited by William Deverell and Greg Hise. Wiley Blackwell, 2010.
Quinn, Arthur. *The Rivals: William Gwin, David Broderick, and the Birth of California*. Crown, 1994.
Quinn, D. Michael. *The Mormon Hierarchy: Origins of Power*. Signature, 1994.
Raboteau, Albert J. *Slave Religion: The "Invisible Institution" in the Antebellum South*. Oxford University Press, 1978.
Rarick, Ethan. *Desperate Passage: The Donner Party Perilous Journey West*. Oxford University Press, 2009.
Ravage, John W. *Black Pioneers: Images of the Black Experience on the North American Frontier*. Second edition. University of Utah Press, 2008.
Reeve, W. Paul. *Religion of a Different Color: Race and the Mormon Struggle for Whiteness*. Oxford University Press, 2015.
Reeve, W. Paul, Christopher B. Rich Jr., and LaJean Purcell Carruth. *This Abominable Slavery: Race, Religion, and the Battle over Human Bondage in Antebellum Utah*. Oxford University Press, 2024.
Regosin, Elizabeth. *Freedom's Promise: Ex-Slave Families and Citizenship in the Age of Emancipation*. University Press of Virginia, 2002.
Reiter, Tonya. "Redd Slave Histories: Family. Race, and Sex in Pioneer Utah." *Utah Historical Quarterly* 85, no. 2 (Spring 2017): 108–26.
Resendez, Andrés. *A Land So Strange: The Epic Journey of Cabeza de Vaca*. Basic Books, 2007.
Resendez, Andrés. *The Other Slavery: The Uncovered Story of Indian Enslavement in America*. Houghton Mifflin Harcourt, 2016.
Richards, Leonard. *The California Gold Rush and the Coming of the Civil War*. Vintage, 2007.

Richards, Thomas, Jr. *Breakaway Americas: The Unmanifest Future of the Jacksonian United States*. Johns Hopkins University Press, 2020.

Robinson, John W. "A California Copperhead: Henry Hamilton and the Los Angeles Star." *Arizona and the West* 23 (Fall 1981): 213–30.

Robinson, John W. "Colonel Edward J.C. Kewen: Los Angeles' Fire-Eating Orator of the Civil War Era." *Southern California Quarterly* 61 (Summer 1979): 159–81.

Robinson, John W. *Los Angeles in Civil War Days, 1860–1865*. University of Oklahoma Press, 1977.

Rothman, Joshua D. *Flush Times and Fever Dreams: A Story of Capitalism and Slavery in the Age of Jackson*. University of Georgia Press, 2012.

Rothman, Joshua D. *The Ledger and the Chain: How Domestic Slave Traders Shaped America*. Basic Books, 2023.

Rowland, Eron. *History of Hinds County, Mississippi, 1821–1922*. Andesite Press, 2017.

Russel, Robert R. *Improvement of Communication with the Pacific Coast as an Issue in American Politics, 1783–1864*. Torch Press, 1948.

Ryan, Mary P. *Women in Public: Between Banners and Ballots, 1825–1880*. Johns Hopkins University Press, 1992.

Saavedra, Yvette J. *Pasadena Before the Roses: Race, Identity, and Land Use in Southern California, 1771–1890*. University of Arizona Press, 2018.

Saunt, Claudio. *Unworthy Republic: The Dispossession of Native Americans and the Road to Indian Territory*. W. W. Norton, 2020.

Savage, W. Sherman. *Blacks in the West*. Greenwood Press, 1976.

Savoy, Lauret. *Trace: Memory, History, Race, and the American Landscape*. Counterpoint, 2015.

Schermerhorn, *The Business of Slavery and the Rise of American Capitalism, 1815–1860*. Yale University Press, 2015.

Schlesinger, Arthur M. "Liberty Tree: A Genealogy." *New England Quarterly* 25, no. 4 (December 1952): 435–58.

Schwartz, Marie Jenkins. *Birthing a Slave: Motherhood and Medicine in the Antebellum South*. Harvard University Press, 2006.

Schwartz, Marie Jenkins. *Born in Bondage: Growing Up Enslaved in the Antebellum South*. Harvard University Press, 2000.

Schoen, Brian. *The Fragile Fabric of Union: Cotton, Federal Politics, and the Global Origins of the Civil War*. Johns Hopkins University Press, 2009.

Schweninger, Loren. *Appealing for Liberty: Freedom Suits in the South*. Oxford University Press, 2019.

Scott, James. *Weapons of the Weak: Everyday Forms of Peasant Resistance*. Yale University Press, 1987.

Scribner, Campbell F. "Surveying the Destruction of African American Schoolhouses in the South, 1864–1876." *Journal of the Civil War Era* 10, no. 4 (December 2020): 469–94.

Shipps, Jan. *Mormonism: The Story of a New Religious Tradition*. University of Illinois Press, 1985.
Shipps, Jan. "The Prophet Puzzle: Suggestions Leading Toward a More Comprehensive Interpretation of Joseph Smith." *Journal of Mormon History* 1 (1974): 3–20.
Shuck, Oscar Tully, ed. *History of the Bench and Bar of California*. Commercial Printing House, 1901.
Shutes, Milton H. *Lincoln and California*. Stanford University Press, 1943.
Sides, Josh. *L.A. City Limits: African American Los Angeles from the Great Depression to the Present*. University of California Press, 2004.
Simmons, LaKisha Michelle. "Black Feminist Theories of Motherhood and Generation: Histories of Black Infant and Child Loss in the United States," *Signs: Journal of Women in Culture and Society* 46, no. 2 (2021): 311–35
Sinha, Manisha. *The Rise and Fall of the Second American Republic: Reconstruction, 1860–1920*. Liveright, 2024.
Sinha, Manisha. *The Slave's Cause: A History of Abolition*. Yale University Press, 2016.
Skinner, Byron R. *Black Origins in the Inland Empire*. Book Attic Press, 1983.
Smith, Cheryl A. *Market Women: Black Women Entrepreneurs, Past, Present, and Future*. Praeger, 2005.
Smith, Stacey L. "*Dred Scott* on the Pacific: African Americans. Citizenship, and Subjecthood in the North American West." *Southern California Quarterly* 100, no. 1 (Spring 2018): 44–68.
Smith, Stacey L. *Freedom's Frontier: California and the Struggle over Unfree Labor, Emancipation, and Reconstruction*. University of North Carolina Press, 2013.
Smith, Stacey L. "Slavery in a Free State: Masters and Slaves in Gold Rush California," *Pacific Historical Review* 80, no. 1 (February 2011): 28–63.
Smith, Suzanne E. *To Serve the Living: Funeral Directors and the African American Way of Death*. Harvard University Press, 2010.
Sneddon, Karen. "In the Name of God. Amen: Language in Last Wills and Testaments." *Quinnipiac Law Review* 29, no. 3 (2011).
Sneddon, Karen. "Speaking for the Dead: Voice in Last Wills and Testaments." *St. Johns Law Review* 85, no. 2 (Spring 2011): 684–754.
St. John, Rachel. "The Unpredictable America of William Gwin: Expansion, Secession, and the Unstable Borders of Nineteenth-Century North America." *Journal of the Civil War Era* 6 (March 2016): 56–84.
Stegner, Wallace. *The Gathering of Zion: The Story of the Mormon Trail*. 1964. Reprint, University of Nebraska Press, 1992.
Smith-Rosenberg, Carroll. *Disorderly Conduct: Visions of Gender in Victorian America*. Oxford University Press, 1986.
Snay, Mitchell. *Gospel of Disunion: Religion and Separatism in the Antebellum South*. University of North Carolina Press, 1997.

Snyder, Christina. *Slavery in Indian Country: The Changing Face of Captivity in Early America*. Harvard University Press, 2010.

Spitzzeri, Paul R. "Judge Lynch in Session: Popular Justice in Los Angeles, 1850–1875." *Southern California Quarterly* 87 (Summer 2005): 83–122.

Spitzzeri, Paul R. *The Workman and Temple Families of Southern California*. Seligson Publishing, 2007.

Splitter, Henry Winfred. "Los Angeles in the 1850's As Told by Early Newspapers." *Historical Society of Southern California Quarterly* 31, nos. 1–2 (March–June 1949): 114–18.

Stampp, Kenneth M. *The Peculiar Institution: Slavery in the Ante-bellum South*. Vintage, 1956.

Stanley, Gerald. "The Politics of the Antebellum Far West: The Impact of the Slavery and Race Issues in California." *Journal of the West* 16 (1977): 19–25.

Starr, Kevin. *Americans and the California Dream*. Oxford University Press, 1973.

Starr, Kevin. *Inventing the Dream: California through the Progressive Era*. Oxford University Press, 1985.

Starr, Kevin. *Material Dreams: Southern California Through the 1920s*. Oxford University Press, 1990.

Steckel, Richard H. "A Dreadful Childhood: The Excess Mortality of American Slaves." *Social Science History* 10 (Winter 1986): 427–65.

Steckel, Richard H. "Slave Mortality: Analysis of Evidence from Plantation Records." *Social Science History* 3, nos. 3–4 (October 1979): 86–114.

Steptoe, Tyina L. *Houston Bound: Culture and Color in a Jim Crow City*. University of California Press, 2015.

Stevenson, Brenda. *The Contested Murder of Latasha Harlins: Justice, Gender, and the Origins of the L.A. Riots*. Oxford University Press, 2013.

Stevenson, Brenda. *Life in Black and White: Family and Community in the Slave South*. Oxford University Press, 1996.

Stevenson, Brenda. "What's Love Got to Do with It? Concubinage and Enslaved Women and Girls in the Antebellum South." *Journal of African American* History 98, no. 1 (Winter 2013): 99–125.

Stewart, Whitney Nell. *This Is Our Home: Slavery and Struggle on Southern Plantations*. University of North Carolina Press, 2023.

Tadman, Michael. *Speculators and Slaves: Masters, Traders, and Slaves in the Old South*. University of Wisconsin Press, 1996.

Taylor, Alan. *The Internal Enemy: Slavery and War in Virginia*. W. W. Norton, 2014.

Taylor, Amy Murrell. *Embattled Freedom: Journeys Through the Civil War's Slave Refugee Camps*. University of North Carolina Press, 2018.

Taylor, Nikki Marie. *Driven Toward Madness: The Fugitive Slave Margaret Garner and Tragedy on the Ohio*. Ohio University Press, 2016.

Taylor, Quintard. *The Forging of a Black Community: Seattle's Central District from 1870 Through the Civil Rights Era*. University of Washington Press, 1994.

Taylor, Quintard. *In Search of the Racial Frontier: African Americans in the American West, 1528–1990*. W. W. Norton, 1998.
Taylor, Quintard, and Shirley Ann Wilson Moore. *African American Women Confront the West, 1600–2000*. University of Oklahoma Press, 2003.
Terborg-Penn, Rosalyn. *African American Women in the Struggle for the Vote, 1850–1920*. Indiana University Press, 1998.
Thiriot, Amy Tanner. *Slavery in Zion: A Documentary and Genealogical History of Black Lives and Black Servitude in Utah Territory, 1847–1862*. University of Utah Press, 2022.
Thomas, William G. *The Iron Way: Railroads, the Civil War, and the Making of Modern America*. Yale University Press, 2011.
Thomas, William G. *A Question of Liberty: The Families Who Challenged Slavery from the Nation's Founding to the Civil War*. Yale University Press, 2020.
Thurman, Sue Bailey. *Pioneers of Negro Origin in California*. Acme, 1952.
Torget, Andrew J. *Seeds of Empire: Cotton, Slavery, and the Transformation of the Texas Borderlands, 1800–1850*. University of North Carolina Press, 2015.
Torres-Rouff, David Samuel. *Before L.A.: Race Space, and Municipal Power in Los Angeles, 1781–1894*. Yale University Press, 2013.
Trouillot, Michel-Rolph. *Silencing the Past: Power and the Production of History*. Reprint, Beacon Press, 2015.
Turner, John G. *Brigham Young: Pioneer Prophet*. Harvard University Press, 2012.
Ulrich, Laurel Thatcher. *A House Full of Females: Plural Marriage and Women's Rights in Early Mormonism, 1835–1870*. Vintage, 2017.
Underwood, Grant. *The Millenarian World of Early Mormonism*. University of Illinois Press, 1993.
Unruh, John D., Jr. *The Plains Across: The Overland Emigrants and the Trans-Mississippi West, 1840–60*. University of Illinois Press, 1979.
Van Hoak, Stephen P. "And Who Shall Have the Children? The Indian Slave Trade in the Southern Great Basin, 1800–1865." *Nevada Historical Society Quarterly* 41, no. 1 (Spring 1998).
Waite, Kevin. "The Brittle West: Secession and Separatism in the Southwest Borderlands during the Civil War Era." *Southwestern Historical Quarterly* 127, no. 1 (July 2023): 8–28.
Waite, Kevin. "The Forgotten History of the Western Klan." *The Atlantic*. April 6, 2021.
Waite, Kevin. "Jefferson Davis and Proslavery Visions of Empire in the Far West." *Journal of the Civil War Era* 6, no. 4 (December 2016): 536–65.
Waite, Kevin. "Lincoln Looks West: California and the Fate of the Nation in the Civil War Era." *Ohio Valley History* (Spring 2026).
Waite, Kevin. "The 'Lost Cause' Goes West: Confederate Culture and Civil War Memory in California." *California History* 97, no. 1 (February 2020): 33–49.

Waite, Kevin. "The Sinister Reason Camels Were Brought to the American West." *National Geographic*. October 26, 2021.

Waite, Kevin. "War in Indian Country." In *Cambridge History of the American Civil War*. Edited by Aaron Sheehan-Dean, vol. 1, 576–600. Cambridge University Press, 2019.

Waite, Kevin. "The West and Reconstruction after the American Civil War." In *The Oxford Handbook on Reconstruction*. Edited by Andrew L. Slap. Oxford University Press, forthcoming.

Waite, Kevin. *West of Slavery: The Southern Dream of a Transcontinental Empire*. University of North Carolina Press, 2021.

Waldstreicher, David. *The Odyssey of Phillis Wheatley: A Poet's Journeys Through American Slavery and Independence*. Farrar, Straus and Giroux, 2023.

Walker, Juliet E. K. *The History of Black Business in America: Capitalism, Race, Entrepreneurship*. 2 vols. Second edition. University of North Carolina Press.

Warren, Wendy. "The Cause of Her Grief: The Rape of a Slave in Early New England." *Journal of American History* 93, no. 4 (March 2007): 1031–49.

Watford, W. H. "Confederate Western Ambitions." *Southwestern Historical Quarterly* 44 (October 1940): 161–87.

Watford, W. H. "The Far-Western Wing of the Rebellion, 1861–1865." *California Historical Society Quarterly* 34 (June 1955): 125–48.

Weiner, Dana Elizabeth. "Debating African Americans' Place in California, 1850–1870." *In Africa and its Diasporas: Rethinking Struggles for Recognition and Empowerment*. Edited by Behnaz A. Mirzai and Bonny Ibhawoh. Africa World Press, 2018.

Weiner, Dana Elizabeth. "Legal Ambiguities on the Ground: Black Californians' Land Claims, 1848–1870." In Beyond the Borders of the Law: Critical Legal Histories of the North American West. Edited by Katrina Jagodinsky and Pablo Mitchell. University Press of Kansas, 2018.

Wertz, Richard W., and Dorothy C Wertz. *Lying-In: A History of Childbirth in America*. Free Press. 1977.

West, Elliott. *Continental Reckoning: The American West in the Age of Expansion* University of Nebraska Press, 2023.

West, Elliott. "Reconstructing Race." *Western Historical Quarterly* 34, no. 1 (Spring 2003): 6–26.

Wexler, Laura. *Tender Violence: Domestic Visions in an Age of US Imperialism*. University of North Carolina Press, 2000.

White, Deborah Gray. *Ar'n't I a Woman? Female Slaves in the Plantation South*. W. W. Norton, 1985.

White, Arisa, Laura Atkins, and Laura Freeman. *Biddy Mason Speaks Up*. Heydey, 2019.

Wigger, John H. *Taking Heaven by Storm: Methodism and the Rise of Popular Christianity in America*. Oxford University Press, 1998.

Wilder, Craig Steven. *Ebony and Ivy: Race, Slavery, and the Troubled History of America's Universities*. Bloomsbury, 2014.

Williams, Heather Andrea. *Help Me to Find My People: The African American Search for Family Lost in Slavery*. University of North Carolina Press, 2012.

Wilson, James A. "Frontier in the Shadows: Prisons in the Far Southwest, 1850–1917." *Arizona and the West* 22, no. 4 (Winter 1980): 323–42.

Wollenberg, Charles. *All Deliberate Speed: Segregation and Exclusion in California Schools, 1855–1975*. University of California Press, 1976.

Woods, Michael E. *Emotional and Sectional Conflict in the Antebellum United States*. Cambridge University Press, 2014.

Woolsey, Ronald C. "Disunion or Dissent? A New Look at an Old Problem in Southern California Attitudes Toward the Civil War." *Southern California Quarterly* 66 (Fall 1984): 185–205.

Woolsey, Ronald C. "Pioneer Views and Frontier Themes: Benjamin Hayes, Horace Bell, and the Southern California Experience." *Southern California Quarterly* 72, no. 3 (1990): 255–74.

Woolsey, Ronald C. "The Politics of a Lost Cause: 'Seceshers' and Democrats in Southern California During the Civil War." *California History* 69 (Winter 1990–91): 372–83.

Wright, Gavin. *Slavery and American Economic Development*. Louisiana State University Press, 2006.

Young, Cory James. "'A Slave in Nebraska' and Other Black Habeas Activism on the Gilded Age Plains." *Western Historical Quarterly* 56, no. 2 (Summer 2025): 117–31.

Zaborney, John J. *Slaves for Hire: Renting Enslaved Laborers in Antebellum Virginia*. Louisiana State University Press, 2012.

Zackodnik, Teresa. "The Green-Backs of Civilization: Sojourner Truth and Portrait Photography." *American Studies* 46, no. 2 (Summer 2005): 117–43.

Zander, Cecily N. *The Army Under Fire: The Politics of Antimilitarism in the Civil War Era*. Louisiana State University Press, 2024.

Zesch, Scott. *The Chinatown War: Chinese Los Angeles and the Massacre of 1871*. Oxford University Press, 2012.

Zesch, Scott. "Chinese Los Angeles in 1870–71: The Makings of a Massacre." *Southern California Quarterly* 90 (Summer 2008): 109–58.

UNPUBLISHED MATERIAL

Bond, J. Max. "The Negro in Los Angeles." PhD dissertation, University of Southern California, 1936.

Dinwoodie, Jane. "Beyond Removal: Indians, States, and Sovereignties in the American South, 1812–1860." PhD dissertation, University of Oxford, 2017.

Dominguez, Laura. "Memory Makers: Tracing Race, Heritage, and Repair in Los Angeles, 1781–2012." PhD dissertation, University of Southern California, 2023.

Gillmer, Jason. "Black. White, and Gold: Litigating Slavery in the American West." Gonzaga University School of Law Research Paper. February 8, 2021.

Hagan, Barney. "Matamoros: Exploring the Relationship Between the Civil War and North American Borderlands in the American Southwest." PhD dissertation, University of Oxford, 2024.

Hart, Charles Ralph Desmond. "Congressmen and the Expansion of Slavery into the Territories: A Study in Attitudes, 1846–1861" (PhD dissertation, University of Washington, 1965)

Horning, Claudia Maureen. "Trailblazing Librarian in the Golden State: A Look at the Life and Career of Miriam Matthews." MA thesis, University of California Los Angeles, 2012.

Jelsing, Kaden. "Sovereign Futures: Indigenous and Settler Prophecies in Two Nineteenth-century American 'Northwests.'" PhD dissertation, University of British Columbia, 2023.

Lappen, Joshua. "Cultures of Power: Electrification. Politics, and Visibility in Greater Los Angeles." PhD dissertation, University of Oxford, 2024.

Lewis, Albert Lucian. "Los Angeles in the Civil War Decades, 1850–1868." PhD dissertation, University of Southern California, 1970.

Lynch, Daniel Brendan. "Southern California Chivalry: The Convergence of Southerners and Californios in the Far Southwest, 1846–1866." PhD dissertation, UCLA, 2015.

Malone, Thomas E. "The Democratic Party in California, 1865–1868." MA thesis, Stanford University, 1949.

Neumann, Alexis Broderick. "American Incest: Kinship, Sex, and Commerce in Slavery and Reconstruction." PhD dissertation, University of Pennsylvania, 2018.

Phipps, Kristen. "Desert Slavery: How the Old Spanish Trail Sustained Captivity and Coerced Labor in the North American West." PhD dissertation, University of Nevada–Las Vegas, 2025.

Smith, Stacey L. "California Bound: Unfree Labor. Race, and the Reconstruction of the Far West, 1848–1870." PhD dissertation, University of Wisconsin–Madison, 2008.

Stanley, Gerald. "The Republican Party in California, 1856–1868." PhD dissertation, University of Arizona, 1973.

Williams, Charnan. "The History of Slavery and Race in California from the Gold Rush to the United States Civil War, 1848–1865." PhD dissertation, University of Michigan, 2022.

Wood, Anthony W. "Forty Years Within the Veil: The Black West and Counternarratives of Race and Place in the Rocky Mountains." PhD dissertation, University of Michigan, 2024.

Yancy, James Walter. "The Negro of Tucson: Past and Present." MA thesis. University of Arizona, 1933.

Index

abduction. *See* kidnapping into slavery
abolitionism: Benjamin Hayes and, 162, 163; LDS Church and, 45, 76 (*see also* Mormonism: slavery and). *See also* allies; antiabolitionism; slave resistance
abolitionist press, 155, 161
Act for the Government and Protection of Indians, 151
Act in Relation to Service, 81–83
Act to Enforce the Fifteenth Amendment to the Constitution, An, 234
Ada Hancock, SS (screw steamer), 208–9
advertising industry, 272–73
Africa and slavery, 15, 37
African Methodist Episcopal (AME) Church, 228; California Conference (1888), 280–81. *See also* First African Methodist Episcopal Church of Los Angeles
agriculture. *See* dairy farming; Jumuba ranch; wheat farming
Alexander, David, 149–50
Allen, Jordan, 266–67
allies, 292; hostility toward, 70, 132–33, 156, 190–92, 215, 243 (*see also* vigilantism); Mason's, 247 (*see also* freedom suit of 1856: allies in). *See also* Owens, Robert Curry: allies
Alston, Charles, 306f, 307
American Civil War, 196–203, 208–12; Benjamin Hayes on, 195–96, 211; Bob Owens and, 198–200, 202; California and, 3, 200; celebrations during, 210, 213; initiation, 196; Lincoln and, 211–12; Los Angeles during, 198, 205, 206, 213; Mason and, 206, 207f, 250; Mexico and, 198; Texas and, 200, 203
American Indians. *See* Native Americans
antiabolitionism, 76, 132, 135, 155, 163, 190, 197, 210. *See also* vigilantism
anti-Mormonism, 45, 75, 76, 113; attacks, 43–45, 47, 49, 76, 94, 98; John Brown and, 43–44, 47–48
Applegate, Jesse, 63

Baker, Edward, 190
Ball, Charles, 16
Ballard, Amanda, 187, 230, 253
Ballard, John, 187, 230, 253–54
Bancroft, Hubert Howe, 109, 255–56
Bankhead, Alex, 72, 73
Bankhead, John H., 57
Banning, Phineas, 209
Barrows, Henry Dwight, 205–6, 211
Bass, Charlotta A., 7, 241, 296, 297, 299, 305

Beal, Israel, 235–36
Beal, Martha Embers (Hannah and Toby's daughter), 79, 102, 125, 127, 147, 234–36
Beasley, Delilah L., 7, 246, 287, 305. See also *Negro Trail Blazers of California*
Bell, Horace, 172, 177, 196, 204, 213, 273; alleged crimes, 269; enemies, 269; libel suit, 269–70; on Mason, 243; Mason and, 269–70; postwar Los Angeles and, 215–17, 253; wife, 269, 270
Bella Union Hotel, 142, 198, 223, 248
Benjamin, R.C.O., 277
Bennet Tract, 271
Benton, Thomas Hart, 74
Bible: slavery and the, 41, 75, 79–81. *See also* Exodus
Biddy Mason Center, 304
Biddy Mason Charitable Foundation, 308
Biddy Mason Foundation, 308
Biddy Mason Memorial Institute, 289–90, 303
Biddy Mason Memorial Park, 308
Biddy Mason Speaks Up (White et al.), 308
big fields, 103
Biggs, Peter, 187, 212–13
Birth of a Nation (film), 296
Black Angelenos, 192, 227, 249, 253, 295–97, 299; finances, 275; paths to survival during Civil War, 213; prosperity, 187; religion, churches, and, 228, 229, 240 (*see also* churches). *See also* Black Los Angeles; *specific topics*
Black Christianity, 40–42, 59–60; in Los Angeles, 227, 230. *See also* Black Mormons
Black Codes, 151. *See also* testimony exclusion laws
Black Los Angeles, 233, 234, 247, 253, 259, 280, 291, 299; associational life, 294; Bob Owens and, 220–21, 290; causes of rapid growth of, 274–75; foundational institutions of, 40; map of early, 262f; Mason-Owens family and, 222, 229, 230, 234; Mason's Spring Street property and, 221; nature of, 223, 229; places of worship in, 227–31, 294; scholarship on, 7, 304–5, 307–8; segregation, 298. *See also* Black Angelenos; *specific topics*
Black Mormons, 80. *See also* Cain and Ham
Black Republicans, 190, 195, 196, 224, 249, 276
Black West, 6, 7, 305
Bond, J. Max, 287
Book of Mormon, 43, 44, 46, 75–76
boom of the eighties, 271–73
Boren, A. D., 189
Bradley, Tom (mayor), 301
Breckinridge, John C., 195
Brent, Joseph Lancaster, 189, 190, 196, 199, 215, 223
British Columbia, 191–92. *See also* Canada
Broadway (Los Angeles), Mason's property on. *See* Spring Street property of Mason
Broderick, David, 191
Brooks, James, 74–75
Brooks, Preston, 132–33
Brown, Elsa Barkley, 232
Brown, Henry Box, 17, 24, 41
Brown, John (fugitive slave), 16, 17, 21–22
Brown, John (Mormon pioneer), 58, 80; anti-Mormonism and, 43–44, 47–48; background and overview, 42; baptisms performed by, 44, 45; Joseph Smith and, 42–44, 47–48; as legislator, 82; as missionary, 42–44; Mormon exodus and, 52–53, 55–58, 61, 65, 66, 68 (*see also under* Mississippi Saints); Native Americans and, 65; Robert Smith and, 42, 56–58, 61; as slaveholder, 45, 53, 55–56, 61, 68, 82; slavery and, 44, 45, 52, 61, 68, 82
Brown, William Wells, 16
Browne, J. Ross, 248
Brunson, Anson, 266
Burns, James F., 218
Butler, Lauretta Green, 243
butter. *See* dairy farming

Caborca, Battle of, 166–67
Cain and Ham, curses of, 71, 79–80
Calafia, Queen, 184
Calhoun, John C., 75
California: bill to divide, 194–95; criminal justice system, 105, 106, 189; enslaved Blacks imported into, 90, 91f; large slaveholding enterprises in, 105–6; in the media, 161–62
California Act Concerning Crimes and Punishments (1850), 157
California antislavery legislation, 157, 161–62; failure to enforce, 89–90, 107–8; legislature and, 106–7; misinformation about, 107; Robert Smith and, 89, 107. *See also* California Fugitive Slave Law; Constitution of California; testimony exclusion laws

California courts: Mason and, 158, 267; Robert Smith and, 2, 165; slavery and, 132–34, 136. *See also specific topics*
California Fugitive Slave Law (1852), 133, 134
California genocide, 108
California Gold Rush, 20, 54, 58, 105–6, 133, 272. *See also* Gold Country
California Indians, 94, 108–9; testimony exclusion laws and, 136, 212. *See also* Native Americans
California Supreme Court, 132–34, 143, 151, 190
Calle de los Negros (Negro Alley), 172, 173f, 237, 238, 248, 279
Camp Drum, 201. *See also* Drum Barracks
Canada, Province of: Blacks fleeing to, 60, 191–93
candy factory that rented space from Mason, 259–61, 261f
Carleton, James Henry, 198
cattle, 64, 99, 117; Biddy and, 63, 64, 73, 99, 121, 157, 161; deaths, 66, 204, 206, 216–17; Robert Smith's, 63, 66, 73, 87, 95, 96, 99–100, 100f, 115, 157, 158
Central Avenue (Los Angeles), 298–99
cheese. *See* dairy farming
Chesnut, Mary Boykin, 25
childcare, 27, 28, 60, 100, 101, 241, 254
children, enslaved, 34, 36; guardianship status, 151–52. *See also* motherhood of slaves
Chinatown (Los Angeles), 279. *See also* Calle de los Negros; Chinese Massacre of 1871
Chinese Americans in Los Angeles, 268, 279–80
Chinese businesses, Mason and, 239, 249, 278
Chinese immigrants: persecution of, 226 (*see also* Chinese Massacre of 1871); testimony ban applied to, 136, 212
Chinese Massacre of 1871 (Los Angeles), 237–39, 238f, 244
Chinese rights, 224–25
Chivalry/Chivs (California's Democratic machine's proslavery wing), 189–90, 194
Christianity, 170–71, 242; slavery and, 41, 42. *See also* Bible; Black Christianity; churches; First African Methodist Episcopal Church of Los Angeles; Mormonism
churches, Black, 40, 227–29, 235, 245, 263, 266, 275, 281; Black churchwomen, 228–29, 233; church-building campaign, 231; Mason's neighbors and, 227, 254, 263. *See also* First African Methodist Episcopal Church of Los Angeles
citizenship rights, 208, 225; *Dred Scott* and, 168, 192, 208
civil rights of Blacks, 136. *See also specific topics*
Civil War. *See* American Civil War
Clark, Anne, 27
Clark, Joseph, 155
coercive labor practices, 108, 109, 136. *See also* convict leasing; involuntary servitude; slavery
Coffey, Alvin A., 64, 66
Cole, Cornelius, 132, 133
Colman, Patty R., 254, 311
Colored Athletic Club, 275
Colored Executive Committee, 192–94
community-building, 183, 186, 221
Compromise of 1850, 77
Confederacy: and the Civil War, 197, 198, 203, 206 (*see also* American Civil War); Lost Cause, 123; Pacific Coast and the, 3. *See also* secession
Confederate Army of New Mexico, 200, 202–3
Confederate secret societies, 196–97
Confederates and Confederate sympathizers: in Southern California, 181, 196–97, 199–200, 201f, 206, 210–13, 223–24 (see also *Los Angeles Star*). *See also* Confederacy
Conness, John, 132
"consent," slave, 82, 157
Constitution, U.S. *See specific amendments*
Constitution of California (1849), 162; Benjamin Hayes and, 139, 147–48, 162, 244; slavery abolished in, 2, 9, 132–34, 147–48, 159, 161, 190–91, 194
Constitution of Mississippi (1832), 19
constitutional rights, 162
convict leasing, 108, 176–77, 183, 184, 291
Cook, John (driver), 55, 58
Cooper, A. H., 125–26, 153–56
cotton: Biddy and, 15, 19–21, 23–24, 27, 28, 34, 36; fatalities from picking, 27; in Mississippi, 13, 19, 20, 22, 71 (*see also under* Hinds County); Robert Smith and, 31–32; slavery and, 13, 15, 19, 21–24, 28, 32, 74, 116; in Southern California, 87, 227
cotton boom, 18–24, 28, 31–32
Cottonwood Heights, Utah, 67, 78; Robert Smith's residence in, 72, 95; settlers in, 67–69, 72, 89, 92
Cottrell, Hartwell, 152–54, 157
Couts, Cave, 151
Crabb, Henry A., 167

Crabb massacre, 167
Cribbs, Stephen, 163
crime, 20, 115; in Los Angeles, 155–56, 166–67. *See also* vigilantism; *specific topics*
Crosby, Sarah Jane (Harmon), 104
Crosby, William, 45, 48, 58, 78, 95; background and overview, 45; Benjamin Hayes and, 135–36; as bishop, 92, 106–7; Brigham Young and, 124; slaves, 45, 57, 92, 94, 101, 104, 107, 123, 136, 158 (*see also under* Embers, Toby)

dairy farming, 73, 95, 96, 99–100
Davis, Jefferson, 196
de Bretteville, Sheila Levrant, 307, 307f
Dean, William Simon (Robert Smith's grandfather), 30–31, 96
Democrats and Democratic Party, 194, 255; California and, 90, 106, 119, 211, 225, 255; Lincoln and, 195
Dennis, William Taylor, 60
Depression of 1873–1896. *See* Great Depression of 1873–1896
desegregation, 245
Deseret, State of, 76–77
disunion. *See* secession
domestic abuse, 253, 269
domestic labor, 27, 28, 249, 293; after emancipation, 178–79, 241; of Biddy Mason, 27, 28, 34, 178–79, 182; new mothers and, 27; Rebecca Smith and, 34, 100; slaveholding mistresses and, 34, 100 (*see also* slaveholding mistresses)
domestic servant jobs, 171, 178–79
Donner Party, 67
Dorn, John, 36
Dorn family, 31, 33, 35–36. *See also* Smith, Rebecca Dorn
Douglas, Stephen A., 195, 212, 213
Douglass, Frederck, 16–17, 27, 191, 208
Dred Scott v. Sanford, 165, 168, 191, 192, 208
Drum Barracks, 201–3, 201f, 208, 213
DuBois, W.E.B., 290, 292, 297; on churches, 228, 229; on Los Angeles, 292, 299; Robert C. Owens's property and, 292, 293f

East Los Angeles, 180
Edgefield, South Carolina, 30, 31
education, 245–47
emancipated Blacks. *See* Black Codes
emancipation(s), 138, 175, 213; Mason, Biddy: emancipation); aftermath, 189, 224, 298 (*see also under* Mason, Biddy); commemorations of, 234; of 1856, 3, 9, 154, 158, 159, 165, 193, 211, 212, 268 (*see also* freedom suit of 1856; Los Angeles and, 216, 224, 234; Mormonism and, 60, 76; and the press, 161, 162, 210. *See also* "freedom"
Emancipation Proclamation, 209–10
Embers, Charles (Hannah and Toby's son), 79, 188, 230, 234, 235
Embers, Grief (Toby's brother), 94, 125, 158
Embers, Hannah. *See* Smiley, Hannah Embers
Embers, Martha. *See* Beal, Martha Embers
Embers, Nathaniel (Hannah's son), 127, 147, 188
Embers, Nelson (Hannah's son), 213, 230, 235
Embers, Toby (Hannah's husband): attacked by thugs, 188–90; children, 79, 102, 104, 125, 166, 188; Hannah and, 78, 79, 102, 104, 125, 166, 188, 234; Mormonism and, 125; in San Bernardino, 166, 188; William Crosby and, 78, 104, 125, 158
employment agency, First AME as, 275
English, William F., 106
evangelists, 41; slavery and, 41. *See also* Mormon evangelists
Evergreen Cemetery (Los Angeles), 286, 301, 302, 302f
Exodus, 41, 59–60. *See also* Mormon exodus

family separation, 17, 35, 60; Biddy's experiences of, 15–18, 284, 286; Frederick Douglass on, 16–17; Mormon pioneers and, 124; resistance to, 17–18
farming. *See* dairy farming; Jumuba ranch; wheat farming
Federation of Black History and Arts in Los Angeles, 304
Fifteenth Amendment, 225, 226, 231–34
First African Methodist Episcopal Church of Los Angeles (First AME), 296, 304; on Azusa Street, 267f; chapel at Eighth and Towne Streets, 287, 294–95, 294f, 304; characterizations of, 231, 294; closed doors in late 1870s, 254, 263–64; finances, 230, 235, 241, 247, 264, 295, 304; functions, 275; gatherings at, 231, 233, 280, 286; Hannah's family and, 235; history and overview, 228–31, 294–95; Los Angeles Forum and, 295; Lucy Gillmore's lawsuit and, 265, 266; Mason honored by, 280, 286, 287, 295, 301, 302f, 304, 306f, 307; Mason's support for, 241, 247, 263–65, 267, 286, 287, 295; membership, 4,

231, 267, 267f, 295; philanthropy, 264, 295; reopened in late 1882, 264
Flake, Green, 52, 53, 78, 124
Flamming, Douglas, 293, 298
floods, 54, 203–4, 206, 257–59
Flores, Juan, 167
Follansbee, Elizabeth, 281
Foote, Henry, 23, 74
Foote, Julia A.J., 233
Fort Laramie, 66
Fort Pillow, Battle of, 197
Fort Street, 218
Fort Street Methodist Church, 229, 230
Fort Sumter, Battle of, 196
Forum of First AME, 296
Fourteenth Amendment, 225, 226
Fowler, John, 302
Franklin County, Mississippi, 32, 39
free Blacks, 33, 83, 117, 134, 154, 207–8; immigration to Texas, 149; who remained with their masters, 123
"free forever," 3, 159, 193, 212. *See also* freedom suit of 1856: emancipations
free states, slaves in, 135–36. *See also* California; California antislavery legislation
"freedom," 224; Biddy's experience and understanding of, 165–66; in California, 3, 107, 109, 192. *See also* emancipation(s)
freedom-seekers. *See* slave escape
freedom suit of 1856, 154, 162; allies in, 79, 119, 122, 125–27, 137, 139, 153–54, 186; coerced testimony, 149, 150; confinement/imprisonment of enslaved persons during, 1–2, 127, 131–32, 137, 154; disappearance and reappearance of Mason's lawyer, 140, 141; emancipations, 3, 9, 154, 158, 159, 165, 193, 211, 212, 268; Hannah's coerced testimony, 149; Hannah's disappearance and reappearance, 148, 149; judge's decision, 147–48, 162; persons who spearheaded, 229; perspectives on and characterizations of, 154; petitioner, 120–22, 126, 140–41, 151, 155; photograph of key sites in, 131f; in the press, 139, 162–63; private testimony, 141–43, 148–51, 159, 163, 182; rescue (operation), 119–27; slaves retained by Smith during, 137; Smith's defense, 135, 136 (*see also* Smith, Robert Mays: claims of benevolence); Smith's disappearance and reappearance, 148, 149; Smith's legal options, 151, 152; Smith's schemes to reclaim slaves, 122–23, 135, 136, 149, 150, 152–57; threats to Biddy's family during, 166; trial, 136–43; writ of habeas corpus initiating, 126, 127, 134, 138, 140, 141, 190. *See also* Hayes, Benjamin Ignatius
Freeman, Tyrone McKinley, 240
Fugitive Slave Act, 77, 133
fugitive slaves, 70, 117–18, 136, 138; capture, 13, 71; legislation regarding, 77, 133–34. *See also* slave escape

Gadsden, James, 106
gender roles, 26–27, 46–47, 228–29
Gillmore, Lucy, 265–66
Givens, Robert, 90, 92
Glorieta Pass, Battle of, 202–3
Glymph, Thavolia, 78
Gold Country: slavery in, 90, 91f, 92, 101, 106. *See also* California Gold Rush
Golden State Mutual Life Insurance Company, 299; murals in lobby of, 299, 306f, 307
Goodwin, Candis, 25
Gorham, George, 224
Grandy, Moses, 21, 27
grasshoppers, 114–15
Great American Desert, 62
Great Basin: Biddy in, 71–73, 86; climate, 67, 89; geography, 60, 66–68; Mormon exodus to, 50, 52, 53, 57, 78, 116; Mormonism and, 59, 60, 68, 71, 79; slave escapes in, 70–71
Great Depression of 1873–1896, 216–17, 220, 252–55, 263
Great Flood of 1862, 203–4, 206; drought following, 206
Great Salt Lake, 59, 67, 69
Great Salt Lake City, 67, 70, 72, 79. *See also* Salt Lake City
Greeley, Horace, 66, 83
Green, Lewis G., 203, 230, 232–34, 264
Green, Peter, 287–88
Green, Thomas Jefferson, 106
Griffin, John Strother, 223; Albert Johnston and, 199; background and early life, 19; Benjamin Hayes and, 167, 179, 181–82; Bob Owens and, 181; as businessman, 180–81, 217; Committee of Safety and, 167; Mason and, 179, 181, 182, 205, 207, 208, 217, 244; medical practice, 179, 182, 207, 208, 242; persecution of Mexicans, 167; photograph of, 180f; pro-Confederate politics, 179, 181, 196, 211; real estate, 179–81, 199, 217, 272; retirement, 242; slavery and, 179; smallpox epidemic and, 205, 207

Griffith, D. W., 296
guardianship status of children, 151–52
Gwin, William McKendree, Jr., 225–26
Gwin, William McKendree, Sr., 90, 106, 199

habeas corpus, writ of, 126, 127, 134, 138, 140, 141, 190
Hahn, Steven, 274
Haight, Henry, 224–25
Hall, John, 254
Hamilton, Henry, 183, 196, 197, 203, 210, 211
Hammond, James Henry, 194
Hancock, Winfield Scott, 170, 195, 198, 202
Hancock County, Georgia, 14, 14f, 170, 212, 235
Hannah. *See* Smiley, Hannah Embers
Harris, H. L., 264
Hayes, Benjamin Ignatius, 126, 143, 151, 156–57; alcoholism, 120, 164; background, 104, 119, 120, 134; Biddy's private testimony and, 141–42, 148; on Bob Owens, 137; California law and, 143, 149, 157 (*see also under* Constitution of California); characterizations of, 119–20, 134, 162, 164; on Civil War, 195–96, 211; constituents, 134–35; daily life, 119; death, 268; elections and, 163, 164, 211; Elizabeth Rowan and, 122; epidemics and, 175, 204; family, 134, 151; final years, 255–56; gratitude for saving his son's life, 160–61, 165, 182; Hannah and, 126, 127, 136, 141–43, 147–50, 152; Hartwell Cottrell and, 154; how he was drawn into Biddy's case, 120–22, 126; Hubert Bancroft and, 255–56; John Griffin and, 167, 179, 181–82; later life, 211; legacy, 165; legal cases, 163–64 (*see also* freedom suit of 1856); life history, 119; Lugo family and, 163–64; Native Americans and, 152, 177; personal safety at risk, 163–64; photograph of, 120f; in the press, 162–63, 165; public opinion on and reputation of, 135, 162, 163, 165, 244; racial attitudes, 104, 134–36, 187; Robert Smith and, 134–36, 141–43, 148–50, 152, 157; ruling, 147–48, 152, 165, 193; slave auctions and, 177; slaves freed by, 160–61; slaves owned by, 104, 134; slaves serving, 134–36; view of Biddy, 182; William Crosby and, 135–36; writings, 120, 136, 139, 162–63, 165, 256. *See also* habeas corpus
Hayes, Chauncy (Benjamin's son), 160–62, 164–65, 182
Hayes, Emily (Benjamin's wife), 164, 171
Henry (John Brown's slave), 52, 53
Hinds County, Mississippi: Biddy in, 20, 23, 24; cotton boom in, 20, 28; Ellen Mason and, 24, 27–28; Mississippi insurrection scare and, 23; slave labor in, 20, 21
"hiring out" (leasing) slaves, 101
Hispanics, 166–67, 172, 279
"History of Medicine in California, The" (mural series), 207, 207f, 304
homeowners, Black, 298; first, 187, 188
homeownership: Black, 222, 235, 292; ethnic discrimination, 297–98
Hopkins, Richard, 111
Hotel Somerville, 298–99
housing in Los Angeles, 292, 297. *See also* homeownership
Huddleston, Ellen Mason Owens (Mason's daughter), 63, 121; Benjamin Hayes and, 142; Biddy and, 24, 26–28, 33, 142, 268; birth, 24; childhood, 24, 26–28, 33–35, 56; children, 184; death, 290; departure from Los Angeles, 246; education, 246; inheritances, 256, 284, 289; Lucy Gillmore's lawsuit against, 265; marriage to Charles Owens, 166, 184; marriage to Granville Huddleston, 265; paternity, 24–26; photographs of, 221–22, 221f, 265f; in postwar years, 222; private testimony, 142; race, 24, 25, 39; real estate investment, 222; residences, 34–35, 138–39, 234–35, 259, 266, 267f, 275; Robert Smith and, 34, 116, 122, 139, 152–53, 157
Huddleston, Granville (Ellen's 2nd husband), 265–66
Hughes, Louis, 27
human rights, 16. *See also specific topics*
human trafficking. *See* kidnapping into slavery; sex trafficking; slave trade
Hunt, Jefferson, 104, 107

independence, 107; slaves fear of, 107. *See also* emancipation(s); "freedom"
Indian Country, 65
Indian Removal, 19, 65
Indian Territory, 19, 24
infant mortality, 27
infectious disease, 51, 53, 64, 175, 205, 207
interracial mixing, 79. *See also* multiracial people
involuntary servitude, 87, 157; abolished by California Constitution, 105, 132, 147–48; abolished by Thirteenth Amendment, 184.

See also coercive labor practices; convict leasing; slavery

Jacobs, Harriet, 25, 107
jail. *See* Los Angeles County Jail
Jane (Hannah's daughter), 127, 147, 235; birth, 39, 56; paternity, 150; race, 39, 150
Jim (fugitive slave), 70
Jim Crow laws, 9, 291
Johnson, Ralph, 107
Johnston, Albert Sidney, 199, 200
Jumuba ranch, 110, 112–13, 153; Biddy at, 95, 99–101, 124–25; characterizations of, 96–97; description and overview of, 95, 96; farming/agriculture, 96, 100, 110; finances, 95–96, 99, 104; Hannah at, 100, 101, 104, 124–25; history, 95; livestock/herding, 95, 96, 99, 110; location, 95, 96; Mormons and, 111–13; Robert Smith on, 112–13; Robert Smith's departure from, 116–17; slave labor at, 95, 96, 99

Kane, Thomas, 75
Kanesville (Council Bluffs), Iowa, 54–57
Keckley, Elizabeth, 17, 26
Kewen, E.J.C., 196, 210–12, 223, 231, 232, 244
kidnapping into slavery, 136, 153, 163; of Indians, 108; *in re Perkins,* 133–34; Robert Smith and, 120–21, 149, 152–54, 157, 158
King, Andrew Jackson: Chinese Massacre of 1871 and, 237–38; Confederate/racist views, 196, 223, 224, 245; positions held by, 196, 223–25; treason, 211, 223, 224
Ku Klux Klan (KKK), 226, 271, 296, 297, 299, 305

labor market: barriers to entry in, 178, 293; for Black women, 178; Los Angeles, 275, 292–93. *See also* coercive labor practices; convict leasing; domestic labor; "servants"; "voluntary" Black labor; work life of Biddy Mason
Latinos, 166–67, 172, 279
Latter-day Saints (LDS/Saints), 42. *See also* Mormonism
Lawrence (Hannah's son), 127, 137, 147, 149
Lee, Archy, 190, 191; similarities between Mason and, 190–91
legacy of Biddy Mason, 6–7, 290, 291, 301, 308; headstone, 170, 236, 301–3, 302f; philanthropy in honor of Mason, 308; sources of information about Mason, 6–8, 14, 15; tributes to Mason, 26, 207, 207f, 236, 286–91, 301, 303–5, 306f, 307–9, 307f (*see also* First African Methodist Episcopal Church of Los Angeles: Mason honored by; "History of Medicine in California, The"); writings on Mason, 5–7
liberty pole, 58–61
Lincoln, Abraham: assassination, 212–14; Civil War and, 211–12; on Mississippi insurrection scare of 1835, 23; presidential elections and, 195, 212; slavery and, 168, 194, 195, 209–10; tributes to, 209, 213, 214, 292
Lincoln Club, 233
livery business, Owens family's, 202, 246; Bob Owens's livery stable on San Pedro Street, 122, 137, 199, 202, 222 (*see also* San Pedro Street); Mason's grandsons' livery stable on Spring Street, 259, 261f, 279
livestock, 55, 86–88, 174; enslaved mothers compared with, 37; Robert Smith's, 55, 63, 73, 99, 115. *See also* cattle
locust, 114–15
Long Depression. *See* Great Depression of 1873–1896
Los Angeles (pueblo), 128–29, 171–72, 303; attitudes toward slavery, 162; Biddy's arrival in, 129–30, 129f; Black origin story, 184–85; Blacks in, 154–55, 274 (*see also* Black Los Angeles); businesses in, 272–73; characterizations of, 166, 257; crime, 155–56, 166–67; growth of and changes in, 278–80; ironies of the post-emancipation history of, 298; law enforcement, 154, 156, 177, 277, 297; Mexican heritage, 248; neighborhoods, 279–80; panorama of, 131f; racism in, 166–68, 224–25 (*see also* Ku Klux Klan; *Los Angeles News*); Robert Smith's journey to, 116–17; transportation, 272. *See also specific topics*
Los Angeles Chinese Massacre of 1871, 237–39, 238f, 244
Los Angeles City Water Company, 180–81
Los Angeles County courthouse, 176, 183
Los Angeles County Jail, 131, 167, 177, 240; Biddy and others imprisoned at, 1–2, 130–32, 137, 154, 157, 158, 166; conditions at, 1, 130, 131, 177, 182–83; Indians in, 65, 176, 177; John Griffin at, 182; philanthropic work for, 178, 182, 183, 240; in the press, 177
Los Angeles County Medical Association, 179, 281
Los Angeles Forum, 295

Los Angeles Home Guard, 198
Los Angeles Mounted Rifles, 199
Los Angeles News (newspaper), 222–24
Los Angeles Plaza, 129f
Los Angeles River, 172–74, 257–58
Los Angeles Star (newspaper), 162–63, 197, 210. *See also* Hamilton, Henry; *specific topics*
Lost Cause of the Confederacy, 123
"loyal slave" myth, 123
Lugo family, 93, 95, 112, 163–64
lumber, 101, 103, 104
Lyman, Amasa Mason: background and overview, 92; and Biddy's name, 169; family, 101; finances, 93, 112; Mormon exodus and, 61; Mormon land and, 93, 112–13; political power, 92, 113; rancho, 93, 112; residence, 103–4; Robert Smith and, 92, 101, 115, 117; slavery and, 61, 92–93, 101, 107; Southerners and, 92
Lyman, William Richard, 61
lynchings, 22, 156. *See also* Chinese Massacre of 1871; vigilantism

manumission, 82
Marion (Hannah's daughter), 102, 127, 147, 235
marriage, forced, 38
Mary, Virgin, 170–71
Mason (Black man who converted to Mormonism), 169
Mason, Ann (Biddy's daughter), 56, 57, 147, 157, 160–61; death, 175, 184, 205; infancy, 33, 34; paternity, 33, 169; race, 33
Mason, Biddy: ambassadorial roles, 280–81; "beatitude," 239; birthdate, 170; characterizations of, 2–5, 39, 162, 181, 186, 223, 236, 239, 241, 264, 274, 277–78, 280–83, 286, 287, 308; in court, 268–70 (*see also* freedom suit of 1856); daily life in early years of freedom, 171; daily life in slavery, 34–35 (*see also* slaves: tasks performed by); daily life in twilight years, 281; death, 286, 289, 291 (*see also* legacy of Biddy Mason); dress, 250, 251f, 252; early life, 14–15; emancipation, 154, 161, 162, 165, 175, 183, 193, 197 (*see also* emancipation(s): of 1856); end of life, 281–82; feelings about legal system, 158, 267–68; finances, 4, 39–40, 171, 182, 240–41, 249–50, 264, 268, 283, 284 (*see also* philanthropy: Mason's; Spring Street property of Mason); funeral, 286, 302; grave, 301–3; hate speech toward, 197; health problems, 281; lawsuit against, 268–69; life history, 2–4, 14–15; map of her transcontinental journey, x–xi; marital status, 169–70; medical training, 178; names, 10, 14–15, 168–70, 169f, 205, 241; personality, 3, 6, 26, 181, 182, 223, 242, 244, 250, 252, 264; photograph of, 2–3; postliberation struggles in Los Angeles, 165; posture, 250, 251f; in the press, 6, 161, 162, 264, 289; reputation, 264, 268; rescue (*see* freedom suit of 1856); residences, 258 (*see also* neighbors of Biddy Mason; Owens home on San Pedro Street; Spring Street home of Mason); separated from family, 16–17; travels, 118–19; will, 283–84, 285f, 286, 289, 301–2. *See also* work life of Biddy Mason
Mason, Ellen. *See* Huddleston, Ellen Mason Owens
Mason, Harriet (Biddy's daughter), 147, 157, 188; on *Ada Hancock,* 208–9; Biddy's death and, 287, 290; birth, 39, 49, 54; death, 290; disabilities in later life, 209; employment, 171, 187, 269; heroism, 209; infancy and early childhood, 56, 64; inheritance, 284, 289; paternity, 39; photograph of, 221f, 222; race, 39; Robert Smith and, 39, 49
Mason, Thomas (plantation slaveholder), 170
Mason Block, 259–60, 260f, 261f, 263; Bob Owens and, 289, 290; finances, 273, 284, 287, 290. *See also* Spring Street property of Mason
matriarchy, Black, 221
Matthews, Benjamin, 70
Matthews, Miriam, 7, 305
McClellan, George B., 212
McFeely, Joseph, 189, 190
McGroarty, John S., 292
McKown, Francis, 70–71
media. *See* press
Meredith (teamster), 152–54
Mesmer, Joseph, 187, 222, 227, 232; Mason and, 181, 187, 241, 243, 244, 263
Mesmer family of California, 243, 244, 260
Methodists, 41, 217, 218, 229. *See also* First African Methodist Episcopal Church of Los Angeles
Mexican California, 186
Mexican Tejas, 116

Mexican-American War, 54, 179, 185
Mexicans, 167, 172
Mexico, 166–67, 185; Blacks fleeing to, 198; California seized from, 54; Los Angeles and, 167, 248
midwifery, 101, 241–42; of Mason, 36–37, 101, 205, 241–44, 263, 270
Miles, Tiya, 219
mining. *See* California Gold Rush; Gold Country
Mississippi, 19, 33; cost and sale of land in, 19–20; cotton in, 13, 19, 20, 22, 71; migration to cotton heartland in 1830s, 13; Panic of 1837 and, 28–29, 33. *See also specific counties*
Mississippi insurrection scare of 1835, 22–23
Mississippi River, 47, 54, 59, 60
Mississippi Saints (LDS), 57, 58, 61, 63, 67, 124; John Brown and, 45, 47–48, 57, 58, 61, 68 (*see also* Brown, John (Mormon pioneer)); Robert Smith and, 47, 57, 63, 67, 72, 75, 78, 83, 89; slavery and, 57, 58, 61, 67–68, 75, 83, 89, 123. *See also* Cottonwood Heights; Mormon exodus
Missouri River, 51, 52, 56, 58, 65; crossing, 51, 52, 57, 58
Mob law, 155, 244. *See also* vigilantism
Mojave Desert, 86, 88–89
"Mormon banknotes," 103
Mormon baptism, 44, 45, 76; of African Americans, 44, 80
Mormon children, 101
Mormon evangelists, 41, 42, 44, 45
Mormon exodus, 49–68, 77–78, 116; biblical Exodus and, 59–60; Biddy and, 49, 50, 52–68; deaths during, 57–58, 64, 65; disease and, 51, 53, 64; John Brown and, 52–53, 55–58, 61, 65, 66, 68. *See also* Great Basin; Mormon pioneers
Mormon leadership: and opposition movement fueled by Robert Smith, 111–13, 125; political influence, 113; priesthood, 46, 80
Mormon pioneers, 98; Brigham Young and, 50–53, 59, 83–84; finances, 93, 112; from Mississippi (*see* Mississippi Saints). *See also* Brown, John (Mormon pioneer); Mormon exodus; *specific topics*
Mormon San Bernardino, 92, 94, 96, 98, 113, 196; elections, 113; history, 114; Mason's midwifery in, 101, 102; naming of, 94; natural disasters, 114–15; politics, 104, 113; Robert Smith in, 96, 102; slavery in, 102, 107, 123; thievery in, 115. *See also* San Bernardino
Mormon Trail, 50, 58, 65. *See also* Mormon exodus
Mormon Zion, 68; Brigham Young and, 52, 71, 76, 83; slavery in, 70, 73, 81, 83, 85; vision of pursuit of, 46, 49, 50, 57
Mormonism: appeal of, 45, 46; Biddy and, 44, 169; Blacks and (*see* Black Mormons; Cain and Ham); history, 45, 50, 51 (*see also* Mormon exodus); patriarchy in, 46–47; slavery and, 45, 52, 59, 60, 71, 76–77, 105 (*see also* Young, Brigham: slavery and); terminology, 42. *See also* anti-Mormonism; Smith, Robert Mays
Moses, 41, 59, 60
motherhood of slaves, 27, 34, 37, 38, 60–61. *See also* childcare; personal life of Biddy Mason; rape: children conceived through
Mott, Thomas T., 232
Mulrein, David, 268, 269
multiracial people, 24, 25, 36, 185–86; "mulattoes," 24, 25, 79, 136
Murray, Hugh C., 132–34, 151

names of slaves and former slaves, 168. *See also* Mason, Biddy: names
National Park Service's National Underground Railroad Network to Freedom, 308
Native Americans, 19, 65, 151; Benjamin Hayes and, 152, 177; Biddy and, 24, 65–66; slavery and, 108–9, 176–77, 183, 184. *See also* California Indians
Native population of Los Angeles, 184. *See also* California Indians
Nauvoo, Illinois, 47, 48; Mormon refugees/exiles from, 49–51, 59; population, 49
Negro Trail Blazers of California (Beasley), 305
neighbors of Biddy Mason, 181, 187, 216, 223, 244, 253, 289; churches and, 227, 254, 263; racism among, 167, 172, 223, 244; secessionist, 210; thugs who later became, 166
New Mexico, slavery in, 77
Newmark, Harris, 103, 171, 172, 187, 202, 204–5, 212, 213, 238, 242, 249, 250, 252, 257, 272, 273
news media. *See* press
Northup, Solomon, 17, 25
nurseries, 241, 294

nurses, 242, 243, 269. *See also* work life of Biddy Mason: nursing

Oakland public schools, 246
Old Spanish Trail (trade route), 86–88
Olmsted, Frederick Law, 35
Ord, Edward O. C., 108–9, 113
"other slavery, the," 108
Owens, Charles (Ellen Mason's 1st husband), 222, 230; Bob Owens and, 122, 139, 222, 246–47; death, 256; Ellen and, 122, 139, 166, 184, 253, 256; Hannah's home and, 234–35; and his son's education, 246–47; in the postwar years, 222
Owens, Ellen Mason. *See* Huddleston, Ellen Mason Owens
Owens, Henry Louis (Ellen and Charles's son), 246, 259; birth, 184; death, 290; inheritance, 256, 284
Owens, Robert "Bob" (Charles's father), 122, 137, 138, 181, 217, 244; Black Los Angeles and, 220–21, 290; characterization of, 137, 220; Civil War and, 198–200, 202; in danger, 152–53; death, 216, 220, 222, 245; as entrepreneur, 137; finances, 138, 153, 202, 206, 283, 292; freedom suit of 1856 and, 138, 152–53; friendships, 137, 181, 187, 197; home (*see* Owens home on San Pedro Street); Robert Smith's teamsters and, 152–53; tribute to, 223. *See also under* livery business
Owens, Robert Curry (Ellen and Charles's son), 186–87, 277; allies, 276–77; awards and honors, 275; birth, 184, 185f; characterizations of, 276, 290; Charles Owens and, 246–47; departure from Los Angeles, 246; finances, 255, 256, 277, 283, 284, 290, 292; Mason and, 246, 255, 268, 269, 277, 303; neighbors, 289, 290; photographs of, 185f, 221, 221f, 276f; in the press, 277, 290, 292; properties, 265, 266, 290–92, 293f; Republican Party of Los Angeles and, 247, 275–77, 276f
Owens, Winnie (Bob's wife), 138, 174, 187, 217, 222; career, 137–38; climbing the social ladder, 137–38; death, 256; emancipation, 138; finances, 283; home (*see* Owens home on San Pedro Street); legacy, 294; life as widow, 222–23, 227, 230, 231; Mason and, 227, 244, 249; photographs of, 138, 221–22, 221f; tributes to, 256
Owens home on San Pedro Street, 256; events at, 138, 227, 309; Masons at, 137–39, 166, 174f, 175, 181, 186; neighbors (*see* neighbors of Biddy Mason); photographs of, 138, 174f, 221–22, 221f; physical characteristics, 137, 175, 202; as refuge for freedom-seekers, 138; targeted by Smith's cronies, 152–55; value, 202

Panic of 1837, 28–29, 33; impact on slaves, 28–29, 33
Panic of 1873, 255
paramilitary patrols, 24–25
Pasadena, 179–80, 272, 275, 292
patriarchy. *See* gender roles; polygamy
Patton, George S., 223
Pauline epistles, 41
Pepper, Ann (Hannah's daughter), 127, 147, 153, 154, 188, 235; interviewed by Benjamin Hayes, 142–43; marriage, 188, 253; motherhood, 102, 116, 188
Pepper, Manuel, 188, 253
Pepper, Mary (Ann's daughter), 102, 127, 147, 153, 170–71
Perkins, in re (1852), 133–34, 151
personal life of Biddy Mason: divine visitation/vision, 217–18; faith/religiosity, 4, 40–41, 44, 170–71, 217, 218, 241, 284, 287–88 (*see also under* First African Methodist Episcopal Church of Los Angeles); marital status, 24, 39–40, 169–70; motherhood, 27, 33, 34, 37 (*see also* Huddleston, Ellen Mason Owens; Mason, Ann; Mason, Harriet); reasons for not pursuing romantic relationship, 39–40; relationships, 26
philanthropy, 239–41; of First AME, 264, 295; Mason's, 4, 239–41, 264, 287, 289; Mason's "gospel of giving," 240; Mason's theory of faith-driven, 239
Pico family of California, 185–86
Pioneer Camp, 52, 53, 66
plantation mistresses, 25. *See also* slaveholding mistresses
Platte River, 59, 61, 66
Platte Valley, 61, 64
Pleasant, Mary Ellen, 271
police, Los Angeles, 154, 156, 177, 277, 297
Polk, James K., 63
polygamy, 46–47, 51
popular sovereignty, 77
Pratt, Orson, 81
prayer meetings, slave, 42
pregnancies, coerced, 108. *See also* rape: children conceived through

pregnant slaves, 38; abuse of, 27
press, 271, 279; abolitionist, 155, 161; Black press of Los Angeles, 291, 296; emancipation and the, 161, 162, 210. *See also specific topics*
priesthood (LDS), 46, 80; ban on Black, 80
prison. *See* Los Angeles County Jail
probate court, 81–82, 151
pueblo. *See* Los Angeles
Purdy, John H., 155

"race war," 166–67
railroad, 272
rancheros (rancho owners), 109, 135, 206, 217
Rancho San Bernardino, 93
Rancho San Pasqual, 179
Rande (slave), 36, 55, 63, 68; allies, 69, 70; escape, 69–72, 83, 85, 123–24
rape, 24–25, 82; blaming the victim of, 25; children conceived through, 24–26, 36, 38, 150, 188; of Hannah, 38–40, 102, 125, 150, 188; perpetrated by Robert Smith, 24, 38, 39, 125, 142, 150; "third-party rape," 38. *See also* sexual abuse
real estate boom of the 1880s, 271–73
Reconstruction, 216, 224, 226, 227, 234, 255; collapse of, 255, 274; Los Angeles and, 165, 216–17, 222, 224, 248, 274; rebellion against, 216, 224. *See also specific topics*
religion. *See* Bible; Christianity; personal life of Biddy Mason: faith/religiosity
Republicans and Republican Party, 190, 210–12, 224, 225, 255; Robert Owens and, 247, 275–77, 276f. *See also* Black Republicans
Resendez, Andrés, 108
Rich, Charles C.: background and overview, 92; finances, 93, 112; Mormon land and, 93, 112–13; political power, 92, 113; rancho, 93, 112; Robert Smith and, 92, 115, 117; slavery and, 92–93, 107
Rocha Adobe, 130
Rocky Mountains (Rockies), crossing the, 51, 54
Rowan, Elizabeth Flake, 125; Agnes Flake and, 123; autobiography, 26; Biddy and, 64, 78, 121, 121f, 125; characterization of, 125; childbirth, 26; Hannah and, 122; photograph of, 121f; Robert Smith and, 122; on the sale of her father, 17; San Bernardino and, 107–8, 121
runaway slaves. *See* fugitive slaves
rust (fungus), 114

Sacramento, 90, 162
Salt Lake City, 53, 70, 72, 80, 87, 112. *See also* Great Salt Lake City
Salt Lake Valley, 53, 54, 66, 71–74, 85
San Bernardino, 104–5; criminal justice system, 105, 106; Elizabeth Flake Rowan and, 107–8, 121; government, 105–7; growth and flourishing of, 102–5; Hannah in, 101, 102, 148, 187; myth of "voluntary" Black labor in, 107 (*see also* "voluntary" Black labor); politics, 105; slavery in, 105–7; Toby Embers in, 166, 188. *See also* Mormon San Bernardino; *specific topics*
San Bernardino House (hotel), 104
San Bernardino Mountains, 92, 93, 103, 104
San Francisco, 90, 234, 271; Blacks in, 90, 191, 227, 234, 271, 274
San Pedro Street (Los Angeles), 249, 266, 309. *See also under* livery business; Owens home on San Pedro Street.
Sanderson, Jeremiah, 246
Santa Ana River, 93, 95, 204, 206; banks of, 95, 97, 109–10
Santa Monica Mountains, 117–18, 118f, 122; Biddy's departure from, 128; Robert Smith in, 117–18, 122, 123, 126, 127, 154
school integration, 245
schools/schoolhouses, 245–47
Scott, Dred. See *Dred Scott v. Sanford*
secession, 74, 168, 194–96; California and, 194–96. *See also* Confederacy
secessionists and secessionism, 196; in California, 196, 198, 199, 201, 203, 210, 211, 223–24
Second Great Awakening, 45–46
Second Middle Passage, 15
segregation, 245, 298
self-emancipations, 9, 158
Sepúlveda, Ygnacio, 233
"servants," 41, 80–82, 104, 107, 135, 165
sex trafficking, 38–39
sexual abuse, 15–16, 25, 26, 40; of Biddy, 15, 24, 38–40, 142; of Hannah, 39, 40, 125, 150, 188; and jealous wives, 25; silence around, 25–26; ubiquity of, 25, 38. *See also* rape
Sherman's March to the Sea, 212
Shore, John W., 152
Sims, James Marion, 243
slave auctions, 15–18, 35, 176, 177, 183, 184
slave-catching, 70, 83, 115, 133–34. *See also* fugitive slaves; slave recapture

slave economy, 18–20. *See also* cotton; slave trade
slave escape: difficulty of and impediments to, 60–61, 72, 77, 92, 117–18, 133 (*see also* slave-catching); to Los Angeles, 117; from Mormon exodus, 60, 70–71. *See also* fugitive slaves; Rande: escape
slave markets, 15, 16, 38–39, 90. *See also* slave auctions; slave trade; slaves: cost of buying
slave marts, 176, 177, 184
slave pens, 15, 16
slave population, growth ("natural increase") of, 19, 37–38
Slave Power, 161, 190, 191
slave rebellion, 22
slave recapture, 71, 133. *See also* fugitive slaves; slave-catching
slave resistance, 17–18, 22, 40
slave trade, 16, 17, 35, 37, 40, 87, 90. *See also* family separation; kidnapping into slavery; slave markets
slaveholders: Black devotion to, 123; lies told to slaves by, 32; stereotypes of and myths about, 32. *See also specific topics*
slaveholding mistresses, 25, 34, 78, 100
slavery, 5–6; conditions of, 13, 15–17, 20–22, 26–28, 34–35, 40 (*see also* sexual abuse); misinformation about, 107; Native Americans and, 108–9, 176–77, 183, 184; portrayed in literature, 21. *See also* coercive labor practices; involuntary servitude; *specific topics*
slaves: ages, 101–2; cost of buying, 16, 18, 29, 35, 38–39, 90, 93, 108, 148; female, 25–27, 36, 37 (*see also* motherhood of slaves; *specific topics*); life expectancy, 102; objectification and dehumanization of, 15–16, 25, 37 (*see also* sexual abuse); reproduction (*see* motherhood of slaves; rape: children conceived through); tasks performed by, 34, 63, 73; use of threats to control, 38, 40. *See also* "servants"; *specific topics*
Sleepy Creek plantation, 31, 35, 36. *See also* Dorn family
smallpox epidemic, 205, 207
Smiley, Hannah Embers, 188; Biddy's friendship with, 40, 188; children, 37–39, 49, 55, 78–79, 102, 104, 137, 150, 235; emancipation, 138, 149; family background, 35–36; medical knowledge and skills, 101, 102; as midwife, 36, 101; pregnancies, 39, 49, 55; private testimony, 149–51; race, 35–36, 150; Rebecca Smith and, 31, 35, 36, 73, 78, 100, 150; Robert Smith and, 35, 36, 138; sexual abuse, 39, 40, 125, 150, 188; work skills, 36. *See also specific topics*
Smith, Henry (Hannah and Robert's son), 147, 149, 203; birth, 127, 137, 188; paternity, 38, 102, 150, 188
Smith, Joseph, 46, 79, 92; assassination, 47–49, 51; Brigham Young and, 50, 51; imprisonment, 47; John Brown and, 42–44, 47–48; overview, 43; personality, 36, 50; presidential campaign (1844), 76; and Robert and Rebecca Smith, 54, 76; slavery and, 45, 76, 79; women, gender roles, and, 46
Smith, Oscar (Crosby), 52, 53, 78, 229
Smith, Rebecca Dorn: Biddy and, 34, 73, 77, 78; childhood, 31; children, 32, 54, 77–78, 100; domestic labor and, 34, 100; family of origin, 31, 33, 35; Hannah and, 31, 35, 36, 73, 78, 100, 150; marriage to Robert, 31, 288; personality, 34, 78; religion and, 42, 44, 54, 288; as slaveholder, 32, 34–36, 77–78, 100, 136–37, 150
Smith, Robert Mays, 2, 48, 158–59, 288; Amasa Lyman, Charles Rich, and, 92, 101, 115, 117; aspirations, 30, 47, 109; background, 30; baptism, 44, 76; Benjamin Hayes and, 134–36, 141–43, 148–50, 152, 157; Biddy sold to, 29, 33; California and, 2, 89, 92, 162; cattle, 63, 66, 73, 87, 95, 96, 99–100, 100f, 115, 157, 158; characterizations of, 29, 30, 32, 60; children, 38, 39, 102, 288; claims of benevolence, 2, 122–23, 135 (*see also under* freedom suit of 1856); cotton and, 31–32; death, 288–89; departure from Los Angeles, 157–59; description of, 29–32; disconnection from LDS Church, 116, 159, 288; Ellen Mason and, 34, 116, 122, 139, 152–53, 157; family background, 30–31, 96; finances, 31–33, 37, 55, 95, 96, 99–101, 112, 113, 148; Hannah and, 35, 36, 138; John Brown and, 42, 56–58, 61; journey from San Bernardino to Los Angeles, 116–17; kidnapping charge (*see under* freedom suit of 1856; kidnapping into slavery); life after the trial, 288–89; marriage to Rebecca, 31, 288; Mississippi Saints and, 47, 57, 63, 67, 72, 75, 78, 83, 89; Mormon conversion, 42, 44; Mormon exodus and, 49–58, 60–61, 63; Mormon faith, 54, 288; Mormon opposition movement fueled by, 111–

13, 125; number of slaves owned by, 33, 36, 37, 45, 55, 57, 77, 79, 87, 102, 115, 127, 136, 137, 148, 288; overview, 29–30; personality, 29, 30, 57, 123; polygamy and, 46–47; portrait of, 31f; positions held by, 107, 111; prospect of selling his slaves, 54–55; reasons for joining LDS Church, 45, 46; reputation and public opinion of, 70, 112; residences and land of, 35, 72, 95–96, 116, 288 (*see also* Jumuba ranch); sexual abuse of slaves, 38, 39, 46, 125; South Carolina and, 30–31, 46, 96; subterfuge, 107 (*see also* freedom suit of 1856: Smith's schemes to reclaim slaves; "voluntary" Black labor); taxation and, 33, 96, 113; testimony exclusion laws and, 2, 136, 151; threats made to, 45, 115; trial (*see* freedom suit of 1856); views of and attitudes toward Biddy, 2, 122–23. *See also under* Texas
Smith, Willy "Seco" (Robert's son), 153, 154, 288
Snyder, Meredith P., 280, 287
South Carolina, Robert Smith and, 30–31, 46, 96
Southern California: movement to reenslave, 194; prospect of independence, 194–95. *See also specific topics*
Southern California real estate boom of the 1880s, 271–73
Spanish Trail. *See* Old Spanish Trail
Spring Street (Los Angeles), 130, 218, 273, 282, 295; Bob Owens's property on, 290, 291; characterizations of, 263
Spring Street home of Mason, 259; Mason's death at, 286; visitors, 308. *See also* neighbors of Biddy Mason
Spring Street property of Mason, 252, 278–80, 284, 289, 291; Bob Owens and, 289–91; businesses at, 249, 259–61, 263 (*see also under* livery business); and the community, 221; cost/value, 219, 220, 249–50, 252, 258, 273, 280, 289; deed to, 219f; disasters that affected, 257–59; gatherings at, 280–81; Mason's children and, 219–20, 259, 284, 289; monument and commemorative wall at site of, 307–8, 307f; photographs of, 260f, 261f, 278f; purchase, 218–21; real estate development, 221, 249, 260f, 261, 261f, 263, 268, 271, 273, 280, 290, 303–4; Robert C. Owens and, 303
squatters, 113
Stanford, Leland, 204, 211–12
Star. See *Los Angeles Star*
Stearns, Abel, 141–42
Stockton, 216, 245, 246
Stovall, Kate Bradley, 241
subterfuge practices to support slavery, 18, 107, 123, 142. *See also* freedom suit of 1856: Smith's schemes to reclaim slaves; "servants"; "voluntary" Black labor
suffrage, 224–25, 231–34, 291. *See also* Fifteenth Amendment
Supreme Court of California, 132–34, 143, 151, 190

Taney, Roger, 168
taxation: in Los Angeles, 194, 206; Robert Smith and, 33, 96, 113
Taylor, Quintard, 296
Temple, Ruth, 295
Temple and Workman Bank, 252, 253
Tennessee, 55–56
Terry, David Smith, 191, 199, 225
testimony: of Blacks, 149 (*see also* testimony exclusion laws); private, 141–43, 148–51, 159, 163, 182. *See also under* freedom suit of 1856
testimony exclusion laws: Benjamin Hayes and, 143, 149, 153; in California, 136, 143, 149, 151, 153, 189, 190, 192, 211–12; overturned, 192, 211–12; Robert Smith and, 2, 136, 151; scope of, 136, 212
Texas: Biddy's testimony regarding trip to, 142; Civil War and, 200, 203; history, 54, 116; immigration of free blacks to, 149; migrants from, 155, 274, 276, 277; Mormons and, 116; Robert Smith's planned trips to, 2, 54, 116–22, 125, 126, 135, 136, 141–42, 148, 152, 153, 157–59; Robert Smith's ranch in, 288; slavery and, 54, 116, 149
"third-party rape," 38
Thirteenth Amendment, 184
Thom, Cameron, 199, 223
Thomas, Alonzo, 140
Thomas, Daniel M., 95–96, 106
Tishomingo County, Mississippi, 54
Toombs, Robert, 75
torture, 22, 23, 27
trial of 1856. *See* freedom suit of 1856
Twelve Years a Slave (Northup), 17, 25

Underground Railroad, Pacific Coast spur of, 138, 220
Union Party, 211

Unionism and Unionists, 198–201, 208, 211. *See also* American Civil War
Utah County, federal census slave schedule for, 84f
Utah Territory, 77, 123; Brigham Young and, 76, 77, 79–81; governance, 77, 79–83; slavery in, 73, 76, 77, 80–83. *See also specific topics*
Utah Territory Slave Code (1852), 83

Valdez Villa, Maria Rita, 185
vaqueros, 99, 122
vigilantism, 133–34, 291; anti-Mormon, 44, 47, 49 (*see also* anti-Mormonism); attack on Toby Embers, 188–90; against Benjamin Hayes, 163–64; against Hispanics, 166–67; in Los Angeles, 155–56, 243–44; during Mississippi insurrection scare, 22–23; Robert Smith and, 152–57. *See also* allies: hostility toward; Chinese Massacre of 1871; Ku Klux Klan
"voluntary" Black labor, 2, 107, 108, 135, 141, 149
voters, Black, 276; in Canada, 191–92. *See also* suffrage

Waite, James S., 162, 163, 197
Wales, Hark (Lay), 52, 53, 124, 158
Walker, Madam C. J., 241
Ward, T.M.D., 229–30
Wasatch Range, 66–67, 72, 88
Webster, Daniel, 63
Wells, G. Wiley, 270–71
Wells, Ida B., 291
westward expansion of slavery, 74, 75, 162. *See also* Mormon exodus; *specific topics*
wheat farming: Biddy and, 73, 100; Robert Smith and, 73, 95, 96, 99, 100; in San Bernardino, 103, 114
white allies. *See* allies
Widney, Robert M., 217, 220, 233, 238
Williams, Rose, 40
Wilson, Benjamin Davis, 211, 216, 220, 272; freedom suit of 1856 and, 163; George McClellan and, 212; and the press, 163; slavery and, 151
Wilson, Christopher "Chinese" North, 266, 268, 269
Winston, James B., 141, 142
Winter Quarters, Nebraska, 51–53, 61, 65
Wolfenstein, Valentin, 250
Woods, James (minister), 228
work life of Biddy Mason, 281; business ethics, 219–20, 239, 261, 263, 268; business savvy, 217–21, 252, 273; domestic servant jobs, 171, 178–79; at Los Angeles County Jail, 178, 182, 183, 240; medical knowledge and skills, 101–2, 178; midwifery, 36–37, 101, 205, 241–44, 263, 270; nursing, 182, 183, 205, 238–39, 242, 253, 263; real estate investment, 4, 217–21, 219f, 241, 252, 258, 283 (*see also* Spring Street property of Mason); retirement, 263; work skills, 36–37. *See also* philanthropy; slaves: tasks performed by
Workman, William, 252
writ of habeas corpus, 126, 127, 134, 138, 140, 141, 190

Young, Brigham: background and overview, 50; California and, 87, 113–14; characterizations of, 50, 51, 60; compared with Moses, 59; Green Flake and, 124; Joseph Smith and, 50, 51; Mormon pioneers and, 50–53, 59, 83–84; personality, 50, 76; on racial politics, 79–81; slavery and, 70–71, 75, 76, 79–83, 124; Utah Territory and, 76–77, 79–81, 83; William Crosby and, 124; wives, 51, 73, 114

Zakheim, Bernard, 207, 207f, 304
zanjas (irrigation canals), 129, 173–75, 174f, 278
Zion. *See* Mormon Zion